THE BIG BOOK OF HOME LEARNING
Volume Three: Teen & Adult

Also by Mary Pride:

The Way Home
All the Way Home
Schoolproof
The Child Abuse Industry
Baby Doe
The Better Butter Battle
The Greenie
Too Many Chickens

With Paul deParrie:

Unholy Sacrifices of the New Age
Ancient Empires of the New Age

THE BIG BOOK OF HOME LEARNING

Volume Three: Teen & Adult

Mary Pride

Crossway Books • Wheaton, Illinois
A Division of Good News Publishers

The Big Book of Home Learning: Volume 3.

Copyright © 1991 by Mary Pride.
Published by Crossway Books, a division of
Good News Publishers, 1300 Crescent Street, Wheaton, Illinois 60187.

Cover Design by Mark Schramm.
Interior Design by Mark Schramm and Mary Pride, based on the
original concept by Karen L. Mulder.
Layout by Bill Pride and Mary Pride.
Cover illustration by Guy Wolek.

First printing, 1991

Printed in the United States of America

Library of Congress Cataloging-in-Publication Data
Pride, Mary
   Big book of home learning / Mary Pride
      v.   cm.
   Includes bibliographic references.
   Contents: v. 1. Getting started — v. 2. Preschool and elementary —
v. 3. Teen and adult — v. 4. Afterschooling and extras.
   1. Home schooling—United States. 2. Home schooling—United
States—Curricula. 3. Education—United States—Parent
participation. 4. Child rearing—United States I. Title.
LC40.P75 1991   649'.68 ' 0973—dc20   89-81254
ISBN 0-89107-550-X (v. 3)

99	98	97	96	95	94	93	92						
15	14	13	12	11	10	9	8	7	6	5	4	3	2

TABLE OF CONTENTS

INTRODUCTION

In the three other volumes of this series you will find resources for getting started with home education (Volume 1), resources for preschool and elementary children (Volume 2), and "fun stuff" for afterschooling (Volume 4). This volume is dedicated to students in grade 7 and up and to those adults preparing for—or trying to improve their chances in—the job market and the Real World. It is also dedicated to those advanced preteen children who have already whizzed through basic math, language arts, social studies, or science, and are ready for *more*!

I do *not* view the teen years as a time to review subjects supposedly taught in elementary school. If your teen has a weak educational foundation, don't make it worse by presenting unlearned concepts in a more complicated way! Too often the difference between teen and elementary courses is just that

(1) the teen courses lack visual appeal,
(2) they are cluttered with extraneous data,
(3) their vocabulary is more complex,
(4) and the explanations are more murky.

For that reason, if your teen's educational background needs strengthening, you probably should start by going over the resources in Volume 2.

Now, what's in *this* volume?

WHAT YOU GET

Bible and character education. In the teen years we have obviously moved beyond the cute rabbits and fluffy hand puppets that infest elementary-grades courses on these subjects. The Bible resources in this volume are more in-depth, challenging, and analytical. The character education courses are *courses* directed to teens.

Language arts. Writing assignments and resources in this volume take on a more professional flavor—including some designed to help you learn to write professionally! Grammar resources are analytical (sentence diagramming) and condensed (reviews of basic grammar). Literature becomes a formal subject. Thinking skills becomes formal logic. You will also find a chapter on remedial phonics for teens and adults. This is the only remedial area where special courses for older learners might really be helpful. Older students have wider life experience and can learn faster and more independently than the little kids for whom elementary and preschool phonics courses are developed. Also, kiddie phonics courses can be humiliating (and stultifying) to older students, who don't particularly enjoy being reminded that they were supposed to learn to read when they were six years old.

Math. I have chosen in this volume to concentrate on the math that truly belongs in junior high, high school, and beginning college courses: consumer math, pre-algebra and algebra, geometry, trigonometry, and calculus. I do also mention a few basic math courses that are especially well suited to teens and adults.

Social studies, life skills, and vocational skills. These subjects are ideally suited for the teen and adult years, when the student has a richer background of reading and life experiences. In fact, some wags hold that nobody under the age of 30 can really begin to understand history, while no practicing historian should be under 50! Thus you'll find in this volume courses and resources that explain in depth how government works (and is *supposed* to work), as opposed to the necessarily more superficial resources in the Preschool & Elementary volume. The topics of money, banking, economic systems, church history, and general history are also gone into more deeply. How to start and run a business, preparation for college entrance tests, vocational training sources, and child training basics are other areas that properly belong in the teen and adult realm, so you'll find them in the Life Skills and Business & Vocational sections of this book.

Science. Science courses in this volume include scientific creationism, biology, chemistry, physics, general high-school science, and a discussion of the proper place of ecology in the home curriculum.

PRODUCTS REVIEWED IN VOLUME 2

Those of you who own Volume 2 will notice that some of the same products are featured in this book. That's because many home-schooling products work equally well in upper-elementary grades and junior high, or

even high school. We chose to repeat the reviews of these products rather than annoy you with continual directions asking you to consult Volume 2. Many of the product reviews that also appear in Volume 2 have been rewritten especially for Volume 3 to stress the products' teen and adult features.

Our goal is to help you do *all* your teen-and-adult educational browsing with just this one book, so you'll only have to buy Volume 2 if you *want* to!

PEOPLE WHO HELPED

Husband Bill, the manager of our home business, did some in-depth testing of resources for the Business chapter. If a review has his name at the end, Bill was there! Bill also put together the indexes and did much of the actual typesetting of the book.

Cathy Duffy, the author of *The Christian Home Educator's Curriculum Manual*, also kindly contributed a number of math and science reviews when she heard how far behind I was with this project. Her reviews are similarly tagged with her name.

Our seven (soon to be eight) children helped by using teen math and literature courses in our home school (although the oldest is only 11), discussing citizenship and economics at the dinner table, demonstrating great creative spelling in their creative writing assignments, and typing those assignments starting at the age of 7. The older ones also helped out from time to time with our home business and all the time with household chores. The little ones helped especially by insisting on crawling into my lap when they thought I was working too long at the computer!

Our children have tested juggling equipment, cookbooks, geography puzzles, and time lines. They have started several businesses using resources in this book, one of which is currently successful (i.e., making more than it costs). They have *willingly* tested *all* the hands-on engineering and science kits I ever received. They have sent away for surplus science goodies from the American Science & Surplus catalog and yukky black caterpillars from Insect Lore Products. They have played educational games, listened to Daddy read *The Yes Minister* at suppertime, and memorized a number of Bobby Horton's *Songs of the CSA*. The Pride kids are the real heroes of this book, even if some of them aren't yet old enough to read it! So to you, Teddy, Joe, Sarah, Magda, Franklin, Mercy Grace, Gregory, and Baby, I gratefully dedicate this book.

HOW TO USE THIS BOOK

You know how to read a resource book. Just turn to the section that interests you and browse through the reviews.

Well, guess what?

You can do the same thing with this book!

The editors and I have, however, incorporated a few innovative features that we hope will make each volume of *The Big Book of Home Learning* more useful than the average resource book.

If you'll flip to the Index of Suppliers you can see that it is more than just names with addresses attached. We're added all sorts of helpful information: toll-free telephone numbers, fax numbers, best times of day to call, methods of payment allowed, refund policy, whether or not the supplier has a free brochure or catalog and what it costs if it *isn't* free, plus a brief description of the supplier's product line.

It is easy to find the address of any given company. Instead of searching through a chapter to find the company, as you have to when full addresses are given in the text, just flip to the index.

What all this means is that you can relax and enjoy *The Big Book of Home Learning* without having to write down reams of information about every product that interests you. Just jot down the name of the supplier, the name of the item, and its price on a handy index card or Post-It™ When you get your whole list together, then you can turn to the index and highlight or underline the companies you intend to contact. Stick the card you were taking notes on in the index and go your merry way. When you are ready to sit down and send away for catalogs, or to call up and order, all the addresses are in one convenient location and you have all the item names and prices handy, too. And you can always find any item whose review you want to reread by turning to the General Index.

The information in *The Big Book of Home Learning* is as current and up to date as we could possibly make it. After the reviews were written, both they and the index information were sent back to the suppliers for verification. Even so, *it is always wise to write or call the supplier to check on prices before ordering.* The prices in this book are included to help you compare different products for value and are not permanently guaranteed. Prices go up and down. Too, you will sometimes have to add state tax (depending on whether you and the supplier are in the same state or not, or whether the supplier has additional offices in your state). Both you and the supplier will feel better if the supplier does not have to return your order because the check you enclosed was not for the right amount.

The four volumes of this third edition of *The Big Book of Home Learning* are not only bigger than the two volumes of the previous edition; we hope they are better as well. Over some product reviews you will see the heading, "**NEW****." This means you are looking at a new *review,* not necessarily a new product. We decided to highlight the new reviews in this way, so that readers of previous editions can immediately turn to the new items. Products that have undergone significant revision, or whose reviews have been significantly expanded, are also highlighted as "updated" or "improved." Product reviews that are essentially the same except for new prices have no special headings. All prices and reviews have been updated, and the Suppliers' Index now includes fax numbers and foreign suppliers.

Among the four volumes of this edition, we have several hundred new suppliers and over a thousand new products reviewed. All this is laid out in a way that should make it easy for you to instantly find the resources you need in any school or after-school subject area.

And the best news of all—the products themselves are better! I keep telling you, people, that education suppliers are listening to you! This edition includes products that are better, more colorful, more educa-tionally sound, simpler to use, and even (sometimes) cheaper than ever before.

So if you need to learn more about education, to set up a home education program (whether home school or after-school), or to find out what's happening in packaged home schooling curriculum—turn to Volume One.

If you are looking for resources for a preschooler or elementary-level child in the basic school subjects —turn to Volume Two.

If you need more advanced resources at the junior high, high school, or adult level—you're in the right place right now!

And if you are looking for the resources to round out your family's education, or just want to have some fun—check out Volume Four.

All four volumes have been designed for the everyday, normal reader. I'm assuming that you are no more interested in boring textbooks and tedious worksheets than I am. Since teen and adult courses often are in textbook format, we can't avoid textbooks altogether in this volume, but I have tried to include plenty of non-textbook resources as well. You'll find lots of videos, kits, tapes, games, and magazines mixed in with the workbooks and textbooks!

One last note. This book would not have been possible without the active cooperation of many of the companies listed. Those who supplied me with samples and free catalogs bravely ran the risks of review, and I have not hesitated to point out their products' shortcomings. I would like them to feel they gained more than a critical going-over by their generosity. Both the publisher and I would be grateful if you would mention *The Big Book of Home Learning* when you contact a supplier whose product is mentioned here.

SOUL FOOD

CHAPTER ONE

BIBLE

The teen and adult years are when a person first comes to grips with the big questions in life. "Who am I? Why am I here? Is this life all there is? Why is the world here? What kind of world should it be?"

The Bible has answers. I'm not saying you're necessarily going to *like* the answers, but you ought to know what they are. Our entire civilization was founded on the belief that certain things the Bible said about people and the world were true. Much of the modern elite and its institutions are more or less self-consciously in revolt against these Bible teachings. You're going to be on one side or the other in every area of your life (and *after* your earthly life, according to the Bible) whether you like it or not. Since this is so, doesn't it make sense to find out what you're defending or opposing?

What other reasons can I give you for wanting to study the Bible? Here are a few:

- The Bible is **the world's greatest literature.** By reading it you absorb this rich sentence structure.

- It also stretches your **vocabulary**, helps you practice **spelling**, and tunes you in to noble **language** with honest words for good and evil.

- **Character development:** learn how God's Word applies to everyday life.

- **Philosophy** and **theology:** covered.

- **History:** ancient world history.

- **Cultural studies:** you get to see that late 20th-century America is not all there is, was, or will be!

- The Bible also includes **death education** (would you believe Resurrection Education?), **sex education** (including instructions on what kind of relationships to avoid and how to get out of bad situations—see the book of Proverbs and the behavior of Joseph with Potiphar's wife), and **logic** (see Ecclesiastes, Proverbs, and the book of Job for examples of logical reasoning contrasted with illogical thinking).

- Not to mention instruction in practical **storytelling**, training in **family living,** practice in **persuasion** and **debate**, and piles of other benefits that the poor kids in age-graded curriculum programs will never get to taste until college, if then.

• All this and eternal life, too! What a wonderful book!

DISCOUNT CHRISTIAN BOOK CLUBS

Before we go any further, let me tell you where to get a lot of your Bible study material at BIG discounts. Although you'll want to visit the Christian bookstore to see what's new and just for the fun of shopping in person, often a bookstore won't have a big stock of in-depth Bible programs and other specialized helps. Or, if you live on Rural Route 2 in Outer Limits, Iowa, chances are you don't get in to the bookstore all that often. So here, for your pocketbook's pleasure, are not one but *two* sources for thousands of topflight Christian materials at up to 90 percent off!

Christian Book Distributors
Annual membership of $5 entitles you to 6 bimonthly catalogs and 6 Members' Newsletters offering additional savings off the catalog prices.

CBD offers a wide range of Christian books written from various theological perspectives, including evangelical, Arminian, conservative, and liberal works. You can get discounts of 20 to 90 percent on over 5,000 titles from 70 publishers, including major sets necessary for the library of every serious Bible student, plus Christian records, cassettes, and CDs. Wide selection of Bibles, Christian bestsellers, youth ministry, and counseling books, all also at discount. First quality books. "Speedy shipping and helpful service." You don't need to be a member to order.

Great Christian Books
$5 for one-year membership (U.S.), $8 (Canada/Mexico), $12 (overseas). Every time you buy, it's automatically extended one year from that date.

GCB changed my life. Bill and I were new Christians, unsteady on our feet, and unable to find a bookstore that had anything but frothy testimonies and Christian cookbooks. (There are many fine Christian bookstores, but we were living in a spiritually deprived neighborhood.) Enter GCB. All of a sudden we had a selection of thousands of the finest Christian books, both classic and modern, at greatly discounted prices. We joined, we read, we learned.

GCB also has a wide selection of Christian music on CDs and cassettes. More, they also have hundreds of children's books. Even more, you can get commen-

taries and books on Hebrew and Greek, plus Bible study aids. Plus the new line of home schooling books and workbooks—name brands like A Beka and Christian Life Workshops, all at discount. This is a great book service to join if you buy any of the above on a regular basis.

Super fast delivery, 5,000 titles, and great prices.

BIBLE VERSIONS

The first hurdle for would-be Bible students to conquer is the alphabet soup of Bible translations. KJV. NIV. RSV. NASB. NKJV. What *are* these strange acronyms?

In the beginning was the KJV (King James Version, named after King James of England, who authorized its translation). Actually, that wasn't the first English Bible, but since Wycliffe's translations and the other versions that informed the KJV went out of print around 1600 A.D., the KJV is the oldest version available today. (We can't count the recent reissue of the original Geneva Bible— the Pilgrims' favorite version—because the publisher messed it up by including some strange new introductory matter that, among other things, appears to sanction polygamy and dwells graphically upon the supposed sexual excesses of King James. Weird!) Next was the ASV (American Standard Version), the NASB (New American Standard Bible), and the RSV (Revised Standard Version). Fast coming on as the evangelical's favorite Bible is the NIV (New International Version), followed by the NKJV (New King James Version). And of course there are the various paraphrases, such as the *Living Bible* and *Good News for Modern Man*. Time fails me to speak of the study Bibles, color-coded Bibles, chronological Bibles . . .

Some people like to make a big deal about the KJV as the only God-inspired translation, while all other translations supposedly are based on faulty Greek texts and humanistic reasoning. I can see their point about the mistranslations in the modern versions—I've found enough of them myself. There's good sense in at least keeping a KJV around, and checking any obvious differences between its version and what another translation says against the original languages. The KJV is also easier to memorize, because of its marvelous, ringing diction and the odd (and therefore memorable) words it uses. We still use the NIV extensively, though, because although it may not be the best translation, it's the world's most accurate Bible story book!

For those who struggle with the old English in the KJV, the New King James Version is a not-altogether-successful attempt to bridge the gap between the classic KJV and modern English. This job was actually done better 150 years ago, as you can see from the writeup below.

NEW★★
Baker Book House
Webster's Bible, $29.95.

In 1833 Noah Webster, the famed American orator and schoolbook-writer, came out with his own edition of the KJV. Webster's Bible was different in three ways from the KJV:

(1) He substituted more up-to-date words for archaic words and words that had changed in meaning.

(2) He organized and standardized the grammar.

(3) He euphemized certain phrases having to do with nursing, childbirth, and elimination of body wastes.

The 10-page introduction to *Webster's Bible* lists every change Webster made, so you can check them for accuracy. Looking these over, my personal opinion is that, like Dan'l Boone, Webster never missed his target. I am not quite so happy about the euphemisms, which actually eliminate some meaning while they seek to eliminate cultural embarrassment. Happily, the euphemisms are few and far between, and each is listed in the introduction, so you can always pencil the originals back into the text if you so desire.

The Baker Book House revival of *Webster's Bible* is a facsimile edition that, like the original, features center notes and smallish print. It looks and sounds even more like a KJV than the New King James Version put out by Thomas Nelson Publishers.

HOW TO TEACH BIBLE

NEW★★
Teaching Home
December 1987, $3.75. Complete six-issue set of 1987 back issues, $17.50, includes free set of 6 plastic magazine holders for your ring binder.

Each *Teaching Home* magazine back issue on a given topic is like a minicourse in teaching that topic. December 1987 the topic was "Bible." It was a "wow" issue, too, with articles on teaching toddlers, Bible memory for little ones, Bible storytelling, Bible study, Bible learning software, two excellent articles by Ruth Beechick and Jonathan Lindvall on how and why to memorize Scripture, children's devotions, increasing your spiritual life, using the Bible as a reader (they did this for 200 years in America), and the Bible and academics. Deep.

BIBLE TIME LINES, CHARTS, & MAPS

Good Things Company
Adam and Eve Family Tree: cassette tapes, $9.50; paper chart, $14.50; laminated chart, $19.50. All prices postpaid.

The Adam and Eve Family Tree is a colorful wall poster that shows who was related to whom and what they were up to for all of Bible history until Christ, plus giving selected Scripture references for further study. Talk about genealogical research! The chart is accurate and easy to use, and will provide hours of educational browsing for any Bible lover. And it's so handy to have a *laminated* chart which the little folks can't shred before they're old enough to appreciate it!

The chart comes in both laminated and plain paper styles, both colorful and very beautiful. You can also get a tape that explains how to use it.

NEW✶✶
Heritage Products, Inc.
The Bible Overview Chart, $5.95. Add $1.50 shipping.

The *Bible Overview Chart* is full-color, 25½ x 11", printed on card stock and laminated on both sides. It folds to 8½ x 11" so you can carry it with your Bible for ready reference. It provides a bird's-eye view of the entire Bible, with a ton of information in an easy-to-follow format. For each book, the chart has a mini map above the time line, color-keyed to the time line itself. The name of the Bible book is on the time line, with its general content, chapter numbers, chapter content, special map references, significant events highlighted, book's author, place of writing, and more! This is not all jumbled together, but presented visually in a way that a seven-year-old can understand. At this price, almost everyone can afford this wonderful resource.

KONOS
Bible characters time line figures $59.95. Add 10% shipping.

KONOS takes a different approach, focusing on Bible characters rather than Bible books. Lots and lots of colorful laminated Bible figures to cut out and staple to a wall time line, each labeled with name and date and carrying a symbol of his or her historical role. Ancestors of Jesus wear a gold cross; kings have crowns; prophets have a staff; Jonah has his big fish (looks suspiciously like a whale!). Lots of fun if you like to cut things out. Requires a long wall—great for Christian schools and Sunday school classrooms.

NEW✶✶
Lion Publishing
Bible Mapbook, $9.95. Add $2 shipping.

In *Bible Mapbook* by Simon Jenkins, bold, primary colors and dramatic graphics are used to create geographical "pictures" of Bible stories. Graphics include uncluttered maps with arrows, computer-generated topographical maps, and graphs.

Bible Mapbook will help those of us who lose track of the comings and goings of armies, the "going ups" and "going downs," and who have trouble figuring out whether they are going up north or going uphill. Bible verses or summaries of Biblical events accompany the illustrations, along with occasional commentary to further clarify events. To keep the maps from getting clut-

tered and confusing, each Biblical event has its own illustration, arranged in chronological/Biblical order.

We have used this 128-page paperback book over and over for both adult and children's Bible studies because it provides geographical information in a way that can be quickly and easily comprehended. The combination of maps and commentary increases our level of understanding beyond where we would be when reading the Bible alone. Recommended for about fourth grade through adult levels.—Cathy Duffy

NEW✶✶
Marcine Bice
Christian Life Plan architectural diagram with Bible verses. Poster, 19 x 25", plus Scripture Schedule, $7.50. Personal chart, $3.50. Study Guide, $2.50. Free shipping.

Ever wonder how to explain to the kids what the Christian life is all about? I bet you never thought of using an architectural blueprint to help in this task! No, it's not as crazy as it sounds. In fact, it's really clever and neat.

Marcine Bice, a creative Christian if there ever was one, has come up with a way to literally walk through the Bible's main teachings about the Christian life, using the metaphor of a building plan. Each architectural feature is numbered, with a corresponding Bible verse on the side of the drawing. Example: you enter through the narrow gate (Matt. 7:13-14). Continuing, you pass through the door (John 10:9—Jesus's saying "I am the door; by Me, if any man enter in, he shall be saved."). In the foyer is a fruit tree, which immediately conjures up the verse about the "fruit of the spirit." You learn more on your way through the living room, fellowship area, dining room, kitchen, and many more rooms and then pass out onto the property, where you visit the lily garden, fountain, bed of spices, pasture, white-unto-harvest field, and so on.

An unforgettable miraculous mystery tour!

Marcine's original plan was simply to offer the oversized blueprint, which you could put up on the wall. After looking at the first version of this product, I suggested that it would also help to have the *Christian Life Plan* shrunk down to a size that is easier to manage when teaching children. So at present, Marcine is offering:

- A 19 x 25" blueprint poster, with the Scriptures on a separate normal-sized sheet of paper. This will make it possible to quiz family members about the verses associated with the building.

- A 10 x 14" personal chart.

- A study guide giving tips for studying the verses and using the plan, and further activities.

BIBLE MEMORY FOR TEENS AND ADULTS

NEW★★
Bible Memory Association
$8/person, with a maximum of $25/family of 4 or more. Deadline to sign up for the January course is November 15; for the May course, April 1; for the September course, August 1.

I know some of you out there have used BMA materials since you were that high—with over 700,000 users since 1944, BMA is not exactly the new kid on the block. But judging by the number of churches who have *no* systematic memory program for either adults or children, the good word could be spread a mite further.

The list of BMA features goes on and on:

- **A Bible memory plan for each age.** Each memory book is divided into 15 assignments, each with its own introduction and explanatory notes. Elementary ages have up to two verses per week; preteens learn three verses per week; teens and weakminded adults like you and me get four. Those who want to tackle an entire book of the New Testament (James, 1 John, 1 Peter, Philippians, and Ephesians are available) learn 7–11 verses per week.

- **Specific requirements and accountability.** Which verses to memorize, when they must be learned, who will check you on your recitation,

and how many errors are allowed are all spelled out in advance. Unlike other disciplines where it makes sense to "go at your own pace," memorization works best when it is systematic and structured. You will know exactly what to do when, *and* when you have done enough.

- **Family memory plans** for families that like to study together. Everyone memorizes the same verses; adults and older children get longer portions. There are three family series, each with a book for children 6–12, a book for youth, and a book for adults. The three series are: Wisdom for Daily Living, Life of Christ, and Our Wonderful God.

- **You can earn a large discount off the price of BMA camp** at one of six North American locations by completing your memory course inside of the twelve months preceding May 31 of any year! This means that a week of camp in 1991 cost as little as $79 per person. Campers must be nine years old or accompanied by parents (yes, BMA has family camp).

- **Prizes for completing memory work.** BMA's *Reward Catalog* lists hundreds of Bibles, coloring books, puzzles, Christian books, posters, and so on. You can pay for these with reward certificates (one certificate is earned per completed assignment) or with cash. *Caution:* some of the newer books feature "slice of life" situations that home-schooled kids don't really need.

- **Doctrinal thoroughness.** The BMA memory plans cover all the basics of salvation, Christian living, and doctrine, without getting into denominational sticky wickets.

- **Depth.** Each memory booklet explains and applies the verses. You go beyond memory to understanding.

How it works: You sign up yourself and/or the kids for a memory course. You select a supervisor who will hear Bible verse recitations (this can be you, in the case of a home-schooling family). Deadline to sign up for the January course is November 15; for the May course, April 1; for the September course, August 1. For the January course, enrollments can be entered up until a month after the deadline date, but fees are increased for late enrollment. You choose which plan you will work on (preschool, beginner, intermediate, youth, adult, family, basic book . . .). Enclose your check, and BMA will send you the memory books, reward certificates, and *Reward Catalog*. BMA provides two scheduling options. Using option one, you memorize one assignment per week for 15 weeks. Option two spreads the 15 assignments over 30 weeks with six more weeks for review, making up a typical 36-week school year.

All BMA memory verses are in the King James Version. The Family Plan books will have card packs with verses printed from the New American Standard Bible and New International Version—available soon!

NEW✱✱
Bob Jones University Press
Two-Edged Sword Memory Program, $15.25/all four volumes or $4 each. Shipping extra.

This Bible memory plan, developed by evangelist Jerry Sivnksty (yes, that's how he spells his name), comes in four topical booklets, each with 130 Bible verses. The booklets are completely independent of each other. Booklet 1 has verses for daily living, booklet 2 has verses about character traits, booklet 3 is for Bible doctrine, and booklet 4 has verses about Christian family life. Each booklet has 26 subjects, with five verses in each subject. If you are using the plan at home, the author suggests that you memorize verses during 26 weeks of the year and review or meditate upon them for the remaining 26. Naturally, he means that you would learn verses one week and review them the next, not that you would take half a year off from Bible memory!

Verses are well chosen, and the booklets include little boxes where you can check off your reviewing.

Verses are supposed to be reviewed daily for five days, then monthly thereafter. All verses are from the King James Version.

NEW✱✱
Church Resource Ministries
Memlok™ Bible Memory System, $39.95 plus $4.50 shipping. Shipping for additionals, $2 each. Pocket cardholder, $3. Ages 4–adult.

Memlok is an exciting new approach to topical Bible memorization based on flash cards with pictures symbolizing the first words of each verse. For example, the front of the card might say, "SOVEREIGNTY. John 1:22." Under this is a picture of an outline "F" with an eye in it. When you turn over the card, you find the verse is, "If I want him to remain until I come, what is that to you? You follow Me!"

As opposed to other visual memory systems, Memlok does not try to present an entire verse in pictures. This means less strain on your brain (in my opinion), and avoids the problem of associating Bible teaching with silly mental images. You are asked to spend only five minutes a day for five days a week, learning one new verse a week. The author calls this a "long range — low pressure" system. By the end, you will have memorized verses from every New Testament chapter, Old Testament book, and every chapter of the book of Proverbs. Memlok is the only topical system I know about that has such complete Bible coverage.

You select your own verses from 48 topics totalling 700 verses. Each topic has an illustrated summary card with a kooky sentence made up of the beginning illustrations from each of the memory verses. All the cards and summary cards are included in the binder in pre-perfed pages of 12 cards per page. Also included are instructions in how to use Memlok, a sample contract of accountability to use with a memory partner, a completion record, memory tips, a complete alphabetical and topical index of all the verses, a plastic Weekly Cardholder with pockets for the cards you are currently learning, five plastic Monthly Cardholders for cards you are reviewing, and of course the cards themselves! The cards are printed on sturdy cardstock, professionally illustrated, and look really sharp.

I am really impressed with Memlok. The packaging is really great, and the cards are kid-appealing. Available in KJV, NIV, and NASB versions. Recommended.

NEW**
The Home Educator
Book by Book, $5 postpaid. Ages 5–adult.

I had planned on coming up with a product like this, but now I don't have to! Brent Allan Winters, a home-schooling dad, has put together a spiral-bound, desktop-published book with themes and key verses from every book of the Bible. By systematically working through this book, your family will gain a bird's-eye view of the entire Bible.

How does it work? Here's an example: the theme and key verse from the book of 2 Samuel.

Theme: The Reason for David's Success
II Samuel 23:3
"The God of Israel said, the Rock of Israel spake to me, He that ruleth over men must be just, ruling in the fear of God."

This isn't too complicated, is it?

Looking through this book, I see that Brent has done a really good job of choosing themes and key verses. I recognize several that my Old Testament prof in seminary used for key verses, proving that great minds think alike. Most verses are from the KJV; three are from the NIV. You, of course, can substitute key verses of your own choosing here and there, as he points out.

Brent has both the M.Div. and Th.M. from Biola University, among other degrees. His majors were Old and New Testament Exegesis. (Just in case you're impressed by such things!)

It's so important to make sure we have an overall view of the Bible before we start narrowly focusing on individual topical verses. Before starting any of the fancier programs in this section, why not try this one? Recommended.

NEW**
The Ten Commandments
Ten Commandments memory sheets; contribution appreciated but not required.

Quick! Name five of the Ten Commandments! They can be in any order. I'll wait . . .

If you're like most people, you had trouble with this assignment. Since the late '50s, when the Supreme Court decided free speech rights didn't apply to God, most American children have grown up never knowing God's simplest rules for people. Now these life-changing rules can be at your fingertips, *without* tedious memorizing! You'll know them in any order, and you'll remember which Commandment is which!

WHAT YOU GET: A set of 10 Ten Commandment sheets, plus one for your personal use. Each lists an abbreviated version of the Commandments on the front, with the unique visualized memory helps on the back. These use pictures associated with numerals to help you remember the Commandments. The pack comes with an introductory page explaining how to use the sheets, and a set of pledge forms people can sign if they get serious about learning and passing on the Ten Commandments.

NEW**
Visual Education Association
Selected Bible Verses, $7.95. Shipping extra.

For those who want the world's most inexpensive, bare-bones Bible memory approach, Visual Education Association's "Selected Bible Verses" flash card set is 1,000 cards with verses from the KJV in the order they appear in the Bible. Each card has book, chapter, and verse number on the front, as well as the topical category, and the verse itself on the back. You also get a pamphlet with study hints and verses by category. The verses are well-chosen; this is a fine resource for parents who believe in teaching key verses from each Bible book. It works equally well as a mini Biblical theology on cards. Work through the cards to get an overview of all the major Bible doctrines that is not prescreened to leave out half the Bible books.

BIBLE COURSES

Here are some questions to ask when shopping for a Bible course.

- Is it **complete**?

- Does it have **depth** and **thoroughness**?

- Does the program **challenge you to grow spiritually**?

- Is it **easy to understand**? Is the teaching systematic? Does one thing follow another in logical sequence, or does the curriculum hop, skip, and jump all over the place? Is the program designed to help you remember the lessons . . . or do the authors simply throw a lot of unorganized data at you?

- **Is preaching substituted for teaching**? Do the curriculum designers prefer to sermonize about, say, the need to avoid drugs rather than to tell us what the difficult words in the Bible passage mean? Are you taught how to handle Scripture study tools like concordances and given a systematic outline of Bible history? Are you given an understanding of Bible cultures (Hebrew, Egyptian, Assyrian, Canaanite, Philistine, Babylonian, Greek, Roman, New Testament Jewish . . .) and a workable Bible memory program? Or does an unbalanced appeal solely to the emotions replace solid teaching for the intellect?

- Does it **trivialize the sacred**? Often Bible courses for teens, in an attempt to be clever or relevant, focus more interest on an activity than on the person or doctrine supposedly being taught. I think,

for example, of the cutesy idea of having students write modern-day news reports about Jesus' birth or other biblical events. Game-show formats, "interviews" with Bible characters, and other such activities all tend to trivialize the Bible's message. Should prophets of God, before whom kings trembled, be reduced to interview subjects for laughing 13-year-olds? (I seem to recall that a gang of irreverent youth once got into serious trouble for taking a prophet—Elisha—lightly.)

The main purpose of Bible teaching is to provide us with enough *understanding* of the Word of God so that the Holy Spirit, through His appointed means of preaching and meditation, can apply it to our hearts.

At home, we parents don't need a load of sermons in workbook form as much as we need resources for sharing the vast amount of *information* in the Bible with our children. Before we go flying off into the air with all kinds of great applications of Scripture, we have to know what the Bible *says*. Seminaries today are forced to provide remedial Bible classes for men who have graduated from Bible college and attended Sunday school all their lives—all because of this overeagerness to get to the preaching and the application before children even know Hosea from Joshua. You don't want this to happen to your family!

Here's what we really need in a Bible curriculum:

- **Chronological knowledge** of Bible events. This includes some understanding of the cultural framework of these events, which the Bible itself readily supplies.

- **Book-by-book knowledge** of what is in the Bible, so you can find your way around in it.

- Knowledge of how to **understand** the Bible (exegesis), how to **apply** its teachings, and **which teaching applies to which situation**. The Bible calls this "wisdom" and says only those who belong to God and practice what they already know of His commandments ever achieve it.

- Knowledge of **the basic Bible teachings** about God, man, sin, redemption, creation, eternity, the meaning of life, etc. We all know what the world teaches about such things. Trust me, the Bible says something different.

The following complete programs are designed to take you through entire books of the Bible, or the whole Bible itself. See how successful they are—or aren't—in the reviews below!

NEW**
A Beka Book Publications
Exodus, Life of Christ, Paul's Missionary Journeys flannel map studies, $18 each. Teacher's kits, $40.45 each. Old Testament, New Testament Bible Survey kits, $17.90 each. Add 10% shipping (minimum $3.25).

A Beka Books, a prominent Christian textbook publisher, has a complete Bible curriculum lineup for nursery school through twelfth grade.

Some noteworthy items: The Junior-High Map Journeys include flannel maps accompanied by removable symbols, labels, and figures, and packed with a lesson guide. Each has a different flannel map. The teacher's kits for the flannel map programs include flannel map, review questions, and teacher's guide.

Intended for grades 11 and 12, A Beka's Bible Survey curriculum covers the whole Bible in two courses. The teacher's kits include a student worktext and teacher's guide.

UPDATED**
Alpha Omega Publications
Bible LIFEPACS, $2.75–$2.95 each or $24.95–$26.95/set of 10 (one course). Bible teacher handbooks, $4.95 per grade. Answer keys, $2.25 each (two per course). LIFEPAC test key (included with teacher handbook), $2.25/course. Shipping extra.

Alpha Omega courses come packaged as sets of 10 "LIFEPAC" workbooks, each with quizzes and tests built in. The first nine LIFEPACS in each course present the material, while the tenth reviews it. Frequent teacher checkpoints in each LIFEPAC indicate where adult feedback is required. Often this is no more complicated than simply checking to make sure the student has done (and understood) the work. Students are

taught to use the SQ3R study method—scan, question, read, recite, and review. In addition, each course includes discussion questions and writing and research assignments, for which you generally need the teacher handbooks.

Alpha Omega's Bible course for grades 1–12 contains seven major themes, each presented from a conservative evangelical perspective: Christian Growth, Theology Themes, Attributes of God, Christian Evidence, Bible Literature, Bible Geography and Archaeology, and Special Themes. All Alpha Omega's products encourage thought—there is little rote fill-in-the-blanks. Each grade ends with a summary unit, in which all the themes covered are gone over once more.

Grade 7 topics include: worship (its meaning, object, and reasons; worship in New and Old Testament times; and standard evangelical thinking on how to do it, featuring prayer, praise, testimonies, Bible reading, preaching, and the Lord's supper as the components of worship, along with teaching against the use of images); the nature and mission of mankind; God's attributes of love, mercy, and grace; prophecies about Christ's advent and offices; "Living the Balanced Life," a unit on personal piety; a study of the book of Psalms; and three units on the life of Christ. Standard evangelical doctrine throughout, combined with vocabulary and word-study emphasis.

Grade 8 studies the following: prayer (Christ's teaching on prayer, how Bible people prayed, types and content of biblical prayer, the results of prayer, how and why God can know what you're going to ask ahead of time and still want you to pray); doctrines of sin and salvation (standard evangelical); God's attributes of justice, immutability, eternity, and love; church leaders from the early church to the Reformation; early church history; a study of the book of Proverbs; "Understanding Today's Problems," a title under which are grouped drug use, developing friendships, and finding God's will; and "Understanding Parents" (learning to be part of the family team).

Grade 9 surveys the entire New Testament, beginning with background historical and geographical information. The Bible survey units are serious, information-packed, and well organized. The Bible literature theme for this grade is "suffering," so you also get into the book of Job and the sufferings of Christ. One whole LIFEPAC is devoted to how-to evangelism tips, while another covers "God's will for my life," especially how to discover your calling.

Grade 10 is an Old Testament survey. As you can expect, this takes the entire year, with no room for anything else. Written by different authors than the New Testament survey in grade 9, the grade 10 course is somewhat less down-to-earth. You get lots of information, but the important information isn't separated as successfully from the merely interesting as in grade 9.

Grade 11 devotes the first LIFEPAC to a study of God's faithfulness. This is followed by a two-LIFEPAC study of the book of Romans, including its historical and geographical background. Next come units on the person and work of Jesus Christ, the historic nation of Israel (including significant archaeological discoveries), and the history of the biblical canon. One LIFEPAC covers friendship, dating, and marriage—a sequence *not* found in the Bible. The next, on "the pursuit of happiness," examines what the book of Ecclesiastes has to say on this subject. Finally, a unit on apologetics explains how to answer agnostics' questions about the Bible's integrity and doctrines. The theological and biblical units in this grade are roughly equivalent to what you could expect from introductory seminary courses in those areas, lacking only the outside source reading assignments from published theologians that seminaries require of their students in order to please the accreditation committees. (I personally don't know anyone who ever found those outside reading assignments terribly beneficial, but supplemental titles and a teacher's bibliography for each section *are* included in the teacher's handbook, for those who like to work harder than they have to!)

Grade 12 leads off with a unit on "knowing yourself" as body, soul, and spirit, particularly emphasizing how to recognize your temperament, spiritual gifts, and vocational skills. Next on the docket is "knowing about Christian ministries," including both career and non-career ministries, and "making your choice of a Christian ministry." After this comes a unit on the doctrine of the Trinity, and another on God's holiness and goodness. The book study is the epistle of James. The Bible literature study is the book of Daniel. A comparative religions unit examines Buddhism, Confucianism, Hinduism, Islam, and Zoroastrianism, with a complete subunit on the occult, including spiritualism, astrology, and a rather vague and unhelpful description of psychic phenomena which gives it credence as "the power of the human mind" and never makes it clear whether it's OK or not. New Age religion as such is not studied. The unit "Wisdom for Today's Youth" looks at David and Solomon, the Psalms and Proverbs, and "the Bible and literature." The whole 12 years of this series are wrapped up by the last LIFEPAC, "Practical Christian Living for Young Adults." Its subtopics include: funda-

mentals of the Christian faith, spiritual growth techniques, and influencing the world for Christ through your life, ministry, and testimony.

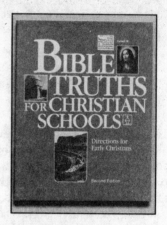

NEW★★
Bob Jones University Press
Teacher's editions, $36.50 each. Student worktexts, $7.95 each. Teacher's edition includes a usable student text. Wall chart for each level, $3.95 each. Shipping extra.

BJUP's secondary Bible education program comes in six levels (A–F), corresponding to grade levels 7–12. Coordinated with each level is a 21 x 35" two-color wall chart.

Level A (grade 7) is "Learning from the Life of Christ." The wall chart is an amplified time line of the life of Christ. Level B (grade 8), "Portraits from the Old Testament," concentrates on role models from this time period. The wall chart for level B is a parallel timetable covering developments in Bible lands during Old Testament times. Level C (grade 9), "Lessons from the Early Church," covers Acts and the early Pauline epistles, with (what else?) a map of the journeys of Paul as the wall chart for this level. Level D (grade 10), "Themes from the Old Testament," introduces principles of Bible interpretation. The wall chart for level D summarizes the Old Testament books. Level E (grade 11), "Directions for Early Christians" covers the remaining New Testament books verse by verse or thematically, depending on which book is being discussed. For this level the wall chart is a table summarizing the New Testament books. Finally, "Patterns for Christian Living," is the level F (grade 12) book. It takes a topical look at major Bible teachings under the two themes of "Loving God Completely" and "Loving My Neighbor As Myself." The level F wall chart is a summary of "fundamental doctrines."

NEW★★
Christian Schools International

Teacher's guides, $36.75 each grade. Student texts, $7.65 each grade except grades 6–8 student texts, which are $15.25 hardbound or $9.80 paperbound. Optional grade 6–8 student workbooks, $6.25 each. Add 12% shipping on orders over $25, $3.50 on orders up to $25. Grades K–8.

The people at Christian Schools International are very excited about their new preschool–grade 8 Bible curriculum, *The Story of God and His People*. Organized chronologically, rather than by Bible themes, and using a historical-literary approach rather than a topical "preaching" approach, it covers the Bible as a whole five times and dips into every book in the Bible at least once. Over 1,600 classroom Bible teachers provided input to this project, which has a strong "covenantal" emphasis.

The Story of God and His People uses the same lesson format from grade to grade but changes the type of lesson activities as students grow older. Each lesson includes a short title summarizing the theme of the Bible passage, a Bible reference, lesson objectives, and list of preparation and materials required. In addition, some lessons have memory work, songs, or background information.

The grades 6–8 courses are quite advanced, covering such things as archaeology (grade 6), intertestamental times (grade 7), and early church history (grade 8). This gets quite graphic, as in the Babylonian account of creation and the flood included in the grade 6 book, and the Albrecht Durer engraving of a naked Adam and Eve with only their genital areas (and not even all their genital hair) covered by two convenient leaves. Although the tone of these books is clearly addressed to teens, the content is right up there with seminary courses I have taken. In these grades students have their own textbooks and optional student workbook, while the teacher's guide is an expanded edition of the student text.

You have to have the teacher's guides to use this program. The student activity books (which are very good, by the way) make no sense without them.

As far as user format goes, this is an excellent program. The spiral-bound teacher's guides are well-organized, graphically clear, and easy to use.

The overall tone is relaxed and bland; you won't find a lot of heart-searing fiery applications or salvation appeals. Students are more likely to be soothed than awed by the Bible as it is presented here.

NEW★★
Covenant Home Curriculum

Doré Bible Pictorial Briefings, $19.95. Copy of *Doré Bible Illustrations* included for $9.95 additional. Add $1.50 shipping. Grades 5–10.

Covenant Home Curriculum is a full-service K–12 home-school curriculum provider with a Reformed bent. Their materials tend to be innovative, beautiful, and thought-provoking, and the new *Doré Bible Pictorial Briefings* are no exception.

You might recognize the name of Gustave Doré. His famous etchings of Bible scenes made the 1860 Doré Bible, which featured these etchings, a financial success. The *Pictorial Briefings* are four-page (8½ x 11") booklets, each with a Doré Bible illustration on the cover. Inside are comments on the illustration, Scripture references, questions based on the illustration, and further questions based on the passage. Example, from the "Creation of Light" booklet:

The eye > What is the focal point of the picture?

The eye focuses first on the light source coming from behind the angry clouds. It then follows the rays and draws down to the surface of the earth. Finally, it circles up into the dark, turbulent clouds, completing a counter-clockwise rotation.

The emotions > Does the bright light convey the idea of great power? Is there something in the clouds that causes you to feel the energy and brooding of the Spirit of God? Do you sense the anticipation in the scene?

1. Why did the artist make the clouds dark and foreboding? . . .

6. Make a list showing the order in which everything was created.

7. Do a word study tracking the word "light" through a book, such as the Psalms. Note all the usages of this key word.

Doré's illustrations are powerful, make no mistake about that. As Dale Dykema, the *Pictorial Briefings* author, says,

Many of the themes which he capably executes are those which are avoided or ignored by modern day Christian teachers and illustrators. The glorious judgments of God upon the disobedient and upon His enemies is one. His awesome vindication of His people is another. . . . These are prominent themes in the Doré drawings. . . . The disarming insights made obvious in many of the pictures by Doré are not the typical fare of religious art today.

The first set of *Doré Pictorial Bible Briefings* includes *The Creation of Light, The Formation of Eve, Adam and Eve Driven Out of Eden, Cain and Abel, The Death of Abel, The Deluge, Noah Cursing Canaan, The Confusion of Tongues, The Flight of Lot, The Trial of Abraham's Faith, Eliezer and Rebekah, Isaac Blessing Jacob, Jacob Wrestling with the Angel, Joseph Sold by His Brethren, Joseph Interpreting Pharaoh's Dream, Joseph Makes Himself Known to His Brethren, The Firstborn Slain, The Egyptians Drowned in the Red Sea, Moses Coming Down from Mt. Sinai, Moses Breaking the Tables of the Law,* and *The Brazen Serpent.* Other sets are in production. These are likely to include one on the period of the Judges and another on the Old Testament prophets and kings.

These sets are very easy to use and an excellent choice for an intellectual, artistically-minded student.

NEW**
Donald and Mary Baker
Bible Study Guide for All Ages, four volumes, $19.95/volume. Add 15% shipping if order is under $50, 10% if over $50. Ages 5–adult.

This program literally does work for all ages, from preschool on up. Each volume of this four-volume program provides a full year of Bible study material for the entire family, if you have two lessons a week. Together, the four volumes cover the entire Bible.

Each lesson includes drill work (e.g., practicing saying the 10 Commandments), review of important questions from previous lessons, seven questions on the Bible chapter for this lesson (you read the chapter aloud), a song, an applicable Bible verse for meditation or memorization, prayer time, and a visual. Some

lessons also have an Additional Scriptures section, with a few verses to read from other sections of the Bible that help explain the passage of the day, and/or an According to the Dictionary section that explains unusual words or customs occurring in the passage. Map work is also included where appropriate. All this is on *just one page for each lesson,* making it super easy to use.

Already this program towers head and shoulders above all others for sheer usefulness. Find me another program that the whole family, from preschooler to Grandpa, can study together at once, let alone one where the entire lesson is so well organized it fits on one page! But there's more. Each volume of *Bible Study Guide for All Ages* also includes all sorts of visual-aid cutouts, flap pages, and drawings, plus literally dozens of suggested Bible games to help pep up your lessons, and (this is what excites me the most) complete plans for an incredibly useful Bible time line and wall map that your kids can both put together and test themselves with. Plus you even get the cutouts to put on the time line! All for (hold your breath) $19.95 per volume!

The program moves back and forth between sections of the Old and New Testaments, with review lessons providing natural transitions. This means you don't have to wait forever to teach your children about Jesus, and since the segments are organized logically—e.g., "Divided and Conquered Kingdoms"—your children won't get confused.

There's no written work required at all for this program—another plus in the eyes of many of us. Designed originally for use in family study times, it is infinitely adaptable to any number of individual or group situations for Bible students of all ages. On a scale of 1 to 100, I give this one a 100.

NEW**
Judah Bible Curriculum
Bible Curriculum Pack, includes teacher training audiocassettes in binder and Curriculum Document, $49.95 plus 10% shipping. Ages 10–18.

The Principle Approach is popping up everywhere these days. This is the first Bible curriculum for school-age children I have seen that uses it.

For the benefit of the uninitiated, the Principle Approach is a method of study based on what some modern researchers say is the way Americans used to study in the early days of the colonies and Republic. It emphasizes a providential view of history (God as the agent making things happen), a "dominion" emphasis

(God's purposes shall prevail on this earth), and the development of student character, especially self-discipline, through a rigorous program of study and creating notebooks.

As this applies to Bible study, Judah Bible Curriculum students are supposed to record in a notebook all the findings they have researched. This finished notebook is supposed to be a model of neatness and organization, not to mention deep thinking. Students are given questions to answer and a way of recording information that forces them to think through Bible principles for themselves.

The curriculum is now in process of revision. I haven't seen the final version, so let's look at the original edition. It consisted of the curriculum document and a set of eight teacher-training audiocassettes in a cassette binder. The cassettes included a curriculum overview (pretty much the same thing said in the document), a cassette on "How God Changes Nations," another on "Internal Government: Creation–Flood," one on "Internal Government: Abraham–Malachi," one on "Internal Government: Matthew–Revelation," one on "Internal Government: Pentecost–Present," a cassette on the unique methods used in the curriculum, and one entitled "Personal Destiny—Studying the Life of Joseph."

The tapes featured an Arminian, as opposed to Calvinist, outlook. The speaker stressed that God has "overall superintendency" over what happens rather than actually causing everything directly to happen. The author tells me that the revised material will take a a stronger approach to God's sovereignty.

I was not able to make it through all the tapes before getting out this book, mainly because all the material is covered so *slowly*. The speaker repeats a lot of the material in the document, speaks slowly, takes long pauses, and spends a lot of time retelling Bible history, often quoting great chunks straight out of the Bible. Since I sincerely wanted to get to the heart of the program, I found all this quite frustrating. Happily, the author told me he plans to write up the material in the tapes along with suggestions on what to teach so that you won't need to listen to the tapes, which will then become optional. I hope he will have finished that project by the time you read this.

Bill Burtness, the curriculum's author, believes that *liberty* is the main theme of the Bible. He put it in the title of his curriculum—"Judah Bible Curriculum: Education for Liberty." Heaven is shown as a situation in which everyone is perfectly self-governed under God. Hell is just the opposite; everyone is totally governed from the outside. Here on earth, society wavers between self-government and outside government, depending strictly on how well we govern ourselves. People and nations who refuse to exercise self-control succumb to tyranny. The history of the Jews and the church is seen to be one of moving towards or away from liberty, depending on whether they (we) were (are) following God or not. All the character emphasis of the course is directed towards helping the student become a self-governing individual who then will be empowered to expand his sphere of influence as a godly servant, like Joseph, the curriculum's hero, who ended up ruling the largest empire of his age.

Now, the curriculum document. These three-hole-punched, photocopied pages break the Bible down into five historical periods called "themes." Each theme is broken down into Biblical keys. Bible portions are studied in terms of key individuals, key events, key institutions, and key documents. Each of these keys has a different key sheet on which the student writes all that he could find about that person, place, or thing. For example, the key sheet for Key Institutions has three sections: Doctrinal Base, Character of the People, and Government. Under Doctrinal Base are the words *foundations*, *truths taught as foundational*, and *controlling ideas*. Under Character of the People you find *physical*, *moral disposition*, and *mental disposition*. Under Government are the phrases *manner of controlling men (internal/external)*, *form of civil government*, *constitution/laws*, *how men are directed/controlled*, and *conduct*. Using these topics and subtopics as a guideline, the student researches and fills out his key sheet. If the institution was "Egypt," for example, he might write down, "Idolatry and the worship of Pharaoh as God" as a controlling idea in the Doctrinal Basis column.

Each week of study is grouped around a weekly theme focus. Students read the Scripture passage themselves and analyze the weekly theme focus using the appropriate key sheets. It's up to the teacher to explain how the key people, places, and things fit into God's plan. It's also up to him to come up with assignments like map making, time lines, art and craft projects, and so on that can further bring out the weekly theme. The student puts one or two of these projects in his notebook each week.

A course overview (scope and sequence) and suggested weekly themes guide for all seven years of the course are included.

The course contents are repeated twice between kindergarten and twelfth grade. All five major "themes" (Bible periods) are covered each year, but different individuals and events are studied each time. Sample blank key sheets are also included that you can photocopy in quantity for your students' use. The appendix includes visuals illustrating the concepts outlined on the teacher tapes, plus samples of filled-out key sheets and a Bible time line. The author says he will also be coming out with a *Curriculum Idea Book* of ideas and resources this year.

The Judah Bible Curriculum is a teacher-directed program. You *will* be using the Bible as your textbook, as the ads say. It requires a scholarly mindset and a lot of commitment on the part of both student and teacher. If you are good at teaching and enjoy coming up with creative ways to present things, and creative assignments for your students, you might very well find this a fascinating program.

Moody Correspondence School
Adult credit courses, $17 each. College credit courses, sample prices: Elements of Bible Study (2 credit hours), $165; New Testament Survey (4 hours), $285.

Adult credit courses for intelligent Christians. Many subjects pertaining to the Bible and the Christian life: for instance, "Basic Christian Doctrine," "The Bible Says," "God's Will for Your Life," and "New Testament Survey." You can earn a certificate for completing each series and with perseverance even earn an Adult Bible Certificate.

An A.B.S. (Associate of Bible Studies) is also available to those who take Moody's college correspondence courses. These should not be confused with the adult credit courses; even though some have the same names (e.g., New Testament Survey), the college-credit courses are a lot more work. V.A. will pay for some college-credit courses. Exams must be proctored.

NEW★★
Rod and Staff Publishers
Truth for Life Bible studies program for grades 7 or 8: pupil book, $2.90; teacher's book, $2.95.

Rod & Staff's *Truth for Life* Bible studies course for grades 7 or 8 includes 35 topical lessons covering basic doctrines from a Mennonite perspective, each with discussion questions and activities.

Their latest catalog announces that a new program is being developed to cover the whole Bible chronologically in grades 5–7, plus another whole new Bible curriculum for grades 8–10, so you might want to write for information about these new programs.

NEW★★
Vision Video
The New Media Bible, $29.95 per tape or $99.95 for 4-tape set of Genesis or Luke.

The New Media Bible is an ambitious project. Using only the text of the Bible itself as narration and dialog, it's a reenactment of the Bible books of Genesis and Luke. The people who did this put a lot of effort and cash into trying to make it historically and culturally accurate, and I would have to say that for the most part they have succeeded. Nobody can ever do a really good job of portraying Jesus, of course, and there is one embarrassing scene when the actor portraying Him swirls through the marketplace while preaching. You also don't get any really awesome special effects like you should when miracles are being shown, but aside from such shortcomings this is an intriguing resource that could help you understand Bible events more vividly.

CHRISTIAN HISTORY AND MUSIC

NEW★★
Christian History Magazine
One year (4 issues), $16. Outside USA, add $6.

Forty-page, quarterly magazine for adults. Each issue is devoted to a single historical person, subject, or theme from church history. Topics covered are intriguing, ranging from the history of the Russian church to the Christian doctrine of money. Illustrations, graphics, charts, and other visual aids help bring the topic to life. A variety of articles cover the topic from different angles—although the underlying point of view generally seems to be what you could call "moderate-left-evangelical." (In other words, fundamentalists will find plenty with which to disagree.) Layout has improved a lot over the last few years; now *Christian History* is beginning to look like a quality magazine.

Christianity Today bought *Christian History* in May 1989. Given *Christianity Today*'s penchant for revising church doctrine to fit secular social trends, it's not surprising that *Christian History* tends to present church history from the viewpoint of current accepted secular scholarship, including a certain materialistic outlook and tone of superiority over those supposedly not-as-enlightened Christians of the past. In fact, it's hard to find the Holy Spirit given credit in the pages of this magazine for *anything* Christians have done in the past. The success of Charles Haddon Spurgeon, "the prince of preachers," for example, is attributed to his "uncanny ability to sense the pulse of his times" and his sensational preaching style, rather than to the Holy Spirit's anointing *combined* with those things. His life with his wife, which in many ways was a great example of love, and the fact that they had clearly defined gender roles are attributed solely to their personal temperaments and the times in which they lived. In other words, *Christian History* is saying that the Spurgeons had no doctrinal reason whatsoever for living as they did—and by implication, neither does anyone else living in a traditional one-wife-for-life, single-income family. (Presumably if Spurgeon had lived today, his Mrs. would have done the preaching, or at least had an outside career!)

The very martyrs themselves come in for criticism, as it turns out (according to *Christian History*) that the Roman despots persecuting them were really reasonable men (or, in the words of the magazine, "humane, cautious, prudent, fair, and pious") simply forced into a persecuting role by the wholly unnecessary stubbornness of the Christians. Thus, while the facts and stories in this magazine are fascinating, its point of view is not altogether inspiring.

NEW★★
Inheritance Publications
Church History, $11.90 U.S., $12.95 Canada. Add $1.50 shipping. Ages 13–adult.

Rev. P. K. Keizer (1906–1985) was minister of the Reformed churches of several cities in the Netherlands. Subsequently he served in the "liberated" Reformed Church of Groningen. The liberation occurred as a protest against what the protesters considered unscriptural and illegal actions of Synod during the years of World War II. Without going heavily into Dutch theology, I'll just tell you that the whole thing is explained in the latter part of this book, of which at least two-thirds is devoted to regular church history.

Dr. Keizer also taught church history in high school for many years. His book, *Church History*, shows the fruit of going over the subject again and again, both in its logical outline and in its content. He neither overloads the student nor skips over anything important.

The book is literally outlined, with numbered points, subpoints, and sub-sub points, but all this actually makes it easier to use. The writing is interesting and pious—from a solidly Reformed Protestant viewpoint—and does the teenager the great service of distilling the lives and teachings of many important people in a form he can remember. Take this passage on Erasmus:

> At first Erasmus was sympathetic toward Luther. He loathed the papal control over the consciences of the people, exercised relentlessly with the help of the infamous Inquisition. He therefore regarded the collapse of the medieval world as a liberation; indeed, Erasmus believed that this freedom of conscience would allow man to reach full human development. He was, therefore, an optimistic humanist. The Roman Inquisition did not trust this man who ridiculed the monks and mercilessly satirized the shortcomings of the Roman Catholic church. But Erasmus never left this church. "I am not made of martyr stuff," he said. Luther commented, "He is as smooth as an eel; he wants to walk over eggs and not break any."

Note how the well-chosen quotes from Erasmus and Luther bring out the personalities of each man. Note also how the author is concerned to tell you what is right and wrong, not only what happened. Thus his section on slavery not only describes the practice, but powerfully condemns it, citing Bible chapter and verse, so the student can know *why* slavery was wrong.

Church History covers the time from the resurrection of Christ to the 1980s. From 1795 on, the focus is on the Netherlands (Holland), but before then we visit the gnostics, Marcionites, Edict of Milan, ecumenical councils, Augustine, the Eastern Orthodox Church, the rise and history of the papacy (with attention to Aquinas, Bernard of Clairvaux, and the Cluniac monastic reform, among other things), the Reformation (in Germany, Switzerland, France, Scotland, England, and Netherlands), the Anabaptists and mystics, the Counter Reformation, the Enlightenment, Jansenists, Pietists, and Methodists. These are only about half of the main topics in the main part of the book, giving you an idea of its breadth of coverage. The index helps you find any topic quickly. An excellent resource.

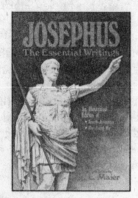

NEW★★
Kregel Publications
Josephus: The Essential Writings, $16.95 hardback.

Seminary students have for hundreds of years been assigned to read two books by the New Testament-age Jewish historian Josephus: his *Jewish Antiquities* and *The Jewish War.* In those two books, Josephus covered the history of the Jewish people from the Creation through his own day, including the part the Bible skips, the Intertestamental period.

The problem with studying Josephus' works has always been their length and the obscure language of some old translations. Now all that has changed! Paul L. Maier, Professor of Ancient History at Western Michigan University, has produced a remarkable new translation, entitled *Josephus: The Essential Writings.* Along with a much more readable text, set in a much more readable typeface, you also get 83 photographs of places and people mentioned in this history (I'm talking about photos of their statues, of course!), 12 maps and illustrations, five charts that explain who

was related to whom, dates of significant events listed in the margins, a bibliography, and a very helpful index. You and your teens can sit down with this book and read it almost as if it were a novel. Which it is—a novel way to increase your understanding of the vital events up to and after the time of Christ.

NEW★★
Kregel Publications
101 Hymn Stories, 101 More Hymn Stories, $9.95 each.

Two absolutely fascinating books by Kenneth W. Osbeck. Each has the stories behind 101 favorite hymns. Each story is accompanied by the complete hymn. Absorbing reading.

Reformed Presbyterian Board of Publications
Book of Psalms for Singing. Hardbound $12.95. Free shipping on prepaid orders. Bulk prices available.

The Bible says we should sing "psalms, hymns, and spiritual songs" (Colossians 3:16). Unhappily, so much time has been spent justifying the use of hymns *in addition* to psalms that nowadays most churches sing hymns *instead* of psalms! The few psalms in the modern hymnbook by no means reflect the Psalms' actual richness. What are we missing? Psalms for times of despair. Psalms for the repentant sinner. Psalms that promise victory in the battle with God's enemies. Psalms about the Messiah. Psalms on every topic of the *real* spiritual life, not the trimmed-down, always-grinning version. They're all here in the *Book of Psalms for Singing*!

Many of the tunes are familiar to hymn-singers, and most of those that aren't are easy to learn. For the convenience of those who don't know how to read music, the RP Board of Publications also offers cassettes of some of the most popular Psalms.

NEW★★
Vision Video
John Wycliffe, John Hus, Standing in the Storm, First Fruits, $49.95 each. *Martin Luther,* $29.95 full-length version, $29.95 abridged version. *Dietrich Bonhoeffer,* $39.95. *C. S. Lewis,* $29.95. Many other videos available.

You want a really fascinating church history project? Try watching Vision Video's biographies of famous Christians in this order:

- *John Wycliffe: The Morningstar*
- *John Hus*
- *Martin Luther*
- *Standing in the Storm: The Story of Jan Amos Comenius*
- *First Fruits*

John Wycliffe, the 14th-century leader commonly remembered as "The Morning Star of the Reformation," influenced both Martin Luther, the German reformer, and John Hus, the Bohemian reformer. Jan Amos Comenius was a Hussite, a descendant of Huss's followers. *First Fruits* then takes up the tale of the Moravians, spiritual descendants of Comenius, who blazed the way for modern missions by taking the gospel to the slaves on St. Thomas Island.

From one video to the next, you find church leaders prophesying what will happen to those who follow them—and it comes true on the next video! Hus, who was burned at the stake, said that his persecutors had succeeded in silencing him, a "silly goose" (*Hus* sounds like the word for *goose* in Czechoslovakia), but that the Lord would bring eagles in his place, men of strong and dauntless will. Enter Martin Luther! Hus talks about his debt to Wycliffe's writings; Comenius talks about his debt to Hus, and prophesies that the gospel

will be spread abroad by those who follow him (Comenius), as in fact happened.

Fascinating stories, beautifully produced and acted. I would only warn you not to let little kids see the Comenius video, since the Czechs who produced it realistically depicted the horrors of Protestants being slaughtered.

The *Dietrich Bonhoeffer* video features interviews with many people who knew him, including his sister and those who attended seminary with him and studied under him. This is a fascinating look at this man who, although a pacifist, both organized a dissident church in Hitler's Germany and joined a plot to assassinate Hitler. Bonhoeffer was killed in a concentration camp. He continues to increase in influence among theologians, and the issues he faced are brought out clearly as we tour the places he studied and worked. Even Bonhoeffer fans may get some surprises, e.g., the revelation that he developed an interest in civil rights for blacks while studying in America (this was in 1940, remember!) as well as in black gospel music. Truly a man for all seasons.

Vision Video has dozens of other videos of interest to thinking Christians. *C.S. Lewis through the Shadowlands,* for example, is the winner of an International Emmy, two British Academy Awards, and 10 other awards from five countries. (I never got to see this one, unhappily; the tape snagged in my VCR and broke it!) *The Cross and the Switchblade* is the classic story of gangleader Nicky Cruz and the skinny white preacher who dared to travel the mean streets of New York and lead desperadoes like Nicky to the Lord. *Hazel's People* is the story of how a visit to Mennonite country changes the life of a bitter fighter for human rights. Many, many more. No need to waste your VCR on watching junk when good stuff like this is around!

MISSIONS EDUCATION & WORLDVIEW

NEW★★
Operation Mobilization Literature
(formerly Send the Light)
Operation World, $12 for complete set. Book alone, $8.95. Prayer cards alone, $2.95. World map alone, $2.95 All prices postpaid.

Operation World began in 1963 as a sheaf of facts, country by country, for use during a week of prayer for the world. Since then, author Patrick Johnstone fell prey to the same syndrome as your loyal *Big Book* writer—he kept adding *more* and *more* facts and up-dating the information while his book got bigger and bigger!

In its present form, *Operation World* provides over 500 pages of densely packed information on every country in the world from a Christian and missionary point of view, plus lots and lots of statistics, historical background information, ethnic information, and prayer needs. This is information you can't find in your friendly *World Book of Facts* or encyclopedia: stuff like, "What is the ratio of missionaries to the number of people in that country?" "How many languages are spoken in the country, and into how many of them is the Bible translated?" "How are Christians treated in that country?" and "What is the history of Christian missionary activity in that country?" Along with this are geographical, social, population, and other facts. The reader is often given specific prayer requests arising from recent history, plus names and addresses of mission groups and a section on special ministries such as medical missions and student ministries.

I didn't find it easy to follow the suggested prayer calendar format (which assigns you a country or ministry to pray for each day of the year), mainly because it takes more than one day to digest all the information about a country or mission! A more promising format for home school use might be to concentrate on one country per week, or even a country of the month. For behind-the-scenes information on that country from a Christian perspective, *Operation World* is un-surpassed.

A complete *Operation World* kit includes not just the book, but also a set of 70 World Prayer Cards, each with facts and prayer requests about a foreign country, and a world map, for locating your country of the day (or week, or month!). It's a really good deal, and I hope a lot of you take advantage of it!

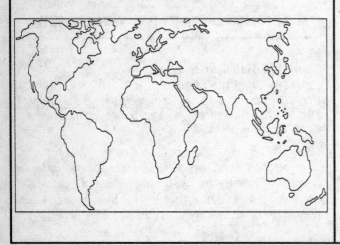

NEW**
William Carey Library

Perspectives on the World Christian Movement, edited by Ralph D. Winter and Steven D. Hawthorne, $13 (discount-ed price when ordering directly from the publisher includes parcel post shipping costs) or $14.95 retail. Add $1 han-dling. Study guide, $8.75 discounted price, $9.95 retail.

Perspectives on the World Christian Movement is a 846-page paperback collection of 87 articles about the Christian movement that, according to the pub-lisher, are "designed to be the missionary platform of essential knowledge for any serious Christian who [has] only a secular education." However, even those with a Christian education are unlikely to have en-countered the breadth of learning available in this one book.

The book is divided into four major sections, all tied together by the thread of the Great Commission: The Biblical Perspective, The Historical Perspective, The Cultural Perspective, and The Strategic Perspective. Articles were contributed by such authors as John R. W. Stott, Don Richardson, Ralph D. Winter, William Carey, J. Hudson Taylor, Donald A. McGavran, and Andrew Murray, along with many others.

Through this book Christians learn about our scriptural responsibility to be a blessing to others. We explore what has already been accomplished. Cross-cultural missionary challenges are discussed and strategies are mapped out.

Thirty-three articles are devoted to strategies under the headings Strategies for World Evangelism, Strategies for Church Planting, Strategies for Develop-ment, World Christian Teamwork, and World Christian Discipleship.

Every Christian will gain from reading this book. Christians with a weak background in church or bib-lical history will especially appreciate the summaries of historical events. Others will broaden their under-standing of how God has moved ceaselessly through our history as He continues to do today. However, this is not just another book for us to read and be blessed by what others have done. The authors hope to motivate us with practical ideas and encourage-ment to be part of the effort to reach all men for Jesus Christ.

Since the book is used in college classes, you will find a few study questions at the end of each article.

Although you can easily pick and choose which articles to read, some of us are easily daunted by such a wealth of information. If this is your problem, get the

174-page study guide. It was written to be used as a course (independent study or classroom) book based upon selected readings from the larger book and from Scripture.

Perspectives is not a book to hand to your average teenager. It's for adults, mature young adults, serious Sunday school classes, or for parents to digest and *then* share with their older children.

As the author of the study guide warns, this study is dangerous—it might change your life. (Note: new articles will be added to the next edition, due in 1991, and the price will also increase.)—Cathy Duffy

CHAPTER TWO

CHARACTER EDUCATION

"Character education," by definition, is training kids to admire and imitate what is right and hate and forsake what is wrong. Now, is the political process and court system the best way to establish it? After all, it was our enlightened judges that ordered the Ten Commandments ripped off classroom walls 'way back in the fifties, thus virtually eliminating public-school character education in the first place!

Teachers used to tell Beaver and Wally that stealing was wrong because "thou shalt not steal." However, as the ripples of the Supreme Court decision spread ever wider, it was felt that to confidently state that *anything* was right or wrong was dangerously close to an "establishment of religion." Thus, the pastiche of values education programs in which Junior was supposed to figure out all by his little self what was right or wrong—with the teacher providing a dose of relativism to help Junior along. References to religion-based behavior were systematically removed from history and literature courses. Teachers were forbidden to even have a Bible on their desks, let alone quote its proverbs about human behavior in class.

Now that it has become embarrassingly obvious that Junior, left to himself, has a good chance of developing into a doper, mugger, or whatever, even folks like Norman Lear are clamoring to put character education back into the public schools, along with information about the role of religion in history. But times have changed since the fifties. Since tolerance is one of the character traits insisted on by the likes of Norman Lear, you can be sure that any new public-school character education programs are going to emphasize the equal goodness of all religions and lifestyles. In other words, by implication human sacrifice to Kali, the Hindu goddess of life and death, will be presented as morally equivalent to a Christian attending church. This new type of character education, in other words, will be the opposite of the old Ten-Commandments-based character education.

Desperate Christian leaders, eager for any crumbs that fall from the government table, undoubtedly hope that they will be able to sneak the Ten Commandments in the back door as "universal human values." That's the way they talk when they are rhapsodizing about the possibilities of reviving public-school character education. Dream on, buddies. The only universal human values will be found to be those held by the guys who booted out the Ten Commandments: egalitarianism, unisexism, "alternative lifestyles," and one-world imperial "democracy." That's what they've been teaching in teachers' colleges for the past 20 years, so in a sense these *are* the new universal values. After all, every new teacher is put through course after course which assumes that these doctrines are true and that the purpose of education is to inculcate them!

I wish I could say that Christian character education materials are immune from the doctrines taught in teachers' colleges. In real life they are often written by the graduates of those institutions. The conflict between extreme secular relativism and personal Christian piety has led to a host of Christian character education materials that are little more than a list of non-threatening ideals (such as Joyfulness), plus Bible verses and simple-minded activities more or less related to these qualities. Typically, kids are urged to be obedient—without a clue as to what God's rules are that we are supposed to obey. Kids are exhorted to be loving (loving what?) and faithful (to what?). Many lessons are spent cultivating the great virtue of self-esteem, the total opposite to the true Bible virtue of humility. Little time is spent talking about suffering for Christ, or denying oneself in any meaningful way, or remaining sexually pure, and even less is spent on the Bible passages which speak of God's wrath and judgment on the impenitent. Instead, kids are told they *can not* love or serve others unless they love and serve themselves first.

In our era the youth program also has come into its own—a little world within a world, where teens are handled with (pardon the expression) kid gloves. Character-molding events like pizza pig-outs and ski retreats are dangled before the pubescent in hopes they will be bribed into retaining some allegiance to the faith of their fathers.

Kids aren't stupid, of course. Sooner or later they realize they can pig out on pizza, listen to rock music, and go skiing without needing to belong to a church. So they have been leaving the church in record numbers. According to current statistics, between 80 and 90 percent of children raised in the church desert it as soon as they leave home. In response, often those in charge of the disaster prescribe another dose of the same: "We need a better youth facility, more youth ministers, and fancier youth retreats." "We need to respect teens' unique needs and culture." "Let's host another Christian rock concert."

A DIFFERENT APPROACH

I would like to suggest a completely different approach. Let's start integrating teens back into *real* culture. Rescue the political prisoners!

This whole "teenage" thing is a scam. Teenagers of the past headed businesses and families, fought in wars, served in monasteries and hospitals, created serious art, and even governed estates and kingdoms.

Today the period of childish irresponsibility has been artificially prolonged by our educational system through high school into college and even graduate school. As a result, lots of 25-year-olds still consider themselves "kids" who are "too young" to get serious about life. What a waste!

Teen culture is another joke. Virtually all teen culture, from the designer jeans to the rock 'n roll, comes straight from Madison Avenue via the shopping mall. Kids mostly don't *make* rock 'n roll music—they buy it and listen to it. They don't *make* their clothes—they buy the "in" fashions down at the mall. Teens don't *have* an indigenous culture—they are just living the fantasies that adults who want their bucks have foisted on them.

Teens *can* learn to live as responsible adults. They *can* control their sex drives, work when they feel like quitting, stand against peer pressure, and lead and provide for a family. They've done it for centuries! Teens worldwide have successfully grown up in the traditional way with adults training them to fit into adult culture, not through special teens-only events like all-night lock-ins for world hunger relief.

Parents of young children have the job of teaching them right and wrong and enforcing it. Parents of older children and teens add to this the job of deciding when the child has learned his lesson well enough to be trusted with greater responsibility. Eventually, if all goes well, the child becomes fully self-motivating. As we keep telling our kids, "Someday we won't be around to check up on you!"

No canned curriculum can do all this for you. However, we could all use some extra support and encouragement . . . and it never hurts to be reminded of what you're aiming for, either. The resources below can't hurt, and they might help!

Harvest House Publishers

Christian Charm Course and *Man in Demand*: teacher's manual for each course is $8.99, and the student manual is $5.99.

Harvest House carries the best-selling *Christian Charm Course* and *Man in Demand Course*, for teenage girls and boys respectively. These provide methods for improving the outer appearance along with spiritual instructions for developing beautiful inner character.

Christian Charm Course topics include diet, posture, personal appearance, cleanliness, wardrobe, and etiquette. The teacher's guide provided expanded lesson information and extra activities for the student. The student manual is an oversized workbook packed with quizzes, illustrations, self-inventory checklists, and challenge sections.

Man in Demand follows a similar format, with an extra emphasis on developing leadership skills. Topics include physical and spiritual fitness, habits, manners, personal cleanliness, dating (traditional evangelical advice), grooming, and wardrobe.

NEW★★
High Noon Books
9–5 Series, $15 postpaid for all five books. Add $2.50 taxable handling. Grades 3 to adult.

The 9–5 Series are small books with easy-reading vocabulary and short sentences. Each is the story of a young man or woman with a summer job who has to solve a mystery concerning his job. The books are intended to teach preteens and teens how to solve problems that might arise in applying for and keeping their first blue-collar job. Some of the problems—like learning to not "talk silly" around the boss—are part of everyday life, and others—like trying to catch the person who is poisoning food at the supermarket—are thrown in to make the books more interesting. The main characters model good character traits like diligence and honesty.

In *Box Girl*, Patty Walker learns to overcome her impetuousness while working as a supermarket box girl. Troy Martin learns he likes nursery work in *A New Leaf*, but are those really mushrooms Pete is growing in his greenhouse with the windows painted black? In *A Nugget of Gold*, Lucy goes to work at the animal shelter, where the dog she likes the best is "adopted" under suspicious circumstances. Jake gets his friend Lee a job at City Auto in *The Set-Up*, only to wonder if Lee is the person ripping cars off from the lot. In my personal favorite, *The Secret Solution*, Jim gets accused of robbing the houses his crew has been painting.

Like the other High Noon books, these are absorbing reading. Kids can painlessly discover which work attitudes lead to rewards and which will get you fired by reading these books.

NEW★★
Human Resource Development Press
Peer Pressure Reversal, Positive Peer Groups, $9.95 each. *How to Say No and Keep Your Friends, How to Say Yes and Make Friends*, $7.95 each. Package price for all four books, $29.95. Add $1.50 shipping per book (maximum $3). Ages 9 and up. Quantity discounts available.

Sharon Scott, author of the books above, spent seven years with the Dallas Police Department as director of the First Offender Program. She "began seeing that the number-one reason why kids were making bad decisions, including breaking laws, was because they did not know what to say to their friends when begged, bribed, dared, or challenged." It's easy to "Just Say No!" to some creepy guy hanging around the schoolyard, but not so easy to say no to your boyfriend, girlfriend, best friend, or the popular kids in school.

Sharon took this as a challenge to train teens in *positive* peer group techniques and peer pressure *reversal* techniques. So far she has trained over 100,000 kids and adults in these techniques and has written several books. Her books have garnered endorsements from such sources as the Boy Scouts of America, the U.S. Department of Education, and the National Federation of Parents.

Mrs. Scott's *Positive Peer Groups* book gives instructions in how to set up a positive peer group program in your school. This book doesn't really apply to the home situation, but may be of interest to those of you with school connections. *When to Say Yes and Make More Friends* likewise is advice for kids on how to reach out and make good friends in school. The kids who most need this advice tend to be from broken or otherwise messed-up homes, as is evident by the case histories given.

Of interest to just about everyone are *Peer Pressure Reversal: An Adult Guide to Developing a Responsible Child* and *How to Say No and Keep Your Friends*, a book with the same message, but directed to teen readers. Mrs. Scott's philosophy is, "You can say no to trouble *and* be liked." She gives specific steps: Check Out the Scene (look and listen, then ask yourself, "Is this trouble?"), Make a Good Decision (think of the consequences on both sides and take action), and Act to Avoid Trouble (what to say and how to say it). This gets really specific. I'll list her 10 peer pressure reversal responses:

1. Just say no
2. Leave
3. Ignore
4. Make an excuse
5. Change the subject
6. Make a joke
7. Act shocked
8. Flattery
9. A better idea
10. Return the challenge

Each one of these responses is presented in detail, with illustrations, examples, and suggestions. Example (under Return the Challenge):

When a peer accuses you with "I thought you were my friend!" several possible comebacks are:

"Yes, I am your best friend, and that's why I'm not going to do this with you."

"If you were my friend, then you wouldn't be trying to talk me into doing something that I don't want to do."

"With friends like you, who needs enemies? If you were really my friend, you'd stop trying to push me around."

"If you were my friend, you wouldn't be so bossy."

And of course, a more stinging comeback could always be: "Who said you were my friend?"

Learn other valuable techniques, such as the Thirty Second Rule (start trying to get out of the situation within thirty seconds or less) and the Two No Rule (never say no more than twice before leaving or changing the subject). This all takes practice, so the book provides numerous role-playing situations for kids to exercise their new skills.

Peer Pressure Reversal, a larger book, explains the Peer Pressure Reversal philosophy to parents and explains how to teach it to the kids (again with role-playing a number of situations). This takes 90-odd pages of the book. Section Four of the book has reinforcement suggestions ranging from the usual behavior modification techniques (positive reinforcement for encouragement and deprivation of privileges for discipline) to organized family activities and influencing the child's circle of friends.

NEW
The Landmark Company
The Lighthouse Adventures 12-cassette series, $39.95 plus $3.50 shipping. Ages 8–adult.

I never encourage people to send me their cassette programs, since it takes so long to listen through even a few cassettes. Happily, the staff at The Landmark Company didn't know this. They sent me the best dramatized Christian cassette series I have ever heard.

It's called *The Lighthouse Adventures,* and briefly, it's the story of Pete and Tim and how they both come to know the Lord, all on 12 cassettes neatly packed into a binder with a fancy little sheet of questions for discussion. Along the way you meet Tony, the tough guy who's into some serious stuff, ever-glib and ever-unreliable Skip and his bonehead pal Danny, old Nathaniel Bolt the lighthouse keeper, sweet sixteen Christy, bombshell Missy—in short a whole raft of unforgettable characters.

Unlike most Christian fiction, this series doesn't miss a beat. The acting is wonderful, as are the sound effects. The story is so gripping you might well hear the whole series through in one sitting. Our kids kept begging for "one more cassette" and we wanted to keep on going, too! The discussion questions and Bible verses are just right: short, sweet, and pointed. Topics covered are important to every child: obedience, trust in God, honesty, standing against peer pressure, the dangers of showing off, true versus false friendship, and so on. Never does the story become cloying. In fact, the characterizations are so realistic that even what I regarded as faults in designing the characters (e.g., the mother's weak failure to control her sons) led to the results you would expect—all without one iota of preaching. There are more lessons in this series than the writers themselves may realize! Even the price is right: it works out to just over $3 per tape.

The big question, "Will the kids listen to this more than once?" was answered immediately in my own family by them requesting it a second time the moment the last cassette was over. I enjoyed it as much the second time—in fact, more, since now I saw more nuances in the plot. I am sure we will play this series again and again.

NEW**
Mantle Ministries

Gaining Favor with God and Man, $14. Add $2.75 shipping. Grades 5–adult.

Only a few generations ago, Americans had vastly different hopes and expectations for their children. Take *Gaining Favor with God and Man,* for instance. Written in 1893, the book instructs children in such character traits as perseverance, self-reliance, industry, and self-control by means of true stories from the lives of successful men and women of that time and earlier. The young reader is exhorted in the best New England Yankee style to become successful by diligently making himself useful in his calling, forsaking evil companions and the society of buffoons, and improving himself by self-education. Christian piety is strongly urged in many places as the self-evident foundation of both public and eternal success.

The book is written in a lively, earnest style. Here's a snippet:

> A young man became clerk in a large warehouse of a New England city. After having served several months acceptably he hinted to his employer that he ought to be paid as much as a certain other clerk received.
>
> "If you will do what he does, you shall be paid as much," replied his employer.
>
> "And what is that?" the young man enquired.
>
> "He takes customers to the theatre, and gives them a drink occasionally, that he may sell them a bill of goods."
>
> Straightening himself up to his full height, and with the fire of indignation flashing in his eyes, our young hero answered, "I thank God that there is a poor-house in my native town, and I will go there and die before I shall do such dirty work," and he left the store. That was principle.

Can't you just see the young Jimmy Stewart in the role, eyes flashing, denouncing the scallywags who want him to fleece a customer?

Principle can get you a job as well as lose you one, too, as the next excerpt shows:

> Nicholas Biddle, president of the first United States Bank, found so much work on hand, at one time, that he asked a portion of his employees to work a few hours on the Sabbath. All but one consented; this one said, "I cannot conscientiously labor on the Sabbath."
>
> "Then you must give up your place to some one who will," answered Biddle.
>
> "Very well, I resign," said the young man, and withdrew. That was principle.
>
> The following day a gentleman waited upon Biddle, saying, "I want a perfectly reliable private secretary, to whom I am obliged to commit great trusts. Can you tell me of one?"
>
> "Yes," Biddle promptly answered. "I dismissed a young man yesterday because he would not work on the Sabbath. He has principle enough for you."

Not only Nicholas Biddle, but also historic luminaries such as George Washington, Abraham Lincoln, John Bunyan, and Edward Burke are represented within the 400-plus gilt-edged pages of this hardbound book. Forgotten heroes like Elihu Burritt, the blacksmith who taught himself classical languages and philosophy while working the forge, and the humble manufacturer of Rising Sun stove polish, who began his industrial empire by selling the product door to door out of a carpet bag, parade through the pages of this book side by side with the Andrew Carnegies and Sir Walter Raleighs. Rich but selfish John Jacob Astor, idle Samuel Coleridge, and foolish Marie Antoinette are held up, along with scores of others, as warnings of how wealth, talent, and beauty alone are not enough to secure the esteem of our fellow man and the benediction of God in heaven.

For a mind-blowing experiment, try reading *People* magazine and *Gaining Favor with God and Man* on the same day. Everything in one contradicts the other. *Inc.* comes a little closer to it, with its exaltation of hard work, perseverance, and upward mobility, but loses out in the personal piety and humility department. Even *Moody Monthly* doesn't come close to the confident I-know-what's-right-and-wrong outlook of *Gaining Favor with God and Man.* (Dwight L. Moody himself gets favorable mention in the book, by the way).

The book does include a fair number of examples of Yankee do-goodism and anti-clannishness masquerading as disinterested philanthropy, as is inevitable. From Emerson and Louisa May Alcott on down, Yankees have been very fond of busybodies. (I was raised in Yankee New England, just outside of Boston, by the way!) The difference is that today the Yankee soul is dedicated to Save the Whales and Feed the Hungry, not Feed the Souls and Save the Hungry, as in times past.

NEW**
Plain Path Publishers
Christian Manhood, $12 for 259-page student text, $6 for 148-page teacher's guide. *Christian Character*, $10, answer key $1. Add 10% shipping (minimum $2.50). Ages 10–14.

> *Christian Character* is a book that provides an intensive examination of the character that should be found in the lives of our young people. *Christian Character* is Scriptural, practical, and convicting; clearly examining the lives of young people who use the book, and then guiding them in setting short-term, specific goals.

That's what the flyer says. Can any book live up to it? This one sure comes close! Designed for kids aged 10–14, *Christian Character: A Guide for Training Young People to Have the Habits That Will Lead to Godly Character* is a series of lessons, in alphabetical order, on 28 major character traits. Each lesson includes a brief introduction defining the character trait in everyday language, with supporting Scripture citations, one or more student exercises, a personal evaluation, and a goal-setting section. One type of student exercise requires the student to answer questions about Bible verses pertaining to the character trait. Another type asks the student to apply what he knows about that character trait to a number of hypothetical situations. The personal evaluation usually is a pretty comprehensive checklist whereby the student can evaluate how well he is doing as far as that character trait is concerned. The questions are quite discerning and interesting to work through. In the goal-setting section, the student is exhorted to set a specific short-term goal for improvement in that area.

The author's point of view is best expressed in his own words:

> After Salvation, the constant indoctrination by example of the "live as you please" philosophy (through

TV, music, adults in the world, etc.) produces young people who lack standards, and therefore are also weak in character. . . . So that provision is not made to fulfill the lusts of the flesh, a young person must be busily engaged in putting into practice principles from God's Word by forming habits of behavior—these behaviors in total forming the various areas of character development. . . . We must teach the Word of God faithfully (Deut. 6:6, 7) and then train young people (Prov. 22:6) by expecting habitual conformity to God's Word as it has been taught. It is a mistake to only teach and then leave the "doing" entirely to the discretion of the child. We . . . cannot produce children with strong character through the philosophy of the world—teach, and then leave them alone to allow them a free choice. . . . Setting goals should become a life-long habit whenever they learn about something that God requires of them and make a decision to do it. A decision without further action is worthless.

Although originally designed by a teacher for classroom use, *Christian Character* works beautifully in the home. The answer key gives the answers to all the exercises that aren't open-ended, and the whole program couldn't be easier to use.

Author Gary Maldaner's point of view is staunchly fundamentalist. He is opposed to rock and contemporary Christian music and is for treating girls and women with special honor (if this be male chauvinism, make the most of it!). He believes in modest dress and the rightness of fighting in a just war. None of these points is beaten to death in *Christian Character*; you could presumably disagree with him on every one of them and still use it by skipping over the questions when they crop up.

Also by the same author, *Christian Manhood: A Guide for Training Boys to be Spiritually Strong Men* is for boys ages 10–14. This 45-lesson text doesn't flinch from any of the tough areas, from homosexuality and sexual identity to a kid's choice of entertainment. Good biblical common sense, along with a fair amount of insight into spiritual warfare.

The author's fundamentalist beliefs are much more basic to the *Christian Manhood* course. The student text has a similar format to the *Christian Character* text, except that lessons are arranged topically rather than alphabetically.

You'll also need the teacher's guide, which includes lesson objectives, suggested memory verses, vocabulary from those verses, explanation of each lesson's goal, introduction, pointers on leading the classroom discussion, additional activities, discussion questions, and answers to the student exercises.

NEW★★
Rod and Staff Publishers
Dear Princess and *Young Man, Be Strong*, $7.75 each. Add $1 if order is under $10.

I really like Rod and Staff Publishers' serious and devout, yet human, approach to the spiritual life. As you know, Rod and Staff publishes an entire line of Christian school textbooks and workbooks, all with a Mennonite emphasis. This means very modest dress, nonresistance to violence, and total nonparticipation in politics. I mention this because you need to know it in order to understand some of the vignettes in Rod and Staff's charming new Christian character-building duo, *Dear Princess* (for girls) and *Young Man, Be Strong* (for teenage boys).

Both books tenderly lead Christian teens to seek a more self-sacrificing, Christ-pleasing life. They warn of the snares that await thoughtless teens. They explain how to recognize in yourself the sprouts of both good and bad character traits, and how to nourish the good while weeding out the bad. All is done with good taste—no graphic descriptions of sinful behavior, but many true tales of teens who made both good and bad choices.

This is the kind of soul-nourishing literature that used to be common in Christian America, but now is as rare as a snowflake in June. When is the last time you heard anyone exhort Christian teens to avoid the sin of vanity, for example?

I'm not a Mennonite, but I found even the specifically Mennonite references useful for challenging my attitudes, which in this hurly-burly world can so easily sink into worldliness. Highly recommended.

NEW★★
Vision Video
Dangerous Journey, $59.95 for set of 2 videos, color story book, teacher's guide, and Scripture guide, all in gift pack. Add $3.95 shipping. All ages.

John Bunyan's all-time bestseller *Pilgrim's Progress* has got to be the greatest character-building book of all time. Based on Bunyan's book, *Dangerous Journey* features the truly excellent, detailed illustrations of Alan Parry and fine narration besides. The art fits the old-fashioned flavor of Bunyan's book, and the length of the series give the narrator plenty of time to cover much of Bunyan's best ground. Instead of animation, the producers used camera angles and special effects to move the story along. I had worried that our children would be bored because of the lack of animation, but what we lost in animation was more than made up for by the vividness of the illustrations. This is one of our children's favorite videos. Warning: the monsters in this series do look monstrous. (Not that it bothers our crowd!)

The new version of *Dangerous Journey* includes nine programs on two full-color VHS videotapes, plus a *Dangerous Journey* 128-page color story book, a teacher's guide, and a Scripture guide, all in a gift pack. Tape 1 includes the Slough of Despond, the Interpreter's House, and the Hill Difficulty, the Fight with Apollyon, and the Valley of the Shadow of Death. Tape 2 takes you to Vanity Fair, Doubting Castle, the Dark River, and the story of Christiana. A good deal, especially since they've dropped the price $20 (it used to be $79.95).

GAMES THAT TEACH CHARACTER

NEW★★
Ornament Publications
The Richest Christian, $23 postpaid. Ages 6–adult.

The Richest Christian is my children's favorite board game, superior in their opinion to *Generosity*. The aim is to learn biblical principles of money—but *The Richest Christian* emphasizes how money is earned as well as how it is spent. The game is for two to six players, who need to know how to read. One player, the cashier, needs to know how to add and subtract large whole numbers.

The large, illustrated game board is easy to read and use. Most spaces have a topic and Bible verse at the top, a picture applying the verse in the middle, and a game action at the bottom. Example:

TOO MUCH TALK
" . . . The talk of the lips tendeth only to poverty."
Proverbs 14:23

[Picture of a man in business clothes, feet up on desk, chatting with a friend holding a cup of coffee]

You are a salesman who wastes too much time talking with other salesmen. Lose $400.

Other spaces tell you to draw a Disaster card or give you a chance to earn game rewards if you have performed a prescribed pious action recently, e.g., if you can quote a Bible verse you learned this month. Opportunity cards may be chosen once you have passed the first round, assuming you aren't in debt at this point. These give you the opportunity to do a good deed with some or all of your game money, thereby earning Eternal Treasures. The game is over when all Eternal Treasures (pretty gold-foil cards with their value printed on them in blue) have been passed out. The player with the most Eternal Treasures wins.

Watch out for the ominous green paths on both sides of the board! If you land on a Shady Transaction space, you make some money on the deal, but then have to suffer through a series of disasters, some brought on by your own evil character (you make unwise investments and lose most of your money, for example) and some visited on you directly by the Lord.

Three of the game cards I could do without. One Disaster card informs you, "If you have $1,000 or more, you are spending too much time trying to make money. Lose your next turn." This comes perilously close to the philosophy of envy, which says having money is a sin. I also would in real life pass up two of the "opportunities": one, to give all my money to help a missionary in poor health and two, to sell some of my jewelry and give $500 to a radio preacher. For one thing, I don't have any jewelry! For another, only in exceptional circumstances and under a direct conviction from the Lord should any of us impoverish himself for another. The goal, as the Apostle Paul points out, is not that we who give should be hard pressed while others live in plenty, but that all who deserve it should have enough.

The Richest Christian admirably teaches principles of diligence, inventiveness, thrift, and generosity, while exposing the pitfalls of get-rich-quick thinking, laziness, dishonesty, show-off giving, and selfishness. It's also

easy to learn and fun to play. Can't ask one board game to do much more than that!

UPDATED**
Rainfall Inc.
Kids' Choices (ages 6–12), *Teen Choices* (ages 13–18), *Adult Choices* (ages 19 and up), $15.99 each.

The *Choices* series of games helps you explore ethical decision making with your children, teens, or other adults. Each game includes 170 real-life dilemmas spelled out on sturdy cards, 20 answer cards, 10 Biblical Principle cards, a reference booklet, an instruction sheet (natch), and a plastic storage tray.

Families, Sunday school classes, and youth or adult groups will find these games illuminating and challenging, as they come face to face with life and sometimes nose to nose with opposing views of it.

Three to ten players can play each *Choices* game (four to eight players are best). Each game is suitable for team play.

Example of a dilemma from the adult game: "You get home from the supermarket only to notice that the check-out clerk charged you less than she should have. Do you go back to the store and correct the error?" You place either a "Yes" or "No" answer card face-down in front of you. Other players guess how you will respond, playing their own answer cards, and you try to justify your answer with various scriptural principles.

Each game includes Biblical Principle cards, as well as a reference booklet which shows what Bible verses the principles are based on and gives recommended principles for resolving every dilemma. Right and wrong answers are not spelled out. This can make for some lively discussions, especially in games played with more players.

Some of the dilemma cards put you in the position of having already committed a sin. Example, from the teen game: "You lied to your parents about where you were going and now you have been in a car accident. Will you tell them the truth?" Others falsely assume that kids are just bound to get into compromising situations. Another example from the teen game: "If you (your girlfriend) became pregnant would you marry the father (mother)?" This is like the old question, "When's the last time you beat your wife?" It doesn't allow for the possibility that any teen playing the game might *not* be sexually involved, since the only allowable answers are "Yes, I would marry him (her)" and "No, I would not." One way to overcome this problem is to allow a third answer, "I wouldn't get in the situation in the first place."

School and home problems appear frequently in the kids' and teen games, and many teen dilemmas also focus on dating and boyfriend/girlfriend dilemmas. Example of a family problem, again from the teen deck: "While cleaning out the garage you found some pornographic magazines on your father's shelf. Will you tell anyone?" This somewhat reduces the games' usefulness for those who home school and have good family lives. I can also see these questions leading to some rather embarrassing moments in the youth group. (Simple solution: pull and toss those cards.)

I like the basic idea of the *Choices* games, and the new format is much more playable than the old "figure out a Bible verse that applies and look it up" format. With 170 dilemma cards to choose from, you can get rid of any that don't apply and still have plenty left to play with. It is a fascinating way to gain insight into the thought processes of family members, and to bring up questions in a family format that might be a lot tougher to face for the first time in real life.

PART II

LANGUAGE ARTS

CHAPTER THREE

CREATIVE WRITING

Every American adult wants to write a book, or at least a letter to the editor that gets published in the local paper. If we can believe Albert Shanker, the president of the second-largest teacher's union in the country, though, most of us are doomed to frustration if we settle for just the writing instruction the local public school offers. In a speech given before a conference of teachers and school administrators in Denver in late September, 1989, he said,

> How many of our 17- to 18-year-old youngsters—the kids who are still there after about 29–30 percent have dropped out—our "successful" kids (not the at-risk kids, not the dropouts)— . . . what percentage of them can write a letter or an essay of one, two, three, four, [or] five pages and do a good job? . . .

> Well, the answer is, depending upon whether you take reading, writing, math, or science, the percentage of those still in school at age 17 and about to graduate who are able to function at that top level is: three, four, five, or six percent.

> *Three, four, five, or six percent.*

> The percentage of those able to write [a] one or two-paragraph letter with lots of errors in it is only 20 percent. In other words, 80 percent of those who have *not* dropped out cannot even write two paragraphs loaded with mistakes [that express] a single idea. . . .

OK. That's our mandate in this book—to increase the percentages! And I'm just the person to help you improve your creative writing. My personal writing style upon graduating college was, to put it charitably, vague and boring. (Not that it's that great now, but at least you can *understand* it!) So I know exactly what you're up against, and believe me, I sympathize.

Getting a cherished idea out of your head and onto paper is considerably similar to childbirth. The struggle . . . the suspense . . . the burdened feeling that finally, miraculously eases as the words come out. Face it, writing well is *tough*. But, with the proper instruction and lots of practice, it will get easier.

FREE SOURCES OF EXCELLENT WRITING INSTRUCTION

Before we get into actual school programs, consider what your local library has to offer. Sheridan Baker's two excellent books, *The Practical Stylist* and *The Complete Stylist and Handbook,* have been a real help to me. I gladly recommend the older editions of both these books. They will help any aspiring writer slash the flab out of his creations. *The Practical Stylist* is shorter and therefore a better book for beginners. *The Complete Stylist* is meant for use as a college text, which means Mr. Baker has to spin things out a bit more.

Another good book is William Zinsser's *On Writing Well.* Zinsser is amusing, instructive, inspiring, approachable, self-congratulatory about his leftward leanings, and less scholastic than Baker.

Still another widely-regarded text is E. B. White's *The Elements of Style.*

Most other books on the subject are, quite honestly, twaddle. Try to avoid those whose titles announce the big bucks you will shortly be earning with your writing. Generally these are hack pieces, written by and for hack writers. Anyway, you won't (let's be honest now) want to work through half-a-dozen books on writing; so just pick one good one from the list above, and start there!

Reading is still the best preparation for writing. If you want to be funny, read everything by P. G. Wodehouse. If drama is your calling, try starting with Dickens and Shakespeare. Soak up the best writing in your field and style, whether it be short story, play, or television scriptwriting. Then try to improve on it.

The children's book market operates by different rules, since children are supposed to be little alien life-forms with peculiar tastes and needs. Thus the never-ending torrent of books convincing children that their parents were doing them a favor by divorcing; the torrid pre-teen sex novelettes; the smarmy stories of bunnies and kittens who discover the yuppie virtue of unconditional self-love. Let me suggest a different path, the road taken by the writers of what we now consider children's classics. If you want to write for children, write a good clean book for adults and then cut its size by 75 percent.

HOW TO TEACH WRITING

NEW★★
Education Services
You CAN Teach Your Child Successfully. $13.70/paperbound, $18.95 hardcover. Each *Teaching* book, $6.45.

Ruth Beechick's new book, titled *You CAN Teach Your Child Successfully,* is (1) designed to help you teach children from 4th to 8th grade and is (2) absolutely wonderful! Like all Beechick books, this has gems on every page. Her comments about time lines and how best to use them are alone worth the price of the book. Considering how little advice on instruction is available for anyone whose children are past the learning-to-read stage, this book is a must-buy for home-schooling parents.

NEW★★
Shekinah Curriculum Cellar
If you're trying to teach kids to write, you've gotta have this book!, $12.95. Add $2.95 shipping. A book for teachers, moms, and dads.

Want to be a success in home schooling? Then realize that your job is to learn the subject you want to teach! Once you know a subject, and know how to teach it, you can use virtually any educational resource successfully.

So, if you want to teach kids creative writing, learn how to teach it first. To learn how to teach it, get Ruth Beechick's *You CAN Teach Your Child Successfully* (from Education Services) and get *If you're trying to teach kids to write, you've gotta have this book!* by Marjorie Frank. The title says it all. Packed into these 220 pages are more thoughts, tips, philosophy, examples, resources, and helps for teaching creative writing than you'll find in any other one spot except Mrs. Beechick's book. Sections like "100 Alternatives to *What I Did on My Summer Vacation*" take you beyond the typical loser writing lesson. Find out how to motivate the reluctant writer, the gifted writer, the very young writer. How to recover from floppo lessons. What to do with the finished writing. How to criticize writing constructively (wish all *my* critics would read that section!). How to start "word collections" of words like *smithereens* and *bamboozle* that are fun just to say. People-watching: an essential skill for writers of fiction and non-fiction alike. Tons more, all shared from the heart of a writer who evidently loves writing and cares about helping you and your children do likewise.

NEW★★
Teaching Home
October/November 1987 issue, $3.75. Complete six-issue set for 1987, $17.50, includes free set of 6 plastic magazine holders for your ring binder.

The October/November 1987 of *Teaching Home* was the issue on creative writing. Article topics included using a word processor, writing readiness, using writing in other subjects, cultivating a lifelong writing habit, poetry, motivation, proofreading and editing, and a great article by Ruth Beechick entitled "The Road to Good Writing."

WRITING COURSES AND RESOURCES

A Beka Book Publications
Handbook of Grammar and Composition: hardbound, $20.15; paperbound, $10. Shipping extra.

A Beka's *Handbook of Grammar and Composition* for grades 11 and 12 is now available in both hardcover and softcover. A Beka says, "This handbook provides a thorough treatment of all of those elements of grammar, mechanics, and usage that are necessary for correct, clear, and effective writing." Topics include The Writing Process, Specific Compositions, The Research Paper, Composing the Sentence, Choosing the Right Word.

NEW**
Alpha Omega Publications
LIFEPACS, $2.75–$2.95 each or $24.95–$26.95/set of 10 (one course). Teacher handbooks, $4.95 per course. Answer keys, $2.25 each (two per course). LIFEPAC test key (included with teacher handbook), $2.25/course. Spelling test booklet, $1.95/course (grades 7 and 8 only). Books available for literature component of courses: *The Hiding Place*, $3.95 (grade 7); *The Miracle Worker*, $3.25, and *20,000 Leagues under the Sea*, $1.95 (grade 9); *In His Steps*, $6.95 (grade 10); *Our Town*, $4.95, and *The Old Man and the Sea*, $3.95 (grade 11); *Hamlet*, $2.95 (grade 12). Shipping extra.

Alpha Omega's language-arts LIFEPACS feature a worktext approach to composition. All forms of writing are covered, including some secular tales, and analyzed from a Christian perspective. The series emphasizes creative thinking, and (unlike some others) actually gets the student writing a goodly number of compositions.

The organization of the courses is a mishmash, with grammar, usage, speaking, and writing mixed in with literature studies in no apparent order. I can understand why courses for schoolchildren keep repeating grammar and usage lessons grade after grade, since you can never be sure what the child was taught in his previous school. However, at home it's much more effective to study grammar separately and get it over with. Therefore, home schoolers might prefer to

pick through these courses on a LIFEPAC by LIFEPAC basis, skipping the grammar and usage units and subunits (which merely interrupt the courses) and concentrating on the excellent literature, composition, and research units.

If you want to do this, it's best to get a copy of the Alpha Omega scope and sequence, which tells you exactly which LIFEPAC covers which subject. I have tried to highlight some of the more successful LIFEPACS below, as well as give you an idea of the basic structure of each grade's language-arts course.

In grade 7, students start off with a review of nouns, pronouns, and other basics. Speaking and listening skills come next, followed by a unit on biographies and one on sentence structure. Then come units on the "nature, structure, and usage of English" and some rinky-dink review, including simple stuff like punctuation and capitalization. The next unit is a study of Corrie ten Boom's book, *The Hiding Place*, about her experiences growing up in Holland, hiding Jews during the Nazi occupation, living in a concentration camp, and rebuilding her life around a new ministry afterwards. Then it's back to non-fiction literature, "learning to listen," and "speaking with gestures," all in the same unit. Finally, you work on writing sentences and paragraphs and pronouncing words correctly.

Grade 8 starts more usefully, with instructions in how to get more out of your reading and how to take notes, among other things. Grammar and usage are woven throughout this entire course, mixed into units on other topics, so I won't bother listing all the numerous places where they appear. Briefly, what you get is an introduction to word-study tools (dictionary and thesaurus), biblical standards for your speech, and critical reading skills. New literary genres studied are essays and autobiography. Composition skills include writing short essays and making an oral report. It's not organized this plainly, unfortunately: a typical unit includes the history of the English language, sentence construction, spelling exercises, and elements of an autobiography!

Grade 9 starts, as usual, with a grammar and usage review, and progresses to reviewing much of the new matter taught in grade 8 (dictionary use, history of languages, etc.). New literary genres introduced are the short story (including "The Slip-Over Sweater" and the very moving science-fiction classic, "Flowers for Algernon"), poetry, drama (*The Miracle Worker*, the story of the woman who taught the blind, deaf, and willful Helen Keller to speak, read, and write), and the novel (*Twenty Thousand Leagues under the Sea* by Jules Verne, starring the infamous Captain Nemo). Students learn to look behind the scenes at conflict, characterization, plot, theme, language, setting, and symbolism, all of which is great. They also learn about using visual aids in both writing and speaking, how to give a speech, and various types of letters. They learn to use the library (we hope this information is not really new to them by now!). You get the idea.

In grade 10, once again we are looking at the history of English. This time it's real history, starting with Anglo-Saxon and the Norman invasion of 1066. More info on how to give a speech follows, ditto on how to listen to a speech. More on writing sentences, grammar (gerunds, participial phrases, etc.), and ways to use words effectively. More on how to write "expository compositions," more on grammar and reading skills. Things perk up with the seventh LIFEPAC, "Oral Reading and Drama," which is followed by "The Short Story" and "Studies in the Novel." Each of these LIFEPACS studies a famous example of its genre: the drama *Everyman*, short stories by Twain and de Maupassant, and the turn-of-the-century Christian novel *In His Steps*. Although we've looked at these literary forms before, we do pick up on a few new ideas, and it's a relief to have three units in a row on the same general topic.

The first four units of grade 11 are all skippable, being yet more grammar and usage review, and even review of how to use a dictionary (normally taught in grades 3–6), for goodness sake! The best units in grade 11 are LIFEPACS 5–9. LIFEPAC 5 is about poetry—its metre, appeal, imagery, and connotations. LIFEPAC 6 looks at nonfiction—its elements, types, topics for reading, and tips for composing it. LIFEPAC 7 looks at American drama—its history, how drama is put together and how it works, and a study of Thornton Wilder's *Our Town*. LIFEPAC 8, "Studies in the American Novel," again summarizes the history of the genre, then looks at a specific novel (Hemingway's *The Old Man and the Sea*). As a bonus this LIFEPAC includes information on how to write a critical essay. LIFEPAC 9 is the most useful of all, being on the topic of research—how to do it, formulating your thesis statement, using the library, preparing a bibliography, taking notes, stating your thesis, outlining the paper, writing the paper and the footnotes, and putting it all together. I see no particular reason why you shouldn't purchase this LIFEPAC separately, for use with younger (seventh-grade and up) students.

The research unit in grade 12 is LIFEPAC 3, which after a skippable subunit on reading for comprehension

has useful information on searching for information in various media (indexes, dictionaries, readers' guides, magazines, directories, and card catalogs) and how to take college-style notes. LIFEPAC 5 has an in-depth introduction to medieval British literature, followed quite sensibly by LIFEPACS on Elizabethan literature and 17th- and 18th-century British literature. For some reason a unit on creative writing is interposed, then we're back to a LIFEPAC on Romantic and Victorian poetry. This is the best grade for literature studies, especially if you leave out the grammar and usage LIFEPACS.

As compared to, say, Bob Jones University Press, whose upper-grades American and British literature courses are so thorough as to be college level, the Alpha Omega courses are quite within the reach of average high-school kids. This is partly because they are not as extensive; you're looking at several literature LIFEPACS per grade instead of two-textbook sequences for both American and British literature. If you are mostly concerned about basic college skills and just want to introduce yourself or your students to literary history and its genres, Alpha Omega is a good choice.

Caddylak Systems
Words that Sell, $26.95.

Words that Sell is one of my favorite books. It's a thickish oversized paperback crammed with advertising terms and slogans. I'll never forget the time we were reading this book, filling in the blanks left for a product name with our family name, and laughing our heads off:

Switch to . . . *Pride*.
Success starts with . . . *Pride*.
Pride spoken here!
Pride means business.
A little *Pride* can go a long way.
The *Pride* advantage.
They don't call us *Pride* for nothing!
A major breakthrough in . . . *Pride*.
Pride is our middle name!
Nothing's built like a *Pride*.
Pride is our business.

I was smothering my giggles on Bill's shoulder in an attempt to avoid waking up our little Prides who do, indeed, go a long way every time my back is turned on them.

But *Words that Sell* also comes in handy for its primary function. Say you need a word that means "classic"—one that has a proven track record of consumer acceptance. How about legendary . . . historic . . . antique . . . from the storied past . . . in the rich tradition of . . . redolent of another age . . . limited edition . . . quaint . . . hallmark of . . . timeless . . . or immortal?

These words are more than mere synonyms. They *sell*. People like to see them. They have good vibes. And that's the point of *Words that Sell*. For every topic you'll find words and phrases culled from thousands of successful ads. You'll even find chapters on how to elegantly knock the competition or how to introduce your product pitch.

Words that Sell is invaluable to anyone who has a business. It could even come in handy for writing book reports and persuasive essays. Anyone who likes or needs to load his words needs this book.

NEW★★
Christian Schools International
Teacher's guides for grades 7 and 8, $52.50 each grade.

CSI's Writing Rainbow series is now available for grades 7 and 8. This popular program not only covers the mechanics of creative writing, but also contains instructions to help children master the writing process. Prewriting, brainstorming, conferencing, peer editing, clustering, and other advanced techniques are made simple and accessible by this program. The program includes instruction in grammar and ethics as well as composition skills, all in an easy-to-use daily lesson format. Grammarwise, the grade 7 course concentrates mainly on sentence structure, while the grade 8 course concentrates on parts of speech.

Here's what you get in grade 7:

Unit 1. Self-Expression
Unit 2. Voices of Others: An Oral History
Unit 3. Describing Places and People
Unit 4. Newspaper Writing (news, editorials, features, columns)
Unit 5. On the Light Side (riddles, fables, tall tales, comic dialogue)
Unit 6. Explaining/Giving Information
Unit 7. Writing Drama
Unit 8. Writing Letters

This is what comes in grade 8:

Unit 1. Preparing to Write
Unit 2. Dreaming and Designing
Unit 3. Writing Poetry
Unit 4. Paragraphing and Summarizing
Unit 5. The Research Paper
Unit 6. Expressing Opinions/Reviewing
Unit 7. Persuading
Unit 8. Creating a Fantasy

Each unit begins with several "skills" lessons. These gradually lead the student through more complex structures and grammar. In grade 8, the year climaxes with the student writing press releases and stories, etc., about an alien who is visiting the earth. The teacher's guides contain background information, daily lesson plans, student activities or worksheets, and follow-up activities.

Creeping faddishness shows itself not only in the "alien" motif, but in some of the exercises and examples. One of the sample student poems which the teacher's manual for grade 8 included as an example to inspire the class listed Madonna, U2, and other teeny-bopper icons as highlights of the year; others mentioned AIDS and the hit tune "We Are the World." This is a far cry from Christian Light Education's farm girls with braids or Bob Jones University Press's suit-jacketed boys. Not that CSI is exactly hip, but if nostalgia is your thing, this series isn't for you.

NEW★★
Family Learning Center
Learning Language Arts through Literature series: Red Book (grade 2), $17.95; Yellow Book (grade 3); $17.95. Tan Book (grade 4–6), $12.95; Grey Book (grades 7–8), $12.95. Add 10% shipping ($2 minimum).

Based on Ruth Beechick's methods, as outlined in her book *You Can Teach Your Child Successfully*, Learning Language Arts through Literature is a program based on excerpts from great children's literature. The original (tan) book was written for ages 10–13, and is now joined by books for children down to age 6 and up to beginning high-school level.

Each of the 25–45 weekly lessons includes a literary passage and five daily learning activities designed to help your student learn thinking and writing skills. You may use either copying (using the Student Editing Model) or dictation. The book itself contains Student Editing Models for all the literary passages. Each is in large print. The student may use the Student Models to check his own work.

Every language art is included: spelling, grammar, vocabulary, writing mechanics, penmanship, and thinking skills. The authors follow Ruth Beechick's sensible approach of only using misspelled words for the spelling list. In fact, the entire series is based on Mrs. Beechick's wonderful teaching methods, as outlined in her book, *You Can Teach Your Child Successfully.* Grammar is taught in the context of writing, not as an isolated subject. For a grammar reference, the authors suggest the Learning Grammar through Writing series from Educators Publishing Service. (See writeup of this program in the Grammar chapter.) Vocabulary is developed through studying English classics and through the dictation/copying exercises. Penmanship is practiced in the same way.

Each dictation lesson also includes a writing activity designed to increase thinking skills. For example, the student might be asked to rewrite an entire passage in the past tense, or change it from third to first person. Doing this with technical correctness and literary flair will take some thought!

Authors Diane Welch, Susan Simpson, and Debbie Strayer have also included instructions on how to use each level of Learning Language Arts through Literature with children of different ages, or with many children at once in a multi-level setting. They also provide instruction in how to dictate properly and a complete bibliography of every book used in the dictation lessons.

All you need is a separate notebook or notebook section for each child for the dictation exercises, and colored pencils to mark the completed lessons according to the program's special directions. You might also want to purchase additional copies of the Student Editing Models. These are the literary dictation selections in large print. Each child uses one to check his own work. One set of the Student Editing Models is provided in the back of the book.

The literature selections are wonderful! (See parallel writeup in the Literature chapter for examples.) Highly recommended.

NEW★★
Hayes School Publishing Co., Inc.
Outlining, Note Taking and Report Writing Skills: A Step-by-Step Guide to Mastery, $4.95. For grade levels 4–8. Add $1.50 postage for first item, 35¢ each additional item.

This wonderful book starts with simple classifying exercises and takes your child right up through all the outlining and note-taking skills he will ever need.

Outlining promotes logical thinking, and helps us get so much more out of what we study and hear. It's absolutely fundamental to real progress in any intellectual endeavor. Knowing this, most textbook companies throw in a unit on outlining somewhere in their English courses. However, almost universally they don't take it slowly enough, explain it enough, or provide enough practice for children to really master this essential skill. The solution: this book. It's a public-school workbook, so some of its text selections have that flavor, but even so, it's the best, easiest-to-use resource on this subject I have yet found. Recommended.

NEW★★
Shekinah Curriculum Cellar
The Write Source handbook (grades 4–9), $8.95. Add 10% shipping (minimum $2.95).

The Write Source, published by the company of the same name, is an excellent English grammar, writing, and general information handbook. I am delighted that Shekinah is carrying it—the publisher was not set up to handle individual orders and I feared I'd have to leave it out of my book!

The Write Source handbook includes a great deal of information useful to students in grades 4–9. Writing skills covered: the writing process, the classroom report, the book review, the short story, the poem, the letter, thinking and study skills, vocabulary and spelling skills, library skills, and speech skills . . . for a start! Other useful information includes: The United States Constitution, U.S. and world maps, computer terms, and more! It's a bit hard to describe such a compendium of everything-you-need-to-know-about-everything. Suffice it to say that this is a great source of information about writing, loaded with facts writers find useful. *The Write Source* has the write stuff, all right!

Writer's Digest Books
Writer's Market, $25.95. *Poet's Market,* $19.95. *Songwriter's Market,* $19.95. *Photographer's Market,* $21.95. *Artist's Market,* $21.95. Each updated annually. These are prices for the 1992 editions, available in September 1991.

The Writer's Digest Books catalog is stuffed with how-to books for budding writers: how to write for magazines, for newspapers, for anyone and everyone. The how-tos of humorous writing . . . short stories . . . poetry . . . novels . . . fillers . . . TV scripts . . . even how to write software user manuals! Plus lots of books on how to find an agent, how to submit proposals, how to collect maximum royalties, and so on.

Each and every one of the Writer's Digest books I have seen (and I have seen a lot) has a bottom-line, dollars-and-cents attitude. Generally this smacks more of the breathless, "I got $50 for my short story and you can, too!" than of the well-paid professional. These books also tend towards a chatty, and even risqué, cuteness familiar to readers of women's magazines. In all, these books are most helpful in their marketing advice and in alerting you to the guidelines for saleable hack writing (e.g., "This is how standard magazine articles look—go and do ye likewise").

The most useful Writer's Digest publication is the deservedly famous *Market* series, which has expanded to now include *Photographer's Market, Artist's Market, Poet's Market,* and *Songwriter's Market,* as well as the original *Writer's Market.* Each of these large, hardbound, annually-updated tomes includes well-organized listings of markets for your work, with plenty of information in each listing to help you find your best opportunities, as well as supplemental listings of clubs, associations, and contests, and advice for how to best prepare and present your work. Each of the latest editions of the *Market* series now include a dozen or so close-up interviews with people in the industry.

If you want to at least try to get published, *Writer's Market* will give you some places to start.

CHAPTER FOUR

GRAMMAR

The following is *not* a list of standard grammar or language materials. Those you can get from any curriculum publisher. Some are good, some not so, but they all share one feature: overkill. Year after year children are drilled in exactly the same material, before going on to a few new lessons . . . which will be part of next year's review.

Home schoolers and parents helping Junior with his schoolwork have no great desire to linger over grammar for years and years. Hence the following collection of one-book grammar tomes and inventive grammar exercises.

NEW★★
Advanced Training Institute of America
Sentence Analysis course, $20/parent set, $26/student set. Extra workbooks, $10 each. Extra sets of *Quizzes and Tests* booklet, $4 each. Shipping extra.

At long last the folks at Bill Gothard's Advanced Training Institute of America are opening up and letting the general public have access to some of their home-school material. I'm referring to their *Sentence Analysis Course*—their wonderful Wisdom Booklets are still available only to those who have attended both IBLP seminars and an on-site parent training course.

The ATIA *Sentence Analysis* curriculum weighs several pounds, due to the many thick books it comes with. The parent set includes a hefty 202-page parent guide and an equally hefty 183-page answer key. Student materials include a textbook, consumable workbook, and a consumable *Quizzes and Tests* booklet. You need *all* these materials to complete the course; don't try to save money by skipping any of them.

In all, you get 18 lessons (each of which might last several weeks) grouped into three units: basic sentence elements, verbals and verbal phrases, and subordinate clauses. Under these topics, all of basic grammar is studied. Easy stuff, like subjects and main verbs. Hard-hitting stuff, like gerunds and participial phrases. In-between stuff, like learning that a sentence *must* contain a subject and a verb (unlike the last two of mine).

In keeping with ATIA's traditional and logical flavor, students get to diagram lots of sentences, starting in lesson 2. They are also expected to memorize definitions of grammatical terms, just like schoolkids did 100 years ago, back when they could both effortlessly create and understand complex sentences, no matter how long the distance between clauses, be the language as ornate as Addison could make it or as energetic as Dickens, even if the sentence went on for what seemed like miles, like this one.

Like other ATIA materials, the *Sentence Analysis* course is beautifully illustrated and replete with charts and lists. Scripture is the subject matter for both examples and practice sentences. Imaginative illustrations from nature are also frequently invoked to explain grammatical features. For example, the butterfly is likened to an action verb, while the chrysalis or pupa stage is likened to a "state of being," in which the pupa's goals are "both to 'exist' against the threat of its enemies and to 'link' one phase to the next."

The textbook for *Sentence Analysis* reads more like a reference book than a regular textbook. It does not really *teach* the material. Teaching requires introducing new information, isolating it from other information for emphasis, and repeating it for retention. Rather, the textbook is so densely packed with information and terminology that each new point is immediately succeeded by the next—sometimes within the same paragraph, or even the same sentence. Example:

> Pronouns are generally classified as *personal, demonstrative, relative, interrogative, indefinite, reflexive,* or *intensive.* Not every category of pronouns can perform all nine noun functions. Neither *relative pronouns* nor *reflexive/intensive pronouns,* for instance, can fulfill the role of a sentence subject. . . .

This sort of prose gives the average reader a headache, unless he is a grammarian to begin with. The extensive glossary section is more useful, especially if you've spent the last 10 years fretting over what on earth an appositive is. However, it seems that the real textbook is the parent guide. That book includes instructions on how to teach each concept, activities to make the concepts clear, and indications of when each practice exercise ought to be completed in the workbook. By contrast with the textbook, the parent guide is clearly written, easy to follow, and the activities are fun. The one thing it does not do is explain where, when, or how you and the student are supposed to use the textbook!

Sentence Analysis covers all the grammar your child is ever likely to need, and does it all in one course. Much more efficient than dragging it out over 12 years, in my opinion. This course is not something to spring on your fourth-grader, but if you have the time to devote to a systematic study of grammar, you and your older children can walk away from *Sentence Analysis* really knowing something.

Alpha Omega Publications
Exploring Truths worktext $5.95, answer key $2.95, grades 6–12. *Exploring Truths Through Diagramming* student text with answer key, $3.95, grades 6–12. *Easy English* $9.95, grades 8–12. Shipping extra.

Did you know that Sunday school was invented to help poor children learn to read, and that their text was the Bible? For centuries the Bible was used as a text for reading, literature, grammar, and composition, and Sunday school is just one of the educational enterprises in this tradition.

Alpha Omega Publications has a series based on this old concept. *Exploring Truths* is subtitled "A systematic approach to learning English through the Bible." Designed to be used by individuals or groups who possess at least sixth grade skills, *Exploring Truths* is for anyone who wants to "learn grammar through studying God's Word." Alpha Omega suggests that the text can be used by individual students for review or enrichment, or by the whole family.

Exploring Truths Through Diagramming revives the honored custom of learning grammar and parts of speech through diagramming, using sentences from the Bible book of Joshua.

Easy English uses a novel way of teaching grammar, sentence structure, and diagramming through Bible passages. Suited for high school students, the publisher recommends it as a review for college entrance exams.

Audio Memory Publishing
Grammar Songs kit (includes cassette, songbook/workbook, answers, progress chart, and teacher's guide), $16.95. *Grammar Songs* workbook without teacher's guide and answers, $4.50. Add $2 shipping. Grades K–12; best suited to younger and remedial students.

"I and You and He and She and We and It and They are all . . . pronouns. Koo koo ka choo." Just call it *Sergeant Pepper's Lonely Grammar Band.* This set of grammar songs does *not* include the aforementioned lyrics, but does have 16 musically professional pop and light rock grammar songs giving you the lowdown about nouns, verbs, adjectives, and so on— even Greek and Latin prefixes and suffixes! The lyrics really educate. For example, part of the first Verb Song goes:

> I'm *running, jumping, singing*—that's because I am a verb.
> I'm *hopping, dancing, ringing*—that's because I am a verb.
> I'm *coming, going, hitting, throwing,*
> *Humming, rowing, sitting, blowing,*
> *Riding, hiding, gliding, sliding*—
> Because I'm a verb.
> I'm a verb, verb, verb—I'm an action word.
> So put me where the action is 'cause I'm an action word.

Other verses list examples of helping verbs and linking verbs, and explain that verbs can describe what you're doing in your head—"The action isn't physical, it's in my mind instead."

The *Grammar Song* kit includes not only this cassette, but also a workbook illustrated with sassy cartoons, a teacher's guide, and answers to the (fairly standard) exercises.

NEW★★
Bob Jones University Press
Basics of Systematic Grammar, $4.95. Teacher's manual, $3.95. Grades 9–12. Shipping extra.

I love books that help you cut through the clutter and *quickly* learn or review the stuff you need to know. *Basics of Systematic Grammar* does just that. It's a programmed text designed to catch high-schoolers up on the basics of grammar. "Programmed" is edu-speak for "self-teaching." Here's how it works: You read the text on the left side of the page, while holding a piece of paper beneath it. Each text box teaches you a little bit, then asks a question about what you were just taught. You try to answer the question, then move your piece of paper down to read the answer. Then on to the next text box, and so on. Very simple, very straightforward.

Like any good programmed text, *Basics of Systematic Grammar* starts by teaching you how to use a programmed text! You then move on to nouns, verbs, and auxiliaries (helping verbs) . . . subjects, pronouns, and noun phrases . . . sentence patterns and adverbs . . . the parts of the noun phrase . . . and other parts of speech, such as conjunctions. At the end of this slim workbook are two checkup sheets for each of the five units. An excellent, quick grammar review for older

students, and not a bad way to introduce the subject to anyone who missed it or muffed it in school.

NEW★★
Crane's Select Educational Materials
Punctuation and Capitalization Flipper, $5.95. Add $2 shipping.

"Flippers" are easy-to-use references with 25 index cards (3½ x 5½") printed on both sides and enclosed in see-through sleeves overlapping each other. Each card has its topic printed on the bottom part that always shows. The whole thing is less than a quarter of an inch thick and can be snapped into a three-ring binder.

The Punctuation and Capitalization Flipper is your ready reference to these quirky topics. It contains over 400 rules, definitions, and examples, with 49 topics in all. Just flip up the appropriate card to find out about, say, where to use commas in a letter or using semicolons in a series. Make up a few more grammar exercises using the sample examples as a starting point, and you have a quick punctuation and capitalization review—or just use it as a handy, inexpensive reference guide.

NEW★★
Educators Publishing Service, Inc.
Rules of the Game: Grammar through Discovery: Books 1, 2, and 3, $4.50 each. Answer key for each book, $2 each. Add 8% shipping ($3 minimum).

Using the inductive approach, the Rules of the Game series leads students to discover grammar rules and definitions. Books 1–3 of this series are intended for grades 6–8 respectively. The exercises use both traditional and innovative approaches. Many exercise sets consist of sentences that form a narrative about a particular subject—for example, Strange but True Baseball Facts or the Underground Railroad. Other exercises ask students to follow sentence patterns, write their own sentences, choose effective modifiers, or combine sentences.

As with all public school workbooks, these workbooks repeat material learned in previous volumes: 18 pages of review on Book 2 and 21 pages in Book 3. Occasional bits of public-school propaganda. Watch out for these and you'll be OK.

NEW★★
Hayes School Publishing Co., Inc.
Learning English, grades 3–8, $3.95 each. Teacher's key for grade 8, $1. Add $1.50 postage for first item, 35¢ each additional item.

We're looking at the Hayes "Learning English" series of cleverly designed, inexpensive 86–156 page workbooks. Books are divided into sections, each with its own diagnostic test, practice lessons to reinforce any skills found wanting on the diagnostic test, and a mastery test to check the student's work after finishing the unit. Diagnostic tests are at the end of the book. Mastery tests are in the middle of the book, pre-perfed for easy removal. All workbooks except that for grade 8 have a pull-to-remove answer key with answers for all tests and practice exercises.

The diagnostic tests are designed to help your child avoid any unnecessary drill work. Each question is linked with a lesson practice page. If the child misses the question, you can assign the exact page to drill that particular skill. This means only necessary practice gets assigned. Lesson practice pages do more than drill; they teach the skill with both rules and examples, as well as with drill exercises, thus quickly bringing your child up to speed.

For further ease of use, each workbook is divided into 6–13 units, each dealing with one topic. For grade 7, the units are: sentence structure; building paragraphs; nouns; pronouns; verbs and their uses; classification of modifiers; adjective modifiers; adverbial modifiers; prepositional phrase modifiers; classification of sentences; punctuation and capitalization; general review; and letter writing. Individual units can be studied in any order. An excellent, clutter-free series for learning or drilling grammar and usage.

Hayes also has an Exercises in English series, with a similar format to their Reading Comprehension series. Exercises in English is much less thought-provoking, more fill-in-the-blankish. I would definitely choose Hayes' Learning English series over their Exercises in English series.

UPDATED★★
Hewitt Research Foundation
Winston Grammar, $29 (grades 3–8). *Advanced Winston Grammar*, $23 (grades 9–12). Shipping extra.

Here's a product that actually makes grammar *fun*, even for students who aren't neat and orderly types. It's called the Winston Grammar series, and it teaches grammatical constructions by pattern-building with colored flash cards, rather than by diagramming.

HOW IT WORKS: You identify the parts of speech in worksheet sentences by laying out their part-of-speech cards in the proper order. For example, in the first lesson, when you have only learned articles and nouns, you would lay out the sentence, "The boy and the girl saw a man eat an apple" as article-noun-blank-article-noun-blank-article-noun-blank-article-noun. Later on, you learn more parts of speech and eventually are able to lay out even complex sentences without using blank cards. (The cards, by the way, have clues on one side and the part-of-speech name on the other, for added learning value.) You also learn to identify parts of speech and constructions by underlining and writing abbreviations above the words in a sentence.

Each Winston Grammar program includes a set of worksheets bound with a pre- and post-test, a teacher's manual, quiz keys, and the color-coded noun function cards and parts-of-speech cards. *Winston Grammar* (the basic course) comes in a really fancy custom molded plastic binder, with space for adding the advanced kit later.

The basic course teaches parts of speech, noun functions, prepositional phrases, and the principles of modification. Parts of speech taught are: article, noun, personal pronoun, verb, adjective, adverb, preposition (and object), coordinating conjunction, and interjection. Noun and pronoun functions are taught in the following sequence: object of preposition, subject, direct object, indirect object, predicate nominative, appositive, and noun of direct address. All in all, it's supposed to take you 50–75 sessions to complete this course, including the frequent review lessons.

Advanced Winston Grammar has 55 worksheets, as opposed to the 30 worksheets in the basic course. After a review of the previous course, it goes on to cover the following: possessive adjectives; pronouns, nouns, and adjectives; reflexives; interrogative pronouns; present and past participles; correlative conjunctions; simple infinitives and gerunds; subject-verb combinations; clause identification; adverb clauses; compound and complex sentences; relative pronouns; adjective clauses; ellipsed relative pronouns; embedded clauses; and noun clauses as direct objects, indirect objects, predicate nominatives, objects of prepositions, appositives, and subjects. The additional cards used in this course are: possessive adjective, possessive pronoun, pronoun/adjective, verbals, Tricky Words, and Tricky Word Clues.

Hewitt tells me the basic kit is good for three to four years of grammar instruction; then the advanced kit takes your student through high school.

UPDATED **
Isha Enterprises
Easy Grammar text (includes all workbook exercises plus teaching instructions), 505 pages, $21. *Easy Grammar Workbook*, $8.95. Daily GRAMS series, $14.50 each. Add 15% shipping.

This might be *the* answer for busy home schoolers. *Easy Grammar* is the easiest complete grammar course around. Minimal effort, maximum results. Workbook for kids, teacher's manual with all the answers and teaching tips. Zero lesson preparation time, easy to teach, easy to understand, easy to correct.

Author Wanda Phillips, a schoolteacher for many years, had the bright idea of teaching children prepositions *first*. Her students crossed out the prepositional phrases in normal sentences, enabling them to easily find nouns, verbs, and so on.

Rather than diagramming, Mrs. Phillips employs a system of underlining and notation.

These big red workbooks really are easy to use and easy to teach. The course is complete, covering everything from antecedent pronouns and appositives through how to write a business letter.

Following the "mastery" system of learning popularized by Madeline Hunter, grammar is introduced step by step. Each unit also contains material from the previous units, for a continuous review.

If you need grammar review more than grammar instruction, you can always get *Daily GRAMS: Guided Review Aiding Mastery Skills*. All *Daily GRAMS* books have the same format. Exercise 1 on each page is always capitalization review. Exercise 2 is always punctuation review, and Exercise 5 is always a sentence combining exercise. Exercises 3 and 4 are general reviews of grammar usage, sentence types, and (in the third and fourth grade levels) dictionary skills. Concepts are repeated every 20–25 days.

There are now four *Daily GRAMS* workbooks: *Daily GRAMS for Second and Third Grades*, *Daily GRAMS for Third and Fourth Grades*, *Daily GRAMS for Fourth and Fifth Grades*, and *Daily GRAMS for Sixth Grade and Up*. All levels of *Daily GRAMS* contain 180 daily reviews, one per teaching day. A GRAM a day only takes 10 minutes or so, including correction time.

Longman Publishing Group
The Slade Short Course, $8.25.

It's a pleasure to find a book like *The Slade Short Course*. Mr. Slade Schuster, a teacher at Shattuck/St. Mary's, one of those exclusive private schools, has produced a slim volume that contains, in his own words,

All ye know on Earth
And all ye need to know
About grammar
In eight lessons.

The book would be too thin if Mr. Schuster had put in nothing but those eight lessons, so he threw in another seven lessons that lead the young author through the mazes of composition.

The book is not a beginning grammar text. You have to know about nouns and verbs in a rudimentary way before embarking on the *Slade Course*. Also, Mr. Schuster has wisely left out the rare exceptions which so litter comprehensive texts. Who cares about appositive phrases anyway (Mr. Schuster assures us that the thingummies are just truncated adjective clauses)? Instead of all this, there's the Grammar Game (you have to ask Veneita Sutherland at Longman Publishing for a copy). Students earn points for identifying all the parts of speech, noun positions, and phrases, clauses, and sentence types. Sample sentences are provided.

In the Composition section, the *Slade Course* concentrates on the sentence by drilling students on the several rhetorical forms. This shows genius. We learn by patterns; why not use them?

IT'S TO LAUGH!

NEW★★
Maupin House Publishing
Caught'Ya!, grades 3–12, $14.95. Available from Shekinah Curriculum Cellar.

Bored middle-school kids. Hate grammar. Frustrated teacher. Wants kids to connect grammar skills taught in class to real life. Serendipitous synergy results in . . . *Caught'Ya: Grammar with a Giggle.* Appalling (but memorable) title, this. (Endless possibilities: *Math with a Mumble. Science with a Sneer. History with a Hiss.*)

Enough of this tomfoolery. Back to real sentences. Believing that "frustration has to be the real mother of invention," teacher Jane Bell Kiester developed a simple, 10-minute-a-day technique that reconnects writing with grammar. *Caught'Ya!* outlines the technique, which has been classroom-tested in Florida public and private schools for 10 years.

Her approach: soap opera. Every day the teacher writes a sentence in the ongoing saga on the blackboard. Each day's sentence contains five to 10 mistakes that must be discovered and corrected. A mistake is only counted wrong if the student doesn't catch it during the self-grading time, when the teacher explains all the mistakes. This means everyone, even the dullest student, has the chance for a perfect score. Result: kids start concentrating on grammar, improving their writing, and enjoying English class!

The book both explains the technique and provides three 100-sentence sample soap opera sagas, complete with a new vocabulary word each day and the corrections needed for each sentence. These soap operas are pretty bad. Romeo and Juliet go to the mall. Students trip about the world with magic purple umbrellas. Hairy Beast suffers from a hopeless crush on a fickle female. Kids learn from these sagas that rudeness pays, revenge is fun, and that kids should keep secrets from their parents. Be glad you don't have to use the prewritten soaps to use the easy, fun, and effective techniques taught in *Caught'Ya!*

NEW★★
McDougal, Littell
Daily Oral Language program, $13.50 each teacher's manual. Grades 1–12 available. Add $4 shipping.

"We wanna use daily oral Language every day, dont you?"

Did you find all the usage errors in the question above? Like the *Caught'Ya!* program, *Daily Oral Language* provides two sentences a day for you to write on the chalkboard. Your students play detective as they solve and recognize the usage and mechanics errors in these sentences. It all takes about five minutes a day, with no blanks to fill in.

Are you a bit rusty on such things as pronoun case and subject-verb agreement? No problem! Each teacher's manual contains the correct sentences for each exercise, plus a list of all the errors in each sentence, all right next to each other on the page.

Unlike *Caught'Ya!*, the *Daily Oral Language* program sentences have no "plot." Each sentence stands alone, totally unconnected to the others. This is a pity, since the anticipation of following an unfolding story does add a lot of interest to daily sentence drills. While I'm complaining, the total lack of capitalization in every single sentence in all 12 grades also gets a bit old. Also, the egregious usage errors the program hopes to correct are unlikely to be a problem outside of the most remote backwoods or derelict inner-city neighborhoods. I seriously doubt any of my children would ever come close to writing anything resembling, "He brang home the most pretty picture him could find" (an actual sentence from Day 3, Level 6).

In my judgment, you should either skip the sentences with usage totally foreign to the way your family normally writes and speaks or rephrase them, so you will be practicing grammar conventions rather than drilling the kids in bad usages they never would have thought of on their own. Example: "The burglar taked these items clothes jewelry and shoes" could become "The burglar took these items clothes jewelry and shoes." In both cases, the correct answer is, "The burglar took these items: clothes, jewelry, and shoes," but in the revised example, you were practicing listing items in a series and how to use a colon instead of puzzling over a weird phrase like "the burglar taked."

Kids do learn a lot better by proofreading and editing sentences than by filling in the blanks in endless workbooks. If you're only teaching one child, he can correct the sentences right at the blackboard. If you have more than one budding grammarian, they will need to write the sentences correctly in their notebooks, so each of them has a chance to solve the sentences' problems. Very simple; you get results in five to ten minutes a day.

Though the sentences in this program may be a bit dull, and the plot element is lacking, the sentences do uphold traditional values and are very easy to use. With the addition of a few commonsense changes, as suggested above, this program could take most of the pain out of grammar drill.

Mott Media
Harvey's Elementary Grammar and Composition, $10.95. *Harvey's Revised English Grammar*, $13.95. Both hardbound.

This duo of classic grammars widely used in the McGuffey era requires (and produces) far more intellectual vigor than any workbooks available today. The teacher is urged to question the student and guide him to discovering the correct answer, rather than either giving him the answer or leaving him to "creatively" thrash it out on his own. As the introduction to the *Elementary Grammar* says,

> Great care has been taken never to define a term or to enunciate a principle without first preparing the mind of the pupil to grasp and comprehend the meaning and use of the term defined or the principle enumerated.

That will give you an idea of what you're in for.

Students begin in the *Elementary Grammar* with the study of words, parts of speech, and sentences (figuring out principles concerning each along the way), and move on in the *Revised English Grammar* to complete sentence analysis and parsing (you may remember this as diagramming). Punctuation, orthography, etymology, syntax, and prosody are thoroughly covered in the latter; some composition is included.

The *Elementary Grammar* is not really "elementary" in the sense of "ridiculously easy." It is intended for grades 4–6, while the *Revised Grammar* goes through junior high and high school.

These are "programmed" texts; that is, everything the teacher is supposed to say and everything the student is supposed to answer is spelled out, albeit in somewhat outdated language. Example:

> In the sentence, "Ellen and Mary study botany," what two words are used as the subject? "Ellen" and "Mary." Why? Because something is affirmed of them: both Ellen and Mary study botany.

Both volumes are notably short on review. Subjects are introduced one after another, and it is assumed that the student has sufficient strength of mind to hang on to each new rule or term while not forgetting the old.

The publisher says two companion volumes are on the way, as are teacher-edition answer keys and a corresponding composition book.

NEW**
Resource Publications
Understanding Grammar, $15 plus $1.75 shipping. All ages.

This slim easy-to-follow spiral-bound book chronicles the highly successful method designed by Mary Schwalm to teach her own four sons grammar at home. Starting with games, your whole family learns the three basic sentence types, the parts of speech, verb tenses, and on to more esoteric stuff. Step follows step in a very simple, clutter-free fashion that concentrates on explaining the *how* and *why* of our English language, often illustrated by sentence diagramming techniques. You will find this book a breeze to use and a wonderful introduction to/accompaniment for a formal grammar handbook such as *Harvey's*.

This is the neatest course in the hows and whys of grammar, including games and diagramming, that I have seen. Super easy to use.

NEW★★
World Book Direct Response
The Student Information Finder, $34.95.

The two volumes of *The Student Information Finder* contain important facts most often taught in school. We're looking at the Language Arts and Social Studies volume right now. (The Math and Science volume is described elsewhere.)

The book has five units: Facts about Writing, Language, and Spelling; Places around the World; Important Dates in History; People Who Made History; and Presidents of the U.S.A. and Prime Ministers of Canada.

Unit 1 has perhaps the shortest parts-of-speech review in print, along with spelling rules, tables of spelling sounds, rules and examples for capitalization and punctuation, and a guide to preparing a paper, including information on outlining, footnoting, and the use of quotes. It's written for teens to use on their own (except for the part about new approaches to grammar, which is a real head-scratcher for non-grammarians). Going through Unit 1 would provide a wonderful review of all the most important information learned in school language-arts courses, while the remaining pictures and data in this book provide fingertip reference to geography and history (from a mainstream perspective, of course).

CHAPTER FIVE

LITERATURE

Is truth stranger than fiction? Or has modern fiction become stranger than truth? As syndicated writer Charley Reese noted recently,

I know it will come as a shock to most scriptwriters, but the majority of Americans do not use four-letter words at a rate of five to the sentence. One does find, too, in contrast to the the world as reflected in movies [and in books—MP], people who talk about subjects other than sex and making money. There are millions of people in business who don't cheat their customers or deliberately pollute the environment. Millions of Americans worship in churches and synagogues whose spiritual leaders are not child molesters or money-grubbing charlatans.

Truth is not only stranger than fiction, but these days is lovelier, healthier, more decent and more inspiring.

THINKING ABOUT LITERATURE

The Bible tells us to seek after what is true, noble, right, pure, lovely, and admirable (Philippians 4:8). I believe that as this applies to art we are to look for what is *true to life*. God does not condemn fiction, for Jesus Himself told parables. The point is that evil should not be glamorized or explicitly described. God tells us, for example, that the men of Sodom were sinners. The Bible does not glamorize their sin, though, or give us graphic details of what exactly the Sodomites were planning to do to the angels who visited Lot. Thus Christians can benefit from stories of heroism, true or fictional, even if the protagonists do not spend their entire time preaching, and also from stories that show the ugliness of evil without dwelling on its techniques.

What you just read is almost a definition of classic literature. As Dale Dykema, headmaster of the Covenant Home Curriculum, writes,

The classics are important for the lessons they teach. Good and evil are in conflict and eternal values are usually shown to win out.

The classics give us good examples of relationships, especially the old English writings. How people should respect and talk with one another is often a part of the work.

The classics, of course, are more than well-written morality plays. As Mr. Dykema also points out, "The classics are important for their language. It is good for us to see proper use of the English language. . . The classic style teaches writing techniques that are imaginative and interesting."

Contrast the opening sentences of *Treasure Island* with the oatmeal of topic-sentence paragraphs as taught in the schools, and you'll begin to glimpse a whole new world of human expression. Eloquence, controlled passion, self-denial, deep thinking, and the effects of a person's actions on others are subjects dealt with more generously in classic literature than elsewhere.

GILDED MEADOW MUFFINS?

Although modern-day writers are not necessarily shut out from the talent club, the awful truth is that literary fads and some disturbing beliefs about literature have crippled most modern writing. For example, porn has become mandatory among both "serious" and "mass" writers. Just as most producers are unwilling to put out a "G" movie, for fear it will die at the box office and be ignored by the critics, so most modern writers put in the obligatory sex scene. Similarly, happy endings are looked down on as naive. A writer who uses happy endings won't be taken seriously or accepted by the literati. P. G. Wodehouse parodied this outlook beautifully: his humor books often took sly pokes at writers whose characters found life "grey."

I'm sure you've had the experience of reading a well-written book about despicable characters you couldn't care less about. In real life, some of us act despicably but others do not. Such visits to the underbelly of society, unrelieved even by the kindness of a Nancy who, social outcast though she is, befriends the orphan Oliver Twist, are mere exercises in self-flagellation. They tell us nothing about ourselves or anyone else. They tell us nothing about life or the realistic results of our actions.

Some people contend that *art* is what counts. A novel might be despicable and patently untrue, but if it's written cleverly it deserves to be read. (Their thinking reminds me of the line from *My Fair Lady*, where the professor says, "The French don't care what you *do*, actually, so long as you pronounce it properly!") This theory applies across all art boundaries. It allows architecture experts (for example) to *ooh* and *aah* over buildings where thousands of people were murdered (e.g., Aztec temples). I believe it should be the other way around. Art is only the handmaid of content. If

the content is no good, the art is no good. If someone has nothing useful to say, who cares how well he says it? You can gild a meadow muffin, but it's still a meadow muffin.

Anyway, why worry about whether we should honor art *or* content, when we can have both? The classics are good art *with* good content. I'll skip the meadow muffins, thank you!

LITERATURE COURSES & CRITICISM

NEW**
A Beka Book Publications
Of People, Of Places, Themes in Literature, $12.55 each. *Backgrounds to World Literature, Masterpieces from World Literature, Beginnings of American Literature, The Literature of the American People, Introduction to English Literature, The Literature of England,* $11.95 each. All texts are paperbound. Student test booklets, teacher keys available for grades 10–12 courses. Shipping extra.

A Beka's literature texts for grades 7–9 are mainly reading anthologies. Each book includes short stories, poems, and essays. Discussion questions are included for each reading selection, as are pronunciation guides where necessary. "Check Your Speed" sections tell you how many words per minute you were reading if you know how long you took at it. Author biographies and a complete glossary in each volume round out these offerings.

The emphasis in these grades is twofold: becoming aware of literary devices authors use in their work (characterization, scene-setting, plot, and theme), and developing a taste for fine literature. In the words of the introduction to the seventh-grade book, "Each book features a rich variety of important short stories, poems, essays, and plays and a good balance of serious and humorous pieces from the finest writers of America, England, and Europe."

Of People, the 576-page seventh-grade book, includes selections chosen for their emphasis on characterization. The selections are grouped under these topic headings: families and friends, people and animals, pilgrims, patriots, time out for Christmas, explorers, pioneers, men and women of genius, sportsmen, and legendary heroes. Some selections are excerpts from longer works such as *Don Quixote, A Christmas Carol, Robinson Crusoe,* and *Pilgrim's Progress.* Many other selections will be familiar to parents, such as the immortal poem "Casey at the Bat," while many others, though well-known in their own way, are likely to be unfamiliar to most readers, like Honoré Willsie Morrow's fascinating true tale of the boy pioneer who led his six younger siblings, including a baby, over 500 miles of the Oregon Trail when the adults in his party gave up because they thought the trip would be too hard! Many of the stories in this book are about Christians (e.g., Isaac Watts, the original martyred missionaries to the Auca Indians, William the Silent, and George Washington Carver). As advertised, each story and poem unfailingly presents us with a strong character. Some of the discussion questions lead the student to observe the literary techniques that spotlight these characters, though I'd like to see them brought out more explicitly. (Perhaps they are in the teacher's guides, which I haven't seen.)

Of Places, for eighth-graders, is supposed to draw students' attention to how each author sets a scene. Its 529 pages include excerpts from *Caddie Woodlawn, The Yearling, The Incredible Journey,* and *The Song of Hiawatha.* ("By the shores of Gitchee Gumee/By the shining Big-Sea-Water/Stood the wigwam of Nokomis . . ."), among dozens of other readings. The selections in this book are grouped by place, it's true—neighborhood, school, home, America, around the world, over all the earth, about the sea, upon the mountains, and in the realm of the imagination—but the questions and selections still focus mainly in on character, whatever the book title might say.

Ninth-graders move on to studying literary themes in a book appropriately titled *Themes in Literature.* This book more successfully carries out its mission, grouping selections in units with titles like "Truth and Wisdom," "Courage," "Humility," "Justice," "Temperance," "Beauty," "Faith and Hope," "Love," and "Time and Eternity" (an entire section on death and dying). Among famous authors anthologized in this volume are Count Tolstoy, Nathaniel Hawthorne (author of *Tanglewood Tales*), Mark Twain, Geoffrey Chaucer, the melancholy William Cowper, the frivolous and sensuous Giovanni Boccaccio,

and Guy de Maupassant—to name just a few. In fact, you'll see a lot more famous names here than you did in the first two books in the series. Here also, for the first time, a large number of the selections dwell on death, dying, loss, and other painful themes.

A Beka's literature course for grades 10–12, called the Classics for Christians series, takes more of a "survey" approach. Grade 10 surveys world literature, grade 11 American literature, and grade 12 English literature. Again, many classics are included or excerpted. Each course has two books. In grade 10, for example, the first book, *Backgrounds to World Literature,* repeats the lessons of grades 7–9 by emphasizing literary devices, while the second book, *Masterpieces from World Literature,* presents reading selections in historical sequence. We then proceed, not to English literature (as one would expect, since it came next chronologically), but to American literature. The two volumes in this course cover American literature in chronological order, with the second one taking up at the later 19th and 20th centuries. Unusual features of this course include a lengthy study of the novel *The Scarlet Letter,* a post-Puritan story of two adulterers (one a minister) and how they deal with their guilt (not entirely in a satisfactory manner). English literature, in the 12th grade, is again presented in chronological order. The first book, *Introduction to English Literature,* includes the entire text of *Macbeth* and *Pilgrim's Progress,* as well as a good chunk of literary history and plenty from the works of early English writers from Venerable Bede through John Milton. *The Literature of England,* the last book of the series, studies English literature "as a reflection of the spiritual state of the British people through the ages," from the Restoration through the modern day. This whole series is *packed* with poetry—far more than I've seen in any other publisher's upper-grades books.

A notable feature of the grades 10–12 books is the integration of art with literature. Each book in this series is illustrated with dozens of full-color reproductions of famous art works. Also worth mentioning is that A Beka prefers to put its main emphasis on the literature itself, rather than the history of literature.

In the Classics for Christians series there are, as in the ninth-grade book, a large number of selections in which major characters die or anticipate the approach of death. This becomes almost ludicrous in places, as in *Masterpieces from World Literature*, where the entire section on classical Greece is so saturated with death that—well, let me just share some of the selection titles in this one section: "The Death of Hector," "Death to the Pagan and to the Christian," "Brevity of Life," "On Early Death," "The Dying Christian to His Soul," "Death Be Not Proud" (a poem by the 17th century Englishman John Donne which only seems to be included here because its subject matter fits the gloomy setting), "The Funeral Oration of Pericles," "The Death of Socrates," and "On Tragedy." Also included in this section is Sophocles' *Antigone*, a play about a sister who attempts to bury her dead brothers and in consequence is given the death penalty herself, the poem "Unhappy Dionysius," and "Elegy for Heraclitus."

This is not an isolated example: depressing tales and poems are found throughout the series. To pick some at random, how about Ambrose Bierce's *An Occurrence at Owl Creek Bridge*, which gave me nightmares after I saw the film in public-school ninth grade, or Poe's *The Pit and the Pendulum*, a classic horror tale, both found (among others) in volume 3 of this series?

In all, I would say that A Beka's upper-grades literature program is somewhat unbalanced. Kids don't need this much tragedy, especially in the suicide-prone teen years. My advice would be to lighten up on the death and misery. Bring on some Ogden Nash and P. G. Wodehouse!

NEW★★
Bob Jones University Press

Explorations in Literature (grade 7), *Excursions in Literature* (grade 8), *Fundamentals of Literature* (grade 9), *Elements of Literature* (grade 10), $17.95 each student textbook, $29.50 each teacher's manual (grades 7 and 8) or teacher's edition (grades 9 and 10). *American Literature* (grade 11), $19.95 each student text, $29.50 each teacher's edition. *British Literature: Early* and *British Literature: Modern* (grade 12), $15.95 each student text, $21 each teacher's edition. All texts are hardbound. Various videos, classic books, and teacher's guides to the classics also available. These are home-school prices. Shipping extra.

Bob Jones University Press takes a slightly different approach to literature than A Beka, with a four-grade series introducing students to literary themes, styles, and devices, followed by a two-grade survey of American and British literature. Reading selections are included in each book, but they are not as anthological in format as the A Beka books, containing more literary history and textual analysis, and are not as heavily loaded with poetry selections. Like the A Beka series, the BJUP series does include many different authors and types of literature. All student texts are hardbound, very nicely laid out, and copiously illustrated.

Explorations in Literature, the seventh-grade book, is organized into six three-week units on the themes of courage, nature and man, generosity, patriotism, humility, and the family. This book is intended to introduce the rudiments of literary discernment, as students move from reading strictly for pleasure to thinking about what they read. Themes in the eighth-grade book, *Excursions in Literature*, are choices, friendships, viewpoints, adventurers, discoveries, and heroes and villains. Again, the book has a character-building emphasis, as the student is asked to identify his own journey through life in terms of these themes. *Fundamentals of Literature*, for grade 9, introduces the student to literary analysis. This text introduces conflict, characterization, theme, structure, point of view, and moral tone, with one unit devoted to each. Finally, *Elements of Literature*, the 10th-grade book, waxes more philosophical by "focusing on those literary details that define and distinguish interpretive literature."

These books are all wholesome and enormous fun to read, containing a great mix of drama, humor, tearjerkers, and whatever else appeals to preteen children. I read several of the stories and poems out loud at the dinner table, and every child in our family read through the books in the next weeks! You can, then, use the books either as the basis of a formal study course, or simply as readers to introduce your children to famous authors and styles.

If you want a formal course, be sure to get the teacher's manual or teacher's edition. The teacher's *manuals* (grades 7 and 8) provide all the daily lessons, activities, and assignments. The teacher's *editions* (grades 9 and 10) include the full student book text on each teacher's page as well as lesson plans and assignments. The teacher's manuals or editions are *absolutely necessary* if you want to teach a formal course, since the student books for these grades *only* include the reading selections and "Reading Check" questions. The teacher's books are really excellent teaching tools, too, opening students' eyes to literature's spiritual, moral, and technical aspects through analysis and discussion of the reading assignments and carefully-chosen writing assignments. One writing assignment, for example, is to turn a story into a drama. The teacher's manual explains the exact steps students need to go through to make the transformation.

After grade 10, the upper-grades literature curriculum now switches over to a chronological study of American and British literature, the same sequence as A Beka presents. Each course examines literary works in the light of the author's life, the historical period and literary movement to which he belonged, and what the Bible has to say about the underlying philosophies of these movements. Lots of *long* reading selections, intermixed with shorter stories, essays, and poems. The British Literature course presently has two separate textbooks, one for early and the other for modern British literature, but its second edition (due out fall 1992) will be one volume. The American Literature course has just been revised into a one-volume form, including a complete modern play. These are *not* "fun" books—frankly, I think they would work well in a college course.

We have been using the upper-grades literature program, and my most severe criticism is that the background political history is so densely packed that it is not always easy to assimilate. This is a common failing of upper-grades material when it deals with history—loading the student with so many names and dates that he can't possibly retain them all. All this encyclopedic information is fascinating, but a broader tracing of background history would suffice, without distracting student attention from the literature itself. Alternatively, you could try first running your student through the *Then and There* series, or the EDC Publishing or Ladybird titles that deal with British history, to acclimate him to the time periods you are about to study.

These books, which emphasize how people lived in each time period, help a lot in avoiding culture shock.

NEW**
Christian Light Publications
Perspectives of Truth in Literature (hardbound, 472 pages), $14.40. Add 20% shipping. Grades 9–12.

Here is an absolutely marvelous literature text that leads your teen to not only discover the different literary forms and styles, but also form some measure of a book's content.

Some quotes from the beginning of Unit 1:

We do not go to literature to find truth, but simply to find truth well expressed and illustrated . . .

The standard of truth is not the man who writes it or the time in which it is written, but rather, truth is judged by the revelation of God . . .

Many men pride themselves on having an open mind. By this they claim to be able to consider any new idea without first rejecting it. They hope they will be able to reject it if it is wrong.

Such men consider persons inferior who have already made up their minds about certain subjects and refuse to entertain any further discussion. But such open-minded persons are often in a dangerous position. For if a person opens his mind to anything, he should not be surprised to discover that his mind is harboring a lot of mental garbage and what truth he has is being corrupted.

But a closed-minded person is also in danger. Much error is quite probably locked on the inside and much truth is knocking in vain from the outside.

How then should we read? We must read with a noble mind like the Bereans of Paul's day. All literature must be tested by the yardstick of God's Word. What measures up is to be accepted and savored; what fails the test is to be rejected without further consideration.

I sat down and read the entire text through. This was a treat, because of the exceedingly high quality of the stories, essays, and poems included in the book, and the excellent thought questions at the end of each selection. Comprehension, reading speed, and writing technique are also covered in this text. With some adaptation (e.g., the parent reading the stories aloud and then discussing the questions with the child) I would think you could begin to use *Perspectives of Truth in Literature* with preteens as well. In any case, it is too good a book for any literature-minded *parent* to miss!

NEW★★
Covenant Home Curriculum

Classic Critiques, $18 postpaid. Specify level: "Short Classics" are for grades 3–6, while "Full Classics" are for grades 5–adult.

How about a home school publisher who does the book reports for you? *Classic Critiques* from Covenant Home Curriculum provide a roadmap through classic literature. Each *Critique* includes a story summary, with attention to the author's worldview. The summaries themselves are rather exciting, and could well serve as interest-sparkers enticing families to read those books. Some *Critiques* also feature discussion questions; others have suggestions for topics to discuss.

Each *Classic Critique* is printed on a single sheet, usually folded in the middle. We're not talking about overwhelming you with tons of data here! They are also attractively printed on parchment-style paper, with a line-drawing illustration of a scene from the book on each cover.

List A includes *Great Expectations, Treasure Island, Macbeth, The Red Badge of Courage, Captains Courageous, Wuthering Heights, Twenty Thousand Leagues under the Sea, Pride and Prejudice, The Call of the Wild, Gulliver's Travels, The Turn of the Screw, Paradise Lost,* and *The Wind in the Willows.* List B includes *Jane Eyre, A Tale of Two Cities, The Last of the Mohicans, Ivanhoe, Canterbury Tales, Hamlet, The Hunchback of Notre Dame, Julius Caesar, Moby Dick, The Iliad, The Odyssey, Alice in Wonderland,* and *Up from Slavery.*

The Covenant Home Curriculum includes all these books, plus much emphasis on creative writing and correct grammar. If you consider in-depth study of great literature from a Christian viewpoint important for your child's education, you might want to look into either *Classic Critiques* or the entire Covenant Home Curriculum program (described in detail in Volume 1).

UPDATED★★
EDC Publishing, Inc.

Greek Myths and Legends, $7.95 paperbound or $13.96 library-bound. *Norse Myths and Legends,* $6.95 paperbound or $12.96 library-bound. Ages 11–15.

Looking for an illustrated introduction to classic mythology? It's here! Top-quality art combines with vibrant illustrations as is usual with EDC series. The legends series for younger children has unfortunately been discontinued, but we still have *Greek Myths and Legends* and *Norse Myths and Legends.* These feature grotesque fantasy art suitable to the actual gloomy myths themselves, and are definitely more suited to upper-elementary and teen readers.

NEW★★
Family Learning Center

Learning Language Arts through Literature: Red Book (grade 2), $17.95; Yellow Book (grade 3), $17.95; Tan Book (grade 4–6), $12.95; Grey Book (grades 7–8), $12.95. Add 10% shipping ($2 minimum).

I wrote this program up in detail in the Creative Writing chapter, although really it belongs in a half-dozen chapters, since it includes *all* the following—spelling, grammar, vocabulary, writing mechanics, literature, penmanship, and thinking skills—all broken down into sensible daily and weekly lessons. Speaking just about its literary side, the literature selections are wonderful! In the Tan Book, for example, you start with Psalm 1, then proceed to *Bambi, The Wheel on the School,* a poem by Tennyson (famous poets are that week's special feature!), *Little House on the Prairie, The Bronze Bow, Caddie Woodlawn, King of the Wind* by Marguerite Henry, *Lassie Come Home, The Hiding Place, Kidnapped,* the Gettysburg Address, *Swallows and Amazons, Anne of Green Gables, Prince Caspian, Rascal, Robinson Crusoe, Star of Light* by Patricia St. John, *The Railway Children, David Copperfield, The Wind in the Willows, Little Women,* and *Big Red* by Jim Kjelgaard. In fact, the literature selections in each *Learning Language Arts through Literature* book would make an excellent reading list, if you are looking for library books to use with your children!

Foundation for American Christian Education

A Family Program for Reading Aloud, second edition, $6.50. Add 10% 4th-class mail, 15% UPS.

A family reading program that reflects American patriotism, the Foundation for American Christian Education's *Family Program for Reading Aloud* contains discussions of more than 200 literary classics.

Part I is mostly directed to parents of elementary-school children. The new second edition now also includes a Part II on reading in depth for high-school students. Some topics: the ocean, pioneers, teaching and learning, and the French Revolution. Some authors covered in depth: Charles Dickens, Sir Walter Scott, Washington Irving, and Nathaniel Hawthorne. A section on restoring heroes and heroines in literature includes Richard E. Byrd, Charles A. Lindbergh, Eddy Rickenbacker, Anne Bradstreet, Lydia Darrah, and Mercy Otis Warren. The last section highlights people who preserve our history.

Jeffrey Norton Publishers

Most cassettes are $12.45 postpaid.

This company, which also owns Audio-Forum and Video-Forum, has a catalog entitled Sound Seminars. Captured on cassette are a host of critics dissecting the works of other people. If this sounds like a good idea to you, Jeffrey Norton has, besides individual cassettes of individual critics, a series by Heywood Hale Broun and another by Gilbert Highet, both of whom have been hailed as provocative, intelligent, and, in Mr. Highet's case, charming. You can also get Norman Mailer talking about existentialism, Stephen Spender talking about everybody, and Shakespeare talked about by everybody. Auden discusses poetry and Frost reads his own poems.

NEW**
Teaching Home

June/July 1988 issue, $3.75. Complete 6-issue set for 1988, $17.50, includes free set of 6 plastic magazine holders for your ring binder.

As I've said before, each *Teaching Home* magazine back issue on a given topic is like a minicourse in teaching that topic. June/July 1988 was the issue on teaching literature. There were several articles on how to teach literature, motivating children to love books, using literature to influence your children's values, lives of great men and women, how to choose and use good books for all ages, and the Bible and literature. This all is a lot livelier than it sounds—these are hands-on ideas and principles from people actually involved in home teaching!

CLASSICS ON CASSETTE

NEW**
Classics on Tape

Purchase prices run from about $4/cassette to $6/cassette; rental is about half that.

Do you or your kids have time spent in the kitchen or the car, walking or showering, eating or dressing, in which you would like to catch up on *unabridged* fiction and nonfiction classics? If your answer is, "Yes!" then here's a catalog for you.

We're not talking your typical two-tape abridgments of *War and Peace* here. Such "Cliff Notes" of book recordings provide only an illusion of having experienced a work, while massacring the author's characters and style. Classics on Tape sells and rents recordings of *unabridged* classics. These range from the gargantuan *Gulag Archipelago* by Nobel Prize-winner Alexander Solzhenitsyn to children's classics like *Robinson Crusoe* and *The Princess and the Goblin.* The catalog is heavy on the conservative-libertarian side of things, with works by Thomas Sowell, Ludwig von Mises, Walter Williams, George Gilder, Clarence Carson, Paul Johnson, and other neo- and paleo-conservative luminaries. The religion section is big on Francis Schaeffer and Malcolm Muggeridge, with a smattering of A.W. Tozer, St. Augustine, and Dr. Martyn Lloyd-Jones. Their literature selections include generally-accepted classics by Jane Austen, Jonathan Swift, Charles Dickens, Dostoevsky, and so on, as well as more traditional children's books like *Pinocchio*. Apparently these folks have never heard that hey-hey, ho-ho, Western culture's gotta go.

These recordings are literature, not entertainment. You won't find music, dramatization with multiple voices, or other gimmicks. One reader reads the entire book straight through. This can, however, have its lighter side. Frederick Davidson's reading of the poetry in *The Princess and the Goblin* put my children in stitches. (I wonder if George MacDonald intended his character's anti-goblin poems to end with a loud, rude, "Blah!"?)

Don't feel you must rush out and get every title carried in this collection. *Tess of the d'Urbervilles*, for example, is a dreary look at "tragic destiny," featuring a pure, innocent heroine who nonetheless finds herself an unwed mom and ends the book by dying miserably. (If you like fuzzy morality and impending doom, that's Thomas Hardy all over.) Such slips are rare, though. Most selections are worth owning by anyone's standards —and the company offers a 30-day money-back guarantee, so you can return any clunkers.

Mind's Eye
Most audiocassettes $7.95 each. Sets are less per cassette. Shipping extra.

This gorgeous, easy-to-use catalog contains mystery, intrigue, horror (those I skip) and set after set of classic tales that I drool over and hope to buy someday. Here you can get fairy tales (fully dramatized), classic children's stories, Mark Twain, Charles Dickens, Tolkien, dramatized biography, radio classics, Greek classics, American novels, the famous BBC Audio Collection, and more!

Jeffrey Norton Publishers
John Bunyan's *Pilgrim's Progress* (1 cassette), $10.95. *Hamlet* (4 cassettes), $22.95. *Henry V* (3 cassettes), $19.95. *Julius Caesar* (3 cassettes), $22.95. *All's Well that Ends Well* (2 cassettes), $15.95. Jane Austen's *Persuasion* (5 cassettes), $25.95; *Emma* (4 cassettes), $22.95. *Jane Eyre* (5 cassettes), $25.95. Shipping extra.

Works by Shakespeare, Jane Austen, Charlotte Brontë, and John Bunyan are available on cassette from this well-known catalog.

Recorded Books
Thirty-day rental or sale. Prices start at $7.50, which includes a "durable bookshelf album with color cover art and contents information."

"Cover to cover studio recordings of the very best in current and classic fiction brought to life on standard-play cassettes by professional narrators." Rental available. Some "adult" cassettes. RB has lots of good stuff, too: P.G. Wodehouse, Tolkien, Jane Austen, James Hamilton narrating the New Testament, Gilbert and Sullivan operas with libretto, and Solzhenitsyn, among others.

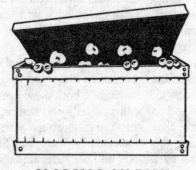

CLASSICS ON DISK

NEW✶✶
DAK Industries
BSR external CD-ROM drive with interface for IBM PC, XT, or AT compatible, plus CD software, $699 plus $19 shipping.

I know, I know . . . this should be in my educational software book (*Pride's Guide to Educational Software*, published by Crossway Books). Nevertheless, I want to open your eyes to something completely different in literature. It's 450 literary, historical, cultural, and religious works on a single CD-ROM disk. The "Library of the Future," which includes full works from Aeschylus, Aristophanes, Bacon, Chaucer, Homer, Milton, Shakespeare, and dozens of others, plus historical documents such as the entire text of Magna Carta and the U.S. Constitution, comes with search-and-retrieve software that lets you instantly find the quote you're looking for. If you've ever wondered *which* Shakespeare play had the line "Methinks the lady doth protest too much," or even if you didn't know it was in Shakespeare, you can pin it down, in context, in a flash. You can pick a topic, such as "liberty," and if you have the time and patience, see what dozens of thinkers had to say about it.

The Library of the Future has a suggested retail price of $695, and I suppose you can buy it all by itself for that. However, you'd be nuts to do so, since DAK has put together a deal whereby you get a CD-ROM drive for your IBM-compatible, a 21-volume encyclopedia (over 33,000 entries and over 1,000 full-color illustrations) on CD-ROM, a "World and U. S. Atlases" CD-ROM with over 320 full-color maps plus related statistical information, an eight-volume reference library on CD-ROM (*Webster's New World Dictionary, Webster's New World Thesaurus, The New York Public Library Desk Reference, Dictionary of Twentieth Century History, Guide to Concise Writing, Webster's New World Dictionary of Quotable Definitions,* and *The 1990 National Directory of Addresses and Telephone Numbers*), and a "Languages of the World" CD-ROM with full text of 17 multilingual dictionaries . . . all for $4 more than the cost of just the Library of the Future by itself!

This all would be a stack of almost 500 books if you bought it in standard paper form, and you could *never* find the information you wanted as quickly with regular books. I'm not saying you just must rush out and buy it, because some selections in the Library of the Future are rather randy (e.g., Giovanni Bocaccio's *Decameron,* which features endless tales of sexual adventures as told by a group of young people enjoying themselves while the Black Plague decimates Renaissance Italy). I have a preteen son for whom I'd love to get this deal, but I don't want him getting libertine sex instruction while he's using his computer!

I shared these concerns with the folks at DAK, and there's a chance that future editions of this software will come with a way for parents to make unwanted selections unreadable. Anyway, this gives you an idea of the open-ended future of literature study. Imagine comparing Shakespeare to Bacon on a topic at the press of a key!

CHAPTER SIX

HANDWRITING AND KEYBOARDING

L et's not waste any time talking about printing, or ball-and-stick manuscript, or precursive. You know how to print. In fact, some of you *only* print, because your cursive hand is illegible!

You teen and adult printers out there are in good company. The transition to cursive writing occurs usually in the third grade—too early for some and too late for others. Children who haven't really become comfortable with writing and reading are asked to switch over to an entirely new alphabet. The cursive *r* doesn't resemble the manuscript *r*. The same can be said about cursive *b*, *f*, *j*, *k*, *l*, *s* and *z*, and virtually *all* the cursive capital letters. As an added bonus, some of the cursive capitals are almost impossible to distinguish from others even when penned correctly: *F*, *G*, and *T*, for example.

One way around this mess is to substitute the newly popular italic hands for cursive. Italic capitals are very like manuscript capitals—you can always add extra swashes just for fun, too. The lowercase letters change less in italic, also. No *f*s with double loops!

Of course, some people just won't be happy without neat cursive handwriting like great-grandma used to have. I have included teen and adult handwriting courses for you, too.

Another way to evade the demands of cursive is to learn to type. Rare is the teacher or boss who would insist that you write out papers or memos by hand rather than typing them. Also, unlike cursive, typing is

a marketable skill. If you call it "keyboarding" and learn a few simple computer commands, it's even *more* marketable!

Without keyboarding skills, a computer is a Stone Age tool. You hunt and peck. With keyboarding skills, it's a rocket. You launch and fly.

HANDWRITING COURSES FOR TEENS & ADULTS

Christian Liberty Press
$4.95 each handwriting workbook. Add 10% shipping (minimum $1.50). Grades K–8.

Christian Liberty Academy's new handwriting program is based on the traditional Palmer method (manuscript and cursive). It takes 15–20 minutes a day, introduces cursive after a year's practice with manuscript, and combines patriotism with scriptural themes and everyday life. Each slim book (60–76 pages) also includes teaching instructions, eliminating the need for separate teacher's manuals. The publishers include a free writing practice pad with each book. Books available:

• Book 1, *In the Beginning*, for four- and five-year-olds.

• Book 2, *Writing with Diligence*, is intended for first- and second-graders

• Book 3, *Writing with Prayer*, starts with manuscript review and finishes up with cursive, introduced in stroke groups.

• Book 4, *Writing with Grace* is designed for third- and fourth-graders.

• Book 5, *Writing with Power*, a new book, provides a review of the principles of advanced cursive for children in grades 4–8.

The advanced books also feature "Home Education Models." These are brief bios of famous people who were educated at home.

These books mix a few language arts activities in with the handwriting practice. Otherwise, the format is simple, logical, and concise.

Collier Books/Macmillan Book Company
The Italic Way to Beautiful Handwriting, $8.95. Add 8% shipping. Available in bookstores.

Fred Eager's book, *The Italic Way to Beautiful Handwriting*, was recommended to me by a home schooling college professor who was using it with his own children. This is the book to use if you want to learn italic yourself and then teach it to your children. The book is very reasonably priced, contains everything you need to know, and is full of inspirational "before and after" examples.

NEW★★
EDC Publishing
Calligraphy, $6.95 paperbound or $13.96 library-bound. Shipping extra. Ages 12 and up.

Calligraphy: From Beginner to Expert is an Usborne book. That means it's highly visual and crammed to

the hilt with full-color illustrations. Text serves the illustrations, explaining how the effects are achieved, what the parts of the pen are, and so on. Topics covered are:

• the history of calligraphy
• basic equipment
• types of letters (capitals, miniscules . . .)
• layout tips
• Gothic and Italic styles
• decoration and illumination
• ways to use calligraphy
• unusual equipment (balsa pens, quills . . .)
• Chinese calligraphy
• stenciling, rubbing, embossing, incising
• careers in calligraphy

The book closes with several pages of sample alphabets, numbers, and borders, and a complete index.

Calligraphy is an excellent introduction to the "pen arts," and actually provides enough information in its 48 pages for the beginner to get started in the style of his choice. Recommended.

NEW★★
Essential Learning Products
Each practice book, $2.95. Buy five and get one free. Add $2 per order for shipping ($3 in Canada).

Want a quick review of cursive? Try the grade 5 handwriting practice book from Essential Learning Products. It's one of a series of drill 'n practice books put out by the people who publish *Highlights* magazine for children. Grade 5 is the "adult" cursive book. Good price, easy to use, nonthreatening format, no busy-work.

Mott Media

Complete Spencerian set, including theory book and all five copy books, $13.95. Individual copy books $2.25, theory book $4.95.

Mott Media has resurrected ye olde Spencerian handwriting books from ye tombe of oblivion. These books were used for over 100 years and are based on the method of Platt Rogers Spencer.

If John Henry was born with a hammer in his hand, young Spencer was born with a pen. A born calligrapher, Spencer greatly admired John Hancock's elegant signature on the Declaration of Independence and desired to design a handwriting system that would produce that kind of grace, yet be easy to learn. The result, carried on by his disciples, was Spencerian writing, a complete system based on a few simple arm movements and seven basic strokes. Every letter is broken down into those strokes. The result is a gorgeous "copperplate" system of writing, quaint and elegant.

Spencer's theory book reads like a catechism, with its questions and answers. "Will you measure and analyze small *r*? . . . How should the small *r* be formed?" The five accompanying consumable copy books take the student from writing the "short" letters on graphed paper to penning such sentences as "Angels are guardian spirits" (this was before the ACLU, remember) and "Modesty always charms." Like all Mott's Classic Curriculum, the books can be used at all age levels and at any pace that fits the student.

UPDATED**
Portland State University
Continuing Education Press

Books A through G and instructor's manual, $4.25 each ($3.25), Specimen set containing all the above, $32 ($25). Basic Blackline Master Practice Sheets for Home-schoolers (covers books A, B, C), Cursive Blackline Master Practice Sheets for Homeschoolers (covers books D, E, F), $10 each. Classroom wall charts, two sets: Basic Italic Alphabet and Numerals, Cursive Italic Alphabet and Numerals, $5.75/set ($4.50). Alphabet desk strips (specify Basic Italic or Cursive Italic), $5.75 set of 30 ($4.50), individual desk strip 50¢ each. New: Movable Alphabet, set of 415 2" high letters with storage box, $37. New videotape, $7 rental, copying permitted. Shipping and handling $4 up to 2 items, then add 25¢ per item. Second price in parentheses is school price. Use school price if your order totals $20 or more. Grades K–6.

Believe it or not, some public school systems are getting into teaching italic handwriting. The series they are using is published by Portland State University. It begins with prewriting exercises in Book A and goes all the way to a very professional italic hand. The series is spread out over seven grades, starting with kindergarten, like most public school courses; but you don't need to buy all the workbooks if you are using them at home.

Barbara Getty and Inga Dubay are the two ladies who invented this simple italic teaching method. Differences between the Getty-Dubay approach and other public-school handwriting programs:

• How many letters change shape when making the transition from manuscript to cursive? Only two capital letters and one manuscript letter change shape in the Getty-Dubay approach. Compare this to the number of letters that change shape in other systems: 18 uppercase letters change in the D'Nealian system and 26 in Palmer, Bowmar-Noble, and Zaner-Bloser; 13 lowercase letters change in D'Nealian and 26 in Palmer, Bowmar-Noble, and Zaner-Bloser.

• Getty-Dubay is the only public-school method in which capital cursive forms are based on the manuscript forms.

• Getty-Dubay uses no loops, aiding both legibility and ease of teaching.

• Capital letters, ascenders, and descenders are in the same proportions as those found in book typefaces, allowing closer writing without tangling letters together. Other methods use ascenders and descenders which frequently become tangled. Example: try writing the word *fly* in cursive handwriting, and then writing *fall* directly underneath. If you learned from one of the other methods, the loops of the *f*s will be getting tangled, and so will the bottom loop of the *y* in *fly* and the top loops of the *l*s. The same words, written in Getty-Dubay script, don't tangle at all.

• Letter slope can be a problem. In Palmer, Bowmar-Noble, and Zaner-Bloser, the slope changes from 0 degrees in the manuscript books to 27 degrees in the cursive books. The D'Nealian slope remains at 17 degrees for both manuscript and cursive. Getty-Dubay script slopes at only 5 degrees, which they feel is a more natural slope better suited to both manuscript and cursive.

Considering I'm talking to teens and adults, the fact is that you've already learned to write using *some* method. True, it may not be legible or pretty. Now's the time to fix that. Cursive italic will do the job; if you want only one book for yourself or an older student, Book G of this series has a self-teaching approach to the whole system.

You can also get an instructor's manual. This includes teaching techniques, a scope and sequence, and the theory behind the course. Blackline masters contain follow-up practice exercises. Portland State University has recently put together two sets of blackline masters (which include permission to photocopy) just for home schoolers.

New: a training video for the parent or teacher explains how to teach handwriting the Getty-Dubay way. It only costs $7 plus shipping to rent, and you can copy it to keep it for your own permanent use.

Rinehart, Inc. Manuscript and Cursive Alphabets

Rinehart, Inc.

Home Study Program, $40. Teacher Training Correspondence Course, $40. State student's grade level when enrolling.

Rinehart's main product is something very useful: a correspondence program for improving your handwriting. The Student Remedial or Home Study Program contains a manual, blackline masters, individual prescriptions, evaluation and diagnosis, remediation, and before-and-after testing. The course takes a minimum of six weeks, but it may span up to six months. Two courses are offered for school-age students: manuscript and cursive.

Rinehart also has a Teacher Training Correspondence Course. This, too, is meant to train teachers in handwriting skills, so they can be an example to their students. Again, choose either manuscript or cursive.

Rinehart also sells handwriting accessories, such as desk tapes, duplicating masters, transparencies, manuscript/cursive cards (8½ x 7", choice of blue or yellow), and pencil grips by the bag.

Rinehart teaches a slanted, precursive manuscript and a classic cursive.

Zaner-Bloser

Handwriting Correspondence Course for adults, $35. Add 8% shipping.

The king of handwriting publishers! Zaner-Bloser sells absolutely everything to do with writing. For younger students, they offer a comprehensive handwriting program including pupil books, teacher editions, and three-ring binders loaded with aids and activities for teaching handwriting. This program pioneered the idea of teaching handwriting through modalities, that is, in accordance with pupils' different learning styles.

Zaner-Bloser has a large selection of handwriting paper for all ages, finger-fitting pens and pencils, an array of handwriting books and filmstrips, even *The Zanerian Manual of Alphabets and Engrossing* for those who are really into handwriting. They also offer a handwriting correspondence course for adults. I don't have space to list all their numerous handwriting accessories. Do get the catalog and see for yourself.

TYPING & KEYBOARDING COURSES

Typing is rapidly becoming the one nonnegotiable business skill. Computer-savvy children need it; housewives whose fingers ache from writing the family correspondence by hand need it; executives need it. Typing can free your children right now from the drudgery of handwriting, making them much more likely to produce creative stories and letters. And in the future, typing can help secure that first job, whether at home or abroad.

A young child will need to learn on either an electric typewriter or computer keyboard. Manual typewriters are difficult for small, weak fingers, and as for typing practice on a piece of paper marked like a keyboard, forget it. Kids in school only put up with this because they have no choice. It's not interactive or useful or fun.

You can find inexpensive used electric typewriters, or even whole computers, in the classified section of the newspaper or your area's equivalent of *Trading Times*. A heavy-duty IBM Selectric that can take anything a child dishes out can now be had for as little as $100, and less-prominent brands may range as low as $25 or less. Consider it an investment in your family's productivity.

Some of the best keyboarding courses are software. Don't forget to check out *Pride's Guide to Educational Software* (due out October 1991) for the best of these!

NEW**
American Christian Schools International (ACSI)
Keyboarding with Scripture, $17.95. Add $3.50 shipping.

It's *Keyboarding with Scripture: A Supplemental Typewriting Book*. It folds out to easel form. You can use it with a typewriter or computer. You're supposed to use it with a standard typewriting course or textbook. It's 120 pages of five-minute timed typing exercises, using the KJV and NIV. Exercises include skill development, warmups, single paragraphs, alphabet concentration practice, keyboarding problems, centering, tabs, letters, and reports. That's about all I can tell you, not having seen anything but the brochure.

Audio-Forum
Touch-Typing: Do It Yourself, $29.50. *Improve Your Typing*, $21.95. Both courses, $47.50. Shipping extra.

Touch Typing: Do It Yourself is designed to teach you to touch type in only four hours. This beginning-level program consists of three cassettes, an "exercise book" (really, a few stapled sheets), and round red stickers to temporarily conceal the keys while you're taking the course. *Improve Your Typing*, with two cassettes and an exercise book, provides warm-up, accuracy, speed, and speed-accuracy drills, plus score sheets for recording your progress. The accuracy drills use the 500 most misspelled words.

NEW**
Beaumont Books
AlphabeTyping, $12.95 plus $2 shipping. Ask for educator's discount price of $10 postpaid. All ages.

Color-code your fingers and keyboard with little colored dots. Learn to type the alphabet letters first, in familiar alphabet order. Then review upper- and lower-case, practice the 70 most-often-occurring words. Practice capitalization and single caps. Learn the top row keys. Practice typing some typical facts and figures (names, addresses, dates, telephone numbers). Learn centering and tabbing. Practice typing state names and abbreviations. Finish with a number of timed-typing exercises.

You get 16 lessons in all, in one spiral-bound book. You can prop the book open, making it easier to use while practicing your typing. The inside back cover is a practice keyboard.

The AlphabeTyping method has worked with regular and intellectually-behind children and adults of all ages. It's *very* simple, starting as it does with something you already know—the alphabet—as opposed to virtually all other typing programs, that start with "home row" keys (ASDF). It's also color-coded. A worthy contender to Educators Publishing Service's *Keyboarding Skills* program (see below).

Educators Publishing Service, Inc.
Keyboarding Skills, $8. Add 8% shipping (minimum $3).

Here's an innovative touch-typing system developed for dyslexics but usable by anyone. Like *AlphabeTyping*, *Keyboarding Skills* starts with the alphabet in its normal sequence, rather than the usual "home row" approach of ASDF and JKL. By saying the name of a letter and pressing its key—a motor process with kinesthetic reinforcement—most students master the alphabet on a typewriter in less than an hour. Next come words of increasing length, phrases, capital letters, and sentences. Numbers, symbols, and punctuation marks complete the course.

Keyboarding Skills is designed for rapid success and ease of use. The spiral-bound top and heavy covers let you stand *Keyboarding Skills* up like an easel, with the copy then in an easy-to-read position. On top of each page is an illustration of the keyboard parts corresponding to the letters freshly introduced. Younger students can use it as soon as their hands are big enough, and the method, though simple, is not too babyish for older students or adults.

NEW★★
Educators Publishing Service, Inc.
Type It, $8. Add 8% shipping (minimum $3).

Type It is a great beginning course in touch typing for those who want to concentrate more on the keyboard and less on the alphabet. This is real touch typing, starting with home row keys and covering the entire keyboard except for the special characters above the numbers. It's also *linguistically-oriented* touch typing. The words chosen for the exercises are phonetically regular, so you can use *Type It* for children as young as six.

Type It now has a bound-in standing easel, so you can simply prop it open at the ideal height for typing. Eight lessons in all, set in large type, with 16 exercise sets per lesson. Kids can check off completed exercises on the progress chart on the inside of the back cover.

There's no magic here—just do the exercises in order, according to the one page of directions at the beginning of the book. You'll need to hover around to make sure your child is using the right fingers, as bad typing habits are easier to prevent than to break. Aside from that, you have nothing to do except *ooh* and *aah* over Junior's newfound typing skills.

CHAPTER SEVEN

LOGIC

*"Like all other arts, the Science of Deduction
and Analysis is one which can only be acquired
by long and patient study . . . Let the inquirer
begin by mastering more elementary problems."*

—Sherlock Holmes

Did you know there really once was a live, breathing Sherlock Holmes? Sir Arthur Conan Doyle, the man who invented the keen-eyed Holmes, was himself the prototype of his own creation. His son, Adrian Conan Doyle, in a fascinating introduction to the International Collectors Library edition of *A Treasury of Sherlock Holmes*, lays the matter before us:

Holmes was to a large extent Conan Doyle himself. Incidentally, and it stands to their credit in view of my father's reticence, this fact was recognized almost from the very first by the police chiefs of the world who, speaking or writing from America, France, Germany, China, India, or Egypt, paid him tribute. The exception was, of course, Scotland Yard, whose silence put to shame even that of the immortal Colonel Bramble. Scotland Yard owed too much to Conan Doyle and it is always painful to acknowledge large debts.

The use of plaster of Paris for preserving marks; the examination of dust in a man's clothing to establish his occupation or locality; the differentiation between tobacco ashes; all these were introduced into the science of criminal detection by my father through the mask of Sherlock Holmes. Far above all else, his own work in the famous Edalji case resulted in the introduction of the Court of Criminal Appeal into the British legal system. And to change the British legal system is almost equivalent to bailing out the English Channel with a teaspoon. The facts are there for all to read, including some noteworthy instances of my fa-

ther rescuing the innocent from the clutches of the police by using the very methods which he had invented for his man in Baker Street.

It appears, then, that Sir Arthur Conan Doyle knew something about how to think, and that the advice of Holmes at the beginning of this chapter can be taken seriously.

"But why should we even care about logic? Everything's relative, anyway. Let's just emote! Let it all hang out! Have a positive mental attitude!" John Robbins, in the introduction to Gordon Clark's *Logic*, has the sufficient answer to these notions:

Logic does not describe what people think about or how they usually reach conclusions; it describes how they *ought* to think if they wish to reason correctly. . . . Logic concerns all thought; it is fundamental to all disciplines. . . . Anyone who disparages or belittles logic must use logic in his attack, thus undercutting his own argument. . . . If one abandons logic, as many people in this century have, than one cannot distinguish good from evil—and everything is permitted. . .

The rejection of logic has led—and must lead—to the abandonment of morality. . . . Once logic is gone, truth is also.

Well, there it is. Would you rather be a lightweight or a heavy hitter? Would you rather be a logical Holmes or a confused Watson? (Actually, even Watson was a heavy hitter compared to most of us today!) Would you rather be a hammer or a nail? Logic makes the difference!

LOGIC COURSES

NEW**
Canon Press
Introductory Logic, $15. Add $2.50 shipping. Grades 8–12.

Introductory Logic for Christian Schools is just what the doctor ordered! At last there's an easy to use, sequential, even (dare I say it?) logical course on logic. The Christian aspect of this book is reflected in the Christian vocabulary (statements about Bible characters and doctrinal positions), examples showing the logical fallacies in popular arguments against Christianity, and the general righteous tone of the book (nothing slimy or stupid). Though the text is sober in tone, the examples are as lively as the real-life samples of false logic you are likely to encounter.

Introductory Logic starts right at the beginning. Students learn to distinguish between true statements, false statements, commands, questions, and nonsense sentences such as, "The round square furiously kicked the green yellowish," which although they have the form of statements don't refer to anything real in this life or the next. From this sound beginning students move on to supported statements and relationships between statements (consistency, implication, logical equivalence, or independence). Next, they learn to translate all statements into sentences using "is." "Paul rebuked Peter at Antioch" becomes "Paul is an Antiochan Peter-rebuker." The reason for mastering this dreadful grammar becomes clear when the text moves on to arguments. Here your student will be learning about premises, conclusions, universals, particulars, abbreviated statements, and a host of other vital logic terms,

all of which in this text are simplified into some form of "all/some/many/few A is B." This enables students to make quick work of tough concepts like subimplication, superimplication, syllogisms, and the like. Kids also learn to detect logical fallacies, diagram arguments, and use propositional and symbolic logic.

This all sounds much more intimidating than it is—any alert preteen ought to be able to master this excellent text.

All *Introductory Logic* needs to be perfect is an answer key for the exercises (the publisher tells me one is now available upon request), and perhaps some more oral practice exercises. Even without them, this is the best logic course for Christian kids currently on the market.

NEW**
The Learning Works
Logical Logic, $5.95. Add $3 shipping for orders under $30, 10% for orders over $30. Grades 7–12.

On the cover: a football player standing in front of a wall poster. The poster is entitled "Syllogisms" and reads as follows:

All football players are mindless hulks.

Watson is a football player.

Watson is a mindless hulk.

Watson's not that mindless, after all, since he is saying "!" and looking cross. However, the syllogism is valid, as *Logical Logic* makes clear in its 48 pages.

As a book on verbal logic, *Logical Logic* starts out studying facts and opinions. It then moves to denotation and connotation (including the common problem of circular definitions), relevance (non sequiturs, *ad hominem* arguments, and *tu quoque* arguments), barriers to logical thinking (double standards, generalities, *post hoc*, improper distributions, false either-ors, and loaded questions), analogies, inferences, deductive reasoning (including matrix logic puzzles), and syllogisms using "all," "no," and "some." Each page has instructions and explanations on the top, followed by practice exercises, and the whole thing is topped by an answer key in the back.

I can't bring myself to like the blockish typeface used in this book, but the content is memorable and broad. I particularly liked the illogical debates between wily Senator Unaware and his challenger, Roger Runamuck. A lot of wallop for 48 pages!

NEW★★
Midwest Publications
Building Thinking Skills series (grades 2–12): student texts $20.95 each, teacher's manuals $18.95 each. Figural series (grades 6–11), $5.95 each book. Mind Benders series (grades 6–11), $5.95 each book. Verbal series (grades 6–11), $5.95 each book. Add 10% shipping.

Midwest's Building Thinking Skills series, a four-books-plus-teacher's-manuals course, covers both mathematical and verbal logic. It works on four basic reasoning skills which the publishers believe will improve your students' academic performance across the curriculum: similarities/differences, sequences, classifications, and analogies. These four skill areas are first introduced figurally (i.e., using geometric figures), then verbally (with word problems).

Book 1 is for little kids (grades 2–4), so let's skip it for the moment. Book 2 (grades 4–7) contains both figural and verbal exercises, using a strictly controlled vocabulary. The series has two Book 3's (grades 7–12): *Figural Book 3* and *Verbal Book 3*. *Figural Book 3* should help in the areas of geometry, science, college entrance exams, engineering, architecture, medicine, etc. *Verbal Book 3* is full of pencil-and-paper exercises in very basic formal logic and covers the same reasoning skills as *Figural Book 3*.

Now let's look at Midwest's Figural lineup of thinking skills workbooks using both word problems and mathematical figures. *Figural Analogies* shows you three figures. You have to figure out the relationship between A and B, and then draw a figure with the same relationship to C. Example: if A is a circle and B a semicircle, then if C is a square, what should D be? The questions rapidly get more difficult, so be glad an answer key is included in the book. Others in this series include *Figural Similarities, Figural Sequences,* and *Figural Classifications*. Except for *Figural Similarities*, a series of four workbooks, each of these comes as a series of three books (titled A-1, B-1, and C-1). The virtue of a figural approach is that the problems are strictly logical, involving no particular political or religious presuppositions. Word problems, in contrast, reflect the particular background of their designer.

Mind Benders is a series of 12 workbooks featuring deductive thinking skills. You might want to invest in the *Mind Benders Instructions and Detailed Solutions* for this series. Books are labeled A-1 through A-4, B-1 through B-4, and C-1 through C-4. Novices should begin with the first series book, *Warm Up Mind Benders*. Mind Benders sets A-1 through A-3 are also available as Apple family or IBM software.

The word problems series includes *Verbal Similarities, Verbal Sequences, Verbal Classifications,* and *Verbal Analogies*. and this just begins to scrape the surface of Midwest's more than 100-book line. What about the five books of syllogisms? Brain Stretchers (two books)? Classroom Quickies (three books)? Etc.

Trinity Foundation
Logic, $8.95. Free shipping on postpaid orders. Grades 10–adult.

The late Gordon Clark, professor extraordinaire and evangelical gadfly, took the time to write this logic textbook (aptly named *Logic*) because he believed Christian children were growing up ignorant of the same. Dr. Clark's erudition is apparent throughout, as is his somewhat caustic humor. The book is logically laid out and covers a lot of ground: unfortunately, not in the most organized way. The student is expected to already know, for example, that NaCl is table salt and how to prove the theorem that in an isosceles triangle the angles opposite the equal sides are equal. Information is densely packed and unformatted. It gets better towards the end, but this is a textbook that needs multiple readings. (Too bad there's no accompanying workbook.)

John Robbins' introduction, "Why Study Logic?," is excellent.

LOGIC AND THINKING EXERCISES

NEW★★
Dale Seymour Publications
Plexers and *More Plexers*, $5.95 each.

What in the world is a "plexer"? As you might guess, "plexer" is derived from the word "perplex."

These are books of fiendishly clever pictorial puzzles, mostly made up of letters. You have to decide what word or phrase the letters bring to mind. Look to the direction, size, and positions of the letters for clues.

Here's an example of a plexer:

THEHABIRDAND

The answer, of course, is "A bird in the hand." Yuk, yuk!

Not surprisingly, my six- and nine-year-olds captured these books the second they arrived in the house. Also not surprisingly, my husband and I fished them out the minute the kids went to bed. I don't know if solving these plexers made us any smarter, but it sure was a lot of fun!

NEW✶✶
Dale Seymour Publications
Quizzles and *More Quizzles*, $8.95 each.

"You're the detective when you solve . . . Quizzles!" Two books with matrix-logic puzzles for seventh-graders and up. Matrix-logic puzzles are this sort of thing:

> Jane, Sue, and Bob each found a job.
> Bob was not the baker.
> The dishwasher was a girl.
> The restaurant needed a dishwasher and a counter manager.
> Jane hated to wash dishes but loved to bake.

I just made that puzzle up, which is why it is so easy to solve! Typically, matrix-logic puzzles come with both the verbal clues and a grid labeled on both sides. In our example above, you'd have a 3 x 3 grid with "Jane," "Sue," and "Bob" across the top and "Dishwasher," "Baker," and "Counter Manager" down the side. You can use the grid to zero in on the answers. For example, since we know Bob is *not* the baker, you could put an "N" in the square for "Bob" and "Baker." We also know Bob is not the dishwasher, since the dishwasher is a girl, so put an "N" in the "Bob" and "Dishwasher" square. That means Bob *must* be the counter manager . . . which means neither girl can be the counter manager . . . and so it goes until you figure the whole puzzle out!

Dale Seymour throws in an extra, though—step by step solutions, so you aren't left wondering how to find out the answers. Lots of fun for teens and their parents!

NEW✶✶
Dale Seymour Publications
Visual Thinking, set A and B, $29.95 per set.

What, you ask, is visual thinking? Good question. In this case, it's the title of two boxes full of colorful task cards (100 per box) designed to teach visual thinking skills. And now, since I have not yet told you what visual thinking really *is*, and I don't want to leave you gnashing your teeth in frustration, here's a definition of visual thinking straight from the teacher's guide included with Set A:

> Visual thinking is an integral part of our society. On any given day we might need to be able to interpret a graph, map, photograph, sculpture, graphic symbol, and/or body language. In order to understand a book or something told to us orally, we must be able to visualize characters, settings, and physical objects from the words that are given. And, in order to efficiently solve a problem, we need to be able to visualize possible approaches to solving it or to draw a picture of the elements of the problem.

So Dale Seymour's *Visual Thinking* series is designed to help fourth-graders and up acquire spatial perception skills. This is important because studies have shown that many students lack these skills. Success in geometry class, engineering, and even in art is based on the ability to interpret, remember, and mentally manipulate visual symbols.

So much for theory. What you get in each box is 100 task cards and a very short teacher's commentary with an answer key for the cards. The box itself, I might add, is very sturdy and attractive, looking as if it were designed by the people who do those upscale cheese popcorn bags. Each task card has a single assignment laid out on it, which should take between three and 15 minutes to complete. These are fun assignments, ranging in Set A from a set of five strings of colored circles with the instruction to "find the two designs that are exactly the same" to card 100 which shows three different views of the same solid and asks how many triangular faces, edges, and vertices (corners) the solid has. (This is not as easy to figure out as you think, since you are looking at two-dimensional pictures of only part of a three-dimensional object!) In between you'll find problems asking you to draw spatial forms, count bricks in a stack (including the ones you *can't* see), find the missing puzzle piece, and all sorts of other ingenious ways to limber up your spatial sense. Problems become more difficult as you move through the cards. Set B is harder than Set A.

These sets are just excellent. The exercises really can improve your spatial skills, and they are lots of fun besides! The task card format means you can use the program just a little bit at a time, or do a whole lot at once—it's up to you. The durable cards should last for years; you can use them with every child in your family, and the grownups, too. Girls should especially benefit, as in general girls have weaker spatial skills than boys. Recommended.

NEW ★ ★
Dale Seymour Publications
Eye-Cue Puzzles, set A and set B, $10.95 each.

Regular jigsaw puzzles are for wimps. You want a *real* challenge? Try the *Eye-Cue Puzzles* from Dale Seymour! First, open the box. You'll find four little zip-lock bags, each containing eight square puzzle pieces adorned with colorful geometric designs. Your job is to "match color and design elements, placing the squares edge to edge" in order to form one of the 10 possible configurations. These range from four-in-a-row to the fiendishly difficult hollow square. With four puzzles sets per box, and 10 configurations into which you are attempting to fit each puzzle set, a little simple math tells us that you have here 40 shots per box at a room in the funny farm. Set B looks a little more user-friendly to me, but then, I struggle with the *easy* configurations! And one last thing: no solutions are provided. For a set of sample solutions you have to send a self-addressed stamped envelope to the publisher. A great gift for people with finely-honed spatial skills; a quick trip to gooney-land for those without.

NEW ★ ★
Fearon Teacher Aids
Playing with Logic (grades 3–5), *Discovering Logic,* (grades 4–6), *Adventures with Logic,* (grades 5–7), $7.95 each. Add $3.50 shipping.

"The activities in this book are divided into five categories. The first is *relationships,* which involves classifying and comparing shapes and ideas. The next three are *sequencing, inference,* and *deduction.* The final section, *group activities,* is a collection of logical games for the entire class to play. These games use the skills developed in the previous sections."

That about sums it up for both books, but it's a bit dry. Let's try to give you a little flavor of the zany exercises and logic puzzles sequentially presented in *Playing with Logic*:

Can you identify these rare animals from the zoo on planet Woo? The zookeeper has identified the first one for you.

A *Scoo* is any animal that has more than two eyes. Put a circle around all Scoos.

A *Frooch* is any animal that has at least one horn. Put a triangle around all Frooches.

A *Ploom* is any animal that does *not* have a beard. Put a square around all Plooms.

[Following are pictures of eight nutty-looking animals. The first has a circle and a triangle about it.]

Just for fun, draw a Scoo Frooch Ploom on the back of this page!

We are only on page 5, and already we're into deep waters. A page or two farther on you get to do picture analogies: This is to that as this 'un is to that 'un. Little circle is to big circle as little square is to big square. Then on to verbal analogies: Herd is to cow as ___ is to ___.

In the Sequencing section, you get to put Captain Pepperoni's map of Pizza Island together in the right order and plan a tour of the amusement park that takes in all four public shows. Again, I'm just giving you a taste of the pages.

The Inference section includes goodies like lists of words with one letter missing. What could that missing letter be?

The Deduction section is your classic logic puzzles. If Violet is between Pinky and Little Red, and Pinky is not first, which duck is where? We work our way up to five-person matrix problems.

The games aren't all that hot, but since they were invented for classrooms, you don't have to feel guilty about not playing them. Better news is the answer key in the back of the book, the court of final resort for desperate beginning logicians. Not a bad start for your logic program.

Adventures with Logic is more of the same—same format and topics—but on a more advanced level. I especially liked the exercise where two newspaper stories were jumbled together and you had to separate the stories and place them in correct sequence. Also fun is the exercise where you find the secret word to replace the word in quotes. Consider these sentences:

1. Tom's mother was elected to the "Pickle" of Representatives.
2. Elaine's theater group played to a full "pickle."

"Pickle" stands for "house," of course, but I love it!. Maybe we *should* rename the House of Representatives the Pickle of Representatives. You and I always get in a pickle when those guys get together . . .

Adventures with Logic also includes word cartoons, Roman number riddles, and other goodies not found in the first book. And it, too, has an answer key at the end of its 59 pages. *Discovering Logic* is quite similar; I couldn't discern much difference between these two books.

NEW**
Fearon Teacher Aids
Digging into Logic, $5.95, grades 5–8. *Logic in the Round,* $7.95, grades 5–8. *Logic, Anyone?,* $11.95, grades 5 and up. *Logic, Anyone?* learning workbook, $3.95. Add $3.50 shipping.

I've described matrix logic puzzles elsewhere. They are a son-of-a-gun to figure out if you've never run across one before. So someone thought of coming up with a book of logic problems for middle school that would actually explain *how to solve them.* Brilliant!

Digging into Logic has 30 matrix logic puzzles—*with* answer key—and excellent, simple instructions. A good first book of logic puzzles.

Logic in the Round, by the same authors, takes the same approach to circle logic puzzles. (These are puzzles in which you try to figure out who is in which position around a circle.) It contains 30 circle puzzles of increasing difficulty and instructions on how to solve this kind of puzzle.

Logic, Anyone? is a bigger book of 165 brain-stretching logic puzzles by the team who brought you *Digging into Logic* and *Logic in the Round.* The puzzles include analogies, matrix logic, table logic, circle logic, syllogisms, and Venn diagrams. Each section includes instructions on how to solve that kind of puzzle, and an answer key is mercifully provided. The book is reproducible, meaning you have permission to photocopy it for every child in your class or family. The *Logic, Anyone?* learning workbook, which is *non-* reproducible, has identical content but only three kinds of problems—matrix logic, syllogisms, and Venn diagrams—for 95 puzzles in all.

NEW**
Penny Press
Original Logic Problems, $11.47/year (6 issues). Add $2 postage outside U.S.A.

Whenever I have trouble finding my husband Bill, he's pretty sure to be huddled in a chair doing the matrix-logic puzzles in his latest issue of *Original Logic Problems* magazine. Each issue includes 45 challenging, brand-new logic problems. Some are easier than others; I've seen our (admittedly advanced) seven-year-old daughter sweating out the answers to the easier ones!

Each issue begins with a page of instructions in how to solve logic problems, and complete solutions are included in the back.

Penny Press also has books of logic puzzles and back issues of an English logic magazine with some *really* tough puzzles. Lots more, all inexpensive!

Wff 'n Proof Learning Games Associates
Propaganda, $27.50 postpaid. Grades 7–adult.

Coauthored by Lorne Greene (remember "Bonanza"?), *Propaganda* defines propaganda devices and provides sample exercises. Players challenge or go along with group consensus as to which statement contains what logical fallacy. The game can be played alone: check yourself with the answer key.

CHESS AND THINKING SKILLS

Studies have shown that kids who play chess improve their grades. How about that! Be sure to log those hours as home school . . .

NEW★★
EDC Publishing
Playing Chess, Advanced Chess, $6.95 each paperbound or $12.96 each library-bound. Shipping extra.

But you don't know *how* to play chess, you say? Or you don't understand the strategy, so you never win?

Take heart! *The Usborne Guide to Playing Chess* explains the basics in its 64 illustrated pages, while the *Usborne Guide to Advanced Chess* takes you through each stage of the game, from opening gambit to endgame, explaining what you're trying to accomplish in each stage and what you're trying to avoid.

The books use algebraic notation, e.g., Ng3 means Knight moves to square g3, where the letters run across the bottom of the board and the numbers run up the side of the board. It takes some mental effort to switch over to algebraic notation if you're used to the old "Knight to King's Knight 3" style, but if you're a beginner, algebraic notation is easier to adopt right from the start.

The advice and examples in these books are absolutely excellent. I can't imagine better beginning instruction books on chess than these.

CHAPTER EIGHT

PHONICS COURSES FOR TEENS AND ADULTS

"If You Can Read This Bumper Sticker, Thank A Teacher." Well, sometimes. Not everyone got all his reading instruction in school. For that matter, lots of people who had years and years of reading instruction in school *can't* read that bumper sticker.

You know, and I know, and everyone ought to know by now how phonics was booted out of the schools starting in the 1950s. We all know Rudolf Flesch wrote his famous book *Why Johnny Can't Read* to explain why "look-say," which replaced phonics and which treats English like a bunch of hieroglyphics, cripples kids' reading ability. As an article in *Collier's* magazine of November 26, 1954 reported,

A thousand times one hears the question, "Why don't they teach my child to read?" How can schools tolerate a method which turns out many children of eight, nine and older who stare helplessly at a word (not on their memory list) and cannot make a stab at reading it? What has happened to the method of teaching reading sound by sound, syllable by syllable, so that a child can at least make a reasonable attempt at reading any word?

Two basic teaching methods are in conflict here. One is the phonetic approach (known as phonics), the old-fashioned way in the view of modern educators. . . . The other method, which the modernists have put into vogue, is the word-memory plan—also known as "sight reading," "total word configuration," or "word

recognition." It has the more friendly nickname of "look and say," since the youngster is supposed simply to look at a word and say it right out. He memorizes the "shape" of the word, the configuration, and identifies it with pictures in his workbook. Often he is taught to recognize phrases or whole sentences in his picture book, or on flash cards, before he can independently sound out and pronounce such simple words as *cat* or *ball*.

In other words, the difference is that phonics teaches kids how to "sound out" words, while all the other methods introduced since the 1950s rely on getting kids to learn each word as an shape. The newer methods make sense for languages such as Chinese and Ancient Egyptian, where each word is a separate picture called a "hieroglyph," but not for English, which is *not* a hieroglyphic language.

PASS THE HIEROGLYPHICS, PLEASE

What a lot of people don't know is that, in spite of the overwhelming evidence shown in study after study that phonics instruction is the *only reliable way* to teach kids to read English, the reading bureaucracy has never bent an inch on this issue. According to Sam Blumenfeld's brilliant article on Whole Language in the February 1991 issue of his *Blumenfeld Education Letter* ($1.50 for that issue from The Blumenfeld Education Letter, P.O. Box 45161, Boise ID 83711, or order by MC or Visa from (208) 322-4440), the International Reading Association was formed, shortly after Flesch's book came out, simply in order to *defend* its members against having to teach phonics (or having to teach future teachers how to teach phonics). In the meantime, these self-styled "reading experts" have tried gimmick after gimmick to avoid teaching phonics, from the "phony phonics" courses which add just a dollop of out-of-sequence phonics instruction in with the dozens of basal readers and picture clues, to the latest fad, Whole Language. (The IRA, who consider themselves the reading experts, have *never* endorsed intensive phonics as their teaching method of choice. And I personally can't see the point of letting people call themselves "reading experts" when the number of children they teach to read successfully keeps *dropping*.)

WHOLE LANGUAGE IS STILL LOOK-SAY

Whole Language, as Sam Blumenfeld points out, is just look-say without the basal readers. Instead of struggling with the hieroglyphics in a Dick-and-Jane style series, kids now struggle with the hieroglyphics in story books. As a Whole Language proponent explained in *Education Week* of March 28, 1990,

> In whole-language classrooms, children read and reread favorite rhymes, songs, and patterned stories with repeated phrases, sentences and stanzas—not single words repeated in unnatural contexts, and gradually . . .

Kids also dictate their stories to the teacher and "read" them back. Teachers are not supposed to correct misreadings as long as the child gets "the general idea" right. In other words, if Johnny reads, "The horse ate a fruit," as "The pony ate an apple," he is reading OK.

By immersing kids in print, the kids are supposed to learn to read without any need for fuddy-duddy old rules like "the short sound of *a* as in *apple*." Instead, they get to see words "in context," meaning as clumps of letters whose sounds they have never learned. Teachers of this method also rely on "Big Books"—not *The Big Book of Home Learning*, but oversized versions of kiddie books, which they read aloud to their story circle, thus motivating the little non-scholars to learn to read by following along with the teacher. Another favored teaching technique is to put on theme plays and events.

THE EMPEROR'S NEW TESTS

Already Whole Language is showing tremendous success at preventing children from learning to read. Reading scores on standard reading tests are dropping wherever it's introduced. But our reading experts have an answer —rewrite the tests! This is actually happening right now. Tests are being changed to measure students' "creative thinking" and inner attitudes rather than reading skills, and a movement has formed to replace all the old tests with these new ones. As an article, "Whole-Language Advocate Says New Tests are Needed," reports in the *American Journal* of October 12, 1988:

> If students taught to read by the new "whole-language" method don't do well in reading tests, the fault is with the tests, not the teaching methods, Dr. Marie Carbo, a leading whole-language teacher, told the New England Reading Association Saturday in Portland [Maine].
>
> New tests better suited to whole-language teaching methods are being introduced into the National Assessment of Educational Progress, Princeton, N.J., she said in printed material distributed with her talk.
>
> State tests in Michigan and Illinois also will be adapted to whole-language, she said.

That was several years ago. The tests are here, and parents are already complaining about them.

I spent all this time telling you about Whole Language because the general public is to this point unaware that Whole Language is really just the same old look-say in a fancy new suit. Its ancestors were educational horse thieves, and it's carrying on the family tradition. Look-say methods failed kids 35 years ago, they're failing kids today, and they'll go on failing kids forever as long as the people who push them manage to keep on escaping accountability for the results of their methods.

In other words, if your son or daughter, husband or wife, mom or dad, neighbor or boss, hasn't learned to read by now, it's not their fault. They're not "dumb" or "unmotivated" or "learning disabled." They haven't learned to read because they were taught *wrong*.

How about a new bumper sticker— "If You Can't Read This Bumper Sticker, Thank the Reading Experts"? Problem is, those who need to read it *can't*. Help them learn to read, with any of the resources in this chapter. Help them register to vote. Then let's all put our heads together and see if we can finally figure out how to get rid of the look-say reading "experts" . . .

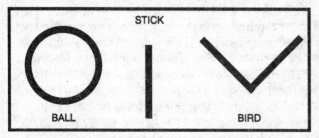

Ball-Stick-Bird
Set #1, Books 1–5 with instructor's manual, $74.95. Set #2, Books 6–10 with instructor's manual, $74.95. Free shipping.

Ball-Stick-Bird, a phonics program invented by research psychologist Dr. Renée Fuller, differs tremendously from every other phonics system. For one thing, it was designed to teach certified, institutionalized retardates to read (people with an IQ of 60 or less). For another thing, it works. No other phonics program, not one, has ever made its debut under such difficult circumstances.

Dr. Fuller's breakthrough, at first sight, might seem to be her system for breaking down the capital letters into three strokes: the Ball (a circle), the Stick (a line), and the Bird (two lines joined at an angle, like the cartoon of a bird in flight). Color-coding these basic forms to make the difference between the strokes even more dramatic, beginning with capital letters presented in a carefully planned sequence, and requiring the student to "build" each letter out of the three basic strokes (thus involving all four sense modalities), Ball-Stick-Bird goes out of its way to make basic phonics mastery painless.

But—and here comes the rub—other phonics programs also feature simplified approaches to reading. Yet nobody dares take them inside institutions for the mentally handicapped and expect success.

Ball-Stick-Bird gets its punch from, of all things, a really different story approach. Dressed up in the for-

mula of a science-fiction story, Dr. Fuller's stories present some heavy-duty moral applications. Her Good Guys and Bad Guys star in fables about human nature: the lust for power, the foolishness of sloganeering, how experts use their authority to stifle criticism of their actions, and so on.

It is easy to see why labeled people—like the "mentally retarded" and "special education" children—lap up these stories. Dr. Fuller tells it like it is. She literally gives them the words that explain their experience as the powerless victims of experts.

I should mention that Ball-Stick-Bird can be used with any person or child mentally old enough to follow a story. Dr. Fuller's contention is that Story Readiness, not some mystical amount of Motor Skill Readiness, is the real preparation for reading, and that successful reading itself grows out of the basic human desire to understand one's own life as a story.

While the science-fiction theme is not exclusively "adult," Ball-Stick-Bird was designed for use with people of all ages.

NEW★★
Educational Products
Winning Home Kit, $109.50. Add $13.69 shipping. Ages 9 to adult.

From the people who brought you *Sing, Spell, Read & Write,* here's a literacy program for teens and adults. Over 150,000 people have already used this program to learn to read.

The heart of the *Winning* program is the sing-along song cassettes. These are essentially the same songs as in *Sing, Spell, Read & Write,* adapted to fit what the publisher perceives are contemporary secular teen and adult tastes. The *SSR&W* ABC Song, for example, is now a black rap instead of a bouncy kiddie tune. Other song tunes feature country and rock styles. The lyrics haven't changed much. The only difference in lyrics between the *SSR&W* version and the *Winning* revision is that *Winning* lyrics occasionally try to make learning to read sound hip.

Songs included on the six cassettes are:

- Phonics Song A–Z (funky rap and comparatively listless jazz versions)
- ABC Echoes (repeating the alphabet sounds)
- Short Vowel Song ("A-a-a-a apple, e-e-e-e-egg . . .")
- Ferris Wheel Blends Song (practicing "ladder letters," e.g., "Ba-be-bi-bo-bu; bu-bo-bi-be-ba")
- Letter Cluster Phonics Song and Letter Cluster Echoes
- All ABC Echoes (a repeat of the ABC Echoes exercise on the first cassette)
- Long Vowel Song ("Ay for apron . . . ee for eagle . . .")
- Two Vowel Song
- Silent E Song
- Mr. GH Song (sounds of GH)

Comparing the cassettes from each version, the *SSR&W* kiddie singers have clearer diction and perform their songs more snappily.

Obviously, just listening to song cassettes isn't going to teach anyone to read, especially someone who's already failed to learn once. That's where the two bingo-like phonics games and the workbooks come in. The *Winning* Home Kit includes four workbooks, with covers resembling those of sports magazines, each with an accompanying (and equally thick) instructor's manual. The workbooks follow the *SSR&W* 36-step approach, teaching all the letters and their "first" sounds, then short vowels, "letter clusters," long vowels, and assorted bothersome mop-up sounds like silent *w* and *k*. By the end of this process, the student will have tackled every important phonics rule there is.

Along with all this come three sets of bingo-like flash cards and a set of green circular chips for playing phonics games, plus two phonics card games that drill letter sounds and clusters.

Book 1 simply introduces the letters—how to read them and write them in pre-cursive manuscript and cursive. Book 2 provides phonics exercises and activities —e.g., writing down the correct starting sounds of words or holding up the right short vowel card—along with simple short-vowel stories in cartoon form. Each book includes pages for handwriting practice. In Book 3, stories break away from the cartoon format and regular

reading comprehension tests are first introduced. (In Book 2, the student was only asked to recognize individual words from the story.) Book 4 continues to teach the rest of the letter clusters, and winds up with instructions on how to read and understand a calendar, table of contents, index, menu, signs and labels, parts of a newspaper. It also tells you how to fill out the following forms: social security application, driver's license, and job application.

In all, the *Winning* Literacy Program has 1,755 spelling words, 70 learn-to-read stories written for older beginners (beginning with cartoon stories and ending with regular-sized newsprint), word recognition tests, word comprehension tests, story comprehension tests, and that optional life skills section I already mentioned. The stories are written to appeal mainly to minority, ESL, and blue-collar teens and adults. No Christian content whatsoever—Christian Broadcasting Network is taking a very low profile as the publisher of this program, presumably to get it into public schools, jails, and other government programs.

The instructor's manual calls *Winning* a "virtually teacher-proof" program, and it is absolutely right. If you can read, you can teach this program. The student mainly teaches himself, only needing occasional help with directions, plus the expected feedback on his work. The instructor's manuals explain how the program works, give a complete programmed "script" for each lesson, and include a copy (on yellow paper) of the student book in the back with correct answers marked for each quiz. In fact, this program is *better* organized that *SSR&W,* and easier to use. All you have to do is pop in a cassette tape and read the instructor's manual. The student follows along doing the work in his book, and there you are! It all adds up to the best teen-and-adult literacy program I've seen.

Educators Publishing Service, Inc.
Starting Over, $15. Add 8% shipping (minimum $3). Ages 16 and up.

"A Combined Teaching Manual and Student Textbook for Reading, Writing, Spelling, Vocabulary, and Handwriting." Large (over 300 pages) spiral-bound manual designed for use with older students and adults who read poorly or are nonreaders, suffer from dyslexia whatever their reading level, or are learning English as a second language. Joan Knight, the author, has many years of experience in adult basic education and presently serves on the New York board of directors of the Orton Dyslexia Society. The Introduction and Foreword both repeatedly refer to *Starting Over's* "humanistic approach."

Starting Over begins with a comprehensive battery of pre-tests. The course itself is "programmed"—that is, everything the teacher does or says is spelled out. Student and teacher can use the same book. Each page is labeled as either a teacher's page, a student's page, or a teacher and student's page.

Spelling rules, blending, and digraphs are mixed in between the introduction of some consonants. The consonants themselves continue to be introduced one at a time throughout the course, ending with consonant *Y* on page 274. Exceptions are included throughout the course, rather than segregated at the end. Vocabulary-building is emphasized within each Consonant Unit. This can be confusing for the novice teacher.

In keeping with the Orton philosophy, *Starting Over* uses a variety of techniques for a variety of learning styles.

St. Ursula Academy, S.U.A. Phonics Department
A Sound Track to Reading, student's book $3.80, manual which includes student's book, $6.80. Add 10% shipping ($2 minimum). Ages 10–adult.

Monica Foltzer, the author of the *Professor Phonics* phonics program (see the review in Volume 2), has also produced something that every reading instructor should be aware of: an incredibly inexpensive advanced phonics program for the older student. It goes by the name *A Sound Track to Reading* and is deliberately adult in its approach. Quickly reviewing (or, in the case of foreign students, introducing) the basic sounds, *Sound Track* quickly moves to words and sentences. By the simple device of adding a few common endings like *ing* and *ed* to root words, which older readers can easily learn to do, babyish vocabulary is eliminated from the start. Now where else can you get all this for under $9?

NEW**
Warren Foundation
English Literacy Introduction (Level 1), $40 for individual package. *English Literacy Development* (Level 2), $50 for individual package. *English Literacy Achievement* (Level 3), $55 for individual package. All levels include tapes and books. Teacher's guide, $5. Add $3 shipping per individual package, $1 for teacher's guide. Classroom prices run even less, as low as $6 to $21 per student. Grade level equivalency: for Level 1, all ages; for Level 2, grade 3; for Level 3, grade 6.

One thing you can see right away about the Warren Foundation program—it's a bargain. See prices above!

Before we go any farther, let's state quite clearly who this program is for, and who it is not for. The brochure for Level 2 states, "Entry level: Third grade equivalency or better." For Level 3, entry level is sixth grade equivalency. This does not mean that the student has to read at a third-grade level before beginning Level 2, but rather that he should have been exposed to the first several grades of school. Both levels take an adult tone, and assume the student is familiar with terminology (such as the words *period, punctuation mark,* and *capital letter*), alphabet letters, and numbers that he would have encountered in the early school grades. He doesn't have to know how to put together any letters yet, but he does need to be able to recognize them and to recognize numerals in order to follow the cassette lessons. The handwriting examples are also given in cursive, which traditionally is taught starting in late second or early third grade. The new *English Literacy Introduction* (Level 1) course assumes much less about its students, requiring only that they understand a basic 200-word vocabulary, and taking the lessons at a slower pace.

Each level gives you 24 one-hour lessons. These are designed to be followed over a course of five weeks, but can be spread out to last a bit longer. When used with the usual remedial population of juvenile delinquents, immigrants, drop-outs, and "slow" students (even some mentally retarded people living in institutions), this program provided one year of grade-equivalency reading growth. When the course was repeated, students added a second year of reading progress. Not bad for just over twenty hours of study! That is why Warren Foundation was one of the 98 recipients of the President's Private Sector Initiatives Award for Summer Jobs for Youth.

This program is designed for the hard-core loser —the preteen, teen, or adult who is just not turned on to traditional schooling. Warren Foundation attempts to capture this population's imagination with humanistic sermonettes scattered throughout the courses. One example: the Three Affirmations, which are:

- "I love everyone all of the time."
- "I like everything about myself."
- "My name is _____ and I know who I am."

Students are asked to imagine their worst enemy, and then visualize (form a mental picture of) him as "the best person he can be." They are asked to do the same for themselves, and to repeat the Three Affirmations in this fashion first thing in the morning and last thing at night.

This is silly stuff for grown people. Anyone who has any sense does *not* like "everything" about himself or herself. You can't improve if you are already perfect —and if you think you are perfect, you'll be the only one who does! Keeping that in mind, the Three Affirmations could be used by adding a couple of phrases. "I love everyone all of the time . . . God helping me." "I like everything about myself . . . except my faults."

Similarly, some of the reading selections promote positive thinking over traditional religion. In "Sir Theodore and the Dragon" knights who prayed for success were defeated by the dragon, whereas Sir Theodore, who made a clever plan first and then prayed "as was the custom" got the victory. "Wonders of the Mind" tells you to "Clear your mind. Relax your body. Be at peace" as if you could achieve spiritual peace as a mere act of the will. It also says, "Who are you? What you say you are. What you *will* yourself to be." This doesn't work—Adolf Hitler *said* he was the first ruler of a 1000-year Reich, and *willed* himself to be that ruler, but he died in a bunker in Berlin.

I'm sure that the Warren Foundation is not nefariously plotting to undermine Christian values. This program was developed for public schools, and rah-rah humanism is about the only motivational technique those schools allow you to use. All the same, you will do well to carefully read through all the selections ahead of time (they are interesting reading, so this will not be too painful) and be prepared to uncover and discuss these sorts of things with your students.

Educationally this is a very good program. Let's look at Level 1 first, the new *English Literacy Introduction* course. This comes with 12 cassettes and a student's book. Whereas the other two levels expect the student to be basically familiar with English, *English Literacy Introduction* does not. If the student can understand the 200 words on the included basic word list, he can complete the first three lessons. After the third lesson, he knows the lesson pattern and can work his way through the remaining lessons, which cover all the sounds of Level 2, but in a simpler way. This may be the best choice for ESL students and those with language deficiencies.

Level 2, *English Literacy Development,* used to be the beginning reading program until *English Literacy Introduction* came long. It comes with 12 cassettes in a nice binder and two fair-sized workbooks. Lesson follows lesson in logical sequence: first consonants and short vowels, then more work with consonants and long vowels, suffixes and diphthongs (two-vowel combinations, and phonograms like *tion* and *tial.* Lessons 11 and 12, titled "How to Pronounce Any Word," top off the initial phonics instruction. Now the student is ready for the anthology, otherwise known as Book 2. This has twelve truly interesting stories, plus an additional eight supplemental stories, intermixed with occasional review exercises and vocabulary improvement work. Stories are a real mix, from fables, to Mark Twain adaptations, to magazine articles. Even the fables and fairy tales included are told in adult language, though. No older student has to feel embarrassed reading this material.

Level 3 follows a similar approach. This package has 12 cassettes, two books, and a Curve of Learning packet. After a review of the Level 2 skills, it gets right into a mix of more readings and additional skills. Covered in this level are such things are dictionary work, good study habits, sentence and paragraph structure, and note-taking. Again, an energetic announcer on cassette takes the student through all his lessons.

The tone of the lessons is unmistakably motivational, very similar in fact to the inspirational programs designed for salesmen. "You can do it! Success is worth the effort!" is the basic message. Think of the narrator, Mr. Rupert K. Shaw, as the Zig Ziglar of literacy, and you've got it.

You do not need to read the teacher's guide to use any of the three courses with your students. The guide does contain teaching tips, reference information, and questions and answers for the reading practice material, though.

For the older student who wants to concentrate and really try to learn to read, this completely self-taught course is the simplest solution I've seen.

CHAPTER NINE

VOCABULARY

Is English your second language? Good news! You don't need a large vocabulary in order to sound like a native-born citizen of the U.S.A. Just master the following expressions with a good regional accent: • *OK* • *Like* • *You know* • *Um* • *Yeah* • *Right* • *No way!* • *Huh?* • *No problem.* In the Midwest, everything is "neat." Up in Maine, "Don't be too sure (pronounced shoo-ah)." Down South, pretend you're chawin' on a wad of cotton (for the country sound) or watch *Gone With the Wind* 20 times for the Melanie-and-Scarlett ladylike effect. (Ignore Clark Gable—he didn't even *try* to sound Southern.) Up North, pinch your nose (the cold will do this for you anyway) to get that Yankee twang. Wherever you are, if anyone asks, "How are you?" or "How's it going?" answer "Fine," even if you're checking your family burial policy as they carry you off to the hospital emergency room. Smile when spoken to, watch a lot of television, eat at greasy fast-food franchises, chirp "Take it easy!" rather than "Good-bye," and everyone will think you were born in the U.S.A.

Those born into a nominally English-speaking country have a different problem. We already know about "Yeah" and "Um." These time-tested friends have seen us through school days, childhood friendships, and on into puberty. However, on graduation or escape from school, we suddenly discover that "Yeah" needs to be replaced with "Yes, sir!" and "Um" with "The proposal will be on your desk first thing tomorrow morning," or at least, "Go ask your father." Suddenly we need to be precise where we had been mellow, and vocal when we had been mute.

Self-employment leaves a little niche in which the mumbler and other strong silent types can hibernate. Ripping the phone out of the wall also helps. But if you ever need to explain anything or persuade anybody, if you feel a need to claw your way up the corporate ladder, if you have been invited to appear on "The Phil Donahue Show," or if having to look up every other word when reading a good book is getting boring, it's time for some vocabulary improvement.

The simplest way to increase your word power is to listen to William F. Buckley, Jr. with a translator by your side. Failing that, you could try playing with the dictionary and a good thesaurus. Boredom not permitting the last option, you could read widely and pick up words in their contexts. (This can be risky, since so many modern writers don't know the proper meanings of words. Try sticking with Dickens and Walter Scott.)

Now, for the rest of us, here are a few vocabulary-improvement programs.

NEW**
A Beka Book Publications

Vocabulary/Spelling/Poetry student books: grades 7 and 8, $5.05 each; grade 9, $3.95; grades 10–12, $7.30 each. Teacher's editions, tests available for some grades. Shipping extra.

A Beka Books integrates vocabulary, spelling, and poetry in its line of books for grades 7–12. Students memorize poetry, learn vocabulary words from the A Beka literature texts they are supposed to be studying at the same time, and learn the "Five Spelling Rules to Master" along with correct spelling of frequently-misspelled words. New vocabulary words are analyzed according to their Greek and Latin prefixes, suffixes, and roots, using the handy Word Analyzer included in each book. Books are fairly slim and not terribly expensive.

Teacher's books, where available, include the entire student text plus answers to all the exercises and explanations for the verbal analogies exercises.

If you're planning on using the A Beka literature series, it won't hurt to get the *Vocabulary/Spelling/Poetry* books as well, especially since I gather this series is being revised, starting with grade 7, to include integrated literature/vocabulary/spelling test booklets.

Advanced Memory Research (AMR)

English Vocabulary series: modules 1–4, $44.95 each.

AMR's English Vocabulary series is designed to increase your word power. Words are presented in groups of four related words and four contrasting words. This method is supposed to help you develop "word sense," the ability to find the exact word you want. Each word is presented with its definition, spelling, pronunciation, category (noun, verb, etc.), and an illustrative sentence. Modules 1 and 2 introduce over 500 words that you can use in your writing

or general conversation. Modules 3 and 4 present "over 500 words in a number of specialized subject categories" such as "Business, Economics, Diplomacy, Debate, Politics, Fine Arts, Sociology . . . Medicine, Law, Psychology, Religion . . ." Each module comes with four C-60 cassettes and a manual containing a transcript of all the recorded material, all attractively bound in a bookshelf-size case.

Arthur Bornstein School of Memory Training

Scott Bornstein's vocabulary course textbook, $25 post-paid. Complete course with textbook, study guide, and tape, $32.50 postpaid. Ages 10–adult.

"Would you be willing to spend as little as 20 minutes a day to learn 40 new words without the grind and repetition?" Scott Bornstein, son of the internationally famous memory expert Arthur Bornstein, has developed a *Vocabulary Mastery Study Course* based on memory techniques, the use of root words, and putting your new vocabulary words to work in daily conversation. The course is designed to "assure your retention of more than 1,600 words," plus increase your reading comprehension of thousands more, thanks to your study of root words, suffixes, and prefixes. Each day's vocabulary lesson ends with a review. You get a deluxe hardcover wire-bound textbook including 84 full-page illustrations. An optional 30-minute cassette tape and study guide round out the program. Excellent preparation for the verbal part of the SAT exam.

NEW**
Bob Jones University Press

Each student worktext, $5.95. Each teacher's edition, $6.50. These are home-school prices. Shipping extra.

BJUP's Vocabulary for Christian Schools series for grades 7–12 is divided up into levels, one level per grade. Levels A–C focus on Latin prefixes, roots, and suffixes. Level D introduces Greek word parts. This is also the book where you find *ack-ack, flip-flop, riffraff, shilly-shally,* and all those other delightfully bumptious words formed by reduplication of a sound within a word. Level E continues with the Greek and Latin, while adding a few words from the French (e.g., *connoisseur*). It also has several chapters on words that allude to the Bible (*shibboleth*), to people in history (*Pyrrhic victory*), to places in history (*marathon*), to literature (*Lilliputian*), and to myths (*jovial*). Those word histories are fascinating! Level F focuses on how words change over time and different types of words (e.g., euphemisms). All levels teach how to discern a word's precise meaning, and how words relate to each other (synonyms, antonyms, homonyms, compounds, etc.).

Words are introduced in a variety of ways. Sometimes they are carefully taken apart and each part defined. Sometimes you are given synonyms for each new word. Sometimes the words are introduced in the context of a text selection. Sometimes an individual word is highlighted and its history given—e.g., *checkmate* comes from the Persian *Shah mat*, meaning "the king is dead."

Each level contains 15 lessons plus cumulative lesson reviews, games, puzzles, and additional enrichment activities. Lessons are designed to only take 10–15 minutes each. From level B on, each book has a cumulative list of word parts learned in the earlier levels. This setup is ideal for every-other-week Friday-morning lessons.

The teacher's edition for each level includes the student text, with additional material, answers to exercises, and so on also included.

Unlike the A Beka series, BJUP's vocabulary series is not integrated with its other courses, so you can use it regardless of what resources you are using for literature study. Some text selections do refer to stories in the BJUP literature program, but you don't need to read the original stories to do the exercises.

I like the tone of this series. It is friendly without being patronizing or silly. Although it is not as strictly organized as it could be—for example, students aren't put through a systematic program of learning Latin roots, then Greek, then French, then Old English—it captures the interest better than such an strict approach is likely to. Every lesson has something new and fresh.

UPDATED✶✶
Educators Publishing Service, Inc.
Wordly Wise series: Books A–C (grades 2–4), $4 each, keys $1 each. Books 1-5 (grades 4–8), $5.35 each; Books 6-9 (grades 9–12), $5.35 each. Teacher's keys, $3 each. Add 8% shipping (minimum $3).

Unlike other alleged vocabulary-building series that I've seen from secular publishers, Educators Publishing Service's *Wordly Wise* is interesting, entertaining, and useful. Several major home school correspondence programs include it in their materials.

Wordly Wise A, B, and *C* are the first books in the series. Each introduces about 100 vocabulary words. Books A and B have 10 lessons each; Book C has 12.

Books 1–5, for grades 4–8, introduce about 375 words each. Each lesson includes about 12 new words, studied in a variety of ways. For each lesson, exercises A–C present words in context, show their multiple meanings (if any), and allow students to practice using the words in sentences. Exercise D reviews the lesson and earlier lessons. Exercise E is self-checking—when completed correctly, the student discovers part of a quotation, poem, or riddle. The Wordly Wise section in each lesson discusses words with interesting histories and distinguishes between commonly confused words. Each third lesson has a crossword puzzle to fill in, using words studied in those three lessons.

Books 1–3 each have word glossaries. Beginning in Book 4, the student needs a separate dictionary, and each lesson has an extra exercise focused on roots, prefixes, and suffixes.

So much for dry, cribbed-from-the-catalog copy. Here's a sample of part of one lesson:

Wordly Wise 4
ABYSS is pronounced *a-BISS*.
NAIVE is pronounced *ny-EVE*.
TUMBREL may also be spelled *tumbril*. The rolling of the *tumbrel* brought fear into the hearts of noblemen during the French Revolution, for this was the cart that carried prisoners to their execution. Its destination was the guillotine (pronounced *GEE-yo-teen* in French, *GIL-a-teen* in English), a machine for chopping off the heads of those sentenced to death.

As you can see, words are not introduced according to common roots or other methods of organization, but they *are* introduced memorably.

If you aren't wedded to the Greek-and-Latin approach to vocabulary study, you could do worse than *Wordly Wise.*

NEW★★
Educators Publishing Service, Inc.

Vocabulary from Classical Roots series: Books A–C, $6 each for book, $3.50 each for teacher's guide and answer key. Add 8% shipping (minimum $3). Grades 7–12.

Now these are *interesting* books. Vocabulary from Classical Roots as a series is intended for students in grades 7–12. Each book can be used at several grade levels. Book A is for grades 7–9, Book B is for grades 8–10, and so on.

The premise: teach kids the Greek and Latin roots they need to decode zillions of English words, especially those lurking on the SAT and in the more literate works of literature. The method: roots are grouped by themes and subthemes. In Book C, for example, the first part, "Who Am I?," has two lessons each on The Person (with roots like *humanus, vir, gyne,* and *anthropos*), Personal Relationships, Feelings, and Creature Comforts. After each root and its definition come a number of English words based on the root. Each English word is defined and used in a sentence. A variety of exercises at the end of each lesson provide practice with the words.

This is not as dull as it sounds. Old woodcuts and engravings liven up the pages, while the sentences and exercises abound with literary, historical, and geographical references designed to improve students' cultural literacy. Example: "In *Pride and Prejudice,* Mrs. Bennet's crude efforts to marry off her five daughters *mortify* Elizabeth Bennet." A classical quotation also introduces each lesson, while special Nota Bene sections provide valuable background information about the words being studied.

This series has a definite paleofeminist flavor (we hear about tons of famous females in the example sentences), but stops short of actual preachments (thank you). Easy to use, will definitely increase vocabulary and aid in social climbing if taken as prescribed.

NEW★★
Educators Publishing Service, Inc.

Analogies series: Book 1 (for grades 8 and 9), 2 (for grades 9 and 10) and 3 (for grades 11 and 12), $4.70 each. Analogy and Vocabulary Quizzes series: Books 1–3, $6 each. Add 8% shipping ($3 minimum).

If you're getting the idea by now that Educators Publishing Service is serious about vocabulary development, you're right! Their Analogies series combines practice in solving analogy problems with opportunities for vocabulary study. Books 2 and 3 are designed to build skills for the Scholastic Aptitude Test and other standardized tests. All three workbooks sharpen students' reasoning powers and their ability to see the relationships between ideas. Accompanying removable quiz booklets with pre-perforated pages are available for each Analogies worktext. Each quiz booklet includes six analogy quizzes and six vocabulary quizzes.

UPDATED★★
Longman Publishing Group

Phenomenon of Language, 2nd edition: $12.81 for text, $8.04 for teacher's manual/answer key. These are school prices. If materials are to be shipped to a non-school location, multiply prices by 4/3.

What do you get when you cross Latin with an introductory course in linguistics? It sounds awful, like pasta with barbecue sauce, but really it's good enough to deserve a separate review of its own. It's *The Phenomenon of Language,* a sprightly text that uses Latin as a vehicle for giving students a method for learning all languages quickly and efficiently. Besides the charming Roman-style cartoons and clever activities, the student spends a lot of time discovering how languages work. The exercises are designed according to the Platonic method: students are gently led to draw the correct conclusions on their own.

The *Phenomenon* approach takes more time than other vocabulary courses, but teaches more Latin. Since it does *not* teach Greek, Old English, or Norman French roots, you might want to follow it up with, say, levels D–F of the Bob Jones University Press program.

The Merry Mountaineer
Thangs Yankees Don' Know, Southern Sayin's for Yankees, Dictionary for Yankees, $1.95 each. Add $1.05 postage.

If you ever wanted to improve your Southern vocabulary, here are the goods. Nationally-published cartoonist Bil (yup, he spells it with one *l*) Dwyer has amassed and illustrated a whole mess of words commonly misused by Northerners in his *Dictionary for Yankees and Other Uneducated People.*

Some of the definitions deserve a second look, as in the definition of *sinner*—"A person in the last year of high school or college, i.e., 'My li'l Polly is goin' to the SINNER prom,'" and *skull*—"What some kids drop out from." The *Dictionary* also includes 900 authentic and possibly never-before-defined words of Southern highland and coastal dialect and two pages of "Select Southern Superstitions," some of which are folk wisdom and some are genuinely superstitious. By the same author, *Thangs Yankees Don' Know* is a laid-back answer to the *Foxfire* series and *Southern Sayin's for Yankees and Other Immigrants* includes a section on Yankee Words That Break Up Southerners. Also available: books of mountain songs and mountain recipes, for that down-home feeling.

MATH

CHAPTER TEN

BASIC AND REMEDIAL MATH

What can I say? You know about basic math. It's addition, subtraction, multiplication, and division. It's also exponents and square roots, fractions, decimals, measurements, graphing, mental math, and calculator math. Add to this checkbook balancing, simple interest, percent-off sales, calculating tips and sales tax, and other real-life math problems that use basic math, and you've got consumer math.

You either love basic math—in which case you probably learned most of it in grades 1–6—or you're checking off the days until graduation when you swear you will *never* use any of this again!

In many ways, standard math courses for grades 7 and 8 are a waste of time. It's like a very long pause to catch your breath before you finally get into algebra or consumer math. Since all decent beginning algebra texts start with a comprehensive review of basic math, I see no reason to meddle with grade 7 and 8 standard math courses at all. These are about as skippable as they come.

What if you or your child had trouble with elementary math the first time around? Do you need the seventh- and eighth-grade courses to "fill in the gaps"? As I have said before, the best way to brush up on basic math is to find a good elementary-school text or workbook series and work through your areas of weakness.

Anyway, here's all the info about where to get your basic and remedial math, and even math manipulatives if you want them for presenting these topics. Maybe your local school district insists you use grade-level texts. Maybe all you really want is a quickie reference tool or overview of some areas. Whatever. It's here!

NEW**
A Beka Book Publications
Basic Mathematics I (grade 7) and *II* (grade 8), $11.50 each. Shipping extra.

Basic Mathematics I and *II* review the math children were supposed to have learned in grades 1–6. Gazillions of practice exercises—the publisher says there are more exercises in these books than in any other math books written on this level for Christian schools. *Basic Mathematics II* pushes on to beginning work in advanced math topics like algebra, geometry, and trigonometry.

Teacher's editions and tests are available for all these books.

NEW★★
Alpha Omega Publications

LIFEPACS, $2.75 each. Complete grade 7 course (set of 12), $29.95. Bible-Based Math LIFEPACS for grade 7, $2.95 each (2 LIFEPACS). Complete grade 8 course (set of 10), $24.95. Teacher handbooks, $4.95 per course. Math solution keys, $2.25 each (two per course). LIFEPAC test key (included with teacher handbook), $2.25/course. Shipping extra.

As you recall, the Alpha Omega system is set up with 10 LIFEPACS per grade. These are consumable workbooks, fairly slim, with full instructions and how-to examples built in.

Alpha Omega is currently revising their entire math program to conform to the typical course of study followed in public schools. Among other changes, they will condense each year's work into two booklets, with one separate teacher's booklet including answer keys, tests, and test answers. The upper-grades revision won't be out for several years yet, though, so let's look at what's here now.

The seventh-grade math course has been beefed up with two new introductory workbooks dedicated to the Christian philosophy of mathematics. From then on, it's a pretty standard review of whole numbers, geometry, fractions, and so on. Eighth-grade math reviews a lot of this material again before introducing some simple probability and statistics, solid geometry, and pre-algebra.

NEW★★
Bob Jones University Press

Student worktexts: grades 7–8 $14.95 each. Teacher's editions, $31.50 each. These are home-school prices. Shipping extra.

BJUP's seventh- and eighth-grade math courses emphasize the use of math in real-world jobs. As usual for math courses at this level, much time is spent in reviewing elementary math, and the eighth-grade book ends with pre-algebra.

NEW★★
Contemporary Books, Inc.

Number Sense, complete set, $53.26. Set includes one copy of each student workbook, one copy of each diagnostic test, one answer key, and one teacher's resource guide. Individual workbooks, $3.93 each. Answer key, $3.93. Teacher's resource guide, $9.26. Pack of 10 diagnostic/mastery tests for a single topic, $13.26. Shipping extra. Grades 4–adult.

This brand-new program was especially designed for students "where traditional methods have failed." It consists of ten 64-page worktexts, diagnostic placement and mastery tests, a separate answer key, and a teacher's resource guide.

Contemporary Books is touting *Number Sense* as the ideal introduction for their best-selling *Number Power* adult math program for GED preparation.

Number Sense was originally designed for use by school teachers who need individualized math help for lots of students, especially those who were already having trouble with math. The "adult" format and easy-reading vocabulary of the program makes it usable for all ages.

Areas covered by *Number Sense* are:

• Whole Numbers—with one workbook for *Addition & Subtraction* and one for *Multiplication & Division*

• Decimals—with one workbook for *Addition & Subtraction* and one for *Multiplication & Division*

• Fractions—with one workbook for *The Meaning of Fractions,* one for *Addition & Subtraction,* and one for *Multiplication & Division*

• *Ratio & Proportion*

• Percent: *Meaning of Percent* and *Percent Applications* are the two workbooks.

The teacher's resource guide has simple, sensible activities for each skill area (e.g., practicing place value by playing a game with straws for "points" and bundling the straws by tens when you have enough) and an "Item Analysis Chart" which helps you find the exact lesson to assign for extra help in a given area. It also includes some basic math teaching philosophy and some good common teaching sense (e.g., don't overdo the praise—praise only genuine success, no matter how small).

Number Sense does not teach the arithmetic facts. You should spend some time working on those before beginning this program. What it does offer is:

- clear, easy-to-follow explanations of each math skill, broken down into bite-sized bits (one skill per page)

- a logical sequence of skills

- highly visual page design, with plenty of white space

- minimal reading load (grade 3–5 reading level)

- plenty of practice

You start by giving the student a simple diagnostic test in a particular area (whole numbers, decimals, fractions, or ratio/proportion/percent). The results of this test show you where to start in the *Number Sense* series, or which particular "gaps" to fill by assigning specific pages. You work your way through the workbook, checking work against the answer key. After all assigned pages have been completed, the student takes a mastery test, to see if he really has mastered it all.

Everything is spelled out and every possible difficulty is anticipated; you don't have to know how to teach math to use this program.

The program's best feature is its excellent explanations. Allan Suter, the program's author, has a real gift for making the complex simple. Problem areas, such as subtracting from a number that contains lots of zeros, or solving multistep problems, are separated out and attended to separately. Nobody has to fail at math with this kind of material.

I could wish that along with the excellent explanations and step-by-step skill building came a continuous review of skills already learned. Home schoolers would be wise to provide some homemade "incremental" review problems from previous lessons along with the new skill of the day to ensure that our students not only understand, but can't forget what they've already learned. Alternatively, if your child is having special trouble with math, you could try using *Number Sense* in tandem with one of the Saxon basic math courses

(*Math 54* or *Math 65*). *Number Sense* has better explanations, and Saxon provides the review!

NEW★★
Crane's Select Educational Materials
Math Flipper, $5.95. Shipping extra.

Another in the Flipper series. These are reference and example cards stored in an innovative set of plastic sleeves, arranged so all the card topics are clearly visible on the front. You flip up the card you want in order to read the information. Each flipper is attached to a sturdy, three-hole-punched card for easy storage.

So much for the packaging. What about the product? After all, how much terminology and how many operations can there be in basic arithmetic? More than you think! The Math Flipper is a gem. It defines all those difficult terms like exponent, prime factor, least common multiple, and so on. It provides the equations for simple geometric calculations like perimeter, area, and volume. It explains how to solve fraction, average, proportion, ratio, and decimal problems (among others). It shows how to solve for percent, sales tax, discount, commission rate, simple and compound interest. It provides all sorts of tables of measure and mathematical symbols.

All is arranged very logically, starting with explanations of the four basic arithmetic operations and proceeding in the order these topics are usually taught in school, or ought to be taught in school (today's teachers spend considerably less time—if any—on topics like calculating compound interest).

If, like me, you're always forgetting how many pints are in a peck, that's reason enough to purchase this inexpensive reference aid. If you need to brush up on the not-so-basics of basic math (square roots, anyone?), you'll find the Basic Math Flipper a wonderful tool.

NEW**
Dale Seymour Publications
Mental Math in the Middle Grades, $8.95. *Mental Math in Junior High*, $9.95. Shipping extra.

Mental math is, quite simply, arithmetic calculations done in your head instead of with fingers, paper and pencil, or calculator. The *McGuffeys* generation used to do lots of mental math, in the belief that it increases both math speed and general mental abilities. *They* could cipher beautifully. Today, most kids can't. Case closed.

So, how do you do mental math with a workbook? Start with chain problems. A chain problem is something like "1 + 4 - 3 + 2 + 5 - 7 . . ." and so on, its length and the size of the numbers used and the choice of operations geared to the skill level of the student. Chain problems can easily become games when you add the element of timing (how fast can I say it and have you get it right?) or competition (which of you can get the answer first?).

Mental Math in the Middle Grades, besides a big, bright format and less teacher busywork, also includes more problem-solving strategies, good for quick solutions of mental math problems. For example, when adding, say, 35 + 48, turn 48 into 45 + 3. Then add 35 + 45 and tack on 3. Presto! 83. Or, if adding 98 to 65, change 98 into 100 - 2 first. Your answer then becomes 100 + 65 - 2 = 163. The book has 36 lessons, enough for one per week for a school year. Each lesson has two reproducible pages: a lesson page for introducing new math strategies and a Power Builder page with two sets of practice problems. You don't have to do all the exercises, but if you want to, the answers are in the back.

Mental Math in Junior High is also an easy-to-use large-format book designed to help you teach or learn the techniques of figuring math problems out in your head. It picks up the techniques of the two earlier books in this series (*Mental Math in the Primary Grades* and *Mental Math in the Middle Grades*) and adds on some flashy junior-high stuff as well. You'll be using a few visual aids: dominoes, a ten frame and counters, and a 100 chart. You'll also be learning all kinds of useful strategies for working with everything from addition problems to fractions, decimals, and percents. Here's one little example of front-end multiplication: "Multiplying in your head is easier if you break a number into parts and multiply the front-end numbers first." So 524 x 3 becomes 500 x 3 + 20 x 3 + 4 x 3 = 1500 + 60 + 12 = 1572. No sweat, right? If this seems too hard, it's only because you missed the first 14 lessons of this very

helpful book. Each lesson has two reproducible pages: a lesson page for introducing new math strategies and a Power Builder page with two sets of practice problems. The book has 50 lessons, enough for one per week for a year. Again, the answers are in the back.

NEW**
Equals
Family Math, $15. Add $4 shipping. Grades K–8.

From a letter by reader Dani Gellatly:

I have discovered a math book I am so thrilled with . . . It's called *Family Math* and it's published by the Lawrence Hall of Science at University of California, Berkeley. Other than drill (we like CalcuLadders), it's just about all you'd need for K–8 general math. . . . at last a family, multi-level math option!

Some of the units included are:

• Word Problems & Logical Reasoning
• Measurement
• Probability & Statistics
• Time & Money
• Geometry & Spatial Thinking
• Patterns & Number Charts

Each unit has several chapters and is so well laid out and easy to understand. There are many games and projects—the kind I can actually envision doing, since on most of them we can all be included!

Family Math is a collection of activities originally invented for community family math classes. The book, however, is definitely meant for use at home. Activities require only common household objects (beans, toothpicks, paper, pencils, etc.), although you may want to photocopy some of the game boards. Sample pages of graph paper for the activities requiring it.

The activities in *Family Math* were chosen because they allow parents and children to play with, discover, and experience math together. An icon at the top of each page indicates which age groups can do the activity.

The activities in *Family Math* are really satisfying. The art, on the other hand, is gross. Many illustrations feature children in threatening situations—e.g., measuring an enormous, ugly snake with a huge bulge in his middle (he has evidently just eaten something or somebody). Tongues, claws, and overwhelming size are recurring features in the illustrations. I don't know whose idea these illustrations were—who needs slasher math?

On balance, this is an excellent math (as opposed to arithmetic) course full of ugly pictures. The first math exercise I'd do with this book is calculate how many stickers it will take to cover up the unappealing portions of the pictures!

UPDATED★★
Hewitt Research Foundation

Pre-Math It (ages 4–6) and *Math It* (grades 2–6), $29 each. *Advanced Math It* (grades 4–8), $15. Math concepts book, $8, covers math learning for all three sets. Shipping extra.

Professor Elmer Brooks' *Math-It* series leads kids through the basic math principles *and* drills them on arithmetic facts. Instead of memorizing tables, kids learn how to derive the answers (e.g., adding nine is the same as adding ten and subtracting one). Kids then practice adding nine (for example), until they can give all the plus-nine math facts instantly.

Pre-Math It involves exercises with dominoes (included). *Math It* tells you "How Stevie Learned His Math" and includes the Addit, Dubblit, and Timzit games. *Advanced Math It* has Percentit and Dividit. Each kit is nonconsumable and covers several years of arithmetic (no time-telling or measurement, etc.).

With *Math It* and *Advanced Math It*, you get pre-perfed math facts cards for each game, color-coded as "facts families"—the +9 family, the +8 family, the doubles, the "neighbors," and the "leftovers" for Addit, for example. You also get game boards, facts sheets, envelopes for storing your cards and games, and an instruction book that covers not only the basic games, but extra math tricks, such as how to quickly "reduce" a complicated multiplication problem to check your answer, or how to add long columns of figures like a flash. The approach gets kids thinking mathematically, and is a lot more motivational than traditional memorization-only methods. (In plain English, it's *fun!*)

Packaging has improved a lot since the first edition of this product. It now comes in a fancy binder, like *Winston Grammar,* with professionally-printed books and materials. If you follow the directions, your student is bound to learn his math facts, and enjoy it, too!

UPDATED★★
Key Curriculum Press

Key to Fractions, $7.40/set of 4 books. *Decimals*, $7.80/set of 4. *Percents*, $5.85/set of 3. Answer books, $1.95 each subject. Reproducible tests, $9.95 for each series. Add 10% shipping ($3 minimum).

You won't beat this guarantee. Steven Rasmussen, the publisher, says, "I unconditionally guarantee that *Key to . . .* worktexts will substantially improve your students' math skills and enjoyment. If, for any reason, you are not satisfied, return your books—even if they're used—and I'll give you a 100% refund. No questions asked."

Why is Mr. Rasmussen so confident? Because these workbooks assume *nothing*. Each page contains only one concept. Sample problems are handwritten to reduce student intimidation. Visual models are used wherever possible, such as shaded-in area when studying fractions. Examples are worked out step by step. New terms are explained and underlined. Students get plenty of workspace and lots of exercises which gradually increase in difficulty. *Everything* you need is in the inexpensive workbook.

Key to Fractions includes:

Book 1: Fraction Concepts
Book 2: Multiplying and Dividing Fractions
Book 3: Adding and Subtracting Fractions
Book 4: Mixed Numbers

Key to Decimals features real-world uses of decimals—such as pricing, sports, metrics, calculators, and science—and includes:

Book 1: Decimal Concepts
Book 2: Adding, Subtracting, and Multiplying Decimals
Book 3: Dividing Decimals
Book 4: Using Decimals

Key to Percents includes:

Book 1: Percent Concepts
Book 2: Percents and Fractions
Book 3: Percents and Decimals

Key to Geometry and *Key to Algebra* are reviewed in the geometry and algebra chapters, respectively, of this book.

These are really good books. Anyone who knows arithmetic can succeed with them.

NEW★★
Mathematics Programs Associates, Inc.
Developmental Math, $140 for a complete set of all 16 student books, 15 teacher books, and all diagnostic tests. Partial set, 3 student workbooks and teacher's editions, $37. Inquire about single workbook prices, as I'm not sure whether MPA is still offering individual workbooks. Shipping extra.

Developmental Math is a series of 16 workbooks. Now don't tune me out, you non-workbook types, because these are different from any other workbook series you have seen. Based on a 10-year research project, they are designed to follow what educators call a "four-step taxonomy." In real life this means that kids are first taught concepts with real objects. In step 2, the concepts are represented with symbols (e.g., circles). Step 3, once the concept is learned, drills for speed using numerals-only problems. Step 4 is application with word problems.

What you get is a really clean, efficient program covering all your child's basic math. Each workbook comes with a diagnostic test, so you can quickly slot your child into the right workbook or figure out which pages of the workbook he needs to work to catch up on concepts he might be shaky on. The series is both "sequential" and "incremental." This means concepts are introduced in logical order, and old concepts are reviewed periodically to make sure they aren't forgotten.

The series explains itself. Teacher's manuals are just student books with the answers in brown—no complicated explanations or projects necessary.

The series is called Developmental Mathematics because it *develops* math concepts rather than presenting them as isolated skills. For example: children are drilled on combinations of numbers that add up to 10, in preparation for teaching them "regrouping," which we used to know as "adding with carrying." They then learn that $7 + 8 = 7 + (3 + 5) = (7 + 3) + 5 = 10 + 5 = 15$. This sounds more complicated than it is, as the workbook presents base 10 addition first with pictures. When I say it's not complicated, I mean that my six-year-old daughter is already at Level 7 (a fourth-grade level), zooming along and really enjoying her math! My non-mathematical 9-year-old is also picking up new math skills more quickly than with any other program I have seen. I expect you could easily achieve similar results with remedial students.

At the rate of two pages per day, your child would be through K–6 arithmetic in 3½ years, starting from scratch. At the still-quite-reasonable rate of four pages a day, it will take less than two years! This is not bad for covering *all* of basic computational math.

Levels 1–7 of the series cover all of addition and subtraction. In Level 8, multiplication is introduced. Level 9 introduces division. In Levels 10–12, kids practice using the four basic math operations on larger numbers. Levels 13–15 introduce decimals, fractions, and the metric system. Level 16 winds everything up by covering the special topics of ratios, percents, graphs, etc.

The series was written by a math teacher with a Ph.D. from the University of Birmingham in England, where they still know how to teach math. It is based on his series of elementary math textbooks that for over 25 years has been the official math series in Egypt, with over 200 million copies in print. The English-language series is the culmination of a 10-year project involving several schools, hundreds of students, and many teachers. I'm not telling you this so you will automatically accept this series, since other ostensibly research-based math courses have been disasters (remember New Math?), but so you will know Developmental Mathematics is not a fly-by-night kitchen-table production. The proof, as always, is in the pudding, which tastes good enough to me that all my younger children have used this series.

Mortensen Math
Algebra, Arithmetic, Problem Solving, Calculus, and Measurement, each 4 levels, each strand per level as low as $3.50 (10 booklets). Teacher's manuals: Level 1, $10; level 2, $12; level 3, $14. Series A manuals, set of 10, $20. Many other manipulatives sets available; see reviews elsewhere in Math section. Add 10% shipping.

Putting math in a box. That's literally what Mortensen Math does. Creator Jerry Mortensen has developed a unique visual math analogy of boxes and rectangles to present not only the basic arithmetic operations, but also such esoteric subjects as algebra and calculus. Workbooks are integrated with their complete line of math manipulatives—see the review of these in the Manipulatives section below.

For multiplication and division, the process is obvious. 3 x 4 is three rows of length four, or a square with surface area 12. Simple. In algebra, simply substitute x and y for any specific numbers. To present $(x + 1)(y + 2)$, you end up with a square of surface area xy flanked on one side by a bar length y and on the other by two bars length x, and two little squares (each valued at 1) in the corner to make up the total square. Clear as mud, right? Maybe you'd better catch the demonstration.

For manipulatives, you get large squares, bars, and tiny unit-value squares. For counting practice, stack the lined bars in order of length . . . 1, 2, 3, and so on. For adding, add the bars. For subtraction, subtract. In multiplication and division life gets a bit more complicated. However, the workbooks creep along at a snail's pace repeating the same sort of problem over and over so your student is not likely to get lost.

The Arithmetic series goes through the basic four operations: adding, subtracting, multiplying, dividing. Algebra goes a bit further with xs and ys. Due to the physical limitations of expressing all algebraic equations as rectangles, you are limited to equations with two factors. Consider this more as pre-algebra and beginning than as a substitute for a real algebra course. Ditto the calculus workbooks, which only in Book 5 get around to introducing the idea of taking delta x to zero. This is pre-calculus, not calculus.

At each level, there are arithmetic, algebra, problem-solving, and calculus workbooks. The teacher's manual for each level follows the workbooks. If you're just trying to understand how to introduce math concepts using Mortensen manipulatives, though, the Series A manuals (a set of 10 books) shows how to introduce addition, subtraction, multiplication, division, fractions, equations, functions and relationships, algebraic operations, and algebraic story problems. The set also includes a games and activities book.

The entire Mortensen series sticks firmly to the math-as-a-rectangle vision. But math is not about making everything into rectangles; it is about solving real-life problems. This entire reliance on an (admittedly helpful) abstract analogy makes it more helpful as a second chance for students with math troubles or an explanatory or introductory tool to accompany regular math lessons than as a complete or primary

teaching tool. Personally, I find the Series A manuals (which explain how to use the manipulatives) much more useful than the workbooks.

New for fall 1991: a story problem/application series. I don't know anything about it yet; we'll wait and see!

NEW**
Providence Project

$15.95 per CalcuLadder unit (specify grade level: grades 1–6 available). It's a good idea to start _below_ your child's grade level to build up confidence and make sure he _really_ knows what he's doing. MasterPak 1 (guides, keys, and copy masters for ReadyWriter and CalcuLadders 1–3), $23.95. MasterPak 2 (guides, keys, and copy masters for AlphaBetter and CalcuLadders 4–6), $23.95. Shipping extra.

Your middle-grader needs math practice? How about sets of calculation drill sheets, starting with numeral recognition in level one and winding up with fractions, percents, and all that other lovely pre-algebra stuff in level six?

Each level consists of 12 copies of 16 different worksheets. Your student works a sheet once a day until he can get it all right in the allotted time (between two and five minutes). Then he gets to tackle the next sheet. Grading is super-simple with the QuicKeys™ grading key (just turn around the sheet, lining up the rows, and instantly see if your answer is correct). An instructor's guide is included for each set. Colored paper, cute visuals in the margins, and a Bible verse on the bottom of each page are freebie extras.

The whole CalcuLadder program only takes about five minutes a day, and let me tell you, it really does increase calculation ability and speed! Plus, each level now comes neatly spiral-bound, so you won't be chasing worksheets all over the house.

I recommend this supplemental program for all home schoolers whose children are anything short of supersonic in their math computation speed and understanding.

- CalcuLadder 1: Basic addition and subtraction for grades 1 and 2 or remedial. 2- and 3-minute drills.

- CalcuLadder 2: Advanced addition and subtraction and basic multiplication. Grades 2 or 3 or remedial, 3- and 4-minute drills.

- CalcuLadder 3: Intermediate and advanced multiplication and basic division. Grades 3 and 4 or remedial, 4- and 5-minute drills.

- CalcuLadder 4: Advanced multiplication review, intermediate and advanced division, place values, product estimation, basic fractions, and decimals. Grades 4 or 5 or remedial. 5-minute drills.

- CalcuLadder 5: Advanced division review, intermediate and advanced fractions. Grades 5–7 or remedial. 5-minute drills.

- CalcuLadder 6: Fractions review, percents, English & metric units, pre-geometry, more. Grades 6–8 or remedial. 5-minute drills.

Saxon Publishers

Math 65, (for sixth-graders or smart fifth-graders), *Math 76,* $35.25 each for student text, answer key, and tests. Coming August 1991: *Math 87.* All prices postpaid.

What modern crusader has upset the math establishment and raised children's math scores by incredible amounts? John Saxon, that's who!

When this ex-Air Force officer took to teaching, he wondered why only 20 percent of his algebra students passed the final exam. Unlike so many modern teachers, who have been trained to blame the students, Saxon blamed the textbook. Moreover, he decided to try an experiment. He invented lesson plans that not only simplified math concepts, but reviewed the same types of problems again and again, once introduced, rather than moving on immediately to new ideas.

This "incremental" approach to math teaching produced unbelievable results. Students, for the first time, had a chance to let math settle into their bones. Instead of desperately treading water, trying to cope with new idea after new idea, Saxon's students had time to become familiar with all the ideas through long-term practice. They also had a chance to experience success, because once they had learned and were required to use a skill, that same skill continued to be included in their problem sets. Math became, as Saxon says, a time for "showing off" instead of for failure. Another Saxon saying: "Time is the elixir that turns things difficult into things familiar."

Dramatic increases in algebra enrollment occur wherever the Saxon texts are used. One high school increased its algebra enrollment by 500 percent!

After all the publicity, I expected to see a very colorful, almost gaudy book. But Saxon's books look quite sombre: black and white, no pictures. The excitement comes from the learning itself. Saxon's texts support and encourage the student, not by babyish Behavior

Modification ("You're doing great! Keep it up!") but by allowing him to go step by step and *rewarding him for learning.* The problems themselves sparkle with wit and display Mr. Saxon's wide reading and awesome vocabulary. Example:

> The goliards sang songs before the banquet. If the ratio of ribald songs to scandalous songs in their repertoire of 3102 songs was 7 to 4, how many ribald songs did they know?

Again:

> Miltiades and his army marched to Marathon, the site of the battle, at 2 miles per hour. After the battle Pheidippides ran back to Athens with the news at 13 miles per hour. If the total traveling time was 15 hours, how far was it from Marathon to Athens?

Saxon also includes lots of problems using chemical terms and measurements in order to try to remove fear of science from his students. One problem starts, "Since knowledge of chemistry is useful even in non-scientific fields, three-eighths of the students elected to take chemistry." This kind of preaching I don't mind!

You have got to admire this man, who in spite of all the opposition and even after having two quadruple heart bypass operations is still working on bringing his incremental method to students in the early grades.

The public-school math establishment hates John Saxon because his methods work and theirs don't. The feminist mafia hates Saxon because he doesn't waste kids' time promoting female careerism. Now, to add to the poor man's woes, some Christian home schoolers are upset at Saxon because a miniscule number of his word problems include fairy-tale creatures like gremlins (in red suits, no less) and fairies (counting toadstools to make sure there are enough seats for all those attending the fairy convention), or refer to characters from Greek and Roman mythology (e.g., two Greek gods guessing at the weight of Athena's armor as she springs full-grown from the forehead of Zeus).

Having read *all* the story problems in these books, and being familiar with the cultural references, I can testify that Saxon is *not* trying to sneak in New Age thinking here. If you look carefully at these word problems, they all treat the fairy-tale and mythological folks *irreverently.* Lacking altogether is that serious, worshipful tone in which those of New Age bent like to refer to such imaginary beings. In any case, the few word problems that refer to myths are only a tiny subset of all the historical, cultural, and scientific references Saxon builds into his problem sets. Two minutes with a Magic Marker can banish the six or ten sentences of this nature from your math book, if they bother you.

Saxon's *Math 54, Math 65,* and *Math 76* are wonderful for home use, with the separate teacher's booklet with problem answers, tests, and test keys all in one place. The incremental approach means our children practically teach themselves, only requiring infrequent explanations of some new concepts.

Bottom line: Saxon Math is the best. Period. We've tried everything else (we *have* to, in order to review it!), and now Saxon Math is the *only* math material our family uses once our children arrive at the fourth- and fifth-grade level (skill level, not age level).

NEW**
Video Tutorial Service
Home version of *Real Life Math Series,* 5 videocassettes, $29.95 each (3 on Fractions, 2 on Decimals) or set of 5 plus two accompanying workbooks for $119.80. Add 4% shipping. Algebra and Integrated Math series (high school through adult) also available.

Colorful, loaded with computer graphics, and hosted by two insufferably vivacious TV-newsroom-style hosts, the Real Life Math series consists of five video cassettes (three on fractions, two on decimals), plus two correlated workbooks covering all the work in these areas tested by college entrance and GED tests. Occasional skits features math used in real-life setting, such as shopping and checkbook balancing, attempt to both entertain and motivate your student. The shopping sequence I saw utterly failed at this—its main message seemed to be that if you are obnoxious to the grocery man and refuse to round your numbers, you'll get a better deal! The meat of the format, however, is the back-and-forth lecture format, which does cover a lot of teaching but is not tremendously entertaining.

This series would be of most value for people who love chatty evening news shows and feel overwhelmed by trying to explain these subjects to their children. Tapes are suitable for use by anyone, child through adult, who has mastered basic arithmetic. Available videotapes: *Fractions 1* (intro to fractions, word problems), *Fractions 2* (adding and subtracting fractions), *Fractions 3* (multiplying and dividing fractions, word problems), *Decimals 1* (intro to decimals; adding, subtracting, multiplying, and dividing), and *Decimals 2* (real life uses of decimals, calculator skills, checkbook balancing). Also available: Algebra and Integrated Math series for high school through adult.

NEW**
Wadsworth Inc.
Mathematics: Its Power and Utility, 3rd Edition, hardbound, $41.95. Instructor's manuals are usually free with classroom orders so no price has been established for individual orders—check with the publisher. Add 7% shipping.

Karl Smith, author of *Mathematics: Its Power and Utility,* is one of the rare mathematicians who recognizes that some people hate mathematics and feel doomed to eternal failure in the subject. Acknowledging that math is a required high school subject, Smith tries to make it more palatable rather than telling his readers to hold their noses and swallow because it's good for them. In the introduction and first chapter he diffuses math anxiety by challenging the student to think about his feelings and attitudes towards math. Throughout the book, he continues to batter away at ill will towards math with silly cartoons and word problems. For example, a hippopotamus tries to convince a little bird that they can play together on the teeter-totter by showing her how he worked it out with algebra. Through a number of steps he shows algebraically that H (hippo's weight) = b (bird's weight). The problem in this exercise is to discover the hippo's error in reasoning!

This one-year 544-page course is designed for beginning high school students who need a firmer background in basic mathematics before proceeding on into any higher math. You'll find a clear and concise review of fractions, decimals, percent, estimation, rounding, negative numbers, and exponents in the first two chapters, along with valuable information on calculators (how to figure out which type to buy and how to use them.) Beginning algebra is covered in chapters 2, 3, and 4. Chapters 5 and 6 introduce geometry. The remaining chapters teach students to use math in a variety of ways—applications of percent, sets and logic, probability, statistics, graphs, and computers (flow charts and BASIC programming.) After the first few chapters, topics can be studied according to student or teacher preference.

The author has purposely written the text for students who benefit more from concrete approaches than from theoretical. Thus, problem solving—applying math in concrete situations—is the main theme throughout the book. As students complete the text the teacher can evaluate their mathematical understanding to determine whether they should move on to algebra and geometry courses or pursue business or practical mathematics.

Supplements available for the text include an instructor's manual (with solutions) and an *Instructor's Resource and Activities Manual* which has an overview, objectives, and activities for each chapter (including games), plus suggested options for the sequence of chapters. Answers to odd-numbered problems are included in the back of the student text.—Cathy Duffy

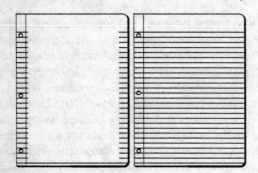

NEW**
World Book Direct Response
Student Information Finder, **$34.95/both volumes.**

Study and review key facts in math, physical science, earth science, and life science with the Math and Science volume of World Book's *Student Information Finder.*

The Math unit in this volume includes a review of arithmetic, algebra, geometry, trigonometry, and the new math.

These truly are "reviews"—you would be hard pressed to teach a subject from this information alone.

One use of the math portion of this volume might be as a quick brushup for parents who will be teaching math at home. If, for example, you are shaky on geometry, the 31 pages devoted to this topic will remind you of what you have forgotten.

The science information in this volume is discussed separately in the Science section.

MATH MANIPULATIVES, TOOLS, AND HANDS-ON LEARNING

NEW**
Cube-It! Manipulative Math
SERIES 1 (grades K–4), $339.80, includes Cube-It! manipulative set. SERIES 2 (grades 5–8), $119.80, is an add-on to SERIES 1. SERIES 3 (grades 9–12), $119.80, is an add-on to SERIES 2.

A math manipulatives program for preschool through grade 12? "Sounds interesting," I told the man on the other end of the telephone line. "Send it along and I'll take a look at it."

I found that Cube-It™ is the best-organized, most complete set of math manipulatives available anywhere. With this one set you can demonstrate *all* the basic arithmetic operations, place value, fractions, measurement, algebra, calculus, and even negative numbers! The 213 pieces, made of an extra-tough, special grade of plastic that wears like iron and handles like wood, are organized in their own durable 7 x 24" blue organizing tray, which is so set up that you can find any piece you need at a glance. Pieces are metric in size, gridded into units, *and labeled.* The last is a very important feature, as it means you can instantly tell the 5 x 5" flat from the 5 x 6" flat or the 4 x 4" flat. Pieces are 1 cm in thickness, meaning you can do 3-D volume work with them as well.

Let's describe this setup.

On the far left back of the tray are two sets of clear gridded plastic squares used in fractions work, from the one-ninths through the one-halfs. Along the back of the tray are labeled yellow fraction strips, ranging from nine one-ninth strips on the far left to two unit squares on the right. Everything neat and in its place so far.

Now, let's talk about the actual positive and negative number flats. On the far left are labeled gridded rectangles of yellow plastic with a layer of black sandwiched in the middle, ranging from 1 x 1 to 1 x 9. At that top of that row are two red, gridded 1 x 10s. The next row goes from 2 x 2 (on the bottom) to 2 x 9 (at the top), with two 2 x 10s at the very top.

Similarly, we have rectangles for every value from 3 x 3 to 3 x 10; from 4 x 4 to 4 x 10; and so on, up to 9 x 9 and the two 9 x 10s in that row. Each rectangle has a clear plastic grid of the same size in front of it—these are used to signify negative numbers of that size. Each rectangle fits into its own individual storage spot, on its end so you can see its label.

Nine extra 1 x 1s are stored in a bin in the front, as are nine extra 1 x 10s. On the right-hand side of the organizing tray are fifteen 10 x 10 flats. These will come in handy when demonstrating operations like 24 x 28 or $(2x + 2)(2x + 5)$.

I've often said that the Mortensen Math method is just turning everything into rectangles. Cube-It uses a very similar approach. Addition becomes "pushing together." Multiplication and division are performed as area operations, making or dividing up rectangles. This "area" approach allows you to go from simple counting to "algebra" (really, only binomials) with breathtaking speed.

It's not practical to *do* all your math problems with these manipulatives. There aren't enough hundred flats, for example, to do 64 x 58. You can, however, *demonstrate* every arithmetic and algebraic operation with Cube-It.

Cube-It! has recently upgraded its "Cubes 'n Crows" blackline masters to include teaching explanations and added a teacher's manual that gives strategies for each concept. This is a welcome change, since the first edition of the blackline masters lacked explanations of what you were supposed to be doing on each page. A teacher's video is also included with each series and explains how to use the Cube-It Concept Cards for that series.

NEW★★
Cuisenaire Company of America
Two-Color Counters, $9.95/set of 200. Grades K–12.

Counters, as you know, are sets of uniform objects used in schools for counting practice. They can be cute little plastic kitty cats, clear poker chips, beans, raisins, forks, spoons, or even children. The Two-Color Counters happen to be thickish plastic circles, one side red and one side yellow. They are especially useful for finding combinations (e.g., "What are all the pairs of numbers that add up to 10?"), single-operator math problems, working with fractions, and simple probability experiments—lots of middle- and upper-grades stuff. You can even use them for your college class on probability! Simple is beautiful.

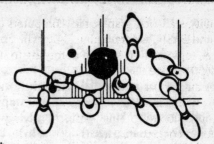

NEW★★
Cuisenaire Company of America
Squared Materials, $18/five sets. Cardboard Thousands Cubes, $7.50/set of 10. Starter Set for Powers of Ten, $37. Base Ten Starter Set (the all-wood version), $27. Thousand Cube, $5.50, has etched lines. *Base Ten Mathematics,* $6.95 (included with Starter Set and Base Ten set). Grades 2–6.

Cuisenaire sells tons of math manipulatives. We're looking at their manipulatives for demonstrating place value, decimals, and powers of 10.

First, the Squared Materials. Each set of these inexpensive materials comes packed in a ziplock bag and includes 20 units, 16 longs, and two flats that reverse to a mini Hundred Board. Materials are plastic, not cardboard, for added durability. Since they come as a package of five sets, you end up with 100 units (enough to cover every numeral on the Hundred Board), 80 longs, and 10 flats. With these you can do all the regular Hundred Board activities, plus work with place value and powers of ten. Since the plastic is thin, not chunky, you can't do volume work; ten flats stacked on top of each other don't resemble a cube. Aware of this, Cuisenaire Company offers cardboard Thousand Cubes, little hollow gridded boxes you build from folded cardboard. No instructions included with the Squared Materials or Thousand Cubes.

In contrast, Cuisenaire's powers-of-ten block sets match the metric size and volume of regular Cuisenaire rods. These are available in either a Starter Set for Powers of Ten (50 natural wood unit cubes, 20 etched orange plastic tens rods, 10 etched orange plastic hundreds squares, *Base Ten Mathematics* book, and 50 Place Value Mats) or the Base Ten Starter Set (identical materials except that the rods and squares are also natural wood).

Personally, I prefer the regular Starter Set. The orange 10 rods match the color coding of my Cuisenaire rods, and the orange flats and rods are more cheerful. Whether you choose all wood or wood and plastic, neither set comes with a Thousand Cube. You can either construct a thousand cube by stacking 10 hundred squares, or (my preferred option) you can buy a Thousand Cube separately.

The *Base Ten Mathematics* book included with Cuisenaire's powers-of-ten material is excellent. It introduces all the natural uses of the material. Learning to build numbers. Adding and subtracting, with and without carrying and borrowing. Multiplying. Primes. Division. Decimals (to the thousands and thousandths). Metric length, area, volume, and mass. Squares and square roots. Basic algebra. Everything you do with Mortensen and Cube-It, except fractions and pre- calculus, is covered in this one 60-page book. It even includes a Hundred Board printed inside the back cover, with some simple Hundred Board activities included in the book. I'd suggest you get *Base Ten Mathematics* if you are using either of these other programs, as neither of them explains how to use powers-of-ten material as well as this book.

It's not easy to compare the Cuisenaire powers-of-ten blocks with Mortensen and Cube-It. Both Mortensen and Cube-It make problems easier to set up by adding rods for 2–9 and 20–90. To represent 99 with Cube-It blocks only takes two blocks, while it takes 18 Cuisenaire powers-of-ten pieces. This Cube-It advantage becomes even more significant when doing problems like 24 x 36. Cube-It is metric like Cuisenaire, extremely well organized, and includes material for negative numbers and fractions. Mortensen blocks are larger (making them easier to use and harder to store), and more colorful, which is fun. The specialized Mortensen kits are either an advantage or a disadvantage, depending on whether you like to present topics separately or whether you prefer one integrated system. *Remember, Mortensen and Cube-It include fractions and pre-calculus, while these Cuisenaire materials don't.*

The larger sets of Cuisenaire powers-of-ten blocks are less expensive than either Mortensen or Cube-It and come with divided storage boxes, but still with only unit cubes. Who wants to solve a problem using 300 unit cubes? On the other hand, the Cuisenaire instructions are easier to follow and require less teacher training.

Bottom line: If all you want to do is *show* kids how the math works, the Cuisenaire Starter Set for Powers of Ten is a great value, covering everything from number recognition to early algebra. Add a set of regular Cuisenaire rods to it for more extensive one-digit addition, subtraction, multiplication, division, and fractions work. If you want the kids to work a lot of complicated problems using your math manipulatives, need to do a lot of work with fractions/algebra/pre-calculus, or just enjoy math manipulatives that are works of art, take a good hard look at Cube-It and Mortensen as well.

NEW**
Mortensen Math

Addition/Subtraction Tray, $25. Addition, Subtraction, or Multiplication facts cards only, $5. Multiplication Facts Tray, $50. All About Fractions Kit, $99. Very Basic Basic Operations Kit, $50. Basic Operations Kit, $350. Combo Kit, $139. Extras Baggie, $28.50. Very Basic Multiple Kit, $89. Decimal Kit Half Tray, $39. Workbooks, $25/level (10 books each in algebra, arithmetic, calculus, problem solving, and measurement). Teacher's manual, $10/level. Home School Kit, regular retail price over $500, only $249 for schools, including home schools. Add 10% shipping. Grades 2–8.

Mortensen Math has *tons* of specialized math manipulatives, plus an entire K–8 math workbook curriculum to accompany them. For space reasons, let's just look at the powers-of-ten material. (You can run your eye down the list above for an idea of what else is available.)

The Combo Kit contains 10 hundred squares, 40 ten bars, 12 unit bars each of values 1 to 6, and nine unit bars each of values 7 to 9. These come packaged in two self-sorting molded trays. You'll have to study the setup for a while, but after you do, it's easy to find the right place for every item.

Like other powers-of-ten material, the Combo Kit doesn't include enough material to demonstrate problems like 52 x 46. For that you would need 20 hundred squares. To solve a problem like 96 x 99 you'd need 81 hundred squares, or more than eight Combo Kits' worth of hundred squares! That's why the Mortensen workbooks tend to use 10, 11, 12, and 21 as the second multiplier. (Note: The Basic Operations Kit can demonstrate all the big problems I mentioned, and more!) You also have to use a large number of 10 rods for each problem, since unlike the Cube-It system the Combo Kit does not include multiple ten bars. However, multiple ten bars *are* included in the Home School Kit.

If you merely want to *demonstrate* decimals, multiplication, algebra, and basic operations, the Combo Kit works very well. The multiple unit bars make life easier than the single unit cubes in most other companies' powers-of-ten material. They do not work as well, however, for simple place value operations like 79 + 86 + 95, where it is beneficial to actually see 79 as seven tens and nine units. For these basic powers-of-ten operations, Mortensen has the Extras Baggie. It includes two whole units (also usable as hundreds), 20 tenths rods (also usable as tens), and 25 hundredths cubes (also usable as units), which is less than you get in the similar set from Cuisenaire Company.

Mortensen's Very Basic Basic Operations Kit helps you take powers of ten concepts up to the ten thousands. The Very Basic Basic Operations Kit contains 10 thousand bars, 10 hundred strips, 10 hundred squares, 20 ten bars, and 20 units. These items are all much smaller in scale than regular Mortensen manipulatives and are made out of thin plastic rather than rodlike in shape. The units are almost impossible to handle, meaning you won't want to use this set for much basic multiplying. Its main virtue is the ability to show 100 as both a square and a strip, and 1000 as 10 hundred squares end-to-end. The set can be used for numbers up to the ten thousands and decimals to the ten thousandth. It can also be used to introduce algebra formulas including x^3 and x^4. The kit comes with a molded plastic tray for storing the units, squares, strips, and bars.

For big-time operations, and big-time spenders, the Basic Operations Kit has multiple hundred bars, gazillions of hundred squares and so on as well as multiple ten bars and units. With this set you ought to be able to solve just about any decent-sized problem, if you can keep track of the teeny-weeny unit pieces.

Both the Combo Kit and pieces from the Very Basic Basic Operations Kit are included in the Home School Kit, along with a Home Fractions Kit, Multiple Tens Kit, Level 1 workbooks and teacher's manual, Apple II or IBM-compatible multiplication software, Multiplication Facts Mastery workbooks, set of Series A (how-to) teaching manuals, and an audiocassette with corresponding coloring book for learning how to skip count. The Home School Kit is definitely the one to get if you want a complete Mortensen Math program that starts at the beginning and does the most for the smallest price.

NEW**
Teachers' Laboratory
Basic Measurement Kit, $18.75. Add $2 shipping.

Teach measurement quickly, efficiently, and thoroughly with this special kit! The Basic Measurement Kit includes three 150 cm plastic measuring tapes marked in both centimeters and millimeters, three triangular plastic meter sticks with different metric measurements on each of the three sides, and *Notes To Teachers*, a simple three-page set of measurement discovery activities. Both the concept of measurement and practical activities are included. As the *Notes* point out, measurement "is . . . an area that many high school students seem to be weak in, indicating that they did not have many opportunities to engage in practical measuring activities in the elementary and middle school years." Sturdy materials, easy to use.

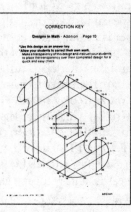

BASIC MATH GAMES

Golden Educational Center
Designs in Math series: *Addition, Subtraction, Multiplication, Division,* $5.95 each. Shipping 10% ($2 minimum). Grades 2–8.

Right-brain math drill. Connect the dots from problems to solutions to create an intriguing design on each page. The correction key on each left-hand page tells you if you did it right. Once successful, color your design in, make it into string art, pound it into submission as a nail sculpture. Reproducible problem pages. A math drill kids will *ask* to do.

KNEXT Card Game Company
KNEXT game, $7 postpaid. Grades 2–adult.

Less than 8; greater than 10; equal to 6; not equal to 12. Mix together 108 colorful playing cards, add some game rules, and what do you have? The *KNEXT* card game, for 2 to 8 players, ages 7 to adult. Each card has a condition (e.g., LT for less than), a number (0–16), and a special instruction in the center of the card. Each player is dealt a number of cards (varies with number of players). The rest of the cards are put in a neat pile, and the top card is turned over to start the discard pile. You then have to meet the condition(s) on that card in order to play a card. First to empty his hand wins. The rules, which include several semicomplicated rules for multiple condition cards (e.g. LT 3 and RED, or GT 4 and LT 9), take a while to master, but then play is both fast and tricky. Professional-quality playing cards, and you get a *lot* of practice in mathematical logic.

NEW★★
Old Fashloned Crafts
Muggins, $29.95. Add $4.50 shipping. Grades 2–adult.

Muggins is an arithmetic drill and thinking skill game played with marbles on a beautiful wooden board. The board has a groove around it (for marble storage while playing), and 36 numbered holes.

The object of *Muggins* is to get your marbles in as many rows as possible, while blocking your opponent's attempts to do the same. You move by rolling three dice . . . adding, subtracting, multiplying, or dividing the numbers on the first two . . . and then to that total doing the same with the third die. E.g., if your numbers are 2, 6, and 3, some possible moves are:

- Divide the 6 by the 2, add the 3. (Answer: 6)

- Multiply the 2 by the 3, multiply by six. (Answer: 36)

- Add the 2 and the 6, subtract the 3. (Answer: 5)

You move your marble into that slot on the board.
There are a few other rules, such as the automatic "bump," where anyone rolling triples gets to remove one of his opponent's marbles, but you get the general idea.

New variations now included in the *Muggins* board game:

- *Muggins, Jr.* (for kids ages 7–9): add and subtract only, using the three included 12-face polyhedrons.

- *Super Muggins* (advanced skill level): add, subtract, multiply, and divide using the polyhedrons.

- *Dishes* (motivational version): dice is thrown only once. Players alternate making totals. First player unable to make a new total has to do the dishes!

- *Bluffing* (optional): encourages players to check each other's math for continual involvement.

Unlike all other math board games I have seen, *Muggins* is fast-paced, uses all the arithmetic operations, and involves a lot of mental math and strategy. Plus it's elegant; the newest version has a furniture-quality walnut finish.

High-class math drill for families with brains who aren't afraid to use them.

Wff 'n Proof Learning Games Associates

Equations game, $22.50. *Real Numbers,* $5.50. *Wff 'n Proof,* $27.50. Imp Kits: 1 kit, $1.50; 5 kits, $6.50; 10 kits, $12.50; set of all 21 kits, $22.50. All prices postpaid. Ages 7 (smart kids) to adult.

Equations is the ultimate math game. You win by never winning, by never making it impossible to win, and by never letting your opponent win. Does this sound just a trifle confusing? *Equations can* be hard to figure out at first, but let's persevere in the knowledge that inner-city fourth graders have figured it out.

Briefly: the game comes with number cubes, symbol cubes, a game mat, an indispensable instruction manual, and an efficient and elegant carrying case. You roll the cubes. One player sets the goal using the cubes. This will be a number, such as 2. On each following move, one cube must be put in the "Forbidden" or "Permitted" or "Required" area of the game mat. The remaining cubes are the "Resources." The idea is to make only moves that don't allow a solution to be built with the addition of only one more cube, and that don't prevent a solution from ever being built. You can challenge another player's previous move as violating these rules, or you can try to trap him by deliberately violating a rule yourself. It's actually not hard to follow, once you've worked through a couple of the sample matches in the manual.

The beauty of *Equations* is that it forces the players to continually make creative arithmetic calculations. You have to consider *all* the possible arithmetic combinations that can be built with the allowed cubes. In the classroom, students quickly develop math strategies in order to help their teams win *Equations* tournaments.

At home, you can discover these strategies with Wff 'n Proof Imp Kits, instructional math play solitaire kits that each teach a specific mathematical lesson from the *Equations* game.

Real Numbers is a handy and very inexpensive introduction to *Equations*. You get colored number and symbol cubes cleverly clipped to a ballpoint pen, plus an instruction booklet that shows you how to play the game with real, rational, irrational, integer, and natural numbers. Smart and motivated kids six years old can play the easiest of the five games that come with it.

And don't let's forget *Wff 'n Proof*. It sounds like the name of a Saturday morning cartoon show, but actually Wff stands for Well Formed Formula and Proof means logical proof. It's a beautiful game for your family or to give as a gift—actually, 21 beautiful games, since the kit comes with an instruction manual listing 21 games of increasing complexity. Six-year-olds can play the first game (*Wff*), and from then on it gets steadily hairier. *Wff 'n Proof* is a game of logic: if this, then that. Physically, it is 36 colored cubes with letters and funny symbols on them and a one-minute timer with pink sand in it. Mentally, it's a real workout and brain organizer that has been shown to *raise IQ by up to 20 points* in dedicated players.

It's only fair to warn you that these are *very* brain-intensive games, nothing like the Milton Bradley games at the teachers' store. If you don't have at least two people in your family who enjoy math logic puzzles, you'll probably try these games for a bit, then put them aside. For those with a mathematical turn of mind, though, or for serious *assigned* math training in your home school, these games are an intellectual order of magnitude above the competition.

CHAPTER ELEVEN

CONSUMER MATH

Consumer math is not basic math. It's about taking the math you mostly already know and applying it to real-life situations—something many elementary texts aren't terrific at, judging from the fact that 60% of American teens can't solve a simple two-step math problem, according to the latest National Research Council study.

A century ago, most school math texts taught consumer math as a matter of course. Teachers knew that Billy and Sally would probably go right to work after graduating the sixth or eighth grade, and they figured that it would help if Billy and Sally could calculate how much principal they still had to pay on their farm mortgage or what Billy's sales commission would be from his day's work as a clerk.

Today, with the increasing emphasis on math for science rather than math for real life, consumer math has become a separate subject. Here's the best and brightest of the consumer math courses I have found.

NEW★★
A Beka Book Publications
Consumer Mathematics (grades 9–12), $11.50, paperbound. Shipping extra.

For older students, A Beka's *Consumer Mathematics* covers what you'd expect, with an emphasis on free enterprise and biblical use of money. Topics covered are buying a car, travel, income, budgeting, housing, food, clothing, calculators and computers for business and personal use, federal taxes and records, banking, investments, and small business. Teacher's editions and tests available.

NEW★★
Alpha Omega Publications
Ten LIFEPACS/course, $2.95 each, or complete Consumer Math course for $26.95. Two answer keys, $2.25 each. LIFEPAC test key, $2.25. Five solution keys, $2.25 each. Shipping extra.

As you recall, the Alpha Omega system is set up with 10 LIFEPACS per grade. These are consumable workbooks, fairly slim, with full instructions and how-to examples built in.

Alpha Omega's *Consumer Mathematics* course takes the same form—10 LIFEPACS, with the last LIFEPAC as a course review. It has a heavy emphasis on family finances, construction and building trades, service occupations, transportation math (figuring currency exchanges and car operating costs, for example), plus some basic business math. One interesting feature is the LIFEPAC on "Occupation Diagrams," such as how to read maps, scale drawings, and house plans, and make calculations based on these diagrams. No separate teacher's handbook.

NEW★★
Bob Jones University Press
Consumer Math (grades 9–12), $18.95 for student book, $31.50 teacher's edition, $7.95 for activity book, $10.65 for activity book teacher's edition. These are home-school prices. Shipping extra.

BJUP's *Consumer Math* begins by reviewing elementary math: adding, subtracting, multiplying, dividing, fractions, simple algebra, percent, and measurement. You spend 125 pages on those topics. Next you learn the math you need to cope with income statements, taxes, borrowing, banking, buying and owning a car, food and clothing, housing (including information on renting or leasing versus buying), home operation and maintenance (utility bills, property taxes, home improvements and repairs), and insurance. Big, thick book, over 500 pages—a whole year's course for schools, but you shouldn't need to spend this much time on it at home.

NEW★★
Christian Light Education
Math at Work, $6.95 plus $2.50 shipping. Grades 5–12.

Is math a practical subject? Adults say it is. Children are supposed to agree. *Math at Work* is a book that *proves* it!

To produce this book, people in a variety of occupations contributed math problems they actually encountered in their work. The result is a 67-page book with over 300 math problems grouped by skill area (e.g., fractions, decimals, percent) and an answer key in the back. Problems cover a range of difficulty and include skills usually taught in grades 5–8.

High school students will enjoy Part 3, in which the student gets to work through a real-life sequence of problems in which he often needs the information from previous problems to solve the present one. These include sequences such as "Carpenter Nathan Patches Mrs. Sauder's Slate Roof," in which he has to figure out how much slate to use, what it will cost to repair the roof with new slate or used slate, how much labor expense is added to the used slate by the time it

takes Nathan to remove it from Richard Eby's house, how much the slate chosen will cost after standard markup, and how much interest Mrs. Sauders has to pay Nathan if he carries a six-month loan on her work at 9.5 percent interest. As the book introduction points out, in this way the student learns that "real-life math does not come prepackaged as fractions or percent."

Problems throughout *Math at Work* are labeled by occupation, such as automobile mechanic, baker, carpenter, electrician, farmer, printer, and so on. This is a refreshing change from the paper-pushing professions or welfare math usually featured in a book of this kind.

The book format is letter-quality dot-matrix printing, double-spaced, with almost no illustrations. But then, real-life math problems often appear in scribbled handwriting on leftover scraps of paper. It may not be fancy, but I like this book.

NEW★★
Hayes School Publishing Co., Inc.
Modern Mastery Drills in Arithmetic series: grades 1–8, $3.50 each. Add $1.50 postage for first item, 35¢ each additional item.

Rule of thumb: Nothing with "modern" in its name really is. Modern, that is! Hayes' Modern Mastery Drills in Arithmetic is no exception. It's a reprint of math drill books originally published decades ago by the Benton Company of Fowler, Indiana. Your parents may have used these books—they are only slightly revised from the original old-timey edition. Nostalgic typography and simple exercises like, "On her way to school this morning, Mary Lou saw 5 robins, 1 kingbird, and 3 song sparrows. How many birds did Mary Lou see?"

To give you an idea of the era in which Hayes' Modern Mastery Drills in Arithmetic was published, consider this question: "Betty mailed two letters for her mother. On one there was a 4-cent stamp and on the other there was a 7-cent stamp. What was the total amount of postage?" Raise your hand if you remember 7-cent first-class stamps! How refreshing to see problem sets that evoke an America that really was kinder and gentler, in which membership in the local Pig Club (for owners of pigs) loomed large in a child's life, when movie tickets cost 45¢, when every boy owned a whittling knife and nobody ever knifed anybody.

As you might recall, in the old days kids really were expected to learn some *serious math*. Thus, although the first-grade book starts charmingly with apples to color in and large numerals to copy, by the time you hit grade 8 you're looking at how to figure percents, commissions, and bank interest, among other things. Strong, practical, consumer-math emphasis.

These books cover *everything*: geometry, graphing, fundamental operations, exponents (called "powers"), units of measure, etc. And they do it all in old-fashioned terms of Mrs. Smith's dress-goods yardage and the capacity of Mr. Jones' cistern. Refreshing!

No effort is required to use these books at all. No teacher's guides; answer keys are built in. Everything is step-by-step and logically arranged. Each new skill is explained in a little box at the top of the page. Problems are well designed for practicing new and old skills. Calm common sense throughout.

Mott Media

Ray's Arithmetic series: complete set with teacher's guide, $89.95. *Primary Arithmetic* (grades 1–3), $5.75. *Intellectual Arithmetic* (grades 3 and 4), $7.95. *Practical Arithmetic* (grades 5 and 6), $16.75. Key for those three books, $11.25. *Test Examples in Arithmetic*, $11.25. *Higher Arithmetic* (grades 7–12), $20.25. Key for *Higher Arithmetic*, $11.25. Parent/teacher guide for all books, $10. Shipping extra.

If you're into classics, you'll be glad to hear that Mott Media has resurrected a whole series of the texts America used in the days of Reverend McGuffey and Laura Ingalls. One of these selections is the Ray's Arithmetic series. The series goes from kindergarten to high school, with a strong consumer-math emphasis in each grade.

Mental arithmetic in this series precedes written, and some of it is tough (your students will have to think!). Example: "If 3 lead pencils cost 18 cents, how many cents will 5 pencils cost?"

Primary Arithmetic starts with counting concrete objects and proceeds to counting, writing, and reading numerals. Word problems appear from the start.

Intellectual Arithmetic, Practical Arithmetic, and *Higher Arithmetic* carry on with old-fashioned word problems and solid business math, right up to compound interest.

Be sure to get the great parent/teacher guide!

CHAPTER TWELVE

ALGEBRA

The ol' gray algebra . . . it ain't what it used to be. Nossir, it ain't. When I went to school, algebra revolved around factoring polynomials. Nowadays, if anyone puts an x in an equation it gets called algebra. So if your eight-year-old can figure out the answer to 4 times x equals 12, he knows algebra.

Right?

Not exactly.

Below are resources for algebra—the real thing, too. Of course, algebra is not really necessary for happiness in life. Nor is geometry. Actual math, of which algebra and geometry are the merest beginnings, is only really useful in a technological career in one of the disciplines that deal with machines. Try as the statisticians will to make math apply to humans, plants, and animals, the living world exists quite nicely without them.

Algebra does, however, unlock doors which otherwise remain firmly shut in your face, such as those technological and professional careers I mentioned above. It's also great for developing reasoning ability and self-confidence, provided you actually manage to learn it. Let's see how you can do with the resources below!

NEW★★
A Beka Books
Alpha Omega Publishers
Bob Jones University Press

These Christian publishers each have algebra courses. A Beka's two-year sequence is designed for grades 9 and 10, while Alpha Omega interrupts its algebra sequence with grade 10 geometry, covering algebra in grades 9 and 11. BJUP follows the same program, with algebra in grade 9, geometry in grade 10, and algebra in grade 11.

Frankly, I haven't had the time to sit down and figure out which program is best: all emphasize Christian values, proceed in more or less logical sequence, and make available teacher's editions, tests, and answer keys.

NEW★★
Barron's Educational Series, Inc.
Algebra the Easy Way, $9.95. Add 10% shipping ($1.75 minimum).

Algebra the Easy Way by Douglas Downing is a really different approach to algebra. It is written as an adventure novel! The characters learn about algebra, why it is used and how it works as the story unfolds.

The author believes that algebra is simply a short-hand way of writing mathematical situations, and that we should all appreciate short cuts and know how to use them. Rules are simply stated with technical terms pointed out but not emphasized.

While I love Downing's approach for its creativity, I am afraid that it might have insufficient explanation and practice for those who have difficulty with math. The author covers concepts from both Algebra I and II in 289 pages, so coverage is rather hurried. It might also be too incomplete for those who need a thorough math foundation to go on to higher math. Concepts are presented in a different order than in most algebra programs, so it's impractical to plan on using part of the book then switching to another publisher for another Algebra II course. However, it should be useful for students who benefit from the user-friendly approach and should certainly satisfy the high school algebra requirement. This would also be a practical book to use for review of previously-learned algebra.

A sequel from the same author, *Calculus the Easy Way*, is reviewed elsewhere in this book. Other books in the Made Easy series are by different authors and lack the creativity of Downing's books. Exercises for practice are included and answers are in the back of the book. The all-in-one format makes this a real bargain.—Cathy Duffy

NEW★★
Crane's Select Educational Materials
Algebra Flipper, $5.95. Shipping extra.

Like the other Flippers, this is a set of reference and instruction cards covering the basic topics of the subject. Instead of a mere box of loose cards, though, the cards are staggered in a set of clear plastic sleeves backed by a three-hole-punched piece of sturdy cardboard. To use, find the topic you want and flip that card up.

The Algebra Flipper contains over 325 rules, definitions, and examples. These begin with definitions of algebraic terms and symbols, how to write algebraic expressions, and the basic properties and run all the way to polynomial operations and coordinate graphing. Excellent clear, simple instructions. You wouldn't want to use this Flipper for your primary algebra teaching tool, but it's great for review and for unscrambling pesky problems.

NEW★★
D.C. Heath
Developmental Mathematics student text, $29, paperbound. Answer key, $2. Instructor's guide with tests, $2. Student guide to margin exercises, $9. Add 10% for UPS shipping.

Although *Developmental Mathematics* by David Novak is sold as a college level text, it covers only a little more than typical high school Algebra I courses in its 992 pages. It teaches how to do the calculations and presents mathematical theory without explaining how or why algebra is used in real life. Students who enjoy math for its own sake will probably succeed much better with this text than concrete learners who need to know *why* they need to learn it.

The somewhat unusual format, designed for use in both classrooms and independent study programs, lends itself to home education. Each page contains instructions with examples. Exercise problems are set up in wide margins along each page so you can work them out right in the book. Bold print within the text directs students when to do which problems. Answers to margin problems are at the end of each section. A review test is at the end of each section. Answers to section problems, chapter review, and chapter tests are in a separate answer key.

Parents ought to get the *Student Guide to Margin Exercises*, a solution manual to the daily problems, if you are weak in math or just don't have the time to work all the problems through in order to check your student's answers. The *Instructor's Guide with Tests* is not absolutely necessary. It contains extra word problems (although there are plenty in the basic text), plus diagnostic, chapter, and review tests, along with answer keys to all tests.

While the review tests at the end of each section in the text might be sufficient, some might want to use the tests provided in the instructor's guide. An answer key to these tests is also in the same instructor's guide.—Cathy Duffy

NEW**
Houghton Mifflin

Unified Mathematics series: Book 1 student hardback text, $22.50; Book 2, $22.65; Book 3, $22.95. Teacher's manual with solutions, $8.25 for each level. Add 8% shipping.

Unified Mathematics is a series of three high school level math texts designed as an alternative to the traditional Algebra I-Geometry-Algebra II sequence. Algebra and geometry are studied through all three years with cross-application of concepts.

So far this sounds like Merrill's Integrated Mathematics (see writeup below). So what makes Unified Mathematics different? Its heavy use of logic. The second chapter of Book 1 is all about logic (heavy duty thinking here!), then logic is used constantly as a means of presenting and unifying algebra and geometry topics. Throughout the presentations, examples, and questions you keep running into the reasoning that "if such and such, then such and such is true."

Probability and statistics are also studied through all three books, with increasing emphasis on probability the second year and on statistics the third year. Computer programming exercises in BASIC are also included to reinforce understanding of mathematical concepts.

While the focus of this series is similar to that of the Merrill series, these books seem much more difficult, requiring well-developed thinking and logic skills. The content coverage is also more advanced. Although the publisher states that the books are for average students, I would recommend them only to those who are above average.

You can tailor the courses to make them easier or more challenging by using the charts of chapter sections in the teacher's guides. You can also assign exercises appropriate to your student' ability. The teacher's

manuals contain commentary on lessons, answers to problems, tests, and suggested course outlines. You will need both the student edition and teacher's manual —however the total cost is much less than most alternatives.—Cathy Duffy

UPDATED**
Key Curriculum Press

Key to Algebra, $12.95/set of 7 workbooks. *Answers and Notes for Books 1–4, Answers and Notes for Books 5–7*, $1.95 each. Add 10% shipping ($3 minimum).

No math teaching experience is required to use the Key to Algebra series. *Everything* you need is in the inexpensive workbooks. Each page contains only one concept. Sample problems are handwritten to reduce student intimidation. Visual models are used wherever possible, such as shaded-in area when studying fractions. Examples are worked out step-by-step. New terms are explained and underlined.

Students get plenty of workspace and lots of exercises which gradually increase in difficulty. An end-of-book review helps insure that new concepts are remembered. Hey, the series is even *guaranteed* to improve your students' math skills and enjoyment, or its publisher promises you'll get your money back!

Key to Algebra has been expanded to seven workbooks. The series now includes:

Book 1: Operations on Integers
Book 2: Variables, Terms and Expressions
Book 3: Equations
Book 4: Polynomials
Book 5: Rational Numbers
Book 6: Multiplying and Dividing Rational
          Expressions
Book 7: Adding and Subtracting Rational
          Expressions

Each book is now 40 pages, rather than 32 pages as previously. Fractions and decimals are not introduced until students have practiced with whole-number variables.

The Key to Algebra series is so designed that your fifth-grader can start on it, yet your twelfth-grader can use it without feeling dumb. This has been the best-selling algebra workbook series for two decades.

The *Key to . . .* lineup also includes Key to Fractions, Key to Decimals, and Key to Percents. See reviews of these series in the Basic Math chapter. Key to Geometry is reviewed in the Geometry chapter of this book.

NEW**
Merrill Publishing Company
Merrill Integrated Mathematics series: Course 1 student edition $20.10, teacher's annotated edition $26.25; Course 2 student edition $20.64, teacher's annotated edition $26.88; and Course 3 student edition $21.12, teacher's annotated edition $27.37. Teacher's resource book, $48.96 each course. Review problem software for each course (Apple computers), $156.

This series of texts covers the content of Algebra I and II and geometry, plus introductory probability and statistics courses. Each of the three volumes is a one-year course.

In some respects these books are not very different from traditional courses. Course 1 concentrates more on algebra while Course 2 concentrates more on geometry. However, algebra concepts are applied to geometry and other topics beginning in Course 1, which helps students to better understand that math subjects are not used in isolation in real life. Geometry, beginning in Course 1, uses columns titled "statements" and "reasons"—essentially formal proofs. Students need to memorize axioms and theorems as in traditional geometry courses. Trigonometry is also introduced in Course 2 and taught in Course 3.

Outlines for using the texts for students of varying skills are included in the teacher's annotated edition. However, the content is equivalent in difficulty to the average algebra and geometry text. (Remedial students will need something easier.)

Lesson presentation is fairly traditional, although the authors have included instruction in problem-solving strategies along with "mathematical excursions" to help students grasp the practical purposes of mathematics. Each lesson includes exercises that practice new concepts and review previously learned material.

You will need both the student edition and the teacher's annotated edition, with its tests, test answer key, and helpful teaching hints. The teacher's resource book is skippable. It contains reproducible handouts and more quizzes and tests which we are unlikely to need. Contact the publisher for more information about the supplemental software programs available for student practice.—Cathy Duffy

NEW**
Saxon Publishers
Algebra 1/2, 2nd edition, $36.50. *Algebra 1*, second edition, $39.75. *Algebra II*, $40.75. *Advanced Mathematics*, $45.25. *Math 87*, TBA. Algebra II and Advanced Math courses come with a hardbound teacher text with answers in back and tests. Algebra 1/2 and 1 come with a student edition and answer key. Prices postpaid.

Algebra without fear. Algebra with topics thoroughly introduced, explained and practiced. Algebra with concepts not mentioned and then forgotten, but drilled again and again until the student knows them as well as he knows his own name. That's the John Saxon approach, and it's made such a difference that students using his books spectacularly outperform those using "traditional" algebra programs.

In "traditional" algebra a concept is introduced, studied, and never seen again until the final exam. In Saxon algebra, every test is treated like a final exam; each includes all the material studied up until that point. Even the chapter exercises include problems from material long ago studied. This both gives kids a boost (since they know they can handle at least some of the questions in every problem set with ease) and tamps material down firmly until the student really masters it. Not only that, but the problems themselves often involve humor and unusual subject areas.

Example (from *Algebra 1/2*):

The freshman class was noted for being prolix. This was a little unfair because only 60 percent of the freshmen suffered from uncontrollable prolixity. If 800 freshmen were not prolix, how many were prolix?

And from *Algebra II*:

Some sparkled and the rest coruscated. Ten times the number of sparklers exceeded 6 times the number that coruscated by 40. But 4 times the number that coruscated exceeded twice the number that sparkled by only 160. How many were in each category?

It was necessary to mix 200 ml of a solution in which the key ingredient made up exactly 63 percent of the total. One container held a solution that contained 70 percent key ingredient and the solution in the other container was only 60 percent key ingredient. How many of each should be used?

Saxon's famous algebra books are a four-year sequence. Each starts at the same place, and then proceeds a little farther than the previous year's book. Starting in *Algebra II*, there is a noticeable emphasis on preparing students for studying chemistry, as seen in the last problem quoted above.

Algebra 1/2, so called because it's mostly an introduction to algebra and review of basic math, builds a foundation for basic algebra skills and concepts, with emphasis on signed numbers, positive and negative exponents, linear equations, and word problems.

Algebra I continues these topics while emphasizing systems of linear equations. Most problem sets include area and volume problems, and many include problems involving similar triangles. Starting with this book, geometry is fully integrated with algebra.

Algebra II goes back to the beginning. Starting with signed numbers, it quickly reviews all of the topics of Algebra I. The purpose of this course is to fully prepare students for the advanced algebra concepts—such as logarithms, the complex plane, probability, and conic sections—that they will encounter in advanced math and applications courses. Topics from geometry, including proofs, are introduced and practiced throughout the book. You will be amazed at how much geometry your students learn from the new edition of this algebra book!

Advanced Mathematics, previously known as *Geometry-Trigonometry-Algebra III*, is the fourth book of the sequence. Again, it reviews fundamental algebra and geometry, and trig skills, while introducing and continually practicing new topics. These include logarithms, determinants, arithmetic and geometric series, conic sections, roots of higher-order polynomial equations, and functions, including curve sketching. The book also includes a lavish helping of word problems, as do all Saxon books. The geometry in this volume includes terminology and proofs.

Each book provides about 125 daily lessons, each followed by a set of 30 problems. The student is expected to work all these problems, plus any practice problems that may be included in the lesson itself.

These texts are ideal for the home learner, not only because Saxon has thoughtfully provided a booklet of tests and test answers keys that you purchase along with the teacher's edition, but because the texts are designed for minimal teacher input. John Saxon believes,

> Since the learning process is often long and slow, students often have difficulty understanding and retaining explanations that are clear to the teacher doing the explaining. Comprehension of abstraction occurs over a period of time and cannot be forced, even by brilliant explanations. This means that presentation by teachers who use this book should be abbreviated as much as possible because students learn by doing and learn much less when the teacher is talking.

Say, "Amen!"

Since skills, once introduced, are repeated in every subsequent lesson, you don't have to be overly concerned if your student doesn't "get" one of these difficult math concepts right away. It will be repeated and reinforced again and again, until sooner or later his mind make the breakthrough and it all starts to make sense to him. It helps, of course, if you know enough of this math to explain any sticky points.

Virtually any teen who is willing to apply himself seriously to these texts will be able to conquer the material. Kids with serious motivation problems need to have the motivation problems dealt with—this is not a fun 'n games course.

The one valid criticism I have ever heard of the Saxon series is that the first algebra course, *Algebra 1/2*, is too big a jump from basic math for some kids. This will no longer be a problem, since Saxon is bringing out *Math 87*, a program covering the same ground as *Algebra 1/2* but with simpler, less abstract language, thus easing the way into full algebraic abstractions. If your preteen or teen can make it through basic math —even by the skin of his teeth—Saxon's *Math 87* book can usher him into the realm of advanced math where nobody thought he would ever go. See the review of other Saxon math books in the Basic Math chapter for yet more glowing comments on this wonderful math program from yours truly.

NEW**
W. H. Freeman and Company
Elementary Algebra, $29.95, hardbound; teacher's guide, $10.95; test masters $11.95. Add $1.95 shipping first copy, $1.25 each additional. Grades 7–11.

Elementary Algebra by Harold Jacobs is an unusual algebra text that invites students to explore standard Algebra 1 concepts in a friendlier environment than other texts. Cartoons, interesting and creative applications, pictures, puzzles, and even poetry capture the interest of students who struggle with abstract mathematics.

Jacobs, the author of *Mathematics: A Human Endeavor* (reviewed in the next chapter) always provides reasons for learning and using what is taught in each lesson, with more real-life illustrations than are found in most algebra texts. My son—still a hands-on, concrete learner in high school—found this text much easier to understand than the Saxon algebra series.

Students can jump around in this text to some extent (although they may not wish to), since all lessons do not build one upon the other.

Four exercise sets are at the end of each lesson, with problems ranging from simple computation through word and application problems to challenging thought problems. By assigning appropriate problems, the text can be used with students of varying capabilities.

Since the answers to questions from Set 2 of each lesson are in the back of the student text, you can avoid purchasing a separate teacher's guide (which includes *all* the answers) by assigning only the Set 2 problems in each chapter and using the student book's answer key. Reasonably-priced test masters are also available with four different tests for each unit, plus answers for the tests.—Cathy Duffy

CHAPTER THIRTEEN

GEOMETRY, TRIGONOMETRY, CALCULUS

D read. Fear. Panic! It's time for the Three Sisters—the math courses without which all technical and many professional careers are closed to you forever.

Actually, geometry, trig, and calculus aren't all *that* hard. The main problem is the lousy textbooks. The higher a person's level of education, the less likely it is that he can both write coherently *and* solve technical problems. At the very tippy-top of technical skill are the very worst writers, some of whom are then tapped to create the next generation of advanced math texts.

It doesn't help a whole lot that fuzzy-wuzzy theories of education are proliferating in the math establishment, as everywhere else. Opaque writing is a dandy way to confuse the reader into thinking he's too dumb to understand what the *writer* doesn't even understand himself! And the technical nature of advanced high-school and college math means that few real writers will be found snickering over (and exposing) the turgid prose in these books.

You can, of course, resort to translating the text into real English (wide margins help here). If you succeed, a promising career as a technical writer lies before you.

Well! It is to be hoped that, in the eventuality that the readability index of math books continues to function as the inverse square of the sum of the educational level of their writers and the years they have worked in the education field, consumption of alternative/traditional mathematical pedagogy will increase exponentially, or on a straight line at the very least, according to the function $f(x) = mx + b$, where m and b are both positive.

Could you translate this? It means, "Look below, buddy, and see what you can find!"

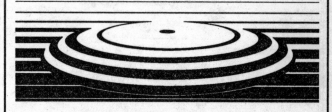

HIGH SCHOOL GEOMETRY

NEW★★
A Beka Book Publications
Alpha Omega Publications
Bob Jones University Press

As I mentioned in the Algebra chapter, these three Christian publishers all offer two years of algebra and one year of geometry. A Beka has a two-year geometry sequence in grades 11 and 12, preceded by two years of algebra, while the other two have an Algebra I - Geometry - Algebra II sequence, with geometry studied in grade 10.

A Beka's new *Plane Geometry: A Traditional Approach* features formal proofs and sounds pretty good, but a reader who has used the program complained to me that the answer book is riddled with errors. Also available from A Beka are *Solid Geometry, Trigonometry with Tables,* and *Analytic Geometry.*

I haven't seen the Alpha Omega geometry course, but from the scope and sequence description it appears to include some proofs, plus regular plane geometry and a smidgin each of solid and coordinate geometry. This all comes in 10 separate LIFEPAC worktexts, unlike the textbook-based A Beka and BJUP courses.

BJUP offers a one-textbook geometry course that ends with an introduction to trigonometry and analytic geometry.

None of these publishers take Saxon's "incremental" approach. A Beka and BJUP books include review sections at the ends of chapters; Alpha Omega has an entire course review in its tenth LIFEPAC.

NEW★★
Crane's Select Educational Materials
Geometry Flipper, $5.95. Shipping extra.

Of all the subjects which cause homework-helping parents to tremble in fear, geometry is one of the worst. It's not that we don't understand it (or so we say!), but there are so many pesky facts and names of things to remember.

To the rescue: the Geometry Flipper. Like the other Flippers, it's a set of reference cards enclosed in flip-up plastic sleeves attached to a sturdy back, prepunched so you can slip it into any three-ring binder.

The Geometry Flipper contains over 350 rules, definitions, and examples—instant help when you need it. Since the plastic sleeves are staggered, you read the topic on the front of the card, and then flip it up to get the details. Example: Topic 8, "Angles," and

Topic 9, "Special Angles," show on the front of the Flipper when all the cards are flipped down. To access these topics, you flip up the cards above. This reveals the information for topic 8 on the front of the card. Flip the card up to read the info for Topic 9, which is on the back of the card.

The information is well illustrated and clearly explained. For example: "Straight angle is an angle of 180 degrees that has opposite rays for sides." A picture of that kind of angle follows.

This Flipper covers just about everything geometrical, from simple set theory (including Venn diagrams) through definitions of all geometric features, theorems, up to and including the laws of sines and cosines.

UPDATED★★
Key Curriculum Press
Key to Geometry, $23.40/set of 8 workbooks. Geometry Starter Set, $5.85/3 books. Circle Master compass, $2.45. Plastic straightedge, 25¢. Answer books for books 1-3, 4-6, 7, and 8, $1.95 each. Add 10% shipping ($3 minimum).

Key to Geometry, another workbook series from Key Curriculum Press, carries the same 100 percent satisfaction guarantee. The publisher is confident you won't cash in on it, because these workbooks assume nothing. Each page contains only one concept. Sample problems are handwritten to reduce student intimidation. Visual models are used wherever possible, such as shaded-in area when studying fractions. Examples are worked out step-by-step. New terms are explained and underlined. Students get plenty of workspace and lots of exercises which gradually increase in difficulty. An end-of-book review helps insure that new concepts are remembered.

No math-teaching experience is required to use the series. *Everything* you need is in the inexpensive workbook.

Key to Geometry covers basic geometry, and includes no proofs. It covers:

Book 1: Lines and Segments
Book 2: Circles
Book 3: Constructions
Book 4: Perpendiculars
Book 5: Squares and Rectangles
Book 6: Angles
Book 7: Perpendiculars and Parallels, Chords and Tangents, Circles
Book 8: Triangles, Parallel Lines, Similar Polygons

For this series, you will also need a compass and straightedge, both also available from Key Curriculum Press.

Key to Geometry is not a full pre-college geometry course, but it works well as a high school or junior high "alternative" course for those not pursuing higher math, or as a supplement to traditional full-menu high-school geometry courses. Younger students can also use it, thanks to the wonderful job the authors have done of simplifying this work, while their basically serious approach won't make even a 12th-grader feel "dumb."

The *Key to . . .* lineup also includes Key to Fractions, Key to Decimals, and Key to Percents. See reviews of these series in the Basic Math chapter. Key to Algebra is reviewed in the Algebra chapter of this volume.

NEW**
Key Curriculum Press
Discovering Geometry course: hardbound student text $24.95, teacher's guide and answer key $24.95, teacher's resource book $54.95, *Mathercise* blackline masters $16.95. Free shipping on prepaid orders, otherwise add 10% shipping and handling ($3 minimum) or 15% shipping and handling to Canada.

Here is a truly different approach to teaching geometry!

Discovering Geometry by Michael Serra is a complete, college-preparatory course that looks more fun, interesting, and inviting than any other text I have seen. The first thing students encounter in the book is art—geometric art. The art leads students into their first investigations about lines and shapes. Investigation by students helps them to discover postulates and theorems by inductive reasoning. Many investigations involve students in activities, including making and working with models. Word problems are imaginative. Real life applications are more true to life than in other texts. Formal proofs are taught only in the last three chapters after students have mastered concepts and understand relationships between theorems.

Discovering Geometry was designed to be used in classrooms and involve students in cooperative learning groups of four students each. Because of this the text will work best in an interactive situation—teacher involvement with one or more students—rather than for independent study.

You will need both the hardback student text and the *Teacher's Guide and Answer Key*. The teacher's guide includes course philosophy, outlines and timetables, classroom organization information, answers to exercises, investigations, projects, puzzles, conjectures (incomplete postulates and theorems), and a glossary. Not quite as essential are the teacher's resource book and *Mathercise* blackline masters. The teacher's resource book contains chapter quizzes and tests, midterm and final exams, computer (LOGO) activities, blackline masters, and an annotated bibliography. *Mathercise* is a set of 50 reproducible exercise pages for 10-minute warmup and review sessions, accompanied by teaching suggestions and answer key.—Cathy Duffy

NEW**
Saxon Publishers

All the upper-grades Saxon math books include geometry right along with the algebra or whatever, so no separate course is needed. For a writeup of Saxon's *Advanced Mathematics,* previously known as *Geometry-Trigonometry-Algebra III,* see the Advanced Math section of this chapter.

NEW**
Timberdoodle
DIME Geometry Build-Up Pack, $25. DIME Geometry 3-D Sketching Project, $26. *3-D Build Up Book 1, 3-D Sketching Book 2, 3-D Sketching Book 3,* $6.50 each. Prices are discounted. Add 10% shipping ($4 minimum).

This geometry/pre-drafting program is based on colorful foam blocks of interlocking shapes. The DIME books start with two-dimensional puzzles even the preschoolers can work and progress to 3-D solids that will give you a challenge. In the process, children (and adults) discover mathematical patterns and relationships and develop amazing spatial skills.

DIME stands for Development of Ideas in Mathematical Education. Naturally, the program was invented by an Australian, pioneered in Scotland, and printed in Canada—Americans today are too strung out over basic skills to pioneer something this fun and effective!

The DIME 3-D Build-Up Pack is described in Volume 2. The Build-Up Pack introduces the program, and you probably should get it even if you are planning to use the program with a teenager. It won't take him long to work through the book (plus it's buckets of fun to make all those solids pictured in the book out of the foam blocks) and he'll have a firm foundation for what is to follow.

Now, the DIME 3-D Sketching Project. Like the Build-Up Pack, it includes a set of DIME solids blocks, so if you're starting with the Build-Up Pack, you might be better off just adding *Book 2* and *Book 3* to the Build-Up Pack. (Exception: since each set only has enough blocks for one child to use at a time, if you plan on using DIME for several children at once, you might want to get both complete kits.)

The focus of the Sketching project set is on learning to sketch 3-D objects. The included book, *3-D Sketching Book 2,* has three sections. In the first, students learn to draw isometric diagrams of solids. This is taken very slowly, one step at a time. Kids first learn to draw solids showing all the cubes. Next, they learn to remove the extra lines. Then they learn to make coded plans. These are overhead views of a solid with the height of each piece shown as a number. A square with *1*s on it, for example, is one story high. A rectangle with a *2* on it is two stories high.

Kids can make their drawings on "dotty" paper, since reproducible master pages of two sizes of isometric drawing paper are included in the book. Also included are master pages for the cubes and cube-tiles (don't ask me to explain these without pictures!) used in this section and the next. In Section 3, sketching skills are further built up.

Throughout the entire process, kids use the solid manipulatives to help visualize the structures they are drawing. The last skills taught in the book are how to sketch reflections and drawing solids *not* made out of cubes. Answers are right in the book, in nonreproducible blue ink—you'll need to photocopy the exercise pages before giving them to your children.

Boys will like the DIME program more; girls, who are normally weaker on spatial skills, need it more. Its virtue as preparation for engineering and inventing of all kinds (landscaping, interior design, small-engine repair, factory design) should be obvious.

ADVANCED MATH

By "advanced math" we here mean trigonometry, analytic geometry, and everything else advanced that's not included in your basic algebra, geometry, and calculus courses. These topics precede calculus and make as much sense as it does, which is precious little for people who have not learned to think abstractly, dealing as they do with imaginary waves, invisible coordinates, the square root of negative 1, and other arcane topics.

NEW**
A Beka Book Publications
Alpha Omega Publications
Bob Jones University Press

Here are our three Christian publishers again. Between them these three heavy hitters account for a large share of the Christian school and home-school textbook and workbook market.

A Beka offers two textbooks in this subject area: *Trigonometry with Tables* and *Analytic Geometry.* I haven't seen either of them, but at least now you know they exist.

Alpha Omega's twelfth-grade course, entitled "Function/Trigonometry," covers (naturally) functions and trigonometry, with one LIFEPAC each devoted to probability and the very first rudiments of calculus. The entire course comes in 10 separate LIFEPAC workbooks, unlike the textbook-based A Beka and BJUP courses.

BJUP twelfth-grade *Advanced Math* textbook reviews algebra, cautiously wades into trigonometry with a lot of repetition, and introduces calculus. You get to graph in both the polar and Cartesian coordinate systems and derive formulas instead of just remembering them. This book provides more of an introduction to calculus than the Alpha Omega course, introducing both differential and integral calculus.

NEW**
Saxon Publishers

Advanced Mathematics, $45.25 postpaid. You get hard-bound teacher text with answers in back and tests.

Advanced Mathematics, previously known as *Geometry-Trigonometry-Algebra III*, is the fourth book of the Saxon algebra sequence. It reviews fundamental algebra and geometry, and trig skills, while introducing and continually practicing new topics. These include logarithms, determinants, arithmetic and geometric series, conic sections, roots of higher-order polynomial equations, and functions, including curve sketching. The book also includes a lavish helping of word problems, as do all Saxon books. The geometry in this volume includes terminology *and* proofs.

The book provides about 125 daily lessons, each followed by a set of 30 problems. The student is expected to work all these problems, plus any practice problems that may be included in the lesson itself. Saxon has thoughtfully provided a booklet of tests and test answers keys, included for home-schooling orders with the teacher's edition.

Like all the Saxon books, *Advanced Mathematics* make difficult concepts as easy as possible by bringing them up again . . . and again . . . and again in the problem sets for all lessons following their introduction. John Saxon calls this the "incremental" approach, and it has been shown to work far better than the traditional tell-em-once-and-move-on method. Enrollment has doubled, tripled, or quadrupled in classes using the advanced Saxon books, as students discover for the first time they really *can* handle—and feel good about—advanced math topics.

With this constant repetition, instead of facing a completely new bunch of problems every time you finish a chapter, you find most of the problems familiar. Those problem types you don't "get" will show up again on the next lesson, and the next, and the next, until they begin to make sense. Kids using Saxon math don't learn a concept just to forget it after the test—they live with it all year, until they *know* it.

NEW**
W. H. Freeman and Company

Mathematics: A Human Endeavor, $31.95, hardbound. Teacher's guide, $12.95. Add $1.95 shipping first copy, $1.25 each additional. Grades 7–12.

Mathematics: A Human Endeavor by Harold Jacobs, subtitled "A Book for Those Who Think They Don't Like the Subject," is not a complete math program that you can label "Geometry," "Trigonometry," or "Calculus." Instead it is a book about math that introduces a variety of advanced mathematics topics in interesting contexts. You learn about inductive reasoning, deductive reasoning, functions and graphs, logarithms, polygons, mathematical curves, permutations, probability, statistics, and more. The math is then applied to problems featuring billiard balls, optical illusions, satellites, and other interesting applications.

Cartoons, mathematical history tidbits, and a friendly writing style make this book inviting to read. Students can choose whatever topics they wish to explore rather than going through chapters in order. Exercises consisting entirely of word problems are included at the end of chapters, with answers to selected problems included at the back of the book.

Mathematics: A Human Endeavor is for the person who wants to understand mathematical thinking and logic in applications, whether or not he wants to devote a few years to the study of higher mathematics. One of the most important features of this book is that you do not need a background in advanced math to understand the concepts.

I personally find this book a wonderful reinforcement to understanding God as a God of order, even though this is not the author's intent, as the book discusses regularity and patterns in math. Some lessons are as simple as examining why bees make their honeycomb cells in hexagonal patterns rather than some other geometric form. Others venture into deeper subjects such as sonic booms, comets, and conic sections.—Cathy Duffy

CALCULUS

NEW★★
Barron's Educational Series, Inc.
Calculus the Easy Way by Douglas Downing, $9.95. Add 10% shipping ($1.75 minimum).

The storm struck my ship with devastating suddenness. Something hit me on the head, and my memory was completely knocked out. The next thing I remember was being washed ashore on a strange land called Camorra. The farmer who first met me . . . decided to take me to the capital city. There it proved to be a time of crisis. Nobody was able to figure out the speed of the new train, which was powered by a friendly giant named Mongol.

So begins the most unusual calculus text I have ever seen. Characters in this fantasy story proceed to solve problems they encounter in the mythical land of Camorra by using calculus. We follow their logic, written as conversations, as they determine the number of roses to get for the elliptical rose garden and the length of banners to be draped from poles for their upcoming celebration.

A substantial amount of the book is dedicated to mathematical explanations. The story serves as glue to hold it all together and keep things moving rather than as a riveting adventure.

Calculus the Easy Way requires a basic knowledge of algebra, geometry, and trigonometry, since it is designed as an introduction to calculus. However, it does not include rigorous proofs and all of the background theory that would normally be included in a calculus text.

Practice exercises, tests, and answers are included in one book.

Students who will be taking more advanced calculus courses will need further study, but others will find this sufficient and will certainly have more fun learning calculus.—Cathy Duffy

NEW★★
Saxon Publishers
Calculus with Trigonometry and Analytic Geometry, $56 for student text and answer key. Solution manual, $18.75. All prices postpaid.

John Saxon makes learning genuine college calculus more painless than anyone else, in my opinion. His calculus text is designed to do most of the teaching; the Saxon philosophy is that the teacher should "be a guide at the side, not a sage on the stage." Saxon also believes students learn from practicing, even before they really understand the concepts behind the problems they are solving. This is good plain common sense—we all need experience with something new before we can integrate it into our data banks. Your job as a parent is simply to make sure the student does every step of every problem in every problem set. The problems are "carefully designed to require the use of the concepts we wish to teach." As students keep on working with them over a long period of time, they will eventually figure out the concepts for themselves.

On the day a new topic is introduced, only one or two problems in the problem set are on that topic. The rest review material from previous lessons. However, the new topic will be reviewed and added to from now on for dozens of problems sets.

For example, the first lesson on limits is Lesson 16. You get at least one problem involving limits in every problem set for the next 111 lessons. Derivatives appear in Lesson 27, and problems involving derivatives are in each of the next 90 problem sets. These problems are carefully designed to incrementally increase the student's proficiency and understanding, not just haphazardly thrown at the student.

The book has a brief, intensive review of the algebra, trig, and analytic geometry needed in calculus class, and then covers "all the topics normally taught in the first two semesters of a three-semester calculus sequence." In all, you get 117 lessons. This works out to four lessons a week, with Friday for testing and math enrichment.

Saxon's famous sense of humor and wide erudition shines through occasionally on the word problems, but not as frequently as in the other Saxon math books, due to the graphical nature of so many of the problems. It's hard to be humorous when asking students to sketch the graph of $y = x$ divided by $(x - 2) (x + 3)$.

Don't even think of trying to do without the solutions manual, unless you're the sort of person who enjoys solving complex differential equations for fun.

Even though my copy of the solutions manual had several blank pages, it's still a lot better than Mom or Dad having to grind through all those problems by hand in order to check Junior's work. Ideally, Junior can check his own work. Since he is supposed to write out every step of the problem, not just the answers, it's pretty easy to tell if he's really doing the work.

Some people feel that even the Saxon course is too much for many indifferent math students. With this I agree—if a student is indifferent to math, e.g., not willing to work hard, this is certainly not the course for him. Neither are the fields of engineering, business, physics, or science for him, all of which require both math knowledge and diligent work.

However, if the problem is that the student is not firm in his pre-calculus work, the solution might be to send him back through the Saxon algebra sequence, to make sure he "gets it" this time. If you've taken him out of public school, you might even want to start him with the Saxon *Math 65* or *Math 76* courses, to ensure that he has basic arithmetic and math concepts down well.

Don't count on the review in the beginning of this book to make up for serious deficiencies—it's designed to refresh kids on what they already know, not teach them basic algebra. Even kids who were strong in algebra might want to slow down the pace and take several days for each of the beginning lessons.

For that matter, if your student wants to take several days for any of the lessons, why not let him? Calculus is not the sort of subject to hop-skip-and-jump through. If your student has a lot of other advanced subjects, it might make sense to take this course at a slower pace. One of the benefits of home teaching is that you can do that sort of thing!

SCIENCE & ENGINEERING

CHAPTER FOURTEEN

CREATION SCIENCE

This is a good place to start. Who made you? Did anyone make you? Are humans really related to the birds and the bees? If so, then a case can be made for pantheism. "Each bug's death diminishes me, for I am involved in bugkind." If as the Bible says God created man, and woman from man, as a direct creative act, making us "a little lower than the angels," we actually have the right to own property and control the plants and animals on it. This becomes important, as you'll see in the next chapter . . .

NEW★★
Center for Scientific Creation
In the Beginning, $9. Add 90¢ shipping. Grades 7 and up.

In the Beginning is a great creation science book for teens and adults. It's easy to read, carefully researched, meticulously documented, and offers answers to the most important questions of the origins controversy.

Besides the usual creation-science approach to questions about the historicity of Genesis and what happened to make the dinosaurs extinct, the book is unique in explaining for the first time how 17 major earth features—including mountains, volcanoes, the Grand Canyon, and "ice ages"—resulted from a worldwide flood. At the same time, it reveals serious yet little-known problems with many evolutionist ideas about earth history and the origin of life—including many ideas that evolutionists themselves have discarded, but are still taught as fact in children's textbooks.

In the Beginning's author, Dr. Walter Brown, has had rather an interesting history of his own. Dr. Brown, who retired from the Air Force in 1980 as a full colonel, received his B.S. from West Point, M.S. from New Mexico State University, and Ph.D. from M.I.T. During his 21 years of military service he served, among other positions, as Chief of Science and Technology at the Air War College, associate professor at the U.S. Air Force Academy, and Director of Benet Research, Engineering, and Development Laboratories in Albany, New York. He is not, in other words, your basic half-baked, undereducated nut. His "hydroplates" theory, whereby he attempts to explain continental drift and a host of other worldwide phenomena more convincingly than the plate-tectonics people do, is absolutely fascinating. Not that you have to be a degreed scientist to follow his thinking—it's laid out in outline form, with charts, graphs, maps, and unobtrusive footnotes.

If you've ever suffered through a mainstream geology course, wherein the profs tried to explain how long, slow, uniform processes caused veins of rock to buckle back on themselves, rivers to dig huge canyons, and marine fossils to appear on the top of the Himalayas, you owe it to yourself to get this book. Everything the profs had trouble explaining is explained more neatly, convincingly, and understandably right here in this wonderful book.

NEW★★
Creation Resource Foundation
Unlocking the Mysteries of Creation, $18.95. Shipping extra. Grades 6–adult can read it on their own; read it aloud to younger children.

Incredible new creation science book. The engaging format combines illustrations, cartoons, text, and graphs; illuminating text unlocks the mysteries of the early earth and early civilizations. A wonderful book for preteens and up, or for reading aloud while your children look over your shoulder.

Unlocking the Mysteries of Creation grew out of author Dennis Petersen's creation science seminars, and thus has both lots of visual impact and an interactive, talk-to-the-reader style. Mr. Petersen evidently likes to keep his audience on the edge of its seat. Let's take a look at the "mysteries" he unlocks.

Section One, "Unlocking the Mysteries of the Early Earth," starts with an explanation of why it matters whether you believe in creation or evolution. It then proceeds to explain what really happened "in the beginning" according to the Bible . . . why the early earth's climate could have been radically different . . . why volcanoes *weren't* present at the beginning . . . and why radiometric dating methods aren't reliable (nor do they verify the approved geologic chart). "What Do Processes in Nature Tell Us About Earth's Age?" is an excellent section, showing the evidence from "geological clocks" such as interplanetary dust buildup, juvenile water, comets, oil deposit pressure, erosion, topsoil, coral reefs, the wearing away of the edge of Niagara Falls, stalactite growth in caves, igneous crust buildup, population studies, the magnetic field, dissolved minerals in the ocean, atmospheric helium, and so on. The section closes by giving evidence against the "Gap Theory" of creation.

Section Two, "Unlocking the Mysteries of Evolution," challenges the Big Bang theory, the idea that nonliving matter produced life, the use of time as the magic factor to make evolution plausible, the idea that random chance can produce increasing complexity, and the idea that simple forms develop into complex forms. In this section, the author examines some famous "fossil links" such as the horse series, and the way geologists date rocks by the fossils while evolutionary biologists date fossils by the rocks. The section concludes with a look at three creatures—the bombardier beetle, the woodpecker, and the giraffe—each of which could not possibly have evolved, since they needed *all* their complex body systems at once in order to survive.

Section Three, "Unlocking the Mysteries of Original Man and the Missing Links," examines the famous "missing links" you learned about in school, and what's happened to this chart since. Why have some ancient human skeletons been ignored? What happened to the dinosaurs? Could man and dinosaurs have lived together? Were there really such things as dragons?

Section Four, "Unlocking the Mysteries of Ancient Civilizations," is my favorite part of the book. The "mystery" seems to keep cropping up: "Why were ancient peoples *so advanced*—when in theory they should be just one step up from cave dwellers?" This section includes amazing information on the technological achievements of ancient man, from the electric battery used by the Mesopotamians to 4,500-year-old examples of electroplating. How did ancient peoples like that race of giants in the Andes Mountains of Bolivia move 100-ton stones across rough terrain from a quarry 60 miles away? That, in turn, pales next to the building stones used in the temple at Baalbek, Lebanon, one of which weighs over 2,000 tons. Even with power equipment, modern engineers can't move anything that big! The list goes on and on, from the achievements of the Maya to those of China, Babylon, Egypt, Greece, and so on. Could it be that, instead of our modern doctrine of "continual progress," our ancestors actually knew more than we did about a lot of things? This section includes a time line showing how long the Bible patriarchs lived, making it clear at a glance that the wisdom of previous generations was around for a *long* time!

None of the stuff in this book is weird *Chariots of the Gods* phoney baloney. Every fact is cited and sourced, often from sources as mainstream as *Reader's Digest* and *National Geographic*.

Unlocking the Mysteries of Creation will profoundly challenge your thinking, even if you already believe in creation science. If you *don't* already believe in creation science, it'll blow you away!

Institute for Creation Research
Scientific Creationism, 2nd edition, $8.95. *Gish/Doolittle Debate,* VHS video, $19.95. Add $4 shipping.

Major source of creation-science materials, all produced by scientists and writers associated with ICR. Large catalog, attractive and professional materials. ICR now has a strong line of creation science books for children.

Adults and older teens might want to start off with the excellent *Scientific Creationism* (available both in public school and uncensored editions) and some of the juicy creationist v. evolutionist debates featuring the hard-hitting Dr. Duane Gish. You'd better send for the catalog, which also includes several audiocassette series, filmstrips, tracts, and slides, plus a large number of other good books, if you're trying to build a strong home science library. Or subscribe to ICR's free periodical *Acts and Facts.* Find out what the ACLU is afraid to let into your public school classrooms!

NEW**
Institute for Creation Research
Back to Genesis video series, $14.95 each video or $150 for all 11. Understanding Genesis video series, $19.95 each video or $200 for all 10; study guide, $2.95. Add 20% shipping.

Back to Genesis is a series of video seminar tapes. Most are for teens and adults. The exception: *What Really Happened to the Dinosaurs?,* led by Ken Ham, is his presentation in front of a large group of elementary age children. (See it written up in Volume 2.)

Other videos in this series include:

• *Ape-Men: Monkey Business Falsely Called Science,* debunking the ape-to-man sequence still taught in textbooks (by Michael Girouard)

• *Ayres Rock and Other Exciting Evidences for the Flood in Australia* (by Andrew Snelling)

• *Creation Evangelism* (Ken Ham)

• *The Dinosaur Mystery Solved* (John D. Morris)

• *Fascinating Design: Evidence for Creation* (Michael Girouard)

• *Genesis and the Decay of the Nation—The Relevance of Creation* (Ken Ham)

• *Genesis 1–11: An Overview—The Most-Asked Questions on Genesis Answered* (Ken Ham)

• *Is Life Just Chemistry?* (Michael Girouard)

• *The Long War Against God* (Henry M. Morris)

• *Why Death and Suffering?—and Six Other Questions Christians Must Answer* (Michael Girouard)

A good buy for your church or home school support group.

Another video seminar series, Understanding Genesis, is a set of 10 talks delivered by Ken Ham and Gary Parker. Topics:

• *Creation: Facts and Bias* (Ken Ham)

• *Why Does Genesis Matter?,* a look at how all biblical doctrines trace their lineage back to Genesis (Ken Ham)

• *Evidence for Creation* (Gary Parker)

• *What's Wrong with Evolution?* (Gary Parker)

• *Fossils: What Do They Mean?,* a look at the evidence for extinction, not evolution (Gary Parker)

• *The True History of the World: Part One,* comparing Genesis to what we know from history and archaeology (Ken Ham)

- *The True History of the World: Part Two*, comparing II Peter 3 to the present day (Ken Ham)

- *Ape-Man: Fact or Fiction?*, a history of "missing links" from the original frauds and hoaxes to recent discoveries in Africa (Gary Parker)

- *From Evolution to Creation*, a personal testimony (Gary Parker)

- *Creation Evangelism for a Pagan World*, demonstrating the links between creation and the

Gospel and between evolution and mysticism (Ken Ham)

Master Books

A division of Creation Life Publishers, the world's largest producer of creation knowledge products. The Master Books catalog contains every book in the ICR catalog, plus some more. Also, the CLP-Video listing contains a wide range of creationist films, videos, and filmstrips.

CHAPTER FIFTEEN

ECOLOGY

Do you and I like litter?
No, of course not!
Do we like smog?
No way!

Do we like smelly factories and polluted water?
You've got to be kidding!

Well, then, we must all be True Green, right?

Well . . . depends what you mean by "green." Is environmental consciousness a matter of personal responsibility, or just another excuse for government bureaucrats to jerk us all around? Is ecology an exact science that can pinpoint precise solutions to actual problems, or a limited statistical model that only works in limited areas? Should ecology become the New American Religion, or is it getting out of hand?

Before you answer these questions, let me tell you a story—the story of Hungarian immigrant John Pozsgai (pronounced *poz-guy*). After working seven days a week for 20 years, Mr. Pozgai managed to find a place to live—right across the street from a 14-acre dump. On the other sides, the Pozsgais' house looked out on two major roads, a tire dealership, and an automobile salvage yard. In his garage he fixed trucks.

Many of us would see this depressing neighborhood as a place to escape. John Pozsgai saw his location as an opportunity. So in 1987 he mortgaged his small house and bought the dump. He wanted to build a garage on that land and expand his business.

First, he had some obstacles to overcome. Seven thousand of them, to be exact. That's how many used tires were cluttering his new property. There was other junk too: rusted auto parts, litter, and scrap. He also noted the existence of a miniscule trickle of a stream, dry most of the year, which flooded part of the dump because the old tired clogged it up. (Once the tires were removed, of course there was no flooding action and therefore no wet land on his property.)

Taking the advice of county officials, Pozsgai installed a protective silt skirt fence around the stream. He also hauled all the old tires and other junk away and placed clean fill and topsoil on five of his 14 acres.

BRING ON THE EPA

And that was his crime. The enlightened folk at the Environmental Protection Agency and Army Corps of Engineers took an interest in the property once it came into Mr. Pozsgai's possession. (I have been unable to find, in the articles I have read about the Pozsgai case, any hint of EPA interest while the site was merely used to warehouse thousands of smelly old tires and heaps of junk.) Though the dump isn't even listed on the Department of Interior's National Wetland Inventory Map, they claimed his new property, smack dab in the middle of an industrial section miles away from any open body of water, was "wetlands" and that John Pozsgai therefore needed a federal permit before he could put fill on his own land.

Annoyed by Pozsgai's attempts to fix up his own property, and probably more by his insistence that spying bureaucrats get the blankety-blank off it, the EPA put him under surveillance. Spending who knows how much of the taxpayers' money, they captured him on film in the act of putting topsoil on his own property. The evidence in hand, in September 1988 John Pozsgai was arrested for "discharging pollutants into waters of the United States."

What makes this case really strange is that the "pollutants" Pozsgai was charged with "discharging" were topsoil, sand, earth, and clean fill . . . and the "waters" into which he was accused of discharging them were *not* the stream on his property (into which he had never dumped *anything*) but the dump site itself, which because of the intermittent flooding due to the old tires was now classified by the EPA as "wetlands." In other words, Pozsgai was arrested for putting topsoil on his own land.

CLEAN A DUMP, GO TO JAIL

All right, now. Tell me, if you can, what the penalty should be for a man cleaning up a dump? Here's what John Pozsgai got:

- Three years in jail (Mr. Pozsgai, by the way, up until this time had no criminal record, and the probation report noted that this sentence would probably be the death of Mrs. Pozsgai, who has a heart condition and depends on her husband as her sole financial support).

- A fine of $202,000.

- Five years of probation after he serves his three years in jail.

- During probation, he must restore the property *not* to its original condition, but to that of a virgin wetland conforming to plans designed by the Corps of Engineers. In other words, Mr. Pozsgai can't just dump the old tires and crud back on his place, say, "OK, now it's the way I found it, are you happy?" but must labor without pay (this is technically known as "slavery") to reconstruct his own property according to the environmental visions of Corps bureaucrats.

Responding to the question, "Why such a stiff sentence for such a trivial action?" the Justice Department's appeals brief notes that the typical arsonist (who typically receives a much lighter sentence) aims his crime "at a limited number of victims," whereas all of us— "the public at large"—are victims of Pozsgai's nefarious tire cleanup and topsoil filling. In the very words of the prosecutor, "a message must be sent to all land owners," meaning you and me if we ever get lucky enough to pay off our mortgages. What is the message they send by destroying John Pozsgai? Presumably that private property no longer exists, stagnant water inside old tires counts as wetlands if the bureaucrats say so, and Hungarian immigrants should move back to Hungary.

NEW DOCTRINES FOR OLD

I am telling you all this, not only because I am ripping mad about the dirty deal they handed to John Pozsgai, but because the presuppositions informing the government handling of this case are even now found in virtually all public school and Christian school science textbooks and workbooks; all science magazines; on the evening news; in the newspaper editorials and letters to the editor; in business advertising (each business vying to be "greener than thou"); on billboards; just about everywhere, in short. Ecology, which started as a scientific attempt to determine the effects of living beings on each other, has become a religion. Here are its doctrines:

(1) Everything on earth is interdependent on everything else. My sneeze in Missouri affects the monkeys in the rain forests. The number of trees in Brazil affects the climate of Siberia. The topsoil on John Pozsgai's property affects "the public at large." (This, by the way, is simply a political statement of pantheistic religion.) Therefore, since my private decisions affect everyone else, I have no right to make my own decisions. *This assumption spells the end of all private property and freedom of action and makes pantheism the de facto state religion.*

(2) The Good Old Days doctrine: John Pozsgai should restore his dump site, not to a dump site, but to a pristine condition it presumably had before the first footfall of the white man (or the red man, for that matter). The best way for things to be is the way they were before people came along.

(3) The Born Free doctrine, otherwise known as Property Rights for Animals: All animals should be allowed to roam free (in their "natural habitat") and all weeds should be allowed to grow where they choose. People, except for those approved by ecologists, should stay away from those habitats. (Part of the Pozsgai prosecution's case for the dump as a "wetland" rested on the presence of "rare vegetation" like skunk cabbage on his property.)

(4) The Preyer Ban: Man is the only predator who should not be allowed to prey (e.g., "animal rights," paint-spraying attacks on ladies with fur coats, etc.) and the only builder who should not be allowed to build (beavers can dam streams without EPA permits but people can't). The whole point of the "wetlands" exercise is to provide free habitat for critters at the expense of the people who own the land—like John Pozsgai.

(5) Who's Afraid of the Big Bad Wolf: Predatory animals should not be controlled. Wolves are "misunderstood." When grizzly bears or coyotes attack farm animals, that's still no excuse for the farmers attacking back. Man-eating tigers "are just weak and old tigers who can't find regular prey." (Note: India protects such tigers even when they have already eaten 30 or so babies and old people, as happened about a year ago in one of its provinces. The villagers were not allowed to kill the tiger—it had to die from old age or indigestion.)

(6) The Hansel and Gretel doctrine: there's not enough food (and other resources) for all of us. Contrariwise, there are too many of us altogether. Thus, we should be sterilized and voluntarily choose to live as if we were poor. Trying to improve your lot in life and get ahead is a no-no.

(7) The Status Quo doctrine: no sub-sub-sub species must ever be allowed to go out of existence. Corollary: the only reason permutations and combinations of bugs and animals disappear is because of people. Rare butterflies, for example, disappear solely because of human collectors, not because birds abound

who like to eat butterflies or because some strains of butterfly just lack the genetic oomph to keep breeding forever. Although it truly was far-fetched of the prosecution to use skunk cabbage as an example of a plant "endangered" by Pozsgai's labors, the fact that it was invoked at all shows how important this point is in their thinking.

(8) The End is Near Prophecy: the by-products of our civilization are about to wipe out all life on earth, unless we immediately repent and start using string shopping bags. This last point provides the eschatological energy to force us into accepting radical changes in our laws and freedoms.

Most of us have accepted these assumptions. They have been dinned into us by educators and the media for years and years. They are in virtually every science textbook—including those published by Christian firms—every science magazine, and every science book. And they are *wrong.*

The Bible clearly teaches we are not as interdependent as all that. The sins of one nation do *not* affect the climate of the next; John Pozsgai's topsoil does *not* change the life of New Jerseyites in general. Furthermore, the sins that lay a land waste are *not* ecological sins (e.g., overpopulation and strip mining) but Ten Commandments sins like adultery and covetousness. (Hosea 4:1–3 couldn't make it any clearer; look it up for yourself.) Further than that, God is not a God of scarcity, but of abundance. His blessing me does not imply there is less blessing to go around for you (Mal. 3:9–12 and hundreds of other verses). Even further than *that,* man is *supposed* to change the face of the earth, to till it and to build our cities (Gen. 1:28 for starters). Getting rid of old tires and putting topsoil on your own property is *good.*

In God's economy, fertility is a good and sterility is a curse (Deut. 28: 4, 18). Wild animals are supposed to be brought under control (Ex. 23:29). Private property is inviolate (Deut. 5:19, otherwise known as the eighth of the Ten Commandments). If my neighbor messes up my air or water, it's an affront against *me,* not the people in the next town, and I have the right (biblically) to sue him for reparations. "The air," "the earth," and "the water" are not corporate entities of their own, with rights of their own. All rights belong to *people.* E.g., in the Pozsgai case, I didn't notice any of his neighbors suing for damages, because *he hadn't harmed any of them.* Government bureaucrats, however much they might have talked about "the general public" were actually suing for the right of "the environment" as such not to be altered by man.

If and when Christians take the time to look into environmental doctrines, Bible in hand, we'll find that virtually *every* environmental tenet is counter to Scripture. It ultimately leads, and will lead, right back to Earth-worship. Paganism. Brother Baal and Mother Astarte.

SCIENCE OR POLITICS?

Environmentalism draws its political legitimacy from the science of ecology. So, what's ecology good for? Within a limited area, it is possible to study the effects of changes in animal and plant populations, including the effects of man-made changes. Even so, one of the elementary rules of logic holds that it is *very hard* to demonstrate that X causes Y. A decrease in the population of bullfrogs could be caused by excessive hunting of bullfrogs, by an increase in the population of frog-eating birds, by the effects of industrial pollution, or simply by an especially cold spring. More fundamentally, the observer may not have noticed all the bullfrogs, or may have failed to note that they had migrated to a nearby marsh.

Thus ecology, like sociology, is inexact and should not really count as a science. You can "prove" anything you like. Simply assert that X causes acid rain, or Y is about to destroy all the sea plankton. All the million *other* factors which might cause acid rain (or even whether acid rain exists, and if so, if it is a problem) need not be examined; whether or not plankton are disappearing need not be proved. What matters is *belief*, not rigorous scientific proof.

Environmentalism, or ecological politics, is simply a bigger and greener type of communism, all of us one big happy interdependent family of organisms, none greater than the other, the cockroach lying down with the lad, in which an elite casts all the votes for the plants and animals. The doctrine of the interdependence of all things leads the way for global busybodies to meddle in the affairs of other people's countries. The doctrine that The End is Near justifies infringement on our basic rights (did you know all printing presses are now supposed to be registered with the government, according to the Clean Air Act?). All of this is overcast with religious terminology and expectations.

DON'T WASH THE CAR

Home schoolers are about to be deluged by a flood of this material. I know, because the people who produce it send it to me, expecting a good word for their products. Take, for instance, the letter I got yesterday, from the publisher of a book urging greenie principles on Christians:

> We feel - - - is a timely resource book that can be used by today's home schoolers. Please review our book and consider it for your next release. We are new publishers, but our editor has had extensive experience with promotion and we are in the process of sending our flyers to a variety of locations. We have had a local (northwest Ohio) booksigning event, articles in the newspapers, a radio interview in San Diego, and the book is available in Christian bookstores in various areas. . .

This particular book exhorts Christians to have "reverence" for the earth. It urges us not to wash our cars, to use the back sides of our white paper, and to wrap our kids' birthday presents in the Sunday funnies.

Other books I have received range from the unabashedly antichild and evolutionary to the more typical "stewardship" tract asserting that we (not the Brazilians) are responsible for the future of the Brazilian rainforest and we ought to buy our clothes at garage sales. In between are those that preach the necessity of regional land management programs (a euphemism for Washington bureaucrats telling you what you can do with your own property, à la John Pozsgai).

Here's how you can tell if any particular science resource is overly "green." The tipoff is the bad guys always discuss environmental issues in terms of *collective* responsibility and guilt. They say things like, "Man has done this or that," or "We have done this or that," or "People have done this or that." They never blame anything on the *individuals* who actually did it: litterbugs, absentee factory owners, people who refuse to tune up their cars, Soviet bureaucrats who covered up the Chernobyl disaster until it was too late, and so on. They also ignore private property rights, using terms like "our resources" or even "the planet's resources." Another tipoff: they deeply exaggerate the problems and attribute all progress that has been made in cleaning up the air and water *solely* to government intervention. The best tipoff of all: when a book, video, or whatever starts crusading for laws to *force* people to do things with their own bodies (e.g., compulsory sterilization), property, or businesses.

Christians are supposed to revere God (not the earth), and respect our neighbor's private property ("Thou shalt not steal. . . . Thou shalt not covet"). Christians are also supposed to *admire* God's handiwork and *garden* the part of it we own, freely enjoying its good blessings. While we are not supposed to heap up great riches for ourselves, we certainly can wash the car and use birthday wrapping paper without guilt. We've got to turn our thinking around in this area— the Earth Goddess is a harsh mistress.

ECOLOGY, SUCH AS IT IS

Ampersand Press
Predator, Krill, Pollination, $7.95 each. *Predator* available in Spanish and French. Games packaged in durable, attractive paperboard boxes. Add $2.75 shipping. Ages 8 and up.

If you want to understand how food webs work (that is, who eats who and how it agrees with them), try playing some of Ampersand Press's inexpensive and classy games. *Predator* is a deck of 40 nice-looking playing cards based on a forest food web. Each card show a plant or animal, tells who eats it and what it eats, and assigns it Energy Points. *Krill* is similar, but it uses an Antarctic Ocean food chain card deck. Both decks have the usual levels in their food webs: producers, three or four consumer levels, and decomposers. Many games can be played with the cards: classification games, *Concentration, Solitaire, Rummy,* and of course the *Predator* and *Krill* food web games.

Pollination is about the birds and the bees, following a similar format.

These games furnish a great introduction to *real* ecology at a very manageable price.

NEW**
EDC Publishing
Ecology, $7.95. *Protecting Endangered Species, Protecting Trees & Forests, Protecting Rivers & Seas,* $4.50 each. *Protecting Our World,* combined volume, $10.95. Add 15% shipping.

Usborne has done us all a great favor by showing us, in full color and with lovely artwork, just exactly what the greenie movement believes and hopes to accomplish. From pages 4 and 9 of *Ecology:* "The connections between all living things stretch into a vast web . . . All life on earth is interlinked in one vast, continuous web." From page 13: "We are upsetting the fine balance of nature, and the results may turn out to be disastrous." From page 22:

> In the natural world there is a fragile balance in plant and animal populations [so fragile it supposedly has already lasted millions of years!—MP]. There are several ways that their numbers are naturally kept in check . . . However, this is no longer true of the human population, the growth of which is fast destroying nature's balance, with alarming consequences for our planet.

From page 31, under the heading "The living planet"

> Some scientists argue that the whole planet and its atmosphere works like a living organism. The idea of a "living" planet is known as the Gaia hypothesis, after the Greek Goddess [capital G in the original] of the Earth [capital E in the original].

On page 3 in *Protecting Endangered Species:* a "Wanted" poster with a smiling man on it, with an arrow pointing to "Human—the most dangerous species." From page 14:

> On the following pages you can find out about some of the ways humans can protect endangered species. The best way is to set aside areas of land or water where animals and plants can live safely. These are called protected areas. They are places such as bird sanctuaries and national parks.

In other words, property rights for animals. On page 22 of that book—and also on the end pages of every book Usborne is now publishing on these topics —are pitches for conservation groups ranging from the World Wide Fund for Nature to Greenpeace. Children are urged strongly to join these groups.

Every environmental bogeyman is trotted out in these books—from the great menace of acid rain, which a $500 million government study now assures us has always been there and doesn't really hurt anything anyway—to the famous "evolutionary embryology" sequence, now scoffed at by every reputable embryologist, where the human embryo in its development is supposed to "mirror [the changes] that took place over billions of years, in which life evolved from tiny, single-celled organisms into the complex structures of today." (It turns out, though the book doesn't tell you, that the guy who invented this theory faked his data.)

So there you have the ecology movement in a nutshell: insulate your water heater, campaign for massive one-world government, dismantle industry, discourage human fertility, property rights for animals, the pantheistic "one vast continuous web" of nature, and Gaia, the earth goddess. Nowhere in all this is the merest suggestion that private property should be respected or that farming of endangered species is one possible way to save them.

NEW★★
Home Life
The Greenie, Too Many Chickens, $9.95 each postpaid.

The Greenie and *Too Many Chickens* are two cartoon children's books by yours truly that point the reader to a more accurate view of ecology. In *The Greenie*, a lovable activist character discovers that personal responsibility is the most fruitful form of environmentalism. In *Too Many Chickens*, barnyard animals learn that resources aren't as scarce as they think and that a large family has its advantages. Both are illustrated by a well-known professional cartoonist, published by Wolgemuth & Hyatt Publishers, and available through Home Life or at your local Christian bookstore.

ALTERNATIVE ENERGY

NEW★★
EDC Publishing
Energy & Power, $7.95. Shipping extra.

The greenie emphasis is creeping into other new Usborne products as well, such as the new book *Energy & Power*. Buried in this otherwise excellent book we find preachments about the "greenhouse effect" (another non-problem disproved by scientific studies) and our old pal acid rain. This book, thankfully, takes a more balanced view of nuclear energy, urging readers to write for information to groups on both sides and make up their own minds. This is then followed, on page 39, by a list of actions we "must" take:

- "The wealthy countries must reduce their energy use, perhaps by 50 percent by the year 2020 . . ."

- "They must also share their knowledge and technology with the poorer countries . . ."

- "Laws must be passed, and help given, to make sure anti-pollution technology is introduced and used in all countries."

- "There must be more co-operation to tackle world problems such as the greenhouse effect. . . ."

All of this "you must do this" stuff is quite unusual for Usborne books. In the past, Usborne books concentrated on facts, not on preaching, and generally showed both sides of an issue. They also did *not* tell readers to join political factions or lobby for particular laws.

Were it not for the gratuitous greenie preaching, this would be an excellent book. Part of Usborne's Science & Experiments lineup, it includes activities and projects scattered throughout which help you understand the science principles so beautifully illustrated on its full-color pages. All types of energy are covered, from oil and gas to geothermal energy and modern alternative energy sources, such as solar power. It's one thing to hear about coppicing (a special way of managing forest land to grow much new wood very quickly), but another to see it in pictures!

Unfortunately, once again the entire book fails to recognize the value of a free-market system and property rights. Sweeping government enactments (with their incredible potential for abuse and for causing huge nation- or even world-wide problems) are seen as the solution to every energy and environmental problem. Evolutionary emphasis, of course.

NEW★★
Real Goods Trading Corporation
Real Goods Alternative Energy Sourcebook—master catalog, $14. Real Goods catalog update to *Sourcebook*, published 4 times yearly: $30/one year subscription includes *Sourcebook* and 4 catalogs.

The *Real Goods* catalog is an excellent education in the high-tech world of alternative energy, for everyone from Junior to Grandpa. For Junior there's a vast array of solar toys and alternative-power educational kits.

Mom and Dad can learn how to take their household offline from the power company. Learn about instantaneous, tankless water heaters and solar water heaters.

Perhaps understandably, the catalog has a certain bias towards the our-rainforests-are-dying school of thought, and their customer base seems to include lots of the sort of people who end their letters with "Goddess Bless." New Age flavor in other areas, too—the catalog I am looking at bills itself as the "Winter Solstice Catalog." This seems to be more a case of California goofiness bleeding into the catalog than an attempt to convert unwary outsiders; the company is there to sell you solar panels, composting toilets, and other "real goods," regardless of your race, sex, religion, or age.

CHAPTER SIXTEEN

NATURE STUDY

When my parents took my brothers and sisters and me camping in Miles Standish State Park on Cape Cod years ago, they always stressed that we should leave the campground cleaner than we found it. We learned how to build fires carefully, first clearing away anything flammable from the surrounding area. We learned that we shouldn't wash our hair in the lake because the fish didn't like the shampoo. We learned to use an outhouse without complaining, how to pump water by hand, and how to find the wild blueberries in the nearby brush patches.

Enjoying God's creation, and taking the time to keep it neat, became a natural part of my life. As I grew older, I often took the time to pick up trash by the roadside when walking home from school. I mourned over every squashed squirrel I found in the road and would never have dreamed of disturbing a nesting bird.

Judging by the condition of the campgrounds back then, most people who liked to camp lived by those rules. Not too surprising: the Boy Scouts and Girl Scouts had been busy for decades teaching our parents and grandparents how to be responsible with God's creation. But this old-fashioned "campground ethic," in which humans live happily and carefully in the world, has unfortunately been replaced with a "flying carpet" ethic, in which the mere touch of a human foot on the soil is supposed to destroy it.

Simply stated, the issue is this: Should nature be left undisturbed or are we humans allowed to garden in it?

THE PAGAN ANSWER

Viewpoint #1, the Hindu response, leaves no room for people. We might, with great difficulty, tiptoe through life without stepping on the ant, but try as we might we can't pass through this world without leaving any traces. We must harvest the Sacred Vegetables to eat (muttering a charm as we do so). Even if we let our babies die of hunger in the streets while the cows and rats eat up the crops, unless we are willing to commit mass suicide we cannot help changing nature somewhat.

At what point is survival allowed? Ask the Africans of Rwanda and other Third-World nations, whose governments, under pressure from Western environmentalists through the World Bank, have passed more advanced environmental-protection laws than we have here in the U.S.A.

In Rwanda, 15 gorilla groups are allowed to roam over 30,000 protected acres (2,000 acres per gorilla family). Guards with guns make sure the people of Rwanda (529 per square mile, or an average of one-fifth acre per human family) are kept out of the gorillas' private property. White people of the greenie persuasion, however, are *encouraged* to enter the gorillas' habitat, since they bring tourist bucks in and pay a fee to the Rwandan bureaucrats for the privilege of gaping at the gorillas. The environmental-minded white tourists can then get back in their jets and fly home, happily polluting the upper atmosphere all the way.

So now we know. May the Africans take the bracken to make their homes? (No, there are guards with guns to protect the gorillas who roam through that bracken.) May they cut down the bracken and farm the land? (No, it is needed for the gorillas' habitat.) Be glad that African eco-freaks aren't visiting America to help us with *our* problems.

THE BIBLICAL ANSWER

Viewpoint #2, the gardener's viewpoint, says that man *is* the lord of creation, but that he is not autonomous. God is the Lord of man, and He will require an accounting. Man is to take control over the physical world, including the animals, and to make it fruitful (*not* keep it static). God's appointed way of managing this was to give humans private property rights, even knowing (as He of all people certainly does) that some will abuse those rights.

Animals don't have property rights; people do. Contrary to greenie thinking, animals *are* property. (The greenie alternative: give animals an unlimited right to "natural habitat," with certified greenies to control and live in majestic solitude on those huge tracts of land . . . all in the animals' name, of course!)

According to the biblical viewpoint, the solution to the problem of poachers decimating elephant herds for their ivory would be to let the Africans herd the elephants. If you want to protect an animal, you do so by giving it an owner, instead of by fencing people out. (Proof: are dogs, cats, cows, and chickens endangered species?) If we want to see both humans and animals thriving, let our fellow humans own the antelopes and gorillas instead of poaching them. Those whose ownership interests incline them towards nonproductive animals can set up zoos and preserves (purchased with *their own* money). They do *not* have a right to megaacres of land they haven't earned, so they can sit and "enjoy wildlife" while the rest of us struggle our whole lives to pay the mortgage on a small house on a quarteracre lot.

Nobody forces us to grow flowers, yet most of my neighbors have a garden. If nobody forced us to keep out of the wild, many would be inclined to tame the wild and bring it home. As long as it's illegal to own hawks, hawks will be endangered. Make hawking legal, bring it back as a sport, and hawks will be everywhere.

IS BAMBI FOR REAL?

I understand how Christopher Robin felt when he lay on his back on an island, looked up at the sky, and said, "There's nobody else in the world, and the world was made for me." It's fun to think of being barefoot, running through the wild grass with the antelope and zebra, unfettered and free, just like it's fun to imagine yourself as Sleeping Beauty (if female) or the Prince (if male).

Of course, such thoughts are mere fantasy: running barefoot through African grass is a great way to slice up your feet, and real-world animals are not nearly as cuddly as the Disney substitutes.

If we study nature, rather than worship it, we will *know* it, and not be as likely to fantasize about it. We all know the failings of mosquitoes and cockroaches, because we all have run into them; but wild animals have their seamy side as well. Nobody who knows wolverines loves them. A liquid-eyed deer can be vicious during mating season. An ostrich can kill you with a well-placed kick (and they are snooty birds), as can a kangaroo. Camels and llamas will spit in your face if annoyed (and they are easily annoyed). Cuddly little rabbits eat their own dung and sometimes their own babies. Elephants destroy whole square miles of vegetation, trampling it down and ripping trees up to get at their leaves. Alligators will eat your granny, or anyone else left lying around.

This doesn't mean you can't appreciate elephants and alligators. It *does* mean that the myth of the Noble Animal deserves to be buried along with the myth of the Noble Savage. Animals aren't poor, helpless victims ravaged by sinful, awful men—a fair number of them would chew your leg off if they could, or destroy your food supply, or poison you, or infect you with diseases. Animals aren't all equal, either—some are a whole lot more worthwhile to have around than others. We don't need large, untamed predators roaming around our backyards or black widow spiders under our baseboards. We don't need wolves at all (coyotes take over quite nicely wherever the wolves move out).

You can search the Bible from one end to the other, and you'll never find God telling anyone to give wild animals their own land. People just aren't ever going to want some types of land, and wild animals are welcome to it: steep mountainsides, deserts, brackish swamps not near industrial areas, and so on. Some people are going to value their woodland and keep it in shape for animals to live in. I, for example, like foxes, rabbits, and birds, and would go out of my way if I ever owned any land to make it possible for these critters to share it with me. (Even here in suburbia we have had a rabbit living in the grass pile near our compost heap, and just this morning I was watching a swarm of sparrows flitting from lawn to lawn on our street.) If you prefer dogs and cats, which chase foxes and kill rabbits, that's your business—unless they wander onto my land, that is! In grape country, though, God Himself tells us to "catch us the foxes, the little foxes, that spoil the vines."

All of which is to say—let's get real, folks. Animals aren't people, and the people who claim to speak for them aren't white knights. You and I can be trusted to run our lives without ruining the world, and we don't need Big Government protecting us from ourselves. Nobody will protect land and animals more fiercely than their owners; if anything out there is being ruined, it's because it doesn't have a private owner. Bambi is cute, but he doesn't exist, and he certainly doesn't need the tons of gush that have been poured out on his behalf.

If only everyone who is uncritically for environmental causes or animal rights had to work on a small ranch or farm for a year or so, making his income solely from the profit (if any) of the ranch or farm! Come to think of it, that would do *all* of us good. Anyone out there want to start a home-schooling farm-or-ranch apprenticeship program?

In the meantime, here are a few resources to help you find out what nature's *really* like (not the Bambi version, but the original, untouched release), and how people can fruitfully work with it and even make it *better.*

NATURE FACTS & STUDIES

NEW✱✱
Blue Heron Press
Each book, $6.95, paperback. Add $1.50 shipping for first book, 50¢ each additional. Ages teen to adult.

Nobody knows as much about nature as someone who has lived and worked in the middle of it. Walt Morey is such a man. Best known as the author of *Gentle Ben,* this 84-year-old's career has included working as a deep sea diver, sawmill worker, orchardist, boxer, and ship building foreman, mostly in the American Northwest. The man knows about sled dogs, select-cut logging, sharks, whales, seals, diving, riding the rails, farming, ranching, horses, cows, cougars, chickens, rivers, salmon, and of course bears, from *experience.* This explains why his adventure books are so full of realism and open skies.

Here's what you get in the Walt Morey Adventure Library. Books about teen boys turning into responsible men. Without sexual adventures. Without agonies about drugs and peer pressure. Without whining.

Without unrealistic teen-worshiping fantasies where the kid knocks out the champ or wins the Big Race.

Some of the main characters have good families. Some are orphans. One has no mom and a drunkard for a dad. One is running away from foster care. Some of them face serious injustices. But these are *not* "problem" books of the type so loved by modern critics, in which the kids are poor helpless victims.

They are *not* "revenge" books, either. Rather, they are completely realistic stories featuring boys, animals, and the great outdoors, in which the boys overcome adversity, reach manhood, and gain respect through perseverance, hard work, and courage, without developing bitter spirits because of the hardships they face.

Because these books are so realistic, you get to meet animals as they really are, in their natural habitat, which often means under the care of humans on their farms and ranches. You get to see how people in real life care for their animals and develop relationships with them. Some people are unpleasant to their animals in these stories; others love them. The books note this, while upholding private property rights and the law in general. The bad guys lose out eventually because of their own sinful qualities, not because the hero beats them up or steals the dog they are mistreating.

School is a comparatively small influence in the heroes' lives—not surprising, since Walt Morey didn't learn to read until he was 13, at which point his mother and brother taught him. He never took any professional writing courses, having learned his craft through self-study. In one book (*Home is the North*) the hero is home-schooled, and in two others (*Scrub Dog of Alaska* and *Angry Waters*) his guardians decide it's not worthwhile enrolling him in mid-term in a new school.

This lack of emphasis on school, dating, and peer-group folderol is refreshing. The kids in these books want to *grow up*, not cocoon in an artificial teen culture.

Titles in this series:

- *Gloomy Gus* —a boy and his bear—also his worthless drunk father and an old prospector who befriends the boy. Life in the Alaskan outdoors and in the circus.

- *Home is the North*—15-year-old Brad Nichols is orphaned, helps fish the salmon run, tracks down a rogue bear, and makes a really tough journey through 60 miles of wilderness.

- *Scrub Dog of Alaska*—half-Indian David Martin saves Scrub, gets orphaned, goes to live with relatives in Anchorage, and sees a lot of dog races and frontier life.

- *Deep Trouble*—my favorite! Joey Bishop's dad dies during a diving accident, and he has to convince the cannery owners he's enough of a man to do his dad's job. Encounters with seals, sharks (one of which he has to remove from a salmon trap), and even whales, plus the book is set during the time Alaska gained its statehood.

- *Angry Waters*—15-year-old Dan Mallory is paroled to a dairy farm, learns to appreciate farming, and shows his true colors when his old thieving buddies break out of prison.

- *Run Far, Run Fast*—on on-the-scene look at hobo life and responsible logging, seen from the point of view of a boy who runs away rather than be sent to a foster home.

- *Runaway Stallion*—small-town Oregon in 1915. Jeff catches a *very* fast horse, faces down the school bully, and watches his family struggle to run the family store in the teeth of opposition from the most powerful man in the valley.

- *Year of the Black Pony*—Chris Fellows' mom, one of the strongest women in all juvenile literature, decides on a marriage of convenience to the man who accidentally killed her husband. Lots of hard ranching work and frontier hazards.

You can't go wrong with any of these books. I will be selling them in my own home business catalog, and I hope a lot of other home-school suppliers follow suit.

NEW**
Children's Small Press Collection
Wintersigns in the Snow, Pond Life, Spring Signs, $5.95 each. Shipping extra. Grades 2 and up.

Years ago we met a man from Wisconsin and got to talking about his home state. When asked why he now was living in Missouri, he complained that Wisconsin was "too cold, too windy, and winter lasts forever."

Well, count your blessings, you Northerners! Kids who live where it hardly ever snows can't use this book, *Wintersigns in the Snow,* to learn to track deer, rabbits, mice, mink, birds, and all sorts of critters.

Wintersigns tells you not only how to recognize animal tracks, but also how to recognize other signs of an animal's presence, such as nesting holes, broken bushes (from deer spurring with their antlers), droppings (how to tell which animal left it), and lots more. The book also is a condensed guide to Northern tree identification in winter and details some winter wonders to watch for in the woods. You even get a special laminated card with the most common animal tracks described. Nothing else like it, especially at the price!

Pond Life, by the same author, helps you identify a wide variety of pond plants and animals, with a special section on easy-to-make gathering equipment. Also by the same author, *Spring Signs* helps you recognize the first, hidden signs of spring about you—the drumming of the ruffled grouse, stirrings of birds, mammals, and reptiles, the first woodland wildflowers to look for, and so on.

NEW★★
EDC Publishing
The Young Naturalist, $6.95 paperback. Ages 10 and up.

If any one book can introduce the entire field of nature studies to kids aged 10 and up, *The Young Naturalist* is the one. With the usual lively Usborne mix of text and illustration, facts and experiments, it covers

- Observing and recording—keeping a bird notebook, making a tree chart, and mapping mole hills, among other activities.

- Collecting natural objects and displaying them.

- Collecting and observing bugs.

- Breeding and observing the life cycles of tiny critters such as butterflies.

Projects include making nesting boxes and bird blinds, building an aquarium and formicarium (ant house), resurrecting an urban plot, pressing leaves, collecting and displaying spider webs, making plaster casts of animal tracks, and lots more.

The Young Naturalist is particularly strong on teaching nature observation skills. Simply reading through the book (not an easy task, with the wealth of information and illustration continually tempting you to browse!) will give you new eyes with which to view the natural world around you.

Don't underestimate this book. All the projects and activities, though worthwhile, require a fair degree of commitment. Country dwellers will also find it easier to do the activities, although the book includes indoor and urban activities as well.

NEW★★
Fearon Teacher Aids
Nature Crafts Workshop, $8.95. Add $3.50 shipping. Grades 3–8.

Nature Crafts Workshop is a collection of more than 40 high-interest study and handicraft projects, all involving the student with living things. Projects span the whole field of nature: bugs, birds, animals, plants of various kinds, trees, reptiles, fish, amphibians, microscopic creatures, and animals. A number of the projects involve observing life processes (seeds and plants, caterpillars and moths, eggs and chicks). Some projects bring nature into your home (e.g., the aquarium and vivarium). Others get kids out in the field observing and collecting data (paw prints, field observations of birds, collecting and observing pond water). In the words of the introduction, "Each project is self-contained and fun, and each one yields a tangible item that kids can hang on the wall, give as a gift, or examine and study."

Teens can follow the illustrated project directions by themselves. Younger children will require more adult supervision.

Every project in the book is a classic. Your grandfather and grandmother probably did most of these things when they were young, from making applehead dolls and pressing wildflowers to making a nesting box and hatching chicks. Great stuff for rainy days and just plain celebrating life.

NEW★★
Reiman Publications
Country, Country Extra, Farm & Ranch Living: Sample issue of any magazine, $2.98. One year (6 issues) of any magazine, $16.98. Ages teen to adult, but even our little nonreaders love the pictures!

I might be prejudiced, but I kinda figure folks who *live* in the country understand it a tad better than city-dwelling greenies who only venture out on back-packing trips. For a *real* taste of the country, you won't find anything better than *Country* magazine. Each issue is a work of art, with gorgeous pictures on glossy paper. Great features include:

- "God's Country"—a family shares the view and culture around their place, and why they think it's the best place to live in the U.S.A.

- A "Daily Diary" section, in which a variety of farm folks from around the country share what they were doing on a particular day.

- Longer photo diaries, in which country families share their life for a month (accompanied with lots of lovely photos!).

- An encouragement section, in which readers send in photos and facts about the folks they think are the "greatest country father-in-law" or "greatest country teen."

- "The Way it Was"—photos of country life from the old days.

I love the "marginal notes," short wise or humor-ous sayings lining the margins of many pages. There's also crafts, recipes, a helping-hands forum where peo-ple can write in with information requests, a Country

Inns & Farm Vacations section that introduces a num-ber of hospitable country bed-and-breakfasts and inns in each issue, and lots more!

If this all sounds kind of cornball to you, you've been breathing smog for too long. These magazines are folksy, but brother, they are *slick*. You could frame any of the photos, and the amount of real-life information in each issue is astonishing.

Country is the most relaxing magazine I know . . . except maybe for *Country Extra* and *Farm & Ranch Living*. *Country Extra* is for people who want *Country* more than six times a year. It comes out in the in-between months, and has some special features of its own (many of which eventually cross over into *Country*). *Farm & Ranch Living*, as the name implies, is about farm and ranch living. It's not a professional journal about the best breed of hogs or how to maximize profits, but another gorgeous photo-'n-life-stories magazine like *Country*. If you subscribe to it, you'll end up tour-ing over 70 farms and ranches a year without leaving your living room. As the blurb says, "Read the others for profit, read ours for pure pleasure."

I might add to this, "Read these magazines to find out what it's *really like* out there, according to the people who take care of the land and animals." This ain't agribiz; it's agrilife.

SPACE & SKY

Ampersand Press
Good Heavens! $7.95 plus $2.75 shipping. Ages 10 and up.

Just what the world has been waiting for—an astronomy trivia game. Lots you never knew about comets, meteors, and other relatively small denizens of the sky. The 54 playing cards each include a question, answer, and informative paragraph as well as (aren't they tricky!) a list of *possible* answers to questions on other cards. You can guess and bluff, but you do better if you really know something. *Good Heavens* also includes a 24-page booklet with tips on celestial observation that introduces you to "the solar system's minor mem-bers." Evolutionary viewpoint.

NEW★★
Charlie Duke Enterprises
Moonwalk videos, $19.95 each. VHS only. Add $3.50 shipping.

Now the Apollo flight is on video, starring Charlie Duke, one of the crew on that historic space mission. So what, you say? Well, aside from the fact that 1990 was the twentieth anniversary of the moon flight, what we have here is an educational space video. Charlie shows how an astronaut gets into his space suit, how he eats (with footage from the flight of astronauts chasing grapes around the capsule), and even explains what every kid wants to know, how they went to the bathroom when there were no bathrooms on the moon. He also shares a lot of behind-the-scenes details of things that went wrong and that *almost* went wrong. Plus you get some fantastic views of the flight itself and the moonwalk.

Since going to the moon, Charlie has become a Christian. That's why Charlie Duke Enterprises has *two* videos available. *Walk on the Moon, Walk with the Son* includes his Christian testimony. *Charlie Duke, Moonwalker* lacks the testimony but in consequence spends more time covering an astronaut's work. We enjoyed them both.

The whole story is also available in book form. Entitled (what else?) *Moonwalker*, it is published by Thomas Nelson Publishers.

NEW★★
EDC Publishing
Young Scientist series: *Jets, Spaceflight, Stars & Planets,* $6.95 each paperbound or $13.96 each library-bound. Shipping extra. Ages 9–13.

The Young Scientist series introduces preteens to a wide variety of science topics. This was one of the first Usborne series, so some of the books feature older artwork and layouts (although the information is up-to-date in all of them). Practical projects and experiments are included wherever possible, along with the cut-away illustrations and fascinating facts.

Jets has an equipment checklist in the front, as does *Stars & Planets,* making it easy to gather materials for the experiments in these books. An older book, *Jets* includes photos as well as drawings. The history of jet flight and the history of basic jet design are covered in a very readable way, making an excellent introduction to the *Spaceflight* volume, which takes us into the age of NASA.

Into the Wind
Kites and accessories for all ages. Kits recommended for children are marked in the catalog with a teddy-bear symbol; ages 8 and up. Octopus kites are good for younger children.

Personally, I'd rather play with the sky than study it. And now that we (oh, thank you Lord) have a backyard bigger than 20 square feet, any gust of air is excuse enough to whip out the Star Octopus or Rainbow Delta kite. These are two economy-but-still-fun kites we bought from Into the Wind (a ready-to-fly Star Octopus with 500 feet of line and a reel is less than $10). Into the Wind sells anything any kite flyer could reasonably want, including glow-in-the-dark gizmos so you can fly a kite at night and power stunt kites that take a real man (or Rosie the Riveter) to haul in. A great hobby—lots of fresh air, no stress, and, just like butterflies, the wind is free.

NEW★★
Rod & Staff Publishers
Discovering God's Stars, $2.95. *Star Guide,* $1.85. Blank star maps, pack of 25, $2.55. Star packet (includes all above), $6.50.

Reader Mrs. Paul Steigerwald of La Pryor, Texas urged me to include Rod and Staff's star materials. *Discovering God's Stars* is a star locator booklet with a devotional air. The *Star Guide* is printed on heavy tyvek (a lightweight, untearable paper used sometimes in catalog envelopes). I don't really know what the Star Maps are. However, the whole packet is quite inexpensive, and coming from Rod and Staff is certain to be reverent and accurate.

NEW★★
Safari, Ltd.
U.S. Space Exploration Quiz, $9.50.

Look! Down on the earth! It's an acrylic box! It's 40 cards in that box! It's 10 questions about space exploration on each card! It's . . . U. S. Space Exploration Quiz!

I bet you don't know the answers to more than 20 of the questions on these cards. That's OK. You'll learn. How? By turning the cards over and reading the answers on the back. You won't want to mess around with trying to look *this* stuff up in encyclopedias and reference books—it's too hard to find! You also may not find it worth the effort memorizing arcane facts like the number of pounds of moon rock that Apollo 11 brought back to earth, or the function of the subsatellite Apollo 15 and 16 put into orbit around the moon. A great Christmas present for the nerd who has everything.

Sky & Telescope
$24/year (domestic), $2.95 single copy.

Latch on to an issue of this magazine and you'll have *no* trouble locating astronomy books and supplies. The ads are often worth more than the articles in a publication of this sort, leading you on to dazzling vistas and brilliant ideas that you would never have discovered on your own. The magazine itself is not glitzy; very technical articles, mixture of black-and-white and color photos. Amateur astronomers do occasionally make serious discoveries, it turns out, and *S & T* is certainly the magazine for the serious amateur.

NEW★★
Super Science, Ltd.
Astropilot, $34.95. 15% discount for teachers and home schoolers. Ages 8–adult.

You've seen star domes before. This isn't one of those. The Astropilot is a patented new system for finding all 88 constellations and more than 860 stars. It shows what is visible from any location on Earth, any day or time. When you get the acrylic dome oriented correctly and turn on the light in the base, you can use it much more easily than a star map. (The Astropilot is prettier, too.)

It takes a while to wade through the setup instructions and all the enclosed "stellar material" (e.g., brochures from *Sky & Telescope*, the Planetary Society, and the Astronomical Workshop), but once you do you have a much better chance of understanding what you're seeing in the night sky.

The Astropilot is endorsed by the Planetary Society. Carl "Cosmos" Sagan helped found this group, which explains its deep interest in extraterrestrial life. Why bother—it's a big enough job searching for signs of intelligence here on earth!

NEW★★
Worldwide Slides
New Space slides, $9/set. Pana-Vue Space slides, $2.50/set. Space videos (VHS only), $29.95 each. Add 10% shipping.

Comedians like to joke about people who go on trips and trap their neighbors into watching all the slides they took. I never thought those jokes were all that funny—I *love* to see other people's slides!

Here's a series of slides your neighbor didn't take on his last trip. The newer sets have 18–20 slides per set and include sets on the Apollo missions, Voyager I and II, Skylab, Space Shuttle missions (including the Challenger disaster), and so on. The original Pana-Vue Man in Space slides are five slides per set and include titles like "John Glenn's Historic 1961 Flight," "Space Walk," and "Moon Landing." Two videos are also available: *The Amazing Space Shuttle* (one hour, with highlights from all flights and lots of space views) and *America's Man in Space,* a 50-minute reprise of 25 years of space travel.

The Worldwide Slides catalog lists exactly what each individual slide is about. An easy way to pep up your space studies unit!

NATURE SUPPLIES

Carolina Biological Supply Company
Huge color catalog, $16.95 postpaid. Supplies for K—college.

From Carolina's Biology/Science Teaching Materials Catalog you can get rabbits, frogs, protozoa, and all sorts of other creepies and crawlies. Plus, of course, food, bedding, and habitats for same. Anyone for leeches? No? Tarantulas (not sexed)? Fiddler crabs? Venus Flytraps? How about unusual corn ears, for studying genetics?

Also of interest are Carolina's wide selection of biology and general science books, records, filmstrips, videos, software, and games. These are geared to public schools and reflect those values.

Educational Insights
Discovering Sea Life, Fossils, Rocks, $24.95 each, grades 3–8. *Discovering Nature,* $9.95, grades 3–8. BrainBoosters™: *Outer Space Adventures, Amazing Animals,* $5.95 each, grades 4–9; Decoder, $1.95. Critter Condo, ages 4 and up, $17.95. Nature Lab, $49.95. Shipping extra.

Nothing is more frustrating than a natural science unit about the ocean when you live in Missouri. Your science text suggests, "Go to the beach and find a starfish, a sand dollar, and a barnacle." "Right," you think. "I'll just slide down to the ol' Mississippi and pick up some floating pop bottles instead." Now, thanks to Educational Insights, you can bring the great outdoors home without going outdoors.

The Nature Collections are boxed sets of labeled specimens plus illustrated activity cards, a full-color illustration of the specimens, and a comprehensive teacher's guide with reproducible worksheets and answer key.

Discovering Sea Life has 26 authentic sea life specimens (goodies like starfish, barnacles, sand dollars, coral, sea fan, conches, murex shells . . .) plus 16 activity cards.

Discovering Fossils provides 12 authentic specimens (like trilobites, dinosaur bone, and petrified wood) from the supposed Paleozoic, Mesozoic, and Cenozoic eras in a sectioned plastic tray, plus 13 activity cards.

Discovering Rocks lets you practice geological identification with 20 neatly packaged and numbered specimens (including the ever-popular quartz, pyrite—"fool's gold," and obsidian), four streak plates, 22 activity cards, and a rock identification game.

If all you really want is a box of suggested activities, EI's *Discovering Nature* activity box might do the trick. 135 activity cards for projects, observations, exhibits, field trips, and ecology study. No specimens included.

If you *love* to get your hands on specimens, EI's Nature Lab has both activities (over 50 of 'em) and lots of fun specimens. Grow living Sea Monkeys from eggs. Grow plants from seeds. Mess around with fossils. Identify rocks. Fiddle with seashells. Lots more included, plus a lovely full-color 32-page activity book.

In a completely different vein, EI's stunning new BrainBoosters series provides lots of fascinating facts and built-in review with the amazing Decoder. Colorful, spiral-bound 32 page books are jam-packed with information and extension activities, not to mention the 10 topic-related questions on each two-page spread. Kids twiddle each of the 10 dials on the Decoder to a circle, triangle, or square in order to answer the 10 questions on the left-hand page. The right-hand page has clues in case you had trouble answering the questions, and also a panel of seemingly random circles, triangles, and squares. Place your Decoder over the panel and the correct answers appear in the Decoder's little see-through boxes. The series contains 10 books in all, two of which have to do with natural science. Hope they add more.

Finally, for you hardy hunters, EI's Critter Condo is a handy home for whatever animal, insect, or whatever your kids bring home. It can be used as a terrarium when the hunting is bad . . . or as an ant theater, a butterfly hatchery, or even an aquarium.

NEW✱✱
Insect Lore Products
Butterfly Garden®, $19.95. Frog hatchery, $14.95. Grow-a-Frog kit, $14.95. Field collector's kit, $19.95. Add 15% shipping. Hundreds of items available. All ages.

For the kid who likes what bugs him. It's not glamorous, but this thick, black-and-white catalog has tons of nature study books, kits, and accessories. Butterfly Garden for raising Painted Lady butterflies. Frog eggs. Silkworm eggs. Praying Mantis eggs. Ant farms. Caterpillars. Chick incubation supplies. Carnivorous plants. Hummingbird nectar and feeders. Field collector's kit (for butterfly collecting) includes everything you need to catch 'em and mount 'em. Nylon butterfly net available separately. Bird feeders. Rock tumbler. Owl pellet kit. Cheesemaking kit.

We've had lots of fun with their Grow-a-Frog kit. This comes complete with tadpole, a supply of chemicals to add to the tad's water, and a tadpole aquarium. As Tad gets bigger, he metamorphoses into a teeny little frog, who you then move to a new aquarium and feed with frog-food pellets. The frog supplies will have to be purchased separately from the manufacturer, but they are not expensive. A nice, quiet pet.

The Insect Lore catalog also includes lots of kits and books from suppliers reviewed in this volume of *Big Book*. The Educational Insights *Adventures in Science* kits and Discovery collections. Mini Labs kits. Usborne nature and science books. Games from Ampersand Press. Plus videos, puzzles, and coloring books, all with a nature theme.

NEW✱✱
Super Science, Ltd.
Critter Emitter, $12.95. Critter Carnival, $12.95. Critter City, $24.50. GEOscope, $39.95. Home schoolers and teachers, take 15% discount.

The first step in observing bugs is to catch 'em. The new Critter Emitter from Super Science helps you discover the tiny critters hiding in a scoop of backyard soil or wet beach sand. This inexpensive kit includes a collecting funnel with detachable vented cover, two strainers, catch basin, scoop, tweezers, dropper, magnifier, and illustrated instructions that explain how to use the Critter Emitter and help you identify common critters. Don't confuse the Critter Emitter with simple collecting tools like nets and scoops. You're not collecting grasshoppers or other large bugs. With the Critter Emitter, you're straining out *very* small, reclusive insects that you otherwise might never notice. Scientists use a version of this apparatus called the Berlese-Tullgren Funnel. Free Curiosity Club membership included.

Once the critters are caught, they need a new home. Low-budget critters can be housed in the Critter Carnival, an imaginative new bug house with seven amusement rides and built-in magnifiers on the sides so you can see your bugs exercising on the rides. Critter Carnival also comes with collecting tools (net, small scoop, and tweezers), a Critter ID wheel, and Critter ID Key silhouette cards. The information on the wheel and silhouette cards is enough to spark a child's interest in insect studies. A great buy; winner of a 1990 Parent's Choice Gold Award.

Upper-class bugs have room to roam in Critter City. This neon-colored futuristic three-domed environment looks like something out of *The Jetsons*. In

Dome 1 there's a mountain scene with sloping ramp to the top. Dome 2 features an apartment building, complete with mini cars in the parking lot. Dome 3 is the homesite—a swanky setup with house, attached buildings, and even a street light that really works! All three polycarbonate domes feature built-in magnifiers and are connected by enclosed tubes, so critters can travel freely between them. You also get two hand-held magnifiers, food basket, a complete activity guide, an offer for two of the best bugs for watching from Carolina Biological Supply, and the same set of collecting tools as in the Critter Carnival. A really fun setup, if you don't mind your bugs living better than you do!

For your field work, Super Science also has the revolutionary new GEOscope. This is the first microscope ever to work on land _and_ underwater! 30x coated glass system, detachable base, focused internal light source, and complete instructions. The beta version I saw wasn't waterproof, but it was a slick piece of work nonetheless.

CHAPTER SEVENTEEN

BASIC SCIENCE

Junior high or middle school—it doesn't matter what you call it or what the exact grade numbers are. It's the place where kids don't exactly learn real high-school science. These are the years generally spent in reviewing first- to sixth-grade science, and getting ready for the *real* biology, chemistry, and physics taught in high school.

I heartily believe in review courses—in place of, not in addition to, the courses they are reviewing. Elementary science courses are an incomprehensible mishmash of topics presented in no significant order. A good middle-school basic science book can bring some order to this chaos. Better to spend the elementary years on reading real books about science and doing real experiments, following it up with one basic science textbook, than to wade through a typical K–6 textbook sequence.

Since life isn't always straightforward, some publishers produce "life science" and "earth science" texts to fill in these years. These are really basic science review courses, with a few extra nibbles thrown in to justify the time you spend on them.

One thing to keep in mind: As Mark Twain said, "Figures don't lie, but liars figure." Since our society worships science, a science textbook makes a marvelous pulpit for anyone with a doctrine to preach, whether it be evolution or safe-sex. Christian texts, when they do preach, are open about it. Secular texts preach just as much, but pretend they don't.

It takes at least 10–20 years after a scientific hypothesis is disproven for the truth to leak into secular textbooks. Java Man still makes appearances, though the eminent gentleman who "discovered" him later admitted he put Java Man together from separate skeletons found far apart and that Java Man wasn't a missing link at all. Human embryos are shown going through "evolutionary stages," although every professional embryologist knows this is hokum and that the originator of this theory faked his data. Pepper moths are shown "evolving" from white to dark forms, although it has clearly been shown that both kinds were present in the original population, which changed from a preponderance of white moths to a preponderance of dark moths after the Industrial Revolution simply because birds could now find the white ones more easily. The "Big Bang" theory is presented as proven fact, though obviously nobody was there to see it and equally obviously nobody can duplicate it in the laboratory. The uniformitarian theory of geology (everything happening very slowly over eons of time) is taught as fact, in spite of the evidence in our own time, from events like the Mt. St. Helens explosion, that fossilization and stratification can occur quite rapidly. Even evolution through inheritance of acquired characteristics shows up from time to time, although Gregor Mendel disproved that over 100 years ago—and the very same text quite likely tells kids about genes and DNA! Not to mention all the "assured results of modern science" involving medical practice, sexual behavior, animal psychology, and so on, many of which are mere attempts to force reality into a politically correct straitjacket.

No textbook is a substitute for wide reading and experience. Most of us don't have wide experience of science principles, especially the more ersatz and unobservable ones. All the more reason to keep an open mind—the history of science is littered with the bones of dead theories!

BASIC SCIENCE COURSES

NEW★★

A Beka Book Publications

General Science series, $11.95 each grade, paperbound. Teacher's guide (includes curriculum), $20/grade. Student test booklet, $3.20 each grade. Teacher key and test booklet, $5.25 each grade. Student quiz booklet (available August 1991), $3.75 each grade. Teacher key and quiz booklet (available August 1991), $7.40 each grade. Video demonstrations (VHS only): grade 8 semester 1, $35; semester 2, $50; grade 9 semester 1, $75; semester 2, $50. Shipping extra.

A Beka's General Science series covers three grades (grades 7–9), with one textbook for each grade. Instead of separate courses in, say, earth science and life science, you get a "building-block" approach, with similar topics presented each year in a "spiral" fashion. This constant repetition, with a little bit new added every year, is supposed to help students digest and remember more.

All books in this series challenge the evolutionary hypothesis, include lots of colorful art and photos, introduce new scientific terms in bold print, and include student experiments and activities. Each gives significant space to creation science and encourages students to both learn and apply the basic principles of science. The books also have a wealth of "in-text learning aids," A Beka's term for sidebars on important concepts, interesting facts, chapter outlines, worked-out examples, and the like. In addition, the grade 8 and 9 courses have optional video demonstrations of lab experiments

(useful for those who aren't able to do all the fancy lab work at home).

The grade 7 book, *Science: Order and Reality*, touches mostly on field biology (with pictorial sections on wildflowers, trees, birds, fish, insects, and weeds), simple physics (with an emphasis on how everyday appliances work), basic principles of science, and scientific creationism.

Science: Matter and Motion, the grade 8 book, has the broadest coverage, with sections on earth and space science, human and cellular biology, chemistry, and physics, as well as the general series emphasis on basic scientific principles and creation science.

Science of the Physical Creation, the ninth-grade book, repeats the grade 8 topics with the exception of human biology, which is not covered in this grade. The section on earth science is greatly expanded, with topics such as atmosphere, weather, oceanography, earthquakes, volcanoes, rocks, and fossils, as well as an extended discussion of why uniformitarian geology (everything happening very slowly over a long time) is wrong. The physics section shows physics at work in modern electronic devices such as computers and lasers.

For each grade, the teacher's curriculum guide includes the lesson plans and teaching information, but not a copy of the student text.

NEW★★

Alpha Omega Publications

LIFEPACS, $2.75 each or $24.95/set of 10 (one course). Teacher handbooks, $4.95 per course. Answer keys, $2.25 each (two per course). LIFEPAC test key (included with teacher handbook), $2.25/course. Elementary Science Kit, $179.95, includes supplies for middle-grades experiments. Specialty items, individual replacement items also available. Shipping extra.

All three of Alpha Omega's grade 7–9 science programs could be considered basic science. These workbook-based courses come in slim LIFEPACS with the lesson text, exercises, and tests all built in.

Grade 7 starts off defining science as a discipline and a career. The second unit covers measurement and graphing. Next come two units on astronomy, one on the atmosphere (slight collective greenie emphasis), one on weather, one on climate, and two on human anatomy. The review unit tries to lend a "careers" viewpoint to the the areas studied. Altogether a decent little course, mostly straight science, with only a minimum of collective guilt tacked on to one unit.

Grade 8 is more concerned with the interplay between science and technology. After this topic is introduced, we move to two units on basic chemistry (the structure of matter, elements, compounds, mixtures, how matter changes, acids, bases, and salts) and one on health and nutrition. Physics is then introduced by two units on energy (mechanical, thermodynamics, magnetism, electricity, and present and future energy sources) and two on machines (simple machines and Newtonian physics). All of this is fine, aside from the environmentalist doomsaying in the latter parts of unit 1. The final unit introduces biology from an strongly environmentalist point of view, as natural cycles disrupted by boorish humans (all of us) who need strong government regulations to force us into more Spartan lifestyles.

The grade 9 course is actually named "General Science." Rather than reviewing the material in grades 7 and 8, it introduces several new topics. Our Atomic World is the first unit, followed by a unit on volume, mass, and density. Two new topics then come up: physical and historical geology (creationist viewpoint). Body Health I, the fifth unit, is an introduction to microbiology from the viewpoint of human health. Body Health II is more of a standard "health" unit (disease prevention, institutional health agencies, and how your body fights disease). Following are units on astronomy (emphasis on telescopes and space exploration) and oceanography (half and half environmentalism and straight science facts). Science and Tomorrow, the ninth unit, then looks at ethical and technical issues in science, while the review unit gives practical applications of the topics studied, from what a libertarian friend of mine likes to call a "statist quo" point of view.

Alpha Omega takes a dim view of population growth ("a serious threat to our world"—grade 9, LIFEPAC 1, p. 27 and numerous other places), even misquoting Scripture in an attempt to justify this outlook. "Read what Isaiah 5:8 says about overpopulation," the ninth-grade review LIFEPAC demands. That verse, which says, "Woe to those who add house to house and field to field until they dwell alone in the land," is actually directed to those who pursue a policy of *under*population, squeezing out all other people by whatever means so they can live *alone* (not surrounded by others)—the greenie ideal.

The LIFEPACS also preach collective action and collective guilt when it comes to environmental matters, e.g., "Too often man has been guilty of abusing the resources that supply his needs." I couldn't say if these books *never* place responsibility for pollution and greed on specific individuals, but after reading through them I can't recall any instance where environmental issues are discussed in any other terms than "man" doing this and that and "man" (collectively) needing to implement policies to take care of "his" (collective) earth and "our" (collective) resources.

Private-property rights and responsibilities are, frankly, not taught; "we" are supposed to solve these problems as a group, through Spartan lifestyles and government policies.

For that matters, the problems are often overblown; I haven't noticed any cattle in Missouri dropping dead from air pollution, as the grade 9 text implies they might (page 7 of LIFEPAC 9).

At times, when dealing with environmental issues Alpha Omega sounds downright New Age. How about this sentence, the concluding sentence of the text of the last science LIFEPAC in ninth grade: "We are one with the earth. If any part suffers, the injury is ours"?

The straight-science units, on the other hand, are quite well done. Unlike other workbook-style science programs, the Alpha Omega offerings actually do a good job of blending teaching with experimentation and observation.

In my opinion, the best way to make use of Alpha Omega science is to purchase the straight-science LIFEPACS, skipping the units given over to greenie preaching (e.g., units 6, 8, 9, and 10 in grade 9) and the subunits on environmentalism tucked into the straight-science units (e.g., the subunit on "Environmental Problems" in the first unit of grade 9). This makes the courses cheaper, more compact, less distressing to read, and a lot more fun to teach.

NEW**
Bob Jones University Press
Middle-grades science series, $19.95 each student text, $31.50 grade 7 teacher's edition, $33.50 each teacher's edition for grades 8 and 9. Teacher's edition includes student text. Student activities, $7.95/grade for student book, $10.50/grade for teacher's edition. TestBank, $9.95/grade. These are home-school prices. Shipping extra.

Like A Beka, BJUP has a series of three textbooks for middle-school general science. Unlike A Beka, these are separate courses in life science (grade 7), earth science (grade 8), and basic science, e.g., an introduction to physical science (grade 9). All three courses are solidly creationist, richly illustrated, well organized and laid out, and loaded with interesting sidelights and supplemental materials. The teacher's edition for each grade includes both a complete student text with special added teacher's notes in red and a separate teacher's guide that shares the course philosophy, provides a master list of materials needed, gives sources for supplemental audiovisual aids, leads the teacher step by step through each chapter with teaching philosophy and methods, and provides answers to the discussion and short-answer questions in the student text. Each teacher's edition comes with a sturdy three-ring binder with labels to identify the subject taught. The teacher's guides are printed on beige paper, so you can easily differentiate between them and the teacher's text in your binder (they fit together in one binder).

In the grade 7 *Life Science for Christian Schools* course, you begin with a Bible-based philosophy of science. The book then gets into classification, cells, creationism, life processes of organisms, and their reproduction. Genetics and evolution are both discussed, followed by a fairly well-balanced unit on ecology. The only thing wrong with the ecology unit is the usual "Man does this" and "Man must do that" collective emphasis that crops up when discussing it; otherwise, the authors maintain a healthy distance from the eco-hysterics, firmly stating that people have a right to live and work on the earth. Finally the book ends with a section on human anatomy and physiology. The section on transplanted organs in this section unfortunately echoes the secular medical position, which promotes any and all transplants while ignoring the fact that some major organ transplants are taken from persons whose hearts are beating and who are breathing (biblically alive persons, in other words) who have *for the purposes of legally cutting out their essential organs* been labeled "brain dead." This is a major problem, on a par with abortion, that Christian texts have yet to acknowledge or deal with. (It takes up little space in the textbook, but I felt it was important enough to mention.)

The grade 8 *Earth Science for Christian Schools* text is really about both space and earth science. After the introductory chapter on science and origins it explores the solar system and universe in seven chapters, including a chapter on space exploration. Next the weather sciences, geology, and oceanography are introduced, with chapters on the Bible and geology, minerals, rocks, volcanoes and earthquakes, mountains, weathering/mass-wasting/erosion, groundwater, glaciers, and oceanography. The final chapter challenges students to apply their Christian beliefs in the scientific world, giving a list of specific areas in which Christians can contribute positively to scientific investigations (e.g., new investigations in creationism and new methods for obtaining minerals from seawater). The book is 469 pages in all, including indexes and glossary, but they go by quickly because the text is so interesting and well organized.

A new edition is due out in fall 1992, though I can't imagine what BJUP felt needed improvement!

"Matter" is the theme of the entire ninth-grade *Basic Science for Christian Schools* course. Units are: What Matters to the Christian, A Description of Matter, The Structure of Matter, The Chemistry of Matter, the Motion of Matter, The Energy of Matter, The Energy of Waves, and Some Matters of Technology. "Christian Men of Science" sections dotted here and there cover Lord Kelvin, Robert Boyle, Johannes Kepler, Michael Faraday, Samuel F. B. Morse, James Clark Maxwell, and Sir John Ambrose Fleming. "Facets of Basic Science" sidebars introduce interesting topics like space stations and how air vehicles fly. Lots of cartoons, graphics, and photos. Environmental issues are raised throughout the book as examples of scientific areas requiring moral decision-making. To BJUP's credit, though they mistakenly repeat the collective-stewardship terminology that has become popular, they stress the importance of technological answers that meet people's needs. Consider this your basic intro to high school science.

The student activity manuals for each grade include experiments, worksheets, reports, and projects. For example, in the life science course you dissect leaves and earthworms, make an insect collection, make observations using a microscope, and make a notebook featuring different kinds of animals, among many other things. In the earth science activity manual a few of the things you do are: draw an ellipse using string and thumb tacks, make a shadow board and record its readings, calculate the distance to the moon using your own homemade equipment, and write an essay on the uniformitarian theory of geology. The investigations in the basic science course are more difficult to do at home, as many of them involve observing a teacher working with specialized equipment and chemicals. "Observe closely as your teacher demonstrates the electrolysis of water" is not quite the same as performing an experiment yourself.

I would definitely urge you to purchase the teacher's editions for each grade along with a student text for your student. The teaching instructions are absolutely excellent—well worth the price—and you need to have the answers in a separate place from the questions.

NEW**
Milliken Publishing Co.
Each transparency/duplicating book, $12.95. Grades 4–9.

The neatest thing about these science workbooks are the 12 jewel-like full-color transparencies included in each one. They're simple to use, too. A teacher's guide in the front of each workbook includes background information, enrichment activities, and an answer key for the 20 worksheets in that book.

Written by the former president of the National Science Teacher's Association, the series includes _Systems of the Human Body, Nutrition, Weather, Fossils & Prehistoric Life, Geology—Rocks & Minerals, Our Solar System & the Universe, Exploring Space, Studying Plants, Studying Insects, Environment & Pollution._ Usual public-school viewpoint: evolutionary, greenie. Good for the facts, not so much for the theories.

NEW**
University of Nebraska-Lincoln
Tuition: $72 resident, $76 nonresident. Add course price to basic tuition. Physical Science, $93/semester (1 and 2). Add $16 handling. Grades 9–12.

UNL's accredited high-school science courses have the additional benefit of including all necessary equipment. Good for those who prefer secular instruction or the feedback of a correspondence-school instructor. The Physical Science course could be considered for the last grade of junior high or middle school or the first year of high school. For more details see the UNL review in the Correspondence Programs section of Volume 1 (it's one of the full-service programs).

SCIENCE EXPERIMENTS & ACTIVITIES FOR MIDDLE GRADES

NEW**
Addison-Wesley Publishing Company, Inc.
Foodworks, $8.95 plus $2.50 shipping.

Addison-Wesley publishes this wonderful book written by the people at the Ontario Science Centre in Toronto, Canada. The Science Centre has three connected buildings filled with more than 500 hands-on exhibits for children to explore, experience, and enjoy science. This book (and others in the series) helps to make hands-on science available to everyone.

Foodworks is subtitled "Over 100 Science Activities and Fascinating Facts That Explore the Magic of Food." The facts are skillfully interwoven in story form. For instance, many of us know that the tomato once was thought to be poisonous, but do you know why people changed their minds? The book introduces us to Colonel Robert G. Johnson of Salem, Oregon who stood on the courthouse steps and ate an entire basket of tomatoes without becoming ill. We also read about Dr. Mile's Compound Extract of Tomato which was *then* sold as a quack cure-all, but *today* is better known and loved as ketchup. Along with the information are plenty of activities in "Try this" form such as the Big Eater experiment:

> How much do you eat each day in relation to your weight? Weigh yourself and weigh your meals. Don't forget the snacks. Divide your weight by the amount of food you eat to find out.

Many of the activities are more involved than this example, but you can easily find the necessary materials around your home or pick them up elsewhere.

While *Foodworks* is written for children, it will appeal to anyone who has reached the age of reason. Humor is generously scattered throughout the writing, and the black-and-white drawings and activities have that light touch that makes learning more enjoyable.
—Cathy Duffy

NEW★★
Dale Seymour Publications
Everyday Science Sourcebook: Ideas for Teachers in Elementary and Middle School, $19.95.

What we have here is a great tool to help you develop science process skills in your children. Need a science activity to correlate with your unit study or textbook? Look no farther . . . it's all here.

First, what the book is not. It is not a science program. It is not a "how to teach science" book. What you get are lots and lots of hands-on activities, organized in ways that make this book really easy to use.

Activities cover the process skills of *observing, communicating, comparing, organizing, relating, inferring,* and *applying.* Activities are arranged numerically by categories: inorganic matter, organic matter, energy, inference models, and technology. These are further subdivided into topics. For example, the category "Inorganic Matter" is broken down into solids, liquids, gases, geology, oceanography, and meteorology. Each activity has a letter code that tells you exactly which skills and age level it is designed for.

The activities in this science sourcebook are designed sequentially for children from ages 1 through 18. Naturally, there is no good reason why your teenager can't do some of the earlier activities too—especially since I doubt he has done all of them already!

UPDATED★★
EDC Publishing
Pocket Scientist series: *Fun with Electronics, Chemistry Experiments, Flight and Floating,* $4.95 each paperbound or $11.96 each library-bound. Shipping extra. Ages 10 and up.

The Usborne Pocket Scientist series includes experiments, projects, and puzzles that explain basic scientific principles. Lots of things to make using readily available components. The chemistry book only uses household materials, for safe experiments. Full-color, fully illustrated, 64-page books, with the famous Usborne visual layout.

NEW★★
Exploratorium Publications
Exploratorium Science Snackbook, introductory price $19.95. Add $4 shipping for first copy, $2 each additional copy. Adaptable for grades 4–12.

I know you're dying to ask, so here are the answers to your questions:

First, the Exploratorium is a hands-on science museum in San Francisco.

Second, they once published a book for science museums explaining how to put together some of their most popular exhibits. That book was called the *Cookbook.*

This book, written for classroom teachers, explains how to make simpler versions of the exhibits—hence the term *Snackbook.* (Get it? Cookbook? Snackbook?) Each project takes somewhere between a minute and an hour to put together, and often kids can do it themselves with just a bit of adult help.

The *Snackbook* is arranged alphabetically, starting with "After Image," a perception and light experiment, and ending with "Whirling Watcher," whatever that is. (I'm reviewing the book in manuscript form, and the last few pages were left off my photocopy.) An index helps you find individual experiments more quickly, as does a cross-reference by subject and phenomenon. Another index, "Sources and Suppliers of Materials," should make it easier for you to come up with the few nonstandard supplies needed.

The *Snackbook* has a really nice layout. At the beginning of each "snack" is a picture of the Exploratorium exhibit and a drawing or picture of what your project should look like when finished. The main difference between the two is that the Exploratorium builds its exhibits to be beaten on by thousands of kids, and its exhibits incorporate fancy stuff like buttons and electronic gear. Your version simply demonstrates the scientific principle without a lot of fuss.

Beneath each picture is a sidebar with a list of materials needed, most of which you have lying around the house. A very short introduction explains what scientific principles your project will demonstrate. Illustrated assembly instructions make it easy to put the project together, "To Do and Notice" provides activity suggestions, and a "What's Going On?" section at the end explains how it works. An "Etc." sidebar shares project extensions and follow-up activities.

The *Snackbook* is heavy on perception and light experiments, as they are flashy and fun and many of them can be done using only a flashlight, index card, paper, and/or mirror. It also includes some simple chemistry, electricity, magnetism, mechanics, sound, heat, and other projects. I would have liked to see a more even spread of projects—when you've seen one optical illusion, you've seen 'em all. All the same, it's a good resource for simple and satisfying Friday afternoon science experiments.

NEW★★
Fearon Teacher Aids
Science Cookbook, $8.95 plus $3.50 shipping. Grades 4–8.

We home schoolers keep telling ourselves that we can teach kids almost anything in our kitchens. Measurement—yeah. Adding and subtracting—no problem. Fractions—piece of cake (pause here to laugh at the joke). Phonics—fingerpainting letters with vanilla pudding. Etiquette—never fingerpainting with vanilla pudding. Social studies—observing the reaction of the guests to Junior's fingerpainting in the vanilla pudding. And so it goes.

We like to talk about kitchen science, too. Nutrition. Observation. Classification. But how about dissolution . . . oxidation . . . evaporation and absorption . . . coagulation . . . softening . . . thickening . . . separation . . . leavening? All this, and more, gallops right into your kitchen with *The Science Cookbook* by Julia B. Waxter.

Let me hasten to inform you that the kitchen science experiments in this book are *not* cutesy rainy-day time-

wasters. Nor are they beat-it-and-eat-it home ec. The terminology is scientific, the methods are scientific, and the goal is scientific.

Gourmets beware: you will have to ruin some good food to carry out these experiments! Overcooking an omelet teaches kids about what heat does to protein. On the other hand, the kids will get to discover which procedures make the omelet fluffier—and why.

Every chapter tackles a different topic (e.g., coagulation) and begins with an explanation of the topic, learning objectives, applied skills used in the experiments, and key ideas to teach. Each experiment likewise includes explanation and teaching tips, scientific vocabulary, materials needed, discussion questions, and related activities. All vocabulary words are indexed, and the book closes with 28 pages of reproducible cookbook experiments. Typical experiment: learn about coagulation by preparing hard-boiled eggs. Bonus knowledge from this experiment: learn about chicken metabolism and life cycle, osmosis, digestion of cooked and raw protein, and why eggs cook better if punctured on the proper side with a pin.

The program was developed for a class of kids with "learning disabilities," and rapidly became one of the most popular courses in that school. This "real" approach to science held the kids' attention, too (keep in mind that we're talking classes of 90 percent boys, many of them labeled hyper).

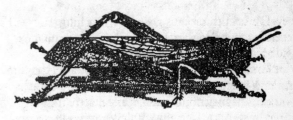

NEW★★
Shekinah Curriculum Cellar
Wall Projects for Students, $2.50 each. Shipping extra. Grades 4–8.

It comes in a pouch, like a baby kangaroo. It goes on your wall when it's done. What is it? (You can tell I've been reviewing too many preschool programs!)

Not to torture you any longer, we're talking about the Wall Projects series carried by Shekinah Curriculum Cellar. You get a long, thin plastic pouch with a folded black-and-white poster inside, plus a teacher's guide and a few extra info sheets. Using the information on the back of the poster and elsewhere, you fill in the blanks on the poster and color it. For example, the *Solar System* poster project requires you to fill in the diameter, distance from sun, revolution time, and rotation time for each planet in the solar system. This information is on the enclosed Planet Information Sheet and the colors you should use are given in the teacher's guide.

The teacher's guides, as usual, overdo things a bit. Don't feel you must burden your child with writing a report on Halley's Comet just become some frenzied teacher stuck this in!

The Wall Projects series includes *U.S. Space Travel and Exploration, The Solar System and Universe, Wonders of the Human Body, Simple Machines,* and *Weather.* The *Weather* project is an especially good deal: it includes eight weather projects, the making of three weather instruments, temperature reading and conversion from Fahrenheit to Celsius, weather forecasting and map reading, and of course the wall poster project itself. (For social studies Wall Projects, see the Social Studies section.) An inexpensive, organized way to learn a lot of information.

UPDATED★★
Things of Science
$36/year for 12 science kits (one mailed each month). Ages 8–14.

The gift that keeps giving all year long. Every month the subscriber gets a science kit in the mail, filled with safe, simple materials and easy instructions for as many as 30 experiments. Each month the topic changes. Recent kits have covered such topics as gravity, magnetism, friction, static electricity, heat, light, sound, surface tension, lever and pulley, and seed growth.

In the past, the kits were designed for older children, but the new kits have been revised and repackaged for preteens. Most of the club members are 10–12 years old.

$3 a month is not a lot to spend for enough Friday science experiments to last that month! I also like the topic-by-topic approach, which helps kids learn more than a scattershot "let's do an experiment and who cares what it's about" approach.

Things of Science has been around for over 50 years, so you can be fairly confident they know what they're doing. Many *Big Book* readers have subscribed to this series in the past, and I haven't heard any complaints.

Wff 'n Proof Learning Games Associates
Queries 'n Theories, $27.50 postpaid. Ages 12–adult.

Queries 'n Theories is a simulation of the scientific method that allows you to create and test hypotheses in the course of trying to break the code your opponent just invented. It's my very favorite Wff 'n Proof game, partly because it develops scientific thinking and partly because I get to play with all those neat little colored chips.

SCIENCE FAIRS

NEW★★
Teacher Created Materials
All About Science Fairs, $9.95. Grades 3–8.

All About Science Fairs is the best workbook I have seen for actually getting home-taught kids rolling with a science fair project. It's not because *All About Science Fairs* was written for home schoolers. Heavens, no! The book was written for school classes and is full of busywork. So what makes it so good?

- The bound-in comic book, in which a goofy alien explains to the earth kids what science fairs are all about and how to design a project. Simple, memorable explanations.

- The Science Project Checklist. Follow the steps for success!

- The list of 120 science project ideas—divided into three ability levels.

- The teacher's guide in the front, which goes through the whole project development process step by step. The guide also neatly explains how to use graphs, data charts, and so on effectively in your science project.

The worksheets, designed to provide practice in scientific procedures, are not the high point of this book. No need to actually fill them out—just read 'em and you'll get the idea.

GENERAL SCIENCE REFERENCE

NEW**
World Book Direct Response
Student Information Finder, $34.95/both volumes (sold only as a two-volume set).

Study and review key facts in math, physical science, earth science, and life science with the Math and Science volume of World Book's *Student Information Finder*.

See the Math section for a description of the math portion of this volume. Now for the science!

The unit "Facts about Chemistry" includes not only the expected—e.g., the periodic table of the elements—but also useful descriptions of basic lab equipment, such as the Bunsen burner, burette, dry cell, compound microscope, and some simple experiments and experimental procedures (e.g., how to set up a distillation apparatus). Chemical processes, such as oxidation and reduction, radiation, and catalysis, are also briefly explained.

"Facts about Physics" whips through Newtonian physics, thermodynamics, light and lasers, magnetism, electricity, and so forth, and includes a useful glossary of physics terms. The explanations, though brief, slice through to the basics kids need to remember.

The information in the Earth Sciences section is somewhat less reliable. Here all geological processes are explained in terms of uniformitarianism, e.g., the hypothesis that geographic features were caused by slow processes over immense lengths of time. A quick look at the landscape around Mt. St. Helens should sufficiently refute this notion.

The climate and weather information is more useful. So is the Life Sciences section. These few pages manage to contain the pith of most of what students should be learning on the subjects from K–12, including basic botany, zoology, and all the systems of the human body.

CHAPTER EIGHTEEN

BIOLOGY

Biology—what can I say? I took chemistry and physics in high school and college, but never biology. The word was out that you had to *dissect a frog* to pass the biology lab. At the time I was a sentimental teenage girl, squeamish about slicing up little green creatures as a scientific experiment. (Not that I'm crazy about slice-'n-dice science even now—see the writeup of Process Skills science in Volume 2.) I also had a fringed vest, bell-bottom pants, and a copper ring that turned my finger green. Guess what era we're talking about. The '60s? Right!

Well, those days are long behind us. Some of us have changed. Some of us haven't. Many of us now have children who need to, or want to, take advanced science courses, of which biology is one.

Good news: at home you don't have to slice up our little amphibious friends unless you feel like it. The KONOS people have kids dissecting cows' eyeballs in grades K–6, which is even yukkier in my opinion— but then, I have a jittery stomach. If this sort of thing is to your taste, see the KONOS review in Volume 2. For the rest of us, good ol' textbook science and a bit of microscope work will suffice.

BIOLOGY COURSES

NEW**
A Beka Book Publications
Biology text, $19.30, paperbound. Teacher's edition (includes student text), $35.95. Student test packet, $5.25. Teacher key with quiz booklet, $7.40 (to be released August 1991). Biology field and lab manual, $10.30, or $19.20 for teacher's edition. Video lab demonstrations (VHS only), $150. Biology transparencies available for school classrooms. Shipping extra.

A Beka's enormous biology text (649 pages!) is quite different from other biology courses. Instead of introducing science topics with philosophy and theory, *Biology: God's Living Creation* starts with the concrete (plants, animals, etc.) and then moves to theory. Again, instead of following an evolutionary sequence (enzymes, to cells, to single-celled organisms, to invertebrates, to fish, etc.) it presents the created world in the order traditionally followed by naturalists.

For example, in the Botany section, students first learn about the familiar flowering-seed plants, then leaf structure and function, flowers/fruits/seeds, stems and roots, and finally less well-known plant varieties. Human anatomy is studied before zoology, and familiar animals are studied before the less familiar animals. In this way, A Beka hopes to avoid the conflict caused by teaching creation science along with evolutionary classification categories.

Other features: a built-in set of TransVision® transparent overlays of the human body, to aid in detailed study of body structures and organs. Easy-to-follow outline format with distinctive typefaces for sections, subsections, etc. Frequent sidebars on "Wonders of the Living Creation" draw attention to God and the marvelous way in which He made things. Lots of excellent drawings, photos, graphs, and charts, many in full color, explain difficult concepts.

Like other A Beka science books, *Biology: God's Living Creation* is like a cross between an encyclopedia and a regular textbook. The contents are accompanied by as much detailed information and as many visual aids as you could expect to find in an expensive encyclopedia—from a Christian viewpoint, which you wouldn't find in the encyclopedia. Unlike the elementary-grade A Beka books, the textbook information is extremely well organized, making it easy to digest and remember.

The book is divided into logical sections: botany, human anatomy and physiology, life science methodology and philosophy, zoology, and cellular and molecular biology. The subsections are equally well organized. For example, under Zoology you find chapters on mammals, birds, reptiles and amphibians, fish, arthropods (invertebrates with jointed feet), and a final chapter on less-familiar invertebrates. The chapter on less-familiar invertebrates includes sections on mollusks, echinoderms and rotifers, hollow-intestined invertebrates, worms of various types, and single-celled protozoa. Underneath the section on mollusks you find subsections on bivalves (two-shelled mollusks), gastropods (stomach-footed mollusks), and cephalopods (head-foot mollusks). The subsection on bivalves is divided up into series of paragraphs, each introduced with a word in boldface. The topics in boldface are shells, locomotion, feeding and respiration, other systems, and edible bivalves. Accompanying the pages on bivalves are a list of study objectives for the section, a three-part line drawing of how clams move about, a beautiful full-color "Anatomy of a Clam" illustration, a photograph of underseas clam shells, and a gorgeous full-page full-color picture of 59 shell types, each numbered, with the name of each given on the side.

I gave this one example to show how well organized the information in this book is, from the section level right down to the paragraph level. The study objectives for each chapter section make it a breeze to learn and review the information. The gorgeous visual

aids tempt you to linger over each topic. The fascinating sidebars don't detract from the main text (as so often happens), but rather complement it. Altogether, an excellent job.

A biology course is, of course, more than just the student textbook. A Beka also offers a teacher's edition that includes the full student text as well as a scope and sequence, daily lesson plans, demonstration ideas, chapter summaries, and teaching strategies. The *Field and Laboratory Manual* is also available in both student's and teacher's editions, and includes complete instructions for completing 27 labs and 3 special projects.

If you think it would be too complicated to actually get the equipment and materials and work through the labs, A Beka has even provided video labs with step-by-step demonstrations of the dissections and biochemical labs in the *Field and Laboratory Manual*. The video lab might be a wise purchase for those with little time or storage space, since the list of required equipment and materials to do all the labs runs on for pages. If you *do* want to work through the labs, much of this material and equipment is available from Bob Jones University Press or Crane's Select Educational Materials. To be even more specific: if you are willing to really put the time into working through this entire biology book, especially as a two-year course, and have a number of children to whom you plan to teach this course (either all at once or one by one), it would indeed be worthwhile to get the equipment and do all the excellent labs and projects. If you simply want to teach the lab techniques and concepts, even though the video lab initially seems expensive you will save a lot of time and money by purchasing it.

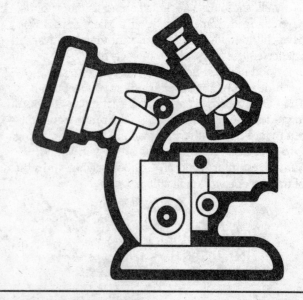

NEW★★
Alpha Omega Publications
LIFEPACS, $2.95 each or $26.95/set of 10 (one course). Teacher handbook, $4.95. Two answer keys, $2.25 each. LIFEPAC test key (included with teacher handbook), $2.25. Elementary Science Kit, $179.95, includes most specialized biological lab equipment and supplies needed for the lab experiments. Slide kit, $16.95, microscope, $97.50. Shipping extra.

Alpha Omega's 10th-grade biology course comes to you as a set of 10 workbooks with the lesson text, exercises, and tests all built in. The design of these LIFEPACS is easy to use, with frequent teacher checkpoints and student experiments right in the book. Here's what you get:

- Taxonomy: The Key to Organization—introduction to classifications and creationism, including the history of taxonomy

- Basis of Life—elements, molecules, chemical reactions, organic compounds, and enzymes

- Microbiology—microscopy techniques and various little beasties of importance to scientists

- Cells—what are they made of and how do they act?

- Plants: Green Factories—structure and growth of plants, plus plants as a "Good Friend" (this is an exact quote)

- Human Anatomy and Physiology—including a *very* restrained explanation of human reproduction that manages not to refer to the sex act at all (instead we hear about eggs, sperm, and the changes pregnancy causes to a woman's body)

- God's Plan for Inheritance—genetics

- Cell Division and Reproduction—asexual and sexual reproduction in cells, plants, and animals

- Ecology, Pollution, and Energy—our old friends the environmentalists share their view of life and righteousness: "everything living is linked to everything else," "every time people do something to the natural environment, reactions happen that are usually more than expected,"

"good management adjusts living things to the environment, not the environment to the living things," "[manmade] poisons [are] everywhere," and so on, plus exhortations to become politically active, ride bikes, and recycle. Man is not seen as playing a part in the balance of nature; rather, nature is presented as *already* perfectly balanced, with you and me as disruptive agents.

- Principles and Applications of Biologists—how to be green in all areas of life.

Alpha Omega has a Science Kit for home schools that includes most of the specialized biological lab equipment and supplies you need for the lab experiments. A separate slide-making kit, with 36 prepared slides, and a microscope are also available to round out your equipment needs for this grade.

As usual, I'd urge you to skip the Politically Correct units (numbers 9 and 10) and stick with the *facts*, ma'am, just the *facts*. The other units are really good, super easy to use, and free of trendy new-ageish doctrine (except the nonsense about plants being our good friends in the end of LIFEPAC 5).

NEW★★
Bob Jones University Press
Biology text, second edition: student text, $21.95; teacher's edition (includes student text with added notes and answers), $33.50. Biology lab manual, $7.95. These are home-school prices. Shipping extra.

If you have a fundamentalist/evangelical point of view and want to find answers in controversial areas like eugenics, drugs, abortion, miracles, euthanasia, homosexuality, genetic engineering, AIDS, animal rights, and so on, as well as the normal 10th-grade biology topics, BJUP has a book for you. It's a hefty 739 pages, but the pages are smaller than those of A Beka's biology text.

Biology for Christian Schools follows the normal public-school textbook sequence, though with a Christian twist. First comes a section on life itself—its chemistry, structure, continuity, and history—all from a creationist viewpoint. Next, the unit entitled "Biology: The Science of Organisms" follows the usual simplest-to-most-complex sequence found in secular biology texts. First there's a chapter on classification techniques. You then start off with bacteria, viruses, and other teeny-tiny organisms; move on to protozoa and algae; follow up with fungi; then move to the plant kingdom, and next the animal kingdom. Animals are covered in four chapters, one each for invertebrates, arthropods, vertebrates, and mammals and birds, in that order. Finally man himself is studied: his anatomy, body systems, and spiritual responsibilities for medical and physical decisions.

The accompanying lab manual not only introduces lab techniques and provides assignments, but even has space for writing the answers and making your lab drawings. Some of the experiments involve feeding one critter to another, bothering a critter, opening an incubated egg, or even dissecting a live critter (an anesthetized earthworm, in this case). You'll be spending a lot of time making and observing microscope slides, dissecting, and testing your own and other people's bodily functions and reactions.

The lab manual was not laid out as well for home use as others I have seen, nor was the visual format as easy to follow. Organizing your lab materials could be a challenge, too, especially if you're trying to live without the teacher's lab manual, which has better-organized materials lists. (Good news: BJUP tells me an improved second edition of the lab manual is due out in fall 1991.) BJUP sells most of the needed supplies; you'll need to ask for their separate Science Supplies catalog.

NEW**
EDC Publishing, Inc.
Introduction to Biology, $6.95. Combined volume, *The Usborne Book of Science,* also includes chemistry and physics, $14.95 hardbound. Add 15% shipping. Ages 12–adult.

EDC Publishing has introductions to electronics, chemistry, biology, and physics that actually *explain* these subjects. Since parents often choke at the point of advanced science instruction, I know you'll like these!

Each book in the series is wholesome and well-balanced. The *Introduction to Biology,* for example, has a much better-balanced perspective on ecology (as the study of small, mostly closed systems) than the newer Usborne titles on conservation and ecology. They also got the story of the pepper moths straight, although they missed the boat slightly on mutations, where the text gives the impression that beneficial mutations have actually been observed, and mixes the phenomenon of natural selection (e.g., penicillin-resistant bacteria surviving) into the topic of mutations (not fair, since some of the bacteria were immune to the penicillin in the first place).

Cheerful cartoon people and critters demonstrate chemical principles throughout the book. Simple experiments and science puzzles are provided, along with gorgeous illustrations (full-color in the first 32 pages, black-and-white in the last 16) and simple explanations of difficult concepts.

Topics include: Definition of biology. What living things have in common. What living things are made of (intro to cell biology). Making food (includes an experiment to prove plants need light and chlorophyll to make starch). Feeding (how different animals do this). What happens to food (includes a jelly-and-pineapple experiment). Getting energy (an experiment with mung beans). How substances move around the body (a "potato chip" experiment which will *not* work unless you remember that the British consider french fries to be "chips"). Plant transport systems (more experiments). Waste disposal. Skeletons and movement. Sensitivity (growing bent-over plants to show how they turn towards a light source). Coordination. Reproduction (birds and the bees emphasis). Life cycles and growth (watch a fly's life cycle—yuk!). Genetics and heredity. The plant kingdom classified. The animal kingdom classified. BASIC computer program to classify living organisms. Ecology and the environment. Mutations and natural selection. Using a microscope. Answers to puzzles found in the book. Short index. A lot in 48 pages!

NEW**
University of Nebraska-Lincoln
Tuition: $72 resident, $76 nonresident. Biology, $53/semester (semesters 1 and 2), $93/semester (3 and 4). Add course price to basic tuition. Add $16 handling. Grades 9–12.

UNL's accredited high school science courses have the additional benefit of including all necessary equipment. Good for those who prefer secular instruction or the feedback of a correspondence-school instructor. For more details see the UNL review in the Correspondence Programs section of Volume 1 (it's one of the full-service programs).

BIOLOGY REFERENCES & HELPS

NEW**
Alpha Omega Publications
Great American Bullfrog Plastic Model Kit, $16.95. Shipping extra.

Now you can dissect a frog without slicing up any little green critters! The Great American Bullfrog Plastic Model is over a foot long and includes organs, snap-fit skeleton, transparent green body, life-cycle display, and anatomical chart. Cheaper than a computer simulation, less smelly and yukky than dissecting a real frog.

NEW**
EDC Publishing, Inc.
Dictionary of Biology, $9.95 paperbound or $15.95 librarybound. Combined volume, Dictionary of Science, also includes chemistry and physics, $21.95 paperbound. Add 15% shipping. Ages 11–adult.

It sometimes seems like half of the work in a science course is learning the *names* of everything. Taking science courses can increase a young person's vocabulary by 50 percent—meaning there's a *lot* of terminology to learn!

The Usborne dictionaries of science are wonderfully designed to serve both as 128-page visual reference works and as explanations of the vocabulary associated with each scientific discipline. Arranged by themes, they present each scientific term in its context, explained with words and full-color pictures. The complex is made simple, justifying the series' slogan: "The facts you need to know—at a glance."

The *Dictionary of Biology* starts off with ecology, including this realistic definition of an ecosystem: "An ecosystem is a self-contained unit, i.e., the plants and animals interact to produce all the material they need." That sounds like the old, sensible ecology we all knew and loved. Next come life and life cycles (brief mention of evolution here), the structure of living things, and cell division. Plants, Animals, and Humans are the three major sections. Each covers anatomy, reproduction, and growth. A final general section in black and white touches on types of reproduction (including cell division), genetics and heredity, fluid movement, food and how it is used, metabolism, energy for life, homeostasis, hormones, digestive juices and enzymes, vitamins and their uses, plant classification, and animal classification. A fairly lengthy index rounds out the book.

You'll find some naked teens standing side by side in the section on human reproduction, and a rather unflattering picture of a baby in the womb. Aside from these minor points, there's nothing in the book to object to, and lots to be thankful for!

I suggest that you use the *Dictionary of Biology* both as a reference work *and* as a handy desk aid for when you run across a concept in your science book that you just don't get. It's also is a great review tool and study aid, since it's so well organized by topic. Recommended.

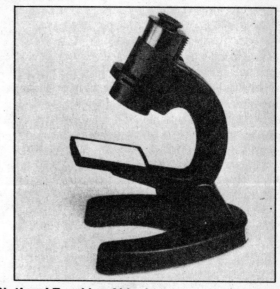

National Teaching Aids, Inc.
$7.25 per viewer, $4.45 per title. Add 15% shipping. Five year guarantee. Grades 3–12.

Here is a nifty idea! Since most schools can't afford high-powered microscopes for every student, why not take pictures of slides as they would appear under ideal viewing conditions and then let children look at those in lieu of expensive specimens? National has a wide range of "photomicrographs" (spell *that* and go to the head of the class!) plus explanatory text folders. You need a viewer, of course, and National also sells those. The viewers are rugged, coming with a five-year guarantee against breakage. These materials have been used by over one hundred and seventy *million* students.

NEW**
National Teaching Aids, Inc.
Micromounts,™ $18/pkg of 150. Includes instruction sheet. Add 15% shipping.

Do glass microscope slides tend to slip and slide out of your fingers and go crash on the floor? Dislike spending big bucks for them? National Teaching Aids has a new alternative: Micromounts. These are made of paper and plastic. Insert your specimen on the clear plastic part of the mount, peel off the protective tape, fold the mount onto itself, and label. Micromounts include a space to indicate specimen number, name, date found, where found, how prepared, main observations, and who prepared the slide. You can use them for both wet and dry mounts.

Let me warn you about one possible pitfall. The peel-off backing is the exact same color as the paper itself: white. I discovered the peel-off portion on the top of the mount by trial and error, but didn't discover the other part at all—which keeps the slide stuck together —until I read the instructions in the catalog and experimented awhile. Just make sure to *read the instructions first* and you'll be fine!

CHAPTER NINETEEN

CHEMISTRY

I f you like bookkeeping, drawing, and mud pies, you'll love chemistry. It's a little bit of all of these. Neat, precise record-keeping. Neat, precise drawings of your lab setups. Doing strange things to laboratory substances.

I *loved* chemistry, which should give you a clue to my personality. (One of the greatest trials of my home schooling career was resisting the urge to get our first-born son Teddy his own set of lab chemicals—at the age of 6!) I love Bunsen burners and Erlenmeyer flasks. What fun to bend glass tubing into weird and useful shapes! Neat rows of chemicals, properly labeled, affect me the same way as neat rows of seedlings in our garden. (My mother has two degrees in chemistry, which might explain a few things.)

Unfortunately, a lot of kids today have the idea that chemistry is difficult. We know this, because we see labored introductions to chemistry texts trying to reassure kids that they will be able to understand chemistry, contrary to their expectations.

If there is any truth at all to the rumor that chemistry is difficult, it's only because kids haven't had good math courses. To cure chemistophobia, run your budding chemist through a few Saxon Math books. John Saxon goes out of his way to make sure kids who graduate from his courses are comfortable with chemistry terminology and that they know all the math they will need for solving chemistry problems. You might also want to give them a few drawing lessons and let them help their little brothers and sisters make mudpies . . .

CHEMISTRY COURSES

NEW**
A Beka Book Publications
Chemistry text, $18.10, paperbound. Teacher's edition (includes student text), $33.50. Solution key, $30. Student test packet, $3.75. Teacher key and test packet, $7.40. Student quiz booklet (available August 1991), $3.75. Teacher key and quiz booklet (available August 1991), $7.40. Chemistry lab manual, $10.55, or $18.30 for teacher's edition. Video lab demonstrations (VHS only), $150 each for first and second semester. Shipping extra.

A Beka believes in giving you a *lot* of pages for your money, and their *Chemistry: Precision and Decision* text for 11th-graders is no exception. Its hefty 655 pages include enough information to take you through high-school chemistry and through the Advanced Placement exam. Most on-site high-school classes won't get through the whole book in one year.

Let's start with the book's content first. Chapters are:

• Chemistry: An Introduction.

• Mathematics in Chemistry. Your typical introduction to scientific notation, significant figures, precision and accuracy, and dimensional analysis (making sure you always end up with the proper units, e.g., feet or inches or ml or kg).

• Matter: The Substance of Chemistry. Properties of matter, how matter changes, ways to separate matter, elements, subatomic particles, the periodic chart, and a fascinating section called "Chemical Elements in Bible Times."

• Stoichiometry: Elements and Compounds. Writing chemical formulas, learning about moles and percentage composition, etc.

• Stoichiometry: Chemical Reactions. In which you learn to balance chemical equations and do various things with them.

• Gases. Everything you are likely to need to know on this subject unless you take a college course in thermodynamics.

• Chemical Thermodynamics. Did I mention thermodynamics? Here it is—but not everything you'd get in a college course (e.g., no adiabatic containers or engineering applications).

• Electronic Structure. Waves! Quantums (quanta?)! Orbitals! The hydrogen spectrum!

• The Periodic Table. Now we really get into it: its historical development, classification, periodicity, electron configurations, atomic sizes, ionization energy, electron affinity, and electronegativity.

• The Chemical Bond and Intermolecular Forces. If the words "ionic" and "covalent" mean anything to you, this is the chapter for that sort of thing.

• Selected Nonmetals and Their Compounds. Hydrogen, oxygen, nitrogen, phosphorus, sulfur, halogens, noble gases. Balanced sidebar on the ozone-layer controversy.

• Selected Metals and Semimetals. Metallurgy, alkali metals, alkaline earth metals, iron, copper, gold and silver, aluminum, and silicon and germanium (very important in manufacturing electronics).

• Solutions and Colloids. You start with definitions, learn everything you can about the properties of soaps and colloids, and end up looking at soaps, detergents, and other common colloids.

• Chemical Kinetics. Reactions, in a nutshell.

• Chemical Equilibrium.

• Acids, Bases, and Salts.

• Ionic Equilibrium in Solution.

• Oxidation-Reduction Reactions: Electrochemistry.

• Nuclear Chemistry.

• Organic Chemistry. Thirty-one pages take you from a definition of organic compounds through chemical bonding, structural formulas, functional groups, alkanes, alkenes, alkynes, aromatic hydrocarbons, alcohols, aldehydes and ketones, carboxylic acids and esters, amines, amides, proteins and amino acids, carbohydrates, and fats.

A lot of the text is taken up with worked examples, exercises keyed to the examples, separate explanations of key concepts, review exercises, chapter summaries, and key term glossaries at the end of each chapter. These all help a *lot*, especially the chapter summaries, which are definitely needed since the text itself is not written in the most uncomplicated language. Let's put it this way—it's obvious that the author is a real scientist!

Chemistry: Precision and Design is not overly rich in graphics. It has more of a normal textbook appearance than, say, A Beka's biology text. In many respects, it reads like a college textbook.

A Beka also offers a teacher's edition that includes the full student text as well as a scope and sequence, daily lesson plans, demonstration ideas, chapter summaries, and teaching strategies.

The *Chemistry Laboratory Manual* is also available in both student's and teacher's editions, and includes complete instructions for completing 36 labs. Be forewarned: the list of required equipment is long (most of it is standard lab equipment readily available from various sources), but the list of required chemicals is *long*!

An alternative to taking the time and money to set up your own home lab and work through the experiments is to purchase A Beka's video chemistry labs. These are video demonstrations of the actual experiments in the *Chemistry Laboratory Manual*. Although the video labs aren't inexpensive, if added to a home school support group library the cost per family would become reasonable. Then you could perhaps just do one or two of the most interesting experiments on-site, for the hands-on experience.

NEW**
Alpha Omega Publications
LIFEPACS, $2.95 each or $26.95/set of 10 (one course). Teacher handbook, $4.95. Two answer keys, $2.25 each. LIFEPAC test key (included with teacher handbook), $2.25. Elementary Science Kit, $179.95, includes some specialized apparatus necessary to do the chemistry lab experiments. Chemicals such as zinc, acids, etc. must be purchased separately from another vendor. Shipping extra.

Alpha Omega presents chemistry as its 11th-grade science course. This comes to you as a set of 10 work-books with the lesson text, exercises, and tests all built in. LIFEPACS are easier to use than textbooks, in my opinion, with frequent teacher checkpoints and student experiments right in the book. Here's what you get:

• Introduction to Chemistry—metric units, length/ volume/mass, the scientific method, scientific notation, and careers in chemistry. The careers subunit is taken from a brochure prepared by the Manufacturing Chemists Association, and (oddly) introduced by a bit of eco-hysteria: "Technology that has brought us hybrid grains has also given us the population explosion." *Au contraire, mes amis*: it's *God* who blesses people with children. "Chemicals for killing pests are

now often more feared than the pests." So why are there bags of pesticide for sale down at my local nursery store? "Everything in this universe is tied to everything else"—a classic statement of pantheism. The careers subunit itself presents the usual skewed picture of all races and sexes equally represented, when in real life most indi-viduals working in professional, chemistry-related fields are white or Asian and male. (Actually, my mother is the only woman I know who has ever worked as a professional chemist.)

• Elements, Compounds, and Mixture—some neat "kitchen science" experiments in this unit

• Gases and Moles
• Atomic Structure and Periodicity—including brief bios of the scientists who discovered all this

• Chemical Formulas, Bonding, and Molecular Architecture

• Chemical Reaction, Rates, and Equilibrium

• Equilibrium Systems

• Two units on introductory organic chemistry

This is mostly a straight science course, and quite a good one at that. Explanations are uncomplicated and everything is well organized. You can figure out what the text is talking about with very little head-scratching.

You need a certain amount of lab equipment and supplies to do the lab experiments—e.g., Erlenmeyer flasks, Bunsen burner, ring stand, tubing, beakers, fil-ters, wire gauze, rubber stop for flask, metal samples, chemicals, test tubes, vacuum apparatus, and so on. Some of this specialized equipment is available in Alpha Omega's Elementary Science Kit. You should get the chemicals from specialized vendors who know how to ship hazardous materials (see Science Equipment chapter).

Wherever feasible, Alpha Omega suggests house-hold objects you can use in place of expensive lab equipment. For example, you may use a hot plate for some experiments instead of a Bunsen burner, or a coin instead of a prepared metal sample. The experi-ments slack off as you approach the end of the course, since the last units mainly concentrate on number-crunching and memorizing vocabulary and concepts.

NEW**
Bob Jones University Press
Chemistry text: student text, $19.95, hardbound; teacher's edition (includes student text with added notes and answers), $33.50. Chemistry lab manual, $7.95. Shipping extra.

BJUP's 11th-grade chemistry course is called *Basic Chemistry for Christian Schools,* not just *Chemistry for Christian Schools,* because, in the words of its own introduction, "it explains complicated theories with simple ideas and it uses an understandable format." The biggest difference you'll notice between a course like this and one like A Beka's is that concepts are explained most frequently with words, not with mathematical equations. The author also does an excellent job of explaining complicated processes in everyday terms, using everyday examples and analogies. Line drawings and cartoons make concepts memorable, while the text is also rich in photographs, graphs, and charts.

Let me give you an example of how clear and straightforward the writing in this book is. From the chapter on chemical equilibrium:

> A chemical equilibrium results when forward and reverse reactions proceed simultaneously. This idea ranks as one of the premier concepts in chemistry. Like the kinetic theory and the atomic theory, it helps to explain many observations. While the study of thermodynamics tries to answer the question "Can the reaction occur?" and kinetics seeks to determine "How fast will the reaction occur?" the study of equilibria seeks to answer "How far will the reaction go?"

All the concepts mentioned in this paragraph, except for chemical equilibrium, have been studied in previous chapters. Yet, although the student already knows about kinetics and thermodynamics, the author provides him or her with the best one-sentence definition of all three topics that I have ever seen.

A little later, chemical equilibrium is illustrated by the fable of Betty and Bob each scooping punch into the other's punch bowl in an attempt to escape their duties as punch servers at Mrs. Tisdale's garden party. (The one who emptied a bowl first could take time off while the other would have to remain and keep serving punch.) When their rates of transfer become equal, they reach dynamic equilibrium and give up the contest. This example is easy to understand and hard to forget—just like the opening definitions in the chapter. The whole book is as good as this!

Don't think for a minute that because the author doesn't indulge in egghead gobbledygook that you're getting anything less than a comprehensive high-school chemistry course. *Basic Chemistry for Christian Schools* has it all, with chapters on:

1. Science, Chemistry, and You. The scientific method, history of chemistry, and what chemistry can mean to a student taking the course.

2. Matter—its classification, energy in matter, and measurement.

3. Atomic Structure—the development of atomic models, including the quantum model.

4. Elements—the periodic table and types of compounds formed by groups within the table.

5. Chemical Bonds.

6. Describing Chemical Composition—how to write the names of compounds, and introducing the mole.

7. Describing Chemical Reactions—writing equations, etc. It's typical of the BJUP approach that "stoichiometry" is a subsection of this chapter rather than the chapter's title, and that the author takes pains to describe exactly what stoichiometry is before launching into the math of how to do it.

8. Gases.

9. Solids and Liquids.

10. Water—as a molecule and in compounds and reactions.

11. Solutions—stuff with other stuff dissolved in it, not "solutions" as in "answers to problems." Colloids are a section in this chapter.

12. Thermodynamics and Kinetics.

13. Chemical Equilibrium.

14. Acids, Bases, and Salts.

15. Oxidation-Reduction.

16. Organic Chemistry. In this chapter you meet all the aromatic hydrocarbons, alkenes, etc. introduced in other textbooks—with the important difference that the minute they are introduced they are defined. E.g., the subsection heading reads "Alkenes: Chains with Double Bonds" not simply "Alkenes."

17. Biochemistry—carbohydrates, proteins, lipids, cellular processes.

18. Nuclear Chemistry.

Note that in all the end chapters major chemical topics are *introduced,* not beaten to death. I heartily applaud this, as there is no profit in throwing more information at students than they can reasonably be expected to retain. These end-chapter topics, from organic chemistry on, are all separate college courses, and even separate degree majors. What high-school chemistry students really need is to find out whether they will want to take any of these college courses later on, rather than to learn half the college material in high school.

The real-life examples in this book are fascinating and the writing is the best I have seen in any chemistry course.

Now what about the lab manual? It's straight lab science, not a mixture of kitchen science and lab science, like Alpha Omega's experiments. The lab manual is just excellent for home use, with a list of all personal lab equipment needed at the beginning of the book and pictures of all the lab equipment at the end, plus illustrated instructions on general safety procedures and how to use the lab equipment. The experiments parallel the textbook. Some have historical significance.

For example, the experiments in which you synthesize mauve dye and soap both are repetitions of the original historic experiments. All the regular "book" experiments give you full instructions on how to set up your equipment and step-by-step procedures for doing the experiments. A Special Labs section at the end provides lab problems *without* procedures, so you have to figure out your own equipment setup and experiment steps.

In all, this looks like an excellent course.

NEW**
EDC Publishing, Inc.
Introduction to Chemistry, $6.95. Combined volume, *The Usborne Book of Science*, also includes biology and physics, $14.95 hardbound. Add 15% shipping. Ages 12–adult.

EDC Publishing has great introductions to electronics, chemistry, biology, and physics that actually *explain* these subjects. Each book in the series is wholesome and well balanced. The *Introduction to Chemistry*, for instance, is pro-industry. It talks about "new, useful substances," which is refreshing to read in an era when all man-made substances are coming under attack.

Cheerful cartoon people demonstrate chemical principles throughout the book. The book also takes a humble view of the history of science, noting how a hypothesis "cannot be conclusively proved true, but if it is never disproved, it comes accepted and can be used in explaining discoveries and forming new hypotheses." Simple experiments are provided, along with gorgeous illustrations (full-color in the first 32 pages, black-and-white in the last 16) and simple explanations of difficult concepts.

Topics include the following (remember, the whole book is only 48 pages long): What is chemistry? Looking at chemicals. What things are made of. Looking at particles (including why a saucepan boils over and how a refrigerator works). Physical changes (includes four separate lab-style experiments for separating substances). What is a chemical reaction? (make a simple compound). Looking for patterns in chemistry. Why chemical reactions happen. Looking at compounds (simple apparatus for testing whether substances conduct when dissolved in water). Valences. Fast and slow reactions (more experiments). Catalysts (lab experiment with hydrogen peroxide, and a simpler one with saliva and starch). How metals react (the flame test is fun!). Acids, bases, and salts (lab and real-life experiments). What is organic chemistry? (Answer: no, it's not about recycling, being the study of compounds containing carbon. Experiments include making wine, then turning it into vinegar.) Organic families (no, it's not about folks who subscribe to *Mother Earth News*—make some molecular models!). Useful organic compounds (make your own plastic out of household ingredients!). Splitting compounds. Identifying substances. Computer program (BASIC text to type in for a program that identifies unknown substances). Formulae and equations. Doing experiments. Answers to puzzles included in the book. Glossary of chemical terms. Short index. Safety instructions are buried on page 45, for some reason: read that page *first!*

This is just a super book. The experiments are super. The text is super. The illustrations are super. Buy it!

NEW**
Globe Book Company
Chemistry Workshop 1, 2, and *3,* $6.65 each. *Teacher's Resource Manual for Chemistry* (one book for all three student books), $4.14. Add 10% shipping.

Those of you who have decided to skip chemistry at home because it is too difficult might want to reconsider. Globe's *Chemistry Workshop* is a chemistry course *with laboratory work* that is practical for the home school. Written as a remedial course, it does not compare with typical high school chemistry courses in scope or depth, but don't let that deter you. You can still grant high school credit for it! If you can cover the basics with such a course, it might be more than equivalent to what your child will retain from a more challenging course. Many of our children will not be pursuing chemistry-related careers, and for them the depth of course coverage will not be crucial. (College preparatory students might need a more challenging course than this one, depending which college they plan to attend and what studies they will be pursuing.)

Chemistry Workshop takes a different approach from traditional chemistry courses, emphasizing learning-by-doing more than learning-by-reading. Its reading level is also easier than that of typical chemistry texts.

Each of the three books is a worktext including instruction, exercises, and activities. The books have short reading passages requiring brief responses. Lots of diagrams and photographs are included with the activities. Throughout each chapter chemistry topics are related to practical applications and science topics in the news.

The first book is introductory—many students will have already covered the content in elementary school or junior high and can skip this book without any problem. Topics in Book 1, *Understanding Matter,* are matter and energy, solids/liquids/gases, atoms, elements, the periodic table, metals/nonmetals, compounds and formulas, physical and chemical changes, mixtures, and oxidation. Book 2, *Understanding Mixtures,* covers mixtures, liquids, freezing and boiling, suspensions/emulsions/colloids, water pollution, acids/bases/neutralization, liquids, and solutions that conduct electricity. Book 3, *Understanding Chemical Change,* includes the substance of matter, classification of elements, atoms, metals, valences, formulas, chemical equations, chemical reactions, oxidation and reduction, alloys, and electroplating metals.—Cathy Duffy

NEW**
University of Nebraska-Lincoln
Tuition: $72 resident, $76 nonresident. Add course price to basic tuition. Chemistry, $148/semester (1 and 2). Add $16 handling. Grades 9–12.

UNL's accredited high school science courses have the additional benefit of including all necessary equipment. This is especially helpful when it comes to their chemistry courses, as it is not easy to find the chemicals and apparatus for home study. Good for those who prefer secular instruction or the feedback of a correspondence-school instructor. For more details see the UNL review in the Correspondence Programs section of Volume 1 (it's one of the full-service programs).

CHEMISTRY REFERENCES

NEW**
Crane's Select Educational Materials
Chemistry Flipper, $5.95. Add $2 shipping.

This easy-to-use reference is 25 double-sided cards in staggered plastic sleeves. Card topics are visible at the bottom; flip up the appropriate card to find information about that topic.

Chemistry Flipper is a great condensed review, as well as a handy reference. The first cards explain how to determine how many significant figures to include in a number, how to use powers of ten, and how to create and interpret graphs. They also include a standard lab report form. Later cards show how to convert moles to lab units and back again, how to balance chemical equations, and lots more.

Like the other Flippers, Chemistry Flipper is fastened to a sturdy 7 x 11" backing that is three-hole punched for easy binder storage.

NEW★★
EDC Publishing, Inc.
Dictionary of Chemistry, $9.95 paperbound or $15.95 library-bound. Combined volume, *Dictionary of Science* also includes biology and physics, $21.95 paperbound. Add 15% shipping. Ages 11–adult.

EDC's *Dictionary of Chemistry* is organized into full-color sections on physical chemistry, inorganic chemistry (stuff that doesn't have carbon in it), organic chemistry, and environmental chemistry (terms referring to climate, water, air, and pollution). A final black-and white general section covers the reactivity series, properties of the

elements, naming rules for simple organic compounds, how six popular gases are prepared in the laboratory (with illustrated equipment setups), laboratory tests used in identifying common substances, various laboratory processes for finding what is in what and how much of it there is (with equipment setups), lab apparatus by name and picture, scientific units, and brief bios of famous chemists (an astounding number of whom were self-taught or home-schooled). A glossary, indexes of substances/symbols/formulae, and a good general index round out the book.

I suggest that you use the *Dictionary of Chemistry* both as a reference work *and* as a handy desk aid for when you run across a concept in your science book that you just don't get. It's also is a great review tool and study aid, since it's so well organized by topic. Recommended.

CHAPTER TWENTY

PHYSICS

Physics is like chemistry, only more so. More math. More pieces of equipment. More graphs and charts for your science notebook.

I had a great high-school physics teacher named Mr. Milne. He taught us Newton's Laws of Motion using polar bears and ice floes. Sample problem:

If a 1000-kg polar bear wearing a bullet-proof vest and ice skates is hit while skating on an ice floe by a one-kg bullet traveling at 100 km/hour, what happens to the bullet and the bear? (Assume zero friction between the skates and ice.) Now take away the bullet-proof vest and shoot the bear again. What happens this time?

We looked at ripples in ripple tanks (reflection and refraction), sat on stools holding spinning bicycle wheels (centrifugal force), and rolled steel balls down inclines coated with carbon paper (acceleration). This was all good fun, and besides I got an A.

College physics was much more dreary. We studied things that exist only in the fevered brains of physicists, such as black holes and quantum levels of energy. For lab experiments, we repeated what we did in high school. (Ever try to concoct a black hole? That's why you can't do lab experiments involving theoretical physics without a particle accelerator.) In a way it was lucky that for four semesters the only lab experiments were reprises of high school, since the teaching assis-

tants no spik English so good. One Japanese gentleman in particular had only two words in his entire vocabulary: "Thissa here" and "Thatta there." For the rest, he tried to make do with math equations and graphs. We applauded his inventiveness and courage, but cut his classes.

Don't shoot the messenger—I'm just telling it like it really is. Once Einstein got his hands on poor Newton's Laws, physics ceased to have much to do with anything that anyone can see or that most people can understand. Take my advice and stick to the polar bears on ice skates.

PHYSICS COURSES

NEW**
A Beka Book Publications
Physics text, $19.95, paperbound. Teacher's guide (does not include student text), $15. Solution key, $30. Student test packet, $4.95. Teacher key and test packet, $8.40. Student quiz booklet (available August 1991), $3.75. Teacher key and quiz booklet (available August 1991), $7.40. Physics lab manual, $10.55. Lab manual teacher's guide, $10.95. Video lab demonstrations (VHS only), $150. Shipping extra.

Did I mention that A Beka believes in giving you a *lot* of pages for your money? It's true of their *Physics: The Foundational Science* text for 12th-graders. It's about the same size as A Beka's chemistry text (649 pages) and includes enough information to take you through high-school physics and through the Advanced Placement exam. (Most on-site high-school classes won't get through the whole book in one year.)

My husband Bill previewed this book for me before I reviewed it myself. His comments were, "It has good explanations, well illustrated; lots of biographical sketches of famous physicists who were Christians; examples are worked out in the text; a logical sequence within each chapter; in sum, the book is all business." To amplify on this a little, what you get are the following sections:

1. Basic concepts in physics. This introduces the nature of science, matter and energy, particles, and the branches of physics, plus a chapter on scientific notation, significant digits, and the other math you need to solve physics problems. (This is the same type of math introduction as in A Beka's chemistry text.)

2. Three states of matter. One chapter each on the liquid, gaseous, and solid state. Consider this a chemistry review.

3. Mechanics. Excellent chapters on velocity and acceleration, Newton's laws and friction, vectors, motion in two dimensions, work and machines, energy and momentum, rotary motion, and gravitation.

4. Thermodynamics. Two chapter that make plain what my expensive one-semester thermo course (which half the class flunked) failed to explain. Good everyday applications of thermodynamic principles.

5 Wave phenomena. Waves, sound, and music.

6. Light. Everything normally studied in a physics course on this topic: the nature of light, the electromagnetic spectrum, color, reflection, refraction, and wave optics.

7. Electricity and magnetism. Includes fields, current, circuits, capacitance, resistance/inductance, and electrical devices.

8. Modern physics. Here's where the rubber really meets the road and all the non-physicists start scratching their heads. I remember the good ol' days when scientists didn't study this stuff until college—and if you're older than me, you might remember the days when even college *professors* didn't claim to understand this stuff! The first two chapters, on quantum theory and special relativity, do what they can to make the invisible and theoretical make some sense. The last two chapters will probably bring a sigh of relief, as they are on technological subjects (modern light and electronics technologies) with which we are familiar from reading popular magazines.

Like the other upper-grades A Beka science courses, the physics course has a wealth of teacher's aids and supplemental resources. The teacher's guide includes daily lesson plans, demonstration ideas, chapter summaries, and teaching strategies. The *Physics Laboratory Manual* includes instructions, record-keeping sheets, equipment lists, etc. for 16 physics labs paralleling the topics in the book. These are not nearly as complicated to set up as the biology and chemistry labs. Besides, the book explains how to make your own experimental devices. A ripple tank, for example, can be as simple as a hole in the ground lined with a plastic sheet with brick side walls holding it in place, or a child's wading pool, or a concrete mixing tub, while you provide the wave action with a simple lattice strip rather than a fancy wave generator. Or, if you really don't want to take the time to set up your own home lab and work through the experiments, you can purchase A Beka's video physics labs. These are video demonstrations of the actual experiments in the *Physics Laboratory Manual*.

Physics: The Foundational Science is an excellent choice for intelligent, well-prepared students who are willing to work steadily through it. Anyone contemplating a future in engineering, technological applications, or science should consider it.

NEW**
Alpha Omega Publications
LIFEPACS, $2.95 each or $26.95/set of 10 (one course). Teacher handbook, $4.95. Two answer keys, $2.25 each. LIFEPAC test key (included with teacher handbook), $2.25. Shipping extra.

Twelfth grade means physics in the Alpha Omega science curriculum. Each science course is a set of 10 workbooks with the lesson text, exercises, and tests all built in. The design of these LIFEPACS is easy to use, with frequent teacher checkpoints and student experiments right in the book. You get a unit each on

- Kinematics—scalars, vectors, velocity, acceleration, and other basic mathematical methods for describing motion. Build your own balance for measuring small items, measure the thickness of a molecular layer, use a percussion timer to measure changes in distance, make a scale model of part of the solar system. You do a report on Galileo and solve problems that involve a caterpillar crawling up a wall.

- Dynamics—Newton's and Kepler's laws. You report (of course) on Newton and Kepler's lives, test Newton's Second Law using your old friend the percussion timer, twirl a rubber stopper around on a string, play bumper cars with two steel spheres (you need tracing and carbon paper plus a bunch of other stuff for this experiment), and so on.

- Work and energy—not human work and human energy, but energy, power, heat, and thermodynamics. You'll need your percussion timer again, to measure the kinetic and potential energy of a homemade pendulum. You'll measure calories (the latent heat of fusion of water) using either a calorimeter or an aluminum tumbler inside a styrofoam cup.

- Wave theory. Play with a Slinky®, build your own ripple tank, make a torsion wave apparatus out of a flexible wire strip and metal rods with weighted ends (they don't tell you this, but you can make weighted ends by soldering on coins or lumps of metal), fiddle with sound, and more!

- Light—refraction, reflection, etc. Write a report on Christaan Huygens. Compare waves to particles (the famous steel-ball-bearing experiment). Lots of experiments with optical equipment: prisms, light pipes, filters, mirrors, etc.

- Static electricity—charges, fields, potential. As you might expect, you'll be rubbing various materials on rubber wands and learning to sketch electrical fields. Some interesting meditations on biblical applications of the ideas of attraction, charge, insulation, and so on.

- Current electricity—resistance and circuits. Write a report on Coulomb, Ampère, Volta, and Ohm. Learn to decipher some simple circuit diagrams and understand simple circuits (serial and parallel). Lots of math. Surprisingly, I didn't see any electrical experiments in this unit.

- Magnetism. Experiments with magnets and iron filings, sketching magnetic fields, simple electromagnetic experiments.

- Atomic and nuclear physics. Lots of terminology, history, and math. No experiments (not that anyone expects you to have radioactive isotopes lying around your house!).

- Review unit.

All these topics are logically presented along with student experiments. The material is at an easier reading level than either the A Beka or Bob Jones University Press courses, and the experiments are easier to set up at home.

If you like to build things and solve math problems —or just like to buy things and solve problems—you'll love this course.

NEW★★
Bob Jones University Press
Physics text: student text, $14.95, softbound; teacher's edition (includes student text with added notes and answers), $29.50. Physics lab manual: student edition, $7.95; teacher's edition, $10.50. Shipping extra.

Here's another BJUP science course we like! Once you get past the first paragraphs of the introduction, in which the authors attempt unconvincingly to reassure the student that physics is not "a form of academic torture" (better not to raise the issue in the first place—it always makes me nervous when the doctor says it isn't going to hurt!) what you have here is a well-written textbook with fascinating sidelights on the history of physics.

Physics for Christian Schools features excellent explanations, examples, and problem sets. The Facets of Physics sidebars make physics real with explanations of the physics of how things work, from fuel cells, to ice skating, to particle accelerators, to diesel trains. Cartoons spice up the text and make the examples more memorable. It's all in two colors: no full-color fancy graphics.

Now, I'm not going to kid you. There's a lot of math here. However, it could be worse. You get a lot of examples worked for you, and the authors do try to make it all make sense in English, using lots of word pictures. Consider this example, introducing the concept of momentum:

> Momentum measures an object's motion. For example, an object with large momentum is harder to stop than an object with small momentum. What properties do you think affect momentum?
>
> The first property affecting momentum should be obvious, after a little thought. Which is easier to stop—a 10,000-kg truck moving at 50 km/hr. or a 0.05-kg tennis ball moving at the same speed? You can stop the tennis ball with one hand, but your whole body would not stop the truck! Therefore, the mass of an object affects its momentum.

The book is divided into units, each made up of several chapters. Unit 1 introduces the scientific method, scientific notation, measurement (the same stuff you studied at the beginning of your chemistry course). Unit 2, on mechanics, covers motion in one, two, and three dimensions (vectors and scalars), dynamics, circular motion, Newton's laws (with lots of word problems), work and energy, conservation of energy, momentum, and periodic motion. Unit 3, on thermal energy, covers properties of matter, expansion and temperature, thermal energy and heat, and the laws of thermodynamics. Unit 4, on electricity and magnetism, introduces fluid mechanics (I don't recall seeing this topic in other high-school courses), electric charge and fields, electrodynamics, magnetism, electromagnetism, and electronics. Unit 5, optics, is the usual light-and-wave properties: reflection, refraction,

and so on. Unit 6, on modern physics, introduces relativity, quantum physics, and nuclear physics. Every other chapter or so is followed by a one- or two-page biography of some famous physicist.

The physics lab manual is pretty standard, with illustrated experiments keyed to the book's chapters. Each experiment has a goal, materials list, explanation, step-by-step procedure, photo or line drawing of the equipment setup, and tables to fill in or calculation sheets to fill out. Finally you write your conclusions on the experiment. Tables, calculations, and conclusions are written right in the lab manual. The teacher's manual does not tell you how to construct any of this equipment, but does has a general equipment list for the year. Some of the equipment is intended to be homemade, judging from the setup illustrations.

The excellent teacher's guide to the text does tell you how to make a bunch of lab equipment (Leyden jars, van de Graff generators, etc.) for in-class demonstrations of the chapter concepts. It also includes teaching objectives and notes for each chapter and answers to all the questions. You absolutely should get the teacher's edition, which includes a regular copy of the student text (no special teacher notes) as well as the teacher's guide to the text, if you plan to use this course.

The First Steam Engine

NEW**
EDC Publishing, Inc.
Introduction to Physics, $6.95. Combined volume, *The Usborne Book of Science*, also includes biology and chemistry, $14.95 hardbound. Add 15% shipping. Ages 12–adult.

Topics in EDC's *Introduction to Physics* include the following (remember, the whole book is only 48 pages long): What is physics? All about energy (includes a neat rubber-band experiment to surprise your friends). Light energy (make a sundial!). How a camera or other lens works. Reflection and refraction. Color (make a color wheel!). Heat energy. How does heat travel (including an experiment on which type spoon handle makes the best conductor). Sounds, noises, and music (sound waves, how to produce them and store the data for replay). Mechanics. Electricity and magnetism (including the ol' lemon-storage-battery experiment and plans for making your own electric motor). Electromagnetic spectrum. BASIC program for calculating how much electricity your appliances use. Glossary. Answers to puzzles. General index.

A lot for your money, and a good browse for anyone thinking of taking or reviewing a physics course.

NEW★★
Harper Collins Publishers
Conceptual Physics 730 pp., hardback, $52. Workbook/practice sheets, $8.50. Add $3 shipping. Check your local college bookstore for better prices.

Conceptual Physics by Paul Hewitt is the most user-friendly physics text I have seen. While it is impossible to teach physics in depth without including logic and mathematics, Hewitt has avoided the common problem of most physics text authors whose books sound like lectures loaded with strings of mathematical equations and conclusions delivered in a monotone voice.

Paul Hewitt feels that physics is more basic than either chemistry or biology. So he has written a text that covers physical concepts that affect all of us, in a format that appeals to even those who are not interested in any further science study. Quantitative math calculations are not stressed, and "equations are seen to be guides to thinking rather than recipes for algebraic manipulation . . . ." Thus, unlike other physics texts, *Conceptual Physics* does not require a background in higher math.

Hewitt uses common examples and familiar illustrations to explain concepts. For example, in explaining the principle behind optical fibers, Hewitt relates it to the hair of polar bears which are actually transparent optical fibers. Physics presented in this way becomes fascinating, understandable, and easy to remember.

Each chapter includes review questions to help students summarize what they have learned, exercises to stimulate thinking and understanding of concepts, and home projects—simple experiments that can serve as lab work. Topics covered are: mechanics, properties of matter, heat, sound, electricity and magnetism, atomic and nuclear physics, and relativity and astrophysics. The instructor's manual, which contains answers to the problems, is not available to home schoolers, unfortunately.

Conceptual Physics is designed for use as either a college text or high school level text. Because Hewitt writes about physics in clear, non-mathematical language, even parents without science backgrounds can read the book and adapt the information to fit all ages.—Cathy Duffy

NEW★★
University of Nebraska-Lincoln
Tuition: $72 resident, $76 nonresident. Add course price to basic tuition. Physics, $193/semester (1 and 2). Add $16 handling. Grades 9–12.

UNL's accredited high school science courses have the additional benefit of including all necessary equipment. You get a ton of mini kits and apparatus: optics, waves, dynamic carts, steel balls, and so on, just to name a smidgin of what comes with your course. Good for those who prefer secular instruction or the feedback of a correspondence-school instructor. For more details see the UNL review in the Correspondence Programs section of Volume 1 (it's one of the full-service programs).

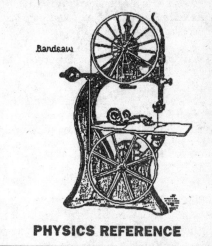

Bandsaw

PHYSICS REFERENCE

NEW★★
EDC Publishing, Inc.
Dictionary of Physics, $9.95 paperbound or $15.95 library-bound. Combined volume, *Dictionary of Science,* also includes biology and chemistry, $21.95 paperbound. Add 15% shipping. Ages 11–adult.

EDC's *Dictionary of Physics* is great for learning or reviewing scientific terminology and basic concepts. The book is organized into full-color sections on mechanics and general physics, heat, waves, electricity and magnetism, and atomic and nuclear physics. The final black-and-white section includes quantities and units, equations/symbols/graphs, measurements, accuracy and errors, fields and forces, vectors and scalars, numbers, circuit symbols, elements and constants, properties of atomic substances, a glossary, and a fine general index.

I suggest that you use the *Dictionary of Physics* both as a reference work *and* as a handy desk aid for when you run across a concept in your science book that you just don't get. It's also is a great review tool and study aid, since it's so well organized by topic. Recommended.

CHAPTER TWENTY-ONE

ENGINEERING

To put it another way, Good Old American Know How. Or should I say, "Good Old American Used to Know How"?

Engineering is science strictly bounded by reality. If you can't build it and test it, it ain't engineering. Scientists can theorize; engineers have to make it work. Dependably. On time. Within budget.

Regular folks may not be able to follow all the latest scientific theories, but we can easily tell if an engineer has done his job or not. I may not understand what those physicist guys are doing with their particle accelerator, but I can tell if my boom box doesn't work. If the dam breaks, or the office building falls down, or the TV set explodes, nobody's going to care about the engineer's wonderful theories as to why it *should* have worked.

Science touches our political lives. Engineering touches our everyday lives. Whether you're for or against nuclear power is likely to, for better or for worse, be a direct reflection of your party politics. Whether you know how to use a fuse box or not doesn't depend on such things.

So why do we spend so much energy teaching kids science, much of which is dubious and riddled with politics, and hardly any time showing them how things work?

ENGINEERING MEANS SOLVING PROBLEMS

Engineering is:

1) Defining your inputs—what goes into this device?

2) Defining the desired outputs—what is it supposed to do?

3) Listing your assumptions—what are your variables? What can go wrong, and what are you assuming will not go wrong? (Hint: Expect *everything* to go wrong!)

4) Designing the "black box" that turns your inputs into the outputs.

5) Finally, testing out the design to see if it works. This includes designing the tests.

As a mindset, engineering is the ability to look at a problem, dissect it without sentimentality, concentrate on the desired result, and make allowances for real-world constraints. The boy who, wanting to play Indian, whittles a tree branch into a bow and tests out different strings to see which works best, is really playing engineer. Other women had dreamed of an easier way to cook, but Lillian Gilbreth, the engineer, invented the efficiency kitchen because she broke down the problem into a series of questions and then answered those questions. People who simply fantasize about what they'd like to see someday, or whose proposed solutions would only work in some nonexistent utopia, are not engineers.

BOOKS ON ENGINEERING

EDC Publishing
Usborne's Electronic World series: *Films & Special Effects, Audio & Radio, TV & Video*, $5.95 each. Young Engineers series: *Superbikes, Supertrains, Supercars*, $5.95 each. *How Machines Work, How Things Began*, $6.95 each paperbound or $13.96 each library-bound. Add 15% shipping.

Absolutely terrific introductions to basic engineering and its applications, for preteens and up. Usborne, an English company represented in the U.S.A. by EDC, has the best, most colorful books around on almost any subject. Each page is artistically laid out with color pictures, diagrams, cutaway illustrations, captions, cartoons, and text to illustrate the principles discussed on that page. All is done with humor and the information conveyed is actually interesting. The overall effect is that of a series of topnotch magazine pieces crossed with a comic book.

If you or your teen don't feel quite ready to tackle heavy-duty engineering, Usborne's *How Machines Work* and *How Things Began* are excellent. Written for ages 7–15, these highly visual books break mechanical pro-

cesses down into simple, illustrated steps. They're also fun to read! (I should mention that *How Things Began* is a look at the history of inventions, not a treatise on origins!)

Not that you need consider the Electronic World or Young Engineers series especially difficult. People of all ages enjoy these books. I'm 35, and I sneak off by myself to read them when they arrive at our house. On the other hand, our sons, at the ages of five and six respectively, chose of their own free will to spend hours with the Usborne Electronic World series. We hand out these books as prizes to our children for special accomplishments. 'Nuff said!

EDC Publishing
Introduction To series: *Electronics, Satellites & Space Stations, Lasers,* and *Robotics*, $6.95 each. Add 15% shipping. Ages 12–adult.

Interested in the physics of engineering—how things work, not just on the snap-this-component-to-that-component level, but in why the components work in the first place? EDC Publishing has great introductions to electronics, lasers, and so on that actually *explain* these subjects. Each book in the series is wholesome and well balanced. Cheerful cartoon people demonstrate scientific principles throughout each book. Simple experiments are provided along with gorgeous illustrations (full-color in the first 32 pages, black-and-white in the last 16) and simple explanations of difficult concepts. You even get a BASIC program to type in at the end of each book!

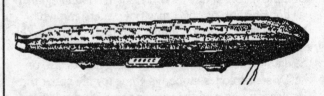

NEW**
Teachers' Laboratory, Inc.
Wheels at Work, Bubbles, Messing Around with Water Pumps and Siphons, Messing Around with Baking Chemistry, Messing Around with Drinking Straw Construction, $7.95 each. Add 10% shipping (minimum $2). Ages 8 and up.

I like Bernie Zubrowski. Since I finished Volume 2 I have been told Bernie is a male (Bernard, not Bernice). So now I can say *he* writes great science books for kids!

Take *Messing Around with Drinking Straw Construction*. In anyone else's hands, a book with that title would have featured some cute patterns for kids to make using drinking straws. Since Bernie wrote it, the book is about using and testing frames made of drinking straws to learn the basic rules of how to design strong structures. First, kids learn how to make frames that don't wiggle. Then they experiment with small and large drinking-straw houses and bridges, eventually graduating to serious-looking structures made out of wooden dowels and large rubber bands. The book is profusely illustrated with drawings illustrating design principles and photographs of kids making these structures. Thanks to the clear directions and drawings, any kid eight and up (better yet, several kids eight and up working together) can make everything in the book. Don't underestimate these books, though. If you're a typical adult, you probably don't know one-tenth of the engineering principles effortlessly taught in *Messing About with Drinking Straw Construction*. After reading it, you'll never look at a bridge or skyscraper the same way again!

Bubbles, also by Bernie, solved a problem at my house. We had bought my daughter Sarah a Bubble Thing for her birthday. This gizmo, advertised as making the world's hugest bubbles, got busted before Sarah had any real fun with it. We don't have to get her a new one, though, since *Bubbles* explains how to make huge bubbles using a couple of tin cans or two drinking straws and about three feet of light string. The book gets into bubble sculpture, soap-film curves, bubble machines, tabletop dome houses made of bubbles, bubble building blocks, bubble sandwiches (picture blowing bubbles between the two layers of a thermal window), measuring bubbles, shrinking bubbles, and observing bubbles. Along the way kids can't help but learn some science and architectural principles. I know this book will be a hit—my kids, bubble fiends all, had invented several of its activities before we ever saw it.

Wheels at Work is perhaps the most obviously educational of the trio of Bernie books Teachers' Laboratory sent me. You will get to build your very own gears, water wheel, windmill, windlass, and paddle wheel. You will use store-bought pulleys to experiment with, discovering which pulley setups work best. All the other gizmos can be manufactured at home out of nothing more complicated than tin cans, paper cups, broomsticks, wire coat hangers, and masking tape. Once you get good at building water wheels, you can build a mechanical music maker and a bubble-blowing machine. Or how about a rubber-band powered paddle boat for the bathtub?

Your kids will learn buckets of real engineering skills from these books

Bernie Zubrowski has also written science activity books entitled *Messing Around with Baking Chemistry* and *Messing Around with Water Pumps and Siphons*. Also activity books on clocks, balloons, tops, and raceways. These I haven't seen, but I can just imagine the skull-popping surprises they must hide.

ENGINEERING KITS AND GAMES

Remember the hours of fun you had with your good ol' Erector set? How dazzled you were when the Christmas wrappings were torn off and it sat revealed in all its glory! The little wheels you could stick onto axles would really turn. Imagine! And although the cheap little all-purpose tool that came with the set was quickly lost, you just as quickly found that Dad's tools worked even better. The happy hours flew by as you built racing cars and space robots.

Or perhaps you were a Lincoln Logs fan. How you pestered for more kits so you could build bigger and better log houses and bigger and better log villages! You hated having to take them apart and zealously guarded your creations from your kid brothers and sisters.

These classic toys of our youth have been joined by an array of proto-engineering devices that would have made Leonardo da Vinci green with envy. Today's construction kit can walk and soon will talk. Some get chummy with your computer. This is serious design material, folks!

UPDATED**
Ampersand Press
AC/DC game, $7.95. Shipping $2.75. Items shipped UPS. Ages 8 and up.

The neatest introduction to the study of electrical wiring and currents that I've seen, Ampersand's *AC/DC*

Electric Circuit Game is played with a deck of special cards. Cards depict energy sources, wires, switches, energy users, and fuses. The object of the game is to construct workable circuits. Players may get "shocked" or "shorted," so watch out! You can't help but learn the rudiments of electricity playing *AC/DC*. I wish someone had given me this game before I went to engineering school (but then, it probably hadn't been invented way back then!).

fischertechnik

No, that's not a typo; fischertechnik is spelled with a small "f." This German company has the highest quality serious engineering construction kits around. See the Timberdoodle review.

NEW ✶✶
LEGO DACTA
TECHNIC 1, $49, ages 7 and up. TECHNIC 2, $66.50, ages 10 and up. Teacher's guide for each set, $10 each. Add 5% shipping.

I love 'em, I love 'em, I love 'em, I love 'em. After years of wishing for a systematic hands-on engineering curriculum, my wish has been granted. The new TECHNIC kits from LEGO DACTA are everything I wished for, and more!

First of all, the kits are beautiful. Pieces are constructed of colorful, sturdy plastic and beautifully engineered. Second, the brilliant designers of this program (God bless 'em!) have put the pieces together in a compartmentalized molded-plastic storage case. This means *no* little TECHNIC pieces crunching underfoot or getting eaten by the vacuum cleaner. In fact, the first exercise in each kit is taking the pieces out of the little plastic bags and learning to put them away neatly in their proper places! Third, the 20 step-by-step Activity Cards included in each kit are *wonderful*. Full-color illustrations show real-life examples of the principles you are learning right along with drawings of the models you are constructing. The accompanying

teacher's guide to each kit explains the assignments, gives in-depth instruction in the engineering principles, and provides numerous follow-up activities. *You need the teacher's guide for each kit,* since there are no words on the cards, just illustrations of the project steps.

Here's how it works. You open the kit. You take out an activity card. You do the activities on the card. After you've finished one card, move on to the next. Can it get any simpler than this? Not only that, individual activities can be completed within 20 minutes!

TECHNIC 1, the "Simple Machines" set for children ages 7 and up, starts with simple frames and how to make frames rigid. Further activities teach principles of levers, moving objects by sliding and rolling, gears, rotation, transference of energy from one form to another, ways of lifting, steering, and wind and water power. No complicated terminology—you *do* things and then discuss them in everyday language. Each model can be built within 20 minutes using some of the 179 pieces!

TECHNIC 2, "Transmission Systems," includes a 4.5 volt motor, worm and differential gears, and chain links among its 278 pieces. This set includes more challenging projects—like models of kitchen mixers, cars, and robots—and is intended for children ages 9 and up. Like the TECHNIC 1 kit, the first cards teach how to put away the kit pieces and the difference between movable and rigid frames. Both kits also include the same theme studies (on different levels): Green Fingers, a theme about garden tools and gardening; Away We Go, a transportation theme; and Home Sweet Home, a theme centered on household utensils and equipment. From here on it gets quite different, as the TECHNIC 2 kit dives into using the provided motor. You'll investigate belt transmissions, build and use a vibrating machine (to study the need for balance and symmetry in machinery), work with chain/gear/worm transmissions, set up drives that use transmission through a right angle, practice translating rotary motion to up-and-down motion, build simple vehicles and a differential, and build cranes, conveyor belts, and robots.

Many of the follow-up activities suggested in the teacher's guides will be a lot easier if you get Bernie Zubrowski's *Drinking Straw Construction* and *Wheels* books from Teachers' Laboratory. These give the principles and steps for building many of the suggested non-kit projects.

Until fischertechnik decides to produce simple, sequential activities *in English* and inexpensive compartmentalized boxes for its kit pieces, these new LEGO DACTA kits will remain, in my opinion, the best engineering education buy. Combine with the *Drinking Straw Construction* and *Wheels* books from Teachers' Laboratory for a full-orbed engineering education!

UPDATED★★
OWI Inc.
Catrat, $59.95. Grand Piano, $38.95. MOVIT WAO II, $109.95. MOVIT Line Tracker, $59.95. Many other kits available. Shipping extra. Ages 10–adult.

While walking in the Heath/Zenith shop one day, in the merry, muggy month of August, we saw to our surprise a display of robot kits. Not just any old robot kits, mind you, but "educational electronic robot kits."

OWI's line of MOVIT kits is a series of computerized, logic-controlled battery robot kits designed to teach the basic principles of robotic sensing and locomotion. Each comes with preassembled PC boards, hardware, and mechanical drive systems. Parts come in little numbered plastic bags. Instructions refer to the numbers on the bag, so you can always tell what part they are talking about. You only need basic hand tools to put these little critters together, and most little human critters over the age of ten are supposed to be able to handle the job.

Each robot uses a different type of movement or has a different sensor. "Mr. Bootsman," for example, has six insectlike legs, two-speed movement, and a control box. He can run or walk forward or backwards, or even turn in circles. You can program him, or use the wired control to make him play slow-mo soccer, etc. "Peppy," a kit we put together as a family project, is lots of fun to run around the room. When its sound sensor comes into contact with a wall or other obstacle or hears a loud noise, such as a hand clap, it automatically reverses direction for a preset time and then zooms off on a new course to the left of its first

one. "Line Tracker" follows a black line drawn on white paper, using a photo-interrupter "eye." "Catrat" moves forward while you are pressing its remote-control button—and changes direction when you release the button! "Grand Piano" has a 47-note memory, and can play 15 preprogrammed tunes. You put it together yourself from kit form. "Robotic Arm" can be programmed to perform simple tasks, using the attached three-button input device. These are just a few of the available kits, with more coming out all the time.

OWI kits are cute as all getout, that is, not cuddly-fuzzy-animal cute but neat-little-buckets-of-gears cute. Only problem is you will want to collect them all!

UPDATED★★
Sanyei American Corporation
(formerly Play-Jour)
Introductory 175, $15.99. Starter 200 (10 projects and models), $21.99. Explorer 250 (20 projects and models), $28.99. Intermediate 400 (22 projects and models), $34.99. Inventor 450 (30 projects and models), $49.99. Advanced 500 (39 projects and models), $46.99. Deluxe 700 (56 projects and models), $69.99. Expert 1000 (100 projects and models), $84.99. Capsela Scientific course: set of Capsela Scientific components, $120; *Capsela Scientific* manual, $30; 3-lesson sampler workshop, $30; hand generator kit with lamp, $20; capsela storage bag, $12. Capsee-Kid Discovery Toys, Capsela Building Discovery Toys series also available. All prices postpaid.

Capsela kits from Sanyei American Corporation are a system of motors and gears housed in see-through capsules with an assortment of moving accessories. You can easily snap together the components to create all sorts of vehicles, devices, and machines: a racing car whose speed you can gear up or down, a vacuum that cleans, a fireboat that sprays water, even a computerized remote control robot with a 96-command memory, and many more that really work. The possibilities are limitless as all sets are totally interchangeable.

Each set also includes the "See How It Works" 32-page science booklet that explains how and why things work. This is an abridged version of the *Capsela Scientific* curriculum guide.

For classroom teachers, Sanyei now offers *Capsela Scientific*, a hands-on science curriculum with a 25-lesson manual written by Dr. Clifford Swartz. The kit includes teacher overviews, notes, and student hand-out masters, along with the Capsela parts to build over 110 high-interest working models. For example, students build a propeller boat to demonstrate buoyancy; a car demonstrates friction, traction, motion, and movement; a blinkmobile demonstrates blinking light behavior; and so on. Lessons also cover the concepts of electricity, Newton's Third Law, work, force, energy, and more.

Capsela is just buckets of fun for kids of all ages—even those with moustaches and beards!

NEW★★
Timberdoodle
Fischertechnik Basic Sets: Start 200 set, $70 (needed with all other sets); Start 200/1 set, $29; Motors & Gears set, $55; Statiks set, $54; all for ages 6 and up. Advanced Sets: Electromechanics set, $105; Pneumatics+ set, $110; Electronics set, $160; all for ages 10 or 12 and up. Robotics, computing, and Geometrix kit prices TBA. Shipping 15% ($4 minimum, $15 maximum).

The Start 200 set is the basis of all fischertechnik sets. You need to buy this one first, no matter which other kits you're interested in, because the items in this one are needed *along with* the items in the other ones to do the projects in the more advanced sets. You can build up to 200 different models with the Start 200 set, which includes nearly 400 pieces ranging from base plates to 100 chain links. Wordless plans for 17 models include a road grader, mobile crane, tractor, catapult, helicopter, and more.

The Start 200/1 is the recommended second step. (You need the Start 200 first, as I said above.) It adds additional pieces—like a universal joint, disc-cams, and bevel gear wheels—plus extras of pieces already included in the Start 200. With it you can build more working models, like a giant forklift, conveyor, and chute.

Motors & Gears, another basic set, also builds on the Start 200. It includes loads of different gears, a six-volt motor, a reduction gear box, a conveyor belt, and much more. Projects include a vertical lift, fan, gearbox, lathe, and more.

The Statik set is for the child who loves to build working models of large cranes, towers, runabouts, bridges, merry-go-rounds, and Ferris wheels. It contains hundreds of struts in various lengths and all the connectors you'll need to build the projects above.

Now, let's look at the advanced sets. Meant for teens or advanced preteens on up to 90-year-olds, these include manuals with instructions in theory and "schematic skills" (e.g., how to read the project diagrams), as well as information on how to control motors through electrical, electronic, or air-control (pneumatic) systems. They include clear demonstrations of technical processes and principles and step-by-step directions that logically progress through these more advanced topics.

The final step? Controlling your project from your home computer! The fischertechnik robotics kits, for those who can afford them, are a great way to introduce robotics just as it is actually used in real-world applications.

The Electromechanics set includes a key, switch, slip ring, magnets, electromagnet, vibratory spring, thermal bimetallic strip, lamps, contacts, leads, and more—everything you need to study circuits and electrical models. Projects range from rotating searchlights to motor control and overload protection for a model crane . . . from thermostats to a Morse code transmitter that also receives code on a paper tape recorder! Lots more.

The Pneumatics+ kit has the special parts you need for air circuits: single and double cylinders, diaphragm cylinders, directional and flow control valves, and tubing and connectors. It even includes a small fischertechnik compressor to supply compressed air to your projects. Projects include an air engine, a pneumatic excavator, and more.

The Electronics kit includes parts for steering and controlling models. You can put together working models of a photoconductive cell, an alarm system, a handclap switch, an automatic flashing light, and more.

Fischertechnik presently has three robotics kits, each available for IBM compatibles, Apple II series (except IIc), and Commodore 64/128 computers. Kits come with software and detailed instructions. The Computing Experimental kit includes experiments using turtle graphics commands, photoresistor light measurement, hot conductor temperature measurement, and more. The Robotics Computing Kit enables you to build 10 projects, from a basic traffic light with pedestrian button to a solar cell tracking platform that will maintain a constant angle to the sun. This one is popular for beginners. The Training Robot Three-Axis Arm kit goes a step farther. You can program this robot arm (which works like those on factory assembly lines) by stepping it through the desired activity or by computer programming in BASIC.

Bill and the boys spent an enthralled couple of weeks testing out one of fischertechnik's robotics kits. The interface to the Apple IIe hooks into the game port on the motherboard. The kit we were testing had four on/off switched inputs, two rheostat inputs, and three on/off switched outputs—enough to run two motors and an electromagnet for picking up objects. The software provided with the set uses a BASIC-like language to program your robot. The model they built solved King Tut's pyramid. Watching the model work was well worth the time it took to build it.

The brand-new fischertechnik Geometrix kits are the fanciest, yet simplest, engineering construction kits I've seen. Not to be confused with fischertechnik's other engineering construction toys, these have no moving parts. No pulleys, no wheels, no gears. Instead, you get beautifully-engineered chunky grey blocks of various intriguing shapes, which you connect with little red strips that slide into slots in the blocks. When put together, they make professional-looking buildings. You can make walls with holes of any shape . . . turrets with pointy cones on the top . . . almost anything you want. Anything you make with these sets looks wonderful. Some of the sets have curved and conical pieces; others have more rectangular-shaped blocks. All come with idea books showing various constructions for your child to model. You really have to see and handle these building pieces to appreciate the beauty and ingenuity of their design.

Timberdoodle is at present the sole importer of these kits for the home-schooling market.

NEW**
Timberdoodle
LEGO™ TECHNIC 1 Activity Center, $75. LEGO TECHNIC 1 Set, $44. Add 10% shipping. Grades 3–12.

What comes in a plastic case that looks like a huge red LEGO brick, includes 110 activity cards, 7 index cards, a 144-page teacher's guide plus a 24-page teacher's supplement, and teaches thinking skills by having kids create and build working models to solve real-world engineering problems? It's the brand-new LEGO TECHNIC 1 Activity Center!

For some reason, the folks at LEGO disbelieve that home schoolers and parents in general would be interested in this program. Timberdoodle thinks they are wrong, so they put the Activity Center in their catalog and sent me a review sample. (They sell the Activity Center and TECHNIC kits at *discount,* by the way, and since LEGO doesn't sell direct to consumers, you might as well buy your TECHNIC stuff from Timberdoodle.)

Let me explain how the plastic case works first. This is itself an intriguing engineering exercise. When shut, grey plastic straps hold it firmly closed. When opened, you can swivel the two side straps around to lock into holes that keep it just as firmly open, turning it into a display case for the cards and manuals. (It only took me five minutes to figure this out!) Nothing in the teacher's manuals, or anywhere else, explains how to set up the display case, by the way!

You will need a LEGO TECHNIC 1 set to use with the Activity Center, since you can't build working models without any components out of which to build them. As you already know, the TECHNIC 1 set includes 20 step-by-step project cards. The Activity Center includes the same 20 cards, so there is some overlap. However, the teacher's manual for the Activity Center gives many additional teaching tips and helps for these cards, and goes much, *much* farther than the TECHNIC 1 set in teaching kids how things work.

Topics covered in this Center are forces and structures, levers, pulleys, gears, wheels and axles, and energy. Each topic is covered in many different ways, and the tops of the cards are color-coded to reflect this.

The green Exploration cards introduce kids to the building materials. Kids play with many different variations of the same device, for example, building lots of different wheeled vehicles or spinning tops. The extension suggestions on these cards often include imaginative writing assignments or add-on features you can build onto your project.

The cards with a blue band across the top are the Guided Investigation cards (same as those in the TECHNIC 1 kit), with step-by-step instructions for building specific models.

Those with a yellow band are Simulation Activity cards. Kids design and build working models of specific items, but the card doesn't show them how. (The teacher's manual lists extra materials to be used, questions to be asked, and has a photo of a finished model, so you can give wise adult guidance as needed.)

The red Invention Activity cards simply give a problem, e.g., "The castle kitchen has a mouse . . . The cook wants to catch it and release it outside." Your child then is supposed to invent and build a device to solve the problem, e.g., a better mousetrap! Since there are hundreds of possible solutions to each invention question, the teacher's manual supplies, along with ways to test each invention, only a rough sketch of some of the main ideas usually built into the inventions.

To make life more interesting, activity cards are grouped around themes like Medieval Castle (build a movable covered ladder so the invading knights can scale the castle walls), Farm (build a working model of a wheelbarrow), The Harbor (invent a machine to help clean up the dock), Amusement Park (build a working model of a gear box to open and close the curtains for the puppet show), Getting Around (build working models of a baby stroller and skateboard), and The Big Race (build your own land yacht and rubber band-powered racing car). I've listed only one or two of the activities under each theme, just to give you a taste of them. All cards have bright graphics, and some have humorous pictures as well, to draw kids into eagerly solving the problems.

COMPARING FISCHERTECHNIK TO LEGO TECHNIC TO CAPSELA TO OWI

Quality engineering construction kits are a serious investment. Most of us can't afford to spend $50, $100 or more on a set that doesn't work out. So I have spent hours pondering the characteristics of fischertechnik v. LEGO TECHNIC v. Capsela v. OWI, while my husband and children spent hundreds of hours playing with them!

Hearing back from our team of experts, plus what I could glean from the folks at Timberdoodle, who have also spent years looking into this, here's what we find.

Fischertechnik invented their engineering modeling kits 40 years ago, not for kiddie use, but for engineering professionals. Today engineers use these components to put together models of new installations, to debug them, and to train the professionals who will operate them. We're talking heavy-duty, quality, realistic design here, good enough for real industrial engineers to use. Fischertechnik provides gears, pulleys, wheels, universal joints, winches, cams, motors, struts, connectors, rivets, gussets, and many other real-world-type goodies. Their components slide together and interlock in uncomplicated ways. When you put the pieces together, they *stay* together until you take them apart. This is important when making motorized or moving models, where cheaper components tend to fly apart.

On the negative side, children are not fischertechnik's primary market, so apart from the wordless manuals included with each set there are currently no other project books. Fischertechnik is used extensively in European schools, and Timberdoodle is pursuing the possibilities of importing English versions of the European textbooks, but that may be a year or more away.

Because children are LEGO's only market, LEGO's support materials for younger ages are matchless. Children are naturally drawn to LEGO's bright colors, and since most of them have been weaned on LEGO's preschool version, DUPLO, working with the pieces comes naturally to them. Major complaints with LEGO TECHNIC are (1) since LEGO has a policy of using the same interconnectable shapes, the finished models aren't as realistic as fischertechnik's and (2) LEGO projects sometimes fall apart (especially when motorized). Also, while their TECHNIC courses touch on a number of different topics, they lack the depth of fischertechnik's separate kits for pneumatics, electromechanics, electronics, and robotics.

Capsela is lots of fun, but isn't as real-world oriented as either LEGO TECHNIC or fischertechnik. On the other hand, it isn't that expensive, either! The new *Capsela Scientific* curriculum makes Capsela a serious educational contender in the realm of teaching physical-science principles, though it isn't an accurate engineering modeling tool.

Finally, if motorized robotniks are what turns you on, you're definitely an OWI Movit customer.

So which is best? You decide!

If you've already invested in regular LEGO kits, you might want to look seriously at their TECHNIC kits and Activity Center for a peerless hands-on thinking skills course. If you are looking mainly for mechanical, practical science, and engineering skills, and especially if it matters to you that your models are as realistic as possible, look seriously at fischertechnik. If you just want to build things and learn simple engineering principles, Capsel and Owi are a lot of fun. Or get them *all*, if you can afford it, and your kids will be able to design everything from bridges to completely automated factories!

CHAPTER TWENTY-TWO

SCIENCE EQUIPMENT

People always ask home schoolers, "But how can you do science at home? Don't you need a lab to do science?" The answer: "It's easy. I just pick up my science supply catalogs and I *have* a lab!"

NEW★★
Alpha Omega Publications
Elementary Science Kit, $179.95 (grades 2–8). Slide kit, $16.95. Microscopes also available. Shipping extra.

Here's a conveniently packaged kit of basic lab equipment designed for use with Alpha Omega courses.

The Elementary Science Kit includes all the basic equipment and supplies you need to set up a home, school, or support group science lab: beakers of various sizes, wire, clamps, a graduated cylinder, pipet droppers, filter paper, Erlenmeyer flask, funnel, stirring rods, test tubes of various sizes, test tube rack, thermometers, tubing, and bunches more. You can add specialty items (which Alpha Omega kindly lists by the LIFEPAC in which they are needed) in order to do all the experiments in Alpha Omega's grades 2–8 courses. You can also buy individual items as needed to replace kit parts that get lost or broken.

Alpha Omega also has the microscope and prepared slides you need for their 10th-grade biology course. Some lab chemicals and specialized lab apparatus for the 11th-grade chemistry course must be purchased elsewhere.

They do have a $299.95 physics-lab kit for regular schools which includes all the materials needed for the 12th-grade physics course, but for some reason they figure most home schoolers can't afford it! (If teaching your kids physics is an important part of your life, and you have that kind of money, you might want to ask for their school science-kit brochure.)

UPDATED★★
American Science & Surplus (formerly Jerryco)

Wonderful widgets from the world of surplus. Only the American Science & Surplus catalog can make a petri dish sound enticing. The man who writes the catalog description has a wry sense of humor and a lot of imagination. Catch this description of a humble petri dish:

CULTURE DISHES

Caviar is of course a culture dish. So is Foie Gras. These are neither. Rather, they are round plastic dishes just under 2" in dia. with tight fitting lids. The notion is to put nutrient agar or another life-sustaining medium into the dish, to add some microbiological life form, and to watch nature produce mold, vaccine, fungus, and other unappetizing life forms. Ralph Petri, or one of his cousins, must have had a hand in the process, as the Becton, Dickinson package insists these are 50 x 9 mm Petri dishes, their style 1006. Packaged in sterile sleeves of (20). You may share the biologist's notion that a swarm of microbes constitute a culture, or you may simply want to understate your Beluga at a plush picnic. Either way, they are culture dishes.

American Science & Surplus not only sells motors and sprockets and gears and everything else, but generously shares ideas about what to do with all these gizmos. Constantly changing inventory as industrial America makes new mistakes. Many items are military surplus, as you may have guessed, but a lot are components of mass-produced items that bombed in the market. Mechanically-minded folks can make something with them. Not-so-mechanical folks can still make use of the educational-product bargains dotted here and there. Everyone will enjoy reading the catalog!

NEW**
Bob Jones University Press

Good selection of basic science equipment and supplies, coordinated to BJUP science textbooks, offered at attractive prices. Great service, too: BJUP is ultra-friendly to home schoolers.

Christian Light Publications

It's not cheap, but if you want science equipment to perform all your science experiments, CLP has it. CLP's lab materials are available in complete sets or as individual components. Sets are correlated with their science worktexts (a Mennonite-approved updating of the original Alpha Omega Publications texts).

NEW**
Crane's Select Educational Materials

Excellent selection of low-cost science lab equipment specifically chosen for home schoolers. Alcohol burners, beakers, test tube brushes, capillary tubes, clamps and clamp holders, crucibles, graduated cylinders, dissecting sets, funnels, filter paper, Erlenmeyer flasks, glass tubing cutter, goggles for children and adults, scalpels, scoops, stoppers, pipettes, test tubes, glass tubing, you name it. Plus a wide variety of lab chemicals, sold by the individual chemical, and microbiological cultures and supplies.

Crane also *rents* microscope slides of uncommon objects often examined in university courses. These slides do *not* include common material such as human hair, fabrics, etc. We're talking sets of algae, bacteria, protozoa, and so on.

Edmund Scientific Company

Every neat scientific widget under the sun. Microscopes, telescopes, stethoscopes, orotoscopes, binoculars, and the ever-popular sextant (don't leave home without one!). Crazy gifts for the child who has everything, from quarters that "blast off" when you tip the waiter to your personal robot. Everything for serious tinkerers and investigators from ages 6–99, plus a pile of science kits with kid-appeal.

Now tell me honestly, where else can you get a giant gyroscope ($8.95) or a fossil collection ($23.95) or a paper clock kit ($10.95)? Sea monkeys! Butterfly collecting! Make your own perfume! Stargaze! Much, much more! Plus survival gear, tools, photography supplies, and everything else far out and technological.

Heathkit

For the novice hobbyist or serious student of electronics, Heathkit has both home-study courses and of course its famous kits. Build your own oscilloscope or IBM PC-compatible computer (Heath swears it's faster than the original). You won't save all that much money, but it's great experience.

The Heathkit course lineup now includes courses in the following categories: basic electronics, linear integrated-circuits, digital techniques, surface-mount technology, laser technology, data communications and networks, amateur radio, microprocessors, and programming. The training devices you use to perform the course experiments can be ordered either assembled, or for greater educational value you can get them in kit form and assemble them yourself! You can also purchase a Heathkit computer kit, tools and test instruments, and various Heath educational kits (AM radio, burglar alarm, speakerphone, etc.).

Heathkit courses are accredited by the National Home Study Council and the Council on the Continuing Education Unit.

UPDATED★★
Learning Things, Inc.

Learning Things, Inc. does its best to supply all your electrical and science lab needs: microscopes, gyroscopes, scales, mineral collections, scales, laboratory equipment like flexible tubing and funnels, electrical equipment like alligator clips and switches, fiber optics, etc. Anatomical models. Photography supplies. Math manipulatives. Pages and pages and pages of biology equipment, electrical equipment, chemistry equipment, magnetism supplies. Now, how about a deck prism—a replica of a special prism laid flush in the wooden decks of old-time sailing vessels to transmit sunlight between decks? Or a periscope for $5? Or a solar system mobile that spans 3½ feet? Then there are kits for building molecular models, crystal growing, or a DNA model. What about the papermaking kit and book? A complete set of cardboard carpentry tools and accessories? Now, the topper, a technological breakthrough in the science of microscopy: an optical light guide (lightpipe) that collects, condenses, and transmits ambient light to the specimen, eliminating the need for a mirror and all the headaches of making constant adjustments. Would you believe it—a 30x model for $11! If you like hands-on learning and experiments, you owe it to yourself to get this catalog.

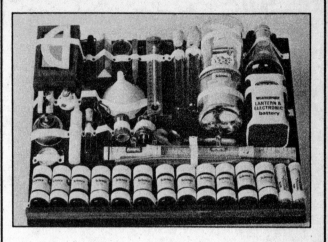

Norris Science Labs and Kits

Mini-Lab, $90. Primary Lab I, $195. Intermediate Lab II, $225. Items may be purchased separately, including the manuals. *Science is Fun* video (VHS or Beta), $50 purchase price. Video rental available. Inquire about discounts for home schoolers.

The ad says, "Now for the first time! ONE SCIENCE LAB equipped for all experiments in any standard science textbook or teacher's guide . . . for elementary and junior high school physical science programs. Ideal For Both Public and Private Schools. Grades K–8."

You have a choice of three lab kits. The Mini-Lab has basic supplies for 50 or so included experiments. Kids can make a thermometer, a friction scale, a steam turbine engine, glass, and a fuse. The Primary Lab I is for grades K–3, and is written up in Volume 2.

Intermediate Lab II contains a formidable array of little labeled bottles holding "safe to use chemicals" (sulfur, starch, soda, white sand, rosin, lime, litmus paper, copper sulfate, borax, acetic acid, and ammonium dichromate for your homemade volcano), along with over 100 items such as a compass, funnel, thermometer, test tubes, flask, battery, measuring cups, beaker, magnets, prism, and test tube rack and clamp. With each of these kits comes a spiral-bound teacher's manual with "easy-to-follow instructions and diagrams."

For those hungry for hands-on demonstrations by a real live science teacher, Norris Science Labs and Kits presents the *Science is Fun* video starring Jack Norris, a man with more than 40 years' experience as a science teacher. Mr. Norris, who has also served as a superintendent of schools and science and math coordinator, demonstrates 19 crowd-pleasing experiments, some correlated with experiments in the various lab kit teacher's manuals.

Norris Science Labs and Kits is a family-owned business willing to answer your questions. Their Mini-Lab "was designed especially for home schoolers—as they do not need a lot of equipment to start, are resourceful enough to make their own, and can add to their science lab apparatus as their interest dictates." Also, Norris Labs will let you purchase items separately. Their catalog contains many fascinating things (live butterfly culture, anyone?) not included in the kits.

SOCIAL STUDIES

CHAPTER TWENTY-THREE

CITIZENSHIP

Kids need to learn how local and state government runs. But the schools aren't teaching them this!

Ever since the days of John Dewey, American schools have required students to take courses in politics. These come labeled as Civics or Government or Citizenship. The idea was to help American children understand their rights and political heritage. This would be a good idea if it were actually carried out. But what good does it do kids to learn about the three branches of the federal government . . . but *not* about how to run for office on their local school board? What good does it do to learn about the histories of the national Republican and Democratic parties . . . but *not* to learn how local parties work?

Most of us, even adults, do not know how local political campaigns are run, much less how to help out in one. We do not understand our state and local government structures or know how to reach the right official when we have a problem. If school textbooks were our only source of information, we wouldn't even know how to register to vote!

Public-school texts fall short in other ways, too. Of the pile of public-school civics texts I have seen, each and every one encouraged dependence on government bureaucrats. The examples given of how "reformers" have "used the American process" always concentrated on how certain people got laws passed that created more bureaucracies. I can't recall a single textbook example of a citizen or group of citizens getting together and *eliminating* a bureaucracy. The "citizenship" taught in these volumes consists of exhorting our children to elect officials who will, in the words of the Declaration of Independence, "erect a Multitude of new Offices, and send hither Swarm of Officers to harass our People, and eat out their Substance."

Christian textbooks have their problems, too. I was only able to find *one* Christian text that devoted more than one or two pages to state and local government (LIFEPACS 2 and 3 of the ninth-grade Alpha Omega social studies course, if you're interested). This helps explain (to me at least) while Christian leaders who get involved in political action invariably end up urging us to spend our leisure hours writing letters to our Congressmen. They must not know that state and local governments *exist!*

You owe it to yourself to become aware of tools for influencing the system. Here in America you can still do a lot more than simply vote for Congressional Candidate A or Congressional Incumbent B. Picketing, lobbying, writing letters to the editor, getting on the media; local party meetings, district canvassing, direct mail; citizens' groups, forums, political conferences—all these and more should be in the political syllabus. It's one thing to choose not to get heavily involved politically. It's another to be unable to do so.

So is this chapter loaded with resources for becoming politically literate? It is not! I just can't find them! Do me a favor, people . . . if you run across a good book or pamphlet written at a high-school level that explains how the state and local political process works, send it to me. In the meantime, it's back to studying the three branches of the federal government. Snore . . .

READ IT FOR YOURSELF

Do you ever get into arguments that go like this:
"XYZ is true!"
"No, it's not!"
"Is!"
"Is not!"
The only way to settle such an argument, we have found in our own family, is to consult an accepted authority. If, for example, we can't agree which land animal is the fastest, we check it out in the encyclopedia. If we are arguing over how to pronounce *progenitor*, we consult the dictionary. If son #1 thinks Ahab was a king of Israel, and son #2 thinks Ahab actually ruled in Judah, a concordance and the Bible will soon settle that question.

Political arguments can be just this dumb. Fur flies back and forth as the debaters fuss over which side has the most voters and which viewpoint ought to prevail. Rarely do they consult the authority—in this case, the United States Constitution—to see what the law of the land *already* says about the subject under discussion.

When it comes to politics, the law in America is supposed to be limited. Our lawgivers, for example, don't have the right to sell the citizens of Massachusetts

into chattel slavery to the Japanese in order to balance the budget. Why? Because slavery is against the Constitution and because the Constitution (even before the anti-slavery amendment) never gave the government the right to enslave free citizens.

Our leaders—whether presidents, congressmen, or judges— have to swear to uphold the Constitution. They do *not* have the right to pass any law they wish, or enforce unwritten laws.

Most political arguments these days tend to ignore the Constitution. The reason is that the vast majority of us have never read it, let alone studied it. It's not even that easy to find a copy—try to the next time you visit a bookstore or library. Failing such knowledge on the part of the citizens, our elected leaders and their unelected bureaucratic friends can, and do, regularly exceed their authority.

Schools go along with this by teaching kids about the "three branches of government," but not about the Constitution's limitations on government. So do educational publishers. Take *World Book Encyclopedia*, for example. Section 8 of Article I of the Constitution gives Congress the power "to coin money, regulate the value thereof, and of foreign coin, and fix the standard of weights and measures." The phrase, "to *coin* money" was deliberately introduced to prevent Congress from issuing paper money, as the Continental Congress had done (with disastrous results) during the Revolutionary War. President after president refused to countenance paper money or any central bank as utterly incompatible with this clear direction in the Constitution. Now see the World Book's comment on this section:

> From this section, along with the section that allows the Congress to regulate commerce and to borrow money, Congress gets its right to charter national banks and to establish the Federal Reserve System.

Tell it to Andy Jackson!
I could go through the Constitution, point by point, showing you how huge swaths of government policy and bureaucracy are illegal according to the highest law of the land. You could then say, "Ain't so! It don't say that!" We could argue back and forth. This gets us nowhere. So I decided instead, as a public service, to pay someone $100 to type the entire Constitution into my computer. Now you can read it *for yourself*. You can see what the Constitution *really* says. Then check out the resources I've slowly gathered together to help us all *understand* our Founding Fathers' long words and sentences. It's culture shock. Guaranteed!

PREAMBLE TO THE CONSTITUTION

We the People of the United States, in Order to form a more perfect Union, establish Justice, insure domestic Tranquility, provide for the common defence, promote the general Welfare, and secure the Blessings of Liberty to ourselves and our Posterity, do ordain and establish this Constitution for the United States of America.

Note: Right here our forefathers made a BIG mistake, and we're still paying for it. They did not acknowledge Christ as the Lord of America. (On the bright side, they also did not acknowledge Mohammed, Buddha, Kali, or the Enlightenment's Goddess of Reason.) Thus, there is no absolute standard underlying the Constitution, unless (as some Supreme Court judges of the past have held) you simply assume that America is a Christian nation. For this very reason, descendants of the Scottish Covenanters for generations refused to take a loyalty oath to the Constitution, thus barring themselves from citizenship and from holding office. Sidelight: the U.S. flag is the first flag of a Western nation NOT to have a cross on it anywhere. This does not mean the Constitution isn't loaded with Christian principles (because it is), or that the Founding Fathers were some sort of deist conspiracy (because they weren't), but that at square one Christians unwittingly disenfranchised themselves from speaking politically in the Name of the Lord.

ARTICLE I [THE LEGISLATIVE BRANCH]

Section 1. All legislative Powers herein granted shall be vested in a Congress of the United States, which shall consist of a Senate and House of Representatives.

Section 2. The House of Representatives shall be composed of Members chosen every second Year by the People of the several States, and the Electors in each State shall have the Qualifications requisite for Electors of the most numerous Branch of the State Legislature.

No Person shall be a Representative who shall not have attained to the Age of twenty five Years, and been seven Years a Citizen of the United States, and who shall not, when elected, be an Inhabitant of that State in which he shall be chosen.

Representative and direct Taxes shall be apportioned among the several States which may be included within this Union, according to their respective Numbers, which shall be determined by adding to the whole Number of free Persons, including those bound to Service for a Term of Years, and excluding Indians not taxed, three fifths of all other Persons. The actual Enumeration shall be made within three Years after the first Meeting of the Congress of the United States, and within every subsequent Term of ten Years, in such Manner as they shall by Law direct. *Note: Federal taxes were to be raised by taxing states, not by taxing individuals. The states were to pay the federal government, thus allowing the states to exercise some control over how their money was spent. This is the opposite of today's "revenue-sharing," where the federal government exercises control over states by threatening to withhold its block grants from those that fail to comply with federal objectives, e.g., seat-belt laws.* The Number of Representatives shall not exceed one for every thirty Thousand, but each State shall have at least one Representative; and until such enumeration shall be made, the State of New Hampshire shall be entitled to chuse three, Massachusetts eight, Rhode-Island and Providence Plantations one, Connecticut five, New-York six, New Jersey four, Pennsylvania eight, Delaware one, Maryland six, Virginia ten, North Carolina five, South Carolina five, and Georgia three.

When vacancies happen in the Representation from any State, the Executive Authority thereof shall issue Writs of Election to fill such Vacancies.

The House of Representatives shall chuse their speaker and other Officers; and shall have the sole Power of Impeachment.

Section 3. The Senate of the United States shall be composed of two Senators from each State, chosen by the Legislature thereof, for six Years; and each Senator shall have one Vote. *Note: Senators were originally appointed by state legislatures, giving the states some con-*

trol in this area also. It also gave rural areas significant power, since state senates had a large proportion of rural representatives.

Immediately after they shall be assembled in Consequence of the first Election, they shall be divided as equally as may be into three Classes. The Seats of the Senators of the first Class shall be vacated at the Expiration of the second Year, of the second Class at the Expiration of the fourth Year, and of the third Class at the Expiration of the sixth Year, so that one third may be chosen every second Year; and if Vacancies happen by Resignation, or otherwise, during the Recess of the Legislature of any State, the Executive thereof may make temporary Appointments until the next Meeting of the Legislature, which shall then fill such Vacancies.

No Person shall be a Senator who shall not have attained to the Age of thirty Years, and been nine Years a citizen of the United States, and who shall not, when elected, be an Inhabitant of that State for which he shall be chosen.

The Vice President of the United States shall be President of the Senate, but shall have no Vote, unless they be equally divided.

The Senate shall chuse their other Officers, and also a President pro tempore, in the Absence of the Vice President, or when he shall exercise the Office of President of the United States.

The Senate shall have the sole Power to try all Impeachments. When sitting for that Purpose, they shall be on Oath or Affirmation. When the President of the United States is tried, the Chief Justice shall preside: And no Person shall be convicted without the Concurrence of two thirds of the Members present.

Judgment in Cases of Impeachment shall not extend further than to removal from Office, and disqualification to hold and enjoy any Office of honor, Trust or Profit under the United States: but the Party convicted shall nevertheless be liable and subject to Indictment, Trial, Judgment and Punishment, according to law.

Section 4. The Times, Places, and Manner of holding Elections for Senators and Representatives, shall be prescribed in each State by the Legislature thereof; but the Congress may at any time by Law make or alter such Regulations, except as to the Places of chusing Senators.

The Congress shall assemble at least once in every Year, and such Meeting shall be on the first Monday in December, unless they shall by Law appoint a different Day.

Section 5. Each House shall be the Judge of the Elections, Returns, and Qualifications of its own Members, and a Majority of each shall constitute a Quorum to do Business; but a smaller Number may adjourn from day to day, and may be authorized to compel the Attendance of absent Members, in such Manner, and under such Penalties as each House may provide.

Each House may determine the Rules of its Proceedings, punish its Members for disorderly Behaviour, and, with the Concurrence of two thirds, expel a Member.

Each House shall keep a journal of its Proceedings, and from time to time publish the same, excepting such Parts as may in their Judgment require Secrecy; and the Yeas and Nays of the Members of either House on any question shall, at the Desire of one fifth of those Present, be entered on the Journal.

Neither House, during the Session of Congress, shall, without the Consent of the other, adjourn for more than three days, nor to any other Place than that in which the two Houses shall be sitting.

Section 6. The Senators and Representatives shall receive a Compensation for their Services, to be ascertained by Law, and paid out of the Treasury of the United States. They shall in all Cases, except Treason, Felony and Breach of the Peace, be privileged from Arrest during their Attendance at the Session of their respective Houses, and in going to and returning from the same; and for any Speech or Debate in either House, they shall not be questioned in any other Place.

No Senator or Representative shall, during the Time for which he was elected, be appointed to any civil Office under the Authority of the United States, which shall have been created, or the Emoluments whereof shall have been increased during such time; and no Person holding any Office under the United States, shall be a Member of either House during his Continuance in Office.

Section 7. All Bills for raising Revenue shall originate in the House of Representatives; but the Senate may propose or concur with Amendments as on other Bills.

Every Bill which shall have passed the House of Representatives and the Senate, shall, before it become a Law, be presented to the President of the United States; If he approve he shall sign it, but if not he shall return it, with his Objections to that House in which it shall have originated, who shall enter the Objections at large on their Journal, and proceed to reconsider it. If after such Reconsideration two thirds of that House shall agree to pass the Bill, it shall be sent, together with the Objections, to the other House, by which it shall likewise be reconsidered, and if approved by two thirds of that House, it shall become a Law. But in all Cases the Votes of both Houses shall be determined by Yeas and Nays, and the Names of the Persons voting for and against the Bill shall be entered on the Journal of each House respectively. If any Bill shall not be returned by the President within ten Days (Sundays excepted) after it shall have been presented to him, the Same shall be a Law, in like Manner as if he had signed it, unless the Congress by their Adjournment prevent its Return, in which Case it shall not be a Law.

Every Order, Resolution, or Vote to which the Concurrence of the Senate and House of Representatives may be necessary (except on a question of Adjournment) shall be presented to the President of the United States; and before the Same shall take Effect, shall be approved by him, or being disapproved by him, shall be repassed by two thirds of the Senate and House of Representatives, according to the Rules and Limitations prescribed in the Case of a Bill.

Section 8. The Congress shall have Power To lay and collect Taxes, Duties, Imposts and Excises, to pay the Debts and provide for the common Defence and general Welfare of the United States; but all Duties, Imposts and Excises shall be uniform throughout the United States;

To borrow Money on the Credit of the United States;

To regulate Commerce with foreign Nations, and among the several states, and with the Indian Tribes; *Note: The "regulating commerce" clause referred to preventing economic warfare between states, not telling individual businessmen how to run their companies.*

To establish an uniform Rule of Naturalization, and uniform Laws on the subject of Bankruptcies throughout the United States;

To coin Money, regulate the Value thereof, and of foreign Coin, and fix the Standard of Weights and Measures; *Note: Congress was specifically forbidden by this section to issue paper money. They had to "coin" money, requiring a precious-metals standard. Coins aren't made out of paper. Nothing here gives Congress the right to give the Federal Reserve (a private bank) the right to create money out of thin air and charge the taxpayers for it.*

To provide for the Punishment of counterfeiting the securities and current Coin of the United States;

To establish Post Offices and post Roads;

To promote the Progress of Science and useful Arts, by securing for limited Times to Authors and Inventors the exclusive Right to their respective Writings and Discoveries;

To constitute Tribunals inferior to the supreme Court;

To define and punish Piracies and Felonies committed on the high Seas, and Offences against the law of Nations;

To declare War, grant Letters of Marque and Reprisal, and make Rules concerning Captures on Land and Water;

To raise and support Armies, but no Appropriation of Money to that Use shall be for a longer Term than two Years; *Note: The Founders were not fond of standing armies. Take that, you hawks!*

To provide and maintain a navy;

To make Rules for the government and Regulation of the land and naval Forces;

To provide for calling forth the Militia to execute the Laws of the Union, suppress Insurrections and repel Invasions;

To provide for organizing, arming, and disciplining the Militia, and for governing such Part of them as may be employed in the Service of the United States, reserving to the States respectively, the Appointment of the Officers, and the Authority of training the Militia according to the discipline prescribed by Congress;

To exercise exclusive Legislation in all Cases whatsoever, over such District (not exceeding ten Miles square) as may, by Cession of particular States, and the Acceptance of Congress, become the Seat of the Government of the United States, and to exercise like Authority over all Places purchased by the Consent of the Legislature of the State in which the Same shall be for the Erection of Forts, magazines, Arsenals, dock-Yards, and other needful Buildings;—And

To make all Laws which shall be necessary and proper for carrying into Execution the foregoing Powers, and all other Powers vested by this Constitution in the Government of the United States, or in any Department or Officer thereof.

Very Important Note: Look through Section 8. See if Congress has the power to transfer money from one group of people to another (welfare programs, entitlement programs, federal medical insurance, etc.); to regulate businesses in their way of doing business (e.g., mandatory parental leave, accommodations for the handicapped); to control education; to establish housing policies and erect public housing; to subsidize milk and tobacco production and to tell farmers what to grow on their own land; and so on. It just isn't there.

Section 9. The Migration or Importation of such Persons as any of the States now existing shall think proper to admit, shall not be prohibited by the Congress prior to the Year one thousand eight hundred and eight, but a Tax or duty may be imposed on such Importation, not exceeding ten dollars for each Person.

The Privilege of the Writ of Habeas Corpus shall not be suspended, unless when in Cases of Rebellion or Invasion the public Safety may require it.

No Bill of Attainder or ex post facto Law shall be passed.

No Capitation, or other direct, Tax shall be laid, unless in Proportion to the Census or Enumeration herein before directed to be taken.

No Tax or Duty shall be laid on Articles exported from any State.

No preference shall be given by any Regulation of Commerce or Revenue to the Ports of one State over those of another: nor shall Vessels bound to, or from, one State, be obliged to enter, clear, or pay Duties in another.

No money shall be drawn from the Treasury, but in Consequence of Appropriations made by Law; and a regular Statement and Account of the Receipts and Expenditures of all public Money shall be published from time to time.

No Title of Nobility shall be granted by the United States: And no Person holding any Office of Profit or Trust under them, shall, without the Consent of the Congress, accept of any present, Emolument, Office, or Title, of any kind whatever, from any King, Prince, or foreign State.

Section 10. No State shall enter into any Treaty, Alliance, or Confederation; grant Letters of Marque and Reprisal; coin Money; emit Bills of Credit; make any Thing but gold and silver Coin a Tender in Payment of Debts; pass any Bill of Attainder, ex post facto Law, or Law impairing the Obligation of Contracts (*In other words, states have no right to water down the marriage*

contract by no-fault divorce laws and other laws changing the status of the marriage covenant after a couple has already wed), or grant any Title of Nobility.

No State shall, without the Consent of the Congress, lay any Imposts or Duties on Imports or Exports, except what may be absolutely necessary for executing its inspection Laws: and the net Produce of all Duties and Imports, laid by any State on Imports or Exports, shall be for the Use of the Treasury of the United States; and all such Laws shall be subject to the Revision and control of the Congress.

No State shall, without the Consent of the Congress, lay any Duty of Tonnage, keep Troops, or Ships of War in time of Peace, enter into any Agreement or Compact with another State, or with a foreign Power, or engage in War, unless actually invaded, or in such imminent Danger as will not admit of delay.

ARTICLE II [THE EXECUTIVE BRANCH]

Section 1. The executive Power shall be vested in a President of the United States of America. He shall hold his Office during the Term of four Years, and, together with the Vice President, chosen for the same term, be elected, as follows.

Each State shall appoint, in such Manner as the Legislature thereof may direct, a Number of Electors, equal to the whole Number of Senators and Representatives to which the State may be entitled in the Congress: but no Senator or Representative, or Person holding an Office of Trust or Profit under the United States, shall be appointed an Elector.

The Electors shall meet in their respective States, and vote by Ballot for two Persons, of whom one at least shall not be an Inhabitant of the same State with themselves. And they shall make a List of all the Persons voted for, and of the Number of Votes for each; which List they shall sign and certify, and transmit sealed to the Seat of the Government of the United States, directed to the President of the Senate. The President of the Senate shall, in the Presence of the Senate and House of Representatives, open all the Certificates, and the Votes shall then be counted. The Person having the greatest Number of Votes shall be the President, if such Number be a Majority of the whole Number of Electors appointed; and if there be more than one who have such Majority, and have an equal Number of Votes, then the House of Representatives shall immediately chuse by Ballot one of them for President: and if no Person have a Majority, then from the five highest on the List the said House shall in like Manner chuse the President. But in chusing the President, the Votes shall be taken by States, the Representation from each State having one Vote; A quorum for this Purpose shall consist of a Member or Members from two thirds of the States, and a Majority of all the States shall be necessary to a Choice. In every Case, after the Choice of the President, the Person having the greatest Number of Votes of the Electors shall be the Vice President. But if there should remain two or more who have equal Votes, the Senate shall chuse from them by Ballot the Vice President.

The Congress may determine the Time of chusing the Electors, and the Day on which they shall give their Votes; which Day shall be the same throughout the United States.

No Person except a natural born Citizen, or a Citizen of the United States, at the time of the Adoption of this Constitution, shall be eligible to the Office of President; neither shall any Person be eligible to that Office who shall not have attained to the Age of thirty five Years, and been fourteen Years a Resident within the United States.

In Case of the Removal of the President from Office, or of his Death, Resignation, or Inability to discharge the Powers and Duties of the said Office, the Same shall devolve on the Vice President, and the Congress may by Law provide for the Case of Removal, Death, Resignation or Inability, both of the President and Vice President, declaring what Officer shall then act as President, and such Officer shall act accordingly, until the Disability be removed, or a President shall be elected.

The President shall, at stated Times, receive for his Services, a Compensation, which shall neither be encreased nor diminished during the Period for which he shall have been elected, and he shall not receive within that Period any other Emolument from the United States, or any of them.

Before he enter on the Execution of his Office, he shall take the following Oath or Affirmation:—"I do solemnly swear (or affirm) that I will faithfully execute the Office of President of the United States, and will to the best of my Ability, preserve, protect and defend the Constitution of the United States."

Section 2. The President shall be Commander in Chief of the Army and Navy of the United States, and of the Militia of the several States, when called into the actual Service of the United States; he may require the Opinion, in writing, of the principal Officer in each of the executive Departments, upon any Subject relating to the Duties of their respective Offices, and he shall have Power to grant Reprieves and Pardons for Offences against the United States, except in Cases of Impeachment.

He shall have Power, by and with the Advice and Consent of the Senate, to make Treaties, provided two thirds of the Senators present concur; and he shall nominate, and by and with the Advice and Consent of the Senate, shall appoint Ambassadors, other public Ministers and Consuls, Judges of the supreme Court, and all other Officers of the United States, whose Appointments are not herein otherwise provided for, and which shall be established by Law: but the Congress may by Law vest the Appointment of such inferior Officers, as they think proper, in the President alone, in the Courts of Law, or in the Heads of Departments.

The President shall have Power to fill up all Vacancies that may happen during the Recess of the Senate, by granting Commissions which shall expire at the End of their next Session.

Section 3. He shall from time to time give to the Congress Information of the State of the Union, and recommend to their Consideration such Measures as he shall judge necessary and expedient; he may, on extraordinary Occasions, convene both Houses, or either of them, and in Case of Disagreement between them, with Respect to the Time of Adjournment, he may adjourn them to such Time as he shall think proper; he shall receive Ambassadors and other public Ministers; he shall take Care that the Laws be faithfully executed, and shall Commission all the Officers of the United States.

Section 4. The President, Vice President, and all civil Officers of the United States, shall be removed from Office on Impeachment for, and conviction of, Treason, Bribery, or other High Crimes and Misdemeanors.

ARTICLE III [THE JUDICIAL BRANCH]

Section 1. The judicial Power of the United States, shall be vested in one supreme Court, and in such inferior Courts as the Congress may from time to time ordain and establish. The Judges, both of the supreme and inferior Courts, shall hold their Offices during good Behaviour, and shall, at stated Times, receive for their Services, a Compensation, which shall not be diminished during their Continuance in Office.

Section 2. The judicial Power shall extend to all Cases, in Law and Equity, arising under this Constitution, the Laws of the United States, and Treaties made, or which shall be made, under their Authority;—to all Cases affecting Ambassadors, other public Ministers and Consuls;—to all Cases of admiralty and maritime Jurisdiction;—to Controversies to which the United States shall be a Party;--to Controversies between two or more States; between a State and Citizens of another State;—between Citizens of different States;—between Citizens of the same State claiming Lands under Grants of different States, and between a State, or the Citizens thereof, and foreign States, Citizens or Subjects.

Note: Doesn't it sound like the Supreme Court is only supposed to mediate in quarrels between jurisdictions? Where is its power to annul duly-passed laws? Nowhere, that's where!

In all Cases affecting Ambassadors, other public Ministers and Consuls, and those in which a State shall be Party, the supreme Court shall have original Jurisdiction. In all the other Cases before mentioned, the supreme Court shall have appellate Jurisdiction, both as to Law and Fact, with such Exceptions, and under such Regulations as the Congress shall make.

The Trial of all Crimes, except in Cases of Impeachment, shall be by Jury; and such Trial shall be held in the State where the said Crimes shall have been committed; but when not committed within any State, the Trial shall be at such Place or Places as the Congress may by Law have directed.

Section 3. Treason against the United States, shall consist only in levying War against them, or in adhering to their Enemies, giving them Aid and Comfort. No Person shall be convicted of Treason unless on the Testimony of two Witnesses to the same overt Act, or on Confession in open Court.

The Congress shall have Power to declare the Punishment of Treason, but no Attainder of Treason shall work Corruption of Blood, or Forfeiture except during the Life of the person Attainted.

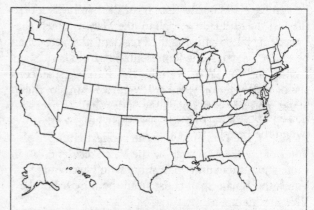

ARTICLE IV
[LAWS CONCERNING THE STATES]

Section 1. Full Faith and Credit shall be given in each State to the public Acts, Records, and judicial Proceedings of every other State. (*Nevada, in other words, should not have the right to cancel marriages made in Nebraska.*) And the Congress may by general Laws prescribe the Manner in which such Acts, Records and Proceedings shall be proved, and the Effect thereof.

Section 2. The Citizens of each State shall be entitled to all Privileges and Immunities of Citizens in the several States.

A Person charged in any State with Treason, Felony, or other Crime, who shall flee from Justice, and be found in another State, shall on Demand of the executive Authority of the State from which he fled, be delivered up, to be removed to the State having Jurisdiction of the Crime.

No Person held to Service or Labour in one State, under the Laws thereof, escaping into another, shall, in Consequence of any Law or Regulation therein, be discharged from such Service or Labour, but shall be delivered up on the Claim of the Party to whom such Service or Labour may be due.

Section 3. New States may be admitted by the Congress into this Union; but no new State shall be formed or erected within the Jurisdiction of any other State; nor any State be formed by the Junction of two or more States, or Parts of States, without the Consent of the Legislatures of the States concerned as well as of the Congress.

The Congress shall have Power to dispose of and make all needful Rules and Regulations respecting the Territory or other Property belonging to the United States; and nothing in this Constitution shall be so construed as to Prejudice any Claims of the United States, or of any particular State.

Section 4. The United States shall guarantee to every State in this Union a Republican Form of Government, and shall protect each of them against Invasion; and on Application of the Legislature, or of the Executive (when the Legislature cannot be convened) against domestic Violence.

ARTICLE V
[HOW TO AMEND THE CONSTITUTION]

The Congress, whenever two thirds of both Houses shall deem it necessary, shall propose Amendments to this Constitution, or, on the Application of the Legislatures of two thirds of the several States, shall call a Convention for proposing Amendments, which, in either Case, shall be valid to all Intents and Purposes, as Part of this Constitution, when ratified by the Legislatures of three fourths of the several States, or by Conventions in three fourths thereof, as the one or the other Mode of Ratification may be proposed by the Congress; Provided that no Amendment which may be made prior to the Year One Thousand eight hundred and eight shall in any Manner affect the first and fourth Clauses in the Ninth Section of the first Article; and that no State, without its Consent, shall be deprived of its equal Suffrage in the Senate.

Note: The Constitution can NOT be amended by majority vote of the Supreme Court, as at least one public-school booklet I saw claims! This, of course, hasn't stopped the Supreme Court, since the days of F.D.R., from doing just that. The judiciary now has open contempt for the people and the legislative process. Law students are even taught that it is a judge's DUTY to "make" laws—since it is so much harder to get policies beloved by the avant-garde through otherwise!

ARTICLE VI [TRANSITION TO AND UPHOLDING THE CONSTITUTION]

All Debts contracted and Engagements entered into, before the Adoption of this Constitution, shall be as valid against the United States under this Constitution, as under the Confederation.

This Constitution, and the Laws of the United States which shall be made in Pursuance thereof; and all Treaties made, or which shall be made, under the Authority of the United States, shall be the supreme Law of the Land; and the Judges in every State shall be bound thereby, any Thing in the Constitution or Laws of any State to the Contrary notwithstanding.

Note: The Founders intended the "Treaties" spoken of to be treaties BETWEEN nations (e.g., a treaty with Britain regarding the rights of American and British shipping). Now that U.N. elites have private conferences at which leaders of many nations get together and sign "treaties" changing the political status of their citizen (example: the U.N. Treaty on the Rights of Children, which makes peer-group dependency and unrestricted access to TV commercials "rights" of children), this proviso has become the most dangerous line in the Constitution.

The Senators and Representatives before mentioned, and the Members of the several State Legislatures, and all executive and judicial Officers, both of the United States and of the several States, shall be bound by Oath of Affirmation, to support this Constitution; but no religious Test shall ever be required as a Qualification to any Office or public Trust under the United States.

ARTICLE VII
[RATIFYING THE CONSTITUTION]

The Ratification of the Conventions of nine States, shall be sufficient for the Establishment of this Constitution between the States so ratifying the Same.

AMENDMENTS TO THE CONSTITUTION

[The first 10 Amendments are called the Bill of Rights. They were ratified Dec. 15, 1791.]

AMENDMENT 1
[FREE SPEECH, RELIGION, PRESS, ASSEMBLY & PETITION]

Congress shall make no law respecting an establishment of religion, or prohibiting the free exercise thereof; or abridging the freedom of speech, or of the press, or the right of the people peaceably to assemble, and to petition the Government for a redress of grievances.

Note: The phrase "no law respecting an establishment of religion" meant, at the time it was written, that Congress should not establish a national religion. States were free to have state religions, as in fact several did for years after this amendment was passed. The amendment does NOT mean that Congress (and the states) must actively suppress all public religion, as the ACLU would have it. This is perhaps the most misunderstood amendment of the Constitution.

AMENDMENT 2
[GUNOWNERS' RIGHTS]

A well regulated Militia being necessary to the security of a free State, the right of the people to keep and bear Arms, shall not be infringed.

Note: A militia, by definition, is a citizen army. In America, historically the militia was organized town by town, not on the state or national level. The American Revolution started when some townsmen in Lexington and Concord refused to hand their guns over to the British.

AMENDMENT 3
[NO QUARTERING SOLDIERS ON THE PEOPLE]

No Soldier shall, in time of peace be quartered in any house, without the consent of the Owner, nor in time of war, but in a manner to be prescribed by law.

AMENDMENT 4
[RIGHT OF PRIVACY AGAINST GOVERNMENT SEARCH & SEIZURE)

The right of the people to be secure in their persons, houses, papers, and effects, against unreasonable searches and seizures, shall not be violated, and no Warrants shall issue, but upon probable cause, supported by Oath or affirmation, and particularly describing the place to be searched, and the persons or things to be seized.

Note: In other words, SWAT teams and IRS guys are supposed to have a case against you and a list of what they want to take before they kick down your front door. They are also not supposed to randomly loot your property in hopes of finding something salable or incriminating.

AMENDMENT 5
[CAPITAL CRIMES, DOUBLE JEOPARDY, SELF-INCRIMINATION, GOVERNMENT "TAKINGS"]

No person shall be held to answer for a capital, or otherwise infamous crime, unless on a presentment or indictment of a Grand Jury, except in cases arising in the land or naval forces, or in the Militia, when in actual service in time of War or public danger; nor shall any person be subject for the same offence to be twice put in jeopardy of life or limb; nor shall be compelled in any criminal case to be a witness against himself, nor be deprived of life, liberty, or property, without due process of law; nor shall private property be taken for public use, without just compensation.

Note: The "takings" clause here is our chief bulwark against the government seizing control of all our land, as per the John Pozsgai case mentioned in the Science chapter, in the name of "the public good." The Constitution does not recognize the doctrine of "our resources" or "the planet's resources" —it respects private ownership of property. Constitutionally speaking, if the government wanted to force John Pozsgai to turn his land into a wildlife reserve, they should have paid him for it instead of fining him $202,000.

AMENDMENT 6
[RULES FOR FAIR TRIALS]

In all criminal prosecutions, the accused shall enjoy the right to a speedy and public trial, by an impartial jury of the State and district wherein the crime shall have been committed, which district shall have been previously ascertained by law, and to be informed of the nature and cause of the accusation; to be confronted with the witnesses against him; to have compulsory process for obtaining witnesses in his favor, and to have the Assistance of Counsel for his defence.

Note: The JURY is supposed to try the case, not the judge. Also note that anonymous hotline tips and the like are not supposed to be cause or evidence for a criminal prosecution.

AMENDMENT 7
(RIGHT TO JURY TRIAL)

In Suits at common law, where the value in controversy shall exceed twenty dollars, the right of trial by jury shall be preserved, and no fact tried by a jury, shall be otherwise re-examined in any Court of the United States, than according to the rules of the common law.

AMENDMENT 8
[BAILS, FINES, PENALTIES]

Excessive bail shall not be required, nor excessive fines imposed, nor cruel and unusual punishments inflicted.

Note: Capital punishment was not considered "cruel and unusual." Torture was.

AMENDMENT 9
[RIGHTS NOT MENTIONED ARE STILL RIGHTS]

The enumeration in the Constitution, of certain rights, shall not be construed to deny or disparage others retained by the people.

Note: Since the Constitution does not mention education, in-state business, charity, and hosts of other subjects, these areas are rights of the people to handle as we wish. We should not have to ask permission to make our own choices in these areas, since WE are the legal authorities over our own choices.

AMENDMENT 10
[PEOPLE AND STATES RETAIN RIGHTS NOT GIVEN TO FEDERAL GOVERNMENT]

The powers not delegated to the United States by the Constitution, nor prohibited by it to the States, are reserved to the States respectively, or to the people.

For example, since education is never mentioned in the Constitution, according to this amendment the control of education is a right reserved to the States or the people. A "national education policy" and a Department of Education in the cabinet are clearly unconstitutional.

AMENDMENT 11
[FEDERAL GOVERNMENT NOT TO DECIDE LAWSUITS AGAINST STATES]

The Judicial power of the United States shall not be construed to extend to any suit in law or equity, commenced or prosecuted against one of the United States by Citizens of another State, or by Citizens or Subjects of any Foreign State. [Ratified Feb. 7, 1795]

AMENDMENT 12
[ELECTION REGULATIONS]

The Electors shall meet in their respective States and vote by ballot for President and Vice President, one of whom, at least, shall not be an inhabitant of the same State with themselves; they shall name in their ballots the person voted for as President, and in distinct ballots the person voted for as Vice-President, and they shall make distinct lists of all persons voted for as President, and of all persons voted for as Vice-President, and of the number of votes for each, which lists they shall sign and certify, and transmit sealed to the seat of the government of the United States, directed to the President of the Senate;—The President of the Senate shall, in the presence of the Senate and House of Representatives, open all the certificates and the votes shall then be counted;—The person having the greatest number of votes for President, shall be the President, if such number be a majority of the whole number of Electors appointed; and if no person have such majority, then from the persons having the highest numbers not exceeding three on the list of those voted for as President, the House of Representatives shall choose immediately, by ballot, the President. But in choosing the President, the votes shall be taken by states, the representation from each state having one vote; a quorum for this purpose shall consist of a member or members from two-thirds of the states, and majority of all the states shall be necessary to a choice. And if the House of Representatives shall not choose a President whenever the right of choice shall devolve upon them, before the fourth day of March next following, then the Vice-President shall act as President, as in the case of the death or other constitutional disability of the President.—The person having the greatest number of votes as Vice-President, shall be the Vice-President, if such number be a majority of the whole number of Electors appointed, and if no person have a majority, then from the two highest numbers on the list, the

Senate shall choose the Vice-President; a quorum for the purpose shall consist of two-thirds of the whole number of Senators, and a majority of the whole number shall be necessary to a choice. But no person constitutionally ineligible to the office of President shall be eligible to that of Vice-President of the United States. [Ratified July 27, 1804]

AMENDMENT 13
[SLAVERY ABOLISHED]

Section 1. Neither Slavery, nor involuntary servitude, except as a punishment for crime whereof the party shall have been duly convicted, shall exist within the United States, or any place subject to their jurisdiction.

Section 2. Congress shall have power to enforce this article by appropriate legislation. [Ratified Dec. 6, 1865]

AMENDMENT 14
[AFTERMATH OF CIVIL WAR]

Section 1. All persons born or naturalized in the United States, and subject to the jurisdiction thereof, are citizens of the United States and of the State wherein they reside. No State shall make or enforce any law which shall abridge the privileges or immunities of citizens of the United States; nor shall any State deprive any person of life, liberty, or property, without due process of law; nor deny to any person within its jurisdiction the equal protection of the laws.

Section 2. Representatives shall be apportioned among the several States according to their respective numbers, counting the whole number of persons in each State, excluding Indians not taxed. But when the right to vote at any election for the choice of electors for President and Vice President of the United States, Representatives in Congress, the Executive and Judicial officers of a State, or the members of the Legislature thereof, is denied to any of the male inhabitants of such State, being twenty-one years of age, and citizens of the United States, or in any way abridged, except for participation in rebellion, or other crime, the basis of representation therein shall be reduced in the proportion which the number of such male citizens shall bear to the whole number of male citizens twenty-one years of age in such State.

Section 3. No person shall be a Senator or Representative in Congress, or elector of President and Vice President, or hold any office, civil or military, under the United States, or under any State, who, having been previously taken an oath, as a member of Congress, or as an officer of the United States, or as a member of any State legislature, or as an executive or judicial officer of any State, to support the Constitution of the United States, shall have engaged in insurrection or rebellion against the same, or given aid or comfort to the enemies thereof. But Congress may by a vote of two-thirds of each House, remove such disability.

Section 4. The validity of the public debt of the United States, authorized by law, including debts incurred for payment of pensions and bounties for services in suppressing insurrection or rebellion, shall not be questioned. But neither the United States nor any State shall assume or pay any debt or obligation incurred in aid of insurrection or rebellion against the United States, or any claim for the loss or emancipation of any slave; but all such debts, obligations and claims shall be held illegal and void.

Section 5. The Congress shall have power to enforce, by appropriate legislation, the provisions of this article. [Ratified July 9, 1868]

AMENDMENT 15
[VOTING RIGHTS FOR MINORITIES]

Section 1. The right of citizens of the United States to vote shall not be denied or abridged by the United States or by any State on account of race, color, or previous condition of servitude.

Section 2. The Congress shall have power to enforce this article by appropriate legislation. [Ratified Feb. 3, 1870]

AMENDMENT 16
[INCOME TAXES]

The Congress shall have power to lay and collect taxes on incomes, from whatever source derived, without apportionment among the several States, and without regard to any census or enumeration. [Ratified Feb. 3, 1913]

Note: There was NO federal income tax before this amendment was ratified. Imagine life without income taxes!

AMENDMENT 17
[SENATORS ELECTED DIRECTLY]

The Senate of the United States shall be composed of two Senators from each State, elected by the people thereof for six years; and each Senator shall have one vote. The electors in each State shall have the qualifications requisite for electors of the most numerous branch of the State legislatures.

When vacancies happen in the representation of any State in the Senate, the executive authority of such State shall issue writs of election to fill such vacancies: *Provided,* That the legislature of any State may empower the executive thereof to make temporary appointments until the people fill the vacancies by election as the legislature may direct.

This amendment shall not be so construed as to affect the election or term of any Senator chosen before it becomes valid as part of the Constitution. [Ratified April 8, 1913]

Note: This amendment destroyed the balance of power between rural areas and cities. From then on, city-based party machines have controlled Congress.

AMENDMENT 18
[PROHIBITION]

Section 1. After one year from the ratification of this article the manufacture, sale, or transportation of intoxicating liquors within, the importation thereof into, or exportation thereof from the United States and all territory subject to the jurisdiction thereof for beverage purposes is hereby prohibited.

Section 2. The Congress and the several States shall have concurrent power to enforce this article by appropriate legislation.

Section 3. This article shall be inoperative unless it shall have been ratified as an amendment to the Constitution by the legislatures of the several States, as provided in the Constitution, within seven years from the date of the submission hereof to the States by the Congress. [Ratified Jan. 16, 1919]

AMENDMENT 19
[VOTING RIGHTS FOR WOMEN]

The right of citizens of the United States to vote shall not be denied or abridged by the United States or by any State on account of sex.

Congress shall have power to enforce this article by appropriate legislation. [Ratified Aug. 26, 1920]

AMENDMENT 20
[LAME DUCK AMENDMENT]

Section 1. The terms of the President and Vice President shall end at noon on the 20th day of January, and the terms of Senators and Representatives at noon on the 3rd day of January, of the years in which such terms would have ended if this article had not been ratified, and the terms of their successors shall then begin.

Section 2. The Congress shall assemble at least once in every year, and such meeting shall begin at noon on the 3rd day of January, unless they shall by law appoint a different day.

Section 3. If, at the time fixed for the beginning of the term of the President, the President elect shall have died, the Vice President elect shall become President. If a President shall not have been chosen before the time fixed for the beginning of his term, or if the President elect shall have failed to qualify, then the Vice President elect shall act as President until a President shall have qualified; and the Congress may by law provide for the case wherein neither a President elect nor a Vice President elect shall have qualified, declaring who shall then act as President, or the manner in which one who is to act shall be selected, and such person shall act accordingly until a President or Vice President shall have qualified.

Section 4. The Congress may by law provide for the case of the death of any of the persons from whom the House of Representatives may choose a President whenever the right of choice shall have devolved upon them, and for the case of the death of any of the persons from whom the Senate may choose a Vice President

whenever the right of choice shall have devolved upon them.

Section 5. Sections 1 and 2 shall take effect on the 15th day of October following the ratification of this article.

Section 6. This article shall be inoperative unless it shall have been ratified as an amendment to the Constitution by the legislatures of three-fourths of the several States within seven years from the date of its submission. [Ratified Jan. 23, l933]

AMENDMENT 21
[REPEAL OF PROHIBITION]

Section 1. The eighteenth article of amendment to the Constitution of the United States is hereby repealed.

Section 2. The transportation or importation into any State, Territory, or possession of the United States for delivery or use therein of intoxicating liquors, in violation of the laws thereof, is hereby prohibited.

Section 3. This article shall be inoperative unless it shall have been ratified as an amendment to the Constitution by conventions in the several States, as provided in the Constitution, within seven years from the date of the submission hereof to the States by the Congress. [Ratified Dec. 5, l933]

AMENDMENT 22
[PRESIDENTS LIMITED TO TWO TERMS]

Section 1. No person shall be elected to the office of the President more than twice, and no person who has held the office of President, or acted as President, for more than two years of a term to which some other person was elected President shall be elected to the office of the President more than once. But this Article shall not apply to any person holding the office of President when this Article was proposed by the Congress, and shall not prevent any person who may be holding the office of President, or acing as President, during the term within which this Article becomes operative from holding the office of President or acting as President during the remainder of such term.

Section 2. This article shall be inoperative unless it shall have been ratified as an amendment to the Constitution by the legislatures of three-fourths of the several States within seven years from the date of its submission to the States by the Congress. [Ratified Feb. 27, 1951]

AMENDMENT 23
[WASHINGTON, D.C. GETS ELECTORAL VOTES AS IF IT WERE A STATE]

Section 1. The District constituting the seat of Government of the United States shall appoint in such manner as the Congress may direct:

A number of electors of President and Vice President equal to the whole number of Senators and Representatives in Congress to which the District would be entitled if it were a State, but in no event more than the least populous State; they shall be in addition to those appointed by the States, but they shall be considered, for the purposes of the election of President and Vice President, to be electors appointed by a State; and they shall meet in the District and perform such duties as provided by the twelfth article of amendment.

Section 2. The Congress shall have power to enforce this article by appropriate legislation. [Ratified March 29, 1961]

AMENDMENT 24
[NON-TAXPAYERS CAN VOTE]

Section 1. The right of citizens of the United States to vote in any primary or other election for President or Vice President, for electors for President or Vice President, or for Senator or Representative in Congress, shall not be denied or abridged by the United States or any State by reason of failure to pay any poll tax or other tax.

Section 2. The Congress shall have power to enforce this article by appropriate legislation. [Ratified Jan. 23, 1964]

AMENDMENT 25
[PRESIDENTIAL REPLACEMENT]

Section 1. In case of the removal of the President from office or of his death or resignation, the Vice President shall become President.

Section 2. Whenever there is a vacancy in the office of the Vice President, the President shall nominate a Vice President who shall take office upon confirmation by a majority vote of both Houses of Congress.

Section 3. Whenever the President transmits to the President pro tempore of the Senate and the Speaker of the House of Representatives his written declaration that he is unable to discharge the powers and duties of his office, and until he transmits to them a written declaration to the contrary, such powers and duties shall be discharged by the Vice President as Acting President.

Section 4. Whenever the Vice President and a majority of either the principal officers of the executive departments or of such other body as Congress may by law provide, transmit to the President pro tempore of the Senate and the Speaker of the House of Representatives their written declaration that the President is unable to discharge the powers and duties of his office, the Vice President shall immediately assume the powers and duties of the office as Acting President.

Thereafter, when the President transmits to the President pro tempore of the Senate and the Speaker of the House of Representatives his written declaration that no inability exists he shall resume the powers and duties of his office unless the Vice President and a majority of either the principal officers of the executive department or of such other body as Congress may by law provide, transmit within four days to the President pro tempore of the Senate and the Speaker of the House of Representatives their written declaration that the President is unable to discharge the powers and duties of his office. Thereupon Congress shall decide the issue, assembling within forty-eight hours for that purpose if not in session. If the Congress, within twenty-one days after receipt of the latter written declaration, or, if Congress is not in session, within twenty-one days after Congress is required to assemble, determines by two-thirds vote of both Houses that the President is unable to discharge the powers and duties of his office, the Vice President shall continue to discharge the same as Acting President; otherwise, the President shall resume the powers and duties of his office. [Ratified Feb. 10, 1967]

AMENDMENT 26
[VOTING RIGHTS FOR 18-YEAR-OLDS]

Section 1. The right of citizens of the United States, who are 18 years of age or older, to vote shall not be denied or abridged by the United States or by any State on account of age.

Section 2. The Congress shall have power to enforce this article by appropriate legislation. [Ratified June 30, 1971]

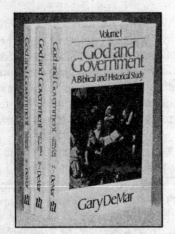

TOOLS FOR UNDERSTANDING THE WAY IT SPOZED TO BE

American Vision
God and Government series, $11.95/volume. Add 12% shipping.

Books and tapes promoting a Biblical worldview. American Vision is in the process of developing a Biblical Worldview Library. The three-volume God and Government series is the first topic covered in the Library. These volumes together comprise the most comprehensive treatment available on biblical principles of government. The series is used by hundreds of home schoolers and several curriculum providers.

NEW**
Educational Insights
American Archives set, $9.95. Minimum order $25. Shipping extra. Ages 9–adult.

Yes, you too can have your very own set of the Declaration of Independence, Constitution, Bill of Rights, and Gettysburg Address. The American Archives collection provides these documents, reproduced on authentically antiqued parchment, all rolled neatly in a plastic tube. The largest document is 12 x 19", if you're thinking of putting them up on the wall.

Foundation for American Christian Education
Christian History, Teaching and Learning, $15 each. *Rudiments,* $7. *Christian Self-Government with Union,* $18. *Consider and Ponder,* $23. Add 10% shipping, or 15% for UPS shipping. Ages 12–adult.

FACE is trying to revive the "Principle Approach" to government, an approach based on biblical law, on which they say the U.S.A. was founded. Their material traces America's roots through source documents. Political freedom begins with self-government, FACE says, and self-government begins in the home.

Before we proceed any farther, let me make it clear that these are *not* workbooks for young children. The theory is that you are going to work through this information yourself and then present it according to a set of complicated teaching suggestions that require you to keep flipping back and forth between books. In practice, I suggest that you invest in the Intrepid Books workbooks for your student's grade level. These use the FACE books as source readings, but are much easier to use than FACE's own study guides.

The Christian History of the Constitution documents that America is a Christian nation (that is, it *was* dedicated to Christ once upon a time) with a Christian Constitution (that is, one based on Christian principles). The "Chain of Christianity" is traced westward to America, as the gospel spread from Israel to the Roman Empire and thence to the uncouth white tribespeople who, once Christianized, spread it over the world. A large book, 8½ x 11", hardbound in red cloth, beautifully gold-stamped, about 500 pages, consisting almost entirely of quotes from source documents.

Teaching and Learning America's Christian History is the original how-to manual of the Principle Approach. Each principle is spelled out, precept on precept, line on line. Likewise beautifully bound and gold-stamped, likewise large, likewise red. Under 400 pages.

Rudiments of America's Christian History and Government is a workbook for students filled with source quotes from distinguished American Christian leaders of the past and questions designed to develop both Christian thinking and an awareness of our Christian heritage. For teens and adults.

Christian Self-Government with Union is red vellum, gold-stamped, eagle-embossed, illustrated, indexed, and 640 pages. More history from source documents, emphasizing the colonist's voluntary union that led to self-government.

Consider and Ponder is the first volume of a projected series on the Christian history of the American Revolution. Covering the Constitutional Debate period of 1765–1775, its 736 pages nestle between blue vellum covers.

NEW*
Intrepid Books
Level A–H books, $10.95 each. Add 10% shipping ($2.50 minimum). Grades 1–8.

Those of you who have felt overwhelmed by the sheer volume of cross-referenced information included in the Foundation for American Christian Education materials (see above) will be glad to know there's now a series of study guides based on their most popular books, *The Christian History of the Constitution* and *Teaching and Learning America's Christian History*. The Level A book is for first-graders, Level B is for second-graders, and so on.

To quote from the brochure:

Does Your Child Know . . .
• What his inalienable rights are?
• How our Founding Fathers felt about taxes?
• Why the Boston Tea Party could only have happened in Boston?
• Who John Locke or William Blackstone were?
• Why America is a Christian nation?
• How the Bible came to be translated into English and thus began the American nation?
• How to contrast the pagan Idea of Man with the Christian Idea of Man?
• That before Christianity, women were regarded as only property to be dealt with as one saw fit?
• What it means to be self-governed?
• That conscience is the most sacred of all property?
• That our Founding Fathers believed God's providence ruled their lives and guided this country?

Each Study Guide is broken into the following sections:

1. God's Principle of Individuality
2. The Christian Principle of Self-Government
3. America's Heritage of Christian Character
4. Conscience is the Most Sacred of All Property
5. The Christian Form of Our Government
6. How the Seed of Local Self-Government is Planted
7. The Christian Principle of American Political Union

Here's how it works. You (the adult) read the recommended portions from FACE's *Teaching and Learning America's Christian History* and *Christian History of the Constitution* listed at the beginning of each section. You also read the Bible portions, definitions, and statements of purpose. Sample, from the Christian Self-Government section:

A man cannot rule our country
Unless he can manage a state,
But . . . A man cannot manage a state
Unless he can lead a county, But . . .
A man cannot lead a county,
Unless he can head a city, But . . .
A man cannot head a city,
Unless he can guide a family, But . . .
A man cannot guide a family,
Unless he can govern himself, But . . .
A man cannot govern himself,
Unless he has reason, But . . .
A man cannot have reason,
Unless he is ruled by and obedient to God!

Each section then speaks right to the student, with historical excerpts and character and Bible lessons designed to teach them about individuality, self-government, America's principled heritage, conscience, Christian form of government, local self-government, and proper political union. The historical events covered differ from level to level, as does the depth of the teaching. Upper-grades books contain proportionately more colonial political philosophy. The Level F book for seventh-graders, for example, has fairly small print, long extracts from historical source documents, and looks at the role geography has played in history, representative government in Virginia and Plymouth colonies, representation and separation of powers, Sam Adams and the Committees of Correspondence, and how the colonists reacted to the closing of Boston Port—among other things!

Each book includes writing and discussion exercises following each historical reading, and ends with a glossary. Lower-level books also include simple art activities and feature more illustrations and graphics.

These books are very pro-Protestant, pro-reasoning, and pro-Founding Fathers style patriotism. The only obviously modern note is the (somewhat misguided, I feel) emphasis on self-esteem in the Individuality sections. Aside from that, you could have taken these books into any 1800s public-school classroom, no questions asked.

LibertyTree: Review and Catalog

Modern-day libertarians split into what some call the "modals"—people who mooch off others and go to the wall for the right to possess child pornography— and the "paleos"—people with moral sense who follow the *original* Christian libertarian ideals of freedom bounded by the Ten Commandments.

The modals have, obviously, given libertarianism a Bad Name. Paleolibertarianism is where it's at. For years those subscribing to the paleolib view have been a small, but literarily acute, minority. And 200 years before that those subscribing to this view were running this country.

LibertyTree is the paleolib catalog, with most of the classics—Tom Paine et al—and a lot of the best modern thinkers. Subject areas include history, economics, literature, education, phonics, humor, political philosophy, and much more. In addition, *LibertyTree* features a lot of books on starting your own business, home schooling, books for children, and a slew of Constitution, bicentennial, and other gewgaws—T-shirts and whatnot.

UPDATED★★
Plymouth Rock Foundation
Biblical Solutions, $6.95. *Fundamentals Guide Book,* $9.95 .

Plymouth Rock's study course in Biblical principles of government, *Fundamentals for American Christians,* is currently used in several thousand Christian day and home schools in the U.S.A. (including Christian Liberty Academy) and in some 14 foreign countries. Designed for upper high school students and adults, it is 400 pages loaded with charts, tables, and study projects, and comes three-hole punched to fit your standard ring binder. Are you *really* a fundamentalist? Get *Fundamentals* and find out!

Another Plymouth Rock entry that has met with great acceptance is *Biblical Solutions to Contemporary Problems: A Handbook.* This is a compendium of Plymouth Rock's scrappy little fact sheets, filled with terse comments on current issues such as abortion, Dungeons 'n Dragons, you name it. First the issue is stated. Next you get facts and statistics. Finally, Plymouth Rock states the biblical position. The previous edition was written in telegraph style to pack as much info as possible in four pages; this new edition is less telegraphic in style, with newer statistics and more topics covered.

Plymouth Rock has more books, booklets, periodicals and cassettes on biblical principles of government, Christian education, and America's Christian heritage. For a free information kit on America's Christian heritage, send 45¢ in stamps to cover postage.

NEW★★
Plymouth Rock Foundation
Institute on the Constitution 10-tape set, $32.50 postpaid, or $27.50 postpaid for COMCORS members. Spiralbound study notes to accompany tapes, $4.95. Add 15% shipping. All orders must be prepaid.

"Oh, no!" you scream. "Just when I thought it was safe to stay inside! Not another multi-cassette series on The Roots of America and all that boring fighting-fundy stuff!" Well, I must admit that renowned Constitutional lawyer John Eidsmoe's mini-course *Institute on the Constitution* does run to 10 audiocassettes. You won't have cassettes spurting all over your house, though, since they come nicely packed in a cassette binder, and thanks to Mr. Eidsmoe's entertaining style and inexhaustible fund of true stories, you won't most likely be reaching for the Stop button and wishing you'd never sent for these tapes either.

The series provides a systematic education in the history and philosophy undergirding the Constitution, and the history of what has happened to it since then. *Institutes on the Constitution* includes:

- The Philosophical Background of the Constitution
- Christian Beliefs of the Framers
- The Miracle at Philadelphia
- An Overview of the Constitution (two tapes)
- Biblical Principles in the Declaration and Constitution
- The Bill of Rights and Other Amendments
- The History of Interpretation of the Constitution: Jay to Rehnquist
- Current Threats to the Constitution
- Questions and Answers, and Reclaiming the Constitution (a summation)

The part on reclaiming the Constitution is the weakest, consisting of the usual "learn, tell others, and write your Congressman." Patrick Henry would have been a little more vigorous in his approach, no doubt!

NEW**
Rothbard-Rockwell Report
One-year subscription (12 issues), $49. High school–adult.

Scrappy paleo-libertarian newsletter that analyzes issues most media don't even discuss. Good-looking, too, with nice paper and two-color printing; this isn't one of your cheap dot-matrix productions.

Sarah Barton digs up the dirt on modal libertarians and their institutions.

Llewellyn Rockwell, "Mr. Anti-Earth Day," comments on news such as the revelation that Pol Pot, the Butcher of Cambodia, has gone green in just the way one would expect—severely punishing starving Cambodians who presume to catch and eat animals on the World Wildlife Fund's endangered-species list. (Mr.

Rockwell contrasts Pol Pot's outlook to that of St. Augustine, who 1500 years ago faced off against a bunch of greenies, Christian heretics called Manicheans.)

LHR also reports on misguided greenie maneuvers such as the crusade to ban helium balloons. (Turns out that there is *no* evidence that a single animal has ever been killed by munching on helium balloon scraps. Doesn't matter to the Balloon Alert Project people: in their own words, there is also "no proof that balloons haven't killed any animals." Meanwhile they have succeeded in outlawing balloon launchings in three states and continue to enlist schoolkids to write letters begging legislators to save the animals from those dreadful balloons. Figure out the logic for yourself.)

Murray Rothbard applies classic libertarian ethics to such diverse topics as the S&L disaster and the recent Gulf war.

Other columnists pop up from time to time, such as Joseph Sobran and the Old Curmudgeon. Mark Twain even got his licks in, in the last issue.

Not much comfort here for military hawks, true-blue greenies (what a color combination!), believers in collective guilt, or libertines. Always fascinating reading.

School of Statesmanship
How To Elect a Statesman, 6-hour video, $21 (VHS or 8 mm). Audiocassettes, $18. Both video and audio run 6 hours. All prices postpaid. Ages 17–adult.

Here are audio and video tapes for anyone who's interested in "restoring our Federal Republic." Lots of theories on how to re-establish a No-Party system, where candidates run solely on their qualifications, not their connections. Topics include the purpose of government, the court system (how it evolved and ideas for reform), regional government (a bad idea), local officials, state officials, "Criminal Deterrents and Crime Breeders," re-elections, and how to reform the electoral system. Part of the instruction is a two-hour course on the history of the U.S. money system.

I have tried and tried to review the video, but although the publisher has kindly sent me several copies, my video player is getting too old to handle ultra slow-play. From what I can glean around the edges, though, the video—which is simply a series of lectures—should breed some lively discussions, whether you agree with the lecturer or not!

Both the audio and video versions come with the same 300 pages of free literature, stories and clippings from a variety of sources. The free literature makes quite interesting reading. I had no idea Davy Crockett once got into trouble for voting relief to a burnt-out area! It's a different point of view: Power to the People, and Bureaucrats Go Home!

NEW★★
Shekinah Curriculum Cellar

United States Constitution, United States Government, Bill of Rights wall projects, $2.50 each. Shipping extra. Ages 10–16.

Pull the folded poster out of the plastic sleeve. *Read* the extensive historical background information. *Use* the enclosed teacher's guide for additional information, projects, vocabulary, and directions on how to complete the wall poster. *Fill in* the requested information on the poster. *Color* it, using colored pencils. *Hang* it on a wall, file it away, or whatever . . . your students will have learned more than they would have from a textbook unit on the topic!

Shekinah carries 10 different history/geography wall projects, of which I have seen three. *United States Constitution* gives historical events leading up to the signing of the Constitution, introduces the signers, and provides an outline of the Constitution. The wall poster shows the famous signing scene, surrounded with state flags to color in and lines for your child to write in the names of the signers from each state.

The Bill of Rights follows the same format, with the entire text of the Bill of Rights included. The wall poster is an illustrated outline of the Bill of Rights, with spaces for children to fill in the topics under each amendment. On the bottom is a historical outline section with more blanks to fill in.

United States Government describes the three branches of government. The wall poster shows past U.S. flags at the top, a fill-in-the-blanks outline of the three branches of government below, a list of U.S. presidents, and the flags of the military agencies. The executive departments included in the president's Cabinet are described on a separate sheet of paper.

All these wall projects include a crossword-puzzle quiz, further research projects, and teaching suggestions.

Others in the series include *United States Map, World Map, Holy Land Map, State Flags and Symbols, California State Map, Christopher Columbus and the Age of Exploration,* and *Presidents and Presidential Elections.* Shekinah has science Wall Projects too: see the Basic Science chapter for details.

NEW★★
Teaching Home

February/March 1989 issue, $3.75. Complete six-issue set for 1989, $17.50, includes free set of 6 plastic magazine holders for your ring binder.

Here's one of the few credible sources I have found for ideas on how to teach political science to your own kids at home. The *Teaching Home* February/March 1989 issue was devoted to just this subject, plus how to teach economics. Articles covered principles of political science, how to make economics and government fun, teaching the Biblical philosophy of government, basic economics, and economics for little kids.

NEW★★
Vic Lockman

Patriotracts sample pack, $5.

Talented cartoonist Vic Lockman is also prolific cartoonist Vic Lockman. Besides free-lance cartooning for major firms, book cartooning, and so on, he's produced dozens of books and tracts of his own, mostly illustrating basic Christian doctrine and classic liberal (as in Founding Fathers liberalism, which now is called conservative or libertarian!) principles of government.

Vic's Patriotracts series takes on bureaucracy, unconstitutional paper money, the New World Order, inflationary politics, the unfunded Social Security system, and power-grabbing judges. He promotes local government, the free-enterprise system (including the right to make a profit), reduced government, gun-owner rights, an end to the income tax (did you know we didn't even *have* an income tax until 1913?), private property rights, and limiting the jurisdiction of the courts.

Vic has a genius for taking complex issues and making them simple enough for kids, and even adults, to understand. While I haven't seen most of these tracts, they ought to be zippy, thought-provoking reading.

TOOLS FOR UNDERSTANDING THE WAY IT IS

NEW**
A Beka Book Publications
American Government and Economics in Christian Perspective: student book, $14.35; teacher's guide/curriculum, $20; student test/review booklet, $5.30; teacher's key/test booklet, $8.45. Shipping extra.

I haven't seen A Beka's government-and-economics text, but can still tell you a few things about it. It's for students in grades 9–12. It's "written from the standpoint of Biblical Christianity and political and economic conservatism." It's pro-limited government and free enterprise. It compares the American system (as set up in the Constitution, although widely evaded by government in practice) to other governmental systems, especially socialism and communism. In other words, it's a completely different point of view than you'll find in public-school texts, which *always* favor making the government bigger, more expensive, and more global.

NEW**
Alpha Omega Publications
LIFEPACS, $2.75–$2.95 each or $24.95–$26.95/set of 10 (one course). Teacher handbooks, $4.95 per course. Answer keys, $2.25 each (two per course). LIFEPAC test key (included with teacher handbook), $2.25/course. Shipping extra.

Alpha Omega's seventh-grade social-studies course tackles a whole bunch of subjects at once: history, geography, economics, politics, sociology, anthropology, you name it. LIFEPAC 6 of this course introduces political science from a historical and philosophical point of view, starting with Jewish and Greek civilization. This is just an excellent unit: you get an introduction to basic philosophy and wind up studying Augustine, Aquinas, Machiavelli, Hobbes, Locke, and Mill! LIFEPAC 9, "The Economics and Politics of Our State," explains how state government is structured and financed.

The first half of Alpha Omega's ninth-grade course introduces many aspects of citizenship. LIFEPAC 1 of this course provides the historical and political background of U.S. society, from a (surprisingly) standard public-school viewpoint (good words about those who brought us compulsory public education, huge government programs, and suffragettes). The second and third LIFEPACS explain how national and state/local government work, respectively. Then comes a skippable unit on planning a career (not terribly necessary if you're using Alpha Omega's Bible course, which deals with many of the same issues) and one on the responsibilities and rights of citizens and how to become a citizen.

If you want to find out more about the history of the American political system, the first LIFEPAC of the grade 11 course has what you want. This traces the history of American democracy (actually, American republicanism) as it developed in the various colonies.

Several LIFEPACS of the grade 12 course, "Democracy and Christian Challenges," also focus on citizenship. LIFEPAC 1 introduces self, family, education, and discrimination from a political perspective. LIFEPAC 2 talks about how the American party system works. LIFEPAC 4 discusses international relations, while the sixth one presents a standard evangelical view of the Christian under authority (you gotta obey, influence, and vote).

NEW**
Bob Jones University Press
American Government (grade 12): student text, $19.95, hardbound; teacher's edition, $29.50; poster, $2.95. Shipping extra.

It's a lovely hardbound text, 465 pages long, designed for serious study. Every chapter section has its own section review questions. Each chapter ends with a list of terms for students to define, content questions, and application questions. Example of a content question: "What five civil liberties are guaranteed by the

Constitution?" Example of an application question: "When parents disagree with the state about the disciplining of their children, which has the final authority? Defend your answer."

Like all Bob Jones texts, *American Government* is well written and well organized. Now, what does it cover, and from what angle? There are sections on "Foundations" (the philosophy behind the American system), the Constitution, party politics, the powers of each branch of government, and economics. What you won't find in here is much discussion of state and local government. (BJUP does have a *State and Local Studies* syllabus to help teachers develop a state-history course for any state, but not having seen it I'm not sure how far it delves into state and local politics.) What you will find is a conservative (not libertarian) outlook on the place of Christianity in politics, the rights and duties of government, and the rights and duties of individuals.

Aristoplay, Ltd.
Hail to the Chief, $25. Add $4.75 shipping. Ages 10–adult.

All the fun of a race for the presidency without the airline meals and Secret Service bodyguards. Game includes U.S. map game board, pad of 25 Candidate Scoresheets, 36 Campaign Cards, President Cards, State Cards, two dice, four playing pieces, instruction booklet written in the style of the U.S. Constitution, free coupons for updates. Two to four players, ages 10 and up, first circulate around the outside of the game board, which is adorned with the pictures of our presidents in chronological order. You amass delegate points in an attempt to become the party candidate by correctly answering the questions on President cards. For the benefit of inexperienced players, the four questions on

each card are in graduated levels of difficulty. Easiest questions are on the top, hardest on the bottom.

Players choose which level they want to try before starting play. The President Card deck also includes some Bonus Move cards, to "duly increase the Speed at which Young and inexperienced Players do move about the Board and win Points," and Bonus Question cards (questions you must answer about the president on whose space you are sitting). Land on a Select-a-Campaign-Card space and you encounter the pitfalls and triumphs of a real campaign trail, from an endorsement by the *New York Times* (add 5 delegate points) to losing a TV debate (lose 5 delegate points).

Once you have the party's vote, your campaign really starts. You hit the campaign trail, laid out as a series of interlocking routes on the U.S. map in the middle of the game board. In order to win a state's electoral votes, you have to land on the state capital on an exact roll of the dice and correctly answer a question from the State Card deck. You now can enter that state's electoral votes on your score sheet (the number of electoral votes are listed for each state) and nobody else can win that state. After winning the required number of electoral votes, which varies depending on how many people are playing, you can try to be the first to reach Washington, D.C. on an exact roll of the dice, thus becoming president.

Hail to the Chief is really quite easy to play, and the element of chance and graduated levels of question difficulty even things out somewhat between political pundits and their younger brethren. The Campaign Cards have a nonconservative slant in that you can win points by endorsements from liberal newspapers and groups and lose them by offending the Sierra Club. This is not quite realistic, as Walter Mondale should have won according to these indicators. Otherwise, an admirably crafted, playable game that can really teach you something about presidential history and politics.

NEW★★
Conservative Book Club
Membership book club. Take one introductory book free or at a bargain price, promise to buy 4 more in the next 2 years. All books discounted. Some superbargains—hardback books for $1 or $2! Occasional close-outs with many superbargains. Prices for *The Complete Yes Minister* and *The Complete Yes Prime Minister* will depend on how many remain in stock at the time you purchase them.

You will laugh, you will howl, you will startle your family with your wild giggling, while you read *The*

Complete YES Minister. Based on the hit British TV show, the only one ever to win a British Academy Award for three years in a row, *Yes Minister* is a fast-paced send-up of bureaucratic statist government, narrated from the diary of fictional Cabinet MP James Hacker.

Poor Jim, a politician with an idealistic streak but also a strong will to political survival, keeps tackling the bureaucracy in his department, personalized by Sir Humphrey Appleby, the Permanent Secretary.

Sometimes Jim wins, sometimes he loses, but he always learns something more about how bureaucracies and government operate, and you will too. It's all done tongue in cheek, with that delicious British sense of humor.

Included are genuine-looking reproductions of official memos, TV news scripts, and other artifacts of day-to-day government life. The authors take care to explain how British Parliamentary government works, which is very helpful to those of us on this side of the sea.

We read it aloud to our children at the dinner table. That way we were able to leave out the infrequent vulgar word that the authors threw in for realism's sake.

If you have been wondering how British Conservatives had managed to not only retain office but be popular for so many years, just read this book and remember that it has been running as a TV series on British television. All we need now is a *Complete Yes Senator* version, and people might finally start understanding what has gone wrong with American government as well.

Since Conservative Book Club's stock changes frequently, I can't guarantee that they'll still have this book when you read this—but I sure hope they do!

Speaking of Conservative Book Club, it's the source for a viewpoint you hardly ever see on TV or in the papers. CBC sells books from what could be called the New Right position (as opposed to the Old Wrong). These run the spectrum from Biblical Christian to atheist libertarian, and cover all issues of interest to thinking people (not just politics).

You join by accepting one of CBC's terrific book offers, which for a while now have been heavily advertised in national conservative magazines. We got a complete hardback set of *McGuffeys* for $10 for joining the Club. Another excellent offer I saw was for Sam Blumenfeld's *Alphaphonics.* Whatever the bait book may be, it's one that's interesting and valuable reading. Once you're in, you need only buy four more books at the discounted club price. Every so often CBC sends

you a mailing about their current specials, along with Neil McCaffrey's terrific reviews.

We have been CBC members for several years now and are well pleased with their service and selection.

EDC Publishing
The Usborne Introduction to Politics and Governments, $6.95 paperbound or $12.96 library-bound. Ages 10 and up.

Like the rest of the Usborne series published in England, *The Usborne Introduction to Politics and Governments* relies on lots of colorful, captioned illustrations and a clever organizational scheme to present you with masses of information in an easy-to-remember format. You will find out about such things as dictators, summits, senates, republics, fascism, Marxism, apartheid, diplomacy, democracy, and elections. Equal emphasis on parliamentary systems (like the British) and presidential systems (like the American). The only strange thing in the book was the way they refused to define fascism.

Fascism is *not* just totalitarianism under a strongman ruler, as the text implied—that's an equally good definition of any number of Marxist African countries. Briefly, fascism is the system under which private owners run their companies, but the government tells them how to do it. Think of fascism as "private-public partnerships," the current buzzword, and you've got it. Big Business in bed with Big Government = fascism.

Fascists emphasize productivity; in fact, *fascism* comes from the Latin root that means "to do." They're also likely to make a lot of noise about balance-of-trade, the need for government help in the import-export economy, the need for planning and wise allocation of scarce resources, and so on. Fascists are not conservative; the "Nazi" in Nazi Party stands for "National Socialist." Lots of flag-waving patriotism and commitment to a New World Order run by technopolitical elites (namely, themselves). Lots of looking for scapegoats on whom to blame the economic messes of the past (Jews and fundamentalist Christians make popular scapegoats). Lots of enthusiasm for well-planned military actions—and even wars—that show off the fascist country's military superiority. Quite similar to the situation now developing in the U.S.A. and other Western countries, actually.

But we digress. This is a fascinating book, covering everything from "What is politics?" to diplomacy and spying. You'll find out how people around the world conduct the business of government. You'll learn about the major political theories. All this in a down-to-earth, amply illustrated, humorous format. Special chart at the end shows each country's main political parties, form of government, and the titles of its leaders. Recommended.

NEW★★
Home School Legal Defense Association
Constitutional Law for Christian Students, $17.50 postpaid. Teacher handbook, $2.50 postpaid. Grades 10–adult.

Want an in-depth introduction to constitutional law for your high-school or college student, or even for yourself? Lawyer Michael Farris, president of the Home School Legal Defense Association and a real nice guy, has what you're looking for! His *Constitutional Law for Christian Students*, subtitled "Original Documents and Decisions of the United States Supreme Court," is a well laid-out, relatively easy-reading summary of constitutional law and theory, written from a sturdy conservative viewpoint. In his own words, "You will find no pretense at neutrality. This book is written to impart what I believe to be the correct views of constitutional law." However, this oversized, 288-page book includes long excerpts from *both* sides of many major decisions.

You get units on the Constitution's historical background, the Constitution as higher law, executive and congressional authority, developing a constitutionally-sound theory of government, and religious freedom. Michael is an acknowledged expert on these areas, especially the area of religious freedom; he has been battling for religious freedom in the courts since 1973, arguing cases before the U. S. Supreme Court and numerous federal and state appellate courts.

The accompanying (and much slimmer) teacher handbook provides questions for each of the book's chapters, along with the correct answers to the questions. These are not discussion questions, but questions

like "State the seven principles of judicial self-restraint" and "Does Congress possess the authority to conduct negotiations of international agreements?" Many questions deal with specific Court decisions summarized and quoted at length in the text. By the time students have finished going through the course, answering all these questions, they will know more about the Supreme Court's interaction with the Constitution than most political shakers and movers do. An excellent way to bring Constitutional studies up to date.

Recommended.

Ideal School Supply
Our Government, $7.95. *Presidential Posters*, $16.95

Our Government is a set of four posters with a simplified explanation of the branches of government. *Presidential Posters* are 8½ x 11 inch full-color portraits with accompanying bios of each man and important events during his presidency. Discussion topics; teacher's guide. Make 'em into a book, or let your kid paper his room with them.

TOOLS FOR DOING SOMETHING ABOUT IT

NEW★★
The Advocate
Advocate subscription, 12 issues/year, $20 suggested donation. Ages 13–adult (anyone who can handle the sight of an aborted baby).

I know this is going to turn some of you off, but the fact is that the main media are *not* covering both sides of the abortion issue fairly. This full-color magazine has the stories Dan Rather and *Newsweek* seem to miss. Supports pro-life direct action ("rescuing"). Strong on the facts: you'll see pictures of babies' bodies found in dumpsters outside abortion clinics and pictures of police officers breaking pro-lifers' arms. You'll also see pictures of babies saved from abortion, held by their now-loving mothers. Strong on historical reporting: the real story behind *Roe v. Wade,* what went on in the planning sessions of the first abortion-rights gang. (Dr. Bernard Nathanson, one of the gang, has defected and now tells all.) Strong on the medical facts: what really happens during the "procedure," how many women are killed in "safe, legal" abortions, how much blood and feces the rescuers found in the clinic before the police dragged them away. Strong on testimonies: women who were persuaded not to abort after all, sidewalk counselors, rescuers, children of rescuers. Strong nondenominational Christian emphasis. Molly Yard will hate you forever if you subscribe.

NEW★★
American Family Association
Journal subscription, 10 issues/year, $15. Bulk subs of 10 or more send $4/name plus name of church and legible mailing list. Adults only.

Read the magazine of "the man the networks love to hate"! The *Journal of the American Family Association* started out as an anti-pornography magazine and is now the best source for what's happening in the media battle. Mini-reviews of offensive TV shows, movies, etc. shine the light on the problem without forcing you to see them for yourself. The AFA is now leading the fight against Christian-bashing, which has developed into a major problem in the media. Issues also include information about current boycotts and how to lobby business leaders. Nondenominational Christian emphasis. Founded by Don Wildmon, a United Methodist minister.

NEW★★
Basil Blackwell, Inc.
How to Win in Washington: Very Practical Advice about Lobbying, the Grassroots and the Media, $21.95.

I know you don't want to go to Washington, the murder capital of the U.S. I don't either. But it *is* kind of interesting to find out how power politics *really* works, and this is the book to tell you. From meeting your elected representatives and their staffs to organizing a lobbying campaign, through the ups and downs of Congressional hearings and working with the media, this little book tells it like it is. Studded with examples of winning lobbying campaigns, *How to Win in Washington* scores high on human interest. You'll also gain

insight into the amazing foolishness of Our Leaders, whose errors often must be undone by intensive lobbying from the grassroots. See how they vow to cripple Toshiba for selling security-sensitive material to the Russians, ignorant of the fact that billions of dollars of American industry depend on Toshiba products. Watch them try to force banks to withhold interest on savings accounts, an idea opposed by roughly 99.9% of the American people. See them posture for political advantage on issues they know nothing about. See how the grassroots are forced into turbulent motion again and again, to defend their rights and property against Congressional enthusiasms. Is this why all roads used to lead to Rome?

NEW★★
Focus on the Family Citizen
One year subscription (12 issues), $20. Older teens and adults.

Of all the many political-action magazines I get each month, Focus on the Family's *Citizen* is the most all-around useful. You not only get pertinent information on current issues of interest to families, but instructions on how to write (and *who* to write), how to lobby, how to approach a store manager, and other essential tools for those who want to exercise their rights as citizens.

Citizen is generally upbeat, featuring (as much as possible) success stories of plain folks who made a difference. At 16 pages, it's also a fairly quick read, and its inviting layout encourages you to make it all the way through.

Wff 'n Proof Learning Games Associates
Propaganda, $22.50 postpaid. Ages 12–adult.

One of the most acute problems when dealing with political issues is recognizing propaganda. The *Propaganda* game, co-authored by Lorne Greene of "Bonanza" fame, consists of definitions of propaganda devices and a series of sample statements, each of which contains one such device. Students play by either challenging the group consensus (in which case the authors' solutions are consulted) or by going along with it. You get points for challenging correctly and lose points for incorrect challenges. You can also play *Solitaire*, checking yourself against the solutions.

Once the basic games have been played several times, students are encouraged to invent their own problems, using the *Congressional Record* or any old newspaper.

Propaganda is an attractive, fun, inexpensive way to bring a little reason to a field that notoriously lacks it.

CHAPTER TWENTY-FOUR

ECONOMICS

Economics is the art of predicting how people will make and spend their money.

That's all there is to it!

Many of us have been dazzled by charts and graphs and statistics into believing economics is a "science." Not so! People in the mass are just like people as individuals—human, not robots. We obey certain laws of our inner nature, and thus our behavior is sometimes predictable, but no scientist will ever be able to predict a new social trend like the Cabbage Patch fad or the computer boom.

Economists nowadays are divided into two main schools. The Keynesian school, as represented by Congress and the New York *Times,* believes that the more you spend the richer you get. Thus they support deficit financing of everything from washing machines to Great Society programs and believe that the piper will never show up demanding to be paid. They also firmly believe that "the economy," meaning your and my decisions about how we spend our money, needs a wise and powerful elite, meaning them, to regulate and control and strangle us into submission.

The other school of economics believes that there ain't no such thing as a free lunch and that "the economy," which you'll recall means you and me, will work out things better for its individual members if said individual members are allowed to make their own decisions. This school, known as Free-Market Economics,

is less than grateful to those who want to "help the people" by plundering those very same people and filtering their money through a bureaucracy. Its members are quick to point out that there can be no such thing as Irresponsible Capitalists Exploiting the People without (a) the Irresponsible Capitalists committing actual crimes, for which they can be punished, or (b) the active cooperation of bureaucrats emitting regulations that stifle small business and entrepreneurial competition.

The two schools, then, divide on the issue of bureaucratic control. The Keynesian side says "Bureaucracy is great! We need more of it!" The Free Market side replies, "Horsefeathers! Bureaucrats *cause* all those scarcities, monopolies, and price problems that you claim we need bureaucrats to solve!" Bureaucracy, for or against, is the main battle line.

There are other areas of conflict. Keynesians love it when the government hemorrhages billions of dollars of unbacked paper money into the economy. Free Marketers hate it. But since the only reason the government is so anxious to spend money it doesn't have is to pay for more bureaucracies, this too is a symptom of the basic conflict.

So economics is not a dull, dry, dreary struggle with dusty statistics, but a full-fledged war. One side believes in itself, and wants all power for itself; the other side believes in the people. One side has its hand in your wallet, the other is trying to get you your wallet back. One side gushes fog and irrelevant statistics to conceal its actions, and hypocritically deplores the sad state of Inflation or The Deficit, both of which it zealously creates every time it gets a chance. The other side writes muscular, readable books and strives to dispel confusion.

SCARCITY OR ABUNDANCE?

Economists are fond of saying that the fundamental problem of economics is how to allocate scarce resources. There's a shortage of everything, and the problem is to make sure either (a) everyone gets the same amount, (b) everyone gets enough, or (c) everyone gets what he deserves, depending on your outlook.

But there's another way of looking at economics.

A friend of mine writes a newsletter about silver and gold (of which, like the apostles, I have none) and current social and economic trends. We swap subscriptions, so I get his newsletter free and he gets mine for the same affordable price. This friend stated in one of his recent letters:

> Scarcity is not chronic and insoluble, but an intermittent problem in time and space, so it seems that the distribution of God's abundance is closer to the heart of economics. (It's the "Tomato Problem"—anyone who has ever raised tomatoes will tell you that the basic concern of economics is not scarcity, but distribution of the abundance in time and space. One week you have nothing but tomato plants; the next you have bushel baskets of tomatoes you can't *give* away.)

> God isn't miserly. He sends His rain on the just and the unjust alike, and he continually tells his people, "Open your mouth and I will fill it with good things . . . I will feed you on the finest wheat and honey from the rock." He shows us in the wilderness that he "opens the windows of heaven" and showers down on

more blessings on us than we can hold. That is His character, and in the 20th century more than ever, with the benefits of several generations of industrialization, we see what lengths that abundance reaches. Man's concern is no longer eating or starving this winter, but whether to buy a new VCR or a new Nintendo. . . .

> In Genesis 3:17 God doesn't say that the ground will produce scarcely, but rather that now the Creation will fight man, that what was easy before will become hard now. However, this doesn't necessarily decree scarcity, simply the extension of the Fall's curse to all creation. God's abundance is poured out, but whereas before it fell off the trees, so to speak, now the ground is cursed and we eat of it in sweat and sorrow, i.e., through much hard work.

An interesting point. God's blessing + hard work = abundance. Scarcity = either laziness, greed (wanting more than is reasonable in the first place), God's judgment on a nation or individual, or some combination of the above. Just because everyone wants something doesn't make it scarce; perhaps some of us need to adjust our wants! Genuine scarcities come from acts of God (famine, plague, disasters, being attacked by strong enemies) or laziness (refusing to reap the abundance that is there). The Pilgrims believed in an outlook very similar to this, and they and their descendants turned America from a Third-World country into the world's most envied nation.

Strangely enough, the "we're running out of everything" viewpoint seems always to come from those who want to limit our freedoms and grow the government. Perhaps an "abundance" viewpoint, besides fitting the facts better, would lead to greater liberty for all. Kinda like what the Pilgrims had in mind. We can hope.

BEGINNING ECONOMICS

NEW★★
A Beka Book Publications
Economics: Work and Prosperity: student book, $12.50; teacher's guide, $21.30; student test packet, $3.20; teacher key/test packet, $7.40. Available August 1991: student quiz booklet, $3.20; teacher key/quiz booklet, $7.40. Shipping extra.

I haven't seen this textbook, but Russell Kirk wrote it, so it has to be good. The catalog description says, "Concepts thought too difficult for high-school students are made thoroughly understandable." The theme: America's market economy versus the loser "command" economies planned by central governments. Conservative introduction to topics such as competition, private-property rights, and how the free marketplace works. The Foundation for Economic Education's *Freeman* newsletter gave this book an outstanding review.

NEW**
Academy for Economic Education

Ump's Fwat: An Annual Report for Young People, 1 copy free, 6 or more copies 50¢ each. Teacher's kit—instructor's guide and 30 copies of *Ump's Fwat*—$15. Instructor's guide alone, $2. 8-minute animated VHS video, $24.95. *The Economic Baseball Game*, $7.

What's a "fwat"? It's the product of Ump's business. Ump is a caveman who excelled with the fwat in the game of fwap, and *Ump's Fwat* is the story of how he made his fortune manufacturing fwats for other cavemen. This fanciful tale is used to illustrate many of the concepts and terms used in business—savings, marketable product, investment, employment, etc.

If I were to criticize anything about this thoroughly winsome booklet, it would be the constant emphasis on how Ump's fwat business is so great at creating jobs. I believe that the ideal is for every man to sit under his own vine and fig tree, i.e., to have his own business and not have to work for someone else's. Since *Ump's Fwat* is written from the entrepreneur's perspective, this is not a major problem.

Also available: an instructor's guide, an eight-minute animated video retelling Ump's success story, and *The Economic Baseball Game*. The latter is a supply-and-demand simulation in which players buy and sell baseballs, and is designed for ages 10 to adult.

I have not seen the instructor's guide, the video, or the *Economic Baseball Game*. Myself, I can get a lot out of the free *Ump's Fwat* book, but if you are not already knowledgeable about free-market economics the in-

structor's guide and game might be helpful. The video is too pricey for single-family viewing.

NEW**
Alpha Omega Publications

LIFEPACS, $2.75–$2.95 each or $24.95–$26.95/set of 10 (one course). Teacher handbooks, $4.95 per course. Answer keys, $2.25 each (two per course). LIFEPAC test key (included with teacher handbook), $2.25/course. Shipping extra.

Alpha Omega's seventh-grade social-studies course tackles a whole bunch of subjects at once: history, geography, economics, politics, sociology, anthropology, you name it. Since we're talking about economics at the moment, you should know that it's mentioned in one of the LIFEPAC units of this course. Unit 5 introduces economic theory of a standard neoconservative variety (e.g., free enterprise is good and so are government regulations and fractional-reserve banking).

You get a smidgin more about economics in grade 12, in LIFEPAC 3, which talks about the basics of a market economy and problems businesses face in a mixed economy from a viewpoint sympathetic to downsizing government. Why the different viewpoints between grades 9 and 12? Because LIFEPACS, even within the same course, are not necessarily written by the same author or authors.

NEW**
American Textbook Committee

Basic Economics by Clarence B. Carson, $29.95 hardbound or $12 paperbound. Shipping extra. Grades 10–adult.

An economics text for "reasonably bright teenagers" and up, from the author of *A Basic History of the United States* (see the History chapter). Solid free-market emphasis with lots of historical nuggets. Lots of handy helps, too: the glossary defines 90 key economics terms, a detailed table of contents tells you exactly what follows what, the index tells you where it is, and a set of 20 profiles of key economic thinkers help you know the players. Almost 400 pages in all.

Aristoplay, Ltd.

Made for Trade, $22. Add $4.75 shipping. Ages 8–adult.

Made for Trade is a historical board game that teaches economics lessons. See full review in the History chapter.

NEW**
Bluestocking Press
Whatever Happened to Penny Candy? 2nd edition, $7.95 plus $2 shipping. Teacher's materials, 75¢ postpaid when purchased with the book or $1.25 postpaid if purchased separately. Canadian supplement, $5.50 postpaid. Prices are in U.S. dollars. Ages 10–adult.

So, whatever *did* happen to penny candy? Inflation, that's what! And where does inflation come from? From governments inflating the money supply. And how do governments inflate the money supply? By "legal tender" laws that force people to treat pieces of paper that can't be redeemed for precious metals as if the pieces of paper were worth something, and by a few other little tricks and quirks that you will fully understand after reading this book.

Whatever Happened to Penny Candy is written as a series of letters from an economist uncle to his teen nephew (or niece) Chris. The origin and history of money, the origin and history of the dollar, the business cycle, inflation, recession, depression, foreign currencies, why and how governments meddle with the value of our money, and so on, are all covered in an easy-to-read style. The author, Richard J. Maybury, has drawn on years of experience explaining these things to his own students and colleagues. What you get is not witty, but it *is* clear and understandable, which is more than you can say for 99% of economics books!

Advantages for home schoolers: the book has a glossary, and words in the glossary are in boldface in the text. It also has an excellent bibliography and Recommended Reading list, with mini-reviews of the books on the list. This will come in extremely handy if you want to pursue further study in economics. Most of the books recommended are available from Liberty-Tree. You also get a fine resources list; a list of cassettes, games, and software; and a list of financial newsletters recommended by the author. The new edition of *Penny Candy* also includes: an excerpt from Laura Ingalls Wilder's *The Long Winter*; an 1846 trade store sign from Sutter's Fort in Sacramento; charts showing dollar supply, federal debt, and real wages; and quotations from the Founding Fathers on numerous subjects.

The author follows the "monetarist" or "Austrian" school of economics, popularized by writers such as Milton Friedman and Friedrich A. Hayek. If you never heard of monetarism or Hayek, don't worry—this is just the book for you!

An excellent introduction to economics for teens and adults that will change the way you read the paper (both the newspaper and the fine print on your dollar bills). Highly recommended.

The teacher's support material is a little brochure with some suggestions, a reproducible quiz with answers printed separately, a set of short reproducible essay questions, and discussion questions.

A Canadian supplement to *Penny Candy* has been published by WindowTreeLearning Project, 9862 - 156A St., Surrey, B.C., Canada V3R 7X7. This 20-page supplement explains the differences between American and Canadian monetary and economic history so that Canadian readers can more easily apply the principles found in *Penny Candy* to their own country. The Canadian supplement can also be purchased from Bluestocking Press.

NEW**
Bob Jones University Press
Economics for Christian Schools (grade 12): student text, $19.95, hardbound; teacher's edition, $29.50, spiralbound. Shipping extra.

This text is so new that I haven't seen it! Since it's from BJUP, you can expect it to be hardbound, well written, and conservative (not libertarian) in outlook. You can also expect the course to begin with the philosophy of economics, as informed by BJUP's biblical convictions, and then progress to teaching you economics terminology and applications. You can also expect the teacher's edition to be the best part of the course, giving background information and answers to the fact and thought questions.

The catalog copy says *Economics for Christian Schools* "explains how [economic] principles work in business firms, financial markets, and government. It also includes a practical analysis of the use of economic principles in managing the finances of the household."

This is meant to be a one-semester course, paired with BJUP's *American Government* book in the first semester. Both books have the same format and style of graphics.

NEW**
Commonsense Press
Alpha Strategy, due out October 1991, $18.95 plus $3 shipping. Grades 10–adult.

This groundbreaking book will change your thinking about money, economy, and the way government and big business cooperate. It also provides you with a bulletproof, productive use for your financial resources that does *not* involve shady ethics, get-rich-quick schemes, or Wall Street gambling with stocks and bonds. Following this advice, we were able (with the blessing of God) to *triple* our income in a few years!

Alpha Strategy is presently being revised, with the new edition due out in October 1991. You'll have to wait for the new edition, because the previous printings have all been sold out. Very highly recommended.

Conservative Book Club
Membership book club. Take one introductory book free or at a bargain price, promise to buy 4 more in the next 2 years. All books discounted. Some superbargains—hardback books for $1 or $2! Occasional close-outs with many superbargains. College and adult.

An unparalleled source for great books on economics at discount prices. Many books are hardbound. I bought *Wealth and Poverty, The Spirit of Enterprise,* and *The Alpha Strategy* from CBC.

Let us now sing the praises of a book CBC sells that actually has the answer to our current tax fiasco. It's *The Big Tax Lie* by William A. Kilpatrick ($17.95 retail, hardbound—CBC price less). After laying out the problems with our current system—the inevitable invasion of privacy caused by government needing to know everything everyone does to verify that it is tax-deductible and to be sure nobody is hiding any income; the plundering mentality of special interests that get loopholes for themselves while siphoning our tax money; the expense of keeping track of it all; the injustice of the IRS's almost unlimited (and unconstitutional) powers of search and seizure; the unfairness of special tax courts where normal rules do not apply, and so on— Mr. Kilpatrick points out a simple, obvious solution.

As Kilpatrick says, "There are two types of taxes, direct and indirect. Both are ultimately taxes on con-

sumption, and no rationalization can change this irrefutable fact." He proves this point—that the consumer ultimately pays *all* taxes, corporate taxes included—and then suggests the obvious solution: substitute a flat-rate sales or use tax on *end products* (those bought and sold retail). Poor people buy less, pay less. IRS no longer needs to know your personal affairs, since tax is between them and the tax-collecting businesses. Special interests can't wiggle out of taxes. Tax courts no longer needed. Bureaucrats no longer control personal affairs by juggling taxes. Most importantly, people finally see what all this huge government bureaucracy we support *really* costs. The more you look at his arguments, the more you see they actually work.

NEW**
Teaching Home
February/March 1989 issue, $3.75. Complete six-issue set for 1989, $17.50, includes free set of 6 plastic magazine holders for your ring binder.

Teaching Home magazine as its usual policy devotes each issue of the magazine to one educational theme. Articles treat the topic in depth, suggesting ideas and profiling methods and resources. It's like a mini-course in teaching that topic! February/March 1989 was the issue on teaching political science and economics. Articles covered principles of political science, how to make economics and government fun, teaching the biblical philosophy of government, basic economics, and economics for little kids.

NEW**
Vic Lockman
Money, Banking, and Usury, $3.95 postpaid. Ages 9–adult.

Easy-reading discussion in cartoon format describes what money is and how it works, how United States money has changed over time, how banks were invented and how they work now, and a biblical case against usury (lending at interest). Same principles as in the books from Theopolis (see reviews later in this chapter), explained more simply. Very engaging and easy to follow.

UPDATED★★
Vic Lockman
Biblical Economics in Comics, $6.95. Add $1 shipping. Ages 8–adult.

Our kids have just about worn the covers off our one and only copy of Vic Lockman's *Biblical Economics in Comics*. This is undoubtedly partly a tribute to Mr. Lockman's cartooning skill—after all, the man has put in more than 30 years in the comic book industry, authoring over 7,000 comic book stories and publishing more than 100 cartoon booklets. The rest of our youngsters' fascination with this 100-plus page small paperback stems from the intriguing storyline. In Vic Lockman's hands, economics is transformed from the "dismal science" into a series of cartoon vignettes featuring mice, rats (Bureau-Rats!), and cats.

Episode One, "The Market," starts with Adam Mouse shipwrecked on an island. There he is joined by a lady mouse, and bingo! the division of labor. They next have a family, which works as a mini-marketplace (more division of labor). When Junior gathers so much fish it begins to spoil, Pop diverts Junior's efforts to chopping wood . . . "and so, production is diverted to fill a greater demand!" The principles of exchange, competition, supply and demand, medium of exchange, capital and savings, loans and interest, profit and productivity, taxes, and even international trade are all explained so clearly a six-year-old can understand them. (I know. I asked him.)

Next, Mr. Lockman starts explaining some of our economic woes. Enter the Bureau-Rats, who, taking their lead from Karl Marx, inflict a graduated income tax on Mouseland. (I say this as someone who most of her life has honestly qualified for one of the bottom tax levels!) This is swiftly followed by a central bank, fiat money, inflation through expansion of printed money, checkbook money (the money printer got tired), tariffs,

immigration quotas, public works, government aid to farms and industry, minimum wage laws, price fixing, rent control, public housing, welfare, monopolies, and that eternal favorite of Keynesian economists for stirring up sluggish economies, war. The rest of the book is devoted (still in cartoon form, but without story plots) to an exposition of the proper roles of government, law, money, and taxes, all from a specifically biblical viewpoint.

The revised edition of *Biblical Economics in Comics* includes a new 12-page cartoon section on usury: what it is, what the Bible says about it, and how to live without it. Excellent teaching on this complex subject, simple enough for a child to follow.

NEW★★
The Weekend Farmer Co.
The Farming Game, $19.95 plus $5 shipping. Ages 10–adult.

Wanna really get into the struggles of family farming in post-New Deal America? Try *The Farming Game* from the Weekend Farmer Company. This very realistic farming simulation game comes with a game board, play money, play promissory notes, peel 'n stick tokens for cows/grain crops/hay crops, fruit crops, and farm implements, player tokens, three sets of cards, and two dice. The game board itself has a map in the middle with the four farm "spreads" on it, surrounded by rangeland where you can run more cattle than will fit on your farm. You move around the outside of the game board, where every square corresponds to a week of the farming year. Every square has directions to follow, e.g., collect an Option to Buy card or get $500 from the bank. When you land on a harvest season space, you roll the dice to find out how much your crop made . . . and how much you have to pay back as operating expenses. Each year has four hay cuttings, two fruit seasons (cherries and apples), one livestock sale, and two grain harvest (wheat and corn). You can only purchase new equipment or acreage between Christmas vacation and the spring planting season, using an Option to Buy card. You can either pay cash or put 20 percent or more down and borrow the rest from the bank.

You start the game with 10 acres of grain, 10 acres of hay, $10,000 cash and a $10,000 debt. Every year on your Christmas vacation you collect $5,000 from your town job. The object of the game is to amass $250,000 in assets, enabling you to shed your town job and become a full-time farmer. Alternatively, you can play a set number of rounds and the winner is the person with the most assets (cash, acreage, livestock, and implements).

The Farming Game teaches you about the realities of farming, finance, and capitalism from a struggler's point of view. It's not big on admiring beautiful rural scenery or going fishing—gotta git them hogs to market! In spite of this, it's fun to play. A real live farmer designed this game on the seat of his tractor and put his weekend farm in hock to produce the game. It's a beautiful game, just as pretty and professional-looking as any sold in the stores, and far more educational and entertaining than most. So let's help him out, folks!

ECONOMICS FOR THE THINKING PERSON

I'm not going to kid you that the following books are all easy reads. Be smart and get the beginner's versions above first. But, for those of you who want *more*, here it is!

NEW★★
Bluestocking Press
The Freedom Philosophy, $5.95 plus $2 shipping. Grades 10–adult.

Two classic essays you absolutely must read in order to understand free-market governing and economics. The first is by Colonel Davy Crockett (yes, *that* Davy Crockett); the second, by a lead pencil.

Davy Crockett relates how, as he was campaigning for reelection to Congressman Horatio Bunce taught him that government ain't in the charity biz. (Stripped to essentials; what gives our elected representatives the right to take money *by force* from person A to give to person B? Where is it in the Constitution? Why don't

these compassionate congressmen ever give any of their *own* money? How can Ted Kennedy weep buckets for the poor, vote for every tax-and-spend idea in sight, and stay so filthy rich? And why do the voters of Massachusetts keep letting him get away with it?)

The lead pencil relates how he is, perhaps not fearfully, but wonderfully made by the cooperative endeavors of hundreds of people who will never meet each other and whose lives are not coordinated by any mastermind other than God.

You also get 12 other essays in this book from libertarianism's best and brightest, but my advice is still to beat your path to Crockett and Pencil first, for indelibly vivid proof that liberty works.

NEW★★
Bluestocking Press
Free Market Economics. Syllabus and Reader, $7.95 each plus $2 shipping each if purchased separately. $15 plus $3 shipping if purchased together. Grades 10–adult.

The *Free Market Economics* reader is a selection of 81 articles by free-market thinkers, all stitched together by Bettina Greave of the Foundation of Economic Education. Articles are arranged in subject categories and run the gamut from simple parables to full-blown treatises. Some authors, such as Abraham Lincoln and Davy Crockett, you will recognize. Others, such as Gary North, you might recognize. Still others, such as Hans F. Sennholz and Sylvester Petro, are only household words at FEE.

I tackled this book prepared to hate it. For one thing, I hate anthologies of every species of literature except fiction. An 81-article anthology offered far more intellectual enrichment than I felt inclined to handle. The book has been saved by its logical layout, which I will describe in a minute, and the sheer fascination of discovering how every day and in every way the Big Boys are stiffing us. I don't mean poor slobs like Donald Trump, trump he never so wisely and boast he never so well. I mean our Noble Leaders, who have obviously never taken the time to read this book.

It can be rattling to find out that just about every assumption the TV pundits operate by isn't worth a Continental. Take "full employment," for example. Do we really want full employment? Think about the Israelites in Egypt, who enjoyed that blessed state as slaves to Pharaoh, before you answer too hastily. You can even find out where the phrase, "it isn't worth a Continental," came from, and why money doesn't grow on *or come from* trees.

Outline of the book: Introduction ("Economics for Boys and Girls," obviously written in the Beaver Cleaver era when being honest and true-blue was still worth something). Economics defined. Human nature defined. Private property and exchange (includes some great advice Abe Lincoln gave his no-good stepbrother). How we can work together in a free market. Why we should let the market determine prices. Savings, tools, and production (in which we find out Karl Marx forgot a few things). Why the entrepreneur is worthy of his wages. Why the worker is also worthy of his wages, and why he should "rob no man by violence." Why we need real money and why its ingredients don't grow as trees. Why Big Biz is no threat until it gets in bed with Uncle Sam. Why free trade works across regional and national boundaries. The history of economic thought. Capitalism v. socialism. The history of economic policies.

The *Free Market Economics Syllabus* is a teacher's manual for a whole course in economics at the high school or college level. It follows the same outline as the *Free Market Economics Reader,* and includes teaching tips, suggested activities, questions (with answers), and lots more references than you'll ever read. This book extensively *teaches* economic principles, while the articles in the *Reader* discuss, argue, and apply them. Although in theory a high schooler could study the syllabus on his own, I think any such brave soul will flounder unless he reads the *Reader* first and finds at least one other person to work through the syllabus with him. Economics studied solo truly is a dismal science!

One last point worth mentioning: Crockett on government aid and the Lead Pencil are in the Reader, too, so if you have the appetite for a larger dose of the Freedom Philosophy, you can skip the book by that name and take the full-course meal right here.

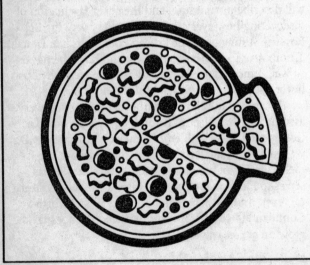

NEW★★
Bluestocking Press
Economics in One Lesson, $7.95 plus $1.75 shipping. Grades 11–adult.

The title says *Economics in One Lesson.* Here's the lesson:

> The art of economics consists in looking not merely at the immediate but at the longer effects of any act or policy; it consists in tracing the consequences of that policy not merely for one group but for all groups.

Oh, if only Henry Hazlitt, who penned those deathless words, had been trained as a copywriter. For then the one lesson would have read:

> If you wanna pass laws that affect how people make and spend their money, Jack, you'd better think about how the laws affect everyone besides the lucky bozo who gets the government handout. And you'd better think about how the laws affect even him, once the first rush from all that cash wears off.

This has been the curse of libertarianism: cloudy words. Abstract nouns. Long strings of them, holding together undeniable truths that nobody will ever bother to read.

I don't mean to imply that Hazlitt is boring. You just have to be an abstract thinker to appreciate him. He does deserve appreciation, for after uttering his one lesson he goes on to explain how it applies to all sorts of loony-tunes economic policies: public works, full employment, spread-the-work schemes, trade wars, saving dying industries, price and wage fixing, rent control, minimum wage laws, employment-killing unionism, inflation, and more.

Someone who can speak or write with sizzle ought to read this book, take all its ideas, massage them till they come back to life, and send them out conquering and to conquer.

Come to think of it, someone *has.* Vic Lockman's *Biblical Economics Through Comics* covers most of Hazlitt's ground, from the broken-window scenario all the way to why trade barriers don't really help protectionist nations. If you can't bear to descend to the comic-book level, you might consider perusing the prewar speeches of Winston Churchill, which made many of the same points. *Economics in One Easy Lesson* is still considered the classic, though; if you want to impress your intellectual pals, read this book.

NEW**
Durell Foundation
Teaching Kit on Money and Banking, $14.95, includes a 28-minute VHS videotape, *It's Only Money*. Grades 9–adult.

What do high school students know about money, anyway? "How to spend it" doesn't count. What do they know about banking? Not much more. Nor do most of them *want* to learn more, until an inspiring teacher shares the fascinating history of these superficially dull subjects. In the terminology of free-market economics, there is a need, but no demand.

Foundations were created to supply demandless needs; thus was born the *Durell Foundation Teaching Kit on Money and Banking*.

This kit gives you a whole lot for your money. Its seven lesson plans cover (1) What are Money and Banking? (2) Money in Colonial America, (3) Money and the Constitution, (4) Money and Banking Before the Civil War, (5) From the Civil War to the Federal Reserve, (6) The Federal Reserve System, and (7) Money and Banking in the Twentieth Century. Nice so far, but there's more. 100 suggested test questions with answer key. A money and banking glossary. A wall poster showing the value of the dollar versus time, with notes indicating historical events that led to rises or dips in the dollar's value. A chronology of American money and banking. Essays and quotable quotes. A copy of *The Durell Journal of Money and Banking* (a formidable repository of economic knowledge with a gold medal embossed on the cover). And last but not least, these books: *Good as Gold: How We Lost Our Gold Reserves and Destroyed the Dollar*, *Money and Freedom* (or *Gold, Greenbacks, and the Constitution*, which may be substituted for *How We Lost*, depending on supplies), and *Coins and Currency*. As with so many other liberty-oriented books and kits, Davy Crockett's famous "Not Yours to Give" essay is included. You also get a 28-minute VHS videotape, which I haven't seen, since I reviewed an earlier copy of the kit.

The lesson plans are easy to use, even for teachers with no previous economic knowledge. Just give your students the reading assignments. When they have completed these, bring out the visual aids included. Each lesson is outlined in simple language, so you and the students can discuss it. After systematically studying your way through all seven lessons, give the test (answer key provided). At this point your student could subscribe to *Reason* or *The Freeman* and understand the economics articles.

The whole package is tremendous value for money and not at all intimidating, with the possible exception of the *Durell Journal* itself. The love of money is the root of all kinds of evil; the Durell kit will prove to your teen that the hatred of honest money is the root of many more kinds of evil.

Foundation for Economic Education
The Freeman, 12 issues/year. Single copy $1. Free subscription in U.S.A.; donation of $15/year to cover shipping outside U.S.A. Bound volumes or microfilmed volumes from earlier years available. *The Law, Mainspring of Human Progress*, $2.95 each. Add $2 shipping. College and adult.

Books from a free-enterprise position. Classics no educated person should miss.

The Law by Frederic Bastiat explains how, under democracy, special interests can use the vote to "plunder" (his word) others . . . and why the redistribution of income via taxes and government aid (as opposed to private charity) is always wrong. Bastiat, a Frenchman writing in the early 1800s, also predicts the Civil War as an outgrowth of tariffs and slavery, two anti-freedom positions respectively adopted by the North and the South. Very easy to read and understand.

Henry Grady Weaver's *The Mainspring of Human Progress* is a breezy history of civilization which explains that the "ups" stem from freedom, the "downs" from the restriction or denial of freedom. Many other books and writers included as well. The Austrian School is well-represented.

FEE publishes a journal called *The Freeman*, "a monthly study journal of free market, private property, limited government ideas and ideals." Recently upgraded to readable print size, it contains fascinating articles like "The Polish Underground." See how the Poles have created a parallel economy in which, as Solidarity's Wiktor Kulerski wrote from hiding, "authorities will control empty stores, but not the market; the employment of workers, but not their livelihood; the official media, but not the circulation of information; printing plants, but not the publishing movement; the mail and telephones, but not communications; and the school system, but not education." That same issue had fine articles on "Native Americans: Victims of Bureaucracy" and "Jamaica: No Free Market, No Miracle," among others. You'll find out a lot about other countries and cultures reading *The Freeman!* Letters to the editor, book reviews also included. FEE also has audio- and videotaped lectures about economics.

If you never understood economics before, it's probably because of that Keynesian fog that glommed up your school texts. FEE has the antidote.

Jeffrey Norton Publishers
Why Socialism Always Fails, A Conversation With Milton Friedman, $10.95 each. *How Government Destroys Our Money*, $10.95. Shipping extra. College and adult.

With enterprising evenhandedness, Jeffrey Norton Publishers carries cassettes both by free-market economists and by the like of John Gailbraith who want to "redirect the system towards the public interest," which naturally means more meddling by public bureaucrats in their own interest.

Ludwig von Mises, rightly titled the dean of Austrian economists, has an innocuous little number called *Why Socialism Always Fails*. Nobel Prize winner Milton Friedman tells us why there ain't no such thing as a free lunch in *A Conversation with Milton Friedman*. Murray Rothbard chimes in, explaining *How Government Destroys Our Money* (by hemorrhages at the printing press and our lend-money-you-haven't-got banking system). Dr. Rothbard also traces the dismal history of government abuse of money. (Q: Why do bureaucrats always want more money? A: Because it's *there!*)

LibertyTree: Review and Catalog

A great source for good books on economics from a free market (libertarian) and "Austrian School" standpoint (e.g. following Ludwig von Mises and F. A. Hayek).

Send for the catalog—once you get into studying economics, history, and citizenship, you'll find it's the best source for many essential books for your whole family, from the little kids to gray old Grandpa.

NEW★★
Ludwig von Mises Institute
The Economics of Liberty, $15. Add $2.75 shipping. Grades 10–adult.

Anthologies usually make me itch. I like to read a book written by a person, not a bunch of articles stitched together.

So I was surprised to find myself picking up *The Economics of Liberty* . . . browsing it . . . flipping to an article . . . reading that article, and the next, and the next . . . and finally going back to the beginning and reading the whole thing through, when I was supposed to be doing something else!

What I discovered, to my amazement, is that every one of the writers in this book can *write*. Furthermore, they are pugnacious, combative, argumentative—in short, a joy to read. If you like bland, this is not the book for you. As Patrick Buchanan says about editor Llewellyn Rockwell's work, "It sends a message: 'Hey, fellas, you've been pushing us around a long time; why don't you come outside, and let's get it on?'"

The Economics of Liberty is, in short, a libertarian book—not left-wing retread-hippy libertarianism, but what is sometimes referred to as "classical liberalism," meaning the political philosophy of America's Founding

Fathers. If you, reading this book, begin to suspect that the reason the libertarians make more sense on all these issues than the TV pundits and mainstream newspaper columnists is that the libertarians are right, feel free to keep thinking it!

Economics of Liberty is divided into five sections:

- Economic Truth v. Political Power—in which we learn the truth about the minimum wage, unions, Keynesian economics, supply-side economics, U.S. trade, and Michael Milliken, among other things.

- Debunking the Bankers—in which we find out that all we ever suspected about fractional-reserve banking, S & L loan insurance, and the World Bank is absolutely true.

- Unmasking the Bureaucrats—in which we tour delightful D.C., NASA, and HUD, and discover why the Federal Emergency Management Agency is less helpful than neighbor Charlie and the Red Cross when it comes to little things like hurricanes.

- The Government Mess—in which we examine the principles of statism and find that they only make things worse.

- Threats and Outrages—in which we see what the bureaucrats are planning for our future, and why we don't like it, from compulsory national service for 18-year-olds to elimination of private property through Greenism.

- The Communist Crackup—in which the libertarians say, "I told you so."

No small print, no doublespeak, no scholarly jargon or mind-deadening graphs.

All in all, *The Economics of Liberty* is a very readable introduction to a fresh viewpoint on a host of economic and political issues.

NEW**
Theopolis
Money: Symbol and Substance by S. C. Mooney, $7.95 postpaid. College and adult.

What is "money"? We know what money is. It's the fancy paper engraved in green ink and the base metal coins which we give to the store clerk when we buy our groceries. Or is it? Why does the store clerk take paper and metal for groceries, anyway? Should we even call these things "money"?

S. C. Mooney gives biblical answers for these questions in his first chapter, "Money and the Bible." He accurately contends that money as we use it was not known in the Old Testament. Money, i.e., weights of silver and gold, was no different than any other good and therefore the law for money was no different than the law governing any other good.

Why silver and gold? Mr. Mooney stipulates that the Bible nowhere specifies that we must use silver and gold, but that the desire for silver and gold is innate in human nature as in the image of God. (God values silver and gold. Didn't He fill His tabernacle and temple with them?) The author contends that money has to be based on something which has that kind of innate broad-based appeal.

Having laid this foundation, he goes on to discuss money and the world, money and the Constitution, and the goal of sound money. This book is just loaded with fascinating insights, and will give you a whole new perspective on this topic.—Bill Pride

NEW**
Theopolis
Usury, Destroyer of Nations, $9.95 postpaid. College and adult.

I'm not going to kid you that this is an easy book to read. It's not. Author S. C. Mooney is too fond of abstract nouns, causing me to pause and scratch my head from time to time trying to puzzle out his meaning.

It's also not an easy book to face, because Mr. Mooney is trying to resurrect the ancient Christian teaching against usury. Usury, in his view (which he defends both from Scripture and history), means *any* interest on loans of *either* money or goods. Rent, for example, qualifies as usury, whereas payment sufficient to cover actual deterioration caused by use of the property would be OK.

This is not what makes *Usury, Destroyer of Nations* so radical, though. Unlike most Christian financial counselors, who counsel their clients not to get *into* debt but don't take it any further, S. C. Mooney calls as loudly as he can for Christians to forego this type of *investment* altogether. We're talking mutual funds, T-bills, rent collections, interest-collecting loans, or investments in any financial instruments or organizations that collect interest.

You've probably heard at least some of the arguments used to justify Christians taking usury from each other and non-believers. S. C. Mooney deals with them all. How well he does so is at the moment beyond me to judge; I'm one of those people to whom a "financial instrument" sounds like a device for bopping people on the head. "Bank president Throckmorton was found unconscious behind his desk. Apparently he had been attacked with a financial instrument." I *can* say that it's obvious America and Americans are being eaten alive by interest payments, and perhaps there's something in this book we Christians ought to think about.

CHAPTER TWENTY-FIVE

GEOGRAPHY

According to a 1988 Gallup Survey undertaken on behalf of the National Geographic Society, "105 million Americans don't have any idea what the population of their own country is." American ranked among the bottom third in an international test of geographic knowledge. Fewer than half of the Americans surveyed were able to identify the United Kingdom, France, South Africa, and Japan on an unlabeled map. Believe it or not, one of four Americans could not pick out the world's largest country or ocean!

Despite heavy U.S. involvement in the Persian Gulf and Central America, 75 percent of adult Americans surveyed could not find the gulf, and 45 percent did not know where Central America is. Only about one-third located Vietnam. One in seven Americans could not even find our own country on a world map!

In announcing the results, Society president Gilbert M. Grosvenor said, "What was most alarming was not only that young Americans did worse than all other 18- to 24-year-olds, but also that they were the only ones in that age group, among all nine countries, who did worse than the oldest group tested."

You can read these results in one of three ways. First, obviously home schoolers hardly need to teach our kids *any* geography for them to know as much as those who have been blessed with 13 years of public-school geography instruction. If your 18-year-old can find the U.S., Japan, France, the U.K., South Africa, the Persian Gulf, Vietnam, and Central America on an unlabeled world map, he's in the top percentiles for geography knowledge. (It should take about three hours of drill and practice to get this under control.)

The second way we can respond is to tear out our hair and run around screaming about how America is going to lose out in international business and politics since our kids don't even know how to *find* the other countries.

The third way is to read farther on down the press release from National Geographic Society, to where it notes that "exposure to maps and globes, travel experiences, and geography courses are also related to degree of geographic knowledge." Aha! Now we know what to do! Take a trip around the world with the kids! (No, too expensive.) OK, how about getting an atlas and a globe and *using* them? How about some simple geography curriculum and drill? (Sounds better.)

If there ever was a subject meant for discovery learning, geography is it. Everything that any person has ever done was done somewhere. Look up that "somewhere" on a map or globe, and the map and globe come to life.

It's boring to watch a hockey game if you don't know anything about the teams or players. It's just as boring to look at places on the map and not know what happened there. Also, when studying shapes (the outlines of nations, states, and continents and the course of rivers, etc.), the best way to get these into the brain is to copy the shapes. I am not a particularly kinesthetic learner, but I will forever remember that Italy looks like a boot because I had to copy its coastline.

Drill has its place, in my opinion, and as far as geography is concerned that place is supplying simple facts and shapes again and again until we are comfortable with then. It then is easier to fill that data with content. When the Sudan comes up in dinner conversation, you'll at least have a vague idea that it's on the other side of the world. You won't think it's one of the fifty states or a province of Mexico!

We are now blessed with a superabundance of colorful and fun geography products. There are books to introduce geographic concepts, hands-on projects, drill products, and maps and atlases and globes. All of these (1) help you get from point A to point B in your personal travels or (2) provide the "where" of "Who did what where?" If these points are kept firmly in mind, geography study can be a thrilling discovery—as it now is for us!

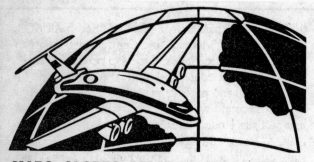

MAPS, GLOBES, ATLASES, AND PUZZLES

NEW★★
Educational Insights
3-D Landform Maps, $14.95. Minimum order $25. Shipping extra. Grades 3–8.

This really is hands-on learning! *3-D Landform Maps* is a set of (1) three full-color raised-relief maps of an imaginary land, showing the 44 most popular geographic features, and (2) a teacher's guide bound together with (3) six reproducible worksheets. Your students literally get their hands on the map and *feel* the shape of a mountain range, peninsula, or delta. You start to feel eerily like a giant looming over the earth after you've used this ingenious educational tool for a while.

A fun way to learn about geographic features, with no sermonizing about how the features may have gotten there.

NEW★★
Educational Insights
Project: Earth, $29.95. Minimum order $25. Shipping extra. Grades 2–8.

Ever want to take over the world? Do it now with the *Project: Earth* kit. There's a catch; you have to make the world first. Yes, it's a do-it-yourself globe kit.

Banish from your mind all thoughts of blowing up balloons, covering them with sloppy papier mâché, waiting what seems like weeks for the goop to dry, and painting continents on the lumpy result. Educational Insights, being a trendsetter, has done away with this Dark Age technology. Instead, you get:

- eight styrofoam globe sections
- a large bottle of blue acrylic paint (the world is mostly covered by water, which is blue)
- smaller flip-top pots of other needed paint colors, all on one handy strip
- a brush
- a cardboard base on which to set your globe
- 112 labeled peel 'n stick country flags
- 11 famous places flags
- 25 resource and manufacturing flags
- 10 numbered but otherwise blank flags
- a set of continent outlines to help you locate and trace these landforms on your globe
- an activity guide with a full-color world map on the cover

Everything is included but the masking tape, flour paste, and papier-mâché strips (yes, you still need these, unfortunately). However, since you are covering sturdy styrofoam, attaching the papier mâché shouldn't be as much of a chore. The excellent step-by-step instructions in the activity guide explain exactly how to attach the styrofoam pieces together, how to cover the globe with papier mâché, how to draw the continents where they should go (a reference map keyed to the continent outlines makes this easy), how to paint the finished product or add extra geographical features, and last but not least, how to add the flags. Simply peel each off its backings, fold in half around a toothpick so the flag's back and front stick together, and push into the styrofoam globe wherever it's supposed to go!

I've looked at globe kits from both sides now—the goop-covered balloon and *Project: Earth*—and believe me, *Project: Earth* wins hands down. With this kit, your kids can make a globe they'll be proud of—and with the flags, they can learn (and be tested on) what goes where on the globe. A great motivational teaching tool.

Golden Educational Center
Forty-eight 11 x 17" maps (2 each of 24), $11.95. Set of 50 of the same map, $5.50. Add $2 shipping. Grades 2–adult.

From the publishers of the Creating Line Designs series and Designs in Math series (see Volume 2), yet another tool for integrating your artistic side with your intellectual one. We're talking about a package of black-and-white outline maps for your students to label and/or color in themselves. The size is a comfortable 11 x 17" —easy for children to work with. Price is right, too.

Let's list the maps you get in the set. World (outline, political boundaries, political with lakes). United States (outline, waterways, state boundaries). Africa, Asia, Australia, Europe, North America, and South America (separate maps for outline, waterways, and political boundaries of each). By looking up and labeling states, countries, rivers, and so on, your student will really learn where these things are. The open-ended format of white spaces to fill in also means you or he can add notes of interest—historical, cultural, or whatever. I haven't found a package with large outline maps like this anywhere else.

UPDATED**
Hammond Inc.
Discovering Maps: A Child's World Atlas, $10.95 plus $3 shipping. Ages 8 and up.

Maps and atlases are Hammond's strong suit. They have great prices for some really fine geography material. *Discovering Maps: A Child's World Atlas* now replaces their previous *The Wonderful World of Maps*

as an introductory atlas for young readers. The first part of the book teaches map skills (symbols, direction, distance, scale, different types of maps, latitude and longitude, time zones, etc.). The second part presents simplified, easy-to-read, full-color political, physical, and special maps of the world, continents, Canada, and the U.S.A. Part three is 16 pages of fun facts and trivia (Why is the ocean blue? What is the world's northernmost piece of land?) plus a glossary of important geographic terms and a digest of world statistics.

(Does this sound too childish for teenagers? Not if you realize how little most of them know about geography to begin with!)

Hammond's World Atlases (which come in models from economy to deluxe) feature an index right next to each map (where you need it the most) as well as a separate master index in the back (in some versions). Hammond also has all sorts of atlases, color relief maps, and hundreds of specialized travel maps (great for unit studies).

An unusual offering is *Hammond's Antique Map Reproductions*. These are full-color repros of the original old-time (mostly before 1700) maps.

Hammond has a separate Education catalog, which I recommend. Hammond's Map Skills program will interest some home schoolers, particularly since it is so inexpensive and well laid out. Student atlases start as low as $4.65. Plus reference maps for less than $3 and a wide selection of other maps.

NEW**
Hayes School Publishing Co., Inc.
Outline Maps of the U.S.A., Outline Maps of the World, $4.95 each. Specify blackline masters. Add $1.50 shipping for first item, 35¢ each additional item. Grades 2–8.

Here's a wonderful resource for learning and testing geographical facts: Hayes' *Outline Maps* series.

These workbooks are just what the name implies: outline maps of various regions. The student can fill in country names, label geographical features, and so on.

Although each book includes a teacher's key, you will need an atlas or globe to check your work.

The teacher's key gives teaching suggestions and lists the names of countries, states, etc. to be filled in on each map.

Both workbooks have maps of the U.S.A. *Outline Maps of the U.S.A. and Other Parts of the World* presents the U.S.A. in more depth, with separate maps for each geographical region. It also covers Europe, South America, and just about everywhere else except Africa and Australia. *Outline Maps of the World* covers the entire world. Maps are drawn rather broadly; not as much fine detail as in the Golden Education Center outline maps. Forty-eight pages of outline maps in each workbook.

Hubbard Scientific
Relief maps start at $15.95. Map Reading Model, $31.

Hubbard is the place for raised relief maps. You can get regional maps (west of the Rockies and some eastern areas), National Park maps, U.S.A., and world maps, all framed or unframed.

For geography study, Hubbard has a map reading model packet that includes a plastic terrain model with five stacking contour sheets, five unprinted stacking contour sheets, a wall map, 50 student project sheets, and even a grease pencil.

Hubbard's catalogs are free, and the map catalog is well worth sending for.

NEW**
Learning at Home
Geographical Terms Charts, $1.80 for a set of 2. Shipping extra.

Learning at Home says that their pair of Geographical Terms Charts is "the best land-water forms learning aid we've ever seen." It ranks right up there with the landforms section of GeoSafari (though not with the *3-D Landforms Kit*), and costs less than $2.

Chart 1 is a full-color composite landscape with each geographic term printed right on its corresponding feature (e.g., *butte, island, delta*). Chart 2 is a blue and white reproduction of this same landscape, but without the printed terms. Kids can use this to test themselves on how well they know the terms.

I found it a little fuzzy to work with, and of course, being blue, it is not reproducible.

National Geographic Society
Membership, $15, includes the magazine. Most maps: $3/paper, $4/plastic.

You know all about *National Geographic* magazine. As befits an originally geographical society, National Geographic Society has maps, maps, and more maps. Lands of the Bible today. Bird migration in the Americas. Mural maps to cover your wall. Ocean floor relief maps. Space maps. U.S. regional maps. Canadian provinces. Antarctica (plan in advance for your trip!)

The Society also has a couple of fancy atlases and a quint of fancy globes.

NEW**
Pacific Puzzle Company
Set of five hardwood continents puzzles, $80. Large World Political/Physical puzzle, $84. U.S. puzzles: small $23, medium $40, large $65, beginner's $40. Dymaxion™ World puzzle, $22. Add $3 shipping for first puzzle, $1 each additional. Shipping for continent set is $7. Add an additional 50% shipping for Canada, AK, HI. Replacement puzzle pieces are available at $5 per piece postpaid, or $7 per piece for large U.S. and World puzzles.

Pacific Puzzle Company has an excellent collection of wood geography puzzles. These utterly gorgeous puzzles are crafted of birch plywood with the best maps available laminated on and cut along political boundaries. Let me tell you about my personal picks from their collection.

The continent puzzles are a set of five gorgeous puzzles covering the five major continents of the world (no Australia or Antarctica). These are great for country studies; see the writeup below under Country Studies!

Pacific Puzzle Company's new World Map puzzle, again, is utterly gorgeous. It requires some large, flat area where you can store it, since it's a huge 19 x 28" and contains about 106 pieces. Some small countries are "doubled up" with other small countries, but otherwise the pieces are cut along country borders. The map shows both longitude and latitude.

Bill says, "This puzzle is absolutely unbelievable. Every time I look at it I am flabbergasted at how beautiful it is." The puzzle assembles in its own frame— you just pop the countries in where they go.(This puzzle should not be confused with Pacific Puzzle Company's small Political World and Physical World puzzles, which have only 15 and 11 pieces, respectively, and which are not nearly as useful.) I really recommend the world puzzle highly!

Pacific Puzzle Company offers a wide variety of United States puzzles: small (8½ x 11"), medium (14 x 19"), and large (19 x 25") puzzles with, respectively, 51, 51, and 45 pieces, or the Beginner's United States, a 51-piece puzzle of stained wood pieces. Lift each piece to see the state name, capital, and outline underneath. The Beginner's U.S. puzzle is a fine testing tool; the other three all use the well-known political map of the U.S. These are PPC's most popular puzzles.

And then there's the Dymaxion puzzle. Based on a the map by Buckminster Fuller, these 20 triangular shapes fit together to present one of the most accurate flat representations of the earth around. However, unlike other map puzzles, you can put it together correctly dozens of different ways, depending on which viewing angle you choose to highlight. Look at the earth from the viewpoint of an Australian or a polar bear! See how the oceans and landmasses connect! There's very little distortion of the shapes and sizes of the continents. Short of using a globe, this puzzle is the best way to gain understanding of the continents and oceans. Its 3½" triangles don't take up much storage space, nor does it take too much room to construct. And since it's manipulative, it has some educational advantages over a globe.

Pacific Puzzle Company also has fun (and relatively inexpensive) alphabet and number puzzles, geometric shape puzzles, and their newest entry, the Apple Puzzle. This 3-D puzzle looks like a real apple, but is actually 35 pieces you put together around the wooden "core." Our kids *love* these puzzles!

NEW**
Vintage Books
The Map Catalog, $16.95. Available in bookstores.

This is it: the ultimate source book for maps of all kinds, in a new revised and expanded second edition. Travel maps. Tourism maps. Special-area maps. Boundary maps. Scientific maps. History through maps. Business maps. Water maps. Sky maps. Atlases and globes, and where to get them. Geography education materials. T-shirts printed with maps. Map software. You may not realize all the possibilities, so let me enumerate some for you. How about a shopping map (where to go for the best buys), a map of Shakespeare's England, or the Ernest Hemingway Adventure Map of the World, the latter featuring more than 200 locations from the H-man's novels and short stores? For a different view of the U.S.A., how about Meridian Graphic's "Portrait of the U.S.A." map, a pictorial map showing

roads, tourist attractions, topographical features (mountains and rivers, mostly), and the skylines of major cities with a 3-D effect?

Sorry, I can't tell you where to get these maps—if you want any of 'em, you'll have to buy *The Map Catalog*!

GEOGRAPHY CURRICULUM

NEW**
Alpha Omega Publications
LIFEPACS, $2.75–$2.95 each or $24.95–$26.95/set of 10 (one course). Teacher handbooks, $4.95 per course. Answer keys, $2.25 each (two per course). LIFEPAC test key (included with teacher handbook), $2.25/course. Shipping extra.

Alpha Omega doesn't have a geography course for middle or upper grades. Instead, geography is added into the social-studies program in a few workbook units (called LIFEPACS) here and there.

Grade 7 touches on geography twice, once defining it as a discipline and the other time as a unit on the history and geography of the U.S.A. The last half of grade 9 discusses man's relationship to the earth, world regions, man and his environment (a greenie emphasis on how we are running out of and ruining everything), and a useful unit called "The Tools of the Geographer" which introduces globes, maps, graphs, charts, and other ways people have found to represent geographical information.

That's about it for separate geographical studies; aside from these units, you'll find geography simply woven into the history units, which are written up in detail in the History chapter.

NEW★★
American Christian History Institute
Physical Geography, $8 postpaid. *Guide to American Christian Education,* $25 postpaid.

Want to teach geography using the Principle Approach?

Physical Geography is a reprint of an 1873 work written by Swiss-born geographer Arnold Guyot. Dr. Guyot was Professor of Geography and Geology at Princeton University. His book attempts to teach geography from a Christian point of view. The new edition has an introduction by Katherine Dang, author of the article "Geography: An American Christian Approach" included in James Rose's *Guide to American Christian Education for the Home and School* (also available from ACHI).

The folks at ACHI suggest you use *Physical Geography* in conjunction with the *Guide to American Christian Education.*

ARKANSAS
LITTLE ROCK

Arthur Bornstein School of Memory Training
States and Capitals Kit, $39.95. Add 10% shipping. Ages 7–adult.

How can a set of 56 8½ x 11" full-color illustrated flash cards help your youngsters memorize the capital of every U.S. state, and each state's general location?

What if I told you that one flash card has a picture of a big ARK on top of a LITTLE ROCK and another shows the BOYS watching while IDA HOES potatoes?

Yes, Arthur Bornstein has struck again. The outrageous associations and goofy scenes in his States and Capitals Kit make it easy to remember which capital goes

with which state. More: the back of each card shows the state's outline and relative size, its abbreviation, nickname, flower, tree, bird, and date of entrance into the Union, plus teaching tips. Accompanying booklet and cassette tape explain whatever else you need to know about using this kit. Then, when your students have finished giggling their way through all fifty states, cards 51–56 feature a map of states and their capitals, and memory associations for the 13 original states, western states, midwestern states, southern states, and northeastern states.

Exaggerated cartoon-style, busty females in low-cut dresses, quite a few Catholic and Christian allusions (Mass for Massachusetts, Ark for Arkansas, St. Paul's Cathedral for St. Paul). Very easy to use.

NEW★★
Audio Memory Publishing
Sing Around the World Geography Kit, $24.95. *Sing Around the World* book, $6.95. Coloring map of world, U.S.A., $3 each. States and Capitals song kit, $9.95. Add $2 shipping. All ages.

Learn what's where by singing along with tapes! Audio Memory Publishing's new *Sing Around the World* kit has two cassettes with 18 songs, a 25 x 26" map of the world to label and color, and a 96-page songbook with all the lyrics plus regional maps to color, crossword puzzles, and several pages with pictures of landmarks to match to their names. Answer keys to the puzzles are in the back of the book. To make things more lively, the book also features many pictures of the people, pastimes, landmarks, and cultural detritus of each area. Song lyrics are also printed on the world map, each near the region it describes. Sample lyrics:

The central plains are called the "outback"
with the sheep and cattle stations.
The aborigines were the first
people in this nation. . . . (from the song "Australia")

Afghanistan, Sri Lanka
Nepal and Bangladesh
Bhutan and India
Maldives and Pakistan
are the countries of South Asia. (The entire song "South Asia")

The French have French Guiana
The British have the Falkland Islands
Brazil is the biggest country
and Chile is the longest. (from "South America")

The two cassettes with 18 upbeat, folksy songs cover the world. Song topics include Southeast Asia, the Middle East, Europe, Australia, New Zealand, Canada, Central America, South Asia, Mexico, Asia, Greenland, Oceania, South America, Africa, West Indies, United States, Continents and Oceans, and the Solar System.

How helpful will these cassettes be? It's all up to you. If you and your kids are the type who like to have music playing, sooner or later you will pick up the lyrics to all of these songs almost unconsciously. They won't *mean* anything, though, until you get out the songbook and start locating the countries you are singing about. They are numbered in the same order as they are sung on the 18 book maps and on the large world map. This has 171 numbers listed on the side, corresponding to numerals on the map.

If you'd like to focus on the United States, Audio Memory Publishing's *States and Capitals Song Kit* comes with a cassette and 25 x 36" map of the U.S.A. with 172 items to label. You can pick a location from the list and find out where it is on the map. "I'll be! So *that's* where the Okefenokee Swamp is!" The songs teach the names and locations of the 50 states and their capitals. The Capitals songs are sung in echo fashion and repeated for self-testing.

NEW**
Bob Jones University Press
Geography for Christian Schools (grade 9): student text, $19.95, hardbound; teacher's edition, $31.50; map packet (25 maps), $3.50; TestBank, $9.95. These are home-school prices. Shipping extra.

Everything you wanted to know about geography from a Christian perspective, and more! Physical geography, political geography, economic geography, and cultural geography, with missionary vision built in.

This takes up the first two units: The World As God Made It is the first unit and The World As Man Subdues It is the second. The first unit deals with the earth's surface, air/climate/weather, vegetation and wildlife, mineral and fuel resources, and water resources. The second has chapters on agriculture, industry and trade, transportation and commerce, population, and nations. In sum, you're looking at what's on the earth and what people are doing with it.

The country-by-country world tour starts on page 242. You travel through North America, Latin America, Europe, Asia, Africa, and Oceania and the polar regions, with one section on each. Each country and region's climate, landscape, and culture are summarized. In all, you get around 640 pages.

Geography for Christian Schools is not 100 percent pro-natal (population growth is presented as a problem) and takes a collectivist view of natural resources in spots. Though anticommunist, it also appears to favor a larger role for government than most of my conservative and libertarian friends would feel comfortable with. The tone of the language when discussing these areas is not much different than what you'd find in one of the better secular textbooks.

NEW**
Crane's Select Educational Materials
Geography Flipper, $5.95. Add $1.50 shipping. Ages 10–adult.

Ever confuse latitude with longitude? Can you tell me whether the Prime Meridian is the same thing as the Greenwich Time Line? Quick, now: spell and define "isthmus." How about estuary? Viaduct?

Unlike the *3-D Landforms* and other geography-at-a-glance teaching tools, the *Geography Flipper* is designed as a ready reference. You don't have to spend long minutes searching for the geographic feature you are trying to define. It's all laid out in overlapping clear pockets filled with 49 handy illustrated reference cards. Starting with maps and globes, rotation, latitude, longitude, circles and topics, degrees, mapping, earth's relationship to the sun, and so on, the cards proceed to describe every type of geographic feature, from islands to highlands. These are laid out very logically, with such categories as "Landforms—Steep Places" and "Water—Inland."

If you know the name of what you're looking for, a short index at the end helps you find it quickly. If you don't, just find the right category and flip until you find what you're looking for.

Not all geographic features are visually illustrated, just those that need it. Definitions are very simple, e.g., "Source: The beginning of a river or stream . . . Bayou: A slow-moving waterway which is a lake's outlet or a river's path through its delta."

The whole thing is mounted on a sturdy, reinforced, three-hole-punched piece of cardboard, the better to fit into your binder, my dear.

A really neat, well-organized condensation of a lot of geographical information.

EDC Publishing
Usborne Book of World Geography, $17.95 hardbound. Ages 8–adult.

More colorful facts than you can imagine about the earth, the seas, people and houses of the world, and maps of the world. Heavily illustrated, with many captioned pictures and short story sequences. Geography is placed in the context of the people who live in each place and the ways they live. Slightly evolutionary in a few spots. Like all Usborne books, the *Book of World Geography* makes fascinating browsing.

NEW★★
Educational Insights
GeoSafari, $99.95. GeoSafari Map Packs, $14.95 each. GeoSafari AC Adaptor, $9.95. Minimum order $25. Shipping extra. Grades 3–adult.

Geography drill is boring. You know this. I know this. But someone at Educational Insights didn't know this. So they invented the GeoSafari teaching machine.

This really neat resource comes equipped with 20 double-sided large (9⅓ x 13") and colorful laminated sheets. Place a sheet on the "screen" area, type in the code on the upper-right-hand corner, tell the computer whether you are playing with a friend or alone and how long you want to be given to answer each question, and go! The computer will flash lights randomly and then flash a light by the question it wants to ask you. You have to quickly look on the sheet for the answer

and type it in. If you miss the answer, it will flash a light by the right answer.

Sheets are such things as a U.S. map with states and capitals or a picture map of geographical terms (island, butte, volcano, delta, etc.). You will learn to identify continents and countries, natural resources, bodies of water, world landmarks, and lots more with just the sheets included in your GeoSafari purchase.

GeoSafari is (I'm warning you) addictive. Reluctant geography students will happily spend hours testing themselves on geography with GeoSafari and learning the facts they missed. Two students can even learn together, thanks to the feature that allows two players to compete!

Additional GeoPacks now available include: U.S. Geography (natural resources and industry, U.S. territorial acquisitions, special points of interest, etc.), World Geography (religions, currencies, cultures, ancient civilizations, literature, natural resources and industries, etc.), Animals of the World, Puzzles, Thinking Games, and Make Your Own. As you can see, this teaching machine is not necessarily limited to teaching geography. Educational Insights plans to keep bringing out more GeoPacks on a regular basis.

Bottom line: GeoSafari is absolutely the best geographic home-teaching resource for anyone who has— or can scrape up— that kind of money to spend.

(Other people think so too: GeoSafari was rated the number one toy in the Great American Toy Test of 1990.) Very highly recommended.

NEW★★
The Learning Works
United States Geography Journey, $24.95 plus $3 shipping. Grades 4–8.

United States Geography Journey is a workbook and game rolled into one. First, the workbook. It's divided into six sections. The first section, General Geographic Facts, teaches kids how to read maps of all kinds. Each of the next four sections focuses on one particular region—southern, northeastern, central, and western— of the U.S.A. Activities include matching states to their outlines, matching states to their geographic features and locations, and a detective story that the reader can follow on his map. The sixth section, Just for Fun, has quiz questions covering all states and regions.

Included with the workbook are six 8½ x 11" Colorprint™ U.S. maps, a large U.S. outline map, and 128 U.S. Geography Grab Bag game cards (printed in sheets of eight questions per sheet). Using the maps, a whole group of students and their teacher can solve the quiz problems at once.

U.S. Geography Grab Bag is a look-it-up game. Categories for the question cards include Using a Map Scale of Miles, Which is Farther?, Rivers-Lakes-and Seas, Latitude and Longitude, North-South-East-or-West, Borders and Boundaries, Comparing Size, and The Name's the Same. Each category includes 16 cards, color-coded to the category. These are not "knowledge" questions, but look-it-up questions, such as "The distance between Columbia and Sumter, South Carolina, is about 50 miles—true or false?"

When you get a card, use your U.S. map to determine whether the information on the card is true or false. If true, place your card in the True box on the game sheet (or in a box labeled "True" on any old plain sheet of paper). If false, place it in the False box. Game variations include moving markers across individual U.S. maps, or claiming states with different-colored markers for each student on a large U.S. map. Answer key is in the back of the workbook.

U.S. Geography Journey has more map work than any other single program I have seen. Good for larger families (who can use more of the maps!) and as a unit to train kids in map work.

NEW*
McDougal, Littell & Co.
Daily Geography program, $13.50 each teacher's manual. Grades 2–11 available. Add $4 shipping.

Can your student answer these questions:

1. What two oceans do not touch Australia?

2. The Prime Meridian passes through which three continents?

3. Two countries in South America are totally land-locked. Bolivia is one; what is the name of the other country?

Dollars to doughnuts he can't. The amount most of us today know about geography is pitiful. You know that. I know that. So what are we going to do about it?

How about a geography program that takes five or ten minutes a day, and teaches not just the simple stuff like, "Find Florida on this labeled U.S. map," but how to answer toughies like the questions above?

Daily Geography from McDougal, Littell & Company is a set of teacher's manuals with geography questions and answers for every week of the school year, plus a scope and sequence, glossary of geography terms, and simple teaching suggestions. The teacher's manuals for grades 2 and 3 have six geography questions a week. The manuals for grades 4–11 have eight questions a week. If you use the entire program, your student will have worked through nearly 2,500 sequenced geography questions.

Here's how it works. You write two geography questions on the chalkboard. (Every home teacher needs a chalkboard, anyway.) Your student then copies the questions into his geography notebook and looks up the answers using maps, globes, and atlases. He then reports his answer orally and/or shows you the answer on the map. Correct answers are recorded in the geography notebook. You can either do one or two geography questions every day or have a single, longer geography session once a week.

The questions for each week fit on a single page of the manual, and are divided according to concept. These are *not* multiple choice—the student has to figure out the answers himself. Concepts taught run the gamut from states and capitals to map reading, relative positions of geographic features (e.g, "Which of the Great Lakes is farthest east?" and "If you were in the Gulf of Bothnia, between what two countries would you be located?"), and "thinking questions" like, "Look at a map of Asia. Why would you find little farming in Northern Asia?" (answer: It's very far north and very cold). The Grade 2 work starts off slowly with questions like, "Is the United States a city, a state, or a country?" and by grade 10 you are finding your way about the Gulf of Bothnia.

The *Daily Geography* program builds on itself. Your average eighth-grader would have trouble jumping right in with the eighth-grade book, in my opinion. The solution is to order all the levels up to and including your student's grade level, and doing extra questions in each geography session until he is caught up.

All the school-age children in a family can learn their geography at once, although you may need to write separate questions for each grade level.

NEW**
Milliken Publishing Co.
Map Skills transparency/blackline series, $12.95 each. Grades 4–9.

Milliken's *United States Map Skills* transparency/blackline workbook is a complete course in U.S. geography. With the aid of 12 colorful full-page transparencies, kids learn about time zones, climate, states and capitals, postal abbreviations, population density, state mottoes, major geographic features, and how to use city, state, and interstate road maps. Twenty-eight workbook pages and a teacher's guide with answer key round out the book.

This book is much easier to use than a traditional geography textbook, partly because of its highly visual approach. Some of the transparencies are fascinating, like the cutaway view of the heights of the waterways included in the St. Lawrence Seaway. Regions of the U.S.A. are briefly introduced, but covered in more detail in the other books in this series: *Eastern U.S.A.*, *Southern U.S.A.*, *Central U.S.A.*, and *Western U.S.A.* The series also includes a book on Canada.

NEW**
Teaching Home
August/September 1988 back issue, $3.75 postpaid. Complete six-issue set of 1988 back issues, $17.50, includes free set of 6 plastic magazine holders for your ring binder.

Want a quick, yet deep mini-course in how to teach geography? Then grab the August/September 1988 issue of *Teaching Home* magazine. *Teaching Home* keeps its back issues continually in print, since each is just crammed with useful information on how to teach the topic-of-the-issue at home. In this issue we find out why modern American schoolkids can't find Florida on a map even when they live there (because geography

was deep-sixed by "social studies," a totally nebulous substitute), how to have fun with geography, how to learn geography through planning and taking imaginary trips, map literacy, and lots more! This issue also has a missions emphasis, with several articles on how to make missions support a part of your child's life.

COUNTRY STUDIES

UPDATED**
Asia Society
Video Letter from Japan (grades 3–7), *Video Letter from Japan II* (grades 9–college), $22.95 each package or $130 for series of 6 prepaid. *Discover Korea* (grades 3–7), $22.95 each package, or $65 for series of 3 prepaid. VHS only. Shipping extra.

I had only slight expectations when writing away for a review copy of the *Video Letter from Japan* series (produced by The Asia Society in cooperation with TDK Corporation). After all, I've seen enough half-baked classroom lectures on video to know that most educational video ain't exactly United Artists quality.

Well, I was really impressed. Beautiful photography, excellent script, state-of-the-art effects (used sparingly where helpful), and a warm understanding of both Japanese culture and the video's intended American audience all combine to make this the *best* educational video I have ever seen, bar none.

A different Japanese child is your host for the 25-minute "letter" on each video. You see Japan through the eyes of this child as he or she attends school, swims in a river, shares a holiday meal with the family, and so on. Each letter illustrates some aspect of Japanese culture. Programs include *My Day*, *Tohoku Diary*, *My Family*, *Making Things*, *Living Arts*, and *Our School* (this was the one we saw). Each package also includes a teacher's manual and a classroom poster.

Beyond this first *Video Letter* series designed for elementary and junior-high school children, another series of six video packages, entitled *Video Letter from Japan II*, is available for high school and early college.

The Asia Society has also produced a similar series on Korea, entitled *Discover Korea*. The first video in this series, *Family and Home*, was just as engaging as the *Video Letter from Japan*. The program is 21 minutes long and comes with a teacher's manual and a double-sided, full-sized instructional poster.

Other titles in the series are *School and Community* and *Geography and Industry*.

NEW**
Audio-Forum
Each LP or cassette, $12.45 postpaid. Minimum order is two titles.

Rise up singing . . . Raise your cultural awareness with Audio-Forum's huge library of authentic music from around the globe. All albums come from the Lyrichord collection of "mostly indigenous and often rare music," and feature annotations by "distinguished ethnomusicologists."

Choose from the music of: Europe, Crete, Cyprus; China, Tibet, and Nepal; India, Asia, and the Pacific; North Africa and the Middle East; the Americas; Black Africa; Japan and Korea. A sample title, *Philippines Gong Music from Lanao,* will give you the flavor of this collection that includes selections as diverse as Eskimo music (two volumes), Jamaican reggae, Persian love songs and chants, and volumes of Indian music divided by caste.

Audio-Forum has prepared a very helpful brochure, "Ethnic Music from Around the World," which lists this music both by region and by instrument or musical format. So if you want to hear lute music, you can easily discover that your choices include Arab music, near-Eastern, Greek, Japanese, and Turkish Sufi albums. Chinese and Vietnamese are into zithers; Africans and Eskimos like drums; and bagpipes venture beyond the confines of the British Isles into such places as Italy and Africa.

NEW**
Capper's Books
Letters from Steven, $14.95. Add $2 shipping. Grades 7–adult.

Nobody in the whole history of the world had ever walked around the world alone. It took 33-year-old Steven Newman four years and 39 million steps to complete his 20,000-mile odyssey, during which he traveled through 20 countries on five continents. All along that route Steven wrote letters that were pub-lished in *Capper's Weekly.* The best of those letters were put together into this book, *Letters from Steven.*

This is not your typical jock tome. You know, "Forty miles outside of Abilene I developed a humongous blister. Well, I stripped off my Nikes and went for the Dr. Scholls. . ." Steven, a trained journalist, spent his time on the road talking to people, visiting them in their homes, observing the countryside, and doing a lot of thinking. The result is a unique look at the world as it really is, minus the political lenses through which we too often view it.

Steven's letters were written to people he knew wanted to hear about what the places he visited were *really* like. As he chronicles his adventures, from a near brush with death at the hands of bushwackers to an encounter with a flock of giant birds in Scotland, you get a feel for the contours of our world quite different from the view preached in travel magazines and on the 6 o'clock news. I'll never be able to forget Steven's description of Thailand:

> "Maybe you like watch American football?" [the Thai waitress] asked. Then pausing as if to wait for my eyes to plunk into my lap, she added, "Today, inside on big screen, we have Super Bowl." . . .
>
> Super . . . Bowl—the Super Bowl? In Pakistan and India hardly anyone had ever heard of such a thing. But now, in a land I had expected to be the most primitive yet, I was being offered the most sacred of all American spectacles as casually as I might have been offered a cup of coffee in a Park Avenue eatery. . . .
>
> Nowhere outside of my own country, not even in London, Rome, or Athens, had I seen such a concentration of consumer and luxury goods from all over the world, particularly America and Japan. It was almost as if those two economic behemoths had found in Thailand a perfect arena in which to do battle for the consumers' bank accounts.

Steven has a gift for making friends and getting invited to unusual places. He also has a gift of extreme spiritual sensitivity, which in his case has made him open to just about every religion he met on the road, with the sole exception of Islam. (His chapter, "Hell in the Shadow of Iran," is one of the most powerful in the book.) You don't have to buy into his philosophy to get his information, fortunately. And the information is really worth having. Steven helps you *see* and *feel* what life is like for everyday people all over the world—and for the world-walking stranger in their midst, whom they invariably befriended. This is a view of our world you simply can't find anywhere else. Recommended, with reservations only because of the occasional universalistic content.

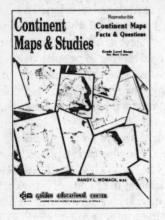

NEW★★
Golden Educational Center
Continent Maps & Studies, $6.95. *South America Country Studies, North America Country Studies*, $9.95 each. *California—Early History*, $9.95. *California—Geography*, $7.95. Add 10% shipping ($2 minimum). Grades 4–8.

Here are some easy-learn, high-interest basic geography and history workbooks. *Continent Maps & Studies* is 64 pages of maps, questions, and additional activities. Recognizing that people have trouble finding information on a map when the map is too loaded with text, Golden has provided separate outline, waterway, and political boundary maps for each continent except (for obvious reasons) Antarctica. The book also includes a World Outline, World Political Boundary map, and World-Pacific view map. Each continent also has a completed political boundary and waterway map. Designed as a supplement for any geography, history, social studies, or world literature course.

The activities are simple, fun, and each can be accomplished in a reasonable amount of time. Example: "Write a paragraph describing the food and clothing of the people" in that country, state, or continent. Other questions and activities can similarly be used for every geographical region studied. The book also provides basic facts about each continent: the number and names of independent countries on that continent; its area; greatest distances north-south and east-west; population; highest and lowest elevations; physical features; waterways; main religions; and other interesting facts. You then can photocopy as many copies of the maps as you need for your own family or classroom and write in the countries, waterways, etc. for a

number of great learning activities. Really nice, clean, nonthreatening format makes this workbook and the others in the series (*South America Country Studies* and *North America Country Studies*) a good choice.

NEW★★
Ladybird Books, Inc.
Each book in the Discovering series, $3.50. Grades 5–9.

Places to go . . . Ladybird's fully illustrated series of little hardcover books takes you on guided tours of famous places. The Discovering series includes *London, Scotland, Tower of London, Shakespeare Country, Castles, Cathedrals,* and *Natural History Museum.* The series also has a book apiece on the Vikings and the Spanish Armada. Text is designed for a preteen reading level.

NEW★★
Operation Mobilization Literature
(formerly Send the Light)
Operation World, $12 for complete set. Book alone, $8.95. Prayer cards alone, $2.95. World map alone, $4.95. All prices postpaid.

Operation World provides over 500 pages of densely packed information on every country in the world, from a Christian and missionary point of view, plus lots and lots of statistics, historical background information, ethnic information, and prayer needs.

A complete *Operation World* kit includes not just the book, but also a set of 70 World Prayer Cards, each with facts and prayer requests about a foreign country, and a world map for locating your country of the day (or week, or month!). A lot of information for a really good price!

NEW★★
Pacific Puzzle Company
Set of five hardwood continents puzzles, $80. Shipping for Continent Set is $7. Add an additional 50% shipping for Canada, AK, HI. Replacement puzzle pieces are available at $5 per piece postpaid, or $7 per piece for large U.S. and World puzzles.

PPC's continent puzzles are a set of five birch plywood puzzles with full-color maps laminated on them and cut along political boundaries for (gasp!) $80. Sounds like a lot? It's really, really worth it. If you want your family to have a real grasp of what is where in the world, this is the best resource I have ever found to teach them. Puzzles are ideal for the purpose, since geography is based on shapes. Pacific Puzzle Company's puzzles are heirloom-quality works of art, making geography study not only fun but also nurturing a sense of beauty. And if all this doesn't convince you, let me just say that I have found these puzzles to be a great starting point for developing a Christian worldview. You can study all the countries on one continent one by one, or have a number of children working several different puzzles at once. They are a size that fits well on a shelf, but big enough to really see the countries and the map details. Pick a country of the day, have the children trace its shape (use the puzzle piece like a stencil), and look it up in the encyclopedia. (Don't have an encyclopedia? Get a cheap one at a yard sale, or invest $10 in a newspaper ad asking for an inexpensive used encyclopedia, e.g., "I'll pay $50 for a used *World Book Encyclopedia*.") Have one child read the encyclopedia entry aloud. Then look up the country in Operation Mobilization's *Operation World* set (see review above). At the rate of one country a day, in just a few months your children will know their way around the world!

One caveat: PPC uses two-sided maps for the Continents series. Some very slight show-through of the map from the other side is unavoidable. I didn't personally notice any show-through until PPC drew it to my attention.

NEW★★
Quantum Communications
Traveloguer videos, $29.95 each. Quantity prices: 3–11 tapes, $24.95 each; 12+ tapes, $19.95 each. Shipping extra. All ages.

Part of a real education includes learning what life is *really* like in other countries. Wealthy parents, under-

standing this, used to send their sons on the Grand Tour, a worldwide tour lasting up to two years after they graduated from the university. Few of us can afford the Grand Tour, but now there's an affordable alterative!

I am really excited about Quantum Communications' fabulous Traveloguer Collection of travel videos. Now, I know what you're thinking. "*Travel videos?!?* What's so great about those?" Too many travel videos are the updated equivalent of Uncle Harry's slide show of Europe, long on tourist attractions and short on descriptions of the real countries and their people.

Not so with the Traveloguer Collection! These 60-minute videos are adapted from films produced by real "traveloguers." Traveloguers are independent film producers who spend years studying what makes a country unique, as well as spotting the best film shots. They then present their films to live audiences of thousands throughout North America. The best of these films of European countries have been brought together into the Traveloguer Collection.

I was really impressed! Not only is this some of the most spectacular film footage I have ever seen, narrated by people who obviously know what they're talking about, but these videos have tremendous educational value (again setting them apart from other travel videos series).

The videos teach you *geography*, as every visit to a new part of the country is introduced by highlighting the parts you are about to visit on a video map, and the videos make a point of showing you each country's distinctive terrain. *Culture* and *history* are introduced through visits to dozens of important cultural events and historic sites. The traveloguers also make a point of introducing us to interesting craftsmen and businesses in each country and showing us in detail how several local crafts are made (e.g., Swedish wooden horses, Irish porcelain baskets).

You find out about the day-to-day life of both urban and rural inhabitants, and what they do for sport and entertainment. The traveloguer narrator gives you a verbal picture of the social and political structure of the country while showing you examples of government buildings and state institutions.

You are also treated to a trip down the major waterway of each country, and taken to the home of a typical inhabitant.

Lest all this sound dull and dry, let me hasten to assure you that these are tremendously entertaining videos, put together with a lot of intelligence and wit. I won't soon forget the spectacle of the kilt-clad Scotsman doing his best to hurl a 300-pound telephone pole end over end! (That's a national sporting event, believe it or not!) You get a real feel for countries that previously were just names on a map.

The videos come in impressive, durable gold-stamped cases that will look lovely on your shelf. And on top of all this, you get a free companion reference guide with each videotape purchased directly from Quantum Communications. It's a gold-imprinted pocket-sized booklet with a map locating the places visited on the video, a representative recipe of the country, a brief history of the country, cultural pointers for visitors, and a recommended reading list for further study of that country.

I can heartily recommend 16 out of the 19 Traveloguer videos. The remaining three require more serious consideration, for the following reasons. *Eternal Greece* starts with a squirrelly sequence featuring a girl posing as Gaia, the earth goddess, and presents paganism throughout in rather too glowing terms to make Christians comfortable. (This is not at all true of the other videos in the series, by the way—they mention each country's Christian heritage in very positive terms.) The *Americans in Paris* video also has a brief nightclub sequence (the only one in all 17 videos), and if you know anything about Paris nightclubs, this is not something you want the children watching. *¡Si Spain!* also has a brief shot of a portrait of the nude wife of a Spanish nobleman. Said portrait created a scandal at the time it was painted, and it doesn't really belong on a family video.

I'm telling you about this only so you are forewarned. I don't want you getting the impression that the rest of the videos suffer from these problems. Even in the case of the Paris and Spain videos, these are only lapses in what are otherwise fine videos. In general, the traveloguers have done a commendable example of showing us what is worth showing and depicting a society honestly, without dragging us through its seamy side or pushing any propaganda. These are videos you can watch again and again, learning more and enjoying them more each time.

Tapes available: *Song of Ireland, The Romance of Vienna, Austrian Odyssey, ¡Si Spain!, A Russian Journey, Treasures of Italy, Bonny Scotland, Byways of Britain, Bonjour France, The Spirit of Sweden, Discovering Denmark, The Glory of England, Romantic Germany, This is Switzerland, The Wonders of Norway, Americans in Paris, Eternal Greece,* and *The Charm of Holland,* and *Portugal and the Azores.* The Germany video has been recently revised, by the way, and is even better than the original. Great footage of those kids taking down the Berlin Wall!

NEW**
TREND Enterprises, Inc.
Famous Places Fun-To-Know Flash Cards, $3.99. *States and Capitals* Fun-To-Know Flash Cards, $4.99. Add $2 shipping. Minimum order $10. Ages 8–14.

Visit 26 exciting landmarks from around the world with *Famous Places* Fun-to-Know Flash Cards. Each landmark is illustrated in color on the front, while on the back it's located on a mini world map and its history is described. A "Think About It!" section provides fun facts about the landmark and asks "thinking" questions about it, e.g., why did the Eiffel Tower take less time to construct than St. Peter's Basilica or the Great Pyramid when it's twice as tall as each of them?

The illustrations aren't all that detailed, but then, look at the price!

TREND has also packed an awful lot of information on the *States and Capitals* Fun-to-Know Flash Cards, while keeping all that information accessible. On the front of each card: state outline, location on a U.S. map, capital location, year of statehood. On the back: the state's capital, nickname, date and number of statehood, flower, bird, industries, attractions, fun facts about the state, and a couple of quiz questions, plus a mini regional map with the state highlighted. Fifty cards in all (if New York State ever gets smart and secedes from New York City, that'll be 51).

Worldwide Slides
Most View-Master packets, $4.25 apiece. Battery-operated projector, $19.95. 3-D Viewer, $4.95. Add 10% shipping.

Do you remember that Christmas you got your first View-Master? Sure you do. Wasn't it fun to click the switch, advance the reel, and see the beautiful color display?

Most of us ended up with packs of cartoon reels as children. But View-Master also developed hundreds of packets of travel reels to go with their viewers. These are now available from Worldwide Slides.

The typical three-reel package includes 21 3-D images, all lovely pictures of famous or important sights. Some packages available: Scenic U.S.A., Alaska, Eskimos of Alaska, Alabama, Grand Canyon , Tour of Canada, Maritime Provinces, Library of Congress, Paris, France, Castles in Europe, Puerto Rico, Luxembourg, Athens, Norway, Disneyland.

This is just the tip of the iceberg, as you can find slides or reels for just about every state and every country. Worldwide Slides also has numerous regular and View-Master slides of the Holy Land, for example, which they report is among their most popular topics.

Another unique line is their series of travel books. Normally sold only at the site of the attraction, but now made available to you by Worldwide Slides, all have 100 percent color pictures and let you "visit" the past by taking an armchair field trip through historic sites and buildings.

NEW
Youth With A Mission
The Personal Prayer Diary & Daily Planner, $11.95, or $13.95 for the looseleaf edition ($9.95 for the looseleaf edition without binder). The new version comes out in September each year. Add $2 postage per item.

For years I have been searching for tools to provide our family with a Christian world view. I may have just found one! Youth With A Mission's *Personal Prayer Diary and Daily Planner* is an integrated prayer journal, planning calendar, and mini social studies curriculum, all bound into an attractive 192-page spiral-bound diary with silver-stamped simulated leather cover (your choice of navy blue, burgundy, or dustry rose) and two-color (blue and black) printing on each page. A looseleaf version is also available.

The introductory section gives elementary instruction on Christian devotion: worship, quiet time, intercessory prayer and prayer for the nations, meditation, memorization, and restoring relationships, among others.

Before each month, another section points out unreached peoples groups that have not yet heard the gospel message or world class cities like Boston and New York that definitely need prayer.

Cultural information about each group and city is supplied, as well as specific prayer requests.

The heart of the diary, the week-at-a-glance planning calendar, provides a place to write notes and "things to do," a nation per day to pray for, a particular Unreached People Group of the day, and a Bible passage to read. These passages are planned to take you through the Old Testament once and Psalms, Proverbs, and the New Testament twice in a year.

And there's more: maps, a country-by-country brief description of each nation's spiritual and material outlook, a prayer journal where you can write down your prayers and their answers, a yearly planner for this year and the next, a listing of weekly prayer responsibilities designed to help you pray systematically for the opinion-molders in every society, etc.

You really can use the *Personal Prayer Diary and Daily Planner* as a daily planner, since its basic week-at-a-glance design resembles the planners used by businessmen. Like the fancier business diaries, it includes a year-at-a-glance planning section for this year and the next as well as an area for notes, addresses, telephone numbers. If you use it conscientiously, you also have a Bible study plan, a nation to pray for, an unreached group to pray for, and a social organization (the church, the family, media, government, education, business, or the arts) to pray for each day. This is not at all an overwhelming task, given the excellent design of this prayer and personal-organization aid.

My one real suggestion for improvement concerns the daily prayers for nations. These are presented in strict alphabetical order, unlike the Unreached Peoples material, which is grouped by region. This diary would be worth far more educationally (meaning that it would be easier for users to remember something about the nations we were praying for) if the nations also were grouped by region, with perhaps a little historical and cultural introduction to each region.

A review of this diary in the now-defunct *Family Resources* magazine suggested that you supplement the diary's maps with globe work and encyclopedia research. I heartily concur. Take the time to look up the country of the day on the globe and read about it in the encyclopedia, taking care to translate the inevitable humanistically-slanted and pro-socialist viewpoint from which modern encyclopedias are written. Also take the time, if possible, to share stories you have heard from that country's history. Your children won't remember all this the first time around, but if you continue to buy and use this prayer diary for several years, they will gain a Christian outlook on the world that is priceless.

GEOGRAPHY GAMES & DRILL

Aristoplay, Ltd.
Where in the World?, $35. Add $6 shipping. Grades 3–adult.

You can really learn some rote geography—what is where and what goes on there—with this colorful set of four games in one. Starting with the simple *Crazy Countries* card game, played like Crazy Eights, you progress to the *Statesman, Diplomat,* and *Ambassador* board games.

First, *Crazy Countries.* As in Crazy Eights, you try to follow suit (region, in this case) or put down a card with the same number. In level 2, you follow suit by putting down a country with the same religion, literacy rate, population level, or whatever. It's doubtful that kids will really bother to stop and memorize much about countries at this level, but they are getting familiar with the idea of different countries, each with its own characteristics.

In level 3, the *Statesman* game, you learn the location and relative sizes of countries. Select the color-coded cards for a particular region, shuffle them, and deal them face down. Then pull out the Region Board for that region. Each country on the board is colored differently than its neighbors and numbered according to size—largest with the lowest number, smallest with the highest number.

Now, draw a card and read the country's name to the player on your left. He must locate the country by either locating its size number on the Region Board or spinning the Spinner and giving the right answer for the category selected. Each correct answer wins you a country. Add up the country numbers at the end. Highest score wins. Since the smaller the country the higher its number, you have much incentive to learn the location of the hard-to-remember little countries.

Diplomat is played the same way, except that you have to provide the answer to a preselected category. The *Ambassador* game takes this to a new level of challenge by making you guess the name of the country from clues, instead of answering questions about a known country. At the Junior level, clues are taken from categories on the cards themselves. At the Senior level, players are supposed to invent their own clues. A clue for U.S.A., for instance, might be "Blue jeans and cowboys."

The categories provided are useful, but somewhat sterile. It would be great if Aristoplay could give us bigger cards with categories like culture, racial and ethnic composition, art, musical instruments and music styles, governmental form (totalitarian, democracy, republic, canton republic . . .), major lifestyles (urban, rural, jungle . . .). I'd gladly trade Literacy Rate and Imports and Exports for some of these.

You get a lot for your money: six durable, colorful Region Boards; 174 playing-card quality Country Cards, each listing capital, population, monetary unit, literacy rate, major languages, major religions, major export, major import, and major seacoasts; five Wild Cards; a Category Spinner; 120 playing pieces in six different colors (for placing on countries you identified); game instructions; and a neat, durable box.

NEW**
Crane's Select Educational Materials
U.S. Geography Game, $9.95. Add $2 shipping. Grades 3–adult.

If you'd like your family to learn a *lot* about U.S. geography and you'd like to only spend a *little* money, the *U.S. Geography Game* is a great resource. Packed in an attractively illustrated box you get five color-coded sets of cards (200 question cards total), five U.S. maps color-coded to the cards, and a set of instructions and answers. The blue State question cards, for example, go with a map on blue paper showing state political boundaries, with the states numbered in random order.

In all there are 50 blue State cards, 50 yellow State Capitals cards, 40 green Geographical Features cards, 30 ivory Large U.S. Cities cards, and 30 pink U.S. Historical Sites cards.

Each card has the same format: three regular questions and a multiple-choice question. If you can figure out the answer from question 1, you get five points. If you figure it out after being asked both question 1 and question 2, you get four points. If you need all three questions to get the answer, you get three points. Finally, after all this, if you pick the right one of the three multiple-choice possibilities, you get one point.

The answer key on the back of the directions gives the answer. The map gives the location. The card's number corresponds to the correct location on the map. To get the answer right, you have to both answer the question and point to the proper location on the map.

Here's a sample question set from the Historical Sites deck:

(1) It is the site of the first permanent English settlement in America. (5 points)
(2) Williamsburg is to the northwest. (4 points)
(3) It is located on the James River. (3 points)
Three Choices: (1 point)
    a. Plymouth b. Jamestown c. Charleston

Notice how the less you know in this game, the more you learn. By the time the geography novice figures out the answer is Jamestown, he has learned that Jamestown was the first permanent English settlement in America, it's to the southeast of Williamsburg, and it's located on the James River. Also notice the breadth of this game, and how it seamlessly integrates history and geography.

You can play *U.S. Geography Game* many ways. The way I like best (not included in the directions) is to pick one category of cards. Take out the map of that color. Shuffle the cards. Players take turns answering the questions, as in a spelling bee. Mom or Dad holds the answer key and exudes curiosity and excitement. Kids try to beat *their own* previous best scores for that deck.

This works a whole lot better than the anxiety of competing with siblings or parents, and the intimidating task of facing all 200 question cards at once.

NEW★★
Educational Insights
GeoSafari, $99.95. GeoSafari Map Packs, $14.95 each. GeoSafari AC Adaptor, $9.95. Minimum order $25. Shipping extra. Grades 3–adult.

It's the world's most super geography-teaching device. It's also the world's most fun geography drill device. It's GeoSafari, and it's written up in detail above under Geography Curriculum.

NEW★★
Educational Insights
Windows of Learning, U.S. Geography or World Geography, $6.95 each. Minimum order $25. Shipping extra. Grades 4–adult.

"Build your knowledge of geography with fun, self-checking quiz wheels!" Here's how it works. Slip one of the compact 7" question-and-answer disks into the circular case. A question will appear in the cutout window at the top. Look in the window on the other side for the answer. Then rotate the disk for the next question! Keep track of how you're doing with the handy scorekeeper. Practice by yourself or with a friend. Each set contains scorekeeper, map case, and five two-sided disks with 10 questions on each side, for 100 questions in all.

The geography sets ask questions about state/country locations and capitals, and other facts usually drilled in geography class. Each circular map case has a full-color political map on the front: a world map for the World Geography *Windows of Learning*, a U.S. map for the U.S. Geography version.

A nice update of the old-fashioned geography drill disks we used to play with when we were children.

Educational Insights
Name That State, $19.95. Minimum order $25. Shipping extra. Grades 3–adult.

Name That State is a board game correlated with a U.S. map. Name the state that corresponds to the number you spin before you can move your marker further on the board. Two to four players. It's painless geography drill, slightly overpriced.

NEW★★
Giant Photos, Inc.
U.S, Geographer, write for current price. Grades 6–adult.

Two flaps with a colorful cardboard disc on each. Each disc has a U.S. map in the middle, pictures of the states on the outside, and a cutout area through which you can view things. What kind of things? Turn the disc and find facts about each state. But there's more: fold back the flaps and—trivia buffs will love this—you'll find all sorts of reference facts in the middle, from the largest gorge in the U.S.A. to a listing of which state joined the Union when, plus fun facts about each state—its history, landscape, and resources. A clever concept that kids can pore over for hours.

NEW★★
Know It All
Know It All, $29.95 plus $3 shipping. Ages 9–adult.

Know It All is a U.S. geography and history board game designed to teach players the states, capitals, state slogans, general U.S. geography, and U.S. history in a fun, systematic way. Drive your car around a colorful playing board with a U.S. map in the middle. Along the way you may help a fellow motorist, get caught in a speed trap, take your car in for repairs, or even get elected Governor!

As in all geography games, you need to learn the answers before you can really play the game. The instruction manual provides lots of help with this. The State Fact and Clue sheets include helpful hints like COW and CAN (California-Oregon-Washington, going north, California-Arizona-New Mexico going east), clues for remembering state capitals like "Nebraska is the 'Linc' between east and west," plus state nicknames and reasons for the nicknames.

For learning general geographic facts (landform descriptions and major geographic features of the U.S.), author Beth Kimmich suggests students research

the answers to three Geography Quiz cards a day until they have studied them all (this takes about a month).

After learning about the states and some basic geography, you can move up to the U.S. History questions. Here you will learn U.S. history—including black and Indian history—in manageable sections from before the white man came through the Reagan administration. Since the U.S. History questions are divided up by time period, a similar approach can be used for mastering these. Going through these cards is a wonderful way to spark mini unit studies through the entire field of U.S. history and geography, which you can then drill by playing the game itself.

Know It All is designed so the whole family can play together, each person at his own level. Since you move around the board by answering questions correctly, there is no need for each person to answer questions from the same card deck. Thus, Dad could be using the entire U.S. History Quiz deck, while Sammy is only tangling with the first 27 cards of that deck, and Suzy is working on Name and Find the State.

Know it All includes:

- colorful duofold game board with road on the outside and U.S. map with each state outlined, capitals shown as stars, and colored by region in the middle
- six sports car playing pieces of different colors
- one die
- 72 clear plastic chips, 12 of each color
- 50 state quiz cards
- 72 U.S. geography quiz cards
- 287 U.S. history quiz cards
- instruction manual with answer keys

What we need now, of course, is a *European Know It All*, *South American Know It All*, *Arab World Know It All*, *African Know It All*, and *Asian Know It All*. (Australia and New Zealand should count as part of Europe for historical reasons, no matter how you Aussies and Kiwis might jibe at this!) While we're at it, how about a *Bible Lands Know It All*? This would give lucky *Know It All*-ers more in-depth understanding of world affairs past and present than most (maybe *all*) presidential candidates!

Know It All, despite its fun appearance, is a serious teaching tool that covers more history and geography than many elementary textbook curricula. It presents and drills the facts in a memorable way. I bet many families end up using *Know It All* as the centerpiece of their social studies program.

NEW★★
Timberdoodle
Take-Off!, $26.95. Shipping extra. Ages 6 to adult (they say); ages 8 to adult (I say).

Take-Off! from Resource Games, Inc. (sold by Timberdoodle at discount) is more absorbing and educational than many other geography games I've seen. For one thing, it's a real game, not just flash cards with a game board. Here's how it works:

(1) Uncork the navy blue tube and pull out the contents. These turn out to be a full-color, laminated 56 x 24" map, two decks of capital city/flag cards, two weird-looking eight-sided dice, and a rules sheet with a pronunciation guide for all those "furrin" places.

(2) Unroll the map. Notice it is about as long as your 10-year-old. You're going to have to clear either the table or the floor to play this game!

(3) Scrap the crummy little plastic bag you ripped apart to get the playing pieces. Replace it with a ziplock bag.

(4) Pick a color . . . any color. You have six fleets of jets to choose from: red, orange, blue, green brown, and yellow. (Incidentally, when will games manufacturers realize that red and orange look very much alike in dim indoor lighting?)

(5) Pick a number from one to four. That's how many jets you will be using per player. (Yeah, the game directions say you have to use at least two jets, but no lightning bolts will zap you if you use only one jet when playing with your four-year-old.)

(6) Roll the dice. If a color comes up, move one of your jets from its present location along a line of that color to the next location. (Some people let you go backwards, if that's the only way you can follow a line of that color. Some prefer to just skip a turn.) If a jet symbol comes up, move along any color route to another city. If a TakeOff! facet comes up, pick a TakeOff! card.

(7) What's this? The TakeOff! card has a city name on it and a flag. But you haven't the faintest idea where Ouagadougou is. Here's where the intellectual stimulation comes in. Around the edges of the map are flags of the countries. Flags of North America are together, as are flags of Central America, South America, Africa, etc. It is merely child's play to match the flag on the card to the right flag on the map. Literally child's play, since this is exactly the sort of matching activity they do in preschool. The country's name is under the flag. So now you know Ougadougou is in—where else?—Burkina Faso. And, since the flag was with the other Africa flags, Burkina Faso is in Africa. A bit of staring at the countries and capitals on the Africa portion of the map, and voila! You can now move your jet to Burkina Faso.

(8) But there's already a jet in Ougadougou. Too bad for him. He has to go back to start.

(9) All jets start in Honolulu. You win by getting your jets around the world and back to Honolulu.

(10) To make your life slightly less complicated, the board is divided into East and West. A line smack down the middle of Africa separates the two. The 169 capitals cards are also divided into two color-coded decks, so you only have 85 (at most) possible flags to check out before you find Burkina Faso.

(11) You will notice there is no well-meant teacherly rubbish about "Tell me how many people live in Burkina Faso and what its chief exports are before you can fly to the next city." Play is fast-paced—you learn directly through playing the game. The game gives its players a need to know where all these places are and satisfies the need, all at once.

Timberdoodle tells us, "Students who played this game only 14 times improved their test scores on the average of 340 percent!"

New: *Take-Off North America* includes Canada and Central America. Less to learn than the full *Take-Off!* game. Ask Timberdoodle for details.

CHAPTER TWENTY-SIX

HISTORY

History is tricky. Unlike mathematics, which follows logical rules no matter who the mathematician is or what his political party, history changes depending on who is telling the story.

We can all memorize (and subsequently forget) dates and places: Columbus sailing the ocean blue in fourteen hundred ninety-two or the Declaration of Independence being signed on July 4, 1776. But even straightforward memorizing is not without its perils. Do we memorize Susan B. Anthony's birthday or Phyllis Schlafly's? Is Mrs. Rosa Parks' refusal to move to the back of the bus more important to the history of America than John Paul Jones bellowing, "I have not yet begun to fight"? Beyond the few major dates on which all agree, there is room for strife aplenty in choosing which events and people are worth our attention and which are not.

Historians wage skirmishes in the halls of academe over more than the relative importance of Date A and Person B. War also rages over the *interpretation* of events. Even if all sides finally agreed that the Pilgrims landed at Plymouth Rock rather than some less photogenic site, that would not be the end of it. Was the Pilgrims' landing a great step for mankind or a disaster for virgin, Indian-populated America? Historians agree that Custer and his men died at the Little Big Horn. But was Custer a hero or a cad? Name your event and you'll find at least two, but more likely ten, different interpretations of its significance and results.

Here's a list of the major theories of history:

- **Cyclical.** Everything repeats itself, and history goes around in circles. This is one ancient view of history, and it is all tied up with bonds of reincarnation and karma. Nothing you or I do will make the slightest difference. The wheel keeps turning around.

- **Random chance.** Everything happens by accident. No historical events have meaning or purpose. Existentialists and nihilists like this view.

- **Marxist.** History is the result of a class struggle between the masses and the wealthy. When class distinctions and religion finally are annihilated, Utopia will arise from the ashes. In the meantime we need censorship and an army of bureaucrats and an army of KGB men and an army of conscripts and an arsenal of nuclear weapons and a first-rate Olympic team. On with the struggle, comrades! Workers of the world unite!

- **Feminist.** History is the result of a struggle between men and women. When sexual distinctions and religion finally are annihilated, Utopia will arise from the ashes. In the meantime we need sexually unbiased textbooks and an army of bureaucrats and an army of social workers and an army of day-care centers and a third chance at the ERA. On with the struggle, sisters! Women of the world unite!

- **Conspiracy.** A group of clever, evil men have plotted for (take your pick) years/decades/centuries to centralize world power in their hands. They are so very clever, and the rest of us are so very innocent and stupid, that every war, recession, bank failure, and crop failure is their doing. Their nefarious plots almost always succeed. Therefore we are heading into another Dark Age.

- **Modernist or Evolutionary.** Things are getting better and better and pretty soon we will end up living in the best of all possible worlds. Why? Cause it just happens that way! Since we are the smartest generation that ever has lived, we don't need to learn from the past. Throw out those history books! Or, if you insist on studying history, make sure it's all stated in terms of today's political program. You know—"The Puritans and Feminism" or "John Adams and Nuclear Disarmament."

- **Great Man.** Individuals with exceptional ability determine the course of history. Some nihilists like this view, too. Most conservative history books sold in America tend to take this position.

- **Providential.** God controls history and is working out His plans on earth. History in this view is cause and effect. If a nation or an individual sins, it or he can expect troubles. If a nation or individual is obedient to God, then in due course God bestows blessing. Some trouble is part of the normal human condition and necessary to keep us from getting soft, but by and large history has grand purposes that the savvy Bible student can discern.

Every one of those viewpoints offends people who believe some other viewpoint. Only the Marxist and feminist theories have ever been known to mix, and that only in the short term until the glorious Revolution actually happens and the women get sent to work hauling bricks and washing dishes. So, you see, there is *no neutral theory of history!* Every history text you read *must* strongly or subtly present one of the views listed above.

There is no harm in reading a history text written from a viewpoint you dislike *as long as you are equipped to recognize points of interpretation and errors of fact.* For this reason, I strongly recommend beginning the official study of history with what are called "source documents." By looking at the books, newspapers, posters, and artwork that people produced in the past we can get inside their heads. We can see what was really important to them and what moved them to action. This view of history is more exciting and earthy than sterile textbook tours guided by a committee of dusty scholars.

Texts have their place. They can provide a framework for us to fill in. To begin with, a simple time line would suffice, but as the history student begins to possess his facts, to really know them, he is ready to venture out into the world of ideas, good and bad, and search for writers of kindred spirit, who he is by now trained to recognize.

HISTORY CURRICULUM

A fascinating study was recently done on how students learn history. Researchers had students in grade 11 read selections from a regular American history text. Other students read from one of three updated versions of the selections. Linguists (people who teach about the nature of language) wrote one version. English composition teachers wrote another. Two professional writers who had worked at *Time* and *Life* wrote the third.

In the words of Suzanne Fields, who reported this study in her syndicated newspaper column of January 20, 1990,

> The results were not ambiguous. Those who read the linguists' version recalled two percent more than the students who read the original; students who got the revision by the composition teachers recalled two percent less. [*That says something about the people we pay to teach our kids to write, doesn't it?*—MP] Students who read the magazine writers' text recalled an astonishing 40 percent more than their classmates who got the original.

In Suzanne's very words, "Textbooks either condescend to make information ludicrously 'relevant' the the life of a teenager, or they cover too much ground in a dull manner without a connecting perspective." How did the professional writers, who had never been paid to patronize their readers or bore them, put the pizzazz back into history? They told all in an interview in *American Educator*, the professional journal of the American Federation of Teachers. As Suzanne reports, the writers used a more conversational tone, chose lively verbs, inserted lively anecdotal "nuggets," and "added a sense of drama."

In other words, there's nothing boring about history that a good writer can't fix. History is really *stories,* and who finds stories boring?

Some of the history books and courses below are written by professional writers. (I co-authored two of them myself.) Others are presented in dramatic or story form, with an unfolding theme or plot. Still others are—well—textbooks.

Keeping what the researchers found in mind, I think we can safely say that students should fill up on source documents and history stories (biographies, videos, theme-oriented history) before attempting to organize the information with a history textbook. All the better if your history text is written dramatically—although you have to look out for bias once the author starts separating people and movements into "good guys" and "bad guys." (There *are* good guys and bad guys, but it takes a bit of pondering to figure out which is which sometimes!)

Students who have followed my suggested course of study for the elementary years will already be chock-full of historical fiction and biographies. These students will profit more from an organized textbook course than those whose only exposure to history thus far has been textbooks. The latter would do better to take time out for history-as-story before plunging back into formal textbook study.

AMERICAN HISTORY

NEW**
A Beka Book Publications
The History of Our United States (grade 4): student book, $10.10; teacher's edition, $17.30. *Heritage of Freedom* (grade 11): student book, $14.75; student test booklet, $3.50; teacher's key/test booklet, $7.40. Available August 1991: student quiz booklet, $3.75; teacher key/quiz booklet, $7.40. Shipping extra.

Social-studies texts for grades 4–6 are ideal for teaching grades 7–9, since they don't assume lots of prior student knowledge and they simplify enough so students have some chance of remembering the material.

This is not always true of A Beka's publications, which tend towards the voluminous rather than the simplified. However, their new *History of Our United States* is just excellent for this sort of history introduction or review for middle (or even upper) grades. It is a fresh, readable, beautifully-illustrated and laid-out book, with good coverage of all the important historic events and *without* a lot of excess dates and other clutter.

Some of the historic interpretations are open to question (e.g., that the Aztecs were merely innocent victims of the greedy Spaniards, that Lincoln was justified in committing the Union to war and Sherman was justified in destroying Georgia, and that John D. Rockefeller Sr. greatly benefited American civilization). Others are a little hard to understand, such as the consistently pro-public school tone taken by this textbook written for Christian schools and home schools!

Otherwise, the book is, as expected, conservative and pro-free market. I'm probably going to use it myself, taking care to give "the other side of the story" where necessary (did you know Cortez preached to the Aztecs that they should give up human sacrifice, and that the other Indian tribes gladly cooperated with him to rid themselves of the hated Aztecs?). It's worth going to a little trouble of this nature, because *History of Our United States* really is about the easiest-to-use, most thorough, elementary-school history text I've seen.

Moving on to A Beka's upper-grades American history book, *Heritage of Freedom,* we have another winner. I stayed up until 2 A.M. reading it—couldn't put it down! This morning I came down to find my son Joseph (age 9, but advanced for his years) attempting to eat breakfast with this book on his lap! Written in a narrative style, it has all the good features that researchers have discovered help students to remember what they have read: crisp writing, interesting anecdotal "nuggets," and lots of interest-building photos, illustrations, maps, and charts. Positive, patriotic approach without hype or overdone flag-waving. The plight of the Indians, for example, is treated fairly. The final 17-page Study Guide for Reading the Constitution presents the entire text of the U.S. Constitution side by side with good, brief explanations of what each section means. There's a wealth of fascinating information here in these 639 pages!

NEW**
Alpha Omega Publications
LIFEPACS, $2.75–$2.95 each or $24.95–$26.95/set of 10 (one course). Teacher handbooks, $4.95 per course. Answer keys, $2.25 each (two per course). LIFEPAC test key (included with teacher handbook), $2.25/course. Shipping extra.

Grade 8 is an American history course, from the European explorers to the modern day. Units include European backgrounds, colonization, the War of Independence, becoming a united nation, the westward movement, the Civil War, industrialism, the early twentieth century, and World War II and its aftermath. The ninth LIFEPAC ends with a section on "challenges

in the United States today" in the areas of technology (usual Alpha Omega greenie emphasis), society, government, and religion.

Some of this history is visited again in greater depth in grade 11. After two units on the birth of our constitutional government, there are units on national expansion (from federalism through Andy Jackson), the emergence of slavery and sectionalism dividing the nation, the Civil War and Reconstruction, industrialism and isolationism, the Depression years, "A Nation at War" (World War II, Korea, and Vietnam), and contemporary America from the Kennedy administration through the Ford administration. The units on earlier American history are absolutely fascinating, giving a wealth of insight into the temper of those times; from Hoover on, you get pretty much the typical public-school view of things.

American Christian History Institute
Guide to American Christian History: Principle Approach, $25. Adults read the book, use the approach when teaching students of all ages.

A huge new book by James B. Rose should contain everything you need to know about what the Principle Approach is and how to teach it. Numerous chapters by various educators currently using this approach show how to present the Principle Approach to all ages in seven school subjects.

NEW**
American Textbook Committee
A Basic History of the United States, 5 paperback volumes, $36.50. Accompanying teacher's guide, free if order with set, $4 if ordered separately. Shipping extra. Ages college and adult.

For the main course, here's help from the ever-clearsighted Clarence Carson. Mr. Carson's insightful, if somewhat dour, reading of American history comes from a solidly Christian background, so he is not over-pleased with recent events since, say, the presidency of Cal Coolidge. From the *Freeman* review of this series:

> For Carson, history is not merely a collection of facts and dates, an account of explorations, settlements, westward expansion, wars, presidents, and elections. History is the product of the actions of countless individuals, each under the influence of certain ideas. And Carson explores those ideas, ideologies, and 'isms.' He shows how they were responsible for the settlement of this continent, the struggle for freedom, the westward expansion, the construction of schools, churches, factories, and the founding of new religious denominations. He explains why our ancestors fought for their beliefs and strove to create a government, limited in scope, with checks and balances, that would not have the power to oppress the people.

Whereas the first volumes show the flourishing results of Christians in control of the culture, the latter reveal what happens when good men do nothing. Here's what you get:

- Volume 1: The Colonial Experience, 1607–1774
- Volume 2: The Beginning of the Republic, 1775–1825
- Volume 3: The Sections and the Civil War, 1826–1877
- Volume 4: The Growth of America, 1878–1928
- Volume 5: The Welfare State, 1929–1985

You will never feel the same about FDR or the Civil War after reading these books! I can't agree with all of Mr. Carson's conclusions, but he certainly has the facts.

NEW★★
Bob Jones University Press
The American Republic (grade 8): student text, $19.95, hardbound; teacher's edition, $31.50; TestBank, $9.95. *United States History* (grade 11): student text, $19.95, hardbound; teacher's manual, $21; map packet (25 maps), $3.50; TestBank, $9.95. These are home-school prices. Shipping extra.

BJUP runs through American history twice at this age level: once in junior high and again in high school. The junior-high text, *The American Republic,* is well written but not particularly exciting. It does have some special helpful features. Early in the book students are given a double-page spread on study techniques, and later on there's another one on map reading. The chapter reviews are good, too. Another special feature: the book contains the entire text of the U.S. Constitution and a brief summary of each section made without any particular comments on the virtues or demerits of the section. The last part of the book regrettably takes a "problem" theme just like secular texts, focusing on the issues the media has labeled as contemporary problems. Patriotic, urbane tone (if you've never seen the two mixed, you'll see them in this book).

United States History, for 11th-graders, is prettier and more interesting. Again, it covers the whole sweep of American history, from the Reformation's influence on politics and the settling of America up until the late 80s. If you could actually master all the information in this book (here the excellent teacher's guide really helps), you would be culturally literate, at least when it comes to American history! The map exercises (in the map packet) are also excellent—if you do *those,* you'll be geographically literate! The book ends with the same "problems" focus as the seventh-grade book, rather than a call to any specific actions. The second edition, due out in fall 1991, has a more upbeat (but only slightly more challenging) ending. In this area, as in its coverage of the history itself, the teacher's guide is far more interesting and challenging than the actual textbook.

NEW★★
Bobby Horton
Songs of the CSA, four volumes. *Songs of the Union Army,* two volumes. $10 each tape. Lyric sheets available for $3 per volume. All prices postpaid. All ages.

Genuine folk songs of the Civil War era, sympathetically rendered by a great singer and musician. For more info, see writeup under Oral History and Source Documents.

NEW★★
Covenant Publications
America: The First 350 Years, 16 cassettes plus nice binder, $49.95. Optional outline (I highly recommend you get it if you can) includes comprehensive bibliography for further study and an index, all in nice binder, $20. Study guide, $5. Complete set of tapes, notebook, and study guide, $69.96. Add 10% shipping. Grades 7–adult.

If you think you've been getting the straight scoop on American history from textbooks—even Christian textbooks—think again! Steven Wilkins, another man with an obvious love of history, has uncovered some fascinating (and forgotten) facts about God's providential guidance of early American history, the Christian roots of the Declaration of Independence and the Constitution, and the *real* issues behind the Civil War—issues we continue to struggle with today.

The lecture format will appeal more to parents and older children. Mr. Wilkins is a master storyteller, so with the exception of the tapes on the Constitution you will find yourself listening with interest to the stories of the men who shaped our history. Did *your* history books, for example, ever tell you that Squanto's first words to the Pilgrims were "Welcome, English! Give me some beer!"? Or that Roger Williams was really an insufferable pest who couldn't work together with *anyone*? Or that Lincoln is on record as saying he didn't care whether the slaves were freed or not, he just wanted to save the Union?

Unlike other history treatments, *America: The First 350 Years* neither puts historical figures on a pedestal nor drags them in the gutter. It is by far the best attempt I have seen to approach history with both realism and

a Christian sense of reverence for the God behind it. The optional outline is very handy, and the study guide is a dream—just enough questions to get the hearers really thinking.

America: The First 350 Years is divided into four segments, one each on the Founding Era, the War of Independence, the Constitution, and the War Between the States (otherwise known as the Civil War), with eight lectures per segment, each lecture more or less filling one side of a cassette tape. Topics are:

• Motives to Discovery I and II—why did the explorers explore? The truth about Cortez and the Aztecs.

• Puritan Foundations I—who were the pilgrims of Plymouth and the Puritans of Massachusetts, what were the differences between them, and why should this matter? Meet Squanto and his beer mug.

• Puritan Foundations II—what six Reformation teachings formed the Puritan worldview?

• Notable Leaders I and II—fascinating background information on colonial leaders.

• The Banishment of Roger Williams—in which we discover that ol' Roger wasn't the 100 percent all-American hero everyone thinks he was.

• The Salem Witch Trials—what really happened?

• The Causes of the War of Independence I, II, III, and IV—economic, constitutional, spiritual, and practical issues.

• The Declaration of Independence I—five things everyone "knows" about the Declaration of Independence which aren't true.

• The Declaration of Independence II—what the Founding Fathers really meant.

• The Pulpit and the War I and II—the part played by preachers, especially Presbyterians and dissenters.

• The Constitutional Convention I and II—the delegates, the historical background, and what it was all about.

- The Text of the Constitution I, II, III, and IV—lectures on what it all originally meant, spiced with explanations of why many modern political institutions really aren't Constitutional.

- The Bill of Rights I and II—In the author's own words, "Why Thomas Jefferson would oppose the ACLU and why Ben Franklin would not like Dan Rather." More surprises.

- The Jeffersonian and Jacksonian Era I and II—when the government had a surplus and the nation looked a lot different.

- Rationalism and Theological Decline—the demise of Calvinism and the rise of theological humanism.

- Humanistic Reform Movements—the ferment of the 1800s that led to all sorts of strange things.

- The Public School Movement—not quite as American as apple pie.

- The Coming of the [Civil] War I—slavery and abolitionism.

- The Coming of the War II—sectional tensions.

- The War and Its Aftermath—what Reconstruction was really like, and how (in the author's view) we're still being reconstructed today.

Loaded with source quotes so you can check things out for yourself, this is one history resource that your family will remember.

Foundation for American Christian Education (FACE)

Christian History of the Constitution, Teaching and Learning America's Christian History, $15 each. *Rudiments,* $7. *Christian Self-Government with Union,* $18. *Consider and Ponder,* $23. Add 10% regular mail, 15% UPS. Ages 16–adult.

Big books full of source documents that trace America's Christian roots. Use along with Intrepid Books' workbooks for best results. See the Citizenship chapter for full details on FACE and Intrepid Books.

NEW✱✱
Mantle Ministries

Tape series, 12 volumes, $16 each, workbooks $4 each. Grades 1–12. *"Little Bear's" Resource Guide,* $4. Shipping extra.

Those of you who attend home school conventions have likely seen Richard "Little Bear" Wheeler doing his historical reenactments wearing period costumes and carrying period artifacts. So have those of you with camp ministries.

Mr. Wheeler has a particular burden for the revival of accurate history. Towards this end he has prepared a series of audiocassettes in which he reads and reenacts historical accounts from the 1300s to the 1800s. Each volume of this series has 20 3–15 minute long historical accounts with biblical application. All are narrated by Mr. Wheeler, with music and accompanying sound effects. Each volume also has an accompanying reproducible workbook with spaces for students to fill in answers to the questions, plus selected color illustrations and/or projects. Here they are:

- Volume 1: 1300s–1620 A.D. Wycliffe, Tyndale, Columbus to the Pilgrims.

- Volume 2: 1607–1775. Jamestown to Paul Revere's ride.

- Volume 3: 1775–1781. God's providence during the American Revolution.

- Volume 4: 1775–1781. Heroes of the American Revolution.

- Volume 5: 1803–1806. Highlights of the Lewis and Clark Expedition.

- Volume 6: 1806–1861. Davy Crockett, Kit Carson, Oregon Trail, and Westward Movement.

• Volume 7: 1861–1865. The Civil War.

• Volume 8: 1865–1890. Cowboys, Indians, soldiers, and gunfighters of the Old West.

• Volume 9: 1620–1880s. Twenty stories from the book *American History and Home Life.*

• Volume 10: 1700s–1900s. Ten godly presidents and ten valiant women of God.

• Volume 11: The Holiday Series. Twenty of our national holidays from a Biblical perspective.

• Volume 12: Highlights of previous volumes.

Mantle Ministries has republished a number of historic books suitable for teens and adults, and is has produced several videos featuring "Little Bear" in his period roles.

"Little Bear" also has a resource catalog, called *"Little Bear's" Resource Guide,* for those of you who'd like to have access to his sources of period clothing and personal effects, instruments, and weaponry.

NEW★★
Midwest Publications
Critical Thinking in American History series: *Evaluating Viewpoints: Colonies to Constitution,* $16.95; teacher's guide, $15.95. *New Republic to Civil War,* $8.95; teacher's guide, $16.95. *Reconstruction to Progressivism,* $16.95; teacher's guide, $15.95. *Spanish-American War to Vietnam War,* $16.95; teacher's guide, $15.95. Add 10% shipping. Grades 8–12.

History texts like to present a single view of history as if it were the infallible truth. Those of us who believe

in serious historical studies can get around this by reading real books written about each historical topic and time period. By comparing historian to historian, and reading source documents for ourselves, it's possible to get a more balanced picture of what actually occurred and what it all means.

Following the same method, *Colonies to Constitution,* the "Evaluating Viewpoints" book in the Critical Thinking in American History series, puts serious historical analysis within reach of high-school kids.

The book's 29 historical lessons *all* present differing interpretations of historical events and even disagreements about basic facts. To avoid prejudice, historians are referred to as "Historian A," Historian B," and so on. Kids are encouraged to analyze the historians' writings logically, according to the rules in the "Guide to Critical Thinking" in the front of the student book. By so doing, they encounter "the gathering and analysis of historical data as selective, fragmentary, and open to question and change."

Yet—and here is the genius of the course's author—they are *not* led to perceive history as unknowable or relativistic. Historical analysis is presented as a search for truth, some of which we can discern and some of which we have to leave as open questions until we have more information.

As you may have guessed, *Colonies to Constitution* is as heavy on teaching logic as it is on history. That portion of our history is blessed with many historical controversies, such as what happened to the lost colony at Roanoke, whether Pocahontas really rescued Captain John Smith, who actually fired "the shot heard round the world," the real reasons behind the Salem witch hysteria and the American Revolution, and whether we made a mistake in exchanging the Articles of Confederation for the Constitution.

Colonies to Constitution not only presents the differing historical views, but also leads kids through analyzing each to discover which is most trustworthy. Along the way they learn rules of evidence, true and false cause and effect, rules of comparison, rules of generalization, types of proof, and how to eliminate alternatives.

You absolutely need the teacher's guide, as it includes both lesson plans and answer keys.

The Critical Thinking in American History series contains another three units, each with student workbook and teacher's guide. Like *Colonies to Constitution,* each analyzes differing viewpoints of specific historical events. The series includes *Exploration to Constitution, New Republic to Civil War, Reconstruction to Progressivism,* and *Spanish-American War to Vietnam.*

NEW**
Peter Marshall
From Sea to Shining Sea, The Light and the Glory, $12.50 each paperbound, $18.50 each hardbound. Study guide for *The Light and the Glory,* $9.50. *America: Roots of Our Nation* video, $52.50. *In God They Trusted,* $32.50/video, $9.50/coffee-table-type book with color pictures and text of video.

Here are two excellent, long books on American history by Peter Marshall, son of author Catherine Marshall and the late Senate chaplain Peter Marshall, and David Manuel.

The Light and the Glory starts with Christopher Columbus and ends with George Washington's last day in office. *From Sea to Shining Sea* picks up the tale and carries it up to the roots of the Civil War.

"Does God have a plan for America?" reads the subtitle in the first book, while the second one continues, "God's plan for America unfolds." American history is read in the light of right or wrong, with the contributions of both Protestants and Catholics noted.

Did you know Christopher Columbus, whose name means "Christ-bearer," thought of himself as a missionary to the Indians? Old Chris was not averse to making big bucks from his discoveries, either, a fact which the book also notes.

This is honest history, in which source quotations are skilfully interwoven with some fine storytelling. Take the slavery question, for instance. We hear from the radical abolitionists, the moderates, the plantation owners, the house slaves, and the field slaves. We learn about the hypocrisy of both South and North, and why the voices of reason were drowned by those shouting for blood. We hear Thomas Jefferson's view of New Englanders and his equally unflattering view of Southerners. We learn about the conflict between Puritans, from whom the New Englanders descended, and Cavaliers, the King's men in the English civil wars, who left their mark on the South. This is a lot deeper treatment of the subject than you'll get in any textbook and much more interesting to read besides. Added benefit: no homework questions at the end of the chapters!

The study guide for *The Light and the Glory* does an excellent job of leading students to see the providential workings of God in early American history, as well as what was good or bad about the colonies and explorations.

From the same source are available a lecture series of two videos on the Christian principles behind the Declaration of Independence and the Constitution (*America: Roots of Our Nation*) and *In God They Trusted,* a video dramatization of five important moments in American history. Both will make more sense if you work through these books first.

NEW**
Reel to Real Ministries
The Story of America's Liberty, $29.95 plus $3.50 shipping. Ages 10–adult.

Reel to Real Ministries, an outgrowth of Maranatha Campus Ministries has produced a video, *The Story of America's Liberty,* that takes you on a tour through the nation's capitol buildings. Your attention is directed to the large number of conspicuously Christian inscriptions, artworks, and so on that surround our devoted legislators and Supreme Court justices while schoolchildren are hermetically sealed off from the same. Learn about the historic events that inspired each of the works of art in our nation's capital and find out why those events so profoundly affected the founding of America.

Teaching Home
Complete six-issue set of 1985 back issues, $12.50, includes free set of 6 plastic magazine holders for your ring binder.

As I've said before, each *Teaching Home* magazine back issue on a given topic is like a course in teaching that topic. August/September 1985 was the issue on teaching history. How about an article on using family storytelling to teach Bible, personal, and national history? Find out about the Principle Approach and the providential view of history. How can old books help your children learn history *painlessly*? Delve into the controversy over how secular texts present history, or find out how to make history relevant to today. Lots more! This back issue is not available separately, but don't let that bother you, since it's really fun to read all those old back issues and see how useful all those articles still are today. Home schoolers are not what you'd call *faddish*. I mean, several issues in '85 carried articles on the Trivium, the classical course of study used in medieval schools and pre-university training, including a reprint of Dorothy Sayers's timeless essay, "The Lost Tools of Learning." (You may remember Miss Sayers as the author of the Lord Peter Wimsey mystery series, and a friend of J. R. R. Tolkien and C. S. Lewis.)

BRITISH HISTORY

British history forms the backdrop to U.S. history. The people who founded the U.S.A. were British subjects who didn't like the practices of the ruling monarch. Their main complaint, in fact, was that King George was trampling on their rights as Englishmen! British literature, law, and culture had a tremendous impact on America. British history is also full of great stories worth knowing just for themselves. So I was very happy to find the resources listed below.

Bob Jones University Press
Each literature textbook, $17.95. Each teacher's manual, $29.50. These are home-school prices. Shipping extra.

As I mentioned in the Literature chapter, BJUP has two textbooks on British literature: once for early literature and one for modern. These include a lot of background British history, from a conservative Christian point of view, and may in some ways be better value as history texts, with literature thrown in, than as literature texts.

Ladybird Books, Inc.
Each book, $3.50. Kings and Queens Wall Chart, $9.50. Grades 5 and up.

Ladybird used to have a series of three dozen small, hardcover history books covering British and ancient history. The old series is almost completely out of print, except for *Kings and Queens of England Book 1* and *Kings and Queens of England Book 2*. These should stay around for awhile.

The new Ladybird History of Britain series is much more up-to-date, with a lavishly illustrated visual format like Usborne books. This series includes *The Romans*, *The Saxons and the Normans*, *The Middle Ages*, *The Tudors*, *The Stuarts*, and *The Georgians*. Lots of fascinating condensed history.

The *Kings and Queens Wall Chart* is an illustrated genealogy of the kings and queens of England. It's approximately 24 x 16" in size, all of which is needed to cover the complex story of who was related to whom!

All the Ladybird history books are designed for a fifth grade and up reading level.

Longman Publishing Group
Then and There Series, $6.45/book. Set of 10 Medieval World titles, $58.29; accompanying teacher's guide and worksheet masters, $25.62. Set of 8 Elizabethan World titles, $45.69; accompanying teacher's guide/worksheet masters, $25.62. These are school prices; individuals should multiply prices by 4/3. Shipping extra.

Longman's Then and There series includes 10 titles on the English Medieval World, eight on the Elizabethan World, and one from a British viewpoint called *The Home Front in the Second World War*.

Good depth, interesting reading. For more information see the writeup below under World History.

WORLD HISTORY

NEW**
A Beka Book Publications

Old World History and Geography (grade 5: 1991 edition): student book, $11.30; teacher's edition, $18.30; maps, tests, review sheets also available. *New World History and Geography* (grade 6): student book, $12.05; teacher's guide/curriculum, $20; maps, tests, review sheets also available. *Since the Beginning* (grade 7), *The Modern Age* (grade 8): student book, $11.95 each grade; teacher's guide/curriculum, $20/grade; teacher key/test booklet, $7.40/grade. *World History and Cultures in Christian Perspective* (grade 10): student book, $14.75; teacher's edition (includes curriculum), $30.70; student test booklet, $3.95; teacher's key/test booklet, $8.45. Available August 1991: student quiz booklet, $3.75; teacher key/quiz booklet, $7.40. Shipping extra.

A Beka has a wealth of world history books and teaching aids written for differing age levels. I'm starting with the fifth- and sixth-grade books, because I believe most middle- and high-schoolers have *not* mastered the history and geography run by them in elementary school.

Old World History and Geography and *New World History and Geography* study the world's history by geographical regions. These books present history and geography in context, introducing the forms of government, important people, national heroes, and culture of each area as they change over time. Both texts are packed with beautiful full-color photographs and illustrations and loaded with maps and other visual aids. Strong Christian and anti-communist emphasis: lots on missionaries. Rather encyclopedic reading; A Beka believes in giving you a *lot* of information.

In the Beginning and *The Modern Age* are the seventh- and eighth-grade world history books, respectively. *In the Beginning* attempts to tell history as "His Story," taking a providential view, from the Garden of

Eden through the Renaissance. *The Modern Age* picks up the threads and follows them from the Reformation to modern U.S. history. Both books are designed for ease of studying. Key events are emphasized in the text, and paragraph headings and summary statements are accented by color or boldface. Lots of support materials available for these books.

Intended for 11th-graders, *World History and Cultures in Christian Perspective* is the most ambitious of A Beka's world history books. It covers African and Asian cultures, not just the Greek and Roman civilizations. The history of ideas gets good coverage, with A Beka at pains to point out the biblical failings of such theories as evolutionism, socialism, humanism, Communism, and so on.

NEW**
Alpha Omega Publications

LIFEPACS, $2.95 each or $26.95 for all 10. Teacher handbook for grade 10, $4.95. Answer keys, $2.25. LIFEPAC test keys, $2.25. Shipping extra.

Alpha Omega's grade 10 social-studies course covers ancient and Western history. It starts at Creation, then moves to the Fertile Crescent, Egypt, Assyria, Babylon, and Persia—all in the first unit! The second unit mentions India and China, but concentrates more on the Greeks and Romans. There then is one unit each on the medieval world (its history and culture), the Renaissance and Reformation, the age of mercantilism and empires, the age of revolution, the Industrial Revolution, the two World Wars, and the contemporary world (focusing mostly on the Cold War and the atomic age). The workbooks are relatively inexpensive, easy to study or teach, and fast-moving.

Though the course content is somewhat uneven, since you don't get the same author writing all the LIFEPACS, by and large this is a good course.

NEW**
Bluestocking Press

The Mainspring of Human Progress, $2.95 plus $1.75 shipping first book, 50¢ each additional. Grades 10–adult.

Here's a little book you never heard of that nevertheless has sold three quarters of a million copies. Who is its author? Henry Grady Weaver (1889–1949), a director of consumer research for General Motors. What's it about? The history of liberty, both its ups and downs, from the Spartan "bee swarm" in which every man's entire life was dictated by state authorities, to the mid-twentieth century. The question: "For 6,000 years people died of hunger. Why don't we?" The style: fast-moving and fascinating, not to mention strongly flavored with the author's own beliefs.

Mr. Weaver contrasts the ancient pagan belief in a static world controlled by statist authorities with what he considers the Christian position—self-government and personal responsibility, with minimum faith invested in any human authority. Along the way we find out why the Moslems were so successful for 800 years, how the English upper classes learned to be jolly good fellows, why the colonists threw the tea into the sea at the Boston Tea Party, why Marx and Engels had absolutely nothing to say that hadn't already been put into practice by the ancient Aztecs, why Spain had the first great trans-world empire and why they lost it, why Good Queen Bess was a better ruler than King George the Third, why of all men the "humanitarian with a guillotine" is most to be feared (and why our bleeding-heart friend always ends up running that guillotine), why even the Pilgrims couldn't make a commune work (they tried!), why advanced thinkers 150 years ago thought the Midwest plains could never be farmed, and so on.

As with any one-person view of history, *The Mainspring of Human Progress* gives you a lot to think about. You can agree or disagree with the author; he does you the honor of saying what he thinks.

NEW★★
Bob Jones University Press
World Studies (grade 7): student text, $19.95 (hardbound) or $12.95 (softbound); teacher's edition, $31.50; Test-Bank, $9.95; activity sheets, $4.95; activity sheets answer key, $1.25. *World History* (grade 10): student text, $19.95, hardbound; teacher's manual, $21; map packet (25 maps), $3.50; TestBank, $9.95. These are home-school prices. Shipping extra.

World Studies for Christian Schools covers the world's history in chronological order and region by region, starting with the ancient Ur of the Chaldees (Abraham's home town). Under Unit 3, "The Medieval World," for example, you find chapters on the golden ages of China and India, medieval Japan, medieval Islam, the Byzantine Empire, the European "dark ages," and the age of feudalism. The book is fundamentalist, missionary-minded, and anti-Catholic in spots (calling the Roman Catholic Church "Satan's tool" in the last chapter, for example). Written at a seventh-grade level, its emphasis on everyday life and culture makes this text interesting reading and a good background introduction to world history for those who share its general outlook.

World History for Christian Schools, the 10th-grade course, is of course deeper than the *World Studies* text. It is also more urbane in tone and more interesting to read. The treatment of the Reformation, for example, while it will not thrill Catholics, dwells mostly on historic facts and source quotes. The book does an excellent job of covering the whole of world history from a traditional Protestant and Western-civilization point of view.

NEW★★
Christian Light Publications
God's World—His Story, $16.80. Add 20% shipping. Grades 6–8.

The Creation and Flood. Sumeria. Egypt. Greece. Rome. Israel and Judah. The Church. Middle Ages. The Reformation. The Spanish Inquisition. Age of Exploration. Age of Colonialism. Age of Missions. Russia. China. India. World Wars. Cold War. This one book, *God's World—His Story,* covers the entire history of the Western world. Written from a staunchly Mennonite viewpoint, it makes very interesting reading, as the trials and tribulations of that group are thrown into relief against the background of the great movements of the time.

History is not only presented, but also analyzed from a conservative Mennonite perspective—including the mistakes of Mennonites and Anabaptists of the past. Topics are covered in reasonable depth, with many intriguing sidelights on how people lived in each age. Each chapter ends with review questions and Bible exercises, in which you either read about the history of the time period or study passages and apply them to the situations people faced at that time. Good, readable writing, presented with both sobriety and feeling. Lots of character-building emphasis on the frequent necessity of suffering for Christ in this world. No uncritical

American patriotism, as in many other Christian textbooks, nor yet any uncritical America-bashing, as in many secular texts.

With all this in mind, I believe *God's World—His Story* provides a good overview of Western world history for this age group while it adds a wholesome balance to the home schooler's history bookshelf, even for those of us who aren't Mennonites.

Warning: lots of religious denominations persecuted the Mennonites (e.g., Lutherans, Anglicans, Catholics . . .), so if you're a member of one of these groups and it bothers you to have the failings of your forebears pointed out, don't say I didn't warn you!

NEW**
Crossway Books
Unholy Sacrifices of the New Age, $8.95. *Ancient Empires of the New Age*, $9.95. Ages 16–adult.

Ancient Empires of the New Age takes a different view of ancient history than that now promoted in typical magazines and textbooks. Instead of lauding the "advanced" Aztecs for their "marvelous works of architecture," for example, *Ancient Empires* explores what the Aztecs actually used their temples *for* (human sacrifice of the vilest kind). You are introduced to the pagan influence in ancient history, and the history of attempts to revive it in modern times (starting as far back as the 1700s and even earlier!), all from a critical, rather than a gee-whiz, perspective.

Unholy Sacrifices of the New Age, while focusing largely on how modern medical practices have changed from "first, do no harm" (the Hippocratic oath) to a pro-death ethic and treating the patient as a potential organ and tissue bank, also includes a lot of forgotten ancient history. The history of surgery, for example, which began with grave-robbing and vivisection. The history of nursing care, which began with Christian

monks and nuns. The history of human-tissue-based medicine, widely practiced along with human sacrifice in ancient cultures. The almost completely suppressed history of the Nazi doctors, which exactly parallels the history of our "modern, compassionate" medical establishment.

We are used to treating all other cultures as tourist attractions: fun places to visit peopled with friendly natives just like us except for the funny clothes and language. These two books show that, with all its defects, the Christian West is *better* than what went before—and that we should not lightly throw it away, as those who would like to return to the ancient "new" age urge us to.

Both *Unholy Sacrifices* and *Ancient Empires* were written by Paul deParrie and yours truly, and published by Crossway Books. You can get 'em in bookstores or through Home Life.

NEW**
EDC Publishing
Time Traveler Series, $6.95 each paperbound or $13.96 each library-bound. Combined volume *The Traveler's Omnibus* $17.95 hardbound. Ages 8 and up. Children's Picture World History series, $6.95 each paperbound or $13.96 each library-bound. Combined volume *The Usborne Book of World History*, $19.95 hardbound. Ages 8 and up.

The most fascinating, appealing history books I have ever seen. Published in Britain by Usborne books in the 80s, brought over to the U.S.A. courtesy of EDC Publishing.

The Usborne Time Traveler series takes you back in time to see how life really was for the high and lowly in ancient Egypt (the *Pharaohs and Pyramids* book), Rome (*Rome and Romans*), Norseland (*Viking Raiders*), and medieval Europe (*Knights and Castles*).

The Children's Picture World History series does the same for *First Civilizations* (strong evolutionary outlook); *Empires and Barbarians; Warriors and Seafarers; Crusaders, Aztecs, and Samurai; Exploration and Discovery;* and *The Age of Revolutions*. All are full-color throughout, 8½ x 11", in quality cartoon style on glossy paper, with plenty of descriptive text. See how Baron Godfrey's castle defenses were designed, or how the Egyptians turned papyrus into paper! Watch the Vikings build their ship, or the Romans prepare a feast! Kids can't put them down (and neither could I). Slight Magic Markering needed in a few places (Cretan ladies dressed like Playboy models).

NEW**
EDC Publishing
Illustrated World History Series includes *The Romans, The Greeks,* and *Early Civilization,* $9.95 each paperbound or $15.96 each library-bound. *The Usborne Illustrated World History Dates,* $11.95 paperbound, $16.95 library-bound. Shipping extra. Ages 12–16.

Usborne's new Illustrated World History series is an ambitious attempt to give teen readers an in-depth look at world history and civilizations.

Like other Usborne books, each book in this series is profusely illustrated , with text and illustrations skilfully interwoven to involve the reader. Books are 96 pages each, most in full color. The last 16 pages of each book are given over to black-and-white maps, glossaries, capsule myths and biographies, history outlines with chronological dates, and general indexes.

Each book contains a wealth of information about life in the ancient world—clothes, jewelry, houses, travel, learning, medicine, music, hairstyles, entertainment, and so on—as well as facts about military life and training, religion, the role of women, and other topics generally covered in textbooks.

Of the two volumes I saw, *The Romans* was unfortunately unbalanced in its treatment of religion. Christianity, which ultimately conquered the Roman Empire and is of immense historical significance, was presented as one of the "alternatives to the state religion," of only equal weight with Mithra-worship, and with a *smaller* writeup than Cybele-worship. Christians' belief in the resurrection of Jesus—the central tenet of the Christian religion—was not even mentioned in the brief capsule description. Christianity is not brought up as a factor in Roman history until the rise of Constantine. Nor are the martyrs mentioned, except in seven words in this sentence about Constantine: "After his victory he granted tolerance to all religious groups,

including Christians (who under Diocletian had been badly persecuted)."

One thing I, and most other home schoolers, dislike about regular school texts is the way they rub kids' noses in the seamy side of life, along with proselytizing for sexual libertinism as a normal way of life. Up until this time, Usborne books have been positive in their outlook, avoiding such material. The Illustrated World History Series marks a departure from this policy. *The Romans* includes a totally unnecessary mention of contraceptive use in Roman times (under the heading "Childbirth"). *The Greeks* devotes part of one page, plus illustrations, to describing the custom of *hetairai,* a social class of girls brought up to be mistresses of wealthy men. There is a quite distressing picture of two wailing abandoned babies, and another of a wife holding her newborn baby and arguing with her husband about being allowed to keep it. Yes, these things did happen, as did a lot of other nastiness *not* mentioned, but I question the value of filling kids' minds with it. If you can leave out descriptions and illustrations of Nero's sex life, temple prostitution, and ritual religious torture, you can leave out this other stuff.

There is no criticism of human sacrifice or totalitarian statism, either. Sample quote: "The Scythians were a very wealthy people. Their graves were filled with rich goods, along with human and horse sacrifices." End of quote. I don't know about you, but this value-free nonchalance about human life gives me the creeps.

World History Dates, as its name suggests, is big on dates. History is presented in chronological sequence. Side-by-side lists of dates and events show what was happening in different places at the same time: Southern/Western Europe, Northern/Eastern Europe, Africa and the Middle East, Asia, and The Americas. Frequent sidebars present important historical events and cultural features. You'll find, for example, capsule writeups on monasticism and feudalism. Especially important dates are pulled out and highlighted in a separate sidebar of their own. Again, Christianity is slighted. Consider this synopsis of Christianity:

Christianity was founded in Palestine by Jesus of Nazareth (c. 5BC–AD29), later known as Jesus Christ. He was arrested and crucified for his teachings. After his death, the faith was spread by his followers . . .

Again, the Resurrection is *not* mentioned, nor is the fact that B.C. means "before Christ" and A.D. stands for Anno Domini, which means "The Year of

Our Lord." The martyrs and persecutions under various Roman emperors are not mentioned either.

Bottom line: These books have a lot of fascinating and useful information. What they leave out is more of a problem than what they put in, as is the change in direction from previous Usborne series. I just hope Usborne, now that it is so successful, doesn't forget the families who *made* it successful and end up as another voice promoting pagan religion and ethics and as a "me-too" evangelist for trendy social fads.

NEW★★
Greenleaf Press
Famous Men of Greece, Famous Men of Rome, Famous Men of the Middle Ages, $15.95 each. Study guides, $7.95 each. *Greenleaf Guide to Ancient Egypt,* $7.95. Ancient Egypt Study Package (includes *Greenleaf Guide*), $36.95. Add $1 shipping per book ($2 minimum). Grades 3 and up (if you read to them, or they are good readers). Public-school reading level: grade 6 and up.

The *Famous Men* series is an attempt "to spread world history over the elementary school years and proceed at a leisurely pace that would allow the child to live with the material for a period of months." They would also make a fine, slower-paced introduction to world history for students in the middle grades.

Famous Men of Greece and *Famous Men of Rome* are reprints of two works originally published in 1904 that present Greek and Roman mythology along with short biographies of famous men from each area.

The books are fairly easy and entertaining reading. Example:

> Besides great philosophers, Athens had some famous painters. Two of the most celebrated were Zeuxis and Parrhasius, who lived about 400 B.C. They were rivals. Once they gave an exhibition of their paintings. Zeuxis exhibited a bunch of grapes which had such a natural look that the birds came and pecked at them. The people exclaimed, "Astonishing! What can be finer than Zeuxis' grapes?"

Zeuxis proudly turned to his rival's picture. A purple curtain hung before it. "Draw aside your curtain, Parrhasius," he said, "and let us look at your picture."

> The artist smiled, but did not move. Someone else stepped toward the curtain to draw it aside, and it was then discovered that the curtain was part of the painting.

> "I yield," said Zeuxis. "It is easy to see who is the better artist. I have deceived birds. Parrhasius has deceived an artist."

> It is said that Zeuxis died of laughing at a funny picture that he had painted of an old woman.

Those who know enough about Greek and Roman history to notice will observe that statism is exalted in these books. Lycurgus, for example, who persuaded the Spartan citizens to divvy up their property and slaves, kill their feeble and deformed babies, and live on the simplest food served in a communal dining hall, is called "one of the wisest and best men that ever lived in Greece." Such were the views common in the early 1900s, proving that yesterday isn't always wiser than today. That's why Greenleaf wrote study guides to highlight some of these problems in Greek and Roman culture and encourage readers to judge ancient customs by biblical attitudes.

My opinion of this series changed dramatically for the better when I read the Greenleaf study guides for Greece and Rome. These books are really well-organized and thorough. Each chapter of the *Famous Men* books is covered separately, with vocabulary word lists and discussion questions. Background information is provided where necessary. The guide for Greece includes supplementary reading assignments from Homer's *Iliad* and *Odyssey* and selections from Plato. The guide for Rome assigns supplementary readings from *Foxe's Book of Martyrs,* Virgil's *Æneid,* Macaulay's *City,* and more. Geography is covered (via salt dough maps), and story characters are analyzed in terms of biblical standards of righteousness. Not only that, but Greenleaf Press's catalog lists supplementary books for each time period, so your children can cut out historically-accurate models, see how cities and towns were built, and read the history of each time period both as straight history and historical fiction.

Here's the Greenleaf philosophy:

> In general, high school level history material is written in a way that assumes some prior knowledge of the stories. If you already know the basic facts about,

say, Charlemagne when you study him in high school, you have less to memorize about him. You can simply add the additional information to what you already know. (One of the things that makes history classes so boring is that very few students come to them with such a background. Because *everything* is new, *everything* must be memorized.)

The Greenleaf way, then, is to get kids familiar with the basic setting and people from each historical time period *before* they enter high school. Perhaps the best example of how this works is the Ancient Egypt Study Package. The *Greenleaf Guide to Ancient Egypt* stands alone, not having a *Famous Men* book to accompany it. To make up for this, the people at Greenleaf have put together several Usborne books (*Time-Traveler Book of Pharaohs and Pyramid* and *Deserts* from the First Travelers series), a book on King Tut's mummy, David Macaulay's great book *Pyramid* that shows the construction of the pyramids, a history book entitled *Pharaohs of Ancient Egypt* written at a fourth-grade reading level, and an illustrated book on Egyptian boats that second-graders can read by themselves.

Using these as the basic texts, the *Greenleaf Guide* pulls it all together with reading assignments, salt dough maps, modeling activities, and discussion questions. It's an absolutely enthralling introduction to this time period, designed so the whole family can study the same lessons at once.

Though guides are not yet available for these time periods, the Greenleaf catalog includes good selections of activity, history, and story books for Middle Ages and Renaissance and Reformation. *Famous Men of the Middle Ages,* another book in the series, should be out by the time you read this.

NEW**
Longman Publishing Group
Then and There Series, $6.45/book. Set of 10 Medieval World titles, $58.29; accompanying teacher's guide and worksheet masters, $25.62. Set of 8 Elizabethan World titles, $45.69; accompanying teacher's guide/worksheet masters, $25.62. These are school prices; individuals should multiply prices by 4/3. Shipping extra.

It's no joke reviewing 28 history books. The job takes days and days. Believe it or not, though, I wasn't even tempted to give up or settle for quick browsing. That's because the Then and There series is so much more interesting than textbooks!

Copiously illustrated from historical sources, each book in this series also draws heavily on source documents for its text. The books are also written as much like stories as possible, which makes a real difference not only for readability but for the likelihood a student will remember what he has read.

(Explanation: they were written in England!)

Words printed in thick black (in the revised editions) or italics (in the old editions) are explained in the glossary of each book. This enables the writers to quote source documents without constantly stopping to explain each old word. This feature should be much appreciated by those of us from outside Britain, for whom many of the terms are strange.

Study questions and activities follow each chapter, but these are unobtrusive enough that you can easily enjoy the books simply as books.

Throughout the series, the authors write as *authors*. They make moral judgments (with which you can agree or disagree) about the behavior of the people about whom they are writing. The authors of the revised editions also take care to point out the areas where historians disagree.

The Then and There series is especially strong in its coverage of British history. All the titles on the Elizabethan World and the Medieval World are excellent. These transport you right back to the times. The *Spanish Armada* book regrettably leaves out the providential nature of the Armada's defeat—both Philip of Spain and the English people considered that God Himself had wiped out the Armada—but aside from that, the books manage to honestly convey what people were thinking at the time.

Since American history series tend to be vague on English history, or leave it out altogether, and since much American history and church history can't be understood without it, these two series deserve a place on the family bookshelf.

Medieval World titles include *The Norman Conquest, The King and Magna Carta, The Medieval Village, The Medieval Town, The Medieval Monastery, The Medieval Castle, The Medieval Knight, Medieval Amusements, The Crusaders,* and *The Black Death.* Fascinating reading!

Elizabethan World titles include *The Elizabethan Village, Elizabethan Citizen, The Elizabethan Country House, The Elizabethan Court, Shakespeare and His Theatre, Mary Queen of Scots, Elizabethan Explorers,* and *Spanish Armada.*

Also available are *The French Revolution, Lenin and the Russian Revolution, The Home Front in the Second World War* (the "home front" in England, that is), *The Chartists* (English working people of the last century who demanded universal male suffrage and other reforms), and *Florence in the Time of the Medici* (lots of nude or partially nude Renaissance statues and artworks in this book).

Unfortunately, those writing about the French revolutionaries seem to subscribe to one degree or another to the idea that it's OK to massacre bunches of innocent people to build a revolution or a great empire. The book on Lenin is also unabashed Bolshevik propaganda. Consider its claims for how well the communists were taking care of Russian children during the civil war, feeding them on *caviar, sausage, and butter,* no less—a quote taken directly from a Bolshevik writer! In spite of its shortcomings of judgment this book still presents the sequence of events surrounding the Russian Revolution in a way schoolchildren can easily remember.

The entire Then and There series is being redone in a more open typeface with nicer covers. The text is also being updated. The Elizabethan and Medieval books are already out in the new style, and the others probably will also be available in the new style by the time you read this.

NEW**
Milliken Publishing Co.
The Hebrews, Phoenicians and Hittites. Byzantine and Moslems. The Italian Renaissance. $12.95 each. Grades 7–adult.

Here's a novel way to study history! Milliken's transparency/duplicating books each contain 12 full-color

transparencies to illustrate the geography, history, and important cultural features of a major historical period. They also include background historical information coordinated to each transparency, and between 4–12 duplicating master quiz pages. Answers to the quizzes are found at the end of the teacher's guide section.

Information in these books is generally reliable, and the full-color transparencies certainly do engage the attention. Although originally designed for use with an overhead projector, their dramatic appearance and clutter-free design works well as a kind of super illustration.

Try using the workbook pages first as a research aid. Students research the answers and check their work against the answers in the teacher's material. The same workbook pages can then be resurrected later as tests, once the student has worked through the material.

I would also recommend that you skip the activities: silly stuff like "Write a newspaper report of David killing Goliath" or time-consuming busywork like "Construct a model of the city of Jerusalem" (the book doesn't even contain enough info for you to construct the model). These are not up to the high standards of the rest of these books.

The workbook study pages and essay questions are excellent; kids will really learn the history working through them. Knowledge is stressed; fill-in-the-blanks is kept to a minimum.

Information in these books is generally reliable. Exceptions: the apparent anti-supernatural bias of the writers of the *Hebrews, Phoenicians, and Hittites* book causes them to ascribe Samuel's anointing of David to Saul's "fits of rage which made him unsuitable as a king" (see I Samuel for the true story), and to question David's authorship of the Psalms bearing his name. Otherwise I have to commend the authors of this series for a well-balanced presentation, even of difficult themes such as *Byzantine and Moslems*.

The transparency pages give you a window into these time periods, showing you how people dressed, what kind of buildings they built, how they worked and played, and so on. None of that gruesome focus on violence and the seamy underside of a civilization that so mars many newer public school histories.

Considering that many traditional history textbooks skip over these periods, ignore their cultural side, or distort the entire time period in favor of preaching some faddish new cultural agenda, the Milliken series is an excellent resource. This series will be available in blackline reproducible version fall 1991–spring 1992, making it even a better deal for home use.

ORAL HISTORY AND SOURCE DOCUMENTS

NEW★★
Bob Jones University Press
American History in Verse, $7.15. Shipping extra. Grades 5–adult.

It's just what the name says: poems about every major incident and personage in American history by a hodgepodge of bards, many contemporaries of the persons or events. You get some queer gems here, as well as many poems rollicking, tender, tragic, and even ludicrous. Find out what the man in the street used to think about American history, back when he used to know enough to think something about it.

NEW★★
Bobby Horton
Songs of the CSA, four volumes. *Songs of the Union Army*, two volumes. $10 each tape. Lyric sheets available for $3 per volume. All prices postpaid. All ages.

For the songsters among us, there can be no greater American history treat than Bobby Horton's four volumes of *Songs of the CSA* (Confederate States of America) and two-volume *Songs of the Union Army*. He sings all the parts and plays all of the about 20 instruments or so featured on these tapes.

Now, I know what you're thinking. Can this be good? You bet it's good! Mr. Horton not only has done a great job of picking the songs, he renders them amazingly authentically. He can go from an Irish Union soldier to a backwoods Georgia hick complaining about his officers, from the comic to the tragic, from toe-tapping hilarity to the powerful *Battle of Shiloh*.

I do want to warn you that, since these are the *real* songs, you will find one or two "bad words" on one or two of the tapes: "h-ll" and "d-mn," as in "I don't give a d-mn," to be precise. I asked Bobby Horton about this, and he explained that he had also thought about possibly censoring them out, but decided against it in favor of historical realism. The whole collection is absolutely true to life, both in its portrayal of the genuine deep piety of both North and South and by its refusal to sanitize the occasional rowdiness of our ancestors. Consequently, you get a *feel* for both sides in the Civil War you just can't get from textbooks, which typically leave out either the piety or the rowdiness or both.

These songs are a kind of "source document" that goes far beyond the written word in evoking the moods

and beliefs of both North and South, black and white, officers and privates, ladies and gents, Christians and not-so-Christians, at a time that marked a watershed in Western history. They are also just about the greatest collection of folk music I have ever been privileged to hear—a real treat to listen to.

Foundation for American Christian Education (FACE)
Christian History of the Constitution, Teaching and Learning America's Christian History, $15 each. *Rudiments*, $7. *Christian Self-Government with Union*, $18. *Consider and Ponder*, $23. Add 10% regular mail, 15% UPS. Ages 16–adult.

Big books full of source documents that trace America's Christian roots. Use along with Intrepid Books' workbooks for best results. See the Citizenship chapter for full details on FACE and Intrepid Books.

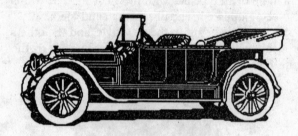

NEW★★
Gallopade Publishing Group
Out of the Mouths of Slaves, The Best Book of Black Biographies, $14.95 each paperbound or $19.95 each hardbound. Grades 4–12.

From the prolific Carole S. Marsh, here are two titles of her *Our Black Heritage* series.

Out of the Mouths of Slaves is billed as "wisdom, trauma, humor—an authentic oral history experience for young readers." Along with a brief history of black civil rights and wrongs, you'll find lots of quotes from a wide spectrum of Southern blacks. Slavery, slave ships, rebellions, the Civil War, and the dreary lives of sharecroppers are chronicled, along with the black community's attempt to withstand the Ku Klux Klan. I was surprised to hear that, in at least one area, the authorities instructed blacks to form a militia and defend themselves—which they did with some success. All in all this is a balanced book, quoting both contented slaves and runaways, success stories and failures. If anything, it gives you an appetite for further reading and a deeper understanding of the financial and emotional frustration that finally boiled over in the Civil Rights Movement.

The Best Book of Black Biographies has an assortment of inspirational long and short biographies of famous and not-so-famous blacks. Slaves. Sopranos. Musicians. Pioneers (including the founder of the city of Chicago). Scientists. Pilots. Symphony conductors. Plus a smattering of the usual politicians, singers, and sports stars. Kudos to Mrs. Marsh for celebrating the diversity of talent in the black community: Michael Jackson gets less space in her book than William Henry Hastie (the first black governor of a U.S. territory, in case you didn't know)!

LibertyTree: Review and Catalog
Documentary History of US (rev. ed.), $7.95. *They Preached Liberty,* $12.95. Audio Classics tape series of abridged and unabridged classics and new books, prices from $17.95–$139.95. Shipping extra.

Upscale catalog of products for your "life, liberty, and prosperity." We're looking now at *LibertyTree's* source document offerings.

The present catalog includes, besides many books about history, several significant volumes of source writings on the Revolutionary War era and an Audio Classics series of important books by historical personages.

First, the books. *A Documentary History of the United States* contains "the documents, speeches, and letters that forged American history," such as the Declaration of Independence, Constitution, Monroe Doctrine, and Emancipation Proclamation. *They Preached Liberty* presents the writings and activities of the New England ministers during the Revolution. *American Political Writings During the Founding Era* is 76 pieces in two volumes. Lots more: Thomas Paine's *Common Sense,* the book that led to the Declaration of Independence; Edmund Burke's *Vindication of Natural Society,* Locke's *Two Treatises on Government,* and *The Life and Selected Writings of Thomas Jefferson,* to name a few.

LibertyTree's Audio Classics series includes *Common Sense/*The Declaration of Independence, *The Federalist Paper, Reflections on the Revolution in France* (by Edmund Burke)/*The Rights of Man* (Tom Paine), *Democracy in America* (Alexis de Tocqueville), *The Wealth of Nations* (Adam Smith), *The Road to Serfdom* (F. A. Hayek), and *Economics in One Lesson* (Henry Hazlitt).

NEW**
Mantle Ministries
Gaining Favor with God and Man, The Plymouth Settlement, Columbus and the New World, $14 each plus $2.75 shipping.

Mantle Ministries, the publishing company founded by Richard "Little Bear" Wheeler, is republishing gorgeous editions of American history classics. Hardcover with gold-edged pages, these books were originally written hundreds of years ago. *Gaining Favor with God and Man* is reviewed in the Character Education chapter.

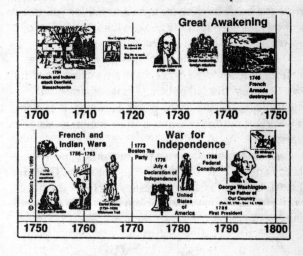

TIME LINES

NEW**
Creation's Child
Chronological World History Chart, $21.95. Prices include 1991 shipping. Grades 4–adult.

S. C. Adams was a man of many talents: pastor, educator, state senator, Oregon pioneer, and farmer. In

1871 he published a time line, and *what* a time line! Over 50 feet long and five feet high, lavished with color engravings, Adams' time line covered the history of the world from creation to his day, including the vicissitudes of nations (with a separate stream for each), discoveries, inventions, alphabets, political events, and much more. Besides Western nations, Mr. Adams' time line also covered China, Persia, Assyria, and a host of other countries normally forgotten in our historical studies. Adams was a bit of a modernist, although still committed to Biblical chronology, and his effusions on the marvels of 1871 technology are amusing.

Mr. Adams made his living for a while traveling around and displaying this monster achievement! Since then, other hands have added some extra years, bringing it up to 1989. The history of nations and their rulers are shown as colored streams, sometimes converging, sometimes disappearing, as one civilization is conquered or superseded by another.

The original chart is on display in a museum in Oregon. But you can get a copy of this beautiful extravaganza from Creation's Child.

The *Chronological World History Chart* comes in book form. It comes in accordian-fold style full-color 12 x 17" cardstock panels, which unfold to one continuous 15-foot panel. The chart may easily be removed from the book binding for use on a wall, or you can do as I do and keep it in the book, where it is easier to store (who has 15 feet of clear wall space?!).

As a data-organizing tool this time line is not as helpful as it could be, since dates are incorporated into the "streams" instead of being firmly separate and viewable on the top of the paper. However, it contains a wealth of information and is an invitation to historical browsing.

As with most Victorian productions, a few naked ladies appear here and there (e.g., Eve in the Garden of Eden). Creation's Child suggests you clothe the naked with crayon or erase the problem areas with fine sandpaper.

"Beach Airie" from Wolff Abel™ Old Earth Almanac. ©1989–9 Bobb-Gibbit Antheart, Inc.

KONOS

Volume 1 Time Line and 176 Figures, Volume 2 (190 figures), Volume 3 (122 figures), $59.95 each. Save $10 if you buy either volume of the time line with corresponding curriculum volume. *Time Line of Bible Characters* (about 190 figures), $59.95. *Artists and Composers* (about 90 artist figures), $20.90. Laminated display lines alone, $9.95. Add 10% shipping. Grades K–8.

The KONOS Time Line and Figures: sturdy, laminated, colored sheets with time lines printed on some pages and little cutout figures on others. The time line covers 2099 B.C. to 1999 A.D., with three lines each for the 1400s on (so much was happening!).

You get the laminated display lines plus 176 people in Volume 1, with dates, some carrying insignia of their profession, others with little colorful stickers to identify them. Prophets carry staffs, mountain men wear coonskin caps, humanitarians have a red heart, preachers and missionaries carry a Bible, and so on.

The people in Volume 1 are those studied in Volume 1 of the KONOS Character Curriculum, which I reviewed in the Curriculum Buyers' Guide in Volume 1 of *The Big Book of Home Learning*! This time line contains a preponderance of Bible figures, along with major cultural leaders like Michelangelo and Martin Luther King, Jr.

Volume 2, corresponding to Volume 2 of the KONOS curriculum, emphasizes American historical figures and scientists with less Bible-times people.

Volume 3 contains a cross-section: Bible-times characters, inventors, singers, Olympic champions, doctors, etc.

Volumes 2 and 3 do *not* come with the laminated display lines, since the publishers figure you most likely got Volume 1 first, which *does* include the lines.

The price reflects the extra cost of providing laminated time strips and figures, which render the product much more attractive and durable. KONOS suggests you mount the time line in ascending and descending steps around a doorway, with B.C. on one side and A.D. on the other. Their time line looks nice enough so your children's room will look decorated rather than defaced.

I should also mention that the kit contains a number of "free" figures, so you can add the people of your choice: family members, for example.

Additional packets and lines are also available: *Bible Characters* and *Artists and Composers*.

Cutting out and setting up the time lines is fun and relatively easy. Cutting out the elaborate figures is neither. Partial solution: instead of cutting out each figure on its outline, why not cut around it in a circle? This speeds the project up considerably.

NEW★★
Rand McNally
Histomap of World History, $6.95. Add 5% shipping. Orders under $50, add an additional $5 handling charge.

What in the blue blazes is a "histomap"? You're gonna love it when you find out! It's a full-color, vertical time line showing the story of civilization.

Unlike other time lines, though, the *Histomap of World History* shows the balance of power at each point in time by the width of the culture's "band" on the chart. See the rise and fall of Egypt's fortunes merely by observing how wide or narrow the pink "Egypt" band is at any time period. Important events in Egypt during that time are printed on its band, too.

Civilizations are presented side by side, so you can easily tell who was more powerful than whom, and what events occurred at the same time but in different places.

The *Histomap* opens to 11½ x 70" for wall display, and folds to 11½ x 9½" if you haven't got that much wall to spare.

HISTORY ATLASES

NEW★★
Bolchazy-Carducci Publishers
Ancient History Atlas, $15. Add $3 shipping. Grades 7–adult.

Ancient History Atlas: 87 Maps of the Ancient World probably sounds as exciting to you as a double dose of Sominex. Wake up, then, because what we have here is actually a fascinating look at the way our cultural forebears lived, fought, traded, worked, and traveled.

Unlike other atlases, which are mainly a boring collection of place names scattered on a map, the maps in this atlas are downright gossipy. Snippets of boxed text point to interesting map features, while textures and map symbols provide more information. The map

entitled "Kingdom of David and Solomon Tenth Century B.C.," for example, shows us the resources provided Israel by the subjected Edomites (oak for ship building, copper and iron), informs us that Hamath was a vassal state under Solomon and that the Philistines were crushed by David and their iron-working and chariot-making taken over. Bethel, we find, was superseded as the capital by Jerusalem; Joppa was David's port city; a tenth-century B.C. calendar has been found at Gezer; Solomon had smelting and refining plants at Ezion-geber. The map even tells us when David took over the city of Jerusalem and when Solomon built the temple.

A similar amount of detail is found in the other 86 maps, which I am tempted to list just to impress you. Suffice it to say that we start with the Near East c. 1700 B.C., follow the travails of the ancient Egyptians, Cretans, Greeks, Phoenicians, Etruscans, Romans, and Hebrews, and finish up with Europe in A.D. 500 and the Byzantine Empire of Justinian I. Along the way, separate maps are dedicated to such things as Roman coinage and trade products, the world according to Ptolemy, the campaigns of Alexander the Great, ancient Athens, and all the other places you need to know about to understand classical literature and world history.

Just browsing through one map—"The Origins of Greek Writers"—is enough to spark interest in everyone from Pytheas (a geographer from Massalia in Gaul) to Zeno (a philosopher from Citium on Cyprus). Clear, clutter-free layout makes these maps a joy to use. This is one neat book!

NEW★★
Rand McNally
Atlas of World History, $18.95. Add 5% shipping. Orders under $50 add additional $5 handling charge.

It's 192 pages long. It's a paperback. It includes 118 full-color maps of the world as you have never seen it before. What is it? Rand McNally's *Atlas of World History*!

The catalog copy says this atlas "examine[s] a wide variety of topics, including early civilizations, economies, trade routes, religions, urbanization, revolutions, and wars" and includes a special section on U.S. history replete with "maps and text dealing with the American colonies, the Revolutionary and Civil wars, immigration, and World War II." Why quote the catalog copy? Because I don't have a copy of the book itself yet!

HISTORY MAGAZINES

NEW★★
Calliope
$17.95/year (5 issues), Back issues, $3.95 each. Foreign subscribers add $6. Grades 5–10.

This magazine used to be called *Classical Calliope* and focus on the ancient classical world. Now it has been rechristened "World History for Young People." With this wider and more updated focus, it looks like a better bet.

From the blurb:

> By showing students that world history is a continuation of events rather than a series of isolated, unrelated occurrences, *Calliope* helps young readers understand how and why those events took place.

> Carefully selected themes explore in-depth circumstances leading up to and following specific events—from ancient times through the Middle Ages and into the Renaissance. Maps and time lines broaden readers' concepts of times and places.

> In recent issues, readers traveled from Byzantium to Constantinople to Istanbul, followed the ancient Egyptian mariners on their trade routes, met with epic heroes, and relived major naval and land battles. Complementary articles, activities, puzzles and illustrations—plus recommendations on further reading —involve young readers in the excitement of past events.

I've looked at a few issues of this magazine, and they've done a good job of putting it together. It's readable, well-laid-out, and interesting. Relativistic flavor, with equal time and acceptance given to Western, African, and Eastern civilizations and all historic world religions. This means, of necessity, that some uncomfortable facts about ancient pagan civilizations are understated

or passed over, since all civilizations and religions are *not* equal (and you think so, too, or we'd have Aztec temples featuring daily human sacrifice in every major city, and you'd have gone back to your ancestors' native countries).

Future issue themes for 1991 and 1992: Major Naval Battles, Lost Cities, Foreign Invasions, Queens of Egypt, Great Explorers to the West, Defenders of France, and Vanished Civilizations.

Cobblestone
$22.95/year (12 issues). $39.95/2 years. Back issues, $3.95 each. Over 135 back issues available. Back issue annual sets, $44.95, include 12 issues, slipcase, and cumulative index. Bulk rate subscriptions available. Foreign subscribers add $8. Grades 4–9.

Would you believe a history magazine for kids? This very professionally done magazine has lots of kid appeal, being loaded with pictures, puzzles, cartoons, and lots of short, zippy stories. Whoever locates the pictures does a terrific job, as they include a lot of rare and apt photos, woodcuts, engravings, and whatnot that truly add to the depth of the stories.

Each issue of *Cobblestone* is organized around one theme. Upcoming issue themes: Andrew Jackson, Jewish Americans, African American Inventors, First Ladies of the White House, and the Sioux. Recent issues: Harlem Renaissance of the '20s and '30s, Chinese Americans, North Pole Exploration. (You can see the melting pot is coming unmelted just from looking at the issue titles.) All are loaded with interesting facts and graphics.

An issue on the theme of Newspapers, for example, featured a two-page time line beginning with Roman slaves sweating out newsletters by hand and ending with the Columbus, Ohio *Dispatch* whipping off the first totally electronic newspaper. Articles took off on tangents: newspaper illustration, war correspondence, rural papers, and specialty presses were some of the unusual subjects covered. The whole issue was held together by several major articles on the history of printing and the freedom of the press. I've described half of that one issue; if it whets your interest, why not send away for a back issue, perhaps choosing one of the themes above?

Back issues, of which there are over 135, are available in boxed annual sets as well as individual copies. The *Cobblestone* brochure thoughtfully lists them in alphabetic order by topic, rather than in order of publishing. So if you're interested in Civil War Reconstruction or Children Who Shaped History, you can quickly find what you're looking for. Baseball? American Theater? The Amish? Cherokee Indians? Great Depression? Jazz? Laura Ingalls Wilder? As you can see, topics can be cultural, famous people, time periods, or groups of people.

All back issue annual sets include the cumulative index to all previously published issues.

HISTORY DRILL

NEW★★
Educational Insights
Windows of Learning, U.S. History or World History, $6.95 each. Minimum order $25. Shipping extra. Grades 4–adult.

"Build your knowledge of history with fun, self-checking quiz wheels!" Here's how it works. Slip one of the compact 7" question-and-answer disks into the circular case. A question will appear in the cutout window at the top. Look in the window on the other side for the answer. Then rotate the disk for the next question! Keep track of how you're doing with the handy scorekeeper. Practice by yourself or with a friend. Each set contains scorekeeper, map case, and five two-sided disks with 10 questions on each side, for 100 questions in all.

NEW★★
Safari, Ltd.
American History Quiz, Presidential Quiz, $9.50 each. Shipping extra.

You need to know something to play these games. *Presidential Quiz,* produced jointly with the Smithsonian Institute, is 40 cards sporting the official presidential portraits, each armed with 10 questions about the president or what was going on in his time, and all

stored tidily in a nice 5½ x 4½ x 1¼" acrylic box. *American History Quiz* is more of the same, this time covering people, events, landmarks (such as the Alamo), and generation (weep for us since we are described as the "TV generation"!) The People category includes inventors, businessmen, pioneers, and ethnic and female personalities, not just political figures.

Answers are on the back of each card, which is good, since you are not likely to know more than 20 percent of them without help.

If you are planning to use these cards in your home educational program, I suggest that you

(1) Give a pre-test using some of the questions (not all 400 at once!). Pick a reasonable subset of the cards to begin with.

(2) Instead of just supplying the answers to the missed questions, let the student discover them himself as a research project. (This works best if you own an encyclopedia or go often to the library.)

(3) Once he has done his research project, he might find all sorts of interesting new historical lines to pursue. For instance, while looking up the purchase of the Louisiana Territory, he might want to find out just why Napoleon was so eager to sell his New World real estate —and get into a study of France, or of emperors!

(4) Give a post-test to see what your student has learned. Then tack the cards up to your time line (loosely, so your student can push them up to peek at the backs), and on to the next set of cards!

NEW★★
TREND Enterprises, Inc.
Presidents of the United States Fun-To-Know Flash Cards, $4.99. Add $2 shipping. Minimum order $10. Ages 9 and up.

A colorful portrait of each president on the front, with his dates in office and the number of his presidency. Biographical details, noteworthy events of his presidency, and fun facts on the back. Forty cards in all. Inexpensive, worth it. Get an extra set for stapling on your time line.

NEW★★
Visual Education Association
 American History I, II, III, $7.95 each. World History I and
II, $7.95 each. Shipping extra.

Visual Education Association has a unique product
in their three boxes of American History flash cards.
These are in chronological question/answer form, with
the questions on one side and the answers on the other.
They make an excellent pre- and post-test for any real
history studies, as well as giving you strongly condensed
answers as a starting point for your own studies. Find
out what you don't know and *look those subjects up* in
the encyclopedia. Presto! Instant history course.
(World History I and II also available.)

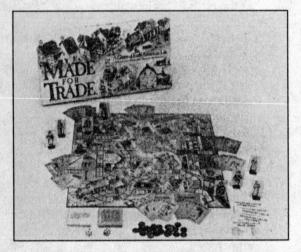

HISTORY GAMES & ACCESSORIES

Aristoplay, Ltd.
Made for Trade, $22. Add $4.75 shipping. Ages 8–adult.

Historical board game that teaches economics
lessons. In *Made for Trade*, you play the part of a character like Makepeace Middleton, a continental soldier, or
Eliza Oglethorpe, a tavern maid. After escaping indentured service, you try to earn shillings and barter for
goods in the town shops while avoiding taxes. Find out
what a free-market economy was like and how taxation
without representation messes things up. Work your
way up from indentured service to colonial prosperity.

Historical events crop up now and then, to which
you must respond. Congress, for example, might au-
thorize the establishment of a navy and you, as
shipowner Christian Fairhill, collect 4 shillings in increased profits. Some fun touches: if you visit the tavern you lose a turn for self-indulgence, and you have

to pay a church tithe every time you pass the meeting
house.

Like other Aristoplay games, *Made for Trade* is a
work of art as well as educational. You get a lot for
your money: the colorful game board (laid out like a
colonial town for atmosphere), eight character cards
with stands, eight inventory lists, 48 object cards
(things you can buy or barter), 30 Event I cards, 30
Event II cards, 60 plastic shillings, and one pair of
dice. In addition, *Made for Trade* includes a special information sheet compiled by the staff of the Winterthur
Museum. This sheet describes all 48 objects and adds
extra historical interest to the game. Two to four characters can play at any of the four play levels.

NEW★★
Bellerophon Books
Each coloring book, $2.95 or $3.95. Quantity discounts
on orders of 25 or more books.

There are coloring books . . . and there are
Bellerophon coloring books. Coloring is permutated,
transmogrified, and otherwise rendered ineffable in
this unique (I can use the word safely) series of over
100 educational coloring books.

Regular coloring books are sold in supermarkets.
Bellerophon coloring books are sold in museum shops.
The reason is that (1) Bellerophon books concentrate
on classical cultural topics such as fine art and ancient
civilizations and (2) the art itself is not designed for little
kids. These are really coloring books for preteens and
right on up to adults.

The art in Bellerophon books is mostly line-drawing
reproductions of original art from the time period covered in the coloring book. Thus, in *A Coloring Book of
Ancient China*, when you see a page-sized picture of a
bird to color in, small print at the bottom of the page
informs you that the bird actually is a line drawing of a
bronze vessel from the Late Chou dynasty. Similarly,
the two-page spread of Chinese men on horses is from
The Tribute Horse, an early Sung painting in the
Metropolitan Museum of Art.

Scattered throughout each Bellerophon book is text explaining historical details of the art and the scenes the art portrays. In a book like *A Coloring Book of Great Composers: Bach to Berlioz*, the text outweighs the pictures. Here again the coloring pictures themselves are based on famous portraits or caricatures of the composers.

A sampling of Bellerophon titles: *A Coloring Book of Rome, A Coloring Book of Great Explorers, Magnificent Helmets in Gold & Silver to Cut Out and Wear, Gorgons, California Missions, Cowgirls, Paper Soldiers of the Middle Ages, A Coloring Book of the Old Testament, Castles to Cut Out and Put Together, Peter and the Wolf,* and *A Coloring Book of Our Presidents*. As I said, this is merely a sampling. You do notice, however, that Bellerophon also sells ornate cut-out books, and that these too have some historico-cultural significance.

These books should be colored with markers or coloring pencils. You'll need watercolor markers, not the heavy-duty permanent kind—these bleed through the paper.

Art of the past often included lots of nudes, sometimes as the subject of the art, other times in the guise of mermaids and other fanciful decorations. Those who object to such decorations (frequently found in these books) can disguise them by overcoloring with the darker shades of felt-tipped markers.

Because Bellerophon art is copied from such diverse sources, flipping through one of these books can be rather unsettling. On one page you might find an ornate, grotesque woodcut, while on the next could be a simple classical line drawing.

For me, accustomed as I am to supermarket coloring books, it took a while to get used to Bellerophon's user interface. Once I did, though, I was really impressed by how much you can learn from one of these books. Remember, these are not just coloring books, but introductions to large hunks of (mostly) Western civilization. You know, as in, "Hey, hey, ho, ho, Western Cultcha's gotta go." (I have news for them. It already has.) And don't forget Bellerophon's trendier titles on non-European cultures, too, even if you're not allergic to WASPs.

NEW**
EDC Publishing
Cut-Out Models series, $8.95 each. Shipping extra. Ages 9–adult.

If you have a pair of scissors and a glue stick, you can put together wonderful accurate historic models of an Egyptian temple, Viking settlement, Roman villa, Roman fort, medieval town, cathedral, castle, and Old English village. Each Cut-Out Models book includes full-color buildings, people, and a baseboard. Bonus: the baseboards of the village, town, castle, and cathedral can be combined to make one *large* medieval setting! Models are compatible with 00/HO scale, so you can add extra figures and scenery pieces from a model shop, if desired. Great fun for those with sufficient shelf or table space to display the finished products!

NEW**
Know It All
Know It All, $29.95 plus $3 shipping. Ages 6–adult.

Know It All is a U.S. geography and history board game designed to teach players states, capitals, state slogans, general U.S. geography, and U.S. history in a fun, systematic way. See detailed writeup in Geography chapter.

NEW**
Safari, Ltd.
Presidential Lotto, $10.90. *Presidential Rummy, American History Rummy, U.S. Space Exploration Rummy*, $5.90 each.

Presidential Lotto is the official portraits of all 40 presidents captured in the format of an educational game.

What you get: Small cards, each with the presidential portrait on it and nothing else. No name to identify who the guy is, no nothing. You also get five collection boards, each with eight presidents (identified by name) and one "free" space with the picture of a historical item—e.g., Teddy Roosevelt's teddy bear. Play it two ways, as memory lotto or regular lotto. Matching the card to the picture on the board soon teaches who is who. A very nice boxed game with excellent lithography. Produced as a joint venture with the Smithsonian Institute. For ages 3 and up.

For somewhat older children, *Presidential Rummy* features the same 40 official portraits on cards and stored in a nice acrylic box. This time you also get the president's name, number, term of office, the major impact of his presidency, his lifespan, home state, political party, first lady, and vice-president. Since you're playing Rummy, you don't need to memorize facts about the presidents in order to win.

American History Rummy is similar, except that the welter of data is less than in *Presidential Rummy*. Here you have a photo of a person, statue, or other historical item, along with its name, date, and a brief paragraph summarizing its historical importance. This format, being less like a reference book, is easier to digest.

U.S. Space Exploration Rummy has the same format as *American History Rummy*. Its 40 cards cover notable events in rocketry history from ancient China to the space shuttle. Find out about the first black man and the first white woman in space (OK, so you know he's Guion Bluford and she's Sally Ride, but did you know how many million miles they each have traveled in space?), the first moon landing, and so on.

To maximize the educational value of the historical rummy games, I would consider buying two sets of each and stapling one to a time line. Then go ahead and play with the other one!

LIFE SKILLS

CHAPTER TWENTY-SEVEN

HEALTH

Why do we teach our kids algebra, chemistry, and how to play soccer, but not emergency medical skills and general family medicine? It's an interesting question. Few of us will go on to use our algebra and chemistry (although those who do definitely benefit), but every one of us will get sick, hurt himself or herself, or have family members who get sick or hurt.

In former days, Mom was the family doctor more often than not. My own mother nursed me at home through chicken pox, measles, colds, flus, semi-serious ear infections, and a continuous parade of skinned knees and bruises. The only times I ever entered a hospital before the age of 20 were to be born, to get a broken arm put in a cast, and a brief five-day stay with the mumps (the treatment at that time required penicillin injections every 15 minutes and Mom wasn't up to giving injections).

Today we are told, "Consult your physician," for everything from colds to our personal diet. This goes against my grain. My grandparents', too. Both my grandmother and grandfather on my mother's side were doctors, and thus properly cynical about the skills and knowledge of medical professionals. I remember learning at my grandmother's knee how the doctors of his time hounded Ignatz Semmelweiss into killing himself, because he had the temerity to suggest that attending birthing women with unwashed hands was the cause of the 98 percent mortality rate in maternal hospitals at that time. This, in spite of the fact that Semmelweiss's patients did *not* die of "childbirth fever" like those of all the other doctors (whose practice was to go straight from dissecting corpses at the morgue to delivering their patients).

Medical history is full of Semmelweisses, slain by the medical profession's unwillingness to give up its own cherished theories and practices. Even Jacob Lister, the father after Semmelweiss of modern hygienic medicine, had to fight his entire life for acceptance.

All this is by way of debunking the idea that only medical experts understand anything about health. Medicine has its fads, just like every other discipline. Hospital birth, for instance. While the AMA cannot produce a single study proving that hospital birth is safer than midwife-attended home birth (for the very good reason that all studies show the opposite), they cling to the doctrine that *all* births should take place in a hospital. Some distinguished AMA types go even farther; one proponent of cesarean sections actually remarked that vaginal birth was child abuse. (The Lord should have designed women's bellies with zippers, no less!)

The opposite extreme, embracing every anti-establishment medical schtick, is no better. "Gorillas eat bushels of bananas every day. Humans are descended from gorillas. So we should all eat a bushel of bananas a day." A little knowledge of biblical teaching will help steer us away from this sort of thing (actually, humans are descended from Adam and Eve), as will a smattering of family medical tradition.

If grandma found a treatment that worked for her, it probably will work for you. At least, it most likely won't hurt. Here's where you learn to cure sore throats by gargling honey or drinking hot lemon-and-honey tea, and find that pressing on a certain spot on your eyebrows will relieve headache. (Note: babies under one year old should *never* be fed honey, as in some cases germs in the honey can poison their immature digestive systems.) Grandma also knew about bandages and splints, and could clean a wound. She might have known that dry skin on the elbows means "eat more carrots" (vitamin A deficiency), and that when your skin turns yellow you've eaten *too many* carrots!

Our health training should include basic nutritional and anatomical information (it helps to know whether you're experiencing early appendicitis or a stomach ache). It also should include the signs of vitamin deficiencies and overdoses—and which foods contain which vitamins. It should include *accurate* information on birth, childhood diseases, and basic nursing care. It should include emergency medical skills, e.g., when you're cutting wood alone and the chain saw kicks back and rips your arm to the bone, step one is to stop the bleeding by holding your arm above your head and pressing *hard* on it with a clean cloth. Some information on which herbs are good for what would be very nice, too, as that was one area in which great-great-grandma excelled. Along with this should be basic information on the different types of medical care and quackery, without the usual bias in favor of allopathy ("standard" medicine, e.g., drugs and knives).

Have I found all this for you? Not this time around! Maybe in two years, when the next edition comes out . . .

HOW TO TEACH HEALTH

NEW**
Teaching Home
October/November 1988 back issue, $3.75. Complete six-issue set of 1988 back issues, $17.50, includes free set of 6 plastic magazine holders for your ring binder.

Once again, *Teaching Home* magazine is your best source for info on how and what to teach on a particular topic. This time it's the October/November 1988 best issue, and the subject is Health Education. Find out about biblical principles of health, 10 topics generally covered in health education, how to teach safety and first aid, a biblical approach to presenting human sexuality, lots more!

NUTRITION

NEW**
Center for Science in the Public Interest
Membership includes *Nutrition Action Healthletter*, $19.95/year (10 issues). Posters $4.95 each, quantity discounts available. Grades 5–adult.

Are you ready for . . . the Food Police? Yes, popular *Chronicles* columnist Jane Greer's worst nightmare has come true. It's . . . the Anti-Twinkie Squad!

The Center for Science in the Public Interest crusades relentlessly for full disclosure of ingredients on packaged and restaurant food, and more healthful ingredients therein. The main thrust is educational, in hopes an aroused electorate will arise and demand Food Reform. Towards this end, they publish a number of amusing and educational materials.

Let's look at their wall posters. These are full color on glossy paper and packed with useful and educational information.

First, the poster you've all been waiting for: CSPI's *Fast Food Eating Guide*! My, it's fun to see the competitors line up to get their GLOOM ratings. The GLOOM index "reflects a food's overall fat, sodium, sugar, and calorie content." And the losers are . . . Arby's Fish Fillet sandwich . . . Arby's cheddar fries . . . Arby's Bac'n Cheddar Deluxe . . . Arby's Steak Deluxe . . . Well, Arby's doesn't lose in *every* category, but they're sure in there pitching! Jack in the Box, Wendy's, Taco Bell, and Dairy Queen manage to pick up a few last and second-to-last places, and even meek and mild Burger King wins the booby prize for their scrambled egg platters with bacon or sausage. In fact, one of those feasts provides *all* the GLOOM points you can get away with in a day! Fat, sodium, and calories per serving are included in every listing, so you can figure out for yourself that a McDonald's Quarter Pounder with cheese is only about half the calories of a Jack-in-the-Box Ultimate Cheeseburger (the loser in that category). A great argument for staying home.

The *Nutrition Scoreboard* rates categories of foods in terms of nutritional value. Fresh spinach is the big winner in the veggie category (see, Popeye knew what he was doing!) and cucumber the relative loser, with avocado hanging in there as the only high-fat veggie. President Bush can relax: broccoli is only #7 on the list, surpassed by spinach, fresh collard greens, sweet potato, potato, fresh kale, and winter squash. Watermelon is the #1 fruit, out of a field of 21 contenders, in which grapes finished last. Raisins, not on the list, would presumably fare even worse. Take that, you California guys! No surprise to find Coca-Cola and "other sodas" in last place on the beverages list, while carrot juice barely beats out unsweetened orange juice for the top spot. This *Scoreboard* is such fascinating reading I am tempted to go on and on. Can you imagine that they found three snacks worse for you than Twinkies? I'll just hint that if you like hominy grits, American cheese, and Sugar Smacks you lose out in three categories. Also covered are condiments, breakfast cereals, dairy, grain foods, and poultry-fish-meat-eggs (a single category). Grading is done, of course, in harmony with CSPI's ideas about what's good for you and what ain't. Unreconstructed Southerners lose big everywhere except in the watermelon and collards categories.

The *Sodium Scoreboard* poster tells you, by food category and brand name, how much sodium is in each, from least to greatest. Wheat Bran has the least sodium of cold cereals listed, while Cheerios packs a walloping 330 mg/serving. That's nothing, though, compared to the 1,700 mg in one serving of Armour

Sloppy Joe Beef or the 4,778 mg in one serving of Banquet Cheese Enchilada Dinner. I hate American cheese, and Velveeta even more, so am not dismayed to find that these two are the biggest sodium carriers under Cheeses. Categories included are Beverages, Condiments, Potpourri, Crackers & Chips, Soups, Natural Foods, Fish, Frozen Foods, Processed Meats, Canned Entrées, Canned Vegetables, Packaged Dishes, Dairy Products, Breads, Cereals, Sweet Baked Goods, Sweets, and Fast Foods (in which you will be gratified to learn that McDonald's french fries come in lowest).

Like the other *Scoreboards*, *Sugar Scoreboard* tells you by category and brand name how much of the goodie is in a serving. Lots of other interesting info, including a graph showing the per-person consumption of sugar in the USA from 1840 to now and descriptions of the different types of sugars found in food.

Fiber Scoreboard shows Granny offering you a salad. ("It's good for you, Sonny! Lots of roughage!") Cereals, nuts & seeds, cakes-pastries-muffins, breads, crackers, fast foods, grains & pasta, frozen dinners and entrees, soups, veggies, fruits & juices, cookies-candies-chips, and beans-peas-tofu are all listed from greatest fiber content per serving to least. Brand name products form the bulk (pardon the pun) of these lists. Unsurprisingly, revolting Kellogg's All Bran with Extra Fiber, a cereal I can barely choke down thanks to its strong resemblance to cardboard shreds, is the high-fiber winner for cereals, while something called Kellogg's Nut & Honey Crunch has absolutely zip (none, zero) fiber per serving unless you eat part of the box. You'll also be delighted to learn that poor Arby's, the big GLOOM factor loser, comes in high in fiber for their baked potato with broccoli and cheese. Granola bars are a fiber joke compared to air-popped popcorn, the poster also reveals. As a bonus, the chart also tells you how much fat is in each serving.

CSPI's *Cholesterol Scoreboard* scores brand-name and regular foods on their cholesterol content. Some foods get negative scores, indicating that they lower blood cholesterol. However, CSPI warns, "Don't gorge yourself on them. Diets high in *any* kind of fat may promote obesity and colon and breast cancer." That's why fat content is also shown for each food. Sometimes foods that are big losers on other scoreboards (for sugar content, for example) turn up as cholesterol winners: marshmallows and jellybeans each have zero cholesterol, for instance! It turns out that Ben and Jerry, the popular ice-cream makers, are Public Enemy Number Two for their superfatted vanilla ice cream. Light 'n Lively Ice Milk has only *one-seventh* the bad cholesterol of Ben & Jerry's offering! It's even worse than gargling eggs—twice as much cholesterol in one serving as an egg, and more than four times the fat. You can also find out the dope on yogurt brands, cereals, and lots more with this handy poster.

The CSPI *Chemical Cuisine* poster has food additives listed in alphabetical order, with a description of each. Each entry is color-coded as "Avoid" (blue), "Caution" (yellow), or "Safe" (green). Lots of interesting info all in one place. Handy for use in home kitchen science research.

The *Anti-Cancer Eating Guide* breaks down current cancer research into easy-to-follow graphs. The Fiber chart, for example, shows grams of fiber for each product, from least to greatest, while telling you current recommendations for dietary fiber. The Fat chart works similarly, as do the Vitamin C and Vitamin A charts. Other categories covered on this poster include Selenium, Contaminants, Vegetables, Food Preparation, Alcohol, Food Additives, Coffee, and Facts to Ponder. The research certainty of each eating suggestion is marked in red, so you can tell whether it is very certain that an eating suggestion prevents cancer or only somewhat certain. Cancer protectors are shown in green, and cancer promoters in red. All together, an excellent job of visualizing and organizing a tremendous amount of data.

The CSPI *Exer-Guide* gives information about the health benefits of exercise, exposes various myths, and lists activities in terms of calories per hour from least (sleeping) to greatest (ice hockey and lacrosse). Juggling, our favorite family exercise, unfortunately is not on the list.

Busy little bees that they are, the people at CSPI gain about 15 percent of their income from selling books, posters, and so on. The rest comes from membership dues, contributions, and non-government and non-food industry grants. Members get the *Nutrition Action Healthletter*, a zippy, colorful 'zine with good graphics and energetic articles written in unpretentious language. At the back are a slew of cookbooks, kiddie toys, and kitchen devices for sale to the members, who presumably want to increase their personal health as much as they want to increase everyone else's.

Do you want to join? It all depends on your religious views about salt, grease, and liquor advertising (CSPI takes a dim view of all three). CSPI's newsletter is very bouncy and earnest, and as long as they don't interfere with Jane Greer's First Amendment to nosh on Twinkies, it's fun as well. Good posters, anyway!

Educational Insights
The Nutrition Box, $9.95. Shipping extra. Minimum order $25. Grades 4–8.

Perhaps the best introduction to public school nutrition ideas is Educational Insight's *Nutrition Box*. "A complete self-contained kit on nutrition," this low-priced kit consists of 50 cards, each with background info and suggested follow-up activities, neatly stored in a handsome box. Topics include vitamins, minerals, and proteins (a more sensible approach than solely concentrating on the Four Food Groups), nutrition around the world, and proper food preparation.

Herald Press
More-With-Less Cookbook, $12.95. Add $2 shipping. Grades 8–adult.

The *More-With-Less Cookbook* is the simplest, handiest introduction to the doctrine of "protein-combining," i.e., eating combinations of foods for your protein instead of munching on steak at every meal. The religious group that put this out has a notion that if Americans eat less, somehow hungry folk on the other side of the world will find more rice in their dinner bowls. You may remember this as the "How can you leave all that food on your plate when there are children starving in

India?" school of thought. Apart from the guilt, it has a lot of useful nutritional data (tables of protein amounts in various foods, etc.) and some very decent recipes.

NEW★★
Milliken Publishing Company
Nutrition transparency workbook, $12.95. Grades 4–9.

Nutrition is another of Milliken's excellent transparency/blackline workbooks. The 12 full-size, full-color transparencies illustrate the basic food groups, protein foods, the fruit and veggie group, the dairy group, the bread and cereal group, foods containing vitamins A and C, vitamin B complex ingredients and foods containing these, vitamins D-E-K, minerals, the digestive process, calorie values of common foods, and common nutrition tips. The built-in teacher's guide gives background information and answers for each of the 20 worksheets, plus optional enrichment activities. Combine this with the CSPI posters for a well-balanced nutrition unit!

ANATOMY

NEW★★
Addison-Wesley Publishing Company, Inc.
Sportworks, 96 pp., paperback, 8.95 plus $2.50 shipping.

This is another book in the series from the Ontario Science Centre. (See the review of *Foodworks* elsewhere.) *Sportworks* will help teens identify their basic body shape, learn how to react intelligently when someone mentions "lats, pecs, and delts," understand the dynamics of movement in different sports, and much more. For example, one activity illustrates the dynamics of balance and counterbalance by having you line your

body up in front of a mirror with a plumb line taped to it. You observe what happens when you lift one leg to the side while keeping your arms at our sides. Then you note the change when you raise the opposite arm. It goes on to offer more tests to help you evaluate your "static" and "dynamic" balance, then offers tips on sports that rely on balance.

More than 50 activities are scattered through the book, along with humorous illustrations and plenty of information.

Sportworks is written for junior and senior high level, but will also appeal to sports-minded children and adults. Teenagers are also more likely to learn sports-related health information from this book than from a text, so consider using it as part of health education. *Sportworks* is also a great book for sports nuts. It will help you understand body mechanics and learn how to prevent common sports injuries.—Cathy Duffy

NEW★★
Apprentice Academics
Baby model, $10.50 postpaid. Price is $5 less than regular retail.

Our kids love this! It's a realistic, flesh-colored plastic model of a 10–12-week-old unborn baby, nestled on a fluffy piece of cotton inside a clear plastic "egg." The little one is curled up, sucking his thumb. Useful for demonstrating what unborn babies really look like, and *darling* to dream over while you're expecting a baby! The model I saw was that of a white baby; you might want to inquire if black baby models are available.

NEW★★
Aristoplay, Ltd.
Some Body, $22. Add $4.75 shipping. Ages 6–10 (they say), but fun for all ages.

Some Body is the simplest, most fun, hands-on body parts instruction I have yet seen, and just as suitable for teaching teens (or adults!) about human anatomy as it is for the preteens for whom it was designed. You can play it right out of the box, after a little time spent parting the peelable vinyl body parts from their storage sheets. Basically, the idea is to place body parts in the correct places and the correct order (from back to front) on the game board.

The *Some Body* game boards, being designed for use with preteens, show a child's body outline. Unless your teen is oversensitive about using "kiddie" materials, he probably won't make an issue about this.

You get four *Some Body* game boards with outlines showing where body parts go, four sheets of labeled vinyl peel 'n stick body-part cutouts, one reference chart showing you where's what in the human body (inside the box top), 40 each illustrated Body Part identification cards and Body Part question cards, four wild cards, and the indispensable instruction sheet.

Savvy home schoolers will immediately think of all kinds of ways to teach anatomy using the peel 'n stick body parts and the game board. Or you can just play the games suggested. Draw cards to find which body part you can place on your Body Board. More difficult version: answer questions about body part functions before you get to place an item on the body board. Cards-only version: match questions and answers about body part functions. Recommended.

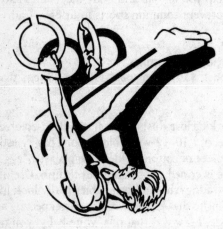

NEW**
EDC Publishing
How Your Body Works, $6.95 paperbound or $13.96 library-bound, ages 7–adult. Young Scientist series, *Human Body*, $6.95 paperbound, $13.96 library-bound, ages 12–adult. Shipping extra.

Take a trip through the Body Machine with *How Your Body Works*, an incredibly visual kids' introduction to the human body and how it works. See the white blood cell "police" chase down germs. Learn how the bones and muscles and reproductive organs function. Terrific cartoon-style illustrations make the concepts vivid. One of our kids' favorite science books.

For older children, the *Human Body* book from the Young Scientist series explains what your body is made of and how every body organ works, right down to the thyroid and pancreas, in its 32 large, dramatically illustrated pages. Explanations and illustrations are more detailed than the *How Your Body Works* book.

Senses, the brain, the skeletal system, genetics, and an explanation of sexual reproduction minus any naked bodies (but plus a brief description of popular contraceptive devices), are also covered.

Two pages on "Things that go wrong," listing common diseases and how they are handled, and an index round out the book.

Educational Insights
Human Body Kit, Pumping Heart Kit, Human Lung Kit, Human Skull, Brain Kit, Heart Kit (non-pumping), Human Ear Kit, Human Tooth Kit, Human Eye Kit, $29.95 each. Models come disassembled. *The Human Body Box*, $9.95. Shipping extra. Minimum order $25. Grades 4–8.

Others must agree that these kits are a good value, since Educational Insights now has twice as many to offer as last year. Each kit contains 25 activity cards, reproducible worksheets, games, student and teacher record sheets, and quizzes.

The Human Body kit includes not only a transparent human form with muscles molded inside, but also a small plastic skeleton with some abdominal organs exposed.

The new Human Tooth model stands on an easel and is hinged to show interior detailing. The Pumping Heart, a rather yukky concept sure to be beloved by preteen boys, is a working model of the heart and circulatory system. Squeeze the bulb and red "blood" wends its ways through veins, arteries, atria, and ventricles.

The regular Heart Model is your normal take-apart plastic model. All models look quite attractive, at least as attractive as this sort of thing can. Color is used where appropriate.

Lastly, just as Educational Insight's *Nutrition Box* is the best deal for public school nutrition, their *Human Body Box* is the most interesting, least expensive substitute for ye boring anatomy text. Fifty durable cards grouped by body parts give info and suggest practical activities.

NEW**
Educational Insights
3-D Human Body Charts, $29.95. Shipping extra. Grades 4–8.

You've seen 3-D maps; the mountain peaks literally stand out. This set of eight Human Body Charts works the same way. You can *see* the body parts in full color, and *feel* them, too, getting an idea of their volume and shape as well as of their outlines. Each chart has exploded views of important features. The Circulatory Systems chart, for example, shows the inside and outside of the heart, as well as a full-body view of the circulatory system. All parts are clearly labeled.

The set includes charts of the circulatory, digestive, muscular, nervous, respiratory, and skeletal systems, plus one each for eye-ear-skin and smell-and-taste. If you purchase it, you'll have hands-on access to more anatomical information than Leonardo da Vinci possessed in his pre-grave-robbing days.

NEW★★
Milliken Publishing Company
Systems of the Human Body transparency/blackline workbook, $12.95. Diagrammatic Prints, $9.95 per package. Grades 4–9.

Systems of the Human Body is a nice thorough overview of the human body, with 12 of Milliken's famous full-size, full-color transparencies. Covered are the following body systems: skeletal, muscular, nervous, brain, eye and ear, circulatory, respiratory, digestive, excretory, endocrine, reproductive, and skin.

The transparency of the reproductive system is tastefully done, focusing on the inner organs. Nothing here to bring the blush of shame to the cheek of modesty. I contrast this to several Christian publishers whose books (unreviewed in this volume) contain anatomy illustrations featuring gobs of pubic hair, women with huge breasts and nipples, and men similarly endowed—pictures well designed for evoking prurient desires in susceptible teenagers.

(Question: why don't anatomy texts ever show fat people or scrawny people? One otherwise well-written book featured bulging male organs on *every* picture, even one of the lymphatic system! Maybe they think they are being avant-garde or something. Maybe they want NEA funding. Jesse Helms, call your office!)

Unlike this anatomically correct but idiotic treatment, Milliken's pictures present only the body systems under discussion, using gender-neutral body outlines to avoid focusing kids' attention where it doesn't belong.

The built-in teacher's guide gives background information and answers for each worksheet, plus optional enrichment activities. Twenty worksheets cover all the topics, plus provide tests and reviews.

For low-cost anatomy studies you might also want to consider Milliken's full-color Diagrammatic Study Prints. *Systems of the Human Body* and *Organs of the Human Body* are each a set of eight poster-size prints with anatomical items clearly labeled. Each comes with four review sheets and a teacher's guide.

NEW★★
National Teaching Aids, Inc.
Human Skeleton Construction Kit, $29.95.

It's only a paper man . . . I am intrigued by the catalog pictures of what National Teaching Aids assures me is a full-size articulated human skeleton made entirely of paper.

The invention of a British professor with the twin hobbies of anatomy and origami, your skeleton comes packaged in a flat box containing 10 die-cut cardboard sheets scored and printed with the name of each bone. Fully illustrated instructions show you how to put Bonzo together—*without* glue or scissors. When completed, your paper man can be moved into every position taken by a real skeleton. Bonzo is supposed to be durable, and he's certainly less ethically upsetting than the real article and less expensive than plastic.

Sycamore Tree
Anatomy coloring book, $13.95. Dover anatomy coloring book, $2.95. Human Body felt set, $25.95. Ages 8–adult.

Sycamore Tree has a great selection of health and anatomy materials for home study. Their anatomy coloring book is meant for high school students. Descriptive text accompanies each drawing. Far cheaper and more suitable for elementary kids is the Dover anatomy coloring book (don't confuse the two!). Sycamore Tree has several other books on the body and health. Skipping over all these, let me tell you about the Betty Lukens felt Human Body Set. When I saw the picture in the brochure I knew this was the teaching tool to get! It is an incredibly beautiful set of felts, containing all the innards and muscle layers, etc. that you'd ever hope to see—even a womb with a little baby inside!

Ten talks accompany this set, plus the "I Am Joe's Body" series from *Reader's Digest*, the most popular series ever printed in their history. The Human Body Set is not overly expensive, and with care it will last almost forever. Where else can you get a life-sized *overlayable* model? Plus anatomical models of everything from teeth to pumping hearts, and even an entire transparent human body model!

SEX EDUCATION

NEW★★
Wolgemuth & Hyatt Publishers
Decent Exposure, $14.95, hardbound.

Connie Marshner's *Decent Exposure: How to Teach Your Children About Sex* is a truly insightful guide to the Youth Culture and to ways parents can rescue our kids from its clutches.

Here is a wide-lens view of sex that ranges far beyond the usual discussion of technique. Technique, in fact, is not discussed at all. She doesn't offer simplistic quick-fix answers, but goes to the root of the problem: our attitudes towards self-control, responsibility, emotions, and child-training, to name just a few. As she says, "The goal is to make your children actively desire to practice virtue."

Some other topics include the wrong way to teach sex ed, why and how parents should take control, God as the creator of life and sex, modesty, peers, and strong advice about dating. You'll also find a question-and-answer section where Mrs. Marshner talks to parents where they are, including we've-already-blown-it scenarios. Tons of valuable information and ideas. The only point I really objected to was Mrs. Marshner's unbiblical condemnation of *all* teen marriage.

FIRST AID & MEDICINE

NEW★★
EDC Publishing
Young Scientist series, *Medicine*, $6.95 paperbound, $13.96 library-bound. Shipping extra. Ages 12–adult.

For a book subtitled "Doctors and Health: How illness can be prevented and cured," *The Young Scientist book of Medicine* is remarkably fair and up-to-date in its treatment of alternative medical techniques. Topics covered: What is medicine? About illness. Things that go wrong with the body. Infections. How your body fights illness. Preventative medicine (a pitch for immunization, public health services, and frequent checkups). Going to see the doctor (includes a flow chart showing how the doctor makes a diagnosis). Treating illnesses and injuries (an excellent description of how drugs, surgery, special diets, and therapy work, including mention of drug side-effects). Alternative medicine (an objective treatment). Operations. How a hospital works (a fantastic capsule description taking just two pages). Technology and medicine. Health and the environment. First aid (splinters, cuts, bandaging, burns, bruises, fainting, artificial respiration, and what to do at an accident scene). Atlas of the body (naked man and woman with arrows pointing out little-known body features like "breasts," plus skeleton and organ models). Amply illustrated, good descriptive text.

NEW★★
Forum for Biblical Ethics in Medicine, Inc.
Journal of Biblical Ethics in Medicine, $18/year (4 issues), U.S. and Canada. All others, $24/year (U.S. funds only). Ages college and adult.

The Journal of Biblical Ethics in Medicine is something we have needed for a long, long time. Here, for the first time in recent history, we find a group of Christian doctors grappling with the real issues of medicine.

What is a Christian doctor? Should doctors share their faith with their patients, and if so, under what circumstances? What's wrong with modern medical training, and how can it be improved? How can Christians recognize that a time does come when God calls us home, without hurrying it along as the euthanasia movement wants to or merely prolonging the dying process as the technophiles wish? How has third-party insurance affected medical care, and how do many doctors abuse it? What about Christian insurance plans, where each member of the group prays for those that are sick and sends a specified amount directly to them? Should medical care be accessible to all, or should it be a free-market institution where the customer gets what he pays for? Why aren't animal rights right? Donor-killing transplants, the coopting of doctors by the social service community, and many other issues that never see the light of day in the big media, are all handled here with grace and insight. No techno-babble, either—these doctors can write!

Merck & Company, Inc.
Merck Manual, $21.50 postpaid. College and adult.

Increase your word power and get a handle on medical procedures with the *Merck Manual of Diagnosis and Therapy*. This is the very same book your doctor uses to help him diagnose and prescribe. The *Merck Manual* is fascinating browsing for those with a large medical vocabulary; extremely helpful in medical emergencies (it's comforting to be able to check out the diagnosis for yourself); and the definitive test of whether Junior really wants to go to med school (can he hardly tear himself away from the *Manual* or does he nod out after reading a paragraph?).

The *Merck Manual* won't tell you about unconventional treatments. Nor will you be able, in many cases, to act on its recommendations without a doctor's prescription. But it will educate and inform you about what is going on in the orthodox medical world for every disease known to man.

NEW★★
SelfCare Catalog

New Agers are strung out on health, but that's no reason why they're the only ones who should get their hands on medical gear! The publishers of *Medical Self Care* magazine, a haven of New Age medical thinking, have assembled a catalog of medical tools 'n stuff for folks who want to keep things medical at home. Up-

scale exercise equipment, simple medical tools, and herbal medicines and how-to training are mixed with greenie editorials and New Age "stress relaxation" tapes. The catalog also contains useful and hard-to-find medical self-tests (e.g., chemical pads to drop in the toilet to test for hidden blood in stools, instant urinanalysis screens, diabetes risk detectors) and food preparation items. Stock changes constantly, so you have to get the most recent catalog to check out the selection and prices.

CHILDBIRTH

UPDATED★★
Apprentice Academics
Midwifery Study Course, $750. New midwifery book, $25. Discounts for NAPSAC members, other discounts. Study guide must be returned at end of course. Course usually takes three years to complete. *Helping Hands*, $24.95 plus $3 shipping.

A systematic study of midwifery, the Apprentice Academics Midwifery Study Course is designed as an integrated curriculum. As the brochure states, "Although the curriculum is not organized by subject, virtually every related subject is very thoroughly covered." Each section covers every aspect of midwifery, so that throughout the course one subject may be covered in a dozen different ways: diagrams, quizzes, research, reading assignments, and so on.

Three-year enrollment includes not only the basic six sections outlined in the study guide (terminology, reading record, optional study, required technical study, research topics, and general study), but 10 issues per year of the *In Touch* newsletter, a resource guide, individualized course assistance and evaluation, and the certification exam leading to a Certificate of Successful Completion or one of two awards. You will have to purchase books and work hard to finish the course. An incentive program helps with this. You can win an award for outstanding work or win in a drawing for midwifery books and supplies only open to those who submit work during a given quarter, among other things.

Suggested for midwives who want to enhance their education, apprentices, childbirth educators, nurses, CNMs, and future midwives who want to "mommy" their young children now and receive their practical training later, the Apprentice Academics course has garnered testimonials from Dr. Robert Mendelsohn, NAPSAC president David Stewart, and others renowned in the home health movement.

Perhaps most importantly, AA's students have written numerous unsolicited testimonials to the course's thoroughness and enjoyableness.

New from Apprentice Academics: a large spiral-bound workbook covering the basics of midwifery, entitled *Helping Hands: The Apprentice Workbook*. This is just an excellent book for anyone considering direct-entry midwifery (e.g., you apprentice to a working midwife while studying on your own rather than attending a nursing college). Along with numerous worksheets and charts are comments from over 150 midwives about all aspects of midwifery, from what it does to your family life, to public relations and politics. Find out what practicing midwives are looking for in an assistant in the "Expectations" section! The "Education" section is loaded with helps for the serious would-be midwifery student, and the rest of the book should discourage anyone who is *not* serious about making the necessary commitment—which is good! Lots of tests to take to see how far along you already are educationally in this area. As author Carla Hartley says, *Helping Hands* is not a midwifery course, but an introduction to midwifery, at which it admirably succeeds.

NEW★★
Fellowship of Christian Midwives and Childbirth Educators, International
The Caul, $15/year. FCM membership, $18/year (includes *Caul* subscription). FCM/NAPSAC membership, $25/year (includes *Caul* subscription). Outside U.S. add $3. Adults.

Theology and techniques for a Christian approach to childbirth. *The Caul* is the newsletter, with legal news, personal stories of birth deliveries, reviews of birthing books/songs/videos/programs, and inspirational editorials. FCM sponsors conferences and midwifery-training seminars. Joel and Renée Stein are the director and president. Dave and Kathy Arns of Spirit-Led Childbirth are editors and do the magazine layout.

NEW★★
Friends of Homebirth
$18/year (6 issues). Free sample issue.

Excellent, good-looking newsletter with news about home birth legalities from state to state, home birth stories, inspirational thoughts, and lots more. *Friends of Homebirth* reminds me a little bit of the early home-schooling newsletters in its earnestness.

Christians and New Agers are both represented among the advertisers.

NAPSAC
Membership includes *NAPSAC NEWS* and special discounts on books and NAPSAC activities: Individual, $20 USA, $22 other countries; Professional, $50 USA, $52 other countries. U.S. funds only. 1986 Summit video "Highlights," $39.95 plus $1.50 shipping—VHS only.

The organization for those interested in childbirth options. NAPSAC, otherwise known as the InterNational Association of Parents and Professionals for Safe Alternatives in Childbirth, a very professional group with many highly-accredited leaders and advisers, is "an umbrella organization supporting and promoting all enlightened childbirth associations," with chapters of its own all over North America and around the world.

NAPSAC issues an excellent quarterly newsletter, *NAPSAC NEWS,* runs a mail-order bookstore with a wide selection of the best books available on childbirth and mothering (including some NAPSAC productions), and sponsors occasional conferences.

The 1986 Summit Conference was an outstanding affair featuring such notables as Dr. Herbert Ratner of *Child and Family Newsletter*, well-known sociologist Dr. Ashley Montagu, LaLeche League founding mothers Marian Tompson and Mary White, French obstetrician Dr. Michel Odent, Dr. Tom Brewer (author of *What Every Pregnant Woman Should Know*), and Dr. Robert Mendelsohn, among others. At this conference, NAPSAC took a prolife stand on abortion, generating heated controversy among some but greatly relieving the minds of others.

NAPSAC's position is that, in order to consistently uphold the goal of nurturing babies and providing the best for them—the original impetus for much of the alternative childbirth movement—the baby must be treated as a person regardless of his or her physical comeliness or "wantedness." NAPSAC's *Position on Abortion and Clarification of Related Questions* (13 pages) is available for $2 postpaid.

Video tapes of the keynote conference speeches, plus a tape of conference highlights, may be purchased from NAPSAC. Audio tapes were also made of all the sessions and workshops and can be ordered from NAPSAC.

Tapes were also made of the 1990 conference, which we attended in person as a family. It was a fun and educational event!

NEW★★
Spirit-Led Childbirth

Run by Christians, Spirit-Led Childbirth is a source for home birthing and midwifery supplies.

The selection is really nice, especially their package deals. You haven't lived until you've had one of their herbal sitz baths after giving birth! I noticed that not only did I heal "down below" much faster, but that the baby (who immediately after birth enjoyed the sitz bath with me) did not suffer from the usual post-birth diaper rash.

It would be a good idea to have one of their home birth kits on hand even if you plan to go to the hospital, just in case things go quicker than expected and you end up with a surprise home birth! Afterwards, the Nursing Tea, Herbal Sitz Bath, inflatable donut for tender fannies, "I'm a Miracle" baby T-shirt, and other goodies can be used when you come home.

NEW★★
Yalad Birthing Supply

Another fine source for home birthing and midwifery supplies, also run by Christians. Yalad Birthing Supply has a similar selection to that of Spirit-Led Childbirth.

CHAPTER TWENTY-EIGHT

HOME ECONOMICS

Cooking. Cleaning. Household crafts. Raising the kids. Everyone needs to know this stuff, preferably before they find themselves, married or not, in an apartment 1000 miles away from Mom and Dad.

Some people are awesomely good at keeping a home neat, orderly, and beautiful. Others are awesomely bad. I fall in the middle. I *used* to fall right off the bottom of the curve, but I'm learning!

BASIC THEORY AND HOW-TOS

NEW**
Home Life
HELP, $15/four issues. Back issues, $4 each except double issue 9/10, $6. Overseas add 25% for ground mail, 60% for air mail.

This is my magazine, which (be grateful) is *not* mostly written by me. *HELP* is a forum where over 5,000 families share their ideas and experiences in every area of Christian family living. It's all organized by topics, with jokes and quickie reviews sprinkled here and there to liven things up. Money-saving tips, inspirational pieces, lots of reader networking.

Almost every issue also includes an article or two on family life in another country. Newer issues will al-

so include reviews of new home-school products, written by yours truly. *HELP* is nicely laid out and professionally printed on quality paper.

Some hot topics lately have included: zippy answers to dumb things people say when you have a big family, alternatives to dating, child training tips, family devotions, good sources for cloth diapers, sterilization reversals, home schooling tips, money-saving ideas, and ideas for family holidays and celebrations. Upcoming issue themes (as of early 1991): courtship alternatives to dating, family health, home business. It's Home Ec for grownups.

CHILD TRAINING, MOTHERING, & FATHERING

I don't believe in "parenting" or "child care." "Parenting" was invented to evade the nurturing connotations of the word "mothering," and to propagate the myth that men and women relate in exactly the same way to their children. "Child care" at best makes it sound like the kid is a package you are trying to keep undamaged. ("This End Up. Handle With Care.") It further implies that taking care of children is a science that you can learn through accredited courses, which it isn't. Furthermore, the title "child care provider" has all the warmth of winter in Siberia. Between them, these two neologisms reduce children's needs to those of a dog in a kennel: correct intakes of food, water, sleep, and exercise . . . plus perhaps an occasional pat on the head, so the dog won't get too discontented.

"Mothering," on the other hand, instantly conjures up warmth. Love. Snuggles on the couch. Gentle hands helping you into your pajamas with the footies. Bedtime stories and kisses. A cool hand on your forehead when you have a fever, and concerned visits in the night to make sure you're still tucked in. Warm cookies and cold milk when you're hungry from playing or studying. Someone who kisses a bruise to make it feel better and who grieves with you when your best friend moves away.

It really is too bad that "fathering" only means "to sire a child," because here's what it *ought* to mean. Strong arms tossing you in the air while you giggle. Horsie rides on Daddy's back. A warm lap and a scratchy cheek to rest your head near while a deep voice reads you a book. Goodies hidden in his pockets when he comes home from a trip. Playing checkers together (and him letting you win now and then). Big hands helping you hold the nail steady while you learn to drive it with a hammer. A car ride home whenever you need it. A wall of protection against anyone who tries to mistreat you.

Mothering and fathering are the "up" side of childhood. Child training seems, to all kids everywhere, like the downside. Nobody likes to be told he can't do this or that . . . and then to have the rules *enforced*. In fact, there's only one thing kids hate more: to have the rules *not* enforced. (Having no rules is not a realistic alternative, however much those hopeful souls who believe in letting kids bloom naturally wish it were. Sooner or later you have to tell Johnny not to run into the road.)

Our generation has been amazingly willing to pay the salaries and royalties of a swarm of "experts" who have taught us everything except how to mother, father, and train our kids. You can learn all you want to about theories of child development, techniques of diaper changing, home birth versus hospital birth, breastfeeding versus bottle feeding, the merits and demerits of pacifiers, how to pick a day care center, ways to amuse toddlers on long trips, and on and on—but almost no one anywhere simply affirms kids' need to be *loved* and *guided*, let alone how to do both at once.

We aren't supposed to need to know any of this, because the preferred way in our culture of handling any childhood needs and problems is to look up the appropriate expert in the Yellow Pages. The parent's job is simply to pick the right experts and write the checks (that's "parenting" in a nutshell for you).

I now have seven kids (going on eight). Here's what I've learned: it's impossible to have a large family without getting serious about learning how to do this child-rearing thing right. Even a yuppie who sends her kids to day care, afterschool programs, and summer camp is hard put to handle more than one full-fledged untrained little monkey. (They'll come up to you on the street and admit it: "I could never handle more than one!") Besides, as my grandmother once told me, "I love my children, so I want everyone else to love them too—and they won't unless the children have learned to be good!"

All I can say is that the following resources have helped us a *lot* in learning to really love and train our children—more than thousands of lookalike magazine articles or child-care textbooks.

NEW**
Bluestocking Press
The Impossible Child, $10.95 plus $2 shipping. Age: adult reader. Applies to: children of all ages.

> There is a subset of children who appear to learn well and easily on one day, but not on another. They seem unable to function consistently well in school. They often act appropriately but suddenly, for no apparent reason, their behavior can exasperate the most patient teacher or parent. Other children appear unable to learn or behave most of the time. Some are too active; others are too tired. . . . Many have recurrent headaches, leg aches, or digestive complaints.

Any of this sound familiar? Then *The Impossible Child* might hold some answers for you. The purpose of this book is to show you how to detect if your youngster is experiencing an unsuspected allergic reaction and what to do if he or she is.

The book does not lay the blame for all bad behavior at the feet of allergies. It does, however, point out that some kids get high on some foods, or bummed out by molds and pollens, and that we all have a much harder time functioning properly under such circumstances.

This is not a superficial book, in spite of its easy-reading style. You are given specific facial or body clues to tip you off to a possible allergic reaction—e.g., red earlobes. The book also includes numerous before-and-after examples of children's work and considerable detail about specific allergies and how to spot and treat them.

Is behavior modification therapy the solution to behavior problems *not* caused by allergies? Author Doris Rapp says yes. I say no. This fairly major disagreement aside, I think this is a good book. We do owe it to our kids to find out if they suffer when exposed to chemicals, pollen, pets, or dairy products. However, no way can the vast increase in kids' rotten behavior today be blamed on allergies. Allergies may indeed provide extra pressure, but even a splitting migraine does not have the power to force any of us to bite, spit, and swear unless we let it.

All this granted, before you give up on a child who is not responding normally to child training it's worthwhile to check out whether he is suffering extra pressure from undetected allergies—and this book can help with that.

NEW✶✶
Christian Liberty Press
Training Children in Godliness, $3.95 plus $1.50 shipping.

Jacob Abbott's *Training Children in Godliness*, revised and edited by Michael J. McHugh, is a delightful 100-year-old book. Its writer was famous in his day as the author of over 200 books, including best-selling children's literature. The book is mostly made up of selections from Abbott's various writings on child training, updated and revised for modern grammatical accuracy. He tells you how to use a child's natural desire for learning and instruction as a means of instructing him in godliness. He tells you *how* to instruct children in a way that keeps them glued to their seats. Abbott, too, stresses "affection and sympathy" as the gentle chains

by which parents bind their children to love and obedience. Abbott reminds us that this is *not* the same thing as indulgence, which "never awakens gratitude or love in the heart of a child."

Now here is his advice on the vexed subject of socialization—advice I guarantee you have never seen in a modern "parenting" manual:

> Keep children as much as possible by themselves, away from evil influences . . . We may go much farther, and almost say, keep them from company, good or bad. Of course this is to be understood with proper limits and restrictions; for to a certain extent, associating with others is of high advantage to them, both intellectually and morally. But this extent is almost universally far exceeded, and it will be generally found that the most virtuous and the most intellectual, are those who have been brought up with few companions. . . .

> In fact, all history and experience shows, and it is rather a dark sign in respect to sinful human nature, that the mutual influence of man upon man, is an influence of deterioration and corruption. . . . Thus densely populated cities, are always most immoral: an army, a ship, a factory, a crowded prison, and great gangs of laborers working in common, always exhibit peculiar tendencies to vice. So with the young. Boys learn more evil than good of their playmates at school . . .

> It is often said that the young must be exposed to the temptations and bad influences of the world, in order to know what they are, by experience, and learn how to resist them. "They must be exposed to them," say these advocates of early temptation, "at some time or other, and they may as well begin in season, so as to get the mastery over them the sooner." But this is not so. The exposure, if avoided in youth, is avoided principally for ever. A virtuous man in any honest pursuit of life comes very little into contact or connection with vice. He sees and hears more or less of it, it is true, every day, but his virtuous habits and associates and principles are such, that it is kept, as it were, at a sort of moral distance. . . . A vast proportion of the vicious and immoral are made so before they reach adulthood, and accordingly, he who goes on safely through the years of his youth, will generally go safely for the rest of the way.

To put this in modern terms, when's the last time anyone tried to sell *you* drugs . . . or double-dared you to commit an act of vandalism? We adults can control our friends and environment, keeping such influences away. But our kids depend on *us* to protect them. The book is loaded with similar forgotten insights into the basics of child training. It also contains a fictional case history, "How to Disciple a Young Person, or The Story of Alonzo," which I found less valuable. Alonzo's experiences and environment have almost no connection to the lives of children today, whereas the principles in this little book will last forever.

NEW✱✱
Christian Life Workshops
21 House Rules Preschooler's Training Kit, Rules for Friends, $10.95 each. *Uncommon Courtesy for Kids*, $12.95. All three kits, including coloring books, posters, and instructions, $29.95. *Child Training God's Way* video rental $25 plus $25 refundable deposit, video purchase $49, cassette tapes $11.95. Add 10% shipping ($2.75 minimum, $7.75 maximum). Ages preschool–early teens.

Want to learn how to teach your kids basic rules of Christian behavior without a lot of fuss? Gregg Harris's *21 House Rules Preschooler's Training Kit* is for you! Yes, I know it's intended to be used with preschoolers, but it's never to late to implement a *simple, sensible* list of house rules for both kids and adults—which this is! It's also never too early to give teens a simple tool for running their future homes—which this also is!

This wonderful kit provides a framework of totally reasonable rules for behavior that children themselves will agree with! Rules like, "We obey our Lord Jesus Christ. . . . We do not hurt one another with unkind words or deeds. . . . When someone is sorry, we forgive him. . . . When we have work to do, we do it without complaining. . . . When we take something out, we put it away." Following these simple rules will eliminate 80 percent of the parent-child strife around your house. Of course, *you will have to obey the rules too!*

The kit comes with a reproducible training manual/ coloring book that illustrates all 21 rules (some great drawings by Gregg's son Joshua), a laminated (jelly-proof) 21 House Rules master sheet to post on your frig or bulletin board, 21 individual rule posters, and

complete instructions. Over 7,000 satisfied families have used it. Very highly recommended.

Rules for Friends is just exactly what every family needs to keep "socialization" from becoming a social disease! Following the same format as CLW's *21 House Rules Preschool Training Kit*, *Rules for Friends* trains your children how to treat their friends and lets the children's friends know what is expected of them when they visit your home. This one is designed for older children.

Just out is the brand-new *Uncommon Courtesy for Kids*, co-authored by Gregg and Joshua. This "training manual for everyone" introduces the concept of courtesy to both kid and adult readers, then gives Six Manners of Speech, Four Words to the Wise, Five Rules for Public Transportation, Six Ways to Be Considerate to Adults, Six Table Manners, Phone Manners, How to Take a Phone Message, Seven Rules for Going to Church, Eight Rules for Traveling in the Car, Four Awkward Things That Happen to Everybody, and more! Each set of rules is illustrated with examples of people of all ages following (or not following!) the rules. Parents are also told how to train kids gently in these rules. Knowing what a wicked world this is, Gregg also includes instructions in when *not* to obey or follow adults.

You'll get a lot more out of *Uncommon Courtesy* if you get the complete kit, which includes not only the basic coloring book manual but a laminated placemat-sized poster listing all the rules and individual "rules" posters, plus instructions in how to use these materials to help your kids actually learn to be courteous. *Very* highly recommended!

Finally, Gregg's *Child Training God's Way* workshop is available both in video and audiocassette formats. In 90 minutes you'll learn how to *train* your child to be "faithful in small things" rather than just reacting to his bad behavior. Extremely highly recommended.

NEW✱✱
Doorposts
"If-Then" chart, $4. Blessing chart and booklet, $4.50. Patterns for "Blessing Chart" rewards, $4. "Service Opportunities" chart, $4. "Armor of God" pattern, $4. Proverbs calendar, $6.50. Add $2 shipping. Ages 2–14.

As you know, child training takes a carrot and a stick. This course provides guidance for both, for children from preschool to early teens.

The "If-Then" chart is the stick. This large (16 x 22") wall chart lists common kid misbehaviors on the left, along with a cute cartoon of each problem area. Next to each misbehavior is a Scripture verse commenting on that misbehavior. For example, next to "Arguing, Complaining, Whining" is the verse, "Do all things without murmurings and disputings" (Phil 2:14). A blank column on the right is where you will fill in the agreed-on consequences of each misbehavior.

The "If-Then" chart comes with a list of suggested consequences for each sin. These include additional work, loss of a privilege, fines, double restitution, asking forgiveness, and a specified number of swats with a spanking spoon. The authors make it clear that these are only their suggestions; each family is free to choose its own disciplinary measures. You can cut out the pre-lettered and illustrated "consequences" and glue them onto your chart, or write in your own.

The "Blessing" chart is the carrot. It's the same size and format as the "If-Then" chart, except that *good* character qualities are listed and illustrated down the left-hand side. The Blessing chart comes with a little booklet, *How to Use the Blessing Chart,* that has some really clever ideas for scriptural methods of rewarding your children. For example, one of the two verses for the character trait of "Truthfulness" is, "Righteous lips are the delight of kings, and they love him who speaks what is right" (Prov 16:13). So here are some of the ideas they associate with that verse: Prince-for-a-Day (with crown, robe, and servants); go to work with Daddy; a family parade in honor of the truthful child; special clothing; special privilege; and a blank space for you to write in your own ideas. Patterns for some of the recurring reward ideas are also available. These include a flag to fly from your front porch with the child's name on it, felt banner and patches, certificates, medals of honor, and a cloth crown.

Also from the same prolific family is the Proverbs calendar. The 1992 calendar will be available September 1991. This has a cartoon illustrating one proverb for each month of the year. You have to figure out what the proverb is for yourself. This is pretty obvious to anyone who knows the Bible. The pig with the ring in his snout reclining on the couch next to the shady lady was a dead giveaway, for example. If you don't know the book of Proverbs very well, though, these illustrations will inspire some digging! Fun for the whole family.

More products from Doorposts: a "Service Opportunities" chart for organizing chore assignments and a set of "Armor of God" patterns, with instructions, so you can make a set of armor for your children like that mentioned in Ephesians 6:10–17.

These materials all look really friendly and professional. Excellent lettering, illustrations in the style of Joshua Harris. Your teens can work through these materials to set up their own expectations and rules for their future families.

NEW**
Home Life
Hints on Child Training, $8.95 plus $1 shipping.

Hints on Child Training was written 100 years ago by Elisabeth Elliot's grandfather, H. Clay Trumbull. I figure this man, a leader in the *original* Sunday School movement and a father of eight, knows something about child training, judging by how his descendants have turned out. Each short chapter contains a wealth of practical, scriptural insights. Why the Bible says we must train our children's wills, not break them. Why scolding is always wrong—and what to do instead. How to train your child to be courteous, to deny himself, and not to pester. How to choose proper amusements and companions. How to nourish your child's faith. How to get *willing* obedience and respect from your children. Just one gem from this great book:

> How many parents there are who are readier to provide playthings for their children than to share the delights of their children with those playthings . . . readier to make good, as far as they can, all losses to their children, than to grieve with their children over those losses. And what a loss of power to those parents, is this lack of sympathy with their children. Parents who sympathize with their children in all things practically train and sway their children as they will: for when there is entire sympathy between two persons, the stronger one is necessarily the controlling force.

Hints on Child Training is published by Wolgemuth & Hyatt Publishers and available in Christian bookstores, as well as from Home Life.

NEW**
Lynn's Bookshelf
Proverbs for Parenting, $15.50 postpaid, hardbound. All ages.

The Christian answer to Dr. Spock. *Proverbs for Parenting* is a handsome hardbound book with all the Bible proverbs in the King James Version or the New International Version pertaining to child raising arranged by topics, such as Fools and Folly, For Boys, For Girls, Marriage and Sex, Anger, Drinking, Boasting, Honesty, and so on—75 topics in all. The categories are Reverence for God, Wisdom and Instruction, Self-Control, Control of Mouth, Relationships, Wrongdoings, Godly Characteristics, and Prosperity.

NEW**
New Moon Records
Each tape, $11.50 postpaid.

More about the incredible singing Lester family: Darlene sent me their latest tape as I was winding up this article, titled *Only My Mama: Songs for Families with Nursing Babies*. If you are the warm, loving type of family (and what home schooling family isn't?) you are going to love this tape. Songs like "Big Wet Baby Kiss," "Don't Hit the Baby/Even Though He Hit You First," and "I Want to Be Close" (the last about how a baby loves to squeeze in between Mommy and Daddy when they're sitting close together) are bound to strike a warm chord in your heart. Let me just give you just one teeny sample:

> Where's the baby?
> Where's the baby, dear?
> I'm awfully suspicious
> Cause it's much too quiet in here . . .

If you like that tape you'll love *One More Person to Love: More Songs for Families with Nursing Babies*. Then perhaps you'd like to branch out and learn family singing with *Traditional Rounds, Canons, and Harmonies* (which teaches your family how to sing traditional rounds) and *Homestyle Harmony* (which teaches you all to sing together in beautiful four-part harmony!).

Keep in mind as you read this that I absolutely *hate* about 95 percent of the song tapes people send me to review. I can't stand anything smarmy, syrupy, adenoidal, show-offy (no cheap Sandi Patti imitations, please!), patronizing, raucous, commercial, or phoney. This eliminates the 95 percent. If I say I like these tapes, you can be *sure* they are fresh, original, down-to-earth, and sound good.

The Lesters and their four sons are all musically talented, without being obnoxious about it, and their hearts are obviously in the right place. Bouncy tunes, no harsh rock, something for the homebody and baby-lover in all of us.

NEW**
Reformed Free Publishing Association
Peaceable Fruit, $9.95. Shipping extra.

Gertrude Hoeksema, who some of you may remember as the author of a Bible-teaching series for younger children reviewed in Volume 2, has also written quite an interesting book for Christian parents, entitled *Peaceable Fruit*. Based on her background as a Dutch Calvinist, this book contains continual references to "covenant children" and the private-school life. You get used to these after a while, and are then able to settle down to ponder her mostly commonsense biblical advice about how to deal with specific challenges in child-rearing, as personified by a character called "Timmy."

Again, the introductory material is take-your-breath-away intellectual. In brief, it is making the point that children are spiritual beings, not mere mechanical machines to program. You know this! Skip it and get to the part about Timmy. I felt at turns challenged, reassured, and ashamed as Mrs. Hoeksema explained how to handle tantrums, toilet training, passive disobedience, and so on right up through the late teens. A really different point of view than you get from the current crop of books down at the bookstore.

HOUSE SAFETY

NEW**
Perfectly Safe
Catalog, $1.

"The Catalog for Parents Who Care," with 32 pages of products for child safety. Electrical outlet protection. Appliance latches. Stove protection. Bathroom protection. Portable monitors for baby's room. First aid kits. Pool safety (alarms, life vests). Bike safety (helmets, pads). Safety skates and trikes. Car booster seats, baby shades. Escape ladders, fire alarms. Choke tube (to check size of child's toys). Books on kid-proofing your house and house-proofing your kids! Simple one-stop shopping.

KEEPING IT CLEAN

UPDATED**
Don Aslett's Cleaning Center
Who Says It's a Woman's Job to Clean?, $5 for a personally autographed copy. *Is There Life After Housework* video, $19.95 plus $2 shipping. Don Aslett's *Clean Report* newsletter plus catalog, free.

Don Aslett is the author of a best-selling series of books on, of all subjects, housecleaning. These books can trim large chunks off your cleaning time—a worthwhile investment for anybody!

Of these, the most suitable for teens and newlyweds is *Who Says It's a Woman's Job to Clean:* not because of the title but because this book, designed to ease recalcitrant hubbies into the cleaning force, is so simple and

so well illustrated with numerous clever cartoons that even a child can understand it. Believe it or not, we frequently find our eight-year-old son Joseph reading it!

You also really ought to get Don Aslett's wonderful *Is There Life After Housework* video, in which he combines comic patter with classy cleaning skills. Our kids love the toilet humor (really, it's *clean* toilet humor), and they've learned to clean windows and bathrooms, vacuum, and wash walls just like Don!

In his books, Don recommends all kinds of work-saving, inexpensive professional tools and equipment. Until recently, these were only available at janitorial supply stores. A few years ago, Bill and I made the trek to one of these stores, endured the hours waiting in line for bored clerks, put up with the inefficient, unhelpful "service," and patiently waited for weeks for some of our ordered materials to arrive. We figured it was worth it—that time—because the products we bought would save us so much time. We also figured we never wanted to go through that again.

Responding to the glaring need for a nicer source for professional cleaning equipment, Don founded Don Aslett's Cleaning Center. This efficient mail-order firm carries the entire line of equipment recommended in Don's books—everything except a bonnet machine for refreshing your carpets. (Anyone know where we can get a bonnet machine?)

We have placed several orders with Don Aslett's Cleaning Center, and are extremely pleased with their service and products. Bathroom cleaning now takes three minutes a day, window-washing is a breeze, and we're seriously considering sealing our concrete basement and garage floors. Our cleaning supplies now fit in one small cabinet, and spray bottles of four basic cleaners (mixed up from concentrate) are all we need to do the entire house.

NEW**
Whirlpool Appliance Information Service
Laundry Tips for Beginners, single copy free. Quantity orders, 15¢/copy. Anyone old enough to get the laundry into and out of the machines.

Laundry Tips for Beginners is an oversized fold-out brochure, completely illustrated, that shows kids exactly how to do the family laundry! Beginning launderers of all ages—including college students and newlyweds—are warned against possible mishaps (e.g., don't put plastics in to dry on a heat setting or they might melt or burn), and the reasons for sorting laundry, cleaning lint traps, and so on are all explained. No ads for Whirlpool washers or dryers, just excellent step-by-step laundering instructions. Need I say more?

COOKING

NEW★★
Eating Better Cookbooks

Main Dishes, $13. *Lunches & Snacks*, $9. *Desserts, Soups & Muffins*, $6 each. *Breakfasts, Casseroles*, $5 each. Complete set, $40. 90-minute VHS video, $20. Video cooking workbook, $4. *Eating Right! A Realistic Approach*, $9. *24-Month Menu Planners, Recipe Organizer, Holiday Menus*, $5 each. 10-day free video rental with cookbook set purchase and refundable deposit check for $20. Add 10% shipping ($2 minimum).

Gotta chew those carob chips . . . Here comes a lady who is going to try to tell you that eating *healthy food* will not only make you feel better but not destroy your pampered taste buds.

Come on, already. I've heard this before. "No," insists Sue Gregg, author of the entire Eating Better with Sue curriculum. "I'm going to show you how to *gradually* switch over to healthier foods."

So, I bite. I read the book. It's called *Eating Right! A Realistic Approach*. What makes it "realistic" is that the author realizes not all husbands and kids (not to mention their choc-chip-chompin' wives) are born in love with the idea of a high-fiber, low-fat diet. This is what she wants us to convert to. But *gradually*, improving the nutritional value of familiar American dishes by

substituting ingredients of higher quality. So you start out by mixing whole-wheat flour with the white flour. Come some happy day, you suddenly realize that you're eating 100 percent whole-wheat bread and liking it!

I'll buy this when it comes to whole-wheat bread. Love the stuff. But carob chips? Bran muffins? Apparently the Pride family is just too far gone. Happily, 98 percent of Sue's recipes don't contain any bran or carob.

So what do we have here? A very impressive series of cookbooks, all written by a lady with a very impressive background in food preparation. Each recipe includes an impressive amount of nutritional information. Not just how many calories the creation has, but the amount of protein, fiber, fat, and suchlike you can expect to get out of it. Sue also includes 200 sample menus (nice to know you can use this dish somewhere), and sample pricing for the dish and menu.

While Sue provides vegetarian meal plans, these cookbooks are not vegetarian.

Emilie (*More Hours in My Day*) Barnes introduces each segment of Sue's *Eating Better* video. This 90-minute tape consists of segments originally prepared for TV, complete with the very same opening sequence and closing ad for Sue's book repeated again and again. In the manner of popular TV chefs, Sue whips up healthy dishes in a sparkling kitchen and serves them to appreciative family members and friends.

A number of women have successfully sponsored video-viewing groups using this video and its accompanying workbook with its step-by-step lesson plans. Kids can join these groups, too, earning a Mother's Helper certificate. You don't have to collect a group to get the video, of course. In fact, if your cooking comes out like mine did, you'd be wise to keep the results to yourself until you improve!

Lunches and Snacks, one of Sue's recipe books, has been totally revised and now includes a children's cookbook section. This might be a good place to start for those of us who aren't overly confident—including teens and newlyweds!

I'll say this for Sue—she knows how to motivate you to stock up on natural food. As for actually *using* all that stuff, if you're a typical junk food junkie, my advice is to take it s-l-o-w and easy. Skip the bran, barley, and carob recipes until you're thoroughly converted —concentrate on the whole wheat and fresh veggies recipes instead. Right now a big threat around our house is, "Eat all your dinner or you'll have to eat a carob chip." . . .

NEW**
Whirlpool Appliance Information Service
Adventures in Basic Cooking, single copy free. Quantity orders, 25¢/copy.

This excellent booklet with 24 illustrated jelly-proof pages belongs in every home.

Adventures in Basic Cooking explains basic safety and economy rules for each appliance covered in the book: stovetop, oven, microwave, refrigerator, dishwasher, and trash compactor. It defines basic food preparation terms such as *slice, chop,* and *roast.* It explains how each appliance works and which pots and pans to use with each. It even includes simple recipes for stovetop, oven, microwave, and refrigerator! A basic home economics course for beginning cooks, and it's *free!*

DRESSMAKING AND SEWING

EDC Publishing
Knitting, Making Clothes, $5.95 each paperbound, $13.96 each ibrary-bound, ages 11–adult. *Beginner's Guide to Sewing and Knitting,* $2.95, ages 8–adult.

The Usborne series from England, published in the U.S.A. by EDC, has recently added a guide to knitting and a guide to making clothes.

Like other Usborne books, these colorful, large (but not thick) glossy paperbacks teach technical terms and techniques in an inventive cartoon style. Each book contains several projects so the novice seamstress or knitter can put theory into practice.

The *Guide to Knitting* and *Guide to Making Clothes* are both excellent introductions to these subjects.

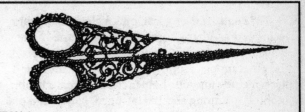

NEW**
Right at Home Productions
The Dorcas Series, $35. Creative Sewing Kits, $2–$6 each. Add 10% shipping ($2 minimum). Grades K–12.

Teach your kids basic sewing skills and Christian character traits with *non-clothes* sewing projects. That's the purpose of *The Dorcas Series,* a set of 60 sewing projects that includes patterns and instructions for both older and younger children, but not fabrics or notions.

The idea behind non-clothes sewing is that

(1) Sewing clothes is expensive . . .

(2) And traumatic, if the clothes don't turn out perfectly the first time . . .

(3) And complicated, if the clothes are to look halfway decent.

Instead, *The Dorcas Series* provides 15 projects in each of these categories:

- "The Growing Disciple"—items like prayer pillows, memory verse treasure chest, a church shoe box (special place to keep shoes ready for churchgoing), tithe purse, Bible book cover, and Scripture banner.

- "The Loving Sibling"—gifts and baby needs like a mini diaper bag, receiving blanket, hooded towel and washcloth set, stroller bag, and crib mobile.

- "The Family Helper"—organizers and gifts like a bread basket, fabric lunch sack, teddy bear pillow for storing pajamas, quilted wallet, and four-sided cleaning cloth.

- "The Playful Learner"—homemade games and toys like a numbered quilt, checkerboard made of glued-on felt squares, magnetic fishing game, fuzzy football for indoor play, juggler's beanbag set, car town play mat, and playhouse table cover.

The entire 60 projects, plus a glossary of fabric terms and another glossary of sewing terms, come in a tabbed three-ring binder. The introduction explains the program philosophy, plus how to organize and keep records for your home school. A reproducible monthly planning sheet is included, so you can plan your excursions to the fabric store and coordinate projects your child might like to give as gifts with upcoming birthdays and holidays. Each pattern is numbered and color-coded, so you can keep it organized after cutting it out and using it the first time.

(Program author Ellen Lyman suggest storing pattern pieces for each project in a ziplock bag, which could be three-hole-punched to keep in the binder with its instructions.)

Each project begins with a character or function objective, e.g., "Designed to encourage your children to spend time each day in prayer with God" or "Designed to encourage your children to store their pajamas where they'll be sure to find them each night!" Next are illustrations of the finished project as completed according to the instructions for younger and older children.

Skills learned are listed separately for both younger and older children, as are supplies required and patterns to cut out. Illustrated directions for younger children are next, followed by illustrated directions for older children, and additional ideas and variations for each project. Color-coded pattern sheets are last (generally, only older children's projects use patterns).

What do kids learn with *The Dorcas Series*? Little kids learn to use a measuring tape, pin and cut out patterns, glue, stitch, decorate, and use pinking shears. Some of the "Playful Learner" projects are also designed to help teach younger kids regular academic skills like counting, time telling, numbers, colors, letters, and shapes. Older children can use a sewing machine for straight seams, finish edges, appliqué, and perform more complicated maneuvers such as turning stuffed pieces inside out before stuffing and then whipstitching the last edge. Older children also use buttons, bias tape, lace, zippers, velcro, batting, fabric paint pens, and other popular sewing notions. They also are supposed to learn to have a pious devotional life, serve their family, love their baby brothers and sisters, and have fun!

Right at Home Productions also sells a number of projects from *The Dorcas Series* as kits. These kits do include pre-cut fabrics and notions, and are just the thing for a quick rainy-day project. Also available: over 50 books on sewing, knitting, crochet, quilting, patchwork, appliqué, embroidery, cross-stitch, and other crafts.

CROSS STITCH

Elijah Company
Covenant Counted Cross Stitch: Books 1 and 2, $5.50 each. Book 3, $3.50.

A simple craft for parents and children.
Each Covenant Counted Cross Stitch book includes clear instructions for those who have never done cross-stitching, clear graphs, and lovely designs with Scripture verses. Between four and 11 designs per book.

DOLLMAKING

NEW★★
HearthSong
Bunting Baby Kit, $18, choice of blue or pink, specify skin color. Real Doll Kit, $28, specify skin and hair color. Shipping extra. Ages 12–adult.

Want to make natural fiber dolls for the young 'uns? HearthSong sells not only the dolls themselves (prices and sizes vary), but a kit to make your very own 12" natural fiber baby doll. Keep in mind that I haven't seen either of these, now—still, the catalog descriptions and illustrations look enticing.

HearthSong's own Bunting Baby Kit comes with cotton velour for the hood and body, carded new wool filling, cotton knit for head and hands, thread, tubular gauze, embroidery thread for features and decorations, pattern, and instructions. Result: one cuddly baby doll. HearthSong also offers a Real Doll kit (all the ingredients for a 16" doll).

We bought HearthSong's wool-filled First Doll a few years ago, and I want to warn you now: when they say "hand-washable" they mean *hand* washable! We put the doll in the washer with some Woolite, and got back a sad little bag full of hard woolen lumps. Don't let this happen to you! Apart from this tragic experience, the doll was a real hit with my then-three-year-old daughter. (And, never fear, we dug out the wadded-up stuffing and replaced it with nice fresh wool lint from our dryer the next time we washed our Superwash wool mattress pad. Happy ending!)

CHAPTER TWENTY-NINE

PHYSICAL EDUCATION

You're not as fat and flabby as you think you are. Just stop comparing yourself to the anorexic models on TV and in magazines—it'll do more for your self-confidence than a two-month diet! All the same, if you're a home-schooled teen, you still need to grunt out the hours at something called Physical Education . . . and if you're not a teen any more, you don't want to entirely lose the Battle of the Bulge!

So here's your choice: an exercise program or a sport. Either will burn off the calories and trim you up. Sports are generally more fun than sheer unvarnished exercise, but often suffer from the disadvantage of needing to find a partner or a team to play with.

The well-rounded citizen (actually, the not-too-rounded citizen) is supposed to be decent at a sport or two and know the rules and basic moves of The Biggies: football, baseball, and basketball. Most Americans have at least an idea of what goes on in soccer and hockey, too, and are familiar with tennis, running, swimming, and diving. Golf and skiing are still mostly upper-middle-class—expensive to play, but not to watch on TV. Most people don't expect you to play polo or know the rules of cricket, although I wish I *did* know the rules of cricket, without which so many English schoolboy stories make no sense. The martial arts are another category, and so are the circus arts.

It's too much to ask a home program to include football, baseball, basketball, hockey, soccer, tennis, running, swimming, diving, golf, and skiing. Even kids in those lavish public-school buildings don't do all of this. For our purposes, it's enough to know the rules of the popular sports, and to pick *one* "lifetime" sport to enjoy for yourself.

Lifetime sports are those, like softball, that you can reasonably expect to still play when you're 45 (or 75!). Boxing, football, and other bone-cracking pastimes are not lifetime sports. Walking, tennis, golf, swimming, and juggling are. Any of these, practiced regularly, provides enough exercise to keep you healthy. With the exception of tennis, which requires another player, all of these lifetime sports can be enjoyed solo.

THE LIFETIME SPORT OF JUGGLING

I am now recommending juggling to anyone who will listen as the ultimate home schooler's lifetime sport. Juggling is fun, impresses your friends, and is great aerobic exercise. The equipment is not expensive, and thanks to the wonderful training and competition videos now available, you can learn at home without an instructor.

Unlike most sports, juggling is very flexible, not only due to the wide range of apparatus used by jugglers (scarves, balls, clubs, rings, unicycles, spinning plates, and balls are just the beginning) but because juggling includes so many sub-sports and styles. You can be a flashy showman, a goofy clown, a technical "numbers" juggler, a balancer, a team juggler (with teams of 2, 3, 4, or more people), a rhythm-stick man, or a club swinger. You can juggle toilet plungers or balance a supermarket cart on your chin! Everyone, whether tall or short, thin or fat, young or old, can find some juggling specialty that fits his style.

Except for numbers juggling—which requires high ceilings—juggling can be done almost anywhere. You don't need special shoes or clothes, or an indoor pool or rink. The whole family can juggle at once, so nobody is left out. Even the littlest baby can chew on the end of a club, while toddlers enjoy tossing up a colorful juggling scarf and trying to catch it! Juggling takes no preparation time; just pick up your beanbags! Nor do you need to have superfast reflexes to master many tricks. Many world-class jugglers do most of their act with just three balls!

You may think I'm prejudiced in favor of juggling because we sell juggling equipment through our home business. Actually, it's the other way around. We started selling juggling equipment when we discovered you can't find it *anywhere* locally except in New York City and a few cities in Southern California (try looking up "Juggling Supplies" in your local Yellow Pages!).

NEW★★
Home Life
Juggling Step by Step video (VHS only): $25 for the half-hour video, $49.95 for the two-hour video. *The Complete Juggler* book, $14.95. Flutterflies scarves (three nylon scarves with complete directions in self-mailer), $9.95. Round beanbags (set of 3), $15. Tough beanbags (lifetime guarantee, set of 3, cubes), $13. Ribbed balls set, $7.50. Bouncy solid rubber balls set, $15. Clubs set, $29. Rings set, $19. Devil Stick set (includes two handsticks), $19. Junior Juggling Kit (3 each of child-sized scarves, ribbed balls, clubs, and rings plus instructions), $35. More kits, new equipment frequently added. Add 10% shipping ($2 minimum) USA/Canada, 25% overseas ground, 60% overseas air mail. Ages 4 and up (scarves), 6 and up (beanbags and balls), 7 and up (clubs, rings, devil sticks).

Here's why none of your friends can juggle—they started out with beanbags (or balls, or oranges). Here's what you should do; pitch the beanbags and try our juggling scarves and *Juggling Step-by-Step* video.

Scarves, the "training wheels of the juggling world," can repair your sagging confidence, and as an added benefit they won't knock over your vases. Once you have mastered scarves, *then* move on to beanbags, but *only after watching the video several times.* Juggling is just too hard to learn from a book for most of us; we need to *see* how it works. Even a juggling friend can't show you the moves in slow motion, but the video can (and does)!

In the *Juggling Step-by-Step* video you meet Professor Confidence (a smooth fellow in top hat and tails who introduces the lessons and performs many of the moves), Won Israel (a colorful little clown), Amy (a beautiful Filipino girl), Andrew (an incredibly talented young juggler), John (a great club juggler), and Robert (a Huck Finn-type kid). Each of these has a particular speciality: balls, clubs, rings, scarves, devil sticks, diabolo, and team juggling are some of the topics covered.

Again, after the first lessons on basic moves, you are expected to pick up more advanced moves from simply watching the tape. The lessons and illustrative performances are set to music. As much fun to watch as a stage show!

The *Juggling Step-by-Step* video is available in both a less-expensive ½ hour version and the full two-hour version. The ½ hour version gives you a basic introduction to juggling scarves, beanbags, balls, rings, and clubs. The full two-hour version includes everything on the ½ hour version, and then goes on to more advanced routines with clubs and balls, unusual equipment like cigar boxes and hats, and even flaming torches! You'll also be introduced to team juggling, juggling with many objects, multiplex juggling, two-in-one-hand, and lots more. Each instruction sequence includes a routine by some really great jugglers. These videos are a quantum leap in juggling education.

Since not every single move on the video is explained in detail, I recommend you also get the *Complete Juggler* book. It includes detailed illustrated directions for all the moves on the two-hour video.

One final word on juggling as the ultimate family sport: When's the last time you saw two guys throwing a football, baseball, soccer ball, or hockey puck back and forth on a street corner, with a hat beside them on the ground, and people throwing money into the hat? Now if they'd been passing *juggling clubs* instead . . . Get the picture?

NEW**
International Juggler's Association
Membership, $25/year. Family membership, $30. Add $5 for membership outside United States. Videos start at $19.99.

The IJA is just what its name says: the International Juggler's Association. A looseknit network of local clubs in the USA and elsewhere provide most of its membership, while the magazine, *Juggler's World*, and the annual festival tie everything together.

Whether or not you decide to join IJA, you should definitely get one of their competition videos. These are highlights of the festival and/or the winning acts of the competitions. The festival-highlights videos give you a great feel for the juggling world, from the sport of "joggling" (juggling while running) to the numbers competitions, obstacle course, junior championships, workshops, and the annual Public Show, which each year features some great professional jugglers. You don't have the faintest idea of the excitement and joy of juggling until you've seen one of these videos. The videos are professionally filmed, with excellent editing and color.

(I should mention here that every IJA video we've ever bought has some spots where the picture tends to jump around. Don't drive them crazy by sending your videos back for an exchange. Live with it.)

Juggler's World has articles on great jugglers past and present, ads for all sorts of ersatz juggling gear (axes, anyone?), news of who's performing where and what club is hosting what event, convention news, and other fascinating stuff for anyone bitten by the juggling bug.

Along with the magazine, members receive the annual roster of membership (even the professional stars have their phone numbers listed!). Right now membership is around 3,000, of whom two-thirds can only juggle three or four balls (or less!). One great big happy family.

SPORTS TRAINING

UPDATED**
EDC Publishing
Ballet and *Dance*, $6.95 each paperbound, $13.96 each library-bound, or $9.95 as a combined paperbound volume. The Superskills series: *Soccer Skills, Running Skills, Swimming and Diving Skills, Tennis Skills, Table Tennis, Racing Bikes, Mountain Bikes*, $5.95 each. *Riding and Pony Care*, $7.95 paperbound or $13.96 library-bound. Shipping extra.

Straight from England, the Usborne sports training books answer the question, "Can you really learn anything about a sport from a book?" *Ballet* and *Dance* both teach simple techniques (and the reasons behind them) as well as presenting the history of these art forms. All volumes in the Superskills series do a wonderful job of explaining technique even to someone like me who knows nothing about these fine points.

Like all other Usborne books, these are lavishly, colorfully illustrated with pictures and text carefully designed to impart information with minimum effort and maximum fun.

NEW**
Human Kinetics Publishers
Sports Rules Encyclopedia, $44.95 ($55.95 Canadian). Shipping extra.

Sports literacy between two covers. *The Sports Rules Encyclopedia* has the official rules for 52 sports in its 744 pages. The new second edition gives the official rules of play as approved by the governing body for that sport, playing area specifications, necessary equipment, and the names and addresses of the governing body or bodies plus the names and addresses of the two top journals for that sport. Some of the more complex rules have been abridged, but most are the complete official rules.

Here's what's covered: Archery (target). Badminton. Baseball. Basketballs. Billiards (pool). Bowling. Boxing. Canoeing. Casting. Cricket (now you can finally find out what those English schoolboys were doing in P. G. Wodehouse's and Rudyard Kipling's schoolboy books). Croquet. Crossbow archery. Curling. Cycling. Darts. Diving. Fencing. Field archery. Field hockey. Flag football (touch). Football. Golf. Handball. Horseshoe pitching. Ice hockey. Lawn bowls. Orienteering. Paddleball. Paddle tennis. Powerlifting. Racquetball. Shuffleboard (get ready for your retirement!). Skiing. Soccer. Softball (separate rules for fast pitch and slow pitch). Speedball. Speedskating. Squash. Swimming. Table tennis (ping pong). Taekwondo. Team handball. Tennis. Track and field (athletics). Trampolining. Tumbling. Volleyball. Water polo. Weightlifting.

I know you're asking yourself, "Why aren't sailing and joggling on this list?" Well, probably you *aren't* asking that, and that's why they aren't in the book. Better luck next time!

SyberVision
Homework Basketball video series, $29.95 each. *Lee Trevino's Golf Tips for Youngsters* video, $19.95. Dennis Van der Meer tennis video series, $29.95 each. Other videos with training guides start at $39.95. Audio/video courses with training guides start at $49.95. VHS only. Shipping extra.

Those who can, do. Those who can't, buy videos. At least that's what SyberVision's developers hope. Their programs are based on the learning theory that (1) we learn best from role models—people who are highly successful at performing the desired behavior, and (2) skills are best learned when key fundamentals are isolated, explained, and either visually presented or vividly described. Thus, SyberVision's *Women's Golf*

course not only features LPGA champion Patty Sheehan, but shows Patty delivering perfect stroke after perfect stroke in a mesmeric rhythm, alternating views of the stroke from in front, on the side, on top, in slow speed and regular, even with an occasional semi-digitized "skeletal shot" of Patty making the stroke in a special suit with the bones drawn on it in luminescent ink. The same stroke is repeated for a long, long time, and then the video goes on to the next—from tee drives to long fairway drives to bunker shots and so on.

Techniques are explained on the accompanying audio cassettes.

Research has shown that seeing a sports maneuver done correctly again and again actually programs your muscles to imitate it—thus the repetition. You don't need to sit to the entire program each time, of course! Sybervision recommends that you spend time with the strokes or moves with which you need the most help.

For younger learners, Pistol Pete Maravich hosts the "Homework Basketball" series, with separate videos on shooting, dribbling, passing, and ball handling. Lee Trevino has golf tips for youngsters on a video of that name.

Older players can learn self-defense for men or women, baseball with Rod Carew, racquetball with Dave Peck, bowling with Jarshall Holman and Johnny Petraglia, tennis with Stan Smith, skiing with Jean-Claude Killy, skiing fundamentals from former U.S. Demonstration Team members, golf from the late great Bobby Jones (introduced by Jack Nicklaus), women's golf with Patty Sheehan, and all sorts of golf specialties from Hale Irwin, Dave Stockton, Mike Dunaway, Greg Norman, and Al Geiberger. If you'd rather learn tennis from the world's #1 tennis instructor than from the world's most famous tennis player, the Dennis Van der Meer series has separate videos on essential strokes, the tactical game, and the attacking game.

Three of SyberVision's products—*Men's Golf*, *Downhill Skiing*, and *Tennis*—have won the Golden Cassette Award for selling more than 100,000 copies.

NEW✱✱
Teaching Home
October/November 1988 back issue, $3.75. Complete six-issue set of 1988 back issues, $17.50, includes free set of 6 plastic magazine holders for your ring binder.

Here's another good reason to buy the October/November 1988 issue of *Teaching Home* magazine. You can get it for its information about teaching health *or* to find out about teaching physical education! (The issue was a twofer, covering both topics at once.)

You might, of course, learn more than you want to. For one thing, I found out I'd *never* get the President's Physical Fitness Award, even if I weren't too old already to compete for it. (My chances are good, however, for the Physical Fatness Award.)

Topics include how to teach phys ed, walking for fitness, indoor P.E., how support groups can fill P.E. needs, and exactly what it takes to win the President's Physical Fitness Award.

Plus, as I said, all that good info on teaching health ed as well!

PART VII

BUSINESS & VOCATIONAL

CHAPTER THIRTY

BUSINESS SKILLS

Academic knowledge is nice. But in the business world, there's no substitute for business savvy. And the "careers" themes in school programs don't provide that savvy!

As I look back on my own business career, I can see so many times when a knowledge of how business works would have come in handy. From my first job in junior high to my last position working for someone else, I was operating off a model that said, "If you don't like the way the boss tells you to do your job, there's nothing you can except to quit." So I let myself (for instance) get trapped in a position where upper management had hired me to beef up the computer department, but my own personal manager, who felt threatened, never gave me any assignments more challenging than, "Change line 1320 in this program from 'If Amount-Payable = 0' to 'If Amount-Payable < $10.'" It never occurred to me to approach the upper manager who had hired me and ask to be transferred to a more challenging position. I knew why I was hired, but not how to get promoted or noticed.

Even more fundamentally, it never occurred to me that I could work for myself. I had never been told, in all my years in public school, that self-employment was an option or that it was possible to start my own business. No class taught me how to pick and price products, how to design displays, how to buy or how to sell. In college, the Placement Department did eventually show me how to apply for a job, but never how to interview prospective employees for a company of my own. I did not receive a single lesson in management techniques throughout my entire educational career, from kindergarten through the Master's degree. This last is especially a shame, since it's impossible to get ahead in business without understanding how to manage people and without knowing when you are being well- or ill-managed yourself. (For that matter, it's hard to run a home and family without management skills!)

So, to fill this gap in American education, I have pulled together below the best of what I've found over the years to help you get a job, start a business, and manage that business (both the money side and the people side). Whether you work at home, work for someone else, or have your own company, the following resources will help you get a better handle on your goals and how to achieve them.

GET A JOB

NEW**
Betterway Books
A Real Job for You, $7.95. Add $2 shipping.

A Real Job for You: An Employment Guide for Teens tells teens what life is really like in the job market and how to get and keep that first job. What do employers want? (Dependable, neat, hard-working, honest workers.) How do you obtain a social security card and work permit? How can you get and use references? How to you make out a resumé and a job application? How should you behave during a job interview?

Somehow I muffed all this stuff and got my first job anyway, but that was back in the '60s, and times (I gather) have changed.

NEW**
High Noon Books
9–5 Series, $15 postpaid for all five books. Add $2.50 taxable handling. Grades 3–adult.

The 9–5 Series are small books with easy-reading vocabulary and sentence lengths. Each is the story of a young man or woman with a summer job who has to solve a mystery concerning his job.

The books are intended to teach preteens and teens how to solve problems that might arise in applying for and keeping their first blue-collar job. Some of the problems—like learning to not "talk silly" around the boss—are part of everyday life, and others—like trying to catch the person who is poisoning food at the supermarket—are thrown in to make the books more interesting. The main characters model good character traits like diligence and honesty (which is why you'll find a more detailed writeup of these books in the Character Education chapter). Kids can painlessly discover which work attitudes lead to rewards and which will get you fired by reading these books.

UPDATED**
New Careers Center
Work Your Way Around the World, $12.95. *International Jobs: Where They Are/How to Get Them*, $12.95. *Jobs in Paradise*, $9.95. *International Employment Hotline* newsletter, $36/year (12 issues). Lots more. Shipping extra.

Have you ever wanted to sail around the world on a yacht? How about living at a ski resort with unlimited free skiing? Or getting a great tan in the Australian Outback?

If you are a flexible single person or enjoy an especially flexible family life, all this is possible. *Work Your Way Around the World* gives you all you need to find fascinating work overseas or at home, including ways to scrounge free transportation to and fro. Some of the more memorable sections:

- Working a Passage includes how to get work on freighters, inland boating, and the invaluable How To Win Friends & Influence Captains, plus salty details on crewing in waters around the world (beware of Caribbean pirates!).

- Travel Ways and Means covers every continent and provides tips for border-passing.

- Enterprise presents local entrepreneurship possibilities, some shady (gambling), most not.

- Work Your Way lays out the possibilities in Tourism, Picking (fruit), Farming, Teaching English, Domestic Work, Business and Industry, and Voluntary Work.

Plus over 170 pages on how to work you way in Europe, country by country, and another 110 pages on how to work your way worldwide, continent by continent. Fascinating personal stories from those who have done it intermingle with practical tips on how to do it.

New Careers Center has more than a dozen books on dream employment opportunites from many different publishers. I listed titles and prices for a few above.

They also sell subscriptions to *International Employment Hotline*, a unique newsletter that devotes about 75 percent of its space to current international job openings.

On top of *that*, they also carry hundreds of the best books on how to make career changes, how to start your own business, how to get hired or moonlight, and lots more!

NEW★★
Peterson's Guides
1991 Internships, $27.95. 1991 Summer Employment Directory of the USA, $14.95. 1991 Directory of Summer Jobs in Britain, $13.95. 1991 Directory of Overseas Summer Jobs, $14.95. The Directory of Jobs and Careers Abroad, $14.95. Teaching English Abroad, $13.95. Shipping extra.

For those needing to break into the job market but not ready to go it on their own, the annual *Internships* and *Summer Employment Directory of the U.S.* books are a terrific resource. The 1991 edition of *Internships* lists more than 50,000 on-the-job training opportunities for college students and adults. Sections include:

- Arts (art, museums and cultural organizations, music, dance, and theater)

- Communications (advertising, PR, film, audio, video, magazine and book publishing, newspapers and journalism, radio, and TV)

- Human Services (career counseling, education, health services, and social service organizations)

- International

- Public Affairs (government, public administration, law, criminal justice, public interest, public service)

- Regional/National Clearinghouses

- Science/Industry (architecture, engineering, business, computer science, environment, retail, science, and research)

Each listing includes the duration and season of the position, pay rates, desired qualifications, duties and training involved, availability of college credit, and application procedures and deadlines, plus helpful quotes from recent interns and articles on career trends written by professionals.

The *Summer Employment Directory,* which like *Internships* is revised yearly, listed 75,000 summer jobs in its 1991 edition, along with whom to contact and where, pay rates and fringes, qualifications required, number of openings, and whether or not you can get college credit for the job, plus articles on how to apply successfully for a summer job. The only drawback to these fine books is the listed companies' continuous discrimination against non-college applicants, who more than anyone else need an initial employment opportunity.

Peterson's also has those of you who want to work overseas covered. *The Directory of Jobs and Careers Abroad* lists permanent career opportunities in trades and professios in Europe, Australia, and New Zealand. The annual directories of summer jobs in Britain and overseas summer jobs are just that: detailed listings of specific job openings and requirements (over 30,000 and 50,000, respectively) in those locations. *Teaching English Abroad* is the book for those of us who would like to pay our way in other countries via word of mouth. Covers opportunities country-by-country, salaries, and even potential red-tape snags.

Peterson's also publishes *Work Your Way Around the World* (written up in the New Careers Center listing).

NEW★★
Teaching Home
April/May 1989 back issue, $3.75. June/July 1986 back issue, $3.50. Complete six-issue set of 1986 back issues, $15; complete set of 1989, $17.50. Each six-issue set includes free set of 6 plastic magazine holders for your ring binder.

Don't ask me detailed questions about what it's like to have your home-taught teens launching out into an apprenticeship or a college program: ask the folks who wrote the articles in these *Teaching Home* issues.

The Work Education issue was June/July 1986, and it dealt both with getting kids to work (in general) and helping them become entrepreneurs (in particular).

The theme of April/May 1989 was Preparing Children for Adulthood. It included articles on careers, homemaking, and college, as well as general growing-up helps.

ARE BUSINESS OWNERS GREEDY?

Most people don't understand how business works. When we hear about 100 percent markups on merchandise, we conclude the retailer is greedy and unethical. If someone tells us that the average manufacturer sets the retail price of his product between seven and 10 times what it costs him to manufacture it, we see red.

Christians have it even worse. If we become Avon ladies or Amway reps, we feel guilty about charging our friends anything more than the product costs us. I have talked to any number of misguided would-be Christian businessfolks who persist in thinking of their business-to-be as a "ministry," in which their sole goal is to undercut all existing competitors by charging the customer a price as close to wholesale as possible.

Another group of people don't understand how businesses *start*. I get letters like this fairly frequently: "I'd like to start a mail-order business just like yours. Please sit down right now and explain exactly how you started your business, who your suppliers are, how much you made last year, and everything else I need to successfully compete with you. I don't actually know anything about which books I would like to sell, so could you help me with this?" (I'm not making this up!)

Most of us have been brought up to believe that business owners can set their profit margin wherever they like and are simply being greedy to charge more than just a few percentage points over their actual product cost. Some of us even believe that our potential competitors have a duty to offer us (at their own

expense for envelopes and postage) the knowledge of business it has cost them years of their life and thousands of dollars to gain.

Rather than fret about it, I've decided to share with anyone who cares to read it the true story of How Business Really Works.

HOW BUSINESS REALLY WORKS

Let's say you have a business and you want to add a new product to your line. You buy 100 of them (to get a bulk discount) at $1 each and plan to sell them at $2 each. Greedy, right? Wrong! It's *hard* to make money on a 100 percent markup. Here's why:

(1) You might not sell all 100. If you sell less than 50, you have lost money on the deal.

(2) If you sell all 100, you then have to buy more. At this point you have received $200 from your customers. $100 of that went to buy the first batch. You now have to spend $100 to purchase the second batch. Having done all the work of advertising to find the customers and then filling their orders, you have made this much: $0. That's assuming your advertising and customer service cost *nothing*.

(3) If you sell part of the second batch without having to reorder, that's your profit. Say you sell only 25 of the second batch. You've spent $200 of your money. You've received $225 from your customers, for a net profit so far of $25, and you have $75 worth of unsellable product you'll have to pay tax on if you can't dump it somewhere by January 1. If your tax rate is 33 percent, you'll have to pay $25. Net gain: zero.

(4) If you sell the entire second batch, you now have to order a third batch. You've made $400 and you've spent $300. Still not big bucks, especially considering that I'm still assuming your advertising and overhead costs at zero.

The moral is that you have to either charge a large markup or turn over your stock very fast and frequently—which means work very hard—in order to make any significant amount of money. And it's *very* easy to *lose* money on an item, by buying larger quantities than your customers want to take off your hands.

Now, the above example isn't really fair. I didn't include the cost of advertising, employee salaries, and office overhead. Advertising alone can cost as much as a product's price. That's why manufacturers—who also have to offer a 50 percent or more discount to resellers —typically set a product's retail price at seven to 10 times a product's cost to them. (Figure it out. Manufacturer's cost, $1. Advertising cost, $1. Employee salaries, $1. Overhead, $1. Price manufacturer gets from reseller, $5. Manufacturer makes $1.) Nor can businesses simply opt out of advertising in many cases. You have to get the customers somehow because without customers you have no sales, whether you own a service typing bureau or sell a national brand of soap.

Huge companies can charge discount prices not because they are less greedy but because they get huge discounts on their huge orders. Mega-Huge Mail Order Books might get a 65% discount on its book orders while my home business only gets a 40% discount. A retail bookstore can rarely hope to match a mail-order discounter unless it is part of a buying chain like Waldenbooks.

Now, philosophy. A Christian friend, to whom I shall be forever thankful, pointed out to me years ago that you aren't doing your customers any good by charging such low prices that you put yourself out of business, thereby destroying all chances of ever serving them in the future. Nor are you doing them any favors by making such a low profit that you have no money to reinvest in better service and products. The costs of keeping in business—including a decent salary for yourself and your workers—and the costs of growth and product development are legitimate business costs. These are the costs that consumers typically forget about when calculating how much the small businesses that serve them are making.

Let's take another example with which I am familiar: a newsletter. Say that, after four years of effort, you manage to get 2,500 people subscribing to your $20 monthly newsletter. A cynical subscriber might guesstimate your paper, printing, and postage costs at 50¢/month, and figure that on that basis you should be making $14 profit for each subscriber, which adds up to a tidy $35,000 per year. On that basis she might write you a letter suggesting that you lower your subscription price, since in her view you can afford to do so.

There are three things wrong with the subscriber's reasoning:

(1) In a free market, the owner of a company has the right to determine what he wants to charge for his products. Since he has no monopoly, the customer can always buy from someone else if they don't like the prices or service. The owner does not have a duty to charge a hypothetical "just" price determined by some outside authority. A letter writer can legitimately point out that the owner is likely to lose customers if the customers as a whole perceive his prices are too high, but she is out of line to demand that the owner lower them because he is making "too much" money.

(2) The subscriber's calculations are off. Short-run printing costs a lot more than long-run printing. The subscriber is also not taking into account the price of salaries (to process subscription orders, inquiries, and mail), equipment (copiers, computers, phones, faxes, desks, and file cabinets), supplies (paper, floppy disks, pens, sticky notes, wastepaper baskets, laser cartridges, and on and on) and advertising (direct mail to existing subscribers when renewal time comes around and prospecting for new subscribers).

(3) The subscriber is also forgetting about the previous years of work which have led to your present success. The typical small businessman loses money, or just barely breaks even, during the first months or years of starting his business. In our newsletter example, your average

newsletter-based income after advertising, printing, and postage expenses over the past years may have been $5,000 the first year (which you immediately reinvested in equipment), $10,000 the second year (half of which went for a copy machine), and $25,000 the third year (during which your increased volume of orders and mail forced you to hire a part-time secretary at $10,000 per year). During the present year, you had to continue paying your secretary's salary. You also invested another $5,000 in software, hard disks, and a larger monitor for your computer. Advertising cost another $3,000. This gives you annual incomes of $0, $5,000, $15,000, and $18,000, all of which averages out to $9,250 per year— poverty level by government standards. If you dropped your newsletter's price by $5/year, as the subscriber requested, you would only make $5,500 next year, assuming that you lost no subscribers. On the other hand, if you continue to charge your present price, keep your costs down, and get more subscribers, maybe by next year you will be making a family wage.

See how the long arm of the Welfare State has infected all our thinking about business? We all tend to have the attitude that a business is perpetual—that its income is assured no matter how it is run—and that businesses therefore "ought" to do all sorts of things. We also assume that a business owner who is making more than his workers is exploiting them, forgetting that it's very likely that for years previously he made *less* than he now pays his workers! This is the era of "mandated benefits," when Congress has discovered that it's possible to increase the welfare state without additional taxes simply by demanding that businesses provide everything from parental leave to AIDS-inclusive health insurance.

In reality most businesses are geese laying golden eggs. As long as you leave the goose alone, she does fine. Try to get all the eggs at once by slicing up the goose and you only get a dead goose.

I don't want to discourage you from starting a business. Golden eggs are nice. But they don't come without some sweat and strain!

Most businesses are run honestly, and most business owners work hard for their money. Let's take the time to learn how business *really* works. Let's respect each other and wish each other success. In a free market, everyone ultimately benefits. Let's keep it free!

SOME SUGGESTED BUSINESS ETHICS

Some business owners *are* greedy, nasty people, just like some employees are greedy, nasty people. Just because, biblically speaking, a business owner is free to set his own prices and policies, it doesn't mean that God has no opinions on how businesses ought to be run.

I would like to suggest the following scriptural business ethics, which have served our family well:

(1) Hold your competitive urges within bounds. Don't start a business competing with anyone who is doing a good job even if you think, thanks to your greater assets or know-how, you could obliterate him in a straight competition. Instead, compete with the lazy, the incompetent, and the unresponsive, or pick a niche that nobody is filling and fill it. Don't fill your mind with greedhead fantasies of starting a monopoly or a business empire. Guiding rules: "Do unto others as you would have them do unto you." "Woe to them who add house to house and field to field until they dwell alone in the land." Application: big businesses should not use their muscle to launch chains that they expect will wipe out hundreds of mom-and-pop businesses unless the mom-and-pop businesses are doing a lousy (not just less efficient) job.

(2) Plan on growing slowly, but continuously, God willing. Guiding rule: "Do not be anxious to

become rich." Application: avoid financing your growth with business debt.

(3) Reinvest in better service and products. Guiding rules: "Do unto others [in this case, your customers] as you would have them do unto you." "The hand of the diligent makes rich." Application: a good product guarantee and a lot of time spent searching for product and service improvements.

(4) When you fail to provide good customer service or a good product (this happens eventually to everyone, thanks to unreliable suppliers or a bad choice when hiring a new employee), apologize profusely and make restitution, e.g., a full refund of their present order or a $5-off coupon for use on their next order. Guiding rules: "Do unto others . . ." and "Gentle words calm strife."

(5) Share your goals with your employees and train each of them to gradually assume more responsibility. Don't just dump the work you hate the most on them. Praise them individually for work well done and give quick feedback on work *not* well done. Don't snap, yell, fume, or threaten—tell them *exactly* what you want, *exactly* what they did wrong, and *exactly* how to do it right next time. Take the time to learn how to be a better manager, especially if you're not naturally a people person. Meanwhile, remember that you hired workers to help you, and you deserve the help you're paying for. Expect high standards (but not hours of unpaid overtime) from both yourself and your employees, and reward them accordingly. If you're blessed, share the blessings with your workers. Guiding rules: "Do unto others . . ." "The worker is worthy of his hire." "If any will not work, let him not eat." "Don't muzzle the ox that treads out the grain."

The biblical ideal is for each man to "sit under his own vine and fig tree, and none shall make them afraid." Enough for me and my family, without huge competitors and huge government bureaucracies conspiring to take it all away. This is a reachable goal, for those with the patience and diligence to achieve it. "Do you see a man skilled in his work? He will serve before kings; he will not serve before obscure men." Believe it!

HOW TO START YOUR OWN BUSINESS

Six steps to a small business of your own:

(1) Learn a skill—how to make something, how to sell something, how to provide a particular service. Actually, learn *lots* of skills! Good all-purpose business skills include typing and keyboarding, computer literacy (use of basic word-processing and database packages), management skills, accounting, and salesmanship. Read lots of how-to business books and magazines.

(2) Pick your business. Ask yourself three questions: "What do I like to do?" "What am I best at?" "What do I think 'they' ought to do—but aren't doing?"

(3) Save up enough money to last through your startup period.

(4) Get your post office box, letterhead, business cards, brochures, and whatever else you need to let the world know you're there.

(5) Get your equipment. It's OK at this stage to finance or lease your basic equipment, in my opinion, since "where there is no ox, the manger is empty, but from the labor of an ox comes an abundance of grain"—in other words, without equipment you don't have expenses but you don't make any money either—but try to avoid debt financing for your salary and day-to-day expenses.

(6) Start selling. This may mean advertising, or calling local businessmen to tell them about your new service, or putting together a direct-mail package, or whatever else you can think of to publicize your product or service.

Starting with step 1, here are enough how-to books and resources to get you serious about a business of your own.

UPDATED★★
Betterway Books
Homemade Money, $16.95. Add $2.50 shipping. College–adult.

The best book for home business details is Barbara Brabec's *Homemade Money: The Definitive Guide to Success in a Homebased Business.* An oversized quality paperback (328 pages, 8½ x 11"), it contains not only the usual lists of business ideas, but tax info, time management helps, pricing and packaging tips, and a tremendous array of publicity and advertising ideas, plus legal, tax, and accounting information. Now in its third edition. Over 50,000 copies now in print.

This is the first book we read when we got serious about starting our home business (which now supports our family). The book's strongest point is the extensive resource lists at the back of the book.

You can't get this information anywhere else.

NEW★★
Betterway Books
The Small Business Information Source Book, $7.95. Add $2 shipping.

"Where and How to Locate Information You Need on Hundreds of Subjects—Everything from Absenteeism, Affirmative Action, and Arbitration to Trademarks, Truth-in-Lending, and Wage and Salary Information . . . More." It sounds great. Haven't ever seen a copy.

NEW★★
Blue Bird Publishing
Home Business Resource Guide, $11.95. Add $1 shipping.
From the people who publish *Home Education Resource Guide* and *Home Schools: An Alternative* comes the *Home Business Resource Guide* by Cheryl Gorder. Its mission: put you in touch with the information you

need to help start a home business, sources for products for home business, and the inspiration you need to consider this seriously. The *Home Business Resource Guide* includes books and courses on how to start a home business, wholesale products available to home businesses, newsletters and magazines on the subject, profiles of successful home businesses, and other essential information.

NEW★★
Busines$ Kids
The Busines$ Kit, $49.95 plus $8.50 shipping. Teacher's guide, 39.95. Ages 10–adult.

Ever wish there were an easy way to start a business? Coming up with the business *idea* is not the problem. It's getting organized . . . getting financed . . . finding out what forms you need to fill out to keep the bureaucrats happy . . . advertising . . . management . . . record-keeping . . . hiring and firing (and whether you *should* hire help) . . . and all those other imponderables that keep would-be entrepreneurs biting their fingernails with frustration. They don't teach this stuff in school!

Nasir M. Ashemimry, a Saudi Arabian airline pilot turned businessman, became aware of this problem when his nine-year-old son Ibrahim asked him for a business card. Little Ibrahim wanted a business card of *his own,* you see, so he could start his own business. Mr. Ashemimry, naturally very proud of his enterprising offspring, started to explain that it takes more than a business card to start a business.

"Like what?" Ibrahim wanted to know.

The answer to Ibrahim's question took a few years to put together, and you'll know why when you see it. From the fancy lacquer-finished cardboard case in which the Busines$ Kit is packaged, to the glossy booklets, to the complete line of Busines$ Kids accessories, this product is first-class. The object is twofold:

(1) Teach American teens that, although we may live in a country where 98 percent of the people work for two percent of the people, they can beat the percentages, and

(2) Set up Busines$ Kids clubs throughout the U.S.A. and (why not?) the world.

Following his empowerment philosophy down the line, Mr. Ashemimry enlisted the aid of a multiethnic teenage board to help finalize the design of his how-to-go-into-business-for-yourself kit. The result has a certain McBiz look about it. Swank. Hip (at least as hip as 90s kids manage to be). The kind of yuppie puppies who would buy a Busines$ Kids "I'M THE BOSS" T-shirt ought to love it.

(Depressing aside: Did you know that sales of California Raisins accessories are larger, dollar-wise, than sales of California raisins? No wonder so many people need Ex-Lax! This definitely proves the smart money should ride on accessories rather than the real thing, or to put it another way, more kids are likely to buy T-shirts announcing their willingness to go into business than are likely to seriously go into business. Even more likely: Mom and Dad will buy the T-shirts, hoping Junior will thus subliminally be motivated to become Bill Gates.)

Now you have an idea of the user interface. What's in the kit?

1. A Business Plan Packet containing: business plan and product/service research worksheets, Going into Business checklist, monthly bookkeeping record, monthly profit/loss statement, official Business Kids IOU, job application form, SS-4 Application for Employer Identification Number, and W-4 Employee's Withholding Allowance Certificate.

2. Template packet containing "A Very Short Course in Advertising" and four sample templates for ads.

3. Appointment calendar.

4. Instruction booklets: "The World of Business" (Introduction, The President's Message, The Business of Business, Business Heroes, Looking Inside a Large Corporation, Small Business Opportunities), "Getting Started" (Getting Started, Some Businesses to Consider, and Some Help with Choosing YOUR Business), "Organizing" (Researching Your Business, Planning Your Business, and Finding Cash), "Mastering Management" (Introduction: The Importance of Management, Setting Up Shop, Hiring People, Managing Your Money, and Taxes), "Marketing" (Marketing Your Business and Satisfying Your Customers), and "Super Index" (Table of Contents, Glossary of Terms, and Index).

5. Stationery and business cards printed with the Busines$ Kids logo.

6. A catalog of everything from cuff-links to backpacks emblazoned with the Busines$ Kids logo.

As you may have guessed, the booklets are the heart of the program—and they are really good. Everything you need to start up and run a growing company is spelled out, right down to such details as the benefits of renting expensive equipment rather than rushing out to buy it, the child labor laws, how to advertise your business, where to get the money to start your business, and even what kind of business to start. It's not a cookie-cutter approach—you're told about the different types of businesses and given brief descriptions of 76 businesses well suited to teens.

Things kids might not realize are covered, like the importance of dressing properly for the job (even kids who mow lawns should keep their shirts on!) and how to find out the pay scale in your area.

Even though the information is well presented, with lively graphics and explanations, a kid will do better to walk through the material with an adult, preferably one with some business experience.

I hear the question you're asking. "Can adults use this kit, too?" Sure! Skip the accessories and try to ignore the teenage success stories. You have enough trouble getting up your nerve to start a business without knowing that some infant has already succeeded more than you ever will! Concentrate on the business plan, product research worksheets, and booklets. As much information is packed in there as you could pick up at hundreds of dollars' worth of seminars.

If Mr. Ashemimry is smart, he'll tweak the Busines$ Kit, add some overheads, and put together his own seminar for grownups. (We adults need these things spelled out, not to mention the support of seeing other people in the room who want to start their own business.)

Did I mention that, included in the purchase of the Busines$ Kit, you get a year's membership, entitling you to participate in the club and get monthly issues of the newsletter? This, again, is a slick production, given to hyping the successes of sundry teen business-folk, and definitely worldly in its outlook (peace, ecology, money, teenage rebellion, and the American Way).

Bottom line: The Busines$ Kit is a good place to start, if you hope to start a business. Even its packaging is a call to excellence. Keep your head screwed on straight, remember that success is not making big bucks but doing what is right, work through the kit, and we'll see what happens!

EDC Publishing
The Usborne Introduction to Business, $6.95. Ages 13–adult.

Other books in this section tell you how to start a business. This is the best one-book introduction to how business *works*. Designed for English children, the *Usborne Introduction to Business* covers all the basics and quite a few more advanced topics, like import/export. The brightly colored cartoons not only entertain, but also explain. If you've never understood how a business worked before, or what goes into starting one, you will after reading this inexpensive book.

Entrepreneurial viewpoint throughout. Not overidealized, but positive viewpoint of business. Very highly recommended.

NEW★★
Entrepreneur
Entrepreneur magazine, $19.97/year U.S., $29.97 Canada, $39.97 other countries (surface mail only). *New Business Opportunities*, $14.97/year U.S., $24.97 Canada, $34.97 other countries. *Entrepreneurial Woman*, $16.95/year U.S. (10 issues), $24.95 Canada, $32.95 other countries surface mail, $92.95 other countries air mail. U.S. funds only. Most business guides are $69.50, with a $10 discount for *Entrepreneur* subscribers. How-to video packages include guide, are $79 for subscribers, $99 for non-subscribers. Specialized business software also available.

Entrepreneur magazine sells over 200 how-to-start-your-own-business guides geared to specific businesses, from advertising agencies, to bed-and-breakfast inns, to consulting businesses, to private investigator, to publishing "Who's Who" guides. Each guide is about 200 pages long and comes in a vinyl-covered loose-leaf binder.

If you get more than one, you'll see that a good chunk of the basic startup information is repeated from guide to guide. This is understandable, since the mechanics of starting up a business are often similar regardless of business type.

Topics covered in each guide include:

• Market considerations—business profit potential, size of the market, who exactly your market is and how to reach them, and a generic how-to-do-your-own-market-research plan.

• Location and facility—types of locations, types of leases available, telephone service options, etc.

• Equipment and supplies—everything from reference dictionaries (for a translation service) to detailed information on dealing with suppliers (for a mail-order business). The information in this section is generally more tailored to the specific business, with the exception of some generic advice on computers and software.

• Personnel—generic advice on hiring and management, plus tailored advice on the kinds of employees needed for your particular business (e.g., freelance translators for a translation business).

• Legal requirements—the advantages and disadvantages of sole proprietorships, partnerships, corporations, S corporations; licenses and permits; copyright and patents; and special laws applying to your business (e.g., Federal Trade Commission regulations for mail-order businesses).

• Recordkeeping and taxes—detailed but generic information applicable to all businesses.

• Financial management—again, this is very detailed information that applies to all businesses, from how to put together a balance sheet, to dealing with banks, to how to collect from delinquent accounts.

• Advertising and promotion—your needs in this area differ from business to business. Some guides go so far as to show you an example of a well-designed brochure; others just give you step-by-step instructions for how to put together your advertising. (Personally, I find how-to examples add a lot, and hope the editors of these guides include more in future editions.)

• Operations—the day-to-day details of running your specific business, from planning and following through on mail-order campaigns (for a mail-order business) to how to estimate and schedule a translating job (for a translation business).

• Startup—a generic section on how to put together your business plan and get financing.

I was frankly skeptical about the value of these guides, mainly because of the breathless hype of the ads for them in *Entrepreneur's* "Be Your Own Boss" catalog. Example: "Ice Cream Store: Profit From the Sweet Taste of Success." Actually, the guides are full of very useful information, especially well suited to the person who has never started or managed a business before. Information that veterans would find simplistic

(e.g., types of leases, how to negotiate one, and why it might be better just to work out of your home at first) can be lifesaving to a new business owner. The information specially tailored to each business type is eye-opening, and can help prospective owners discern whether they should even get into that particular business in the first place.

Now, *Entrepreneur* magazine itself. *Entrepreneur* deals with both starting a business and running it once it's up. Rah-rah tone, with many products and companies profiled that advertise in the magazine. Heavy involvement in franchise promotion—lots of franchisors advertise. Articles typically start out in a whirl of breathless excitement, but sometimes simmer down around the third paragraph and begin to impart useful information. The "Advertising Workshop" section, in which ad pro Jerry Fisher does a before-and-after job on an ad written by an *Entrepreneur* subscriber, is the best feature in the magazine. If you want to find out about new franchise operations and business ideas, and don't care a whole lot about classic journalistic techniques, *Entrepreneur* has it all, from the downright dubious to the commercially viable.

New Business Opportunities, an *Entrepreneur* spinoff, is a much slimmer magazine solely devoted to profiling new industries and franchises. Again, breathless enthusiasm and lots of ads from businesses profiled.

Entrepreneurial Woman falls somewhere lower down the spectrum, in my opinion. Remember *Gidget Goes Hawaiian*? Well, this glossy magazine reads like *The Cosmo Girl Starts Her Own Business.* Lots of positive thinking, yuppie morality, virtually no critical analysis of any of the businesses profiled, no philosophizing whatsoever.

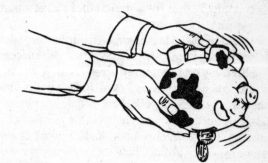

Home Life
Extra Cash for Kids, $9.95. Add 10% shipping ($2 minimum). Ages 8–adult.

Extra Cash for Kids is just the best book around for starting kids aged 8–16 in their own simple businesses. One hundred mini chapters on kid-sized jobs.

Workable ideas, entrepreneurial tips, and lots of invaluable details on equipment, pricing, scheduling, and how to do the job right. The Special Notes tips include ideas on how to expand some of the businesses into other areas. *SuperIdeas,* a mini-menu of general business tips like how to keep records or how to clean up on school fads, are scattered throughout the book, along with inviting cartoons and graphics.

Actually, *grownups* who want to ease their way into home business on a shoestring might want to test the waters with some of these ideas! *Extra Cash* inspired our sons to start *two* businesses! Less hype, more solid help than any other book of this kind.

NEW★★
Inc. Business Products
How to Succeed in a Home Business, Women in Business, $39.95 each. Add $2.50 shipping each. VHS only.

It finally happened! *Inc.* sent me a copy of one of their how-to-start-and-succeed-in-business videos! The video in question: *How to Succeed in a Home Business,* a subject naturally dear to my heart since I have a home business.

Hosted by *Inc.* editor George Gendron, the video is drawn mostly from at-home interviews with successful home business owners. Advertising, catering, public relations, cosmetic sales, and even coffee wholesaling are among the lines of work these people are pursuing at home. A tax advisor also shares some pertinent information. Topics touched upon include what kind of business you should start, how to combine your business with the rest of your life, legal and tax issues, marketing, and the place of technology in your home business (with sample office setups).

The business owners' advice is honest, nitty-gritty, helpful, and directed mostly to the person considered starting a business, not the home business owner with years of experience. If you're looking for help starting a

business, don't skim over this tape—some of the most obvious-sounding advice will save you the most grief, if you take the time to note and follow it!

How to Succeed in a Home Business was very interesting to watch as well—the real test of an educational product! However, I did find it strange that not one of the home businesses profiled fit the fairly common model of a mom-and-pop or family-team operation. In each case, the business owner was going it solo, either lacking a spouse or simply doing all the work himself or herself.

Women in Business costs the same and is published by the same company, so I presume it follows the same people-centered format. Maybe next time I'll get to review that one, too!

NEW★★
New Careers Center
Whole Work Catalog, $1. *Homemade Money,* 3rd edition, $16.95. *Small-Time Operator,* $12.95. *Marketing Without Advertising,* $14.95. *Starting and Operating a Business in . . .,* $29.95 each state. *The Work-at-Home Sourcebook,* 3rd edition, $14.95. Shipping extra. College and adult.

Here is the business that will put you in business! Send these folks $1 and ask for their "Whole Work Catalog." It offers books, cassette tapes, newsletter subscriptions and other materials in the categories of alternative careers, working from home, self-employment, and "better ways of working." Tom and Sue Ellison, the catalog publishers, have done a great job of bringing together the best secular books on these topics. Everything you need to find your family's money-making calling and start up your own business is right there. For the less entrepreneurially minded, the catalog also has resources to help you locate employers who will let you work at home.

My personal picks from this catalog, as the best books to start with, are:

• *Homemade Money: The Definitive Guide to Success in a Home Business.* Excellent first book on this subject. Provides an overview of everything involved, gives hundreds of ways to connect (organizations, newsletters, books, etc.). See Betterway Books review.

• *Small-Time Operator: How to Start Your Own Small Business, Keep Your Books, Pay Your Taxes, and Stay Out of Trouble.* The title says it all. Demystifies the dreaded record-keeping.

- *Marketing Without Advertising.* Since a huge percentage of most business's outlay goes to advertising, this book can make a BIG difference in your chances of success!

- *Starting and Operating a Business in . . .* This authoritative guide comes in different versions for each state. You'll appreciate the handy helps, like the tear-out postcards already addressed to the various state bureaucracies you need to get forms from.

- *The Work-At-Home Sourcebook.* Detailed info on specific jobs that allow you to work from your home. Over 1,000 companies listed that actually hire people to work at home. By the editor of *The Worksteader News.*

NEW★★
Surrey Books
The Teenage Entrepreneur's Guide, **$12.95 postpaid.**
Ages 12–18.

Nearly 80% of all teens will work this year. But two out of five employed teens will work in low paying, unrewarding jobs at fast food joints, convenience stores, and service stations.

All too often, convenience sector jobs require long, late night hours for work that is boring, stressful, and sometimes dangerous. Such jobs can conflict with school work, and most offer little preparation for a meaningful career.

Teens can escape this rut by being their own bosses, says Sarah Riehm, author of *The Teenage Entrepreneur's Guide: 50 Money-Making Business Ideas.* Her 1990 revised edition features 50 tested business ideas that teens can start and run on their own with a minimum investment of time and money. Most of the businesses can be run from home or around the neighborhood, eliminating the need to commute to and from work.

Mrs. Riehm recommends that any business young people start should

- generate at least minimum wage
- be flexible enough to schedule around school or other activities
- succeed with 5–15 hours a week
- provide a steady income
- teach valuable business skills
- be run out of the teen's home
- require little or no expertise, capital, or transportation

Some of the businesses she picks violate these guidelines—e.g., professional musicians, clowns, and tutors need excellent skills and holiday businesses don't provide year-round income—but hey, this is the real world, and even house cleaners need to be great at what they do.

The descriptions of each business are amazingly complete. Here's an example:

Job Description: Baker
Personal Traits Required: You must love to cook and have an outgoing personality to market your wares.
Experience Required: Depends upon product selected
Materials Required: Recipe ingredients, a reliable oven and stove, baking pans and utensils
Marketing Method: Direct sales
Expected Wages: $4 and up per hour.

This is followed by three paragraphs of advice and tips about the baking biz in general, a page of more detailed advice broken down under the categories of muffins, cookies, fancy cheesecakes, specialty bread, international desserts, and cakes, two detailed examples of pricing scenarios (Cora selling muffins at school and Tom selling fancy cheesecakes to restaurants), and yet another page of marketing advice by type of outlet supplied. And she provides this level of detail for *all* 50 jobs!

The Teenage Entrepreneur's Guide also includes a quiz for determining your entrepreneurial I.Q., a step-by-step approach to setting up your own business (how to pick a business that's right for you, how to determine the price for your service or product, how to register with the government), and separate sections on marketing and accounting.

You'll find some marked similarities between Mrs. Riehm's list and the list of jobs in the Busine$ Kit, probably because these same jobs *are* the most obvious choices for teens. Her job descriptions are much more detailed and practical, however. The marketing, business plan, and accounting advice is actually more detailed in *The Teenage Entrepreneur's Guide*. This book takes a more conservative approach than the Busines$ Kit, urging teens *not* to hire employees while the Busines$ Kit includes an entire section on how to hire and fire. The book is nowhere near as pretty or easy to use as the kit, due to its more cramped format. You have to *study* your way through this book; you can't just read it and go.

I think the *Teenage Entrepreneur's Guide* and the Busines$ Kit balance each other nicely. The Busines$ Kit inspires and teaches, while the *Teenage Entrepreneur's Guide* gives more details and keeps reminding you to not overschedule, not overbuy, and not overhire.

In both cases, you shouldn't just throw the material at your teen. Look it over yourself first. Then you will be able to offer intelligent advice and support, based on your wider experience of life. You will also see why I suggest you run your teen through the Busines$ Kit *first* (for inspiration and to get the main points clear) and the *Teenage Entrepreneur's Guide* second (for more details and a second viewpoint).

A kid whose parents have bought and worked through both has a much better chance of starting—and succeeding—at a business of his own.

MINDING YOUR BUSINESS: MONEY

Starting a business isn't even half the battle. You've still got to *manage* the pesky thing!

Don't wait until you've started to find out how to run your business's finances. Load up on the resources below *first*.

NEW**
Christian Financial Concepts

The Complete Financial Guide for Young Couples, Debt-Free Living, $11 each, hardbound. *Your Finances in Changing Times*: 4-tape video set with syllabus & leader's guide, $99.95; 5-tape audiocassette soundtrack set with syllabus & leader's guide, $30; additional workbook, $2; paperback book, $7. *How to Manage Your Money*: 4-tape video set with workbook & manual, $99.95; 6-tape audiocassette soundtrack set with workbook & manual, $30; additional workbook, $7; additional instructor's manual, $6. *The Financial Planning Workshop*: 3-tape video set, $99.95; 4-tape audiocassette soundtrack including workbook and instructor's manual, $30; additional workbook, $7; additional instructor's manual, $6. *Two Masters* video, $19.95. *Business by THE BOOK*, $12 hardbound. *God's Principles for Operating a Business*, 11-tape audiocassette series with outline, $50. *Surviving the Money Jungle*: student guide, $7.50; leader's guide, $9.50. Shipping extra. Video series are designed for adults; *Surviving the Money Jungle* is a high school/young adult study. Shipping extra. 15% discount when purchasing 10 or more of any item.

Larry Burkett's organization, Christian Financial Concepts, has prepared a slew of material on personal finances, debt-free living, marriage and money, and the like. Much of this material is now available in your choice of video seminars or audio soundtracks of those seminars.

Both audio and video seminars come complete with the needed workbooks and instructor's guides.

Larry Burkett is generally considered the premier Christian speaker on this topic. He certainly is interesting to listen to, with a wealth of practical and biblical tips on how to get your financial life under control and make it productive for the Lord.

His *How to Manage Your Money* seminar, for example, starts out by defining wealth biblically, then delves into God's will for your finances, the perils of money, how to get out of debt, financial planning with a Christian perspective, motives for accumulating wealth, how much is enough, sharing the wealth (including how to tell the difference between those who deserve and *don't* deserve your help), and instruction in a basic Christian approach to making financial decisions.

Sound too philosophical and boring to you? Believe me, it's not! Larry sprinkles his presentation with dozens of true-life examples, good and bad, of the principles he is teaching, and gets *really* specific about the types of behavior that lead to good—or disastrous—financial results. There's plenty for business owners here, as well as for wage earners and homeworkers.

That's not to say that I agree with every jot and tittle in this seminar, but that it's an excellent place to start. If you can't afford to buy the video seminar, talk your church into it.

Those who prefer a more dramatic presentation should start off with the *Two Masters* video. This is a dramatized look at two couples who get themselves in a sad financial pickle, and then attend a home meeting where Larry Burkett is speaking. Flashbacks at the meeting show how his message addresses their exact situation, and what they can do to get out of their financial hole. The video is well acted, quite interesting, and absolutely right-on in its analysis of how so many Baby Boomers (and older people, too) get into marital and financial difficulties. Just about every young couple would benefit from watching this video—preferably *before* getting married.

The best Burkett book and tape set for would-be business owners (*Business by THE BOOK* and *God's Principles for Operating a Business*) are also available from Timberdoodle, a popular home-school supplier—the tape set at $5 discount! See the Timberdoodle writeup in the next section.

NEW**
The Economics Press, Inc.

Beyond the Bottom Line is a painless look at finance and accounting for the nonfinancial executive. It consists of a professional looking looseleaf binder and 32 four-page lessons sent one each week. Most lessons end with a quickie quiz, with the correct answers thoroughly explained.

The topics cover the whole range of financial considerations, from reading balance sheets and income statements to limiting tax liability. Each unit is well-written and assumes no prior knowledge of the material. All terms used are carefully defined and the concepts are all carefully explained. I found I could read and take in one of their lessons in about 15 minutes. The once a week pace was just right to let me digest one lesson before moving on to the next.

This course is particularly valuable for those to whom business finance seems more like a black art than a science. One of us in this family (naming no names) has never been able to understand how banking works, which is why she (oops! a hint!) sent away for this course. Even folks who are "accounting disabled" can understand the clear explanations and illustrations in this excellent program.

I would highly recommend *Beyond the Bottom Line* for anyone contemplating starting a business and for anyone already in the business world who wants to understand those hard-to-handle numbers.—Bill Pride

NEW**
The Hume Company, Inc.
Successful Business Management, $15/lesson plus shipping.

Extremely attractive, slick self-instruction program for fledgling entrepreneurs. Once you sign up for this program, every month an envelope arrives in your mailbox. Inside you'll find two lessons on aspects of business management. The fancy binder and a free Special Report come with the first issue. You also get a comprehensive guide to key business terms and concepts, and a problem-solver index. The latter is a topical index to the whole course, and is obviously designed to whet your appetite for continuing all the way through with this program.

The program's whole title is *Successful Business Management: How to Make Money in an Independently-Owned Business*. (It sounds like they've been reading Jeffrey Lant's books, doesn't it?) Now, let's list the lesson titles. Strategies for Success. Other People's Money (how to raise capital). Planning for Success (defining and achieving your business goals). Why Keep Records (with simple how-tos). Avoiding the Cash Crunch (cash flow budgeting and forecasting). Maximizing Your Marketing Power (whatcha gonna sell, and to whom?). Working with Your Banker. Successful Tax Strategies. Negotiating the Best Deal. Building Your Organization (personnel how-tos). Business Growth and Management Style (how to lead and delegate). How to Improve Your Sales. Dealing with Your Employees. Location Can Mean Everything. Successful Advertising Strategies. Organizing Your Business (partnership, corporation, or what?). Buying a Business: The Perils and Profits. Improving Your Financial Profile (using financial statements and ratios). Computerizing Your Business. Your Business and the Law. Making the Best Use of Your Advisors. Credit and Collection Techniques (my hint: don't *give* credit!). How to Franchise. Protecting Your Assets (business insurance howtos). Working Effectively with Your Vendors. Remove the Guesswork from Decision-Making. Effective Sales Techniques. Product Profitability (controlling production costs). Reducing Purchasing Costs. You can also order some optional follow-up units: Why When and How to Sell Your Business, Your Family and Your Business, Improving Your Lifestyle, and How to Protect Your Business.

As you can see, the writers assume you have put yourself in hock to finance this enterprise. For advice on debt-free business operations, you'll have to look to a handful of Christian writers and speakers (Bill Gothard springs to mind). For the best of mainstream managerial advice, though, this is a relatively inexpensive (compared to seminars and learning by doing) and effective way to pick up on a lot of what you need to know. If you're ready to quit dreaming about your own business and get serious, *Successful Business Management* is a good investment.—Bill Pride

NEW★★
Jeffrey Lant Associates
Cash Copy, $28.95 postpaid, includes free year's subscription to the *Sure-Fire Business Success Catalog*.

Cash Copy: How to Offer Your Products and Services So Your Prospect Buy Them . . . Now! is not the book you think it is. You think *Cash Copy* is just about how to write sizzling ad copy. Wrong. It's actually—and perhaps even unintentionally—a complete Christian approach to marketing allied with a powerful persuasive-writing a course.

Author Jeffrey Lant, writer of the "Sure-Fire Business Success" column and publisher of a catalog of books by the same name, gets into his pulpit and preaches with fierce abandon against what he calls "Selfish Marketing, Arrogant, Self-Absorbed Marketing." Marketing that talks about *you* and *your product* and *your image* and tells everyone how wonderful *you* are is a no-no, according to Mr. Lant. Client-centered copy and getting down to reality is where it's at. Client-centered copy means telling people exactly what your product is going to do for *them*, not how great your product or company is. It means selling more by having an attitude of serving, rather than a bullheaded obsession with selling.

This paradox may seem almost painfully self-evident, but believe me, it isn't. For example: "$25 OFF!" is not the same as "You can have $25 more in your pocket for Christmas presents if you take advantage of our special offer!"

Cash Copy is full of real-life examples in which Mr. Lant rips apart some all-too-typical examples of lackluster (yet seemingly OK) advertising. Learn to overcome the Professional Syndrome, the Bald Assertion, the Big Bad Words Complex. Learn the proper use of testimonials, how to repeat sell, how to lead with benefits instead of features. There's a whole lot more in the 480 pages, but (if you're like me) the pages will just fly by. It's fun to see this man in action!

Don't think of writing another brochure, flyer, business plan, response coupon, flyer, cover letter, proposal, catalog, ad, resumé, or even another begging letter home to Mom and Dad without reading this book *several* times. Since marketing is what makes or breaks businesses, don't even think of starting, or continuing to run, a business without getting and *studying* this book. Someday it's going to be a classic. Right now it's merely the best.

Visual Education Association
Compact Facts sets: *Accounting, Investments, Marketing,* and *Economics*, $4.95 each. Shipping extra. Grades 10–adult.

Basic information about each of these business areas presented in plain talk in sets of about 60 pocket-sized 2½ x 3½" cards each. Ideas, rules, formulas. At the price, you just can't lose!

MINDING YOUR BUSINESS: PEOPLE

NEW★★
Bits & Pieces
One year (12 issues), $17.55. Bulk subscriptions available. Ages 10–adult.

How do you describe a magazine like *Bits & Pieces*? For one thing, it doesn't look like anything else. Each issue is 4 x 6½" in size, 24 pages of two-color printing, loaded with maxims, stories, jokes, and inspiration all more or less on the topic of how to manage and get along with other people. Varying typefaces and line drawings—plus little lines separating each selection—make it easy to read a "bit" or a "piece" at a time. Clever sayings from famous people, good business ideas, folksy stories, lots of common sense in every issue. Some short samples from the latest issue:

> The trouble with telling a good story is that it always reminds the other guy of a dull one.

> Keep both feet on the ground and you'll be less likely to jump to a conclusion.

> You can't save face if you lose your head.

> Four out of five potential litigants will settle their disputes the first day they come together, if you will put the idea of arbitration into their heads.—Moses H. Grossman

> Someone once approached Helen Hayes on the set of a disaster movie called *Airport*.
> "Why, Miss Hayes, what are you doing in this picture?" she asked.
> "My dear," replied the first lady of the stage, "I supply the sexagenarian appeal."

That issue also has some words from Ralph Waldo Emerson on the subject of courage, the story of why the top-paid executive in the world (in 1901) voluntarily tore up his employment contract and settled for a smaller salary, Thomas Edison's tribute to his mother, how an apple grower managed to turn hail damage into a selling point for his apples, how a clever toastmaster managed to pay a nice-sounding tribute to a figurehead committee chairman, Julia Ward Howe and Norman Vincent Peale on curing boredom with imagination, advice on how to motivate workers to want training, a fable about how to make the unbearable seem more bearable, a seven-point plan for how to make more friends in a week, and another fable about how fearing the worst can make it happen . . . plus dozens more anecdotes, proverbs, and funny sayings.

The idea behind *Bit & Pieces* is that people will soak up management theory and skills more readily if they enjoy what they're reading. The general thrust of the material is to nudge the reader to a balanced mixture of hard-driving work and appreciation for other people and life. Dependability, creativity, perseverance, and self-confidence are frequent themes of the selections. It's low-key, it's fun to read, and my kids have started a

Bit & Pieces collection, proving that you're never too young to start learning to manage!

NEW★★
The Economics Press, Inc.
Supervisory Styles video: 3-day preview, $45; 7-day rental, $145; purchase price, $395.

Are you about to become a supervisor or manager? Then you'd better take a quick inventory of your personality, according to the folks at The Economics Press. They have produced a 25-minute video demonstrating four flawed character roles into which many people fall when trying to deal with subordinates. The scolding parent. The aggressive bully. The nice-guy pushover. The old-fashioned authoritarian boss. The video shows these characters in action, including the reactions of employees to these character types, then gives advice on how to overcome these negative management styles. I can't tell you if the video is worth the money or not, since I haven't seen it.

NEW★★
Executive Strategies
Executive Strategies newsletter subscription includes free *Black Book of Executive Politics*.

How to get ahead in the corporation. That's the subject of *Executive Strategies* (the newsletter) and *The Black Book of Executive Politics* (the book). Don't kid yourself: it's a rat race, and you'd better know what you're doing before diving into it. The focus is on problems—corporate shakeups, credit-grabbing bosses, backstabbing peers, insubordinate underlings, rumormongers, impossible deadlines—and how to survive and thrive in this high-pressure environment.

Executive Strategies is not another winning-through-intimidation rag, but it's not exactly a Mr. Nice Guy newsletter either. You're not supposed to undermine your boss or fellow workers, but you aren't supposed to automatically trust them, either. It's for competitive, ambitious people with a pragmatic outlook, not for those who see their mission in life as helping other people succeed.

NEW★★
The Hume Company, Inc.
Successful Business Management, $15/lesson plus shipping.

We described the *Successful Business Management* course above. Besides information on money management and financial decision-making, it includes several units on negotiating, personnel how-tos, leadership, delegation, employee relations, and other "people" issues.

UPDATED★★
INC. Magazine
One year (12 issues), $24.

INC. magazine is a practical source of information for wannabe fast-track execs and sole proprietors, and real help for the real thing. Lots of articles and advice for owners and execs of small and mid-sized businesses. Real-life stories about the trials and tribulations of various company founders. Big emphasis on managing your workers so they *want* to produce, rather than management by fear or bribes. Book reviews, how-to tips, tax info. No "new product" press releases or photos. Lots of small ads from franchise operators in the back of the magazine. Muscular writing. Fun to read. Find out about the pitfalls of doing business before you fall in the pits! Slight greedhead emphasis from time to time—inevitable, I suppose, in a magazine focusing on business success—countered by laid-back subscribers who write letters objecting to what they see as too much emphasis on fast growth.

Compared to magazines like *Success* and *Entrepreneur,* *INC.* is a bastion of intelligence and old-fashioned journalistic values. The editors and writers dig deep to uncover both sides of each business's story: its successes *and* its failures. *INC.* also philosophizes about such things as how to treat workers fairly and whether companies should practice "social responsibility" by running welfare-like programs or just by hiring a lot of people and doing a good job. Plus deeply researched articles like the famous annual *INC.* 500 report on the 500 fastest-growing small companies in America, or the annual report on the business climate in each state in the Union.

Unlike some other magazines I could mention, *INC.* is not loaded with breathless ads promising untold millions if you send in TODAY for the SPECIAL REPORT on HOW TO MAKE MILLIONS!!!! Rather, it's loaded with ads for expensive cars, expensive liquors, and expensive business equipment. The average subscriber makes over $90,000/year, according to *INC.*'s own figures—and *INC.* has over 640,000 subscribers.

INC., in brief, is the magazine for those who are really making it in business, as opposed to those who just hope they will. Of course, you don't have to be rich to subscribe—I've had a subscription for years!

NEW★★
Timberdoodle
Business by the Book, $12.95. *God's Principles of Operating a Business*, $45. Shipping extra.

Timberdoodle carries Larry Burkett's business management advice at a discount. *Business by the Book: The Complete Guide of Biblical Principles for Business Men and Women* is Larry's comprehensive guide to biblical management principles.

Larry Burkett, a well-known Christian business and financial counselor with an organization of his own, covers issues like what goals we should have for our businesses, the role of the spouse, keeping business promises, hiring and firing, employee pay, borrowing, lending, tithing, retirement, and so on. The book is enlivened with numerous true anecdotes.

Now, I'm going to tell you that I don't agree with everything in this book. I think Larry is a bit too quick to cede authority to the government. Nowhere in his book does he suggest Christian businessmen should challenge *any* government laws or rulings, no matter how egregiously unbiblical or unfair. He also believes it's OK to employ mothers of preschoolers, thus throwing the poor kids into day care, without any attempt to grapple with the business owner's responsibility for this situation. Even under slavery the owner had to take care of the kids of his slaves! Nor is there any serious discussion of how scriptural principles regarding slaves and slave owners apply to modern employers and employees, or any suggestions for how modern Christians can help buy each other out of economic slavery. (Startup capital, anyone?) Even with all these gaps, this is a fun read, and on the areas he emphasizes most, Larry Burkett is rock-solid. Truth is, there's nothing better out there on this subject.

If you'd rather listen than read, Larry's audiocassette series, *God's Principles of Operating a Business*, covers similar ground. His speaking style has more impact than mere words on a page, and if you're the sort who likes to "read" while driving or jogging, it'll only take you 15 hours or so to go through the 11 cassettes. They come attractively packaged in a case, with a minimalist outline to jog your memory. I listened most of the way through this series while exercising on our treadmill, and found the tapes so interesting that I had incentive to exceed my planned exercise time again and again! The only problem with listening to these tapes solo is that you'll have to replay them to share the good points with your spouse or business colleagues, as you're sure to want to.

AUDIO AND VIDEO BUSINESS COURSES

Audio-Forum

Listen Your Way to Success, $39.50. *Effective Speaking for Managers*, $49.95. *Speed Learning* modules, $125 each. *Please Come to Order*, $49.50. *Giving a Good Speech/The Art of Conversation*, $10.95. *Learning from the World's Worst Salesmen*, $10.95. Steve Allen's *How to Make a Speech*, $10.95. *Make Time Work for You*, $34.50. *Successful Entrepreneurship*, $69.50. *How to Start a Home Business*, *Great Home Businesses*, *Teenage Business Opportunities*, $10.95 each. *How to Start and Manage Your Own Business* , $79.50. *Public Relations: Do It Yourself*, *Advertising: Do It Yourself* , $59.50 each. *Profitable Spare-Time Hours*, $10.95. *Tax-Saver Accounting System*, $79.50. Shipping extra.

Much wider selection of business self-help courses than I've found elsewhere, tucked among a potpourri of New Age teaching and pop psychology. Once you've fought your way past *Romantic Love and Sexuality*, *Power of Self-Esteem*, and *Self-Transformation Through the New Hypnosis*, you find some truly interesting stuff. Audio-Forum has *Listen Your Way to Success*, *Effective Speaking for Managers*, and all the *Speed Learning* modules. Now hear this: *Please Come to Order* (on the art of managing meetings), *Giving a Good Speech/The Art of Conversation*, *Learning from the World's Worst Salesmen* (sounds like fun!), Steve Allen's *How to Make a Speech* (this I've heard: it's a good tape), and *Make Time Work for You*.

OK, that was just for starters.

Successful Entrepreneurship by A. David Silver includes a 200-page book and six cassettes on the following subjects: Characteristics of Successful Entrepreneurs, The Entrepreneurial Process, Survival Plans for Entrepreneurs, Financing Strategies for the New Business, What Kind of New Business to Start, and Entrepreneurial Growth Techniques.

If you're not playing in this league, *How to Start a Home Business* by Gary Null is only $10.95 for one cassette. *Great Home Businesses*, by the same author at the same price, includes case histories. Richard Berman also has several tapes. His *Teenage Business Opportunities* might interest you. According to the blurb "this cassette is packed with solid, practical information about how teenagers can make as much as $200 a week after school and during vacations."

Also for entrepreneurs: *How to Start and Manage Your Own Business*, *Public Relations: Do It Yourself*, *Advertising: Do It Yourself*, *Profitable Spare-Time Hours*, and the *Tax-Saver Accounting System*. You want more? Then ask for their Personal Development catalog.

Learn, Inc.

Top Selling, Listen Your Way to Success, $39.95 each. *Effective Speaking for Managers,* $59.95. *Speed Learning,* $145 for each of these modules: Medical, Data Processing, Science/Engineering, Management, and Finance/Accounting. *Speed Learning* video (VHS or Beta), $195 for each module listed above. Standard Edition of *Speed Learning,* $120 audio, $170 video.

Another catalog of self-help and business tapes, with a slant toward language usage training (including foreign languages) and learning techniques.

Speed Learning, billed as "much more than speed reading," is supposed to help you understand, remember, and use more of what you read. Not a rehash of the eye-training exercises and speed drills offered by other programs, *Speed Learning* concentrates on improving your thinking and memory skills. Special modules are available containing an additional workbook with reading material and exercises from particular professional fields. Two hundred thousand people have taken this course.

Listen Your Way to Success focuses on listening skills for managers. It comes with three cassettes, guidebook, listening test, and workbook and a promise that it will "improve your comprehension and retention by at least 100 percent!"

Top Selling, yet another Learn, Inc. product, is directly geared to salesmen. The ad says, "People hate to be sold—but love to buy! They buy because they think we understand them, not because they understand our products or services!" All the same, the course tells you how to professionally handle an interview as well as how to psyche out the prospect.

Effective Speaking for Managers is just one of Learn, Inc.'s product aimed at corporate dundermouths. Mainly focusing on public speaking, it also covers telephone technique and one-to-one conversations.

Learn, Inc. has lots more, some mentioned elsewhere in this book and some not.

NEW★★
Personal Progress Library
Annual membership fee, $199/division.

It's my own fault for not sending back the little card, but I don't have all the details on this business and self-help audio- and videocassette lending program. From the little card, it sounds good. To quote:

NEVER BUY ANOTHER AUDIO CASSETTE!
Borrow them instead!

The nation's largest LENDING LIBRARY of self-help programs NOW OFFERS all of today's most popular audio and video programs on personal and professional success.

Nominal Membership Fee provides you with:
• Personalized Curriculums
• Unbiased Program Recommendations
• Unlimited exchange of Sybervision, Nightingale-Conant, and Career Track programs plus hundreds more nationally acclaimed audio and video programs for free!

Convenient delivery and pick-up.

The library comes in three "divisions": Personal Development, Professional Success, and Real Estate.

If you like to listen more than you like to read, and if you have a large appetite for business advice, this might be worth looking into.

Soundview Executive Business Summaries
One year subscription, $69.50.

Who reads those thick business books? Do you? Do I? If you'd like the info in the books, but don't have time to struggle through 500 pages to get to the choice stuff, here's a possible solution. Executive Business Summaries is a subscription service of eight-page book summaries. They pick what they think are the best books and assign each to a professional writer who prepares a summary. "*Not* a review (someone's opinion). *Not* a digest (book excerpts strung together). A skillful distillation that preserves the content and spirit of the *entire* book." So says the promo piece.

You receive a minimum of 30 summaries—two or three a month. You can also purchase back issues to catch up on what's not quite new but still is relevant. Back issues are only available to subscribers.

Books summarized in the past include *Successful Direct Marketing Methods, Getting to Yes, How to Become a Successful Consultant in Your Own Field, Entrepreneurial Management, How to Succeed in Your Own Business, The Organized Executive, The Art of Managing People, In Search of Excellence, Service America, Robert Half on Hiring . . .*

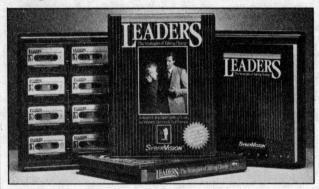

NEW**
SyberVision
Achievement, Leaders, $69.95 each for 8 audiocassettes and study guide. The Effective Managers series, $95/module. Shipping extra.

SyberVision's philosophy is to find the winners and let them tell and model how they did it. The *Achievement* and *Leaders* tape sets are all based on former Stanford University neuropsychology researcher Dr.

Karl Pribram's studies of those who excel in these attributes. Each includes "a fascinating series of exercises that will teach you to saturate your own nervous system with sensory-rich images of success." Hm. It's true that if you can't even imagine where you are going, you are unlikely to get there. On the other hand, I suspect that the parts of these tapes that deal with the nitty-gritties of actually doing something, as opposed to just thinking about it, however fiercely, are what really provides any success on the part of the user. "If wishes were horses, beggars would ride."

Somewhat more standard is the Effective Manager series by Brian Tracy. Each module is a short seminar in itself, with two audiocassettes, one 60-minute video covering the same material, and two workbooks with full program notes and study guide. The series of 14 modules covers everything from how to hire and fire, to motivating people toward peak performance, to executive time management, to selling skills. You get a 25 percent discount if you purchase the entire 14-program library at once.

Sybervision has tons more business self-help and management video and audio courses, some of which look frankly New Age and others of which are more traditional. Beware of psychological "think 'n be rich" approaches and overrated experts and stick with the courses that focus on how-tos, is my advice.

CHAPTER THIRTY-ONE

TEST PREPARATION AND COLLEGE ENTRANCE

Personally, I think college today is overpriced and overrated. This is not sour grapes: I have two college degrees myself and my father is a college professor. The problem is that almost immediately after I graduated, college tuition went through the roof and college faculties fell under the spell of Political Correctness. To quote from Brad Miner and Charles Sykes, two guys who edited the *National Review College Guide* and who know a lot about life on campus:

> American higher education is in crisis: admissions standards have been lowered, curricula debased, and courses trivialized. Many professors have put aside teaching in favor of research and writing, leaving their students in the hands of graduate teaching assistants (T.A.s), who have little more education than undergraduates and no classroom experience (let alone tested skill); and restrictions on free speech have been imposed on students in the name of diversity, with the result that the educational environment has become highly politicized. Universities that were once bastions of Western civilization are today centers of deconstruction and despair.

If you are a high school student who has yet to visit a college, or a parent whose last days on campus were twenty years ago, you may be shocked to discover how far the intellectual environment at some schools has deteriorated, how politicized things are. Feminism (including its lesbian subspecies) and feminist studies, black studies and affirmative action, gay rights and "sensitivity" rules—these are few of the enthusiasms that now parade in academia under the banner of diversity. . . . [Some] professors and administrators have taken to using the classroom—almost no matter what subject is supposed to be taught—as a propaganda cell.

One might be able to live with that if students were being well educated, but in many cases they are not. As the Gallup Organization recently reported, 25 percent of America's college seniors could not tell the difference between the words of Stalin and Churchill; could not distinguish the language of *Das Kapital* [Karl Marx's communist opus] from the U.S. Constitution; could not even recall that Christopher Columbus first reached the New World before 1500. . . . The Gallup report concluded: "Using the standard 'A' to 'F' scale . . . 55 percent of the students would have received a grade of 'F' and another 20 percent a 'D.'"

Meanwhile, *Reader's Digest* runs articles with titles like "Who Says College Campuses are Safe?," in which we discover that

> Despite the idyllic images college brochures present, violence is a fact of life on the nation's campuses. Last year colleges reported to the FBI a total of 1990 violent crimes—robbery, aggravated assault, rape, and murder. This is a startling number, considering the fact that about 90 percent of U.S. colleges do not report crime statistics. [In other words, the *real* number

of violent crimes was at least 19,900, and since the college who don't report are likely to be those with the greatest crime rate, it may be a whole lot higher than that.—MP] The incidence of property crime was even greater—more than 107,000 cases of burglary, larceny, arson, and motor-vehicle theft at reporting schools alone. [Again, you need to multiply by 10 or more to get the true number of property crimes—a startling 1,000,000-plus.—MP] Shockingly, 78 percent of the violent crimes were committed by students, according to the Center for the Study and Prevention of Campus Violence.

Well, I'm not all that shocked, because human nature being what it is, once people get the idea that they can commit crime with impunity, it's natural for them to do so. When I went to college, kids knew that you could do almost anything on campus and get away with it, from smoking pot to stealing food from dorm refrigerators. Even rape and assault aren't handled the same way on campus as they are in the real world.

Since the downfall of *locus parentis* rules, when colleges took responsibility for acting as students' parents and monitoring their behavior, colleges have gone to the other extreme of avoiding all responsibility for keeping students in line. The new solutions to the crime problem on campus still do not include holding the culprits personally responsible; that would mean up to a million kids expelled from college per year, according to the crime statistics.

REFOMING COLLEGE

Colleges have no real incentive to change for the better, because they exercise a virtual monopoly on the granting of lifetime success to young people—at least in the public mind. (Interesting note: a large percentage of company founders never graduated from college.) Everybody is convinced that the road to success lies through college, which is why we keep putting up with the outrageous tuition and the dumbing-down of

the curriculum, not to mention the infantile political fads of faculties and administrators. Parents don't want to inquire too closely into what's really going on; they just want Junior to own that scrap of parchment with B.S., M.S., or Ph.D. on it. Students are delighted with the booze, sex, drugs, and party atmosphere. (Students who *aren't* delighted may not even get in; admissions counselors admit to searching for "well-rounded" students who enjoy partying. I've heard of Asians with straight A's being rejected because they were "too narrowly focused on academics.") Employers, the vital link in upholding the university/college educational monopoly, persist in requiring a college degree as a prerequisite for almost any worthwhile position. (This is *really* stupid, since business has to expand its own training programs every year to compensate for the decreasing skills of college graduates.)

What today's colleges need is a good stiff dose of competition, which they aren't likely to get anytime soon because of all the gazillion federal and state regulations forcing any new college to hire people whose philosophies and lifestyles are at odds with any credible conservative or Christian position. Strictly religious institutions have a small dispensation of grace—my husband's seminary, for example, in order to keep its accreditation had to hire a female professor to teach the all-male ministry students, but she didn't *have* to be a feminist. To be accredited, seminaries also have to subject their students to large doses of liberal theology ("current modern scholarship"). In contrast, during their entire seminary course the students at my husband's Presbyterian seminary never were required to read one book that Calvin, the father of Reformed theology, wrote. Between federal and state requirements and accreditation-committee requirements, hardly any higher-education institution can call its soul its own.

An obvious solution would be for large industries to start hiring kids straight out of high school and training them themselves. Since kids *pay* to go to college, it's hard to see why they should squawk at a free, or cheaper, education leading to an assured job. Another solution would be for our churches to finally take their discipling job seriously, realize this includes academics as well as personal Bible-study tips, and set up church university systems run according to church principles. (This has been done before. All the major universities in the U.S.A. were founded by churches.) Another solution is for large numbers of us to start our own companies, teach ourselves what we need to know on our own (using resources like *Big Book*), and then *not* require college degrees from the people we hire.

I am not against education; I'm all for it. I just hope that the colleges of America will start providing real educations sometime soon, instead of serving as Ministries of Partying and Propaganda, and in the meantime I don't feel obligated to spend our my family's time or money where it isn't deserved. A mind is a terrible thing to waste.

WHAT COLLEGE IS LIKE, HOW COLLEGE HAS CHANGED

NEW★★
American Association of Bible Colleges
Annual directory, $7.50 postpaid.

This is the place to call or write if you're interested in attending a Bible college. AABC is the government-recognized accrediting agency for undergraduate Bible-college education, and has information on these colleges not found in typical college guides.

The latest (1990–91) version of the AABC's *Directory* is a 142-page spiral-bound handbook. Sections include: Accredited Institutions (the bulk of the book), Candidates for Accreditation, Applicants for Accreditation, AABC Board/Commisions/Staff, Closures/Merges/Name Changes/Withdrawals, and two indexes of colleges, one alphabetical and one geographical.

The information about institutions includes their names, addresses, and telephone numbers . . . year established, accredited, reaffirmed, and the date of the next AABC review . . . denominational affiliation . . . schoolyear schedule (e.g., "semester" or "4-1-4"), fall full-time equivalent enrollment . . . staff members, with titles . . . and degrees and majors offered.

This is obviously not enough information to enable you to choose a college, but it should at least help you narrow down the prospects.

American College Testing Program (ACT)
College Planning/Search Book, $10 postpaid. Updated yearly.

If you absolutely can't live without a college experience, ACT's *College Planning/Search Book* is an excellent place to start. The Planning Section helps you decide what you're looking for in a college, and guides you through the application process. The Search Section displays up-to-date information about more than 3,000 colleges in several helpful ways. You can, for example, look up schools that offer Forestry, or colleges in Wisconsin, or the student profile of St. Louis U. Vital facts such as cost, religious affiliation, and composition of student body are laid out straightforwardly.

NEW★★
American Vision
Surviving College Successfully, $10 postpaid. Free newsletter, *The Biblical Worldview*, is well worth getting.

Gary DeMar's *Surviving College Successfully* comes out swinging. Your kids, Gary says, are going to face real battles in college. That kindly college professor may (and probably will) try to destroy their religious faith. Those great guys at the frat house may (and probably will) apply pressure to fornicate, swear, get drunk, and other ungood things. (Can we call this "beer pressure"?) Get wise, kid, before they get you.

Surviving College comes in two parts. Part One is a very clear and helpful explanation of what young Junior from Oshkosh will find lurking in the halls of Harvard or even good ol' State U. Gary not only tells you that your Christian worldview will be challenged; he goes beyond that and explains *what those other worldviews are* and *why they matter*. This information is better and more useful than what Junior is likely to get in his philosophy courses. Gary also includes a section on how to keep the faith even though Junior is submerged in (and subsidizing) the anti-Christian collegiate culture. Part Two tells how to be a better student: how to study, research, memorize, take tests, etc. more effectively.

I'll tell you the truth—the main effect of this book on parents should be to make us question the dubious value of four or more years at $5,000–$10,000 or more per year with the Thought Police thundering away at our offspring's head. Gary doesn't even tell the worst of it, either. Such as the feminist profs who persecute students who even *ask questions* in class. Or the proposed (and installed, in some places) courses in "sensitivity" that require you to *affirm* (not just study about) a non-Christian belief in the equal goodness of, say, homosexuality and Christian marriage. Not to mention the courses in witchcraft, porn films, and so on funded with your and my tax dollars.

The one question this book never answers, and that I hope Gary will answer in a sequel, is: What can Christians do to change the university? Why do we just have to "survive," taking it on the chin all the time? And if we *can't* change the university, why should we subsidize it? If Christians let the present crowd keep running higher education, how long until a university degree is nothing but proof the bearer has denied Christ and burned incense to Caesar? Questions that demand a verdict, to paraphrase Josh McDowell (who, by the way, has been barred from many college campuses because his message is "too Christian").

NEW★★
Conservative Book Club
Choosing a College: a Guide for Parents and Students by Thomas Sowell, $7.95. *Profscam* by Charles J. Syke, $18.95.

Choosing a College is aptly subtitled "An Outspoken Look at Admissions, Campus Life, & the Academic World by a Professor & Scholar." Thomas Sowell does a masterful job of raising the questions that ought to go into a parent's decision of what college his son or

daughter should attend. He does discuss all the obvious questions about scholastic ability, finances, type of college, etc. But he goes well beyond these to questions you might not have thought to ask, like, "Can my Florida-born and -raised daughter stand the cold, long nights at University of Minnesota?" or "Will the smog in Los Angeles be too much for Junior's asthma?"

Unlike other "how to send your kid to college" writers, Sowell pulls no punches. He digs out the dirt that colleges and universities like to keep hidden under the rug. Is the college you or your children are considering shot through with Marxism in the required courses? Are Feminist Thought Police running the English department? Are the dorms set up like freebie brothels? Are homosexuals openly recruiting on campus? How about the amount of rape and robbery on campus? Are you willing to live with a social environment in which robbers and rapists are dealt with by student-run ethics committees instead of by the courts? These are questions you should ask, before a member of your family gets more out of his or her college experience than your family bargained for.

Mr. Sowell (who is black) has a whole chapter on special considerations for minority students. Again he deals with realities. He demonstrates how top universities sabotage minority students when to meet artificial minority quotas they accept students who, if they were WASPs, would have been rejected. This results in a ripple effect. Top-grade minority students (who would do well at B-level colleges) get drafted by A-level colleges, where only a few can academically survive. Then the B-level colleges accept the next best group of minority students—those who would have done well at C-level colleges, but for whom B-level work is just too much. And so it goes on down the line, with each batch of students accepted at schools where they are unlikely to make it. This constant misfitting of students and schools results in enormously high drop-out rates for minority students and the perpetuation of an unfair stereotype that "these people just can't do the work," when in fact they would do fine work if the recruiting process weren't skewed against reality. His solution is for minority students to accurately appraise their academic background and either pick an institution that fits it or do extra work *ahead* of time to prepare themselves for the college world.

This book is a must for any parent who wants to send his child to college.

Another book you shouldn't miss is *Profscam*, in which author Charles J. Syke, who like me is the child of a college professor, proves beyond a shadow of a doubt that the direct and ultimate reason for the collapse of higher education in the U.S.A.—which has led directly to the collapse of K–12 education as well—is "the selfish, wayward, and corrupt American university professor." Harsh words, yes? But Sykes (a former editor of *Milwaukee* magazine) proves, in a very readable and not at all hysterical style, that what used to be Higher Education has become Hire Education. Thanks to tenure, professional peer review, and above all the university professor's built-in financial incentive to prefer research to teaching, the concept of Christian civilization that used to underpin university education has given way to trendier-than-thou civilization-bashing.

College kids, Sykes proves, are *not,* in most cases, receiving the education their parents have sacrificed to provide. Instead, they are being "educated" in mass classes and by graduate students, many incompetent as English-speakers, who themselves are controlled by what amounts to an academic Thought Police.

This all has tremendous implications for Christian parents, and particularly home-schooling parents, who persist in setting a college education as their children's *summum bonum.*

There are still some good colleges out there, but you are not likely to find or recognize them until you read this book. *Profscam* shows you how to tell the turkeys from the winners.

Crossway Books
This Present Darkness, $9.95.

Bestselling Christian novel that explores what happens when nogoodniks decide to take over a town by capturing its university. Dramatic conflict between angels and demons, spiritualist Mafia types and small-town Christians. Fast-moving plot, muscular dialogue. No sci-fi stuff: the book is based on what's happening now, brother. Would *you* send *your* daughter to Whitmore College?

NEW★★
Wolgemuth & Hyatt Publishers
The National Review College Guide, $14.95.

This book is a real find! Since it is subtitled "America's 50 Top Liberal Arts Schools," I wasn't terribly interested in it at first, figuring it would be about places like Harvard and Radcliffe. (I'm from Boston. Yawn.) Actually, it's about the colleges the editors of *National Review* consider the best. This is a whole different ball of wax!

When Charles Sykes (author of *ProfScam*) and Brad Miner (literary editor at *NR*) go looking for colleges, they are looking for traditional academic excellence. "Oppression studies" courses, indoctrination seminars like "Goddess Worship: The Philosophy of Women's Religion," and guts like Brown University's "Rock 'n Roll is Here to Stay" earn no brownie points in their blue book. On the other hand, colleges with a core curriculum that attempts to educate students in the great works and thoughts of Western culture are praised and exalted. And they have actually found some such colleges—50 of them—to describe in detail.

The colleges in *The National Review College Guide* are not picked just because of their conservative orthodoxy. Some of them, like Columbia, aren't conservative at all. (A preponderance do have and enforce at least semi-sane standards of conduct and philosophy, though.)

Nor are they inferior in the ways that count to the Ivy League. Whether you're measuring percent of graduates who go on to earn doctorates, or percent accepted at the medical and law schools of their choice, often the colleges in this book *beat* the Ivy Leaguers. Grove City College graduates, for example, average an incredible *99 percent* acceptance rate at the law, medical, and graduate schools to which they have applied, as the guide is delighted to point out!

This is not a "quantitative" guide like the elephantine tomes at the high school counselor's office. The only stats for each school are its year founded, total cost (room, board, tuition, etc.), total enrollment, total applicants (including percent accepted and percent of those that graduate), SAT averages, financial aid (percent who apply and get it), and whether or not the college has a ROTC program. Addresses and enrollment schedule are of course also provided.

Aside from that, the book is made up mainly of insightful reviews of the institutions themselves: their histories, core curriculums (described in detail), religious and social atmosphere, special programs (such as student years abroad), and any current power struggles agitating the faculty and administration. The authors, university insiders, know if a liberal coup is in the offing or has just been foiled, giving you clues to the future of each institution as well as to its past.

Rereading what I've written so far, it seems somewhat lackluster and ho-hum. So let's give you a sip of the book itself. From the writeup of Saint Anselm College:

> In addition to the Portraits program, Saint Anselm has an impressive core curriculum that includes a two-semester freshmen English course, three courses in philosophy, including "philosophy of Nature and Man" and "Ethics"; three courses in theology, including "Biblical Theology"; two semesters of a foreign language beyond elementary work; and two semesters of laboratory science. Students must also pass a comprehensive examination in their major field before graduating. There are no junk courses at Saint Anselm and each of the various programs appears strong.

> Particular note should be taken of Saint Anselm's major in "Liberal Studies in the Great Books," which includes six seminars as a preceptorial. How good is this program? Just consider. Students in the first seminar, on ancient authors, begin by reading selections from among a list of authors that includes Homer, Aeschylus, Sophocles, Xenophone, Thucydides, Plato, Aristophanes, Plutarch, and Aristotle. The seminar on Roman literature exposes them to Vergil, Lucretius, Cicero, Tacitus, Seneca, Plutarch, St. John the Evangelist, St. Ignatius of Antioch, and Plotinus. Turning to medieval writers: the Great Books seminar focuses on Boethius, St. Augustine, St. Bede, St. Anselm, *Beowulf*, *The Cloud of Unknowing*, St. Bonaventure, and St. Thomas Aquinas. The seminar on the Renaissance draws from Erasmus, Bacon, St. Thomas More, Machiavelli, Montaigne, Shakespeare, and Milton. The seminar on modern writers chooses from among Galileo, Hobbes, Descartes, Locke, Molière, Hume, Kant, Pope, and Goethe. Late modern writers studied include Madison, Hamilton, De Tocqueville, Hegel, Dostoevsky, Kierkegaard, Nietzsche, Tolstoy, and Newman. The seminars are rounded out by a preceptorial that studies a single book or author. With the help of several individual conferences with the professor, students write a long essay on a topic related to the material being studied . . . .

> If this were not impressive enough, students in the major are also required to take a fine arts elective, two English literature courses, and five philosophy courses, including "Formal Logic," "Metaphysics," and "Philosophy of Science."

> This entire picture is all the more remarkable when one considers that while students at Saint Anselm are seeking out "what is true, what is good, and what is beautiful," students are taking "The Sociology of Sport" at Dartmouth, "Television as Culture" at Middlebury, and "Women's Lives and Women's Lyrics" at Amherst.

There's pages and pages more on Saint Anselm; I've only quoted a fraction of the writeup (just enough to help you see how hopelessly sick Yale and Brown look next to Saint Anselm!) And remember there are 49 more colleges of similar calibre featured in this guide!

Remember, we're talking about *liberal arts* colleges. Many of these colleges are strong in science and math, though, and all of them have at least some courses in those areas. Some even have arrangements with affiliated engineering colleges, so don't skip this book just because you're technically oriented.

Bible institutes are not included, although Wheaton, Baylor, and a whole group of Roman Catholic institutions made it in. The editors' definition of "sectarian" also somehow allows them to include Brigham Young University while leaving out Bob Jones University (whose graduates also have impressive records).

The reason why "many religious schools are missing from *NR*'s recommended list" is that "although these schools are conservative, they fail effectively to educate their students in the full spirit of academic freedom." Another reason: many Christian colleges are more strongly vocational than the liberal arts schools the guide intends to profile. Yet another reason: students who wish to attend a Christian school presumably find it easy to discover those schools, thanks to knowledgeable pastors.

The authors of *The National Review College Guide* expect you to browse, skipping only to the colleges of your interest. (To make this easier, all colleges are listed alphabetically in the book, and by geographical location on a separate list.) However, I'd urge you to read it *straight through* if you have a child of college age or are contemplating attending college yourself. Nowhere else can you get such a wonderful overview of what's available in college today and of the war for our culture's soul that is being waged in the no-longer-sacred halls of academe.

COLLEGE ALTERNATIVES, ALTERNATIVE WAYS TO GO TO COLLEGE

NEW**
Betterway Books
Home Study Opportunities, $9.95. Shipping extra.

"The Complete Guide to Going to School by Mail." Detailed school and program listings. Information on accreditation, admission requirements, program completion times, costs, and financial aid. A small section with information on K–12 programs as well as much larger sections on career, certificate, and degree programs. Advice on how to keep from being fleeced by unscrupulous fly-by-night practitioners.

Author Laurie M. Carlson has put her finger squarely on the legitimate frustrations many people feel about their educational experiences:

> I began this book because of my frustration with traditional institutions and their refusal to accept similar courses taken at other schools, along with the fact that graduate level courses I took more than six years ago are not transferable into any traditional graduate program. . . . I refuse to accept their opinion that knowledge "expires" after six years. . . .

> In years past, the only older students on campuses were bored housewives seeking to study something cultural or enriching, who had a husband more than

happy to oblige with supporting the costs. . . . I have a hunch that those of you reading this book are not so lucky as to have a financial backer ready to "spend you to college." You're probably like most of us, who work at a full-time job, wrangle kids and a home life, and seek to improve your lot in life through education. The problem for us is that the average State U is out of the question. Most colleges and universities do not tailor their programs to the likes of us in the "real world." We cannot fit our schedules to theirs. The fact is that we cannot obtain a degree without taking Philosophy 103, and Philosophy 103 is only offered spring semesters every other year, and only at 10:00 in the morning. How can you juggle a 10 A.M. class with your employer, even if he is very supportive? . . .

> Home study also fits the needs of so many who are unable to get to class because of physical limitations, or because they must remain at home to care for others, or to handle other responsibilities that prevent them from spending hours sitting at a desk in a traditional classroom. . . .

> I had some incredibly lousy courses at large universities, which I later supplemented with private home study courses of superior quality. . . . I guess what I enjoy about home study is that, compared to on-campus classes where you are largely at the mercy of the teacher's ability, in home study you are in charge, and you can get out of it what you put into it.

Since the book was published in 1989, you'd better verify the tuition prices and accreditation information for any school that interests you. However, *Home Study Opportunities* is an inexpensive, easy-to-use source for more information about individual National Home Study Council-accredited schools than you get in the NHSC brochure, plus a number of programs not accredited by NHSC.

NEW**
Bluestocking Press
Careers Without College, $7.95 plus $2 shipping.

Careers Without College: No B.S. Necessary has more going for it than a great title. It's an in-depth look at 10 open-ended careers you can get into without a college degree: advertising . . . banking . . . commercial art . . . data processing . . . fashion merchandising . . . finance . . . nursing . . . publishing . . . retail and restaurant management . . . and travel. Author Russo believes not every family is going to want to spring $35,000 to $70,000 for a college degree, especially when the quality of the educational product is sagging.

This is not a rah-rah book. Author Jo Ann Russo states,

> It sometimes seems that everyone is eager to give young people all kinds of advice about school, work, and life in general. Some advice can be very valuable; a lot must be taken with the proverbial grain of salt. But almost all of it concerns what you should do—where you *should* go to school, what companies you *should* apply to, what offers you *should* accept . . . I have absolutely no feelings one way or the other about what you *should* do, and the book is meant to reflect his objectivity. Read it. Sit down and think about what you *want* to do. Then do it.

Everything you need to know to embark on one of these careers is included. How to prepare for each career. Entry level jobs. Work environment. Career paths. Specialties in each field. What you can expect to make. What will be expected of you. How to compete with degreed applicants for the job. It's like a long chat with 10 experienced mentors, one from each field.

Is her advice good? I haven't personally worked in all of those fields, but as the sister of a woman who started working at a bank as a temporary secretary and ended up as a vice president, I know upward mobility still exists. Sure, she had a college degree or two, but they probably didn't know that when they hired her as a temp! The main thing is to get your foot in the door and show what you can do, and *Careers Without College* will help you do just that.

UPDATED**
Ten Speed Press
College Degrees by Mail (11th edition), $11.95. Over-sized, paperbound. Updated yearly.

BUY THIS BOOK!!! Dr. John Bear has put together the ultimate handbook of nontraditional education. "Nontraditional" means you don't spend four years in a stuffy classroom. Included are correspondence programs, short-term residency programs, after-hours and week-end programs, and even a section listing every known degree mill in the U.S.A. (just in case you want to buy Fido a Degree of Canine Knowledge for his birthday). This completely legitimate, incredibly well-researched book tells you how to get the degree you want, the way you want.

In the 11th edition of what used to be called *Bear's Guide to Non-Traditional College Degrees,* you discover Dr. Bear's choice of the 100 best schools that offer Bachelor's, Master's, doctorates, and law degrees by

home study. He devotes an entire page to each school, giving a full description, address, phone, fax number, key person to contact, cost, programs offered, accreditation status, and a personal evaluation.

Unlike so many resource books, *College Degrees by Mail* is delightful to read. Bear's descriptions of the colleges and universities are lively as well as informative. Dr. Bear also includes information on getting personalized counseling and assistance, equivalency and entrance exams, and advice for people in prison who want to earn college degrees.

Bear gets his information both from extensive questionnaires and phone calls, and from the letters readers write telling him about their educational experiences. You can't find a better guide. Someone you know could save thousands of dollars by reading this book.

GETTING IN & DOING WELL

NEW**
Louis Publishing
The Overnight Student, $4.95 plus 95¢ shipping. Ages 11–adult.

The Overnight Student by Dr. Michael L. Jones is a small volume of 63 pages. Yet it has the potential to *revolutionize* your children's higher education. Why? Because it presents a study method that literally enables college and high-school students to go from straight F's to straight A's, *without* any faddy gimmickry.

The *Overnight Student* method has been tested for years. It worked for its author, who failed every college class he was taking for two semesters in a row before he discovered it. After using this method, he went on to earn a doctorate! It also has worked for hundreds of people he has taught. It works for students, teachers, businessmen . . . anyone who needs to quickly master *and retain* a large amount of information.

Did you know that "we remember 14 percent of what we hear, 22 percent of what we both see and hear, 70 percent of the movies in our mind, and 91 percent of what we teach others"? OK, so *how* do we put this knowledge to use? This is where Dr. Jones excels. In a winsome, easy-reading fashion he eliminates all the obstacles you place between yourself and successful study habits. If you can read and write, you can read this book and *instantly* begin to excel in your studies.

Dr. Jones' study method is not only easy to implement, but scripturally-based. It involves a special, simple system of note-taking, plus instruction in how to teach yourself the content of what you are studying. Along with this come tips and inspiration that can dramatically improve your study abilities.

As I said, the method was designed for college and high-school students. Dr. Jones assumes you are attending classes in which the teacher lectures and expects you to take notes. Home-schooled teens *will* need to learn these skills, even if at present their education consists of self-study from books and informal instruction from parents. Sooner or later, all of us end up taking some kind of class. Sunday school. Bible classes. On-the-job training classes. Even the weekly sermon at your church provides an excellent opportunity to practice the skills taught in this book.

The Overnight Student can help students studying from books, too, provided the students are good at outlining their textbooks' contents. I have already suggested to Dr. Jones that he include information about outlining books in a future edition. In the meantime, it can help anyone who has organized information before him that he needs to learn.

NEW✱✱
Poppyseed Press
College Admissions: A Guide for Homeschoolers. $7.95 plus $1.20 postage.

I am not wildly enthusiastic about modern college "education." But if you're determined that Junior should have a college degree and aren't willing to save time and energy by getting one through the mail, Poppyseed Press can tell you how to get Junior into the college of his choice.

College Admissions: A Guide for Homeschoolers was written by a home-schooling mom. This book answers all your questions (and some you don't even know you should be asking) about how to get Junior through his tests, which standardized test(s) to take, how to jolly

along the admissions officer, and so on. Home schoolers have some special obstacles to hurdle, since we have no guidance counselors holding our hands and filling out forms for us. Find out what the obstacles are, and how to overcome them, from this book.

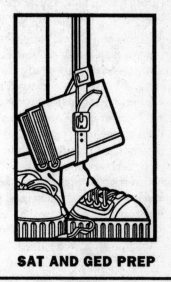

SAT AND GED PREP

In spite of all that our infinitely wise leaders have done to ensure that every kid, no matter how lazy and undisciplined, can get into a college *somewhere*, preferably at taxpayer expense, it's still true that your chances of getting into a "good" college improve if you produce a fancy performance on a college entrance test.

The SAT, whatever its failings, is about the last bastion resembling an objective standard of educational measurement that we have today. That being so, it provides a golden opportunity for home-schooled students to prove their merit. Many home schoolers have found that a good SAT score vindicates their entire home school program in many colleges' eyes.

The GED, while not an early-graduation option (see Appendix C), also provides a much-needed alternative to the common institutional high school diploma.

While you're considering the test preparation materials below, don't forget to check *Pride's Guide to Educational Software* for test-prep software, too!

UPDATED✱✱
Arthur Bornstein School of Memory Training
College Passport, 8 one-hour cassette tapes and 52-page workbook, $89.95 plus $4 shipping.

"How to Get Top SAT and GRE Scores." Strategies and memory techniques to help students prepare for the verbal and math challenges of these tests, presented by memory expert Scott Bornstein and a phenomenal female whose background includes teaching math in high school at the age of 19 (after having already received her college degree, of course!)

College Passport is very attractively packaged, and just as attractive in its teaching. No useless razzmatazz, but a lot of good, honest information about how the tests are administered and scored, coupled with vocabulary-building segments and math skill-building segments. You don't just review what you already knew. You learn the Greek and Latin roots and word parts from which tens of thousands of English words are formed. You also learn a number of important vocabulary words often used on the tests, using clever memory techniques. You walk through the math you'll be tested on. High interest, no boredom.

The workbook contains examples of major test questions, so you can test yourself. A really good program.

UPDATED**
Contemporary Books, Inc.
The New GED: How to Prepare, $10.75. GED Satellite Program books—*Writing Skills, Social Studies, Science, Literature and the Arts, Math*—$8.73 each. GED exercise books, $5.27 each.

Contemporary's GED prep series has review, instruction, exercises, explanations, practice tests, and strategies. Useful as a supplement for high-school juniors and seniors who want to be sure they *really* learned something, or as a core instructional program for adults pursuing the GED. The blurb says that Contemporary's *New GED: How to Prepare for the High School Equivalency Examination* has been "used by hundreds of thousands of GED candidates to earn their high school diploma."

The Satellite Program provides instruction and exercises for each of the five test areas. Sold directly by the publisher and through bookstores.

Educational Design
Inside Strategies for the SAT, $6.95. *GED Math, Reading Skills, Writing Skills, Science Test, Social Studies*, $5.95 each. Add 10% shipping.

The cover of Gary R. Gruber's *Inside Strategies for the S.A.T.* announces "Scores on the actual SAT have been raised an average of *133 points* and up to *300 points* by using the strategies in this book!" Dr. Gruber analyzed over 2,500 actual SAT questions, and came up with thinking strategies for decoding the questions and answering them quickly and correctly.

Educational Design's GED series doesn't come with so much advertising hype. I hope that this is because it is so great it needs no introduction. The *GED General Review* is not tremendously expensive, and it might be a good idea to see how well your home-schooled teen does on it. Just think how silly the state would look hassling you if your 13-year-old had already passed the GED!

NEW**
Educators Publishing Service, Inc.
Analogies 1, 2 and *3*, $4.70 each. *Analogies 1—6 Analogy and 6 Vocabulary Quizzes; Analogies 2—6 Analogy and 6 Vocabulary Quizzes;* and *Analogies 3—8 Analogy and 4 Vocabulary Quizzes*, $6.00 each. Add 8% shipping (minimum $3).

Can you remember back to your pre-college days (for some of us it's *way* back) to the SAT? I remember sweating through that long Saturday in one of the classrooms in my high school. The problems which gave me the most grief were verbal analogies:

> 6. ARMADA : SHIPS : :
>   a. herd : cattle
>   b. magazine : pages
>   c. wall : bricks
>   d. college : undergraduate
>   e. sweater : fabrics

Here is a way to get a little of the grief out of the way before the day of the test.

Analogies 2 and *Analogies 3* provide strategies and exercises for the potential SAT-taker. *Analogies 2* demonstrates techniques such as the bridge sentence, checking for multiple meanings, and handling two step analogies. *Analogies 3* is more of the same with harder problems. Each book contains extensive practice sets with vocabulary lists and answers. (*Analogies 1*, for junior high school, is not really SAT prep, but preliminary practice for this age level in solving analogy problems and adding vocabulary words.)

Analogies 1—6 Analogy and 6 Vocabulary Quizzes and *Analogies 2—6 Analogy and 6 Vocabulary Quizzes* are exactly what their name suggests. Not to be confused with the basic Analogies series reviewed above, these are booklets of analogy tests and vocabulary quizzes.

Anyone who is unfamiliar with the SAT would do well to master these books first.—Bill Pride

Jeffrey Norton Publishers
How to Take the SAT & PSAT, $26.95. Add $3.50 shipping.

Two cassette tapes plus 372-page book on test-taking strategies tuned to the SAT and PSAT. Basic advice on techniques like spotting key clues, avoiding wrong answers, and unearthing built-in answers.

For general test-taking strategies and study skills also see Jeffrey Norton's *Study for Success!,* reviewed in the "Study Skills" chapter in Volume 1 of this series.

NEW**
Learning at Home
Strategies for Success Reading, Strategies for Success Social Studies, Strategies for Success Science, Strategies for Success Mathematics, Strategies for Success Writing, $9 each. *GED Comprehensive Review Book,* $20. Shipping extra.

This *Strategies for Success* series is designed with the GED in mind. The sections in each book correspond to the topics covered in the GED.

Each 136-page book starts with a diagnostic test to point out the student's weak areas. You check off any incorrect answers on a skill preview chart. This points the student to the section in the book that deal with that topic.

Topics covered are: Reading—Finding Information, The Meaning of Words, The Main Idea, Organizing a Paragraph, and Interpreting What You Read. Social Studies—Geography, History, Political Science, Economics, and Behavioral Science. Science—Biology, Earth Science, Chemistry, and Physics. Mathematics—Whole Numbers—Addition and subtraction, Whole Numbers—Multiplication and Division, Fractions, Decimals, Percent, and Measurement. Writing—Capitalizing Correctly, Using Punctuation, Writing Clear Sentences, Nouns, Pronouns, and Adjectives, Using Verbs and Adverbs, and Correcting Your Spelling.

Each instructional section gives a brief lesson on its topic. Each section ends with a self test with questions similar to those the student would find on a GED test. The answers are given with explanations of why that particular answer is correct and the others aren't.

GED Comprehensive Review Book, as its name suggests, is a more complete version of the *Strategies for Success* series, all in one 640 page volume. It begins with a diagnostic test in all five subject areas. The results of the test show which subjects you need to spend the most time on.

Each section of the book gives a brief lesson and a sample. For example, the poetry section gives a sample poem. This is followed by a strategies section. In math, the strategies sections have to do with problem solving, such as eliminating unnecessary data or using estimation. In literature, the strategies are things like identifying elements of style or how to get the main idea out of a paragraph. The strategies section is followed by examples, a practice test, and a GED mini-test. Each section give the answers to the questions with thorough explanations.

These books do not come close to completely covering any of the topics. The whole numbers addition section in the mathematics book, for example, starts with addition of two digit numbers, assuming the student knows his addition facts. Having said this, these books still look like a great way to get your feet wet in preparing for the GED.—Bill Pride

NEW★★
Visual Education Association
SAT Prep Set, $7.95. All other vocabulary sets also $7.95 each. Shipping extra.

From Vis Ed Association, "The Study Card People Since 1950," now comes a set of their special self-study flash cards called the *SAT Prep Set*, or, more formally,

Preparatory Study Cards for SAT-Verbal. Inside the box you'll find 340 antonym question cards, 290 sentence-completion question cards, and 260 analogy question cards.

Each pocket-sized card has a typical SAT-style question on the front, with the correct answer on the back.

The included study guide gives tips on how to analyze each problem type and how the SAT-Verbal test works.

If this isn't enough, you can improve your vocabulary even more with the Vis Ed *English Vocabulary 1* and *2* sets, *Scientific & Technical Vocabulary* set, *Medical Terminology* set, *Computer Terminology* set, and *Legal Terminology* set.

CHAPTER THIRTY-TWO

CAREERS FROM ACCIDENT INVESTIGATION TO ZOOLOGY

Money, money, money. It's not the *only* reason adults sign up for educational programs! Knowledge is power, but it is also satisfaction, confidence, and even entertainment.

Adult education has come a long way from the rows of high-school dropouts bent over dog-eared textbooks under the fluorescent lights of an after-hours high school classroom. For many people, adult education still means pursuing a diploma, but in your home, not a classroom. Nor are high school diplomas the only credentials available to after-hours scholars. You can get a college degree, a Master's, or even a legitimate Ph.D. at home!

Academic degrees are not the whole story, either. You can learn hundreds of marketable skills at home, from accident investigation to zookeeping. Upgrade your present job, or change jobs, *without* wearing yourself to a frazzle with late-night classes!

And then there's the sheer joy of learning. Dazzle your friends with your wok cookery! Learn how to make new slipcovers! Design your own clothes! Immerse yourself in history! Develop a gorgeous calligraphic handwriting style! Study French and read Blaise Pascal in the original, or Russian and grapple with Dostoyevski and Solzhenitsyn.

I'm not saying you should try to "reach your potential." You can *never* reach your potential! If you lived a thousand years, you could still be learning new things in your tenth century. And wouldn't it be *fun!*

NOW, YOUR ULTIMATE SOURCE OF ADULT HOME LEARNING

Home education is much more than college degrees. It's vocational training, and hobbies, and religious instruction. It's courses on writing and art and fashion design. Where can you go to not only find academic degree programs, but also vocational programs and self-improvement courses? And if you spend 100 to 1,000 bucks by mail, how do you know you are getting a good product?

I firmly support the entrepreneurial spirit which moves people to set up new mail order courses. And it's true that not every reputable home study course is accredited by the National Home Study Council. Calvert School, for example, although it is accredited by the Maryland Department of Education has not sought NHSC accreditation. But the National Home Study Council's *voluntary* accreditation program can increase a shopper's confidence, especially when you are unacquainted with the companies that offer the program you need.

The National Home Study Council has very kindly given me permission to reprint their listing of accredited home study courses, and information about accreditation, for your information. The rest of this chapter is reprinted from their brochure, *NHSC 1990–91 Directory of Accredited Home Study Schools.* To receive a free brochure of your own, just write to the National Home Study Council office.

COMMENTS FROM THE NATIONAL HOME STUDY COUNCIL

WHAT IS HOME STUDY?

Home study is enrollment and study with an educational institution which provides lesson materials prepared in a sequential and logical order for study by students on their own. When each lesson is completed the student mails, or otherwise makes available to the school, the assigned work for correction, grading, comment, and subject matter guidance by qualified instructors. Corrected assignments are returned immediately to the student. This exchange provides a personalized student-teacher relationship.

Home study courses vary greatly in scope, level, and length. Some have a few lessons and require only weeks to complete, while others have a hundred or more assignments requiring three or four years of conscientious study.

ADVANTAGES OF HOME STUDY

Many courses provide complete vocational training. Others prepare you for upgrading in your present job, without losing experience or seniority. Avocational and hobby courses are also available.

Emphasis is on learning what you need to know. Instructional materials from accredited schools are up-to-date, clearly written and easy to understand.

Home study is especially suited for busy people who wish to increase their knowledge and skills.

With home study, you do not have to give up your job, leave home or lose income. You learn as you earn. The school comes to you. You receive individual attention, and you work at your own pace.

WHAT HOME STUDY ACCREDITATION MEANS

For more than 60 years the National Home Study Council has been the standard-setting agency for home study schools. The Council has progressively raised its standards. Its accrediting program employs procedures similar to those of other recognized educational accrediting associations.

Each accredited school meets the following standards:

It has a competent faculty.

It offers educationally sound and up-to-date courses.

It carefully screens students for admission.

It provides satisfactory educational services.

It has demonstrated ample student success and satisfaction.

It advertises its courses truthfully.

It is financially able to deliver high quality educational service.

To become accredited each school has made an intensive study of its own operations, opened its doors to a thorough investigation by an outside examining committee, supplied all information required by the Accrediting Commission, and submitted its instructional materials for a thorough review by competent subject-matter specialists. The process is repeated every five years.

DIRECTORY OF ACCREDITED HOME STUDY COURSES

1. **American Academy of Nutrition,** 3408 Sausalito Drive, Corona del Mar, California 92625. Founded 1985. Diploma course in human nutrition.

2. **American Educational Institute,** 3787 Main Street, Bridgeport, Connecticut 06606. Founded 1988. Courses in airline/travel career training and hotel-motel career training.

3. **American Institute of Music,** 56 Chadwick Drive, Richmond Hill, Ontario L4B 2V9, Canada. A division of Tritone Music. Founded 1977. College credit courses in Music Teacher career training in music theory, harmony, music history, and the teaching of music. Send inquiries to MPO, Box 1706, Niagara Falls, New York 14302-1706.

4. **American Medical Record Association,** 919 North Michigan Avenue, Suite 1400, Chicago, Illinois 60611. Founded 1928. Course in medical record technology.

5. **American School,** 850 East 58th Street, Chicago, Illinois 60637. Founded 1897. Complete high school diploma course.

6. **Army Institute for Professional Development (IPD),** U.S. Army Training Support Center, Fort Eustis, Virginia, 23604-5168. Founded 1976. U.S. Army specialist and professional development courses. Enrollment is restricted to Active and Reserve Component military personnel, Federal civil service personnel, ROTC cadets, and allied military students.

7. **Art Instruction Schools,** 500 South Fourth Street, Minneapolis, Minnesota 55415. Founded 1914. Courses in art, poetry, fiction and nonfiction writing.

8. **Aubrey Willis School,** 1212 West Camelback Road, Suite 100, Phoenix, Arizona 85013. Founded 1970. A division of Career One Home Study Corporation. Courses in piano tuning, regulating and repairing.

9. **The Barton School,** Scranton, Pennsylvania 18515. A division of North American Correspondence Schools—National Education Corporation. Founded 1977. Courses in medical and dental office assisting.

10. **Berean College,** 1445 Boonville Ave., Springfield, Missouri 65802. Founded 1948. A division of Assemblies of God. Degree and non-degree courses in Bible studies, evangelism, and theological areas.

11. **The Boyd School,** One Chatham Center, Pittsburgh, Pennsylvania 15219. A division of Wilma Boyd Career Schools, Inc. Founded 1968. Combination home study-resident course in airline/travel training.

12. **California College for Health Sciences,** 222 West 24th Street, National City, California 92050. Founded 1978. Degree program and non-degree courses in respiratory therapy, health-related fields, and child care.

13. **Cambridge Academy,** Highway 316, P.O. Box 1290, Ft. McCoy, Florida 32134. Founded in 1978. Complete high school diploma curriculum.

14. **Canadian School of Management,** Suite 1003, 121 Bloor Street East, Toronto, Ontario, Canada M4W 3M5. Founded 1976. Bachelor and Master level courses in management, business administration, health services administration, and travel counselling.

15. **Career One Home Study Corporation,** 1212 West Camelback Road, Suite 100, Phoenix, Arizona 85013. Founded 1989. Course in computer-based office skills.

16. **The Catholic Home Study Institute,** 9 Loudoun Street, S.E., Leesburg, Virginia 22075. Founded 1983. Catechetical Diploma and college credit options. Courses in Catholic doctrine, moral theology, sacraments, scripture, history, spirituality, medical ethics, philosophy, and mariology.

17. **Citizens' High School,** 5115 New Peachtree Road, Atlanta, Georgia 30341. Founded 1981. Complete high school diploma course.

18. **Cleveland Institute of Electronics, Inc.** 1776 East 17th Street, Cleveland, Ohio 44114. Founded 1934. Degree and non-degree courses in electronics engineering, electronics technology, broadcast engineering, color TV troubleshooting, electronic communications, and digital and microprocessor technology.

19. **Columbia School of Broadcasting,** 5858 Hollywood Boulevard, 4th Floor, Hollywood, California 90028. A division of Broadcast Training, Inc. Founded 1964. Courses in radio announcing (English and Spanish), radio announcing/basic radio production combination production resident, radio/television advertising sales, radio/television commercial copywriting, FCC general class radiotelephone operator's license, including basic electricity and electronics.

20. **Columbia School of Computer Science,** 5858 Hollywood Boulevard, Suite 216, Hollywood, California 90028. A division of Broadcast Training, Inc. Founded 1989. Course in PC computer skills and concepts.

21. **Computer Home Study Institute,** 1605 North Cahuenga Boulevard, Suite 216, Hollywood, California 90028. Founded in 1988. Course in computer literacy.

22. **County Schools, Inc.,** 3787 Main Street, Bridgeport, Connecticut 06606. Founded 1959. Courses in accounting/bookkeeping, airline/travel, travel agent preparation, hotel-motel management, hotel-motel operations, tractor trailer driving, and nurse's aide.

23. **Country Schools, Inc.**—Tractor Trailer Training Site, 44-120 River Street, Bridgeport, Connecticut 06604. Send inquiries to number 22 above.

24. **County Schools, Inc.**—Nurse's Aide Training Site, Barnett Multi-Health Care Facility, 2875 Main Street, Bridgeport, Connecticut 06606. Send inquiries to number 22 above.

26. **Diamond Council of America,** 9140 Ward Parkway, Kansas City, Missouri 64114. Founded in 1944. Courses in Diamontology and Gemology leading to certificates of Certified Diamontologist and Guild Gemologist offered to members of the Diamond Council of America and their employees.

27. **Educational Institute of the American Hotel & Motel Association,** Steven S. Nisbet Building, 1407 South Harrison Road, P.O. Box 1240, East Lansing, Michigan 48826. Founded 1951. Courses and certification programs in hotel-motel, restaurant and food service operations.

28. **Emergency Management Institute,** Federal Emergency Management Agency, 16825 South Seton Avenue, Emmitsburg, Maryland 21727. Founded 1967. Federally sponsored courses in emergency preparedness.

29. **English Language Institute of America,** 332 South Michigan Avenue, Suite 1058, Chicago, Illinois 60604. Founded 1942. Course entitled Practical English and the Command of Words.

30. **Executive Security International, Ltd.,** 605 West Main Street, Suite 103, Aspen, Colorado 81611. Founded 1981. Combination home study-resident courses in executive security training and investigations training.

31. **Extension Course Institute,** United States Air Force, Gunter Air Force Station, Alabama 36118-5643. Founded 1950. U.S. Air Force professional military education, career development, and specialized technical courses. Enrollment is restricted to active duty military, Air Force Reserve, Air National Guard, civil service, and other specified personnel.

32. **Futures in Education, Inc.,** 1249 F Street, San Diego, California 92101. Founded 1985. Complete high school diploma course.

33. **Gemological Institute of America,** 1660 Stewart Street, Santa Monica, California 90404-4088. Founded 1931. Courses in diamonds, diamond grading, colored stones, gem identification, colored stone grading, pearls, jewelry design, jewelry display, and jewelry sales.

34. **Global Academy,** 4840 Roswell Road, Building E., Suite 200, Atlanta, Georgia 30342. Founded 1986. Courses in training for positions in the travel and tourism industry, including airlines, travel agencies, hotels, tour operators, and cruise lines.

35. **Grantham College of Engineering,** 34641 I-12 Frontage Road, P.O. Box 5700, Slidell, Louisiana 70469-5700. Founded 1951. Associate and Bachelor degrees in electronics engineering technology and computer engineering technology.

36. **The Hadley School for the Blind,** 700 Elm Street, Winnetka, Illinois 60093. Founded 1920. Over 100 courses offered. Courses for the blind in braille, high school, vocational, avocational, and technical subjects. Taught by braille or audio cassettes. Also

offers courses for sighted parents of blind infants and children. No tuition charged.

37. **Heathkit/Zenith Educational Systems,** Hilltop Road, St. Joseph, Michigan 49085. A division of Heath Company, subsidiary of Groupe Bull, Inc. Founded 1975. Courses in electricity and electronic fundamentals, advanced electronics, digital electronics, microprocessors and minicomputers, robotics, computer programming, CAD, and computer graphics.

38. **Hemphill Schools,** 510 S. Alvarado Street, Los Angeles, California 90057-2998. Founded 1920. Spanish language courses in art, sewing, photography, automotive repair, radio-TV repair, electricity, air conditioning, computer programming, video repair, refrigeration, accounting and English (ESL).

39. **Hollywood Scriptwriting Institute,** 1605 North Cahuenga Boulevard, Suite 216, Hollywood, California 90028. Founded 1976. Courses in professional screenwriting and computer literacy. Optional resident training available.

40. **Home Study International,** P.O. Box 4437, 12501 Old Columbia Pike, Silver Spring, Maryland 20914-4437. Founded 1909. Correspondence courses for preschool, kindergarten, elementary (grades 1–6), junior high, secondary (with diploma), college and adult education, and independent study. (Send inquiries to P.O. Box number.)

41. **Hospitality Training Center, Inc.,** 220 N. Main Street, Hudson, Ohio 44236. Founded 1961. Combination home study-resident training motel management program, and home study course in airline and travel career training.

42. **Hospitality Training Center, Inc.**—Motel Management Training Site, Aurora Inn, Routes 306 & 82, Aurora, Ohio 44202. Send inquiries to number 41 above.

43. **Hypnosis Motivation Institute,** 18607 Ventura Boulevard, Suite 310, Tarzana, California 91356. Founded 1967. Professional training in hypnosis and hypnotherapy.

44. **International Aviation and Travel Academy,** 300 W. Arbrook Boulevard, Arlington, Texas 76014-3199. Founded 1971. Home study and combination home study-resident courses in airline/travel industry fields.

45. **International Correspondence Institute**, Chaussee de Waterloo 45, 1640 Rhode-St Genese (Brussels) Belgium. A division of the Foreign Missions of the Assemblies of God, Springfield, Missouri. Founded 1967. Degree and non-degree courses in Bible studies, evangelism, and theological areas.

46. **ICS—International Correspondence Schools,** Scranton, Pennsylvania 18515. Founded 1890. A division of National Education Corporation. Courses at the secondary and postsecondary levels in technology, engineering, business, vocational trades, practical arts, and specialized industrial subjects. (See subject listings.)

47. **ICS Center for Degree Studies,** Scranton, Pennsylvania 18515. Founded 1974. A division of International Correspondence Schools—National Education Corporation. Specialized Associate degree programs in business, engineering technology, and electronics technology.

48. **ICS-Newport/Pacific High School,** Scranton, Pennsylvania 18515. Founded 1926. A division of International Correspondence Schools—National Education Corporation. Complete high school diploma course.

49. **IMC—International Management Centres,** Castle Street, Buckingham, England MK18 1BS. Founded 1964. Courses in general management and all major fields of professional management.

50. **John Tracy Clinic,** 806 West Adams Boulevard, Los Angeles, California 90007. Founded 1942. Courses for parents of deaf children and deaf-blind children. No tuition charged.

51. **Laurel School,** 2538 North 8th Street, P.O. Box 5338, Phoenix, Arizona 85010-5338. Founded 1978. Courses in medical and dental assisting, medical and dental receptionist, administrative secretary, executive secretary, general business secretary, legal secretary, and medical secretary.

52. **Learning and Evaluation Center,** 515 Market Street, P.O. Box 616, Bloomsburg, Pennsylvania 17815. Founded 1972. A home study "summer school"

offering extensions in general subject areas to 5th to 12th grade students who fail during their regular school year. Student's school approval required.

53. **Lifetime Career Schools,** 2251 Barry Avenue, Los Angeles, California 90064. Founded 1944. Courses in landscaping, floristry, dressmaking, and doll technology.

54. **Marine Corps Institute,** Marine Barracks, 8th and "I" Streets, S. E., Washington, D. C. 20390. Founded 1920. Courses to improve the general military and technical proficiency of Marines. Enrollment is restricted to active duty military personnel, retired Marines, reserve Marines, civilian employees of the armed forces, NROTC midshipmen, and allied military students.

55. **McGraw-Hill Continuing Education Center,** 4401 Connecticut Avenue, N.W., Washington, D.C. 20008. Founded 1971. Courses in computers, electronics, automotive technology, air conditioning, appliance servicing, construction, photography and video production, small engine repair, bookkeeping, paralegal, and travel.

56. **Modern Schools of America, Inc.,** 2538 North 8th Street, P.O. Box 5338, Phoenix, Arizona 85010-5338. Founded 1946. Courses in gun repair and small engine repair.

57. **MTA School,** 1801 Oberlin Road, Middletown, Pennsylvania 17057. A division of CareerCom. Founded 1968.

58. **Napolean Hill Foundation,** 1440 Paddock Drive, Northbrook, Illinois 60062. Founded in 1962. Course in PMA (Positive Mental Attitude) Science of Success.

59. **National Center for Logistic Management,** 819 Meetinghouse Road, Cinnaminson, New Jersey 08077. Founded 1923. Courses in transportation and traffic management.

60. **National Safety Council,** Safety Training Institute, 444 North Michigan Avenue, Chicago, Illinois 60611. Founded 1913. Courses in safety supervision and human relations for first line supervisors.

61. **National Tax Training School,** 4 Melnick Drive, P.O. Box 382, Monsey, New York 10952. Founded 1952.

Basic and advanced federal income tax preparation courses.

62. **National Training, Inc.,** 188 College Drive, P.O. Box 1899, Orange Park, Florida 32067-1899. Founded 1978. Combination home study-resident courses in truck driving training and heavy equipment operation.

63. **National Training, Inc.,**—Truck and Heavy Equipment Operator Training Site, SR 209, Green Cove Springs, Florida 32043. Send inquiries to number 62 above.

64. **National Training, Inc.,**—Truck and Heavy Equipment Operator Training Site, Southeastern Louisiana University, Hammond, Louisiana 70402. Send inquiries to number 62 above.

65. **National Training, Inc.,**—Truck Driver Training Site, 9600 E. 104th Avenue, Henderson, Colorado 80640. Send inquiries to number 62 above.

66. **National Training Systems, Inc.,** 7140 Virginia Manor Court, P.O. Box 2719, Laurel, Maryland 20708. Founded 1976. Combination home study-resident courses in truck driving training and diesel mechanics, and home study course in applied computer technology teaching spreadsheet, database and word processing applications on a minicomputer.

67. **National Training Systems, Inc.**—Truck Driving Training Site, 2031 Jennie Scher Road, Richmond, Virginia 23231. Send inquiries to number 66 above.

68. **New England Tractor Trailer Training School,** P.O. Box 326, Field Road, Somers, Connecticut 06071. Founded 1965. Combination home study-resident course in tractor trailer driving.

69. **NHAW Home Study Institute,** 1389 Dublin Road, P.O. Box 16790, Columbus, Ohio 43216. A division of Northamerican Heating & Airconditioning Wholesalers Association. Founded 1962. Not-for-profit industry program. Courses in heating, air conditioning, and financial management for contractors.

70. **North American Correspondence Schools,** Scranton, Pennsylvania 18515. A division of National Education Corporation. Founded 1959. Courses in accounting, conservation, drafting, firearms, legal secretary, secretarial, and travel.

71. **Northwest Schools,** 1221 Northwest 21st Avenue, Portland, Oregon 97209. Founded 1946. Courses in airline/travel reservations, ticketing and sales, hotel-motel management, and computer learning.

72. **NRI Schools,** 4401 Connecticut Avenue, N.W., Washington, D.C. 20008. A division of McGraw-Hill Continuing Education Center. Founded 1914. Courses in air conditioning, appliance servicing, bookkeeping, TV-audio repair, microcomputers, electronic communications, automotive, building construction, locksmithing, robotics, telephone servicing, music technology, photography, small engine repair, paralegal, and travel.

73. **Paralegal Institute, Inc.,** 2922 N. 35th Avenue, Suite 4, Drawer 11408, Phoenix, Arizona 85061-1408. Founded 1974. Course in paralegal assistant training.

74. **Pathfinder High School of Independent Studies, Inc.,** 26440 La Alameda, Suite 350, Mission Viejo, California, 92691. Founded 1982. A division of Futures In Education. Complete high school diploma course.

75. **Peoples College of Independent Studies,** 233 Academy Drive, Drawer 1768, Kissimmee, Florida 32742-1768. A division of Southeastern Academy, Inc. Founded 1985. Specialized Associate Degree in travel and tourism; computer programming, and electronics technology; non-degree courses in computer programming, electronics technology, seamanship, and small boat handling.

76. **Police Sciences Institute,** Scranton, Pennsylvania 18515. A division of North American Correspondence Schools—National Education Corporation. Founded 1977. Course in police sciences and investigation.

77. **The Rouse School of Special Detective Training,** 3410-G West MacArthur Boulevard, Santa Ana, California 92799-5750. Founded 1976. Course in special detective training.

78. **Seminary Extension Independent Study Institute,** 901 Commerce Street, Suite 500, Nashville, Tennessee 37203-3697. Founded 1951. Courses in Bible, Christian doctrine, Christian history, religious education, and pastoral work.

79. **Seton Home Study School**, 612 Crosby Road, Front Royal, Virginia 22630. Founded 1982. Complete Catholic school curriculum for kindergarten, elementary (grades 1–6), junior high and high school.

80. **Southeastern Academy, Inc.,** 233 Academy Drive, Drawer 1768, Kissimmee, Florida 32742-1768. Founded 1974. Combination home study-resident courses in airline/travel career training and hotel/motel front desk training.

81. **Southern Career Institute,** 164 West Royal Palm Way, P.O. Drawer 2158, Boca Raton, Florida 33427-2158. Founded 1976. Courses in legal assistant/paralegal assistant training and professional photography. Advanced specialty programs for legal assistants.

82. **Stenotype Institute of Jacksonville, Inc.,** 500 9th Avenue North, P.O. Box 50009, Jacksonville Beach, Florida 32250. Founded 1940. Courses in court reporting, convention reporting, notereading, and stenotype machine shorthand.

83. **Trans World Travel Academy,** 502 Earth City Plaza, Suite 204, St. Louis, Missouri 63045-1315. A department of Trans World Airlines, Inc. Founded 1978. Combination home study-resident courses in airline/travel career training.

84. **Travel Lab**, One Chatham Center, Pittsburgh, Pennsylvania 15219. A division of Wilma Boyd Career Schools, Inc. Founded 1968. Combination home study-resident course in airline/travel career training.

85. **Travel Lab**—Travel Agent/Career Training Site, Concourse Tower II, Suite 200, 2090 Palm Beach Lakes Boulevard, West Palm Beach, Florida 33409. Send inquiries to number 84 above.

86. **Tritone Music**, 56 Chadwick Crescent, Richmond Hill, Ontario, L4B 2V9, Canada. Founded 1977. College credit courses and Music Teacher career training in music theory, harmony, music history, and the teaching of music.

87. **Truck Marketing Institute,** 1090 Eugenia Place, P.O. Box 5000, Carpinteria, California 93014-5000. Founded 1964. Courses in truck selection, application, and sales.

88. **United Training Institute, Inc.,** 9966 Dolores Street, Suite 203, Spring Valley, California 92077. Founded 1985. Course in law enforcement and security.

89. **USA Training Academy, Inc.,** 955 South Chapel Street, P.O. Box 6032, Newark, Delaware 19714-6032. Founded 1970. Combination home study-resident course in truck driving training.

90. **U. S. Coast Guard Institute,** P.O. Substation 18, Oklahoma City, Oklahoma 73169-6999. Founded 1928. U.S. Coast Guard military and technical training courses. Enrollment restricted to active duty and reserve military, Coast Guard Auxiliarists, retired Coast Guard personnel, civilian employees of Coast Guard, and other specified personnel.

91. **WORLDSPAN Travel Academy,** 7310 Tiffany Springs Parkway, Kansas City, Missouri 64153. Founded 1978. Wholly owned by Delta Airlines, Northwest Airlines and Trans World Airlines. Course in travel agency and airline reservations sales.

92. **Westlawn Institute of Marine Technology,** 733 Summer Street, Stamford, Connecticut 06901. A division of National Marine Manufacturers Association. Founded 1930. Courses in boat and yacht design and related marine technology subjects.

SUBJECTS TAUGHT BY ACCREDITED SCHOOLS

This is a PARTIAL list of subjects offered by accredited home study schools.

In many cases, courses on a given topic are available from more than one school. However, each school presents its courses in its own way. Therefore the content may vary in intent, range, and length.

Because of this it is important that prospective students write to each of the schools which offer courses in the desired subject field. Each student should obtain from each of the schools complete descriptions of course offerings including course objectives, the quality of materials to be furnished by the schools, and obligations of both the student and the school.

NUMBERS refer to schools listed above in the Directory of Accredited Home Study Courses.

APPENDIXES

SUGGESTED COURSE OF STUDY, GRADES 1–6

What should your child study when?

Until this point, most of us have been more-or-less following the typical course of study devised by the public-school curriculum designers. (For those of you who are interested, it is outlined in *Typical Course of Study,* a booklet published by World Book, Inc., and available from them for a nominal price.) Most published curriculum, whether Christian or secular, uses *Typical Course of Study* or some similar guide as a rule for what should be taught when.

Looking at *Typical Course of Study,* the first thing that strikes you is the large number of skills taught in each subject at each grade level. The second thing that strikes you is the totally arbitrary nature of where many of these skills are placed. The third thing that strikes you is how often many of these skill and content areas are repeated from grade to grade.

Let's look at some examples. "Presenting original plays" is listed as a grade 5 language arts skill. "Introduction to mythology" is listed as a grade 6 learning area. The two could easily be reversed, presented at lower grades, presented at later grades, or skipped altogether (especially since the mythology presented in public schools is no longer just classic Greek and Roman mythology). Under Health and Safety, "sewage disposal" makes its one and only appearance in grade 5 (why grade 5?), while "dental health" or "dental hygiene" is presented and re-presented eight years in a row (does it take that long to learn to floss and brush your teeth?). Sentence grammar is first presented in grade 3 (simple punctuation), skipped altogether in grade 4, and then spread out over grades 5–8, only to pop up once again in grades 10 and 11. As one girl complained to me, "They keep teaching us this stuff again and again, and I *learned* it three years ago!" Science topics appear in an equally capricious fashion, with a dozen or more topics presented each year, some of which are repeated almost every year while others are not. The solar system, in various forms, is studied every year in grades K–5. Simple machines, on the other hand, pop up only in grades 1 and 3.

Another thing worth noting about the typical course of study is that *each skill and topic is given equal emphasis.* Learning to read and write are just *part* of the language-arts program, which before children can even read already includes "simple pantomimes and dramatic play" and 15 other topics, including "development of class newspaper." "Dressing for weather and activity" and "neighborhood helpers" are not shown in any obvious way to be lower priority than "establishing sight vocabulary." This undoubtedly accounts for the huge number of cluttered projects teachers are always publishing in teachers' magazines, where first-grade kids spend a whole week making a cardboard box village in order to learn about "me and my neighborhood" rather than working on reading, writing, and arithmetic.

Our children need more than better educational resources. They need a better educational schedule. Here are what I see as the basic steps in that schedule:

1. First give kids the tools of learning (Bible, reading, writing, and arithmetic).

2. Second, present them informally with lots of data in all the subject areas.

3. Third, tie it together with organizing devices like time lines.

4. Once steps 1–3 have been accomplished, *then* introduce formal study of science, history, geography, art, and so on, while continuing to read voraciously and *discuss* what is read.

Now, before we discuss a suggested curriculum for our teens, let's look first at the background we'd like to give them.

STEP ONE: THE TOOLS OF LEARNING (GRADES 1–3)

No matter how young or old your child is, here's where he needs to start once he's passed the "readiness" stage (can use crayons, scissors, hold a pencil properly, knows left from right, etc.).

1. Bible
   A. Memorize books of the Bible in order by name.
   B. Read through the entire Bible, with explanations of the difficult parts (many times).
   C. Memorize the Ten Commandments.
2. Learn to read *well*.
3. Learn printing and handwriting.
4. Learn to write *well* (creative writing), including proper grammar and spelling.
5. Learn summarizing and narrating (child is able to recount a story well).
6. Learn basic arithmetic, from numeral recognition up to decimals and fractions.

These are the *real* basics, to be studied together until mastered. Don't assume just because he's in fifth grade that he's on top of all these areas. Check him out with Step One skills first.

If your child can't read or write well, *don't worry* about teaching him Civil War history or cell biology.

Get the reading and writing under control *first*, without distracting him with hours of studies in areas he can't handle due to his lack of language-arts skills.

STEP TWO: THE FACTS (GRADES 1–3)

You don't have to let the science and social studies vanish during the time your children are mastering the basics. Here's some simple ways to provide social studies and science facts and experiences during the first three grades of school:

1. History
   A. Read historical biographies and fiction aloud. Good readers can read them to themselves. Try to focus on explorers, inventors, entrepreneurs, scientists, artists, musicians, preachers and evangelists, mothers, writers, and so on, not just on political figures. "Daily life" books that give a feel for the cultural setting of each time period are also good.
   B. Rent historical videos.
   C. Discuss the history of each holiday as it comes up.
2. Geography
   A. Look up locations on the map or globe as they come up in family conversation.
   B. Teach the kids to use a map and globe.
   C. U. S. and world puzzles.
   D. Geography games (optional, if you have the time) .
3. Science
   A. Read science books aloud, or have the child read them alone. Topics to cover: plants, animals, farming, rocks, weather, seasons, solar system and universe, measurement, human anatomy and senses, dinosaurs, magnetism, electricity, and simple machines.
   B. Nature walks and field trips (as time permits).
   C. Pet care (if desired).
   D. Simple experiments (if time permits).
   E. Basic personal hygiene (washing, brushing, flossing, putting dirty clothes in the hamper, etc.).

Here's what *not* to bother with:

• Any K–3 formal social studies or science courses. Without exception, these are all rinky-dink.

- Units on transportation. You could with equal justification study clothing, food preparation, architecture, or cosmetics (none of which I recommend bothering with). As your child studies history and drives in your car, he is bound to pick up transportation information without any special effort.

- Units on "community helpers," "interdependence of people," "basic human needs and wants," and other code words for statism. Community helpers units teach careerism (only paid jobs are represented, never volunteers or people who serve their families and neighborhoods) and subservience (self-employment and leadership positions are rarely presented). Units on interdependence and human needs invariably present gigantic institutional structures as *the* way to live.

- All collective-guilt studies, whether the guilt be racial, ecological, religious, economic, or whatever. These sometimes come disguised as "cultural appreciation" or "conservation" studies.

- Complicated, cluttered projects that "integrate skill areas" (e.g., handwriting assignments that include spelling words). It's safer to keep those skill areas separate until you're sure your child has actually mastered the skills!

If you want to integrate Bible with social studies and science, you can use Christian books or take the time to discuss what your children are reading (a good idea anyway!). It's always interesting to look up what the Bible has to say on a subject, too. Just pick your topic (e.g., "ear" or "liberty") and look up the references found under that topic in your concordance. You can pursue such studies further by adding cross-references. Example: "hearing" and "listening" fit naturally with a study of what the Bible says about ears, just as "freedom," "slave," "slavery," and "subjection" go along with a study of liberty. This can be done on Sundays or during family devotions time, if your regular home-school time is too short. You can also draw on the Bible for reading, literature, history, handwriting, drama, narrating, science (developing a proper attitude toward creation and the Creator), and even grammar assignments—McGuffey did!

The first three grades are also a good time to introduce the rudiments of baking, sewing, housecleaning, child care, and other daily-life skills. Again, with the exception of personal cleanliness and picking up after oneself, these can be fit in as time allows.

STEP THREE: PUTTING IT ALL TOGETHER WITH FORMAL STUDIES (GRADES 4–6)

We're only in the fourth grade at this point, so there is no reason to panic just because your son or daughter isn't sure whether Columbus discovered America in 1492 or 1776. (Let's keep this in perspective: a hefty minority of high-school graduates aren't sure about the dates either!) Up to this point we've been working on stories, not dates. Does your child know Columbus discovered America? Good: that's the first step! Now's the time to start your history time line, if you haven't already, and to perhaps work through a beginning history textbook. Now is also the time to get a bit more systematic about science (if desired), although serious science studies can really wait until junior high or even high school without major educational consequences.

I am not suggesting "dumbing down" the curriculum. I am suggesting that it's dumb to suffocate kids with more information than they are able to remember. Keep in mind also that the public schools teach kids all the information from this age onwards at least *twice*. The assumption is that they will *not* learn or remember most of it the first time around. My position is that we shouldn't teach them material we don't expect them to remember in the first place. Thus, it makes more sense to present the excellent fourth- through sixth-grade history and geography texts to seventh- through ninth-graders, who will actually be able to retain all that information, than to the age group for which they were written.

Therefore, here's what I suggest for grades 4–6:

1. Bible studies
   A. Time line.
   B. Maps (Middle Eastern geography).
   C. Memorizing the theme and a key verse for each book of the Bible.
   D. Knowing how to quickly look up any given Bible verse.
   E. Hebrew and Greek alphabets.
   F. Use of the basic Bible tools (dictionary, concordance).
2. Reading: a lot. Include good classic literature. Some Nancy Drew and Hardy Boys won't hurt, but don't let that level of book be *all* they read. If a child reads a lot, you can almost get away with skipping everything else except math. (I am *not* suggesting that you do this!)
3. Handwriting: developing a beautiful hand. Typing can be taught now, but is optional (do only if time permits).

4. Creative writing: all literary types (letters, journals, poems, stories, essays, plays, memos, reports, newspaper articles). Pen pals are great, as is writing for one of the homemade homeschool-kids newsletters.
5. Oral presentation skills.
6. Grammar: formal study. It should only take a year or so to cover *all* of it at this age level.
7. Spelling: formal study if necessary (some children are naturally almost-perfect spellers). Rule-based program and child's own misspelled words, not canned "word lists."
8. Arithmetic: continue. If finished, proceed on to pre-algebra, etc.
9. Geometry.
10. History.
    A. Time line of U.S. history.
    B. Time line of world history.
    C. First history textbook (if desired: semi-formal study; read it as a book and *discuss* it).
    D. More mature history-oriented books from the library or EDC Publishing, etc.
11. Geography: continue as above. Add geography quizzes and drills, if desired.
12. Science.
    A. Engineering with construction kits (e.g., LEGO Dacta, fishertechnik).
    B. Simple experiments every now and then (child has more responsibility for setting up experiments on his own, calls you over to see the results).
    C. First science textbook (if desired; semi-formal study; do exercises, but don't worry about keeping up a standard classroom pace).
    D. History of science (through biographies or as a separate study). Can also be done later.
13. Health and safety: totally informal, as family situations arise (e.g., washing wound and putting on bandage, using Desitin on diaper rash, pointing pot handle to the back of the stove, etc.).
14. Physical education: pick a lifetime sport and get good at it.
15. Home economics: assign chores, let kids bake using simple recipe books. Weaving, knitting, and woodworking kits are also popular with this age group.

Of the above list, only Bible, grammar, and math actually need formal preparation time. Handwriting, creative writing, oral presentation, spelling, and engineering and science experiments require adult feedback, but not necessarily a lot of up-front teaching. If your child reads well and you get him good resources, he is able at this age to follow the instructions by himself.

FOR THOSE WHO WANT MORE

I personally feel that the elementary grades are also a fine time to introduce art, music, and foreign languages (all covered in Volume 4). Other subjects worth introducing in grades 4–6 are business, economics, and citizenship (covered in this volume). Consider adding those subjects if any of the following apply:

- Your family considers such studies part of family play time, so they don't take any extra time from your day.

- Your family has a history of being musical (or artistic, or good at languages, or owning your own business) and you feel one of these subjects is likely to become your child's vocation.

- You are using resources that don't require you to prepare for the lessons.

- You are willing to take several weeks at a time off from your normal studies to really get into these new areas and get comfortable with them, or you have the basic studies under control and can afford the extra time for regular instruction in these areas.

Remember, the more time you spend on the basics, the more time you'll have later on to spend on everything else!

SUGGESTED COURSE OF STUDY, GRADES 7–12

Has your teen student mastered the tools of learning and the basic content areas outlined in the Suggested Course of Study for grades 1–6? You might want to take a minute or two and read that appendix first (that's why I included it again in this volume!). Remember, we are going to be talking about an *ideal* course of study for the teen and college years—at least, one as ideal as I can think of at the present time—and this assumes an excellent educational background for grades 1–6.

My suggestions for the teen years boil down to the following:

(1) Spend enough time with important subjects to make sure the student learns *and remembers* the material he invested the time on studying.

(2) Condense sequential material (such as math course) as much as possible, and introduce serious math earlier, thus opening up access to serious science and engineering courses earlier.

(3) Skip all trendy, irrelevant, and faddish subjects.

(4) Explore unit studies in areas of special interest.

(5) Take advantage of hands-on and real-world learning wherever possible

(6) Recognize that the dividing line between high school and college isn't always obvious. Don't be afraid to tackle "college" material (which in yesterday's world would have been high-school material anyway) during the teen years.

In contrast to these suggestions, I believe the present typical course of study followed in the schools (both public and private) doesn't do a good job of equipping students with the tools of learning or of presenting them with useful knowledge. The typical high-school curriculum wastes hours, days, and weeks on political propaganda about women's role in society, ethnic and racial "studies," peace education, sex education, nuclear education, and other cause-oriented trendy stuff. This leaves little time for the serious intellectual work students of this age are capable of doing.

Most fundamentally, the very reasons for studying the subjects required are outdated. Example: *all* high school students now must take science courses, because American leaders of the 1950s were frightened by the Russians beating us into space. This makes as much sense as forcing *all* students to take three years of gymnastics, because Eastern Bloc nations wipe the floor with us in international gymnastics competitions!

SUBJECT CHECKLIST

Who should decide, after all, the relative importance of sports, science, math, practical life skills, literature, history, and so on for every single student in the country? I believe that *families* should decide these issues, not educational bureaucrats. So here's a handy checklist to help you determine which subjects make the most sense for a teen to study.

Ask yourself the following questions:

(1) Will it prepare me for my future work?

(2) Will it prepare me for my future ministry (unpaid service to others)?

(3) Will it prepare me for leadership in the business world or my community?

(4) Will it prepare me for my future home life?

(5) Will it enrich my life?

Any subject that flunks all five of these tests has obviously little reason for taking up your time. Unhappily, such subjects often are the very ones required by states and colleges.

Let's walk through an example. You are, let's say, a people person with a decided artistic flair. Math has always bored you. So has science: you studied it in grade school, but you have no intention of going into a technical career of any sort. The value of a series of high-school science courses is obviously small in your case, let alone both biology *and* chemistry with their associated lab work. However, most colleges require just such a science sequence as an entrance requirement.

Now, it may happen that you have very little initial interest in an area, but yet that area would be extremely valuable for you later on. It's fair to say, for example, that few high-school students are wild about history. Yet a knowledge of history is indispensable for wise leadership. Those who don't learn from the mistakes of the past are doomed to repeat them, as it has been said, and those who are responsible for the welfare of others shouldn't make more mistakes than they can help. (This explains something about our current congressfolks, few of whom have any significant knowledge of even American history.) However, studying history from the angle of "what did these people do wrong?" and "what did this other bunch do right?" is a whole different approach from typical school history courses, which either skip such issues entirely or fail to present an absolute moral base by which to judge past leaders and movements.

Whether you can follow your own ideal course of study or not, though, it's worthwhile going through the exercise of determining what it would be if you had the choice. You can then sculpt the actual graduation requirements to fit your particular needs and abilities. If you're technically oriented, you might want to take math and science to the max while taking it easier on your literature studies. If, on the other hand, you foresee more use for the liberal arts in your future, you might be content to satisfy the minimum science requirements with some all-purpose science courses.

GRADUATION REQUIREMENTS

Before we get too excited about the educational possibilities of the teen years, let's look first at the standard graduation requirements set up by the various states.

Junior high still can be very much what you make it in most places, but by high school things start to get serious.

In general, states require three years of English, two years of math (can be consumer or survival math), two years of science (can be basic science with no lab work), a year of U.S. history, a year of world history, one semester each of government (citizenship) and economics, one year of either foreign language or fine arts (art appreciation, music, drama, etc.), and two years of physical education. These are *minimum* graduation requirements. Most students also take driver's education. The smart ones take typing class.

For college entrance, somewhat more is required. Generally colleges require four full years of English, three years of math (including at least algebra and geometry), biology and chemistry plus lab work, and a year of fine arts. Some colleges also require two years of the same foreign language. Driver's education and typing are virtual necessities for the college-bound. On top of *this*, Christian families will try to include Bible education as well.

For specific high-school graduation suggestions, forms to fill out, and all the other record-keeping details home schoolers need, I suggest you get a copy of Cathy Duffy's *Christian Home Educator's Curriculum Manual for Junior/Senior High.* Cathy has spent more time researching this area than just about anyone else, and for $15 plus $2 shipping, her book is a bargain that will save you a lot of grief when it comes time to issue diplomas and/or send transcripts to colleges. Cathy's book is available from Home Run Enterprises (address in the Suppliers Index).

ENGLISH

Are we having fun yet? No? Then let's get into a better way of doing things!

Studying grammar in high school is boring. Thus, suggestion #1 is to teach it *before* high school. Failing that, give your student a *condensed* one-book grammar course instead of spinning out grammar instruction into 12th grade.

The tools of learning needed in high school are note-taking, outlining, and research skills. (We assume your student is already an excellent reader; if not, see the Suggested Course of Study for grades 1–6.) Teaching these skills can be accomplished in less than a month.

Now's also the time to teach typing. Word processing is even better. Either of these will make your high school and college work much speedier and neater.

Handwriting: teach cursive italic, if you haven't by now.

Creative writing: now we're really starting to have fun! Here's a menu of creative-writing assignments to complete before graduation:

- Poems—traditional, blank verse, limericks, haiku, epic, ballads
- Essays—persuasive, how-to, factual, humorous
- Short stories—tragic, humorous, adventure, first-person, third-person, historic, mystery, fantasy/science fiction (if desired)
- Drama—one-act plays
- Journalism—articles, reviews, editorials

All writing assignments should be edited for spelling and grammatical correctness, as that is exactly what happens to authors in real life!

For extra fun, have your student write assignments in the styles of the authors you are studying in Literature class!

Oral presentation skills: the Middle Ages curriculum emphasized what was called "rhetoric," the art of persuasive speaking. Aside from formal vocabulary studies, this skill is more readily caught than taught. However, you can provide opportunities for public speaking, from helping out in a Sunday school class to emceeing a neighborhood talent show.

Now, Literature with a capital *L.* High-school literature typically includes American, British, and World literature: one course each. This just isn't enough time. I suggest you start your serious literature studies in grade 7 and take *two* years per course. This will give you enough time to thoroughly enjoy the reading selections *and* to branch out into unit studies on the authors that particularly interest you.

It just makes no sense to "study" Shakespeare for two weeks (if that long) and then rush on to someone else. How much better to read the biographical information about Shakespeare in a good literature textbook (or encyclopedia or library book) and then read several of his plays and poems aloud as a family! The same goes for any other major author. You can't really *know* a writer by gobbling 10 pages of his writings, so let's take the time and do it right!

Basically, what I'm suggesting is that you give your teen a college literature course. The only difference is that the college prides itself on assigning 100 pages to read per night, which guarantees your child won't remember most of it, and that the college forces him to write umpteen reports and papers on what he read, which guarantees he won't enjoy it. I'm suggesting that you let him read the same amount *at his own pace*, and that you discuss what he read (with perhaps an *occasional* writing assignment thrown in) rather than overdoing the writing.

If the student in question is one of the strong, silent types who is much happier tinkering with a machine, there's no need to beat him over the head with Shakespeare. Looking back at our five-point checklist, such a student is not likely to use advanced literary knowledge in his lifework, ministry, or home life. Although being able to quote the notables does add points to your leadership quotient, generally such people are *not* the glib, crowd-pleasing orators who could make maximum use of a wide literary background. You would accomplish more in such a case by giving him just a good taste of the classics than by making him hate them forever by pushing him too far beyond his interest level.

MATHEMATICS

Every child in this country except those with major physical brain damage could know algebra by ninth grade. Math is a totally sequential subject; A leads to B leads to C leads to D. When it's taught properly, that is!

Math class is *not* the time for units on careers, hands-on experiments with thermometers, lectures on behavior, and so on. The more you interrupt math with measuring, experimenting, graphing, and other scientific studies, the less obvious its sequential nature becomes. Ditto for non-math-related topics of all sorts.

If math is taken at a reasonable speed, your student will have finished at least a year of real algebra by the end of eighth grade. He then has plenty of time for trigonometry, geometry, advanced math topics, and calculus, if desired.

The reason it's good to speed up math instruction is that you then will be able to have a really excellent six-year course of science instruction. See below!

SCIENCE

What's true of high-school and college literature goes double for high-school and college science. Typically, science teachers don't even expect to finish the textbook by the end of the course. They move rapidly through the material—rapidly enough to leave a lot of their students scratching their heads—but it doesn't help, because there's just too much material in the typical text to be covered in the hours of the typical course.

Here's how to change all that. Instead of twiddling with basic science/physical science/life science for three years in junior high, *take two years each* for biology, chemistry, and physics in grades 7–12. That will give you enough time to digest all the material, enjoy all the experiments, add some unit studies on areas of special interest, and finish the textbook!

Of course, you need basic algebra to do the work in a good chemistry course—which is why it's good to speed up the math studies to the level expected of average Japanese kids, as per my suggestions in the Math section above.

Christians will want to introduce some serious creation science in these grades. This is easy, thanks to the excellent videos, books, and seminars now available. We also should make a serious effort to apply biblical thinking to these areas rather than just regurgitating the man-manipulates-objects point of view of secular science texts, or the man-is-a-destroyer view of

New Age and ecology texts, or even the no-growth man-is-a-steward view of the Christian ecology popularizers. (For the record's sake, you and I are supposed to build and be fruitful, not keep things in some supposedly utopian static state. The Creation is *fallen,* just like the rest of us, and keeps needing to be brought back into order.)

Remember, again, there is no transcendent reason why teens must take all these science courses in the first place, other than arbitrary college-entrance and high-school graduation requirements. However, if we're going to do it at all, why not do it *right?*

SOCIAL STUDIES

You may have noticed that geography isn't even on the list of high school graduation requirements. That's because it's presumably being taught right along with the history—which, once again, is zipped through too rapidly for the students to digest.

Yes, I know kids have been taking U.S. history over and over and over again since kindergarten. I also know they haven't learned it, because at each level the schools throw more material at them than they can retain. We, however, can do it right. How? By, once again, *taking two years* each for U.S. and world history instead of the one year in the high school curriculum. That leaves one year each for economics and citizenship—which are excellent introductions to philosophy, if tackled right.

FINE ART AND FOREIGN LANGUAGES

No problem. You just move to France and do your school lessons on a bench in the Louvre art museum!

Impractical, you say? Well, that's not really a problem. If you own Volume 4 of *The Big Book of Home Learning,* you know that there are dozens of great resources for at-home fine arts and foreign language study.

Learning to draw or learning to play a musical instrument are two fun ways to fulfill a fine-arts requirement. Seriously, I don't expect home schoolers, who accumulate more arts 'n music 'n crafts goodies than anyone else, to have any problems in this area.

If you plan to go to Bible college, Biblical Greek might be a good language choice. Latin is also a good choice, as it helps with many other school disciplines (vocabulary, science, grammar, etc.). Or go wherever your fancy leads!

PRACTICAL LIFE SKILLS

Beryl Singer, a reader of my HELP newsletter, had the brilliant idea of making a checklist of household management skills for teens. (Of course, some of these skills could be learned much earlier!) Here's Beryl's list:

Cleaning Kitchen
—set table
—clear table
—dry dishes
—wash dishes
—wipe off table
—clean highchair
—clean sink
—clean stove top
—clean oven
—clean burner drip pans
—clean refrigerator, outside
—clean refrigerator, inside
—clean refrigerator drip pan
—defrost freezer

Bathroom
—clean sink
—clean toilet
—clean bathtub
—clean shower walls
—clean tile walls
—wash shower curtain
—clean brushes and combs
—clean mirrors

Living room
—clean upholstery
—clean fireplace doors
—clean fireplace brick
—remove ashes
—build a fire in fireplace

Floors
—mop vinyl floor
—strip and wax vinyl floor
—vacuum carpets
—clean throw rugs
—clean door mats
—change vacuum cleaner bags
—shampoo carpets
—remove carpet stains
—dust mop wood floor
—strip and wax wood floors

Windows
—wash windows
—wash window frames
—wash curtains
—lubricate sliding parts
—wash exterior windows

Other
—dust furniture
—dust high places
—make beds
—change bed linens
—empty waste baskets
—clean wastebaskets
—clean telephones
—clean doorknobs
—clean light fixtures
—clean walls
—paint walls

Housecleaning
—houseclean bedroom
—houseclean bathroom
—houseclean living room
—houseclean kitchen

Plan and execute one week cleaning schedule, including delegation and follow-up.

Wash
—put away clothes
—fold clothes
—sort clothes to wash
—load and set washing machine
—clean lint trap—washer
—load and set dryer
—clean lint trap—dryer
—mend straight seams
—sew on a button
—patch a hole
—wash hand washables
—hang wash on clothesline

Handle the family wash for one week.

Food Preparation
—read recipe and follow directions
—measure ingredients
—set oven temperature
—set oven timer
—operate crockpot

Menu Planning
—plan week's menus
—write up shopping list
—shop for groceries

Plan one week's menus, plan shopping list within regular food budget, shop for groceries, and do the cooking for the week.

Organizing Skills
—sort belongings—things to keep and things to discard
—sort belongings—store like things together
—sort belongings by frequency of use
—store belongings by frequency of use (most used belongings in most accessible places)
—know and use the four storage alternatives (on a shelf, in a drawer, on the floor, on the wall)
—sort the mail

Baby Care
—change a diaper
—dress baby
—wash diapers
—bathe baby

Simple Repairs
—change light bulb
—turn off main water supply
—oil squeaky door
—use fire extinguisher
—reset digital clock
—unstop clogged drain
—unstop clogged toilet
—check circuit breakers
—shut off main power
—install curtain rods
—find studs
—hang picture
—replace faucet washer

Telephone
—know phone number
—know address
—place local calls
—make emergency calls—fire, 911, etc.
—take phone messages
—handle telephone solicitation
—place long distance calls
—place collect calls

Financial
—write a check
—fill out mail order
—pay bills
—read bank statement
—read electric meter
—balance checkbook
—plan budget
—open a checking or savings account

Breakfast
—cold cereal
—toast
—granola
—scrambled eggs
—pancakes
—french toast

Lunch
—peanut butter and jelly sandwiches
—lunchmeat and cheese sandwiches

Supper
—hot dogs
—hamburgers
—meat loaf
—barbecued chicken
—chili
—baked beans
—mashed potatoes
—rice
—corn
—green beans

Other
—instant pudding
—hard boiled eggs
—tea
—biscuits
—bread
—cookies

This list is only a beginning—but a very good one! Add to it any skills particularly applicable to your household. One hundred percent hands-on learning!

BIBLE

We will assume that your teen is thoroughly familiar with the Bible's contents. If he or she isn't, go back to the Suggested Course of Study for grades 1–6!

Once basic Bible knowledge is under control, it's time for the Bible study tools. Learning the Greek and Hebrew alphabets only takes a few weeks. Learning to use Bible dictionaries, concordances, interlinear translations, and other helps can take up to a year of relaxed study. The goal is to have your student able to find things for himself and answer his own questions straight from the Book.

Now is also the time for a serious study of church history, a topic on which virtually all Christians are ignorant. It's also time to start learning how to teach others: how to lead a Bible study, how to teach a flannel lesson, how to lead family worship, how to evangelize, and so on.

(You're not a Christian. You're sitting here gritting your teeth, totally disgusted at the thought of all those hundreds of thousands of home-schooled Christian students who are going to be out there teaching other people about the Bible. Well, look at it this way. Who would you rather meet in a dark alley: a teenager with a Bible in his hand who wants to tell you about the Ten Commandments, or a teenager with a knife in his hand who wants to break them?)

NON-COLLEGE-BOUND STUDENTS

The course I've outlined above may seem overwhelming to someone who doesn't plan to go on to college in the first place. That's a *lot* of writing and reading and science and math!

Fair enough. The beauty of home school is that you don't have to do what other people think you "ought" to do. I'm all for the traditional core curriculum that people used to study back in the good old days—but if God made you to be a carpenter, or a juggler, or a farmer, who am I to dictate to you?

Those who already have a calling firmly in mind should feel free to cut and paste my suggestions above to fit the demands of their callings. After all, they *are* just suggestions, and they *are* rather strongly tilted toward higher education. If you're going to play in a symphony orchestra, I agree that you need music and foreign language studies more than you need calculus. (Orchestras travel a lot.) If you're going to farm, soil chemistry would be more helpful than abstract studies of covalence and oxidation-reduction. If you absolutely can't stand Shakespeare and Chaucer—if they don't enrich your life at all—then read someone who does! (You can't go wrong with P. G. Wodehouse.)

Don't sweat it. You can always pick up anything you missed later on—maybe when you're teaching your own children! In the meantime, if you can read and write and find Japan on an unlabeled world map, you're better off than a large minority of high school graduates!

COLLEGE-BOUND STUDENTS

You've followed the suggested course of study outlined above, which means you've had a really strong educational experience in the last six years. So, what's left for college? You've already had college-level math, science, theology, history, and literature!

College is properly the time for serious studies in philosophy and theology. It's also time for formal logic, learning languages in order to do research, specialized courses in the major disciplines, and vocational courses.

Before you study philosophy and theology, you ought to know right from wrong and know why you know. Before you take advanced or specialized courses like Advanced Physics or Topology, you ought to have mastered basic physics and mathematics. The same goes for intensive study of Jane Austen's literature or a history course on the French colonies: you should have a basic background in literature and history before tackling specialized courses in those areas.

Happily, you can often pass out of basic college courses by taking Advanced Placement tests. This then frees you up to spend less time (and money) on your basic college education, and make the most use of the specialized facilities and courses. Assuming you want to bother at all—see the Test Preparation and College Entrance chapter for some reasons to consider alternatives to the traditional on-site college degree!

REAL-WORLD LEARNING

Now's the time to talk about *emphasis*—what gets the most attention and what gets the least.

If you're mainly concerned about graduation and college-entrance requirements, the course of studies outlined above ought to satisfy these while providing a superior academic education.

However, if you are also concerned about bringing a Christian worldview to your educational program, and are not convinced that academics are the entire heart and soul of an education, then it's time to bring up a few more points.

The literature-science-history-etc. content of the better high school programs (note that we are *not* talking about fad programs and Mickey Mouse courses) tends to virtually exclude the real world entirely. In biology class, students handle only dead plants and creatures, or creatures so small you can only see them through a microscope. In chemistry class, they deal with purified materials and specialized equipment. History is learned through textbooks rather than through discussions with older people who lived through the times in question, or lectures by historians, or visits to historic sites. Literary excerpts are read in isolation from the cultural history of the times. During the entire process, students live in a specialized world of their own, cut off from the daily life of the community.

I don't think that this obsession with lab science and with manipulating regulated objects is balanced. You could make a pretty strong biblical case for teaching all teens the hands-on principles of gardening, farming, and animal husbandry, for example, rather than abstract biology from a textbook. According to the Bible, the human race's original assignment *was* gardening and animal husbandry! This would be an entirely different approach, focusing on nurturing plants and animals and helping the good ones be fruitful rather than on observing and manipulating dead plants and animals. Yes, you would end up studying microscopy, but from the viewpoint of analyzing and controlling plant and animal diseases and parasites rather than as a sheer abstraction.

Nurturing, as opposed to theorizing, is a hands-on process. Taking care of a baby is quite different from filling out workbook pages on child development. Building a toolshed is quite different from theorizing about architecture or physics. The real world, including the local community, is different from the classroom.

Biblically, the church and the home are supposed to prepare teens for independent life in the community. One way we can do this is to give teens opportunities for genuine community involvement, from helping out at the State Fair, to passing out political flyers at voting places, to starting a business.

Teens need a variety of non-institutional experiences with people *not* their own age, from the very young to the very old. This is more difficult because of our segregated society in which the old live in nursing homes or retirement communities and the babies are warehoused in daycare centers. The family and the church, however, both provide natural age-integrated environments, as does the business world to a lesser degree.

Teens also need real-world experiences: weeding a garden, baking a cake, sawing wood, sewing a dress. Ancient societies used to emphasize these real-world skills almost exclusively. Ours ignores them, relegating them to a small section of the revised Home Economics syllabus. We reward people for memorizing other people's theories, not for knowing how to make things work themselves.

I sometimes wonder: if all our expensive economic infrastructure were removed, how many of us could even survive? How many could find water, grow food, make their own clothes and shelter, raise our own children? How many could survive in a situation where we were suddenly cut off from police and fire protection? Surely such basic human wisdom counts as the *real* survival skills.

FINAL THOUGHTS

Home-schooled students have a great advantage over classroom-based students when it comes to following these suggestions. At the present time, it's doubtful that many of these ideas even could be implemented in traditional classrooms. Group education, especially age-segregated group education, is a whole different process from individual instruction and self-study.

But, on the other hand, if you've got it, why not flaunt it? I firmly believe that home-based instruction has potential to provide the *best* possible education for our children—if, that is, we have the courage to look at *all* our options, and not just keep treading on the same old tired K–12 treadmill! Let's all start thinking seriously about what we really *want* to learn and *want* to teach. Then go out, give it your best shot, and share your experiences with the rest of us!

GED REQUIREMENTS BY STATE

I f you're thinking of the GED as a handy way to have your child graduate high school early, think again. Although most of us think of the GED just as "the test you take to get your high school diploma," actually it has always been intended solely as a second-chance test for adults.

I spent a fascinating half-hour recently on the phone with Jean Lowe, the Assistant Director of the General Educational Development Testing Service. This is the private, non-profit group which owns and leases the GED tests. Let me share some of the history of this organization with you, as Jean shared it with me.

During World War I, a group of university presidents got together and decided to do something to help out the servicemen. Recognizing that the soldiers had their education interrupted by the war, and figuring that surely serving under Uncle Sam was an educational experience, the presidents decided to offer one semester of college credit for every year a man fought overseas. This idea was, of course, a disaster! Many of the soldiers had little more than a fourth-grade education and were totally unable to cope in the college environment.

By the time World War II rolled along, the university community had come up with a better idea. In 1942 they founded the Veterans Testing Service, with the mission of creating and disseminating a test of high-school equivalence. Now servicemen could prove that they had finished out their high school studies, and colleges would know they were getting acceptable students. This second venture was naturally a huge success, since all the colleges accepted the test from the start.

In the mid-1950s, New York state officials began to see that civilian adults would also benefit from the chance to obtain a "second chance" high school diploma. After some deliberation, the Veterans Testing Service decided to agree to the plan. Its name was then changed to the General Educational Development Testing Service. In due course, all 50 states, all provinces of Canada, and all U.S. territories acknowledged and adopted the GED test as a high-school equivalence exam for adults.

Since the GED Testing Service owns the tests, its board decides who gets to take the tests. Each state leases the tests from the GED Testing Service and negotiates the terms under which it will administer the tests. The GED Testing Service has certain minimum requirements which all states must follow. These terms have traditionally been designed to, in Jean's words, "not subvert the states' attendance laws." In most cases, you can't obtain a diploma from your state via the GED route until you are at least as old as the class in which you would normally have graduated.

Bottom line: if you don't mind waiting until your child is graduation age, the GED is an excellent way to validate your home school program's success. If you need this validation earlier, at present you'll have to look elsewhere.

REQUIREMENTS FOR ISSUANCE OF CERTIFICATE/DIPLOMA

Location	Minimum Test Score	Minimum Age For Credential	Residency Requirement	Minimum Age For Testing	Testing Fee Per Battery	Title of Credential
UNITED STATES						
Alabama	35 min & 45 avg	18[1]	30 days	18[1]	$20.00[2]	Certificate of High School Equivalency
Alaska	35 min & 45 avg	no minimum[1]	resident	no minimum[1]	maximum $15.00	High School Diploma
Arizona	35 min & 45 avg	18[1]	physically present[1]	18[1]	maximum $15.00[2]	High School Certificate of Equivalency
Arkansas	40 min & 45 avg	18	legal resident	18[1]	no charge	High School Diploma
California	40 min & 45 avg	18[1]	resident	18[1]	varies	High School Equivalency Certificate
Colorado	35 min & 45 avg	17	resident[1]	17	varies	High School Equivalency Certificate
Connecticut	35 min & 45 avg	19[1]	resident	19[1]	over 21, $13.00 otherwise free	High School Diploma
Delaware	40 min & 45 avg	18	resident	18[1]	$20.00	State Board of Education Endorsement
District of Columbia	35 min & 45 avg	18	resident[1]	18[1]	$9.00[2]	High School Equivalency
Florida	40 min & 45 avg	18	resident	18[1]	maximum $25.00	High School Diploma
Georgia	35 min & 45 avg	18[1]	resident	18[1]	$25.00	High School Equivalency Certificate
Hawaii	35 min & 45 avg	17	resident[1]	17[1]	$15.00	Department of Education High School Diploma
Idaho	35 min & 45 avg	19	resident[1]	19[1]	$30.00[2]	High School Equivalency Certificate
Illinois	35 min & 45 avg	18[1]	30 days	18[1]	$15.00[2]	High School Equivalency Certificate
Indiana	35 min & 45 avg	18[1]	30 days	18[1]	maximum $18.00	High School Equivalency Certificate
Iowa	35 min & 45 avg	18[1]	none	18[1]	$20.00[2]	High School Equivalency Diploma

---

[1] See jurisdictional requirements for exceptions and limitations

[2] See jurisdictional requirements for credential and other fees

REQUIREMENTS FOR ISSUANCE OF CERTIFICATE/DIPLOMA

Location	Minimum Test Score	Minimum Age For Credential	Residency Requirement	Minimum Age For Testing	Testing Fee Per Battery	Title of Credential
Kansas	35 min & 45 avg	18[1]	resident[1]	18[1]	$30.00	High School Equivalency Diploma
Kentucky	35 min & 45 avg	17	resident	17[1]	$10.00	High School Equivalency Diploma
Louisiana	40 min & 45 avg	17[1]	resident[1]	17[1]	varies	High School Equivalency Diploma[1]
Maine	35 min & 45 avg	18[1]	resident[1]	18[1]	$20.00[1]	High School Equivalency Diploma
Maryland	40 min & 45 avg	16[1]	30 days	16[1]	$12.00[2]	High School Diploma
Massachusetts	35 min & 45 avg	19[1]	6 months	19[1]	maximum $30.00	High School Equivalency Certificate
Michigan	35 min & 45 avg	18[1]	30 days	18[1]	varies	High School Equivalency Certificate
Minnesota	35 min & 45 avg	19[1]	resident	19[1]	$15.00-$35.00	Secondary School Equivalency Certificate
Mississippi	40 min or 45 avg	17	30 days[1]	17[1]	$15.00	High School Equivalency Diploma
Missouri	35 min & 45 avg	18[1]	resident[1]	18[1]	maximum $17.00	Certificate of High School Equivalence
Montana	35 min & 45 avg	18[1]	resident[1]	18[1]	$8.00	High School Equivalency Certificate
Nebraska	40 min or 45 avg	18	30 days[1]	18[1]	$20.00-$30.00[1]	Department of Education High School Diploma
Nevada	35 min & 45 avg	17	resident	17	$20.00	Certificate of High School Equivalency
New Hampshire	35 min & 45 avg	17	resident	17	$20.00	Certificate of High School Equivalency
New Jersey	see requirement	18[1]	none	18[1]	$20.00	High School Diploma
New Mexico	40 min or 50 avg	21[1]	resident	18[1]	varies[2]	High School Diploma
New York	40 min & 45 avg	19[1]	1 month	19[1]	no charge	High School Equivalency Diploma

[1] See jurisdictional requirements for exceptions and limitations
[2] See jurisdictional requirements for credential and other fees

REQUIREMENTS FOR ISSUANCE OF CERTIFICATE/DIPLOMA

Location	Minimum Test Score	Minimum Age For Credential	Residency Requirement	Minimum Age For Testing	Testing Fee Per Battery	Title of Credential
North Carolina	35 min & 45 avg	16	resident[1]	16[1]	$7.50[2]	High School Diploma Equivalency
North Dakota	45 min or 50 avg	18[1]	30 days[1]	18[1]	varies	High School Equivalency Diploma
Ohio	35 min & 45 avg	19[1]	resident	19[1]	$30.00[1,2]	Certificate of High School Equivalence
Oklahoma	40 min & 45 avg	18[1]	resident	18[1]	varies[2]	Certificate of High School Equivalency
Oregon	40 each test	18[1]	resident[1]	18[1]	varies	Certificate of General Educational Development
Pennsylvania	35 min & 45 avg[1]	18[1]	resident[1]	18[1]	varies	Commonwealth Secondary School Diploma
Rhode Island	35 min & 45 avg	18[1]	resident[1]	18[1]	$15.00	High School Equivalency Diploma
South Carolina	45 average	17	see state requirement	17[1]	$15.00	High School Equivalency Certificate
South Dakota	40 min & 45 avg	18[1]	resident[1]	18[1]	maximum $20.00	High School Equivalency Certificate
Tennessee	35 min & 45 avg	18	resident	18[1]	varies	Equivalency High School Diploma
Texas	40 min or 45 avg	18[1]	resident[1]	18[1]	varies[2]	Certificate of High School Equivalency
Utah	40 min & 45 avg	18[1]	resident[1]	18[1]	varies[2]	Certificate of General Educational Development
Vermont	35 min & 45 avg	16	resident	18[1]	$25.00	Secondary School Equivalency Certificate
Virginia	35 min & 45 avg	18[1]	30 days	18[1]	$20.00[2]	Commonwealth General Educational Development Certificate
Washington	40 min & 45 avg	19[1]	resident	18[1]	$22.00	Certificate of Educational Competence
West Virginia	40 min & 45 avg	18[1]	30 days	18[1]	varies	High School Equivalent Diploma

[1] See jurisdictional requirements for exceptions and limitations

[2] See jurisdictional requirements for credential and other fees

REQUIREMENTS FOR ISSUANCE OF CERTIFICATE/DIPLOMA

Location	Minimum Test Score	Minimum Age For Credential	Residency Requirement	Minimum Age For Testing	Testing Fee Per Battery	Title of Credential
Wisconsin	40 min & 50 avg	18.5	resident	18[1]	varies	High School Equivalency Diploma
Wyoming	35 min & 45 avg	18	resident[1]	see state requirement	maximum $20.00	High School Equivalency Certificate
CANADA - PROVINCES & TERRITORIES						
Alberta	45 each test	18[1]	resident	18	$40.00	High School Equivalency Diploma
British Columbia	45 each test	19[1]	resident	19	$25.00	Secondary School Equivalency Certificate
Manitoba	45 each test	19[1]	resident	19	$22.00	High School Equivalency Diploma
New Brunswick	45 each test[1]	19	3 months	19	$10.00	12th Year High School Equivalency Diploma
Newfoundland	40 min & 45 avg	19[1]	3 months	19	$20.00	High School Equivalency Diploma
Northwest Territories	40 min & 45 avg	18[1]	6 months	18[1]	$5.00	High School Equivalency Certificate
Nova Scotia	45 each test	19[1]	none	19	$20.00	High School Equivalency Diploma
Prince Edward Island	45 each test	19[1]	resident	19[1]	$20.00	High School Equivalency Certificate
Saskatchewan	45 each test[1]	19	resident	19[1]	$25.00	High School Equivalency Certificate
Yukon	45 each test	19[1]	resident	19[1]	$25.00	Secondary School Equivalency Certificate
U.S. TERRITORIES						
American Samoa	40 each test	18	resident	18[1]	$10.00	High School Diploma of Equivalency
Canal Zone	40 min & 45 avg	17	resident[1]	17	$35.00	Certificate of High School Equivalency
Guam	35 min & 45 avg	18	resident	18[1]	$10.00	High School Equivalency Diploma

[1] See jurisdictional requirements for exceptions and limitations
[2] See jurisdictional requirements for credential and other fees

REQUIREMENTS FOR ISSUANCE OF CERTIFICATE/DIPLOMA

Location	Minimum Test Score	Minimum Age For Credential	Residency Requirement	Minimum Age For Testing	Testing Fee Per Battery	Title of Credential
Kwajalein	35 min & 45 avg	18		18	$22.25	Certificate of Equivalency
Mariana Isls.	40 min or 45 avg	18	30 days	18[1]	$5.00	High School Equivalency Diploma
Marshall Isls.	40 min or 45 avg	18	30 days	18[1]	$7.50[2]	High School Equivalency Certificate
Palau	40 min & 45 avg	16		16[1]	$10.00	Certificate of Equivalency
Puerto Rico	35 min & 45 avg	18	resident	18	no charge	High School Equivalency Diploma
Virgin Isls.	35 min & 45 avg	18	3 months	17	$20.00	Certificate of Equivalency

[1] See jurisdictional requirements for exceptions and limitations
[2] See jurisdictional requirements for credential and other fees

INDEXES

HOW TO USE THE INDEX OF SUPPLIERS

These indexes were designed to give you both the necessary information to order products and catalogs, and to give you an idea of each company's services and policies. Besides addresses, the indexes of suppliers contain telephone numbers, types of payment accepted, price of catalog or brochure (if any), refund policy, and a general description of the company's product line. This information will (we hope!) help you become a more informed shopper.

HOW TO BE A PERFECT CUSTOMER

First, please do not call a toll-free number except to order, unless the index entry specifically says that the supplier is willing to use his toll-free line for inquiries.

Each call on a 800 number costs the supplier a substantial amount, and it is frustrating to have callers rack up your phone bill for questions that could have been answered just as well by letter.

A number of suppliers have asked me to mention that it is necessary to add state sales tax when you order from a supplier in your home state. Not sure what the tax is? The supplier's order form will tell you.

It is always wise to get the supplier's catalog or brochure before ordering. Prices change, and so do refund policies. You are less likely to be disappointed if you carefully check these out before ordering.

When requesting information by letter, an SASE (self-addressed stamped envelope) is always appreciated. This does not apply to requests for free catalogs, since these seldom fit in a standard envelope.

Companies that offer free catalogs do so in the hope that we will become interested in and buy their products. By all means, send for any catalogs you think might be useful. Just remember that catalogs are expensive to print and mail, so give the supplier a fair chance to sell you something in return!

If you experience a problem with a supplier, please contact them about it more than once before assuming they have deliberately mishandled your order. Errors do happen. The Post Office may not have delivered the letter containing your original order, or may have lost the letter you wrote complaining about your order. Phone messages can be mislaid. Verify all information: enclose copies of your cancelled checks, product invoices, and packing slips.

Remember the rule of charity, even when dealing with businesses: "Do unto others as you would have them do unto you." Then you will be a Perfect Customer!

EXPLANATION OF CODES USED IN THIS INDEX

Credit card information: we list credit cards accepted by each supplier. "VISA" means (of course) they take the VISA card. "MC" means they take MasterCard. "AmEx" means they take American Express. "CB" stands for "Carte Blanche." Some companies also take Discover, OPTIMA, and other lesser-known cards.

Please note that many suppliers *only* allow the use of their toll-free lines for credit card orders. In-state calls must also be made on the local telephone number rather than the toll-free number. You may also need to have a certain minimum size of order to qualify for ordering over the toll-free line.

Local telephone number: when you see a toll-free number followed by two letters, a colon, and another number, that means that callers from that state must use that local number. Example: "OR: (503) 343-0123" means Oregon callers must use the (503) number.

Other methods of payment: "Check or M.O." means the company *only* takes checks or money orders; they do not take credit cards. All companies that take credit cards also take checks and money orders. "School P.O." means they accept purchase orders from *legitimate, institutional* schools. Do not try to get around this by sending a P.O. on your home school's letterhead! (Home schoolers who do this give us all a bad name.) Similarly, "Business P.O." means they accept purchase orders from *legitimate* businesses.

Although it is not explicitly stated in many instances, most suppliers offer wholesale terms to retailers and catalogers. Call or write the supplier for information if you are interested in retailing their products.

Some suppliers list office hours during which they answer their phone. In such cases, "EST" stands for Eastern Standard Time; "PST" stands for "Pacific [West Coast] Standard Time"; and "CST" stands for "Central Standard Time."

SASE stands for "self-addressed stamped envelope." "Long SASE" means a self-addressed business-size (#10) envelope.

Catalog/brochure prices: many catalogs and brochures are free. Some companies charge for their catalogs, though. A number of those who charge for their catalogs refund the catalog price on the first order you place with them. Thus, "Catalog, $1, refundable on first order," means that although you have to send $1 in advance to get the catalog, you get to deduct $1 from your first order from that catalog.

Returns policy: generally, companies either offer unconditional guarantees (return product within the time limit for any reason), or have a guarantee that applies only to products returned in "resalable condition." This means the product must not be tattered, written on, or look used, since the supplier expects to sell it again.

Sometimes you are also required to return the product in its original packaging or with a copy of your invoice. This is to ensure that it does not arrive back damaged and to help the supplier quickly locate and refund your account on his computer system.

Some suppliers' guarantees require you to get permission first to return the item. This means you must call or write first and receive a return authorization from the company *before* sending the item back.

We sincerely hope you find this index information helpful. Please keep in mind that businesses do move and change their telephone numbers and order policies; that's one reason why the *Big Book* is periodically revised! Generally, if a successful business moves, it arranges to have its mail forwarded. If there is no forwarding address, or it has expired, the company very likely has ceased to exist. (All companies in this index were verified shortly before the book was printed.)

WHERE TO FIND MORE HELP

Please also be kind to your humble reviewer. I no longer have the resources to answer requests for new business addresses, or to give personalized curriculum consultations. (Did I mention we're expecting our eighth child?)

Your local home school support group, on the other hand, exists to offer this very kind of help. Go ahead and give them a try!

INDEX OF AMERICAN SUPPLIERS

A Beka Book Publications
Box 18000
Pensacola, FL 32523-9160
1-800-874-BEKA (2352) M-F 8-4:30 CT VISA,MC
(904) 478-8480
Fax: (904) 478-8558
Free catalog, order form, and brochures.
Returns: In resalable condition, in original packaging, within 120 days.
Christian texts and supplies (Preschool-Grade 12).

Academy for Economic Education
125 Sovran Center
Richmond, VA 23277
(804) 643-0071 Check or M.O.
Returns: With permission
Economics education programs.

Addison-Wesley Publishing Co.
Jacob Way
Reading, MA 01867
1-800-447-2226 VISA, MC, C.O.D.
(617) 944-3700

Fax: (617) 942-1117
Free catalog.
Textbook and trade publisher.

Advance Memory Research, Inc. (AMR)
2601 Ulmerton Rd., E.
Suite 106B
Largo, FL 34641-3822
1-800-323-2500 VISA, MC, AmEx, Discover.
FL: (813) 539-6555
Free brochure. Call toll-free for info.
Foreign language and speaking courses.

Advanced Training Institute of America
see Institute in Basic Life Principles

Advocate, The
P.O. Box 13656
Portland, OR 97213
(503) 257-7023 Check or M.O.
Fax: (503) 255-6164
Pro-life news and issues magazine.

Alpha Omega Publications
P.O. Box 3153
Tempe, AZ 85280
1-800-622-3070 Orders VISA, MC, C.O.D.
1-800-821-4443 Information
AZ: (602) 438-2717
Fax: (602) 438-2702
Free catalog.
Returns: Unconditional guarantee, within 30 days.
Christian curriculum.
Home school program.

American Association of Bible Colleges
P.O. Box 1523
Fayetteville, AR 72702
(501) 521-8164 Check or M.O.
Fax: (501) 521-9202
Directory $7.50.
Information about Bible colleges.

American Christian History Institute
P.O. Box 648
Palo Cedro, CA 96073
(916) 547-3535 Check or M.O.
Free brochure. Returns: In resalable condition.
Principle Approach by James Rose.
Books on Teaching and Learning

American Christian Schools International
P.O. Box 4097
Whittier, CA 90607-4097
1-800-367-0798 VISA, MC.
CA: (213) 694-4791
Fax: (213) 690-6234
School association, curriculum publisher.

American College Testing Program (ACT)
2201 N. Dodge St.
P.O. Box 168
Iowa City, IA 52243
(319) 337-1429 Check or M.O.
Returns: With permission, in resalable condition.
Tests, career planning software, college guide, study guides.

American Family Association
P.O. Drawer 2440
Tupelo, MS 38803
(601) 844-5036 Check or M.O.
Family issues magazine.

American Science & Surplus
601 Linden Place
Evanston, IL 60202
(708) 475-8440 VISA, MC.
Fax: (708) 864-1589
$12.50 minimum. Flat $4 shipping/order.
Catalog $1 first class, free otherwise.
Returns: Unconditional, within 15 days, doesn't include shipping and handling.
Surplus stuff described with wit.

American Textbook Committee
100 Union Hill Drive
Suite 101
Birmingham, AL 35209
(205) 879-9222 Check or M.O.
Postage paid on prepaid orders. Returns: With permission, in resalable condition.

American Vision
P.O. Box 724088
Atlanta, GA 30339
1-800-628-9460 VISA, MC.
(404) 988-0555 (office)
Fax: (404) 952-2587
Free brochure. Returns: With permission.
Christian worldview organization.

Ampersand Press
691 26th St.
Oakland, CA 94612
(415) 832-6669 Check or M.O., C.O.D.
Fax: (415) 832-3918
Free brochure. Returns: In original packaging.
Educational games publisher.

AMR
see Advanced Memory Research

Apprentice Academics
P.O. Box 788
Claremore, OK 74018-0788
(918) 342-1335 VISA, MC
Free full-page sized info pak.
Returns: Books and Baby Model in resalable condition, within 30 days. No refund on course.
Midwifery course, book, baby model.

Aristoplay, Ltd.
P.O. Box 7028
Ann Arbor, MI 48107
1-800-634-7738 VISA, MC. School P.O.'s net 30.
(313) 995-4353
Fax: (313) 995-4611
Free color catalog.
Refund or exchange of damaged or defective games.
Educational games publisher.

Arthur Bornstein School of Memory Training
11693 San Vicente Blvd.
Los Angeles, CA 90049
1-800-468-2058 VISA, MC, AmEx
(213) 478-2056
Fax: (213) 207-2433
Free brochures.
Returns: With permission, in resalable condition, within 14 days.
Memory training materials.

Asia Society, The
725 Park Avenue
New York, NY 10021
(212) 288-6400 Check or M.O. or school P.O.
Fax: (212) 517-7246
Free brochure and materials list.
Educational videos about Japan and Korea.

Association of Christian Schools International
P.O. Box 4097
Whittier, CA 90607
(213) 694-4791
School association. Publishes some curriculum materials, including typing book.

Audio Forum
Division of Jeffrey Norton Publishers, Inc.
96 Broad Street
Guilford, CT 06437
1-800-243-1234 VISA, MC, AmEx, DC, CB, Institutional P.O.
(203) 453-9794
Fax: (203) 453-9774
Free catalogs.
Returns: Unconditional, within 3 weeks.
Self-study audio and video tapes.

Audio Memory Publishing
1433 E. 9th St.
Long Beach, CA 90813
1-800-365-SING VISA, MC.
(213) 591-1548
Free catalog. Returns: Unconditional.
Audio cassettes and related educational materials.

Baker Book House
P.O. Box 6287
Grand Rapids, MI 49516-6287
(616) 957-3110 VISA, MC
Fax: (616) 676-9573
Christian book publisher.

Ball-Stick-Bird Publications, Inc.
P.O. Box 592
Stony Brook, NY 11790
(516) 331-9164 Check or M.O.
Free color brochure.
No returns.
Reading system that even works for labeled children.

Barron's Educational Series, Inc.
250 Wireless Blvd.
Hauppauge, NY 11788
1-800-645-3476 VISA, MC. $10 minimum.
NY: 1-800-257-5729
Fax: (516) 434-3723
No catalog. No returns.
Textbook publisher.

Basil Blackwell, Inc.
American International Distribution Corp.
64 Depot Road
Colchester, VT 05446
1-800-445-6638
Fax: (617) 494-1437
Free catalog.
Returns: In resalable condition, within 60 days.
Publisher.

Beaumont Books
P.O. Box 551
Westminster, CO 80030
(303) 433-9192 Check or M.O.
Free brochure with Long SASE.
Returns: In resalable condition, within 90 days.
Publishes a typing program.

Bellerophon Books
36 Anacapa St.
Santa Barbara, CA 93101
(805) 965-7034 Check or M.O.
Fax: (805) 965-8286
Free catalog with SASE.
Returns: For credit, within a year, in resalable condition.
Educational coloring books and cutout books.

Betterway Publications
P.O. Box 219
Crozet, VA 22932
1-800-522-2782 8-6 EST. Check or M.O.
(804) 823-5661
Fax: (804) 823-2047
Free catalog with long SASE (.89 postage).
Returns: In resalable condition, within 30 days.
Publisher.

Bible Memory Association
P.O. Box 12000
Ringgold, LA 71068-2000
(318) 894-9154 VISA, MC.
Fax: (318) 894-9189
Free brochure. Returns: In resalable condition.
Bible memorization course.

Bits & Pieces
12 Daniel Rd.
Fairfield, NJ 07006
1-800-526-2554 VISA, MC, AmEx.
(201) 227-1224
Fax: (201) 227-9742
Free catalog.
Returns: Will refund balance of subscription if you are dissatisfied.
Common sense wisdom magazine.

Blue Bird Publishing
1713 E. Broadway #306
Tempe, AZ 85282
1-800-654-1993 for orders. VISA, MC.
(602) 968-4088
Fax: (602) 983-7319
Free brochure with long SASE.
Returns: With permission.
Publisher of home-school and home-business books.

Blue Heron Publishing, Inc.
Rt. 3 Box 376
Hillsboro, OR 97124
(503) 621-3911 Check or M.O.
Publishes Walt Morey Adventure Library.

Bluestocking Press
P.O. Box 1014
Placerville, CA 95667-1014
(916) 621-1123 VISA, MC. U.S. funds only.
Free info with large SASE and 2 first class stamps.
Returns: In resalable condition, within 30 days.
Free-market economics and business books for children and adults.

Blumenfeld Education Letter
P.O. Box 41561
Boise, ID 83711
(208) 322-4440 7 days, 24 hours. VISA, MC.
Newsletter.

Bob Jones University Press
Customer Services
Greenville, SC 29614
1-800-845-5731 E.S.T. weekdays. VISA, MC.
Free catalog. Orders and info on toll-free line.
Returns: Resalable condition, with permission, within 30 days.
Christian textbook publisher.

Bobby Horton
3430 Sagebrook Lane
Birmingham, AL 35243
(205) 967-6426 Check or M.O. or he will bill you.
Free brochures. Returns: Within 30 days.
Civil war songs.

Bolchazy-Carducci Publishers
1000 Brown Street, Unit 101
Wauconda, IL 60084
(708) 526-4344 VISA, MC, AmEx.
Fax: (708) 526-2867
Free catalog includes ordering info for many other magazines, publishers.
Must request buttons catalog separately.
Returns: Resalable condition, within 30 days.
Classical language materials, ancient world studies.

Busines$ Kids
301 Almeria Ave., Suite 330
Coral Gables, FL 33134
1-800-852-4544 VISA, MC, AmEx.
Fax: (305) 445-8869
Free catalog. No returns.
The Busines$ Kit.

Caddylak Systems, Inc.
131 Heartland Blvd.
P.O. Box W1322
Brentwood, NY 11717-0698
1-800-523-8060 VISA, MC, AmEx
Fax: (516) 254-2018
Free catalog.
Returns: In resalable condition, within 30 days.
They will bill your business.
Office organizers, *Words that Sell*.

Calliope
30 Grove St.
Peterborough, NH 03458
(603) 924-7209 VISA, MC. $10 minimum.
Fax: (603) 924-7380
Free catalog.
Children's world history magazine.

Canon Press
P.O. Box 8741
Moscow, ID 83843
1-800-488-2034 VISA, MC.
(208) 799-8511
Free catalog and brochure with long SASE.
Returns: In resalable condition, within 30 days.
Publishes ogic book for Christians.

Capper's Books
616 Jefferson
Topeka, KS 66607
1-800-777-7171, ext. 107 VISA, MC.
Free catalog.
Authentic pioneer, old-time stories.

Capsela Engineering Kits
see Sanyei American Corporation

Carolina Biological Supply Company
2700 York Rd.
Burlington, NC 27215
1-800-334-5551 VISA, MC, Discover, AmEx.
(919) 584-0381 Fax: (919) 584-3399

Catalog $16.95, free to science teachers.
Returns: Unconditional, within 30 days.
Supplies and resources for teaching science and
mathematics at all levels.

Cathy Duffy
see Home Run Enterprises

Center for Science in the Public Interest
Suite 300
1875 Connecticut Ave. N.W.
Washington, DC 20009-5728
(202) 332-9110 VISA, MC.
Fax: (202) 265-4954
Free catalog. Returns: Within 30 days.
Nutrition Action Healthletter. Membership $19.95.

Center for Scientific Creationism
5612 N. 20th Pl.
Phoenix, AZ 85016
(602) 955-7663 Check or M.O.
Fax: (602) 955-7663
Creation science books, videos, and seminars.

Charlie Duke Enterprises
P.O. Box 310345
New Braunfels, TX 78131-0345
(512) 629-1223 Visa, MC
Fax: (512) 620-1255
Moonwalk videos.

Children's Small Press Collection
719 North Fourth Avenue
Ann Arbor, MI 48104
1-800-221-8056 VISA, MC.
MI: (313) 668-8056
Free catalog. Returns: In resalable condition.
Children's books, records, and games.

Christian Book Distributors
Box 6000
Peabody, MA 01961-6000
(508) 977-4500 VISA, MC.
Fax: (508) 531-8146
Free sample catalog.
Returns: Shipping mistakes, defective products.
Membership $5/year.
You don't have to be a member to order.
Discount Christian books/Bibles.

Christian Financial Concepts
601 Broad Street
Gainesville, GA 30501
1-800-722-1976 (orders)
GA: (404) 534-1000
Fax: (404) 536-7226
Free catalog.
Returns: No questions asked within 30 days.
Larry Burkett videos, tapes, books.

Christian History Back Issues
P.O. Box 627
Holmes, PA 19043
(215) 532-6190 VISA, MC.
US funds only. All orders prepaid.
Magazine of church history, back issue orders.

Christian History Magazine
P.O. Box 627
Holmes, PA 19043
(215) 532-6190 VISA, MC.
U.S. Funds only. All orders prepaid.
For back issues see Christian History Back Issues.
Magazine of church history.

Christian Liberty Press
502 W. Euclid Ave.
Arlington Heights, IL 60004
(708) 259-8736 Check or M.O.
Free catalog and brochure. Returns: Within 30 days, 10% restocking charge.
Full service homeschool program and Christian book publisher/distributor.

Christian Life Workshops
P.O. Box 2250
Gresham, OR 97030
(503) 667-3942 VISA, MC.
Catalog and brochure $1.
Returns: 100% refund, except shipping and handling, in resalable condition, within 30 days.
Gregg Harris seminars.
Home schooling resources.

Christian Light Education
see Christian Light Publications

Christian Light Publications
1066 Chicago Ave.
P.O. Box 1126
Harrisonburg, VA 22801-1126
(703) 434-0750 VISA, MC, C.O.D.
Free catalog, brochure, and samples.
Returns: With permission, in resalable condition, within 30 days for 100% refund.
Science equipment, curriculum, and school supplies, Mennonite-approved books.

Christian Schools International
3350 E. Paris Ave., S.E.
Grand Rapids, MI 49512
1-800-635-8288 VISA, MC.
Canada: 1-800-637-8288
(616) 957-1070
Fax: (616) 957-5022
Free catalog.
Returns: Within 60 days, in resalable condition, with authorization.
Christian textbooks.

Church Resource Ministries
420 East Montwood Ave.
La Habra, CA 90631
(714) 738-0949 Check or M.O.
Fax: (714) 879-6076
Free brochure. Returns: In resalable condition.
MEMLOK Bible memory system.

Classics on Tape
P.O. Box 969
Ashland, OR 97520
1-800-729-2665 VISA, MC.
OR: (503) 776-5179
Fax: (503) 734-2537
Free catalog. Free replacement or broken cassettes.
Returns: within 30 days.
Unabridged cassette tapes of classic books.

Cobblestone Publishing
30 Grove St.
Peterborough, NH 03458
(603) 924-7209 VISA, MC. $10 minimum.
Fax: (603) 924-7380
Free catalog.
Children's magazines.

Collier/Macmillan
100 Front Street
Riverside, NJ 08075
(212) 702-2000 VISA, MC, AmEx.
Returns: In resalable condition, with receipt, within 1 year.
Publisher.

Commonsense Press
PO Box 471
Corona del Mar, CA 92625
(714) 673-6136 Check or M.O.
Returns: Within 30 days.
Publisher of *Alpha Strategy*.

Conservative Book Club
15 Oakland Ave.
Harrison, NY 10528
Check or M.O.
Returns: With permission.
Monthly reviews to members.
Discount book club.

Contemporary Books, Inc.
180 N. Michigan Ave.
Chicago, IL 60601
Attn: Wendy Harris
1-800-621-1918 VISA, MC, AmEx
(312) 782-9181
Fax: (312) 782-2157
Free catalog. Returns: In resalable condition, with invoice, within 60 days.
Number Sense math program.

Covenant Home Curriculum
Stonewood Village
17700 West Capitol Drive
Brookfield, WI 53045
(414) 781-2171 VISA, MC.
Free information packet. Catalog $9.50, refunded with first order.
Returns: With permission, within 30 days.
K–12 curriculum. Quarterly tests.

Covenant Publications
224 Auburn Ave.
Monroe, LA 71201
(318) 323-3061 Check or M.O.
Free brochure with long SASE.
Returns: In resalable condition, within 30 days.
American history cassette series.

Crane's Select Educational Materials
P.O. Box 124
Bedford, IN 47421
(812) 279-3434 Check or M.O., C.O.D.
Catalog $1, refunded with first order.
Returns: Unconditional, in resalable condition, within 30 days.
Supplemental teaching materials catalog.

Creation Resource Foundation
P.O. Box 16100
South Lake Tahoe, CA 95706
(916) 542-1509 Check or M.O.
Fax: (916) 541-7980
Publisher of creationist materials.

Creation's Child
P.O. Box 3004 #44
Corvallis, OR 97339
(503) 758-3413 Check or M.O.
Free brochure with SASE.
Returns: In resalable condtion, within 30 days.
Home school supplies.

Crossway Books
1300 Crescent St.
Wheaton, IL 60187
(708) 682-4300 Check or M.O.
Fax: (708) 682-4785
Free brochure.
Publisher.

CUBE-IT! Manipulative Math
P.O. Box 141411
Spokane, WA 99214
(509) 928-6843 8-5 M-Sat PST. VISA, MC, budget plan available (for Series 1, 2 or 3).
Free catalog.
Returns: With permission, in resalable condition, in original packaging, within 5 days.
Publisher of Cube-It! Manipulative Math.

Cuisenaire Company of America
12 Church Street, Box D
New Rochelle, NY 10802
1-800-237-3142 VISA, MC, C.O.D.
(914) 235-0900
Fax: (914) 576-3480
Free catalog and brochure with SASE.
Manufacturer of math manipulatives.

D. C. Heath and Company
125 Spring St.
Lexington, MA 02173
1-800-428-8071 VISA, MC.
Identify your home as a home school to receive
the school price listed in this book.
Textbook publisher.

DAK Industries Incorporated
8200 Remmet Ave.
Canoga Park, CA 91304
1-800-325-0800 (orders) 1-800-888-6703 (for the
hearing impaired) VISA, MC, Amex, Institutional P.O.
1-800-888-7808 (inquiries)
Fax: (818) 340-3069
Free catalog.
Returns: In original packaging, within 30 days.
Discount electronics supplier.

Dale Seymour Publications
P.O. Box 10888
Palo Alto, CA 94303
1-800-872-1100 VISA, MC. (orders)
(415) 324-2800
Fax: (415) 324-3424
Free catalog.
Returns: In resalable condition, within 30 days,
call first.
Publisher of supplemental teaching materials K–12.

Don Aslett's Cleaning Center
P.O. Box 39
311 S. 5th
Pocatello, ID 83204
1-800-451-2402 (orders) VISA, MC, Discover,
C.O.D.
ID: (208) 232-6212 (inquiries)
Free catalog and brochure.
Returns: Unconditional, within 60 days.
House cleaning supplies and books.

Donald and Mary Baker
37 Delsie Street
Clarksville, AR 72830
(501) 754-2223 or 754-3309 Check or M.O.
Free brochure with SASE.
Returns: In resalable condition.
Publisher of *Bible Study Guide for All Ages.*

Doorposts
Suite 372
P.O. Box 1610
Clackamas, OR 97015
(503) 698-8127 Ext. 372 Check or M.O.
Free brochure with long SASE.
Returns: In resalable condition, within 10 days.
Character education materials.

Durell Foundation
P.O. Box 847
Berryville, VA 22611
(703) 955-4939 Check or M.O.
Fax: (703) 955-4943
Free catalog. Returns: Unconditional.
Teaching kit on money and banking

Eating Better Cookbooks
8830 Glencoe Drive
Riverside, CA 92503
(714) 687-5491 Check or M.O.
Returns: Resalable condition, within 10 days.
Natural foods cookbooks.

Economics Press, Inc.
12 Daniel Rd.
Fairfield, NJ 07006
(201) 227-1224   Fax: (201) 227-9742
Beyond the Bottom Line financial managament
course.

EDC Publishing
Division of educational development corporation
P.O. Box 470663
Tulsa, OK 74147
(918) 622-4522 VISA, MC, C.O.D.
Fax: (918) 663-4509
Catalog $2, rebated on first order.
Returns: With permission in resalable condition,
after 60 days, before 360 days.
10% shipping, $2.50 minimum.
Usborne books.

Edmund Scientific Company
101 East Gloucester Pike
Barrington, NJ 08007
(609) 573-6250 VISA, MC, AmEx, Discover, OPTIMA.
Fax: (609) 573-6295
Free catalog.
Returns: Unconditional, within 45 days.
Science supplies, optics, kits for all ages.

Education Services
6410 Raleigh St.
Arvada, CO 80003
Biblical Psychology of Learning (a great book),
How-to teaching books by Ruth Beechick.

Educational Design, Inc.
47 W. 13th St.
New York, NY 10011
1-800-221-9372 Check or M.O.
(212) 255-7900
Free catalog. Returns: Within 30 days.
Skillbooks, various subjects.

Educational Insights
19560 S. Rancho Way
Dominguez Hills, CA 90220
1-800-933-3277 VISA, MC.
(213) 637-2131 or 979-1955
Fax: (213) 605-5048
Free catalog. Returns: With permission.
Minimum order $25.
10% shipping, $2.50 minimum.
Producer of innovative, hands-on materials for
grades K–12.

Educational Products
(CBN Center)
CSB336
Virginia Beach, VA 23463
1-800-288-4769 VISA, MC.
Fax: (804) 523-7990
Free color brochure.
Returns: Within 30 days, in resalable condition.
Total language arts K–adult.

Educators Publishing Service, Inc.
75 Moulton St.
Cambridge, MA 02138-1104
1-800-225-5750 VISA, MC, Discover, AmEx.
MA: (617) 547-6706
Fax: (617) 547-0412
Free catalogs and brochures.
Returns: In resalable condition, within 30 days.
Indicate grade level you need.
Language arts, math, college prep, and parent
helps.

Elijah Company, The
P.O. Box 12483
Knoxville, TN 37912-0483
(615) 691-1310 Check or M.O.
Catalog $1, refunded with first order.
Returns: In resalable condition, within 30 days.
Shipping 10%, $2.50 minimum.
Home school catalog.

Entrepreneur
2392 Morse Ave.
P.O. Box 19787
Irvine, CA 92713-9438
1-800-421-2300 or 2345 MC, Visa, AmX
CA: 1-800-352-7449 or (714) 261-2325
Fax: (714) 755-4211
Free catalog.
Returns: In original packaging, within 30 days.
Magazines, business startup guides.

Equals
Lawrence Hall of Science
University of California
Berkeley, CA 94720
(415) 642-1823 Check or M.O. or Purchase Order
for amounts over $25.00.
Fax: (415) 642-1055
Free brochure. Non-returnable.
Activities for families at home, mathematics in-
service classes, or family math K–8.

Essential Learning Products Co.
2300 W. Fifth Ave.
P.O. Box 2607
Columbus, OH 43216-2607
(614) 486-0631 VISA, MC, Discover.
Fax: (614) 486-0762
Free catalog.
Returns: With permission, in resalable condition.
Math and language arts practice books.

Executive Strategies
1328 Broadway
New York, NY 10001
Newsletter and books for corporate executives.

Exploratorium Mail Order
3601 Lyon St.
San Francisco, CA 94123
1-800-359-9899 VISA, MC.
(415) 563-7337 Fax: (415) 561-0307
Science museum and publisher.

Family Learning Center
Rt. 2, Box 264
Hawthorne, FL 32640
(904) 475-5869 Check or M.O.
Free catalog. Returns:
Resalable condition, within 30 days.
Home-school curriculum and widgets.

Fearon Teacher Aids
PO Box 280
Carthage, IL 62321
1-800-242-7272 VISA, MC.
(217) 357-3900 Fax: (217) 357-3908
Free catalog.
Publisher.

**Fellowship of Christian Midwives
and Childbirth Educators, International**
7661 Deertrail Drive
Parker, CO 80134
Check or M.O.
Christian childbirth and midwifery magazine.

Focus on the Family
P.O. Box 500
Pomona, CA 91769
VISA, MC.
Publisher *Focus on the Family Citizen.*

Forum for Biblical Ethics in Medicine, Inc.
P.O. Box 13231
Florence, SC 29504-3231
Check or M.O.
Publisher of *Journal of Biblical Ethics in Medicine.*

**Foundation for American Christian Education
(FACE)**
Box 27035
San Francisco, CA 94127
(415) 661-1775 VISA, MC.
Free catalog and brochure.
Returns: In resalable condition. Principle Approach
to America's Christian history and education.
Reference volumes and literature curriculum.

Foundation for Economic Education
Irvington-on-Hudson, NY 10533
(914) 591-7230 VISA, MC.
Fax: (914) 591-8910
Free catalog.
Returns: With permission, in resalable condition.
Free enterprise literature.

Friends of Homebirth
103 N. Pearl St.
Big Sandy, TX 75755
(903) 636-4014 Check or M.O.
Fax: (903) 636-2288
Free sample issue.
Home birth newsletter.

Gallopade Publishing Group
235 E. Ponce de Leon Avenue
Suite 100
Decatur, GA 30030
(404) 370-0420
Check or M.O. or school purchase order.
Free brochure. Satisfaction guaranteed.
Publisher.

GED Testing Service
see General Educational Development Testing
Service of the American Council on Education

**General Educational Development Testing
Service of the American Council on Education**
One Dupont Circle, Suite 20
Washington, DC 20036-1193
(202) 939-9490 Fax: (202) 775-8578
GED requirements by state.

Giant Photos, Inc.
P.O. Box 406
Rockford, IL 61105
1-800-826-2139 (orders).
VISA, MC, C.O.D. ($4.00 charge).
(815) 964-7927 Free brochure.
Returns: Resalable condition within 30 days.
History and geography resources.

Globe Book Company
Simon & Schuster School Group
4350 Equity Drive
Columbus, OH 43216
1-800-848-9500
Textbook publisher.

Golden Educational Center
P.O. Box 12
Bothell, WA 98041-0012
(206) 481-1395 Check or M.O.
Free catalog. Returns: Damaged merchandise only.
Innovative math and geography materials.

Good Things Company
Drawer 'N'
Norman, OK 73070-70130
(405) 329-7797 Check or M.O.
Free brochure.
"Adam and Eve Family Tree."

Great Christian Books, Inc.
229 S. Bridge St.
P.O. Box 8000
Elkton, MD 21922-8000
(301) 392-0800 VISA, MC, Discover, C.O.D.
(U.P.S.)
Fax: (301) 392-3103
Free catalog. No returns unless defective.
Discount Christian books, music and home-schooling supplies.

Greenleaf Press
1570 Old Laguardo Rd.
Lebanon, TN 37087
(615) 449-1617 Check or M.O.
Catalog $1 (refunded with first order). Returns:
With permission, in resalable condition.
"History for the thoughtful child."

Hammond Inc.
515 Valley St.
Maplewood, NJ 07040
1-800-526-4953 Check or M.O.
NJ: (201) 763-6000
Free catalog. Returns with permission.
Geography and other school supplies.

Harper Collins Publishers
1900 East Lake Ave.
Glenview, IL 60025
1-800-782-2665 VISA, MC.
(708) 729-3000
Returns: Within one year, in resalable condition,
with invoice.
Policy: "Teacher's answer keys, guidebooks, etc.,
are available only at request of teachers or school
officials where books or tests are adopted for
class use." Contact the publisher to establish
acceptable verification.
Public school textbooks.

Harvest House Publishers
1075 Arrowsmith
Eugene, OR 97402-9197
1-800-547-8979 (including Oregon) VISA, MC.
OR: (503) 343-0123 Fax: (503) 342-6410
Free catalog and brochure.
Returns: With permission, in resalable condition,
within 365 days.
Christian publisher.

Hayes School Publishing Co., Inc.
321 Pennwood Ave.
Wilkinsburg, PA 15221-3398
1-800-245-6234 VISA, MC.
PA: (412) 371-2370
Fax: (412) 371-6408
Free full-color catalog. Minimum phone order $15.
Supplemental materials.

HearthSong
P.O. Box B
Sebastopol, CA 95473
1-800-325-2502 VISA, MC, AmEx, Discover.
Fax: 1-800-872-0331 (For Orders Only)
Free 48-page full-color catalog.
Returns: Unconditional.
"A catalog for families." Toys, natural art materials,
craft kits.

Heathkit
Heath Company
455 Riverview Dr.
Benton Harbor, MI 49022
1-800-253-0570 VISA, MC, AmEx.
MI, AK: (616) 925-3650
Fax: (616) 925-4876
Free catalog. Unconditional guarantee.
Electronics courses.

Herald Press
616 Walnut Avenue
Scottdale, PA 15683-1999
(412) 887-8500 VISA, MC, Discover.
Fax: (412) 887-3111
Free catalog. Returns: With permission, in
resalable condition, within 365 days.
Mennonite publisher.

Heritage Products, Inc.
P.O. Box 246
Glencoe, IL 60022
1-800-346-2395 Check or M.O, C.O.D.
Fax: (708) 577-1681
Free brochure with SASE. Returns: In resalable
condition, within 30 days.
Bible overview chart.

Hewitt Research Foundation
P.O. Box 9
Washougal, WA 98671
1-800-348-1750 VISA, MC.
(206) 835-8708
Fax: (206) 835-8697
Free catalog and brochure. Returns: With
permission, in resalable condition, within 10 days.
Innovative home-school materials.

High Noon Books
20 Commercial Blvd.
Novato, CA 94949-6191
1-800-422-7249 VISA, MC, AmEx
(415) 883-3314
Fax: (415) 883-3720
Free catalog. Returns: With permission, in
resalable condition, with 6 months.
Call or write for address of one of their Canadian
or overseas distributors.
Hi-lo mystery novels and language arts teaching
aids.

Home Educator, The
C.M. Hudson Academy Press
R.R. 1 Box 41
Martinsville, IL 62442
(217)932-4406 Check or M.O.
Free flyer with SASE.
Bible memory program.

Home Life
P.O. Box 1250
Fenton, Mo 63026-1250
Check or M.O.
Fax: (314) 225-0743
Free catalog.
Returns: Resalable condition, within 30 days.
Our home business.
HELP newsletter ($15/4 issues): tips, reviews,
resources for growing families. Juggling equipment.
Books. Organizers. TV-free video systems.

Home Run Enterprises
12531 Aristocrat Ave.
Garden Grove, CA 92641
No phone orders.
Brochure w/SASE.
Returns: In resalable condition, within 10 days
Christian Home Educator's Curriculum Manual by
Cathy Duffy. Math games for home schoolers.

Home School Legal Defense Association
P. O. Box 159
Paeonian Springs, VA 22129
(703) 882-3838 Check, M.O., C.O.D.
Fax: (703) 882-3628
Free brochure.
Returns: Within 60 days, in resalable condition.
Home school legal defense.

Houghton Mifflin
Ordering Office
Wayside Road
Burlington, MA 01803
1-800-225-3362 VISA, MC.
Free catalog.
Returns: In resalable condition.
Public school textbook publisher.

**Hubbard Scientific Division of Spectrum
Industries**
P.O. Box 104
Northbrook, IL 60065-9976
1-800-323-8368 VISA, MC, AmEx.
IL: (312) 272-7810
Fax: (312) 272-9894
Free catalogs.
Maps. Science supplies.

Human Kinetics Publishers, Inc.
Box 5076
Champaign, IL 61825-5076
1-800-747-4457 (credit card orders only) VISA,
MC, AmEx, Business P.O.
(217) 351-5076
Fax: (217) 351-2674
Free catalog.
Returns: Within 30 days, in resalable condition.
Sports Rules Encyclopedia.

Human Resource Development Press
22 Amherst Rd.
Amherst, MA 01002
1-800-822-2801 MC, VISA, AmEx.
(413) 253-3488
Fax: (413) 253-3490
Free catalog.
Returns: In resalable condition, within 30 days.
No shipping/handling on prepaid orders over $25.
Books about peer pressure.

Hume Financial Education Services
835 Franklin Court
Box 105627
Atlanta, GA 30348
1-800-222-4863 VISA, MC, AmEx.
Free brochure. Returns: Within 15 days.
Successful Business Management Program.

Ideal School Supply Company
11000 S. Lavergne Ave.
Oak Lawn, IL 60453
1-800-323-5131
IL: (708) 425-0800
School supplies, all subject areas, K-8.
Order from school suppliers.

INC Magazine
38 Commercial Wharf
Boston, MA 02110
1-800-234-0999 (subscriptions)
(617) 248-8000 (editorial)
Business magazine.

Inc. Business Products
P.O. Box 1365
Willkes-Barre, PA 18703-1365
1-800-372-0018 X-4082 (orders only) 24 hours 7
days. VISA, MC, AmEx.
Fax: (717) 822-8226
Satisfaction guaranteed.
Sales and management audio and video tapes
and booklets.

Inheritance Publications
2207 - 76th St.
Caledonia, MI 49316
(616) 698-0186 Check or M.O.
Free brochure.
Returns: In resalable condition, within 30 days.
Christian publisher and distributor.

Insect Lore Products
P.O. Box 1535
132 S. Beech
Shafter, CA 93263
1-800-Live Bug (548-3284) VISA, MC, school
purchase orders by mail or fax only.
(805) 746-6047
Fax: (805) 746-0334
Free catalog. Returns: In resalable condition, in
original packaging, within 10 days.

Institute for Creation Research
10946 Woodside Ave. N.
Santee, CA 92071
(619) 448-0900
Fax: (619) 448-3469
Creation science resources.

Institute in Basic Life Principles
Box One
Oak Brook, IL 60522-3001
(708) 323-9800 Check or M.O.
Fax: (708) 323-6394
Seminars. Supplier of ATIA curriculum.

International Juggler's Association
Box 3707
Akron, OH 44314-3707
(216) 745-3552 after 5 P.M. EST weekdays.
VISA, MC.
International juggling organization.

Into the Wind Kites
1408 Pearl
Boulder, CO 80302
(303) 449-5356 M-Sat 10-6, credit card orders
only. VISA, MC, AmEx, Discover, CB, C.O.D.
Fax: (303) 449-7315
Free catalog. Complete refund or exchange. You
return prepaid and insured.
Kites, wind-play supplies.

Intrepid Books
P.O. Box 179
Rough and Ready, CA 95975
(916) 432-3197 Check or M.O, C.O.D.
Free brochure. Returns: In resalable condition.
Principle-Approach history workbooks.

ISHA Enterprises
5503 East Beck Lane
Scottsdale, AZ 85254
(602) 482-1346 VISA, MC.
Free brochure with SASE.
Returns: In resalable condition, within 30 days.
Grammar materials.

Jeffrey Lant Associates
50 Follen Street, Suite 507
Cambridge, MA 02138
(617) 547-6372 VISA, MC.
Free catalog.
Business books and reports.

Jeffrey Norton Publishers, Inc.
96 Broad St.
Guilford, CT 06437
1-800-243-1234 (USA and Canada) VISA, MC,
AmEx, DC, CB, institutional P.O.
(203) 453-9794 Fax: (203) 453-9774
Free catalogs.
Returns: within 3 weeks, unconditional.
Various cassette-of-the-month plans.
Spoken-word cassettes, videos.

Judah Bible Curriculum
P. O. Box 122
Urbana, IL 61801
(217) 344-5672 VISA, MC.
Free brochure.
Returns: Resaleable condition only, within 60
days.
Bible curriculum.

Key Curriculum Press
P.O. Box 2304
Berkeley, CA 94702
1-800-338-7638 VISA, MC.
CA, AK, HI: (415) 548-2304
Fax: (415) 548-0755
Free catalog. Orders under $25 from individuals
must be prepaid.
Math workbooks.

KNEXT Card Game Company
P.O. Box 368
Englewood, OH 45322
Check or M.O.
Math game.

Know It All
733 West Naomi Ave.
Unit I, Suite 165
Arcadia, CA 91007
1-800-I-KNOW-IT (456-6948) Check, M.O., or C.O.D.
(818) 287-0158 Fax: (818) 447-5667
Free brochure with SASE.
Returns: Within 30 days in resalable condition.
Geography game.

KONOS
P.O. Box 1534
Richardson, TX 75083
(214) 669-8337 Check or M.O.
Fax: (214) 699-7922
U. S. funds only. No phone orders.
Free brochure. Catalog $1.
Returns: Within 21 days, in resalable condition,
10% restocking fee.
Homeschool curriculum, seminars.

Kregel Publications
P.O. Box 2607
Grand Rapids, MI 49501-2607
(616) 451-4775 VISA, MC.
Fax: (616) 459-6049
Free catalog.
Returns: With permission, in resalable condition,
within a year.
Christian publisher.

Ladybird Books, Inc.
49 Omni Circle
P.O. Box 1690
Auburn, ME 04210
1-800-523-9247 VISA, MC, C.O.D.
Open account for established businesses.
(207) 783-6329
Fax: (207) 783-6130
Free catalog.
Returns: With permission, in resalable condition,
for account holders only.
Educational books, readers.

Landmark Company
1580 Raven Hill
Wheaton, IL 60187
(312) 690-9978 VISA, MC.
Returns: Within 15 days, in resalable condition.
Lighthouse Adventures tape series.

Learn, Inc.
113 Gaither Dr.
Mt. Laurel, NJ 08054-9987
1-800-729-7323 Ext. 120 VISA, MC, AmEx,
Discover.
Inquiries: (609) 234-6100
Fax: (609) 273-7766
Free catalog. Returns: Within 30 days.
Self-study and classroom audio and video courses.

Learning at Home
P.O. Box 270bb
Honaunau, HI 96726
(808) 328-9669 VISA, MC.
Free catalog.
Returns: Within 15 days, in resalable condition.
Home-school catalog.

Learning Things, Inc.
P.O. Box 436
Arlington, MA 02174
(617) 646-0093 Check or M.O.
Fax: (617) 646-0135
Minimum order, $15. Free catalog.
Returns: In resalable condition.
Science apparatus, math aids, cardboard carpentry,
tools and construction kits for kids K–12.

Learning Works
P.O. Box 6187
Santa Barbara, CA 93160
(805) 964-4220 Check or M.O.
Fax: (805) 964-1466
Free catalog. Returns: Resalable condition within
10 days.
Supplemental materials.

LEGO DACTA, Inc.
555 Taylor Rd.
P.O. Box 1600
Enfield, CT 06083-1600
1-800-527-8339
CT: (203) 749-2291
Fax: (203) 763-2466
Sold only through educational distributors and
teacher stores. Available directly from LEGO DACTA
in certain states. Please call for details.

LibertyTree: Review and Catalog
The Independent Institute
134 - 98th Ave.
Oakland, CA 94603
1-800-927-8733 (credit card orders only) VISA,
MC, AmEx. 24 hrs 7 days.
Inquiries: (415) 568-6047 M-F 8:30-5:30 PST
Fax: (415) 568-6040
Free catalog.
Returns: In resalable condition, in original
packaging, within 10 days of receipt.
Store Hours: M-F 8:30-5:30, Sat. by appointment.
Libertarian books 'n gifts.

Lion Publishing
1705 Hubbard Ave.
Batavia, IL 60510
1-800-447-5466 Check or M.O.
IL: (708) 879-0707
Free catalog.
Returns: Within 1 year, with permission, in
resalable condition.
Christian publisher.

Longman Publishing Group
95 Church St.
White Plains, NY 10601
1-800-447-2226 (orders and customer service)
Visa, MC, AmEx.
(914) 993-5095
Fax: (914) 997-8115
Free catalog.
Returns: Within 30 days, in resalable condition.
Publisher.

Louis Publishing
1105 Inverness Lane
Bellingham, WA 98226
(206) 647-3229 Check or M.O.
Returns: In resalable condition.
Publisher of *The Overnight Student*.

Ludwig von Mises Institute
Auburn University
Auburn, AL 36849
(205) 844-2500 Check or M.O.
Fax: (205) 844-2583
Free catalog.
Returns: Within 90 days, in resalable condition.
Free-market economics publisher.

THE BIG BOOK OF HOME LEARNING — VOLUME III

Lynn's Bookshelf
P.O. Box 2224
Boise, ID 83701-2224
Check or M.O.
Free brochure with SASE.
Returns: In resalable condition.
Proverbs for Parenting.

Mantle Ministries
140 Grand Oak Drive
San Antonio, TX 78232
(512) 490-BEAR Check or M.O.
Free catalog. Returns: Within 30 days.
History resources by "Little Bear" Wheeler.

Marcine Bice
1908 Ave. F
Kearney, NE 68847
Check or M.O.
Christian life plan architectural diagram.

Master Books
P.O. Box 1606
El Cajon, CA 92022
1-800-999-3777 VISA, MC.
CA: (619) 448-1121
Free brochure.
Creation Science books, videos.

Mathematics Programs Associates, Inc.
P.O. Box 118
Halesite, NY 11743
(516) 588-4391 or 549-9061 Check or M.O.
Free catalog and brochure.
Developmental Mathematics series.

Maupin House Publishing
P.O. Box 90148
Gainesville, FL 32607
(904) 336-9290 VISA, MC, purchase order.
Returns: In resalable condition, within 30 days.
Publisher of *Caught 'Ya!: Grammar with a Giggle.*

McDougal, Littell & Company
P.O. Box 8000
St. Charles, IL 60174
1-800-225-3809 VISA, MC.
(312) 869-2300
Free catalog. Returns: Within 30 days, with
permission, in resalable condition.
Public school textbook publisher.

Merck & Company
P.O. Box 2000
Rahway, NJ 07065
1-800-659-6598 VISA, MC.
(908) 855-4558
Fax: (908) 750-8746
Unconditionally guaranteed.
Doctor's diagonostic manual.

Merrill Publishers
1300 Alum Creek Dr.
P.O. Box 508
Columbus, OH 43216-9886
1-800-848-6205
OH: 1-800-445-6409
Require some sort of evidence that you are a
legitimate school or certified teacher (e.g, copy of
affidavit or teacher credential) for purchase of
teacher materials.
Public school textbook publisher.

Merry Mountaineers
P. O. Box 667
Highlands, NC 28741
Check or M.O.
Free brochure.
Publisher of Southern humor books.

Midwest Publications
Critical Thinking Press and Software
P. O. Box 448
Pacific Grove, CA 93950
1-800-458-4849 VISA, MC.
(408) 375-2455
Fax: (408) 372-3230
Free catalog.
Returns: Unconditional.
Thinking-skill materials.

Milliken Publishing Company
1100 Research Blvd.
St. Louis, MO 63132-0579
1-800-325-4136 MO: 1-800-333-READ.
VISA, MC, AmEx, C.O.D.
(314) 991-4220
Fax: (314) 991-4807
Free catalogs. Available catalogs: PreK–8, 7–12,
Computer Software, Reading, Early Childhood,
Childhood Literature.
Educational publisher PreK–12.

Mind's Eye
P.O. Box 1060
Petaluma, CA 94953
1-800-227-2020 VISA, MC, AmEx, Discover.
CA: (415) 883-7701
Fax: (415) 883-1849
Free gorgeous catalog. Unconditional guarantee.
Stories on tape.

Moody Correspondence School
820 N. LaSalle St.
Chicago, IL 60610
1-800-955-1123 VISA, MC.
IL: (312) 329-2080
Free catalog and brochure. 15-day free trial.
Returns: Within 30 days, with permission, in
resalable condition.
Self-study adult Bible courses.

Mortensen Math
see V.J. Mortensen Co.

Mott Media
1000 E. Huron St.
Milford, MI 48042
MI: (313) 685-8773 VISA, MC.
Free catalog. Returns: In resalable condition,
prepaid and traceable, within 90 days of shipping
date, on new material for 80% credit.
Classic texts, McGuffeys.

MOVIT Electronic Kits
see OWI Inc.

NAPSAC
Rt. 1 Box 646
Marble Hill, MO 63764
(314) 238-2010 (NAPSAC) Check or M.O. US
funds only.
Free book catalog for large SASE.
Membership organization. Supports alternatives
in childbirth. Publishes NAPSAC NEWS and several
excellent works on childbirth and medicine.
Video/audio conference tapes.

National Geographic Society
P.O. Box 2895
Washington, DC 20013
(202) 857-7000 or 857-7589 (301) 948-8970:
8971 for books & globes
Geography supplies.

National Home Study Council
1601 Eighteenth Street, N. W.
Washington, DC 20009
Accrediting agency for home study schools.

National Teaching Aids, Inc.
1845 Highland Ave.
New Hyde Park, NY 11040
(516) 326-2555 Check or M.O.
Fax: (516) 326-2560
Catalog $1. Returns: 60 days, permission.
Teaching aids for science and health.

New Careers Center
P.O. Box 297
Boulder, CO 80306
(303) 447-1087 M-F 8-5 (orders) Visa, MC
Catalog $1.
Returns: In resalable condition, within 365 days.
The Whole Work Catalog.

New Moon Records
P.O. Box 203
Joshua Tree, CA 92252
(619) 366-9684 Check or M.O.
Free catalog. Unconditional guarantee.
Cassettes of original family music.

Norris Science Labs and Kits
P. O. Box 61281
Las Vegas, NV 89160
(702) 458-6427 Check or M.O. or school P.O.
Catalog $2, refunded on first order.
Returns: In resalable condition, within 30 days.
Science lab equipment, supplies.

Old Fashioned Crafts
Route 2 Box 2091
Ellijay, GA 30540
1-800-962-8849 VISA, MC.
(404) 635-7612
Free brochure. Returns: With permission.
Wooden board games for the whole family.

Operation Mobilization Literature
P.O. Box 28
Waynesboro, GA 30830
(404) 554-5827 VISA, MC, Fax: (404) 554-7444
Free catalog. Free brochure. Returns: With permission, in resalable condition, within 90 days.
Publishes Operation World kit.

Ornament Publications
2301 Country Club Road
Garland, TX 75041
Check or M.O.
Free brochure.
Publishes *The Richest Christian* game.

OWI, Inc.
1160 Mahalo Place
Compton, CA 90220
(213) 638-4732
Fax: (213) 638-8347
Free brochure.
Electronic robot kits.

Pacific Puzzle Company
378B Guemes Island Rd.
Anacortes, WA 98221
(206) 293-7034 VISA, MC, C.O.D. U.S. funds only.
Free catalog. Refund or exchange if dissatisfied.
Beautiful hardwood puzzles.

Paradigm Company
P.O. Box 45161
Boise, ID 83711
(208) 322-4440 VISA, MC.
Sam Blumenfeld's publisher.

Penny Press
6 Prowitt Street
Norwalk, CT 06855
Check or M.O.
Logic problem puzzles.

Perfectly Safe
7245 Whipple Ave. N.W.
North Canton, OH 44720
1-800-837-KIDS VISA, MC, AmEx, minimum $10.
(216) 494-2323
Fax: (216) 494-0265
Free catalog. Returns: Within 30 days.
Children's safety products.

Personal Progress Library
7657 Winnetka Avenue
Winnetka, CA 91306
1-800-748-6245 VISA, MC, AmEx.
(818) 700-0818
Fax: (818) 700-0631
Free brochure.
Audio and video lending library.

Peter Marshall
36 Nickerson Road
Orleans, MA 02653
(508) 255-7705 (office) (508) 255-7570
American history resources.

Peterson's Guides
P.O. Box 2123
Princeton, NJ 08543-2123
1-800-EDU-DATA (338-3282) VISA, MC, AmEx
($25 minimum credit card order)
NJ: (609) 243-9111
Fax: (609) 243-9150
Free catalog. Returns: Within 30 days, in resalable
condition, with original invoice.
Book publisher.

Plain Path Publishers
P.O. Box 830
Columbus, NC 28722
Check or M.O.
Free brochure.
Returns: In resalable condition, within 10 days.
Christian character and manhood training for
young people.

Plymouth Rock Foundation
Fiskmill, P.O. Box 577
Marlborough, NH 03455-0425
(603) 876-4505 VISA, MC.
Fax: (603) 876-4128
Free catalog. Returns: In resalable condition.
Books on Christian world view.

Poppyseed Press
P.O. Box 85
Sedalia, CO 80135
(303) 688-4136 Check or M.O.
Free brochure with SASE. Returns: Unconditional.
College entrance for home-schoolers.

Portland State University
Continuing Education Press
Box 1394
Portland, OR 97207
1-800-547-8887 X 4891 VISA, MC.
(503) 725-4891
Free brochure.
Returns: With permission, in resalable condition,
within 90 days.
Italic handwriting series.

Providence Project
P.O. Box 1760
Wichita, KS 67201
(316) 265-0321 VISA, MC.
Catalog $2, refunded with first order.
Returns: Unconditional, within 1 year.
Learning Vitamins-CalcuLadder, ReadyWriter,
AlphaBetter.

Quantum Communications
3301 West Hampden Ave., Suite N
Englewood, CO 80110
(303) 781-0679 Check or M.O. (Made payable to
Traveloguer Collection) VISA, MC, AmEx.
Fax: (303) 761-8556
Returns: Within 15 days.
Traveloguer videos.

Rainfall Inc.
1534 College Ave. S.E.
Grand Rapids, MI 49507
1-800-437-4337 VISA, MC.
(616) 245-5985
Fax: (616) 245-2127
Free brochure for large SASE.
Returns: With permission.
Bible games, toys, gifts, and videos.

Rand McNally & Company
PO Box 7600
Chicago, IL 60680
1-800-451-7266 except KY. They will bill you.
Free catalog.
Returns: With permission, in resalable condition.
Atlas and map publisher.

Real Goods Trading Company
966 Mazzoni Street
Ukiah, CA 95482
1-800-762-7325 7 AM to 7 PM PST. VISA, MC,
AmEx, Discover.
CA: (707) 468-9292
Fax: (707) 468-0301
Catalog: Quarterly, subscription $30 American,
$35 Canadian.
Returns: In resalable condition, within 90 days.
Educational solar powered kits. Catalog of offline
power equipment and energy saving devices.

Recorded Books
270 Skipjack Road
Prince Frederick, MD 20678
1-800-638-1304 VISA, MC.
(301) 535-5590
Fax: (301) 535-5499
Free catalog. Free brochure.
Returns: Unconditional.
Books on tape.

Reel to Real Ministries
P.O. Box 4145
Gainesville, FL 32613
(904) 371-2466 VISA, MC, C.O.D.
Fax: (904) 375-0327
Free brochure. Returns: Unconditional.
Christian videos.

Reformed Free Publishing Association
Box 2006
Grand Rapids, MI 49501
(616) 534-1927
Bible helps.

Reformed Presbyterian Board of Publications
Board of Education and Publication
7408 Penn Avenue
Pittsburgh, PA 15208-2531
(412) 241-0436 Check or M.O. or they bill you. No
postage and handling charges on prepaid orders.
Fax: (412) 731-8861 5 P.M. - 8 A.M.
Free catalog.
Returns: Within 30 days, in resalable condition.
Quantity discounts for bookstores and churches.
Psalm books, cassettes.

Reiman Publications
5925 Country Lane
Box 572
Milwaukee, WI 53201
1-800-344-6913 VISA, MC, or they will bill you.
(They will not bill for sample issues.)
Fax: (414) 423-1143
Publisher of country and ranching magazines.

Resource Publications
9403 Winding Ridge
Dallas, TX 75238
(214) 341-1157 Check or M.O.
Free brochure with SASE.
Grammar book.

Right at Home Productions
6628 - 193rd Street, S.W.
Lynnwood, WA 98036
Check or M.O.
Free brochure.
Returns: Unconditional, within 10 days.
Non-clothing sewing projects.

Rinehart Incorporated Handwriting System
Allen Drive
P.O. Box 441
Barre, MA 01005
(508) 355-2727 Check or M.O.
Free brochure.
Returns: In resalable condition, within 10 days.
Handwriting correspondence courses.

Rod and Staff Publishers
Crockett, KY 41413
(606) 522-4348 Check or M.O.
Fax: (606) 522-4896
Free catalog listing texts. Returns: With
permission, 10 percent restocking charge.
Christian schoolbooks. Mennonite.

Rothbard-Rockwell Report
Center for Libertarian Studies
P.O. Box 4091
Burlingame, CA 94011
1-800-325-7257
VISA, MC.
Fax: (415) 692-8459
Libertarian newsletter.

Safari Ltd.
P.O. Box 630685
Miami, FL 33163
1-800-554-5414 VISA, MC, AmEx, Carte Blanche
(305) 621-1000
Fax: (305) 621-6894
Free catalog.
Returns: With permission, in resalable condition,
in original packaging, within 45 days.
Educational games.

Sanyei America Corporation
Capsela Division
450 Harmon Meadow Blvd.
Secaucus, NJ 07094
(212) 864-4848   Fax: (201) 864-5770
Capsela Scientific kits.

Saxon Publishers, Inc.
1320 West Lindsey, Suite 100
Norman, OK 73069
(405) 329-7071 Check or M.O.
Fax: (405) 360-4205
Call or write for free brochure.
Returns: In resalable condition, within 30 days,
10% restocking fee.
Math and algebra texts.

School of Statesmanship
1235 Newport Road
Manheim, PA 17545
(717) 665-3157 Check or M.O. Free brochure.
30 day money-back gurantee.
Political science course.

SelfCare Catalog
349 Healdsburg Avenue
Healdsburg, CA 95448
1-800-345-3371 6:00 A.M.-6:00 P.M. CT (orders
only). VISA, MC, AmEx.
(504) 893-1195
Free catalog. Returns: Unconditional.
Medical self-care products.

Shekinah Curriculum Cellar
967 Junipero Drive
Costa Mesa, CA 92626
(714) 751-7767 Check or M.O.
Catalog $1.
Refunds: Resealable condition, within 15 days.
Co-op buying plan.
"Quality books and teaching aids for home
educators."

Sky & Telescope Magazine
P.O. Box 9111
Belmont, MA 02178
1-800-253-0245 VISA, MC.
(617) 864-7360 Fax: (617) 864-6117
Free catalog.
Magazine and astronomy resources.

Soundview Executive Book Summaries
5 Main Street
Bristol, VT 05443
1-800-521-1227 VT: (802) 453-4062
Fax: (802) 453-5062
Business books summarized.
By subscription only.

Spirit-Led Childbirth
6413 N. Lunar Ct.
Fort Collins, CO 80525
(303) 226-5079 8-5 M-F MT. VISA, MC, C.O.D.
(additional charge for C.O.D.)
Free catalog.
Returns: With permission, in resalable condition, within 7 days.
"Birthing and Parenting Supplies."

St. Ursula Academy, S.U.A.
Phonics Department
1339 E. McMillan St.
Cincinnatti, OH 45206-2180
(513) 961-4877 or 961-3410 Check or M.O.
Free brochure.
Returns: In resalable condition, within 30 days.
"Professor Phonics" reading program.

Super Science Ltd., Inc.
1133 E. Francisco Blvd, Suite E
San Rafael, CA 94901
1-800-284-4775
(415) 454-1407 Fax: (415) 454-0172
Science tools and resources.

Surrey Books
230 East Ohio Street, Suite 120
Chicago, IL 60611
1-800-326-4430 IL: (312) 751-7330
Publisher.

SyberVision Systems, Inc.
7133 Koll Center Parkway
Pleasanton, CA 94566
1-800-678-0887 VISA, MC, Discover, AmEx.
(415) 846-2244 Fax: (415) 426-0256
Free catalog. Quantity discounts.
Returns: With permission, in resalable condition, in original packaging, within 30 days.
Cassette and video courses.

Sycamore Tree
2179 Meyer Place
Costa Mesa, CA 92627
(714) 650-4466 (info) (714) 642-6750 (orders)
VISA, MC.
Fax: (714) 642-6750
Catalog $3, refundable on first purchase.
Returns: In resalable condition, within 15 days.
Full-service home-school supplier.

Teacher Created Materials
5445 Oceanus Drive, #106
Huntington Beach, CA 92649
1-800-662-4321 Visa, MC.
(714) 891-7895
Fax: (714) 892-0283
Supplementary materials for public schools.
Student activity workbooks.

Teachers' Laboratory, Inc.
104 Canal Street
P.O. Box 6480
Brattleboro, VT 05302-6480
(802) 254-3457 VISA, MC.
Fax: (802) 254-5233
Free catalog.
Returns: With permission, in resalable condition.
Math and science supplies.

Teaching Home
P.O. Box 20219
Portland, OR 97220-0219
(503) 253-9633 Check or M.O.
Fax: (503) 253-7345
Free brochure. Satisfaction guaranteed.
Christian home-schooling magazine.

Ten Commandments, The
P.O. Box 577
Marlborough, NH 03455
(603) 876-4685 (603) 876-4505
A contribution is appreciated but not required.
Fax: (603) 876-4128
Ten Commandment packet.

Ten Speed Press
P.O. Box 7123
Berkeley, CA 94707
1-800-841-2665 Check or M.O.
Include $2 shipping.
(415) 845-8414
Fax: (415) 524-1052
Free catalog.
Publisher.

Theopolis
P.O. Box 198
Warsaw, OH 43844
(614) 824-3616 Check or M.O.
Publisher of books about money.

Things of Science
P.O. Box 579
Sarasota, FL 34230-0579
(813) 951-1688 Check or M.O.
Free brochure. 100% guarantee.
Monthly science kits.
Secular.

Timberdoodle
E. 1610 Spencer Lake Road
Shelton, WA 98584
(206) 426-0672 Check or M.O., or COD.
Free catalog. Returns: In resalable condition, in
original packaging, within 60 days.
Educational materials.
Fischertechnik kits.

TREND Enterprises, Inc.
P.O. Box 64073
St. Paul, MN 55164-0073
1-800-328-5540 Check or M.O.
MN: (612) 631-2850
Fax: (612) 631-2861
Free catalog. Satisfaction guaranteed.
$10 minimum order. Add $2 for shipping, orders
over $15 add 10% shipping.
Stickers, wipe-off books, bulletin board cut-outs,
flash cards, more.

Trinity Foundation
P.O. Box 700
Jefferson, MD 21755
1-800-594-4588 U.S. Check or M.O.
(301) 371-7155
Free catalog, brochures.
Returns: only defective books.
Newsletter, tapes, books.
Publisher.

University of Nebraska-Lincoln
Independent Study Department
Division of Continuing Studies
Lincoln, NE 68583-0900
(402) 472-1926
Fax: (402) 472-1901
Full service high school diploma course.
Science equipment, courses.

V.J. Mortensen Co.
P.O. Box 98
Hayden Lake, ID 83835-0098

1-800-777-0930 VISA, MC, AmEx
(208) 667-1580
Fax: (208) 667-4787
Free catalog and brochure.
Returns: Within 30 days, with authorization.
Math manipulatives and methodology.

Vic Lockman
P. O. Box 1916
Ramona, CA 92065
Check or M.O. Minimum order $5.
Fax: (619) 739-0537 (files)
Free brochure with long SASE.
Returns: Wholesale buyers only, with permission,
in resalable condition.
Cartoon booklets on drawing, economics,
government, catechism, etc.

Video Tutorial Service, Inc.
1840 52nd St., Suite 11
Brooklyn, NY 11204
(718) 232-7551
Fax: (718) 236-4960
Video workbook series.

Vintage Books
201 East 50th St.
New York, NY 10022
(212) 572-2080 Check or M.O.
The Map Catalog.

Vision Video
2030 Wentz Church Rd.
Worcester, PA 19490
1-800-523-0226 VISA, MC.
(215) 584-1893
Fax: (215) 584-4610
Free catalog and brochure.
Returns: In resalable condition, within 30 days.
Church history and Bible story videos.

Visual Education Association
581 W. Leffel Lane
P.O. Box 1666
Springfield, OH 45501
1-800-243-7070 VISA, MC.
Fax: (513) 324-5697
Free brochure. Returns: In resalable condition, in
original packaging, within 1 year.
Flash card sets in all subjects.

W. H. Freeman and Company
4419 West 1980 South
Salt Lake City, UT 84104
(801) 973-4660
Fax: (212) 689-2383
Textbook publisher.

Wadsworth Inc.
7625 Empire Drive
Florence, KY 41042-2978
(606) 525-2230 VISA, MC, AmEx.
Free catalog. This publisher has not yet established policy for home school orders. It might be possible for some to receive a school discount. Availability of Instructor's Manuals will depend upon evidence that the purchaser is a valid school. Call the publisher for clarification. Returns: With permission, in resalable condition, with receipt. Public school textbook publisher.

Warren Foundation
13751 Lake City Way, N.E. Suite 220
Seattle, WA 98125-8612
1-800-877-0370
(206) 361-1934
Fax: (206) 365-9351
Literacy in English for education and business.

Weekend Farmer Company, The
P.O Box 896
Goldendale, WA 98620
1-800-222-GAME (4263) VISA, MC.
WA: (509) 773-5374
Free brochure. Returns: In resalable condition, in original packaging, within 30 days.
Farming game.

Wff 'n Proof Learning Games Associates
1490-FS South Blvd
Ann Arbor, MI 48104-4699
(313) 665-2269 VISA, MC, C.O.D.
Free catalog.
Games for school subjects.

Whirlpool Redemption Center
P.O. Box 85
St. Joseph, MI 49085
1-800-253-1301 Check or M.O.
Fax: (616) 926-3164
Free pamphlets (single copy). No returns.
Cleaning instruction pamphlets.

William Carey Library
P.O. Box 40129
Pasadena, CA 91114
1-800-777-6371 VISA, MC, Billing available.
(818) 798-0819
Fax: (818) 794-0477 (credit card orders only).
Free catalog.
Returns: With permission, in resalable condition.
Christian publisher.

Wolgemuth & Hyatt Publishers
P.O. Box 1941
Brentwood, TN 37027
Order through Christian bookstores.
Christian book publisher.

World Book Educational Products
Educational Services Department
101 Northwest Point Boulevard
Elk Grove, IL 60007
(708) 290-5431 Check or M.O.
Orders over $25 may be billed.
Fax: (708) 290-5403
Free catalog with long SASE.
Encyclopedia. Workbooks. Learning aids. Posters.
Typical Course of Study.

World Book Direct Response
1560 Sherman, Suite 1111
Evanston, IL 60201
(708) 570-8899
Educational handbooks and helps.

Worldwide Slides
7427 Washburn Avenue South
Minneapolis, MN 55423
(612) 869-6482 Check or M.O, C.O.D.
Pana-Vue catalog $1, refunded on first order.
Returns: In original packaging.
Minimum 5-packet order.
Free View-Master catalog.
Travel slides, videos, books.

Writer's Digest Books
1507 Dana Ave
Cincinnati, OH 45207
1-800-289-0963 VISA, MC
Fax: (513) 531-4744
Free catalog.
Returns: 30 days, resalable condition.
Publisher.

Yalad Birthing Supply
P.O. Box 8111
Canton, OH 44711-8111
(216) 499-0679 VISA, MC.
Free catalog. Returns: With permission, within 30 days, 15% restocking charge after 30 days.
Birth supplies catalog.

Youth With A Mission
Box 55787
Seattle, WA 98155

1-800-922-2143 8-5 PST M-F. VISA, MC.
WA: (206) 771-1153
Fax: (206) 775-2383
Free brochure.

Zaner-Bloser
2200 West Fifth Avenue
PO Box 16764
Columbus, OH 43216-6764
(614) 486-0221 VISA, MC, C.O.D.
Spelling and handwriting resoures publisher.

INDEX OF FOREIGN SUPPLIERS

Realizing that you overseas and Canadian readers prefer to shop in your own countries, I asked every distributor listed in this book for a list of their non-USA distributors. The results, while scanty, might be of help to some of you. The American company is listed first, with its distributor's name (and where available, address) second.

As you can see, any of you who are interested in starting an importing business featuring American home-education materials have a wide-open market. Most other countries do not have as well-developed home-schooling movements as the U.S.A., and consequently Americans are blessed with more than our fair share of innovative products designed for home use. Why not even things out a bit? And when you get your business going, let me know so I can list it in the next edition!

ASIA PACIFIC

Betterway Publications
Graham Brash (PTE) Ltd.
227 Rangoon Road
Singapore 0821

AUSTRALIA

Baker Book House
S. John Bacon Pty., Ltd.
P.O. Box 223
9 Kingston Town Close
Oakleigh, Victoria, 3166
(03) 563-1044

Children's Small Press Collection
The Book Garden
Unit E3 Cnr. Windsor Rd.
Castle Hill, N.S.W. 2154
(02) 634-2558

Harvest House Publishers
Hodder and Stoughton
10-16 South St.
Rydalmere, N.S.W. 2116

Human Kinetics Publishers, Inc.
Human Kinetics Publishers Australia
2 Ingrid Street
Clapham, SC 5062
(08) 374-0433 Fax: (08) 232-2136

Human Resource Development Press
Power Human Resource Development
443 Victoria Ave. 1st Floor
Chatswood, N.S.W. 2067
(02) 411-4811

Kregel Publications
S. John Bacon Pty., Ltd.
9 Kingston Town Close
P.O. Box 223
Oakleigh, Victoria, 3166
(03) 563-1044

Learning Works
Hawker Brownlow Educational Pty., Ltd.
235 Bay Road
Cheltenham, Victoria 3192
(03) 555-1344
Fax: (03) 553-4538

Midwest Publications
Hawker Brownlow Education Pty., Ltd.
235 Bay Road
Cheltenham, Victoria 3192
(03) 555-1344
Fax: (03) 553-4538

Milliken Publishing Company
Encyclopaedia Britannica (Australia) Inc.
Britannica Center 12 Anella Ave.
Castle Hill, N.S.W. 2154
(02) 680-5607
FAX: (02) 899-3231

Rainfall Inc.
Care and Share
44B Harley Crescent
Condell Park, Bankstown, N.S.W. 2200
(02) 707-3111

Teacher Created Materials
Southern Cross Educational
348 Orrong Road, P.O. Box 161
Caulfield, Victoria 3161

Vic Lockman
Light Educational Ministries
PO Box 101
Booleroo Centre 5482

Vic Lockman
Reformation Book Centre
119 Adelaide Arcade
Adelaide, SA 5000

Vision Video
Australian Religious FilmSociety/Esdras Giddy
Blenham Road and Warwick Street
(02) 888-2511
Fax: (02) 958-2812

CANADA

Alpha Omega Publications
Academic Distribution Services
528 Carnarvon St.
New Westminster, B. C. V3L 1C4
(604) 524-9758

Baker Book House
G. R. Welch Co. Ltd.
960 Gateway
Burlington, Ontario L7L 5K7
(416) 681-2760

Betterway Publications
Raincoast Book Distribution, Ltd.
112 East 3rd Ave.
Vancouver, B.C. V5T 1C8
(604) 873-6581

Children's Small Press Collection
Books and Toys to Learn On
1745 Golfview Drive
Windsor, Ontario
(519) 978-0999

Contemporary Books, Inc.
Beaver Books
195 Allstate Parkway
Markham, Ontario L3R 4T8
(416) 477-0030

D. C. Heath and Company
D. C. Heath and Company
100 Adelaide Street W.
Suite 1600
Toronto, Ontario M5H 1S9
(416) 362-6483

Educators Publishing Service, Inc.
Educators Publishing Service
1100 Birchmount Road
Scarborough, Ontario M1K 5H9
(416) 755-0591

Harvest House Publishers
R. G. Mitchell Family Books
565 Gordon Baker Rd.
North York, Ontario M2H 2W2

Herald Press
Herald Press
490 Dutton Drive
Waterloo, Ontario N2L 6H7
(519) 747-5722 Fax: (519) 747-5721

Home Run Enterprises
Window Tree Learning Project
9862 - 156 A Street
Surrey, B.C. V3R-7X7
(604) 583-2882

Human Kinetics Publishers, Inc.
Human Kinetics Publishers, Inc.
Box 2503
Windsor, Ontario N8Y-4S2
1-800-465-7301 or (519) 944-7774

Human Resource Development Press
Pride Canada
2220 College Ave.
Regina, Saskatchewan
(306) 975-3755

Inheritance Publications
Inheritance Publications
Box 154
Neerlandia, Alberta T0G 1R0
(403) 674-3949

Kregel Publications
R. G. Mitchell Family Books, Ltd.
565 Gordon Baker Road
North York, Ontario M2H 2W2

Learn, Inc.
Hume Publ.
4100 Yonge Street
Willowdale, Ontario M2P 2B9
(416) 221-4596 Fax: (416) 221-4968

Midwest Publications
Western Ed. Activities, Ltd.
10929-101 St.
Edmonton, Alberta T5H 2S7

Midwest Publications
Educational Resources Ltd.
109-8475 Ontario St.
Vancouver, B.C. V5X 3E8

Midwest Publications
Kahl's Inc.
Box 126
Kitchener, Ontario N2G 3W9

Milliken Publishing Company
Encyclopedia Britannica Publications
175 Holiday Drive
Cambridge, Ontario N3C 3N4
(519) 658-4621

National Teaching Aids, Inc.
Concepts in Learning
302 Broadway Avenue
Toronto, Ontario M4P 1W3
(416) 486-3331

OWI, Inc.
Mitsutani International
(604) 984-2421

Rainfall Inc.
Main Roads Productions
55 Woodslee Avenue
Paris, Ontario N3L 3X5
(519) 442-1303

Real Goods Trading Company
Bob McCormack
Northern Alternative Power Systems
P.O. Box 14
Pink Mountain, B.C. V0C 2B0
1-800-688-9288 or (604) 827-3547

Teacher Created Materials
Educator Supplies Limited
2323 Trafalgar Street
London, Ontario N5W 5H2

Vic Lockman
Discount Christian Books
12719 126th St.
Edmonton T5L 0X9
 or
Still Waters Revival Books
12810 - 126 Street
Edmonton T5L 0Y1

Writer's Digest Books
Prentice-Hall Canada
1870 Birchmont Rd.
Scarborough, Ontario M1P 2J7
(416) 293-3621

ENGLAND

Audio Forum
Audio Forum
31 Kensington Church Street
London W8-4LL
01-937-1647

Basil Blackwell, Inc.
Basil Blackwell Publisher Ltd.
108 Cowley Rd.
Oxford, OX4 1J5
011-44-865-791100 (for calls from America)

Betterway Publications
Gazelle Book Services Limited
Falcon House, Queen Square
Lancaster LA1 1RN

Harvest House Publishers
Nova Distributors
29 Milber Industrial Estate
Newton Abbott, Devon TQ12 43G

Herald Press
Metanoia Book Service
14 Shepherds Hill
Highgate, London N6 5AQ
0134-08775

Human Kinetics Publishers, Inc.
Human Kinetics Publishers (U.K.) Ltd.
c/o Eddington Hook
406 Vale Rd.
Tonbridge, Kent TN9-1XR
(0732) 357755 Fax: (0732) 770219

Milliken Publishing Company
Gemini Teaching Aids
19 Kirkgate
Sherburn-in-Elmet
Leeds, LS25 6BH
0977-684524

OWI, Inc.
Vector Products
0686-24870

Rainfall Inc.
New Wine Ministries
Unit 22, Arun Business Park
Bognor Regis
Chichester, West Sussex P022 95X
0243-683000

Teacher Created Materials
Gemini Teaching Aids
19 Kirkgate
Sherburn-in-Elmet
Leeds, LS25 6BH
0977-684524

Vision Video
Bagster Video/West Brooke House
76 High Street
Alton, Hampshire, GU341EN
0420-89141
Fax 0420-541160

Writer's Digest Books
Freelance Press
5/9 Bexley Square
Salford Wanshester M3 6DB

INTERNATIONAL

Lion Publishing
Lion Publishing
PLC Sandy Lane
West Littlemore, Oxford OX4 5GH
0865-747550

NEW ZEALAND

Baker Book House
Omega Distributors, Inc.
Box 26-222
69 Great South Road
Remuera, Aukland
548-283

Harvest House Publishers
Omega Distributors
P.O. 26-222 Epsom
Aukland 3

Human Kinetics Publishers, Inc.
David Bateman Ltd.
Box 65062
Auckland 10
Mairangi Bay
(09) 444-4688 Fax: (09) 444-0389

Kregel Publications
Omega Distributors, Ltd.
69 Great South Road
P.O. Box 26-222
Remuera, Epcom, Aukland

Rainfall Inc.
Heyes Enterprises
P. O. Box 24-086 Royal Oak
Auckland
(64) 665-5951

SCOTLAND

Kregel Publications
John Ritchie, Ltd.
40 Beansburn
Kilmarnock KA3 1RH
Ayeshire

SINGAPORE

Midwest Publications
Global Educational Services
3 Irving Road
#03-06 Irving Industrial Building
Singapore 1336

SOUTH AFRICA

Baker Book House
Harvest House Publishers
Kregel Publications
Christian Art Wholesalers
20 Smuts Ave., Box 1599
P.O. Box/Postbus 1599
Vereeniging, 1930
(016) 21-4781/5

Vic Lockman
Signposts
PO Box 26148
0007 Arcadia